PROPERTY

By
Calvin Massey

Professor of Law
University of California
Hasings College of the Law

THE PROFESSOR SERIES

Published by

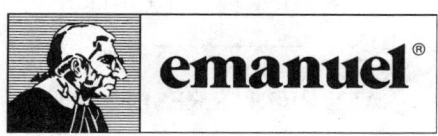

Property, 1st Edition (1998)
Emanuel Publishing Corp. • 1865 Palmer Avenue • Larchmont, NY 10538

Copyright © 1998

By EMANUEL PUBLISHING CORP.
1865 PALMER AVENUE
LARCHMONT, NY 10538

ALL RIGHTS RESERVED

No part of this book may be reproduced, stored in a retrieval system, or transmitted in any form, or by any means, electronic, mechanical, photocopying, recording, or otherwise, without the prior written permission of the copyright holder.

ISBN 1-56542-130-2

DEDICATION

To Ellen

CASEBOOK CORRELATION CHART

You may download a free copy of the Casebook Correlation Chart for this book from the Emanuel website at **http://www.emanuel.com**.

TABLE OF CONTENTS

CAPSULE SUMMARY C-1

CHAPTER 1
CONCEPTUAL BASICS, POSSESSION, AND PERSONAL PROPERTY

I. WHAT IS PROPERTY?	1
II. POSSESSION	3
A. Introduction	3
B. Two meanings of possession	4
C. Of "unowned" things — wild animals, discovery and creation	4
1. Wild animals	4
2. Discovery	5
3. Creation	6
D. Finders keepers	7
1. Abandoned property — general rule	8
2. Lost and mislaid property — general rule	8
3. Statutory modification	12
E. Adverse possession	13
1. Rationales for adverse possession	13
2. Elements of adverse possession	14
3. Property acquired by adverse possession	21
4. Statutory issues	23
5. Adverse possession by tenants and co-owners	25
6. Adverse possession of personal property	25
7. Title acquired by adverse possessor	25
8. Alternatives to adverse possession in boundary disputes	26
F. Accession	27
III. PERSONAL PROPERTY	27
A. Introduction	27
B. Bailments	27
C. Gifts	30
1. Intent	30
2. Delivery	31
3. Acceptance	34
4. Trusts	34
5. Bank accounts	35
D. Transfers for value	36

Chapter 2
FREEHOLD ESTATES

I. ORIGINS AND TAXONOMY OF FREEHOLD ESTATES 40
    A. Estates generally 40
    B. Feudal tenures 40
    C. A taxonomy of freehold estates 42

II. FEE SIMPLE 43
    A. Introduction 43
    B. Fee simple absolute 43
    C. Alienability and inheritance of the fee simple absolute 44

III. FEE TAIL 45
    A. Introduction 45
    B. Origin and operation of the fee tail 45
        1. The fee simple conditional 45
    C. Elimination of the fee tail 47

IV. DEFEASIBLE FEES 50
    A. Introduction 50
    B. Fee simple determinable 50
    C. Fee simple subject to condition subsequent 52
    D. Fee simple subject to executory limitation 55
    E. Some consequences of classification of defeasible fees 56
        1. Transferability of the interest retained by the grantor 56
        2. Accrual of a cause of action for recovery of possession 57
        3. Effect under the Rule Against Perpetuities 58

V. LIFE ESTATES 58
    A. The nature of a life estate 58
    B. Relationship to fee tail 61
    C. The modern life estate 61
    D. Waste 63

VI. RESTRAINTS ON ALIENATION OF FREEHOLD ESTATES 65
    A. Types of restraints 65
    B. Total restraints on a fee interest 66
    C. Partial restraints on a fee interest 66
    D. Restraints on life estates 68

Chapter 3
LEASEHOLD ESTATES

I. THE NATURE OF LEASES 69
    A. Origins and development 69

- **B. Dual nature — estate and contract** 69
  - **1.** The traditional view — estate 69
  - **2.** The contemporary view — contract 70
- **C. The general requirement of a written lease** 70
- **D. What makes it a lease?** 70

II. THE TYPES OF LEASEHOLDS 71
- **A. Term of years** 71
- **B. Periodic tenancy** 72
- **C. Tenancy at will** 75
- **D. Holdovers — the tenancy at sufferance** 76
  - **1.** What constitutes holding over? 76
  - **2.** Eviction and damages 78
  - **3.** Election of a new term 78
  - **4.** Statutory alterations 80

III. DELIVERY OF POSSESSION 81
- **A. Introduction** 81
- **B. Implied obligation to deliver legal right of possession** 81
- **C. Obligation to deliver actual possession** 82
  - **1.** The English Rule 82
  - **2.** The American Rule 83
- **D. Tenant obligation to take possession** 84

IV. SUBLEASES AND ASSIGNMENTS 85
- **A. Introduction** 85
- **B. Assignment** 85
  - **1.** Privity of estate 85
  - **2.** Privity of contract 87
  - **3.** Assignor tenant as surety 89
  - **4.** Multiple assignments 89
- **C. Subleases** 90
- **D. Distinguishing an assignment from a sublease** 91
- **E. Lease provisions restricting assignment or sublease** 93
  - **1.** Strict construction of restrictive covenants 93
  - **2.** Limits on landlord power to deny consent 93
  - **3.** Landlord waiver 94

V. TENANT'S OBLIGATIONS 95
- **A. Introduction** 95
- **B. Pay the rent** 95
- **C. Waste avoidance** 96
- **D. Refrain from illegal uses** 97
- **E. Honesty as to intended purpose** 97
- **F. Duty not to commit nuisance** 98
- **G. Duties from express lease provisions** 98
- **H. Common law — no excusing tenant of obligations** 98

  I. Modern circumstances excusing tenant of obligations 98
VI. **LANDLORD'S REMEDIES** 100
  A. Introduction 100
  B. Remedies typically derived from lease provisions 100
  C. Remedies derived from statute and common law 101
    1. Eviction 101
    2. Tenant abandonment 103
    3. Seizure of the tenant's personal property 105
VII. **LANDLORD'S OBLIGATIONS AND TENANT'S REMEDIES** 105
  A. Introduction 105
  B. Quiet enjoyment 106
  C. Warranty of habitability 109
  D. Tort liability of landlords 115
VIII. **FIXTURES** 117
  A. Introduction 117
  B. Fixtures 117
  C. Attached chattels, but not fixtures 118
IX. **SOCIAL REGULATIONS OF LEASEHOLDS** 118
  A. Introduction 118
  B. Rent control 118
  C. Anti-discrimination statutes 119

CHAPTER 4

FUTURE INTERESTS

I. **INTRODUCTION** 122
II. **FUTURE INTERESTS RETAINED BY THE GRANTOR** 122
  A. Reversion 122
  B. Possibility of reverter 125
  C. Power of termination or right of entry 127
III. **FUTURE INTERESTS CREATED IN GRANTEES** 128
  A. Remainders 128
  B. Executory interests 136
    1. A note on history 136
    2. Springing executory interests 138
    3. Shifting executory interests 139
    4. The executory interest following a fee simple determinable 139
IV. **THE MARKETABILITY RULES** 139
  A. Introduction 139
  B. Destructibility of contingent remainders 140
  C. The Rule in Shelley's Case 143
  D. The Doctrine of Worthier Title 146

TABLE OF CONTENTS

- E. **The Rule Against Perpetuities** 148
  1. Brief summary of the rule 149
  2. Vesting 151
  3. Measuring or validating lives 152
  4. The curious problem of defeasible fees 154
  5. Classic traps for the unwary 156
  6. Reform doctrines 158
  7. Drafting issues 161
  8. Applicability of the Rule Against Perpetuities to commercial transactions 161

CHAPTER 5
CONCURRENT OWNERSHIP AND MARITAL INTERESTS

- I. **FORMS OF CONCURRENT OWNERSHIP** 163
  - A. **Introduction** 163
  - B. **Tenancy in common** 163
  - C. **Joint tenancy** 164
    1. Nature of joint tenancy 164
    2. The four unities of joint tenancy 165
    3. Creation of joint tenancy 167
    4. Severance of joint tenancy 168
  - D. **Tenancy by the entirety** 173
    1. Nature of tenancy by the entirety 173
    2. Creation 173
    3. Operation of the tenancy by the entirety 174
    4. Termination 176
    5. Personal property 176
  - E. **Partnerships and coparceny** 176
- II. **RIGHTS AND OBLIGATIONS OF CONCURRENT OWNERS** 177
  - A. **Introduction** 177
  - B. **Partition** 177
    1. Partition in kind 177
    2. Partition by sale 178
    3. Agreement not to partition 179
  - C. **Rents, profits, and possession** 179
    1. Exclusive possession by one co-owner 179
    2. Rents from third parties 181
    3. Profits from the land 181
  - D. **Accounting for the costs of ownership** 181
  - E. **Adverse possession** 183
  - F. **Implied fiduciaries** 183

III. MARITAL INTERESTS ... 183
   A. **Introduction** ... 183
   B. **The common law system** ... 183
      1. *Femme sole* and *femme covert* ... 183
      2. Husband *uber alles* ... 184
      3. Wife's rights ... 184
      4. Curtesy ... 186
   C. **The modern (mostly statutory) "common law" system** ... 186
      1. Rights on divorce ... 186
      2. Rights on death ... 187
      3. Antenuptial agreements and spousal contracts ... 188
   D. **Community property** ... 188
      1. Origins and concept ... 188
      2. Definition of community property; ... 189
      3. Management of community property ... 192
      4. Rights upon divorce ... 193
      5. Rights upon death ... 193
      6. Creditors' rights ... 193
   E. **"Quasi-marital" property — unmarried cohabitants** ... 193

IV. CONDOMINIUMS AND COOPERATIVES ... 194
   A. **Introduction** ... 194
   B. **Condominiums** ... 194
   C. **Cooperatives** ... 195

CHAPTER 6

SERVITUDES: LAND USE LIMITS CREATED BY PRIVATE BARGAIN

I. INTRODUCTION ... 197
II. EASEMENTS ... 198
   A. **Introduction** ... 198
      1. Defined and distinguished from fee simple ... 198
      2. Types of easements ... 199
      3. *Profits a prendre* ... 202
      4. Licenses ... 202
   B. **Creation of easements** ... 205
      1. Easements by grant ... 205
      2. Easements by estoppel ... 206
      3. Easements by implication ... 206
      4. Easements by prescription ... 210
   C. **Scope of easements** ... 215
      1. Parties' intentions control ... 215
      2. How easement was created ... 216
      3. Change in location of easement ... 217

4. Enlargement of the dominant estate 218
5. Division of an easement's benefit 219
6. Use or interference by servient estate owner 220
- D. **Transfer of easements** 221
- E. **Termination of easements** 222
   1. Expiration 223
   2. Merger 223
   3. Actions of the easement holder 223
   4. Cessation of purpose 225
   5. Actions of the servient estate holder 226
   6. Changed circumstances in the surrounding area 226

III. REAL COVENANTS 227
- A. **Introduction** 227
- B. **Creation of real covenants** 229
- C. **Enforceability by or against successors** 229
- D. **"Running elements" — intent** 230
- E. **"Running elements" — privity of estate** 231
   1. Horizontal privity 231
   2. Vertical privity 233
- F. **"Running elements" — touch and concern the land** 235
   1. Essential meaning of touch and concern 235
   2. Negative covenants 236
   3. Affirmative covenants 237
   4. Benefit in gross 238
   5. Burden in gross 239

IV. EQUITABLE SERVITUDES 239
- A. **Introduction** 239
- B. **Creation** 241
- C. **Enforceability by or against successors** 243
- D. **Identifying the benefited land** 245

V. INTERPRETATION OF COVENANTS 249
- A. **General rule** 249
- B. **Building restriction or use restriction** 249
- C. **Residential purposes** 249
- D. **Architectural approval** 250

VI. TERMINATION OF REAL COVENANTS AND EQUITABLE SERVITUDES 251

Chapter 7
COMMON LAW CONTROL OF LAND USE: NUISANCE AND SUPPORT

I. THE SUBSTANCE OF NUISANCE	255
A. The general principle	255
B. Private nuisances	255
C. Public nuisances	257
D. Relationship to trespass	258
II. REMEDIES — FOUR VIEWS OF NUISANCE	258
A. Introduction — the economic theory of modern nuisance law	258
B. No nuisance — continue the activity	262
C. Nuisance — enjoin and abate the activity	262
D. Nuisance — pay damages and continue the activity	263
E. Nuisance or not — enjoin the activity but award damages to the enjoined actor	263
III. SUPPORT RIGHTS	264
A. Introduction	264
B. Lateral support	264
C. Subjacent support	265

Chapter 8
PUBLIC CONTROL OF LAND USE: ZONING

I. ZONING BASICS	266
II. AUTHORIZATION FOR ZONING	268
A. Enabling legislation	268
1. Defective enabling act	268
2. *Ultra vires* local action	269
B. Comprehensive plan	272
III. STATUTORY DISCRETION AND RESTRAINT	272
A. Introduction	272
B. Nonconforming uses	273
C. Amendments — spot zoning and abusive amendments	274
D. Administrative discretion — variances, conditional uses, floating zones, conditional zoning, and cluster zoning	275
E. Voter discretion — initiative and referendum	279
IV. CONSTITUTIONAL LIMITS ON ZONING	279
A. Introduction	279
B. Equal protection	279
C. Due process	281
D. The takings clause	287

V. PLANNED DEVELOPMENTS: SUBDIVISIONS AND THEIR KIN 288
   A. Introduction 288
   B. Subdivisions 289
   C. Planned unit developments (PUD) 290

VI. WHO NEEDS ZONING? 290
   A. Theoretical objections to zoning 290
   B. Houston — the empirical example 291

CHAPTER 9
TRANSFERS OF REAL PROPERTY

I. CONTRACTS OF SALE 292
   A. Introduction 292
   B. Statute of Frauds 293
      1. Formal contract not necessary 293
      2. Single instrument not necessary 294
      3. Conditions 294
      4. Exceptions to the Statute of Frauds 294
      5. Revocation of contracts 296
   C. Implied obligations 296
   D. Default and remedies 298
   E. Duties of disclosure and implied warranties 301
      1. Duties of disclosure 301
      2. Implied warranty of quality 303
   F. Risk of loss and equitable title 304
      1. Equitable title 304
      2. Risk of loss goes with possession 306

II. DEEDS 306
   A. Formal requirements and component parts 306
   B. Delivery 309
      1. Presumed delivery 309
      2. Attempted delivery at death 309
      3. Commercial escrows 311
      4. Delivery by estoppel 311
   C. Warranties of title 312
      1. General warranty deed 312
      2. Special warranty deed 313
      3. Quitclaim deed 314
      4. Merger doctrine 314
      5. Breach of covenants of title 314
      6. After-acquired title (estoppel by deed) 318

III. FINANCING DEVICES: MORTGAGES, DEEDS OF TRUST, AND INSTALLMENT CONTRACTS ... 319
   A. Mortgages ... 319
   B. Deeds of trust ... 323
   C. Installment sale contracts ... 323

CHAPTER 10
ASSURING GOOD TITLE TO LAND

I. INTRODUCTION ... 325
II. RECORDING ACTS AND CHAIN OF TITLE PROBLEMS ... 326
   A. The recording system ... 326
      1. What the recorder does ... 326
      2. What the title searcher does ... 327
   B. Race acts ... 328
   C. Notice acts ... 329
   D. Race-notice acts ... 329
   E. The consequences of recordation ... 330
   F. When is an instrument recorded ... 331
   G. Scope of protection afforded by recording acts ... 332
   H. Notice ... 334
      1. Actual notice ... 334
      2. Constructive notice ... 334
   I. Common chain of title problems ... 336
      1. Instrument made by a complete stranger to the chain of title ... 336
      2. After-acquired title ... 336
      3. Deed recorded after grantor has parted with record title ... 337
      4. Deeds from a common grantor ... 338
   J. Marketable title acts ... 338
      1. Validity of pre-root interests ... 339
      2. Twin chains of title ... 339
III. TITLE REGISTRATION — THE TORRENS SYSTEM ... 340
   A. Introduction ... 340
   B. Adjudication of title ... 340
   C. Public records and title transfers in the Torrens system ... 341
   D. The practical realities of Torrens registration ... 342
   E. Possessory title registration ... 343
IV. TITLE INSURANCE ... 343
   A. Introduction ... 343
   B. Coverage ... 343

Chapter 11

TAKINGS: THE POWER OF EMINENT DOMAIN AND REGULATORY TAKINGS

I. INTRODUCTION 345

II. THE PUBLIC USE REQUIREMENT 347

III. REGULATORY TAKINGS: HOW MUCH REGULATION OF PROPERTY IS TOO MUCH? 348
    A. Introduction 348
    B. The *per se* rules 348
        1. Nuisance abatement 348
        2. Permanent dispossession 350
        3. Loss of all economically viable use 350
    C. **Balancing public benefits and private costs** 351
    D. **Remedies** 353

ESSAY EXAM QUESTIONS & ANSWERS 355

TABLE OF CASES 380

TABLE OF REFERENCES TO THE RESTATEMENTS OF PROPERTY 386

TABLE OF REFERENCES TO THE UNIFORM RESIDENTIAL LANDLORD & TENANT ACT (URLTA) 387

SUBJECT MATTER INDEX 388

CAPSULE SUMMARY

This Capsule Summary is intended for review at the end of the semester. Reading it is not a substitute for mastering the material in the main outline. The order of topics is occasionally somewhat different from that in the main outline; that's because this Capsule Summary is meant to be a separate outline for night-before-the exam review, not just a summary of the main outline.

Chapter 1
CONCEPTUAL BASICS, POSSESSION, AND PERSONAL PROPERTY

I. WHAT IS PROPERTY?

A. Introduction: Property is ***socially contingent.*** Its meaning varies across cultures and, over time, within cultures. At bottom, property is whatever interest in a thing that the legal system protects against invasion by others. But that definition merely describes a result; it does not explain how we get there. Moreover, property rights are not absolute. Property is relative — it describes the relationship between people with respect to things, not the relationship between persons and things.

B. Theory: The principal theoretical explanations of property are the ***labor theory, utilitarianism, economic efficiency,*** and ***custom.***

1. **Labor theory:** John Locke is the originator of the idea that by mixing your labor with something unowned (e.g., catching a wild fish) you own the resulting mixture of labor and object.

2. **Utilitarianism:** David Hume and Jeremy Bentham argued that property was utilitarian — we protect others' possessions as property because we desire the same protection for our possessions. The implicit root of property in this theory is possession.

3. **Economic efficiency:** Property is economically efficient. If everything is unowned, or owned communally, people will unduly deplete the resource because the individual gain from depletion is greater than the individual cost. But from the society's perspective, the gains from depletion are less than the cost. To an individual the cost is **external.** Property helps to internalize these costs, so that individuals make economically efficient judgments. If the Atlantic cod fishery is unowned individual fishers will take as much cod as they can, since the cost of overfishing is borne by others — external to them. Eventually there will be no more cod, which is pretty much the case today. But if each fisher had an individual property interest in the fish, the incentive to overfish would be reduced, to the long-run benefit of the fisher and to the society as a whole.

4. **Custom:** Property has a customary root. People engaged in a common activity (e.g., whaling or cattle ranching) often develop customs that govern their relationships between themselves and towards their objects of acquisition or husbandry (e.g., whales or cattle). Some customs acquire force of law.

C. Legal doctrine: Property may be broken up into constituent elements: the right to ***use,*** the right to ***exclusive possession,*** and the right to ***dispose or transfer.*** These elements are important, but it is not possible to say, for example, that the combination of any two makes property.

II. POSSESSION

A. **Introduction:** Possession of an object implies its ownership. "Possession" has a dual quality — it can mean the *physical act* of possession and it can mean the *legal conclusion* that someone is in possession of an object.

B. **Unowned things:** There are several methods of acquiring property rights in unowned things.

1. **Possession:** Usually, the first actual physical possession of an unowned object makes you its owner. But this must be qualified, since property is relative. You are not free to trespass upon another's property to hunt wild pheasants and reduce them to property by killing and possessing them.

2. **Discovery:** Acquisition by discovery is related to first possession. If you discover a rare shell on an unowned beach you are simultaneously its discoverer and first possessor.

3. **Creation:** Lots of property is acquired by creation, as Bill Gates will surely tell you. A key issue with respect to intellectual property is the degree of exclusivity the creator ought to have.

C. **Finders:** When property is *lost, mislaid,* or *abandoned,* and then is found by another, a problem of relative title emerges. Finders law attempts to restore property to the true owner, reward honest finders, deliver the reasonable expectations of landowners, and discourage trespassers and other wrongdoers

1. **Abandoned property:** When the true owner intends to give up ownership of property it is abandoned. Abandoned property is unowned and the first possessor becomes its owner unless the circumstances of that possession are wrongful (e.g., the finder is a trespasser).

2. **Lost and mislaid property:** If your wallet slides out of a hole in your pocket without your knowledge, it is lost. But if you place the wallet down on the grocer's counter, intending to put it back in your purse, but forget to do so, it is mislaid. Generally, the finder of lost or mislaid property has a better title to it than anyone else except the true owner. But the owner of the property where the object is found may have a better title than the finder in some circumstances.

   a. **Finder vs. landowner:** If the object is lost and the finder is not a trespasser, the finder prevails. If the object is mislaid, the landowner prevails, on the theory that the owner of mislaid property is more apt to retrace her steps to locate where it was misplaced. But even with respect to lost property, the finder loses out to the landowner if the finder is an employee or invitee of the landowner, or the object is embedded in the soil.

3. **Statutory modification:** These rules are often modified by statute, typically by awarding all found property to the finder if, after a reasonable search for the true owner, the true owner cannot be found.

D. **Adverse possession:** If a person wrongfully possesses land long enough, he may well acquire title from the true owner. Statutes of limitation prescribe the period within which a suit to recover possession of real property must be brought. If a wrongful possessor has occupied the property for longer than the prescribed period in a fashion that meets the requirements of adverse possession, the true owner is barred from recovering possession. The adverse possessor has effectively acquired title.

1. **Elements of adverse possession:** For the true owner's claim of possession to be time-barred the adverse possessor's occupation must meet the following elements.

   a. **Actual entry:** The adverse possessor must actually enter and take exclusive possession of the property. Exclusive possession means to exclude the world, except by permission of the possessor.

   b. **Open and notorious:** The adverse possession must be readily visible and be the type of occupation a true owner would make of the property.

   c. **Hostile or under claim of right:** There are three different views of hostility.

i. **Good faith:** The adverse possessor must actually believe, in good faith, that he is entitled to possess the property.

ii. **Objective:** The adverse possessor's acts and statements germane to his occupation objectively appear to be claims of ownership.

iii. **"Aggressive trespass":** The adverse possessor must know that his occupation is wrongful but still intend to claim the property.

d. **Continuous:** The adverse possessor must continuously occupy for the limitations period. This means that the occupation must be as continuous as a true owner's occupation would be, without voluntary abandonment by the adverse possessor. An adverse possessor may tack his possession onto that of a prior adverse possessor so long as the two adverse possessors are in ***privity*** — they have voluntarily transferred possession from one to the other.

e. **Taxes:** A few jurisdictions require also that the adverse possessor have paid the property taxes for the requisite limitations period.

2. **Color of title:** An adverse possessor who enters under a defective deed or some other defective writing that purports to deliver title to the adverse possessor has entered under color of title. Color of title is usually not necessary to establish adverse possession (although some states require it), but an adverse possessor who enters under color of title is deemed to possess all the property described in the deed so long as it is physically contiguous and owned by the person against whom the actual entry was made.

3. **When the limitations period begins:** The statute of limitations starts to run when the adverse possession first begins. But if at that moment the owner is legally disabled (typically imprisoned, insane, or under the age of majority) the owner is given an extended period of time (after the disability ends) in which to bring suit.

4. **By tenants or co-owners:** A tenant or one co-owner has a right to possession, so their occupation is not wrongful until and unless there has been a very clear repudiation of the lease (by a tenant) or assertion of exclusive ownership (by a co-owner). At that moment, possession becomes wrongful and adverse possession starts.

5. **Boundary disputes:** Boundary disputes are sometimes resolved by adverse possession, but the doctrines of ***agreed boundaries, acquiescence,*** and ***equitable estoppel*** are also employed to resolve these problems.

6. **Personal property:** Adverse possession was developed to deal with wrongful occupation of real property which, of course, has a fixed location. Adverse possession is not well suited to deal with wrongful occupation of personal property, since most personal property is highly portable and easily concealed. A shorter statute of limitations usually applies and some states have discarded adverse possession altogether, in favor of a rule that triggers the limitations period when the owner first discovers, or reasonably should have discovered, the facts that constitute the cause of action.

III. PERSONAL PROPERTY

A. **Bailments:** A bailment is a legitimate possession of personal property by someone who is not the owner of the property. The bailor is the owner and the bailee is the legitimate possessor.

1. **Elements of bailment:** A bailment is created when the bailee has ***actual control*** of the property and ***intends to possess*** the property.

2. **Bailee's rights and obligations:** A bailee has a better right to the property than any third party (other than the bailor, of course). Modern cases require bailees to exercise ordinary care — they are liable for negligence. Older cases make the bailee exercise utmost care over property entrusted for the bailee's benefit, ordinary care over property

entrusted for mutual benefit of the bailee and bailor, and minimal care over involuntary bailments and property entrusted for the bailor's benefit. A bailee must, of course, return the property.

3. **Bailor's rights and obligations:** The bailor is entitled to receive the property back and is obligated by contract to pay any contractual charges associated with the bailment. If the bailment is involuntary, the bailor can sue third parties for property damage even if the third party has already paid the bailee. But if the bailment is voluntary, the bailor must look to the bailee, and cannot sue third parties who have already paid the bailee.

4. **Variation by contract:** These rules may be altered by contract.

B. **Gifts:** A gift is a voluntary transfer for no consideration. A gift is made when the donor intends to make a gift, the property is delivered to the donee, and the donee accepts the property.

1. **Gifts causa mortis:** A gift causa mortis is a gift in contemplation of death. A gift causa mortis is revocable if the donor recovers from the specific threat of death that prompted the gift.

2. **Gifts inter vivos:** An inter vivos gift is one made during life while not under any specific contemplation of death. Inter vivos gifts are irrevocable.

3. **Intent:** A donor must intend to transfer title, not just possession.

4. **Delivery:** The subject of the gift must be delivered to the donee. This usually means physical possession, but possession of some property is not easily transportable. Property may be delivered by ***deed,*** by ***symbolic delivery,*** or by ***constructive delivery.*** When actual physical possession is impossible or impractical, the delivery of something symbolic of possession is symbolic delivery. When actual physical possession is possible but impractical, delivery of an object that is the means of obtaining possession (e.g., a safe deposit key) is constructive delivery.

5. **Acceptance:** Delivery triggers a presumption of acceptance, which can be rebutted by the donee upon proof of the donee's rejection of the gift.

6. **Trusts:** Gifts to trusts are subject to special rules. The settlor/donor may create an irrevocable or revocable trust by conveying property to a trustee (the legal owner) for the benefit of named beneficiaries. While inter vivos gifts are normally irrevocable, a gift to a revocable trust is indeed revocable.

7. **Bank accounts:** There are special rules to govern the gift of bank accounts.

   a. **Power of attorney:** A depositor may give another person power of attorney to withdraw funds from the account, but banks often refuse to open such accounts.

   b. **Pay-on-death accounts:** POD accounts are payable on the depositor's death to a named person. These accounts were usually void at common law for want of delivery until death, when a will would be required to transfer title. But this rule has been altered by statute in many states.

   c. **Totten trusts:** A Totten trust is a POD account in the form of a trust, with the depositor as trustee for the death beneficiary but with the sole right to deal with the account during life. It was popular when POD accounts were generally void because the gift to the depositor as trustee was completed during life.

   d. **Joint tenancy:** Two or more people may own a bank account as joint tenants, which creates a right of survivorship. But the joint tenants have equal right to the funds during life, which may not be the depositor's desire.

C. **Bona fide purchasers:** Generally, a person may only transfer the title he has. But a bona fide purchaser may acquire better title than the seller had. A BFP is somebody who pays good value, does not know that the seller lacks good title, and has a good faith belief that the seller is a true owner. The exceptions to the general rule in favor of BFPs include negotiable instruments, purchases from a merchant who deals in the type of goods if the property has been entrusted to the merchant for sale, and where the seller has voidable title.

CHAPTER 2
FREEHOLD ESTATES

I. POSSESSORY ESTATES

A. Introduction: An owner of land owns an *estate in land,* not the land itself. A possessory estate is the right to possess the land now, as opposed to a future interest, which is a present right to possess the land at some time in the future. Possessory estates are divided into *freehold estates* and *non-freehold* or *leasehold* estates.

B. The types of freehold estates: There are four basic types of freehold estates: the *fee simple,* the *fee tail,* the two *defeasible fees,* and the *life estate.* The most important of these is the fee simple, closely followed by the life estate. The principal difference between each of these types of freehold estates is the *duration of the estate.*

II. FEE SIMPLE ABSOLUTE

A fee simple absolute is of perpetual duration. It has no natural end. It is the form of ownership that non-lawyers think of when they think of ownership.

A. Creation: At common law a fee simple absolute was created only by use of words indicating that the estate was capable of indefinite inheritance — "to A and her heirs." The words "to A" are words of purchase (indicating who owns the estate created) and the words "and her heirs" are words of limitation (indicating the perpetual duration of the estate created). Today, no magic words are required. A grantor conveys his entire estate unless the grant is to the contrary.

B. Alienability and inheritance: A fee simple absolute is freely alienable, inheritable through intestacy, and can be devised by will. Inheritance is a term of art that refers to intestate succession — the succession that occurs by operation of law when a person dies intestate, or without a will. If a person dies with a will, his takers under the will are called devisees.

III. FEE TAIL

The fee tail is virtually extinct. Only a few states recognize it. Most of the problems surrounding the fee tail involve how to treat a grant that would at common law have created a fee tail.

A. Creation: The fee tail was created by a grant "to A and the heirs of his body." The words "to A" described the owner of the fee tail estate. The words "and the heirs of his body" described the duration of the estate — until all the lineal descendants of A have died. A fee tail endures until the bloodline of the initial taker has run out. Because there is a natural end to this estate every fee tail is followed by a future interest — either a reversion in the grantor or a remainder in somebody else.

B. Modern destruction: There are five methods by which American states today either destroy the fee tail or permit its destruction.

  1. **Fee simple absolute:** Most states statutorily convert anything that would have been a fee tail into fee simple absolute and simply destroy any remainders or reversions.

  2. **Fee simple subject to executory limitation:** Some states convert the fee tail into a fee simple, and convert any remainder into an executory interest that lapses if the first

taker of the fee simple dies with surviving issue, leaving the first taker's estate with fee simple absolute. If the first taker dies without surviving issue, the executory interest becomes a possessory fee simple absolute.

3. **Life estate with remainder in life tenant's heirs:** A few states convert the fee tail into a life estate in the first taker, followed by a remainder in the first taker's heirs. This essentially allows the fee tail to persist for one generation only.

4. **Fee simple conditional:** Two or three states hold that a fee tail is, instead, a fee simple conditional, an estate that predated the fee tail. The fee simple conditional is identical to a fee tail except that if a child is born to the estate holder the estate holder has the power to convey fee simple absolute by an ordinary conveyance. Once a child is born to the owner of a fee simple conditional, it is easy to convert title into fee simple absolute by conveyance to a straw man and back again.

5. **Fee tail subject to the disentailing conveyance:** A handful of states continue to recognize the fee tail, but they provide that the holder of a fee tail can destroy it by a conveyance during life. Unlike fee simple conditional, the holder need not have children to do so.

IV. DEFEASIBLE FEES

Any estate may be defeasible — subject to termination — upon the happening of a specified event. There are two types of defeasible fees simple — the ***fee simple determinable*** and the ***fee simple subject to a condition subsequent.*** The basic difference is that the fee simple determinable ***terminates automatically*** when the future event occurs and the fee simple subject to a condition subsequent ***terminates only when the holder of the power of termination or executory interest exercises it.***

A. **Fee simple determinable:** This interest is created when the grantor conveys the property only for a limited time — until the specified future event occurs. "You can have this property only for so long as you farm it." This intent is usually implied from the language of the grant. If the grant is only "for so long as ..." or only "until ...," the grantor is thought to have parted with title only provisionally. When a fee simple determinable is carved out of a fee simple absolute something necessarily is left over. If that leftover is kept by the grantor it is called a ***possibility of reverter.*** If it is sent to a third party it is an ***executory interest.*** A fee simple determinable is freely transferable. It has been abolished in two states.

B. **Fee simple subject to a condition subsequent:** This interest is created when the grantor makes an unrestricted grant and then follows it with an attached string. "Here's your property. Oh, by the way, I want it back if you ever stop farming it." In form it looks like a grant of fee absolute followed by a condition subsequent. Telltale language includes such usage as "provided, however ..." or "but if ..." or "but in the event ..." or "on condition that ...." When a fee simple subject to a condition subsequent is carved out of a fee simple absolute, the interest left over is called a ***power of termination*** or ***right of entry*** if retained by the grantor. It is an executory interest if created in a third party. The holder of the power of termination or executory interest following this fee must take substantial steps to recover possession and title in order to terminate the defeasible fee. When the grant is ambiguous, most courts prefer the fee simple subject to a condition subsequent because it avoids the automatic forfeiture of the fee simple determinable. The fee simple subject to a condition subsequent is freely transferable.

C. **Fee simple subject to executory limitation:** Either form of defeasible fee, when subject to an executory interest, is called a fee simple subject to executory limitation.

D. **Some consequences of defeasible fees:** The type of defeasible fee created may have some significant consequences.

1. **Limited transferability of the grantor's interest:** At common law neither a possibility of reverter nor power of termination could be alienated or devised. They were only inheritable. These restrictions still exist in some states.

2. **Running of the adverse possession limitations statute:** The statute of limitations for adverse possession begins to run at different times.

   a. **Determinable fee:** Once the limitation occurs the determinable fee immediately expires. Continued possession by the holder of the determinable fee is wrongful, so the owner's cause of action accrues and the limitations statute starts to run at that moment.

   b. **Fee simple subject to a condition subsequent:** Even though the condition has occurred, continued possession is not wrongful until and unless the holder of the power of termination has exercised it. Unless the limitations statute specifies to the contrary, it starts to run only when the power of termination is exercised. But the equitable doctrine of laches may cut off the ability of the holder of power of termination to exercise it if she fails to do so for an unduly long time.

3. **Rule Against Perpetuities:** A possibility of reverter and a power of termination are each exempt from the Rule Against Perpetuities. But the analogous executory interests are not, and will likely be destroyed by the Rule.

V. LIFE ESTATES

A. **Nature:** A life estate is a possessory estate that expires on the death of a specified person. A life estate is usually for the life of the holder of the estate but can be for the life of somebody other than the owner of the life estate, in which case it is called a life estate *pur autre vie*. A life estate, being less than a fee simple, is always followed by either a **reversion** in the grantor or a **remainder** in a third party. As with any estate, a life estate may be defeasible. A life estate is freely alienable. Of course, only the life estate *pur autre vie* may be inherited or devised.

B. **Legal and equitable life estates:** Almost all life estates today are *equitable* — they consist of a beneficial or economic interest in assets legally owned by a trustee. Legal life estates are rare and a bad idea, because a life estate is simply not as easily marketable as a fee simple absolute. A trustee owns fee simple absolute, albeit for the benefit of the trust beneficiaries. So the trustee can sell trust assets and buy new ones, thus achieving more flexibility and greater economic returns for the trust beneficiaries.

   1. **Judicial intervention into legal life estates:** Courts may order sale of the legal life estate and the remainder (which together form fee simple absolute) if sale is (1) in the best interest of all parties and consistent with the grantor's intent, or (2) necessary to avoid waste.

C. **Waste:** When ownership is divided between a life tenant and a remainderman, interests conflict. The life tenant has the economic use of property for life, and the remainderman owns its future economic value. A life tenant commits waste if she uses the property now in a fashion that permanently impairs its future economic value. A life tenant is liable to the remainderman for waste.

VI. RESTRAINTS ON ALIENATION OF FREEHOLD ESTATES

A. **General rule:** Restraints on alienation of freehold estates are generally void. Total restraints are always void. Partial restraints may be valid if they are for a reasonable purpose and limited in duration.

B. **Types of restraints:** Restraints may be couched in the form of a **forfeiture** if alienation is attempted, as a **disabling** restraint (no power to convey granted), or as a **promissory** restraint (grantee promises not to alienate). The forfeiture restraint is viewed with most skepticism. Restrictions on use can be so restrictive that they amount to a restraint on alienation. Some restraints on alienation are unenforceable because they violate constitutional law (e.g., racial restrictions on alienation).

C. Spendthrift trusts: An exception to the general rule against restraints on alienation is the *spendthrift trust*. Assets are conveyed to a trustee for the benefit of a "spendthrift," subject to the disabling restraint that the spendthrift cannot alienate the trust assets until they are disbursed to him by the trustee. This makes the trust assets unreachable by the spendthrift's creditors.

Chapter 3
LEASEHOLD ESTATES

I. THE NATURE OF LEASES

A. Non-freehold estate and contract: The lease started out as a non-freehold estate, probably a device to avoid usury limits. Now it is a hybrid — both a non-freehold property estate and a contract. A lease is thus simultaneously a conveyance of an estate and a package of bilateral promises. Leases of residential property are more apt to be seen as primarily contracts than commercial leases, but all leases have the dual quality of both property estate and contract.

B. The requirement of a writing: By statute, all American states require that long-term leases (usually for a year or more) must be in writing to be valid. But if possession is transferred under an invalid oral lease, and rent is tendered and accepted, some form of tenancy has been created by those actions.

C. The possessory interest of the lessee: A lessee has all the rights of possession that the fee owner has. A lessee may recover for invasion of his possession through ejectment, trespass, or nuisance.

II. TYPES OF LEASEHOLDS

A. Term of years: A lease for a single, fixed term of any length is a lease for a term of years. A term may be "indeterminate" in the sense that it is not precisely stated, so long as the length of the term can be readily computed by reference to some formula. But if the term is of indefinite duration a tenancy at will may be created. But a term of years may be made defeasible on the occurrence of some uncertain future event.

B. Periodic tenancy: A periodic tenancy is a lease for a recurring period of time and continues in existence until either party gives advance notice to the other of termination. Common law required 6 months advance notice to terminate a year-to-year tenancy and notice equal to the period for periods of 6 months or less. These advance notice requirements have been significantly altered by statute, usually to make the notice period no more than a month. Periodic tenancies may be created by agreement or by operation of law. When created by operation of law there is often difficulty in deciding what the period is, but the issue is usually resolved by observing how frequently the rent is paid and using that recurring period.

C. Tenancy at will: A tenancy at will is a leasehold for no fixed time or period and lasts only as long as both parties desire. It may be terminated at any time by either party. It may be created by agreement or by operation of law. A tenancy for a defined period — either periodic of for a term of years — that is terminable whenever one party wishes is a determinable periodic tenancy or term, but is ***not a tenancy at will***. But a tenancy of uncertain duration that is terminable whenever one party wishes may be a tenancy at will, though many courts regard such a tenancy as a determinable leasehold life estate.

D. Holdovers:

1. **Tenancy at sufferance:** A tenant that stays on in possession after the term has expired is no longer a lawful tenant. The "holdover" is a tenant at sufferance — a legal limbo between the status of trespasser and lawful tenant — until the landlord decides how to treat the holdover. Within a reasonable time the landlord must elect either (1) to ***evict and recover dam-***

ages for lost possession or (2) to **bind the holdover to a new term as a tenant**. A tenant is a holdover unless the tenant's continued possession after expiration of the term is due to circumstances beyond the tenant's control. If the landlord elects to evict and recover damages the general measure of damages is the fair market value of possession. If the landlord elects to bind the tenant to a new term most states treat the new tenancy as a periodic tenancy defined by the rent payment period. Once made, an election of remedies is irrevocable. A few states provide for a double or treble rent penalty as the exclusive landlord remedy for holdovers.

III. DELIVERY OF POSSESSION

A. **Landlord obligation to deliver legal right to possession:** A landlord must deliver to the tenant the legal right to possess the leased premises. This means that the landlord promises that the tenant will not be evicted by somebody with a better title to the premises than the landlord. The tenant can waive this right, either explicitly or by taking possession with knowledge of a paramount title.

B. **Landlord obligation to deliver actual possession:** The English rule (adopted by most American states) imposes on landlords the obligation to deliver actual possession to the tenant. The so-called American rule (but a minority rule in the U.S.) holds that a landlord is not obliged to deliver actual possession. Under the English rule a landlord has the right and duty to evict holdovers and is liable to the new tenant for damages for lack of possession. Under the American rule the burden of evicting a holdover falls entirely on the new tenant.

C. **Tenant obligation to take possession:** A tenant has no obligation to take possession, unless the lease expressly requires a tenant to do so.

IV. SUBLEASES AND ASSIGNMENTS

A. **Essential distinction between the two:** An *assignment* places the assignee in *privity of estate* with the landlord, which means that the assignee is personally responsible for performance of those obligations in the assigned lease that "run" with the leasehold estate. A *sublease*, by contrast, does not create privity of estate between the landlord and the subtenant, so the subtenant is liable only to the sublessor for performance of the sublease. An assignment occurs when the assignor conveys his entire remaining estate to the assignee. A sublease occurs when the original tenant transfers anything less than his entire remaining interest in the leasehold estate. In both cases, however, the assignor or sublessor remains in *privity of contract* with the landlord and thus continues to be liable for performance of the original lease, unless the landlord has released the original tenant from his obligations. Neither an assignee nor sublessee is in privity of contract with the landlord unless the assignee or sublessee *assumes* the obligations of the original lease.

B. **Lease covenants that run:** A lease covenant runs with the leasehold estate and thus binds the assignee if the promise is *intended to run*, the assignee is in *privity* of estate or contract with the party seeking to enforce the covenant, the substance of the covenant *touches and concerns* the use or enjoyment of the estate, and the assignee has *notice* of the covenant. Personal promises do not run.

C. **Restrictions on transfer:** A tenant is free to transfer his leasehold unless the lease restricts that right. Landlords commonly condition assignment or sublease on their consent to the transfer. But landlords may not deny consent for reasons that constitute unlawful discrimination, nor may landlords in commercial leases unreasonably deny consent. The test of "reasonableness" is objective; at the very least landlords may not deny consent to reap an unrelated commercial advantage.

V. TENANT'S OBLIGATIONS

A. **Defined by the lease:** A tenant's obligations are defined by the lease. The principal duties follow, but just about any duty can be imposed by the lease.

1. **Pay the rent:** This used to be an *independent obligation,* which meant that the tenant had to pay rent no matter what the landlord failed to do. Most American states today treat this obligation as *dependent* upon the landlord's performance of his obligations. This is especially true of residential leases. The amount of the rent is almost always stipulated; otherwise it is the reasonable rental value.

2. **Avoid waste:** The tenant is obligated to avoid waste. This consists of two components — the *duty to repair* and the *duty to avoid damage.*

   a. **Duty to repair:** This was a tenant obligation at common law but most states today have, by statute, made it a landlord obligation in residential leases. Otherwise it may be apportioned however the parties wish.

   b. **Duty to avoid damage:** Voluntary acts of the tenant that substantially damage the premises constitute waste. The tenant is liable for such actions.

3. **Refrain from illegal uses:** A tenant may not use the premises for illegal purposes. If the landlord either intends such use or knows of it the lease is unenforceable. If a landlord is ignorant of illegal use he may terminate the lease once he learns of the activity.

4. **No nuisance:** A tenant has the duty not to use the premises to commit a nuisance.

B. **Excuse:** At common law there were no excuses permitted, but today a tenant is excused from his obligations under a variety of circumstances. The most important ones follow.

1. **Sole use becomes illegal:** If the tenant has bargained for one specific use that later becomes illegal the tenant is excused from further performance. This excuse is not available if the tenant has not bargained for one specific use (now illegal) and the premises may reasonably be used in a legal manner.

2. **Destruction of the premises:** A tenant may terminate the lease if the premises are destroyed, unless either (1) the destruction was caused by the tenant, or (2) the tenant has agreed in the lease that destruction is no excuse.

3. **Eminent domain:** A governmental taking of the premises automatically terminates the lease. The tenant is entitled to share in the compensation only to the extent the fair market value of the leasehold exceeds the rent obligation.

4. **Frustration of intended purpose:** In commercial leases only, a tenant may be excused if (1) *extreme hardship* would result from (2) a third party's *unforeseeable action* that (3) makes the *mutually intended purpose* (4) *virtually impossible* to accomplish.

VI. LANDLORD REMEDIES

A. **Remedies usually derived from the lease:** Landlords create many of their remedies in the lease. Some important ones follow.

1. **Rent acceleration:** A rent acceleration clause makes the entire remaining rent for the term of the lease immediately payable upon a tenant default under the lease. Usually these clauses give the landlord the option of accelerating rent.

2. **Security deposits:** The landlord may demand a deposit from the tenant, at the inception of the lease, as security for the tenant's performance of the lease obligations.

3. **Liquidated damages:** A lease may provide for liquidated damages. Such clauses are valid if the amount of liquidated damages is reasonably related to the probable damages but the actual damages are capable of easy determination.

4. **Confession of judgment:** These clauses, which stipulate that upon default the tenant waives service of process and authorizes a landlord nominee to confess judgment, are widely prohibited by statute and of doubtful validity even where permitted.

B. **Remedies derived from statute or common law:** Statutory and common law provide a number of additional remedies, summarized here.

1. **Eviction:** By statute, a landlord is permitted to terminate the lease and evict the tenant for non-payment of rent and occasionally for breach of other lease covenants.

    a. **Unlawful detainer:** The usual method of eviction is by a summary judicial proceeding known as unlawful detainer or forcible entry and detainer. In this proceeding, which is handled expeditiously, the only issue is entitlement to possession.

    b. **Ejectment:** The old common law action for ejectment is also available but this suit is not a summary proceeding, which means that there is no calendar preference and the tenant can raise issues that go beyond the right to possession.

    c. **Landlord self-help:** Some states absolutely forbid self-help, while others permit it so long as the landlord acts peaceably or does not use unreasonable force.

2. **Tenant abandonment:** A tenant abandonment is an offer to surrender the lease, which the landlord may (1) accept and thus terminate the lease, (2) reject and leave the premises untouched, or (3) reject but retake possession and relet the premises on behalf of the tenant. If the landlord accepts the surrender and terminates, the tenant is liable for unpaid rent up to the moment of termination plus damages created by the abandonment. If the landlord rejects and leaves the premises untouched the tenant remains liable for the rent. Some jurisdictions require the landlord, even if he rejects surrender, to retake possession and relet the premises to mitigate damages.

3. **Seizure of tenant's personal property:** Common law permitted landlords to seize and hold the tenant's personal property until the tenant cured his default. This right is substantially limited by statute today.

VII. LANDLORD'S OBLIGATIONS AND TENANT'S REMEDIES

A. **Source of obligations and remedies:** These landlord obligations and correlative tenant remedies are rooted in the lease, or imposed by law.

1. **Quiet enjoyment:** A landlord has a duty imposed by law to refrain from the wrongful actual or constructive eviction of the tenant.

    a. **Actual total eviction:** A tenant who is wrongfully physically ousted from the entire premises may terminate the lease with no further liability.

    b. **Actual partial eviction:** The traditional rule is that a wrongful eviction from any part of the premises entitles the tenant to abate rent entirely until the tenant is restored to full possession. The modern view is that the tenant should be entitled to a partial rent abatement, reflecting the reasonable value of the lost possession.

    c. **Constructive eviction:** If a landlord wrongly interferes with the tenant's use and enjoyment of the premises so substantially that the intended purpose of the tenant's occupation is frustrated, a ***constructive eviction*** has occurred. The tenant may move out and thus terminate the lease with no further liability. The landlord must interfere, not someone else. Before vacating the premises the tenant must notify the landlord and give him a reasonable chance to fix the problem. Of course, if a tenant vacates and a court later determines that there was no constructive eviction the tenant has abandoned.

2. **Warranty of habitability:** The traditional rule is that the landlord makes no warranty that the premises are suitable for the tenant's purposes. The modern (albeit minority) trend is to imply into every residential lease a warranty that the premises are habitable.

This implied warranty consists of a warranty of habitability at the inception of the lease and a continued obligation to repair as necessary to maintain habitability. The tenant may not waive this warranty. The implied warranty of habitability is often codified by statute.

  a. **Tenant remedies:** Upon breach of the implied warranty of habitability a tenant has the following remedies.

    i. **Terminate and leave:** In addition, the tenant may recover damages, if any.

    ii. **Stay and withhold rent:** If the tenant exercises this remedy, he must deposit rent into an escrow account pending landlord repair of the defects.

    iii. **Stay and repair:** The tenant may stay in possession and use a reasonable portion of the rent to make repairs.

    iv. **Stay and recover damages:** The tenant may remain in possession and recover damages in the form of a rent abatement or deduction. The measure of damages is either (1) the difference between the warranted value and actual "as-is" value, (2) the difference between stated rent and actual "as-is" value, or (3) a reduction in stated rent equal to the proportion by which warranted value has been reduced.

    v. **Stay and defend:** The tenant can stay and prove the uninhabitable condition as a complete defense to an eviction action based on tenant failure to pay rent.

3. **Retaliatory eviction:** Usually the landlord's motivation for seeking eviction is irrelevant, but if a landlord seeks eviction in retaliation for a tenant's assertion of the habitability warranty, many jurisdictions will deny eviction. The tenant must prove retaliatory motive and the remedy is available only to a tenant who is not in default. A landlord may evict after a retaliatory motive has been found only if the landlord can prove an independent good business reason for it. Nor may a landlord use indirect methods of eviction, like drastic reductions of services.

4. **Tort liability of landlords:** Modern law places greater duties on landlords to maintain leased premises in a fashion that avoids foreseeable injury to others. This is merely a subset of the tort doctrine of negligence.

  a. **Pre-existing dangerous conditions:** At common law a landlord had no tort liability for pre-existing dangerous conditions unless they were *latent defects* known to the landlord, and the landlord had failed to warn of the defects.

  b. **Conditions occurring during lease term:** A landlord generally has no liability for injuries resulting from conditions occurring after the tenant has taken possession, unless the landlord has undertaken a duty of repair.

  c. **Common areas:** Landlords are liable for injuries resulting from their negligence with respect to common areas that remain under landlord control.

  d. **Landlord duty to repair:** Many jurisdictions impose on the landlord a duty to repair, especially in residential leases.

  e. **No special rules:** About ten states hold landlords to the same duties as anyone else, finding landlords liable when they have failed to act as a reasonable person under the circumstances.

VIII. FIXTURES

Fixtures — personal property permanently attached to the premises — belong to the landlord, but *trade fixtures* — personal property that is used in carrying on a trade or business, may be removed by the tenant, who retains ownership.

IX. SOCIAL REGULATIONS OF LEASEHOLDS

A. Rent control: Rent control laws, usually adopted at the local level, consist of price controls often augmented by limitations on the landlord's ability to evict tenants at the end of the lease term. So long as the landlord is able to earn a reasonable rate of return on his investment, rent control statutes do not constitute a governmental taking of property without just compensation.

B. Anti-discrimination statutes: Federal, state, and local laws substantially restrict the landlord's common law right to decide with whom he wished to deal. These laws prohibit most private acts of racial discrimination in the sale or rental of real property. Probably the most important such statute is the federal Fair Housing Act, which exempts (1) the sale or lease of a single family house without use of brokers or public advertisements that reveal discriminatory motive and (2) rentals of residential housing in owner-occupied units of four units or less.

CHAPTER 4

FUTURE INTERESTS

I. INTRODUCTION

A. Definitions: A future interest is a legal interest in property that is *not possessory* but which is *capable of becoming possessory some time in the future.* A future interest is a *presently existing* property interest to a *future right to possession.* Future interests may be created in the transferor or the transferee. Future interests created in the transferor are one of three types: a *reversion,* a *possibility of reverter,* or a *right of entry* (also known as a *power of termination*). Future interests created in a transferee may be either a *remainder* or an *executory interest.* A remainder may be either *vested* or *contingent.* A contingent remainder is subject to one or both of two uncertainties: (1) its owner is *unknown* or (2) there is a *condition precedent* to ultimate possession (other than the natural expiration of the preceding possessory estate). Executory interests are either *shifting* or *springing.* A shifting executory interest *divests* (cuts off) a future or possessory interest of another transferee. A springing executory interest divests the grantor's interest at some future time.

II. FUTURE INTERESTS RETAINED BY THE GRANTOR

A. Reversion: When a grantor conveys a lesser estate than what he originally owned, a reversion in the grantor is created. Reversions are freely alienable, inheritable, and devisable. Reversions are always vested when created.

B. Possibility of reverter: A possibility of reverter is created whenever the grantor conveys his estate upon a *determinable limitation.* A determinable limitation is a limit upon the duration of the conveyance, as when the grantor conveys for only "so long as" a given event does not occur or, phrased positively, only "until" the occurrence of a given event. The estate conveyed "determines" or *expires automatically* when the limiting event occurs. A possibility of reverter is created only in the grantor, never in a transferee. The analogous interest in a transferee is called an executory interest.

1. **Transferability:** At common law a possibility of reverter could *only be inherited*; it could not be transferred inter vivos or by will. Today, most (but not all) states permit a possibility of reverter to be freely transferred or devised.

2. **Termination:** Because a possibility of reverter is vested when created it cannot be destroyed by the Rule Against Perpetuities, and so can endure forever. Some states have, by statute, provided that a possibility of reverter expires some specified number of years

after its creation. A few of those states permit a possibility of reverter to be kept alive for an additional period by recording a notice of its continuation.

3. **Eminent domain:** When property in which there is a possibility of reverter is taken by eminent domain, most states give the entire condemnation award to the owner of the fee, but a few require sharing.

4. **Abolition:** A few states have abolished the possibility of reverter and its correlative possessory estate. In these states, attempts to create a determinable possessory estate will result in a possessory estate subject to a condition subsequent. The possibility of reverter that would otherwise result is turned into a right of entry (a/k/a power of termination).

C. **Right of entry (power of termination):** A right of entry (power of termination) is created whenever the grantor conveys his estate subject to a retained right to cut short the transferred interest upon the occurrence of some specified future event. This interest may only be created in the grantor. The analogous interest created in a transferee is called an executory interest. Issues of transferability, termination, and eminent domain are the same as for the possibility of reverter.

III. FUTURE INTERESTS CREATED IN GRANTEES

A. **Remainders:** A remainder is a future interest created in a grantee that will become possessory (if at all) upon the *natural expiration* of the preceding possessory estate. Remainders never divest another interest. A *vested remainder* is certain to become possessory. A *contingent remainder* has only the possibility of becoming possessory. The term "remainder" identifies the type of future interest, but a remainder is a future interest in some estate, whether it be fee simple, fee tail, a life estate, or a term of years.

1. **Vested remainders:** A remainder is vested if it is created in a known person and ultimate possession is not subject to any condition subsequent. It must necessarily become possessory upon the natural expiration of the preceding estate.

    a. **Indefeasibly vested remainders:** An indefeasibly vested remainder is certain to become and remain possessory. It cannot be divested in whole or in part.

    b. **Vested remainders subject to complete divestment:** A vested remainder subject to complete divestment is one created in a known person and not subject to any condition precedent, but which is either (1) subject to a condition subsequent that, upon occurrence, will completely divest the remainderman of his interest or (2) subject to destruction because of some inherent limit in the estate held in remainder.

    c. **Vested remainders subject to partial divestment:** A vested remainder subject to open (also called partial divestment) is a remainder created in a class (or group) of people, at least one of whom is known and presently entitled to possession as soon as the preceding estate expires. Because the class of grantees is capable of including others, the class is "open" and so the vested remainder is subject to partial divestment in favor of possible new entrants into the open class.

        i. **Class-closing rules:** A class closes upon the sooner of two events: (1) it is no longer possible to have new entrants or (2) under the *"rule of convenience"* any member of the class is entitled to immediate possession. The rule of convenience is a presumption that the grantor intended this consequence and can be rebutted by contrary evidence. When it applies it causes a class to close around all living members of the class, whether or not they are all entitled to immediate possession.

2. **Contingent remainders:** A contingent remainder is a remainder created in an unknown person or that has a condition precedent to ultimate possession. The natural expiration of the preceding estate is not a condition precedent. The condition must be expressed. Sometimes the same condition precedent can be used in the alternative (e.g., "to Jane if she marries, but if she never marries, to Elizabeth"). This formulation creates *alternative contingent*

remainders. Although the common law did not generally permit contingent remainders to be transferred, that is no longer the case.

B. **Executory interests:** Executory interests are future interests in a grantee that divest either (1) another grantee's possessory or future interest (a ***"shifting executory interest"***), or (2) the grantor's interest at some future time (a ***"springing executory interest"***). By nature, the possibility of possession inherent in an executory interest is contingent upon the occurrence of an uncertain future event — the divesting condition.

   1. **Shifting executory interest:** A shifting executory interest divests an interest held by another transferee from the grantor. It cuts short, or divests, that other interest. It "shifts" the interest from one transferee to another.

   2. **Springing executory interest:** A springing executory interest is a future interest created in a grantee that cuts short the grantor's interest at some future time after the conveyance. It "springs" out of the grantor.

IV. MARKETABILITY RULES

A. **Destructibility of contingent remainders:** At common law, a contingent remainder in land was destroyed if, at the expiration of the preceding freehold estate, it was still contingent. This rule is virtually extinct today. Its function — increasing the marketability of land — has been supplanted by the Rule Against Perpetuities. It was never very effective because there were a number of ways to avoid its application.

B. **The Rule in Shelley's Case:** This rule dates from the 16th century and was designed to stop avoidance of feudal death taxes. That function is of no modern relevance. To the extent that the rule improved the marketability of land its function has been supplanted by the Rule Against Perpetuities. It is virtually extinct today.

   1. **The rule:** If (1) one instrument (2) creates a freehold in real property and (3) a remainder in the freeholder's ***heirs*** (or the heirs of his body), and (4) the freehold estate and the remainder are ***both equitable or both legal,*** then (5) the remainder becomes a remainder in the freeholder.

   2. **The practical effect of the rule:** The merger doctrine — under which the possessory estate and the immediately following future interest (if vested) are merged together — caused the destruction of most remainders subject to the Rule. But not all — like destructibility, the Rule in Shelley's Case was riddled with exceptions.

C. **Worthier title:** This doctrine is still observed by many American states. If an ***inter vivos*** conveyance creates ***any future interest*** in the ***heirs of the grantor*** the future interest is ***void.*** The grantor retains a ***reversion*** instead. The doctrine is a rule of construction, raising a rebuttable presumption that the grantor did not intend to create a future interest in her heirs. By contrast, the destructibility rule and the Rule in Shelley's Case are rules of law. Worthier title is very broad — it applies to both real and personal property, to any kind of future interest regardless of the nature of the preceding estate.

D. **Rule Against Perpetuities:** This is today's all purpose rule of law, designed to destroy any future interest that could remain uncertain of ultimate possession after the elapse of a defined period of time from its creation.

   1. **The rule:** A future interest is void unless all uncertainty as to whether it will ultimately become possessory is removed no later than twenty-one years after the end of some life in being at the creation of the interest. The classic statement of the rule is: "No interest is good unless it must vest, if at all, not later than twenty-one years after some life in being at the creation of the interest."

      a. **Possibilities, not probabilities:** In its common law form, the rule is concerned with the ***possibility*** of remote vesting, not its probability. Put another way, the rule is concerned about the mere possibility that uncertainty as to whether the future interest will ultimately become possessory will continue past the permitted period of the rule.

- **b. Vesting in interest, not possession:** The rule is concerned about when future interests *vest in interest* — when uncertainty as to *ultimate possession is removed* — rather than when they actually become possessory, or vest in possession.

- **c. Vesting — removal of uncertainty:** A vested interest is certain to become possessory, so no uncertainty attaches to its ownership. With one exception, a vested interest means the same thing for purposes of the Rule Against Perpetuities as it does for purposes of classification of future interests. However, a *vested remainder subject to open* is *not vested for perpetuities purposes until the interest of every possible member of the open class is vested.* This rule is but an application of a more general rule that *no interest in any member of a class is good unless the interest of every possible member of the class is good.*

- **d. Permitted period of uncertainty:** An interest is good under the Rule if it will *certainly vest or certainly fail to vest* within (1) 21 years from its creation, or (2) during the life of some person alive at its creation, or (3) upon the death of some person alive at its creation, or (4) within 21 years after the death of some person alive at its creation. You must prove that the interest in question will vest *or* fail to vest within this period. If you cannot, or if you can illustrate any possible way in which the uncertainty might persist longer than the perpetuities period, the interest is void.

    - **i. Validating life:** To prove validity, you must identify some person (or class of persons) alive on the effective date of the grant whose life (or lives) can serve to validate the interest. If you use a class of persons the class must be closed on the effective date of the grant in order to be a life in being. If there is any possibility that the class could include someone born after the grant, the class is not a life in being. The validating life is almost always someone who is germane to the interests created by the grant.

- **e. All future interests covered:** The rule applies to all future interests, though some future interests (e.g., those retained by the grantor) are vested at creation and so always valid under the Rule. By contrast, executory interests are always contingent, since ultimate possession hinges on occurrence of the divesting event.

- **f. Validity tested at creation:** The common law Rule tests the validity of the interests created at the moment of their creation, even if the actual moment of judicial decision is years later. The common law Rule is only concerned about *possibilities*, not about probabilities, nor even about what has actually happened.

2. **Defeasible fees and the following future interests:** A defeasible fee creates a retained interest in the grantor, which interest is vested and thus valid under the Rule. But the same fee can be followed by an executory interest instead of a retained interest in the grantor. That executory interest is not vested, and thus subject to the Rule. There are three statutory remedies to this inconsistency.

    - **a. Apply the Rule to everything:** The U.K. applies the Rule to possibilities of reverter and rights of entry as well as to executory interests following a defeasible fee.

    - **b. Statutory destruction of the grantor's interest:** Some American states continue to regard the grantor's retained interest as vested but destroy it by a statute, independent of the Rule, that voids possibilities of reverter or rights of entry some specified number of years after their creation. Some states vary this theme by permitting the grantor to keep the interest alive by periodic recordation of a notice of continuation. In this scheme, executory interests following a defeasible fee remain subject to the Rule.

    - **c. Statutory destruction of all interests:** Some American states exempt all interests following a defeasible fee (whether retained by the grantor or created in a transferee) but subject them all to a statutory rule of destruction. These states also permit the holder of

 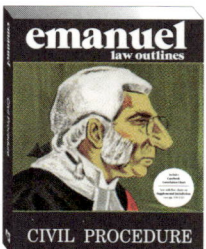 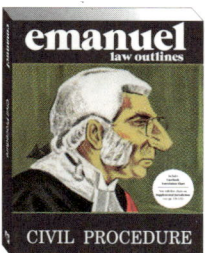

Thank you for purchasing an Emanuel title!

These bookmarks can be detached and used as you read.

If you have any comments on any of our books or flashcards, please feel free to e-mail them to **comments@emanuel.com**.

Send in the card at right to to receive our current catalog, to get on our mailing list, or for information on becoming an **Emanuel Student Rep** at your school!

Emanuel does not sell its mailing lists to anyone.

 I want to learn more about Emanuel!

❏ **Send me your current catalog**
❏ **Add me to your regular mailing list**
❏ **Add me to your e-mail list**
❏ **I'd like information about becoming an Emanuel Student Rep at my school**

|_____|_____|
Name   E-mail address (e.g., johndoe@school.edu)

|_____|_____|_____|_____|
Address   City   State   ZIP Code

|_____|_____|
Law school attended   Graduation Year

|_____|
Telephone Number

Visit us on the Internet at http://www.emanuel.com

emanuel®

First Year Products   E L S P
- Civil Procedure
- Civil Procedure 2
- Constitutional Law
- Contracts
- Criminal Law
- Criminal Procedure
- Future Interests
- Property
- Torts

Upper Year Products
- Agency & Partnership
- Bankruptcy
- Constitutional Law
- Corporations
- Criminal Procedure
- Environmental Law
- Evidence
- Family Law
- Federal Income Taxation
- Future Interests
- Intellectual Property
- International Law
- Labor Law
- Neg. Inst. & Pmt. Systems
- Products Liability
- Prof. Responsibility
- Sales (UCC Art. 2)
- Secured Transactions
- Wills & Trusts

E - Emanuel Law Outlines
L - Law In A Flash flashcards & software
S - Siegel's Essay & M/C Q&A's
P - The Professor Series

Strategies & Tactics Series
Strategies & Tactics for First Year Law
Strategies & Tactics for the MBE
Strategies & Tactics for the MPRE
The Finz Multistate Method

Steve Emanuel's 1st Year Q&A's

emanuel®

First Year Products   E L S P
- Civil Procedure
- Civil Procedure 2
- Constitutional Law
- Contracts
- Criminal Law
- Criminal Procedure
- Future Interests
- Property
- Torts

Upper Year Products
- Agency & Partnership
- Bankruptcy
- Constitutional Law
- Corporations
- Criminal Procedure
- Environmental Law
- Evidence
- Family Law
- Federal Income Taxation
- Future Interests
- Intellectual Property
- International Law
- Labor Law
- Neg. Inst. & Pmt. Systems
- Products Liability
- Prof. Responsibility
- Sales (UCC Art. 2)
- Secured Transactions
- Wills & Trusts

E - Emanuel Law Outlines
L - Law In A Flash flashcards & software
S - Siegel's Essay & M/C Q&A's
P - The Professor Series

Strategies & Tactics Series
Strategies & Tactics for First Year Law
Strategies & Tactics for the MBE
Strategies & Tactics for the MPRE
The Finz Multistate Method

Steve Emanuel's 1st Year Q&A's

emanuel®

First Year Products   E L S P
- Civil Procedure
- Civil Procedure 2
- Constitutional Law
- Contracts
- Criminal Law
- Criminal Procedure
- Future Interests
- Property
- Torts

Upper Year Products
- Agency & Partnership
- Bankruptcy
- Constitutional Law
- Corporations
- Criminal Procedure
- Environmental Law
- Evidence
- Family Law
- Federal Income Taxation
- Future Interests
- Intellectual Property
- International Law
- Labor Law
- Neg. Inst. & Pmt. Systems
- Products Liability
- Prof. Responsibility
- Sales (UCC Art. 2)
- Secured Transactions
- Wills & Trusts

E - Emanuel Law Outlines
L - Law In A Flash flashcards & software
S - Siegel's Essay & M/C Q&A's
P - The Professor Series

Strategies & Tactics Series
Strategies & Tactics for First Year Law
Strategies & Tactics for the MBE
Strategies & Tactics for the MPRE
The Finz Multistate Method

Steve Emanuel's 1st Year Q&A's

---

name: _____
address: _____
city: _____
state: _____ zip: _____

Place postage here.
The Post Office will not deliver without postage.

To: Emanuel Publishing Corp.
1865 Palmer Avenue, Suite 202
Larchmont, NY 10538
ATTN: BRC

the future interest to keep it alive indefinitely so long as a notice of continuation is recorded within each statutory period.

   d. **Charity-to-charity exemption:** By statute or judicial decision, many states exempt from the Rule an executory interest in a charity if the divested interest is also held by a charity.

3. **Reform doctrines:** There are several doctrines that ameliorate the harsh effects of the common law rule.

   a. **Wait-and-see:** This statutory reform, adopted in some form by about half the states, evaluates the validity of future interests as events actually unfold, rather than at the time the interests are created. "What-might-happen" is replaced by "what-did-happen." The most common form of "wait-and-see" is to wait for the period permitted by the common law Rule, if necessary. This means that you must wait, if necessary, for the expiration of all relevant lives in being at the creation of the grant, plus 21 years. Of course, if the uncertainty is removed before then, there is no need to wait any longer.

   b. **USRAP:** The Uniform Statutory Rule Against Perpetuities provides for waiting for up to 90 years after the creation of the future interest to see if it has vested within that time period. USRAP also provides that a future interest is valid if it will timely vest under either the common law rule or USRAP's wait-and-see for 90 years rule.

   c. **Construction:** Most modern courts will construe the instrument creating the future interests in a way that will avoid destruction of future interests by the Rule, if that construction is at all plausible.

   d. **Reformation:** Some modern courts will outright alter the instrument to make the interests created under it conform to the Rule, if such reformation is at all possible.

4. **Drafting issues:** Perpetuities problems can often be avoided in trusts by the simple expedient of a "savings clause," which provides for termination of the trust no later than 21 years after the expiration of all relevant lives in being at the creation of the trust.

5. **Commercial transactions:** The Rule applies to commercial option agreements that are open-ended. If an option is created with no fixed date for exercise it may well be void under the Rule because of the possibility that the option may not be exercised within the perpetuities period. A commercial option should always be tied to the life of somebody in existence, and if that is not possible, ought to expire by its terms no later than 21 years after creation.

CHAPTER 5
CONCURRENT OWNERSHIP AND MARITAL INTERESTS

I. FORMS OF CONCURRENT OWNERSHIP

Concurrent ownership occurs when the same property is owned by more than one person at the same time.

A. Tenancy in common: Tenants in common own separate but undivided interests in the same property. Each tenant in common has a fractional interest in the entire property, each is entitled to use and possess the property, but none can exclude her fellow owners. A tenancy in common interest may be alienated, devised, or inherited separately from the other tenancy in common interests. By statute or judicial decision, a tenancy in common is the presumed form of co-ownership, rebuttable by clear evidence of intention to create some other form of co-ownership. Property passing by intestacy to two or more heirs is always taken as tenants in common. There is a rebuttable presumption that tenants in common have equal shares.

B. Joint tenancy: The distinctive feature of a joint tenancy is the *right of survivorship. Upon the death of a joint tenant, the interest of the deceased joint tenant terminates.* Thus, if Blackacre is owned by A and B as joint tenants, upon the death of A Blackacre is owned solely by B. If Blackacre was owned by A, B, and C as joint tenants, upon the death of B Blackacre is owned by A and C as joint tenants. The theory of the joint tenancy is that each joint tenant owns an equal share in all of the property, so when one joint tenant dies nothing passes to the other joint tenants. The dead joint tenant's interest simply dies with him.

1. **The four unities:** At common law, the interests of joint tenants must be equal in every respect. To create a joint tenancy at common law, four unities must be present: (1) *time,* (2) *title,* (3) *interest,* and (4) *possession.*

   a. **Time:** Each joint tenant must acquire his interest at the same time.

   b. **Title:** All joint tenants must receive their interests under the same instrument. At common law it was impossible for a sole owner to convey to himself and another in joint tenancy, since the conveyance to himself was a nullity. This is commonly permitted by statute today.

   c. **Interest:** Each joint tenant must have the identical interest in the property, which means that each joint tenant must have (1) the same share of the undivided whole and (2) the same durational estate. However, it is possible for one fractional interest in property (e.g., 2/3) to be held by joint tenants and the remaining fractional interest to be held in tenancy in common, so long as the four unities are met as to the joint tenancy fraction. Thus, A and B can be joint tenants as to a 2/3 interest in Blackacre and tenants in common with C as to the remaining 1/3 interest.

   d. **Possession:** Upon creation of a joint tenancy each joint tenant must have the same right to possession of the whole property. After creation, joint tenants are free to allocate possession rights as they wish.

2. **Presumption against joint tenancy:** Today, every American state presumes that a conveyance to two or more people creates a tenancy in common, unless there is clear evidence of intent to create a joint tenancy.

3. **Severance of joint tenancy:** A joint tenant may destroy the joint tenancy at any time by conveyance of the joint tenant's interest. This severs the joint tenancy and creates a tenancy in common in its place.

   a. **Unilateral conveyance:** A conveyance by a joint tenant from himself to himself was not effective at common law to sever the joint tenancy, because such a conveyance was an empty act. At common law, you could not convey to yourself what you already owned. By statute or judicial decision, some American states now permit the unilateral conveyance.

   b. **Mortgages:** States differ as to whether the mortgage by one joint tenant of her interest severs the joint tenancy. States following the *title theory* of mortgages (a mortgage is a transfer of title subject to a condition subsequent) often (but not always) conclude that severance has occurred. States following the *lien theory* of mortgages (a mortgage is simply a lien on title) rule that no severance has occurred.

   c. **Leases:** Contrary to common law, most jurisdictions today hold that a lease by one joint tenant does not sever the joint tenancy. A corollary to that conclusion is that a lease from one joint tenant endures no longer than the life of the lessor joint tenant, even if the leasehold term purports to be longer.

   d. **Agreement:** A joint tenancy my be severed by agreement if the agreement is clear.

   e. **Operation of law:** In a few instances (e.g., when one joint tenant murders another) the joint tenancy is severed by operation of law, to avoid injustice.

C. **Tenancy by the entirety:** A tenancy by the entirety is a variant form of joint tenancy that is only available to a husband and wife. The four unities are required for creation, plus a fifth unity of marriage.

  1. **Differences from the joint tenancy:** There are two important difference from the joint tenancy.

     a. **One owner:** The common law indulged in the fiction that there was only one owner of a tenancy by the entirety — the fictional marital person. Never mind that it takes two to make a marriage. This fiction has consequences concerning the ability of creditors of one marital partner to seize his or her interest in a tenancy by the entirety.

     b. **No severance:** A tenancy by the entirety may not be severed by one tenant acting alone. This rule makes the right of survivorship indestructible unless both partners join in a conveyance.

  2. **Presumption of creation:** Most American states that recognize the tenancy by the entirety observe a rebuttable presumption that a conveyance to a husband and wife creates a tenancy by the entirety.

  3. **Modern operation of the tenancy by the entirety:** Unlike common law, which gave the husband exclusive power to control a tenancy by the entirety, both spouses are equal today. But there are two ways to achieve equality: (1) Endow the wife with equal rights to alienate her possession and survivorship rights, or (2) prevent either spouse from doing so.

     a. **Equal right to alienate:** The effect of this view is to enable the creditors of either spouse to seize the debtor spouse's possessory interest in a tenancy by the entirety, but not the survivorship interest.

     b. **Neither spouse may alienate:** The effect of this view is that the creditors of either spouse may *not* seize the possessory or survivorship interests of the debtor spouse.

     c. **Variation:** A few states permit the creditors of either spouse to seize the *survivorship right* of the debtor spouse but not the possessory right.

  4. **Termination:** A tenancy by the entirety is terminated by death, divorce, or conveyance by both spouses acting together.

II. RIGHTS AND OBLIGATIONS OF CONCURRENT OWNERS

A. **Partition:** A joint tenant or a tenant in common may demand partition at any time and for any reason. A tenant by the entirety is not entitled to partition — the effective remedy is divorce. Partition is accomplished by a judicial proceeding resulting in either (1) *physical division* of the property or (2) *sale and division of the sale proceeds.*

  1. **Partition in kind:** A physical division of the property is called *partition in kind.* This is the preferred method, but if it is (1) *impossible or very impractical* or (2) *not in the best interest of all parties* a court will order partition by sale.

  2. **Partition by sale:** This method is actually quite common because it is impractical or impossible physically to divide most property in America today. The property is sold and the proceeds divided among the co-owners in proportion to their ownership interests.

  3. **Agreements not to partition:** Such agreements are enforceable if they are clear, fair and equitable, and limited to a reasonable period of time.

B. **Rents, profits, and possession:** Absent agreement to the contrary, each co-owner has the right to possess the property and no co-owner may exclude the others. These contradictory principles invite conflict, which is resolved (in the absence of an agreement) as follows.

  1. **Exclusive possession by one co-owner:** If exclusive possession is not by agreement the owner in possession has the following obligations to owners not in possession.

a. **Rent:** Most jurisdictions hold that the owner in possession has no obligation to pay rent unless the other owners have been *ousted,* or the owner in possession has a *special duty* to the other owners, or there is an agreement to pay rent. *Ouster* is a term of art — it occurs if the owner in possession either (1) *prevents the other owners from possession,* or (2) *denies the other owners' claim to title.* A minority of states hold that the owner in possession is obligated to pay the fair rental value to the other owners whether or not there has been ouster.

2. **Rents from third parties:** A co-owner who receives rents from a third party is obligated to account to his co-tenants for those rents and share them pro rata.

C. **Accounting for the costs of ownership:** Generally, each co-tenant is liable for his proportionate share of the costs of ownership, e.g., mortgage payments, taxes, repairs, and maintenance.

1. **Exceptions:** There are several exceptions to this rule.

a. **Repairs:** A co-tenant has no obligation to repair property, since owners are free to let their property fall into ruin. Thus, a co-owner who voluntarily repairs the property may not recover repair costs from other owners, except by deduction from rent due the other owners or upon partition.

b. **Improvements:** No co-owner is obliged to improve property. Thus, an improving co-owner may not recover improvement costs from her fellow owners, but upon partition or by way of deduction from rent owed to the other owners the improving co-owner may recover the *value added* by the improvements.

D. **Adverse possession by one co-owner:** In order for one co-owner to occupy adversely to his fellow owners, it is essential that he give the other owners absolutely clear and unequivocal notice that he *claims exclusive and sole title.* Otherwise, the possession is not wrongful.

E. **Implied fiduciary duty:** Generally, co-tenants do not owe each other fiduciary duties, unless they are voluntarily assumed. A fiduciary duty is implied in law, however, when one co-owner acts to gain an advantage of title over his fellow owners.

III. MARITAL INTERESTS

A. **Common law:** The *pure* common law system of marital property is extinct, but aspects of it continue to exist. Upon marriage a woman lost all legal control over her property to her husband, but acquired some inchoate property rights — a right of lifetime support from her husband and a *dower* right.

1. **Dower:** Dower was the right given a widow to a life estate in 1/3 of each and every possessory freehold estate the husband had owned at any point during marriage that was capable of inheritance by children born of the marriage. Once dower attached it could only be removed by divorce or with the wife's consent. Dower is largely abolished today. The modern analogue is the spousal elective share, which guarantees a surviving spouse a specified portion of the decedent spouse's estate.

2. **Curtesy:** Curtesy was the common law's sibling to dower. A husband acquired a life estate in his wife's property upon marriage, measured by the first to die of husband or wife. But upon the birth of a child the life estate ripened into one measured by the husband's life alone. Curtesy has been abolished.

B. **The modern version of the common law system:** The common law system of marital property has been altered considerably by statute.

1. **Divorce:** Most states have some form of *equitable distribution* statute. These statutes define marital property and make that property subject to equal division.

a. **Increased earning power:** States split over how to treat the increased earning power one spouse may obtain during marriage (e.g. a professional degree). Some states say it is *not property* and thus not subject to division. Others treat the increased earnings potential as property ***subject to equitable division.*** Others take a middling course of requiring the benefited spouse to reimburse the contributing spouse for the support he or she supplied.

   2. **Death:** Today's substitute for dower is the spousal ***elective share,*** created by statute. The surviving spouse is entitled to elect either the statutory share (usually half) of the deceased spouse's estate or to take under the deceased spouse's will.

   3. **Spousal agreements:** Common law did not generally enforce agreements made between spouses before marriage that were intended to govern property division upon divorce. Today, many states will enforce such agreements so long as the parties fully disclosed their financial condition and the substance of the agreement is not unconscionable. The enforceability of contracts between spouses after marriage depends on the subject matter.

C. **Community property:** Community property is a civil law institution inherited from French and Spanish colonization of portions of America. The fundamental idea is that a marriage is a partnership of equals, and that the property acquired during marriage by the efforts of either spouse belongs to that marital community. Each spouse has an equal claim to the assets of the marital community. The Uniform Marital Property Act is, for all practical purposes, a statutory replica of community property.

   1. **Definition of community property:** Community property consists of earnings during marriage of either spouse and all property acquired from such earnings. This excludes ***separate property*** — property acquired before marriage or, during marriage, by gift, inheritance, or devise. Property can be transmuted from one form to the other only by agreement of both spouses. Courts use a rebuttable presumption that property acquired during marriage is community property.

   2. **Commingled property:** Once separate and community property is commingled it becomes community property unless one spouse can trace the source of some discrete portion to separate property. When a partially paid-for asset is brought to marriage and the remainder of the purchase is made by community funds, states employ three different approaches.

      a. **Inception of right:** Some states hold that the character of the property is fixed at the inception of legal right to possession.

      b. **Time of vesting:** Some states hold that the character of the property is determined when title passes.

      c. **Pro-rata apportionment:** Some states hold that the percentage of the purchase price paid prior to marriage establishes the portion of the property that is separate; the remainder is community property.

   3. **Management of community property:** Husband and wife have equal management powers. Either spouse can transfer community property but neither spouse, acting alone, can convey their interest in the community to a stranger.

   4. **Divorce:** At divorce, each spouse is entitled to half the community property and all of their separate property.

   5. **Death:** At death, the half interest of the deceased spouse in the community property is disposed of according to the deceased spouse's will. It does not automatically go to the surviving spouse.

   6. **Creditors:** Generally, debts incurred during marriage are presumed to be community obligations and the community property is subject to seizure to satisfy such debts.

D. **"Quasi-marital" property:** Lots of people live together without marriage. Their property rights depend mostly on whatever agreements they have between themselves as to their shared property. Otherwise, title to property determines ownership.

1. **Common law marriage:** Common law conferred marital status on a man and woman who openly lived together as husband and wife, even though they were not ceremonially married. This status was the same as any ceremonial marriage. But many states have abandoned common law marriage and, even in jurisdictions recognizing the doctrine, it does not extend to same-sex couples.
2. **Contracts:** Unmarried cohabitants may create express contracts to govern their property upon death or termination of the cohabitation. These agreements are generally enforceable, unless they are explicitly founded on illegal consideration.

IV. CONDOMINIUMS AND COOPERATIVES

A. **Condominiums:** The condominium consists of fee ownership of an individual unit and a fractional interest as a tenant in common with all other condominium owners of the common areas of the building. The condominium is a creature of statute. Creation is by compliance with the statute. Each condominium may be sold and financed separately. Each condominium owner is jointly and severally liable for the common areas. No owner can partition the common areas. Condominium owners are members of an association which elects a board of directors, empowered to run the association and make important financial and other decisions about the condominium development.

B. **Cooperatives:** A cooperative apartment building is owned by a corporation. Each apartment "owner" owns shares in the corporation and has a lease to the apartment from the corporation. Thus, each dweller is simultaneously part owner (by virtue of owning shares in the corporate building owner) and a tenant. The corporation's board of directors is elected by its shareholders. Lease rentals are set to recover the operating costs of the building, which include mortgage service and taxes. Transferability of the corporate stock and the lease are restricted to be sure that any transferee is financially capable of discharging the obligations of ownership and tenancy.

CHAPTER 6
SERVITUDES: LAND USE LIMITS CREATED BY PRIVATE BARGAIN

I. TYPES OF SERVITUDES

Servitudes are private arrangements concerning the use of land. Some servitudes give a person the right to **use somebody else's land** in a specific and limited manner. These servitudes are either **easements** or **profits.** Other servitudes consist of promises that a landowner **will use her own land (or not use her own land)** in a specific way. These servitudes are called **real covenants** if damages are sought as the enforcement remedy and **equitable servitudes** if an injunction is the method of enforcement.

II. EASEMENTS

A. **Defined:** An *affirmative* easement is an interest in land that entitles its owner to use another's land. A *negative* easement, though rarely recognized, entitles its owner to restrain the use another makes of his land. Courts employ a rebuttable presumption that an ambiguous grant conveys an easement rather than a freehold.

B. **Types of easements:** Easements may be *appurtenant* or *in gross* and also may be *affirmative* or *negative.*

1. **Appurtenant:** An easement appurtenant is one that benefits the owner of another parcel of land, rather than conferring a personal benefit. The benefited parcel is the **dominant estate**

and the burdened parcel is the *servient estate.* In cases of ambiguity, courts prefer to find easements to be appurtenant.

2. **In gross:** An easement in gross benefits its owner personally, and not as an owner of land. That personal right may be transferred if the parties so intended.

3. **Affirmative:** Almost all easements are affirmative. An affirmative easement permits a person to use the servient estate in a specific manner. Affirmative easements can be appurtenant or in gross.

4. **Negative:** A negative easement confers only the right to prevent specified uses of the servient estate. It confers no right to use the servient estate. Very few negative easements exist. Common law recognized only four appurtenant negative easements — for light, for air, for support, and for the continuing flow of an artificial stream. A few modern courts recognize appurtenant negative easements for view and for solar collection. Today, by statute, many states permit the creation of negative easements in gross for purposes of conservation or preservation. And if a negative promise does not create a negative easement it may create a real covenant or equitable servitude.

C. **Profit distinguished:** A profit is the right to take a natural resource or crop from the land of another. Profits are always in gross and are freely transferable.

D. **Licenses:** A license is simply permission to enter the licensor's land. Licenses are ubiquitous, may be oral or written, and are revocable at any time unless the licensor makes the license irrevocable, either expressly or by his conduct. The same promise may be seen as a license or an easement in gross; courts prefer to treat the ambiguous promise as a license. Licenses are assignable if the parties so intend, or if the license becomes irrevocable through equitable estoppel.

1. **Irrevocable licenses:** A license may become irrevocable by *intention,* by *equitable estoppel,* or when *"coupled with an interest."*

    a. **Equitable estoppel:** If a license is granted and the licensee reasonably relies on it to make substantial improvements to property, equity requires that the licensor be estopped from revoking the license until the value of the improvements has been entirely exhausted. A few states do not recognize these "easements by estoppel."

    b. **License "coupled with an interest:"** When a license is tied together with some other independently legally recognized interest the license is irrevocable until that other interest is vindicated.

E. **Creation of easements:** Easements may be created by *grant,* by *estoppel* (an irrevocable license), by *implication* (in two different ways), and by *prescription* (an easement version of adverse possession).

1. **Grant:** An easement by grant must be in a writing signed by the grantor.

    a. **By reservation:** A grant that "reserves" an easement from the grant creates an easement by reservation. By contrast, an "exception" in a grant excepts from the grant a pre-existing easement. States recognize the validity of easements reserved in favor of the grantor, but most do not recognize easements reserved in favor of a third party. This rule makes little sense but only a few states have rejected it.

2. **Estoppel:** The license made irrevocable by equitable estoppel is the same as an easement by estoppel. Whatever the name, this easement expires when the detrimental reliance expenditures have been exhausted.

3. **Easements by implication:** There are two circumstances in which easements are created by implication.

    a. **Implied from prior use:** When the following elements are proved, an easement is impliedly created from prior use.

i. **Common owner:** A common owner of land must use some part of it for the benefit of the remaining part, and then divide ownership of the "quasi-servient" estate and the "quasi-dominant" estate.

ii. **Reasonable necessity:** The prior use must be reasonably necessary for the use and enjoyment of the "quasi-dominant" estate. Some states require that, if the "quasi-dominant" estate is retained by the common owner and creator, the prior use must be "strictly necessary" for the use and enjoyment of the "quasi-dominant" estate.

iii. **Continuous use:** The prior use must be continuous and the parties must intend, at division, to continue the use.

iv. **Apparent existing use:** At division, the use must be in existence and must be apparent, which does not necessarily mean that it is visible.

b. **Implied from necessity:** An easement is implied from necessity only when an owner divides his property in such a way that one of the resulting parcels is left without access to a public roadway. An easement for right of way between the landlocked parcel and a public road, across the original owner's remaining land, is then implied. The necessity must be present at the time of severance and at the time the easement is asserted. If the necessity is later removed (e.g., by creation of a new public road) the easement implied by necessity terminates.

4. **Easements by prescription:** Prescription is analogous to adverse possession. Adverse *use* for a sufficient period of time can ripen into an easement by prescription. The adverse use must be ***actual, open and notorious, continuous,*** under an ***adverse claim of right,*** and ***exclusive*** for the limitations period applicable to adverse possession.

    a. **Adverse claim of right:** The use must *not* be *permissive.* The objective version of this element is that a neutral, objective observer would conclude that the use is not permissive. The subjective version requires the adverse user to prove that she harbored a good faith belief that she had a right to use the property without permission from the owner.

    b. **Exclusive use:** Exclusive use does not mean that the adverse user was the only user; rather, it means that the adverse user's claim does not depend on somebody else's claim. The adverse user's claim is his own, not part of a public claim.

    c. **Public prescriptive easements:** Many states permit the public to acquire a prescriptive easement. Other states achieve the same result through implied dedication, custom, or the public trust doctrine. Some states, however, reject all these doctrines.

    d. **No prescriptive easements:** There are two types of easements that may not be acquired by prescription.

        i. **Negative easements:** A negative easement may not be acquired by prescription because there is no cause of action that is cut off by the limitations statute.

        ii. **Easements upon public land:** As with adverse possession, it is not possible to obtain a prescriptive easement in public land.

F. **Scope of easements:** Two separate issues are raised by consideration of the scope of an easement: (1) How extensively and intensively may the easement holder use the easement, and (2) To what degree may the servient estate owner use or interfere with the easement?

  1. **Parties' intentions control:** The parties' intentions control the scope of any easement, but intentions are not always easy to identify. Other factors, considered below, are thus used to help infer intentions.

  2. **How easement was created:** The scope of easements by grant is governed by the express language of the grant, to the extent that can be dispositive. The scope of easements implied from prior use is whatever was within the reasonable contemplation of the parties at the time of division. The scope of an easement implied by necessity is identical to the necessity. The scope of prescriptive easements is generally confined to the particular prescriptive use.

3. **Change in location:** Easements with a specified location are permanently fixed, unless both parties agree to a change. But some modifications, within that location, may be made if they do not increase the burden on the servient estate.

4. **Enlargement of the dominant estate:** An easement, however created, cannot be used for the benefit of land that is not part of the dominant estate. A landowner who attempts to do so may usually be enjoined, though a few courts have awarded damages instead.

5. **Division of an easement's benefit:** The benefit of an easement may not be divided if it will produce an unintended increase in the burden on the servient estate.

   a. **Division of a dominant estate:** The benefit of an appurtenant estate may be divided into smaller portions so long as the burden on the servient estate is not greater than what the parties initially intended.

   b. **Division of profits and easements in gross:** If a profit or easement in gross is shared with the servient estate it may ***not be divided.*** But if the profit or easement in gross is exclusively held by ***one person*** it ***may be divided.*** If it is exclusively held by ***several persons*** it may be divided but it ***must be used as a single unit.*** This ***"one-stock"*** rule is intended to prevent the burden on the servient estate from being materially increased beyond the initial intent. Thus, some courts ignore the "one-stock" rule and look only at the increased burden.

6. **Use or interference by servient estate owner:** Unless the easement grants to the holder a right of ***exclusive use*** the servient estate owner may also reasonably use the easement. In any case, a servient estate owner may not unreasonably interfere with the easement holder's use of the easement.

G. **Transfer of easements:** Transferability of easements depends on the type of easement. Appurtenant easements are as freely transferable as the estates to which they are attached. In general, ***commercial easements in gross*** are freely transferable but ***non-commercial easements in gross*** are transferable only if the parties so intended. Profits have always been freely transferable.

H. **Termination of easements:** An easement may terminate in one of five different ways: (1) ***expiration by its terms,*** (2) by ***merger*** of the dominant and servient estates, (3) by ***some act of the easement holder,*** (4) upon ***complete cessation of purpose,*** and (5) by ***some act of the servient estate owner.***

   1. **Acts of the easement holder:** The easement holder may voluntarily ***release*** the easement. An easement will be extinguished if its owner manifests a ***clear and unequivocal intention to abandon*** the easement, but mere lack of use is not sufficient proof of abandonment. If the dominant estate owner so alters the dominant estate that the easement may no longer be used it is extinguished.

   2. **Cessation of purpose:** Easements end when their purpose is completely extinguished. An easement implied from necessity terminates when the necessity ceases. An easement by estoppel (also known as an irrevocable license) terminates when the benefit of the reliance expenditures have been fully reaped. Acts of third parties that wholly destroy the easement's purpose cause an easement to terminate. The accidental destruction of the servient estate destroys the easement, but this rule only applies to easements in structures and not in the ground itself.

   3. **Acts of the servient estate owner:** If the servient estate owner uses the easement adversely to the easement holder for the prescription period the easement is extinguished by prescription. In a few states, an easement burdening a structure (not the land) is extinguished if the structure is intentionally destroyed by its owner because its continued existence is not economically feasible.

III. REAL COVENANTS

A. **Defined:** A *real covenant* is a contractual promise about land usage that runs with an estate in land so that it binds subsequent owners of that estate. The promise may be affirmative or negative. The promise that forms the substance of a real covenant will benefit some land and burden other land. Either or both the benefit and burden of the promise may run with an estate in land. The remedy available for breach of a real covenant is damages. If an injunction is sought, the identical promise is treated as an *equitable servitude* and different rules apply to determine whether the benefit or burden of the promise runs to later holders.

B. **Creation of real covenants:** A real covenant may only be created in writing and may not be created by implication or prescription.

C. **Enforceability by and against successors:** The elements necessary to enforce the *burden* of a real covenant against later owners of the burdened estate differ from the elements necessary for a later owner to assert the *benefit* of a real covenant.

   1. **Burden running with an estate in land:** For the burden of a real covenant to run with the estate, the following elements must be proven.

      a. **Intent:** The original parties must have intended the burden to run.

      b. **Horizontal privity of estate:** Most courts still insist on the presence of *privity of estate* between the original parties. An ever growing number of states dispense with this requirement altogether. Horizontal privity of estate is generally satisfied whenever the two original parties either (1) have a *pre-existing mutual interest in each other's estates* or (2) the real covenant is created in the instrument by which *one owner transfers title to the other owner.*

      c. **Vertical privity of estate:** Virtually all courts require *privity of estate* between the original promisor and the successor to the burdened estate. Vertical privity of estate is generally satisfied when the successor acquires an estate of *at least the same duration as the original promisor.*

      d. **Touch and concern:** The substance of the promise must *touch and concern* the burdened land and, in most cases, the benefited land as well. This means that the promise must affect the use and enjoyment of land, or must affect the advantages and burdens of land ownership. The underlying theory is to identify those promises that are so economically beneficial to land ownership that successor owners might well impose them voluntarily if given the chance to do so.

      e. **Notice:** The successor to the burdened estate must have notice of the real covenant when she acquires the estate. Notice may be actual or constructive. Notice is most often constructive — the covenant is recorded in the chain of title to the estate.

   2. **Benefit running with an estate in land:** For the benefit of a real covenant to run with the estate, the following elements must be proven.

      a. **Intent:** The original parties must have intended the benefit to run.

      b. **Vertical privity of estate:** Virtually all courts require *privity of estate* between the original promisor and the successor to the benefited estate, but privity is satisfied so long as the successor acquires *some interest* in the originally benefited estate. Note that *horizontal privity is not required for the benefit to run.*

      c. **Touch and concern:** The substance of the promise must *touch and concern* the benefited land. The traditional rule is that "if the benefit is in gross, the burden will not run." This rule is breaking down, partly by statute (to facilitate conservation or historical preservation covenants) and partly be judicial decision, but is still the overwhelming majority rule. By contrast if the burden is in gross, the benefit may still run.

IV. EQUITABLE SERVITUDES

A. Defined: An equitable servitude is a promise about land use that will be enforced in equity (by an injunction) against a successor to the burdened estate who acquired it with notice of the promise. Equitable servitudes are more common than real covenants because most people prefer to enjoin an offending use rather than simply receive damages for its existence.

1. **Differences from the real covenant:** There are three important differences: (1) the remedy for an equitable servitude is an injunction, not damages, (2) neither vertical nor horizontal privity is needed for either the burden or benefit of an equitable servitude to bind or benefit successors, and (3) an equitable servitude may be created by implication in some states, but a real covenant may never be created by implication.

B. Creation: Generally, a writing is required to create an equitable servitude since it is an interest in land and the Statute of Frauds applies. Some states recognize an exception to this rule, permitting creation of *negative equitable servitudes* by implication from a common development scheme. Other states reject this doctrine and require that all equitable servitudes be created in writing.

1. **Implied from common development scheme:** If a single landowner develops property by selling off lots subject to an identical servitude (e.g., residential use only) and on the explicit or implicit promise that all the lots in the development will be similarly burdened, some states create an equitable servitude by implication. Of course, if the developer follows through on his promise, there is no need to create an equitable servitude by implication. The equitable servitude thus created must be *reciprocal* (it must cover all lots in the common development) and *negative* (it must restrict use). The development must be of a common and uniform character. An implied equitable servitude only applies to lots conveyed after the beginning of the common scheme.

C. Enforceability by or against successors: In order for an equitable servitude to be enforceable by or against successors the original covenant must have been *intended to run to successors,* the successor must *acquire with notice* of the servitude, and the substance of the promise must *touch and concern* the affected property.

1. **Notice:** Notice may be *actual, constructive,* or *inquiry.*

    a. **Constructive notice:** If the covenant is in the chain of title of the property, constructive notice is satisfied. Some states include in the chain of title deeds from a common grantor to grantees other than a direct ancestor of title. This requires title searchers to determine if any prior grantor conveyed other property under a deed by which he burdened his retained property with a servitude. Most states reject this rule and limit the chain of title (and constructive notice that stems from it) to the direct lineal succession of owners.

    b. **Inquiry notice:** A few courts have ruled that a purchaser has an obligation to inquire about the existence of servitudes if the neighborhood exhibits a common character and there is record evidence of a possible common development scheme.

D. Identifying the benefited land: Courts identify the benefited land by (1) looking to the parties' intentions and (2) determining whether the land purportedly benefited has actually received a benefit. If the party imposing the covenant owns nearby land, it is rebuttably presumed that that land was intended to be benefited.

1. **Enforceability by third parties:** Land owned by a third party — neither a party to the covenant nor a successor to land benefited by the covenant — may still be benefited under the following circumstances.

    a. **Purchaser before common scheme begins:** A lot owner who purchases before a common development scheme begins is benefited by the common scheme equitable servitude and may enforce it (1) if the prior purchaser acquired title from the person imposing the servitude (the developer), or (2) if the prior purchaser was an expressly intended beneficiary of the servitude, or (3) if the property was an implied beneficiary of a common scheme of development (whether or not the servitude is created by the common scheme).

   b. Complete stranger but intended beneficiary: Some states permit any intended beneficiary to enforce the benefit of a servitude. In these states it does not matter whether the intended beneficiary acquired title from a person imposing the servitude, or whether the intended beneficiary was intended to be benefited by a common scheme of development.

V. INTERPRETATION OF COVENANTS

Courts attempt to implement the parties' intentions, but in cases of ambiguity some judicially created presumptions may apply. Courts prefer to interpret covenants that may restrict either a use or a type of structure to refer to the structure rather than the use. Covenants restricting use to "residential use" create particular problems because people use their residences for a variety of purposes. Commercial uses are sometimes (but not always) found to violate such covenants. Use as a "group home" (e.g., for the handicapped or juvenile delinquents) does not generally violate a "residential use only" covenant but might violate a "single family use only" covenant.

VI. TERMINATION OF REAL COVENANTS AND EQUITABLE SERVITUDES

A. Merger: If title to all of the burdened land and benefited land is united in a single owner the covenant — whether real covenant or equitable servitude — is extinguished.

B. Eminent domain: If the government takes the burdened land for a purpose inconsistent with the restrictive covenant the covenant is extinguished. Most states require that the owner of the benefited land be compensated for loss of the benefit.

C. Express waiver or release: If all holders of the benefit expressly waive or release the benefit of the covenant it is extinguished.

D. Expiration by its terms: If a covenant has an express expiration date it, of course, expires by its terms.

E. Doctrines terminating equitable servitudes: Equitable defenses may be asserted against enforcement of an equitable servitude, but not as against a real covenant. These defenses, when successfully asserted, effectively terminate an equitable servitude.

   1. Changed conditions: If conditions *within the area affected by the servitude* have so radically and thoroughly changed that the servitude cannot accomplish its purposes it will be extinguished. If the change occurs in the *area adjacent to, but outside, the area affected by the servitude,* the servitude is extinguished *only if all of the benefited land has lost the benefit of the servitude.*

   2. Abandonment: When a servitude is frequently and persistently violated without enforcement it may be treated as having been abandoned by the benefit holders. One test of such abandonment is whether the *average person would reasonably conclude that the use restriction has been abandoned.* The competing test is whether the servitude's purpose has been so frustrated that enforcement would seriously impair the value of burdened properties without producing any substantial benefit.

   3. Equitable estoppel: If the party seeking to enforce an equitable servitude has knowingly lied to a defendant ignorant of the true facts, intending to and actually inducing reliance on the lie, he will be estopped from enforcing the servitude.

   4. Laches: Unreasonable delay in enforcing an equitable servitude, coupled with some resulting prejudice to the defendant, will bar enforcement.

5. **Unclean hands:** A plaintiff guilty of the same violation of which he complains may not enforce an equitable servitude.

6. **Balance of hardships:** As with all injunctions, a court is free to deny an injunction if the hardship thereby imposed on the enjoined party greatly outweigh the benefits of the injunction.

Chapter 7
COMMON LAW CONTROL OF LAND USE: NUISANCE AND SUPPORT

I. THE SUBSTANCE OF NUISANCE

A. **General principle:** No person may use his own land in an *unreasonable manner* that *substantially* lessens another person's *use and enjoyment* of his land. A nuisance may be public or private. A private nuisance involves interference with the rights of one or more private landowners. A public nuisance involves interference with rights of the entire public.

B. **Private nuisance:** A private nuisance occurs when there is **substantial interference** with private rights to use and enjoy land, produced by either (1) *intentional and unreasonable conduct,* or (2) *unintentional conduct* that is either *negligent, reckless,* or *inherently dangerous.*

   1. **Substantial interference:** To constitute a nuisance the offending use must substantially impair use and enjoyment to the average person, not to the specific owner affected. An unusually sensitive person has no augmented power to cry "nuisance."

   2. **Intentional conduct:** Intentional interference occurs when the activity is known by its maker to interfere with another's use of his land. The key focus is on whether the interference is *unreasonable.* It is if the *gravity of the harm inflicted by the activity outweighs its social utility.* This judgment is highly contextual. A nuisance may often be the right thing in the wrong place — hot tar on the carpet instead of the roof.

   3. **Unintentional conduct:** When the interference is not known by its maker to interfere the focus is on whether the activity poses an unreasonable risk of harm to others — either because the actor is careless or the action is inherently dangerous.

C. **Public nuisance:** A public nuisance affects rights held in common by everybody (e.g., to the municipal water supply). A pure public nuisance is rare. Usually, a public nuisance is also a private nuisance. The substantive test for public nuisance is the same as for a private nuisance, A private citizen may enforce a public nuisance if he has suffered special injury — some particularized and personalized injury.

D. **Relationship to trespass:** Trespass involves a physical invasion of a person's land — an interference with the *exclusive right to possession.* Nuisance involves an interference with *use and enjoyment* but does not necessarily involve any interference with the exclusive right to possession.

II. REMEDIES: FOUR VIEWS OF NUISANCE

A. **Economic theory of nuisance remedies:** Nuisance presents a problem of conflicting uses — each land user's desired use prevents the other use from occurring. Each use produces externalities — costs that are not imposed on somebody other than the person producing them. Economic theory suggests that it doesn't matter who gets the initial right of use, because the parties will reallocate the right to whoever values it more. But *transaction costs* — the costs of moving the right — are not negligible and so inhibit this efficient transfer. When there are only two possible rightholders the problem is *bilateral monopoly* —

only one buyer and one seller — and the possibility that the gains from transfer will be frittered away by expensive bargaining. When there are numerous parties to the negotiation the problem is either *free riders* or *holdouts* — people who won't consent in the hopes of getting something for nothing or in the hopes of extracting an exorbitant payment for their consent.

1. **Economic theory's effect on nuisance law:** In allocating the use right, nuisance law pays attention to the fact of transaction cost. In doing so, nuisance law also recognizes that any legal right may be protected by a *property rule* (which makes the right immune from forced transfer) or a *liability rule* (which permits the right to be taken away upon payment of damages). Thus, there are four possible outcomes to any nuisance suit.

    a. **No nuisance:** The use attacked is not a nuisance and so continues without restraint. The attacked use is protected by a property rule. It will stop only if the plaintiff's use is more valuable and the parties can reach an efficient agreement to shift the right to the plaintiff.

    b. **Nuisance enjoined:** The attacked use is found to be a nuisance and its continuation is enjoined. The plaintiff landowner's use is protected by a property rule. The nuisance use will continue only if the nuisance use is more valuable and the parties can reach an efficient agreement to shift the right to the nuisance user.

    c. **Nuisance permitted to continue upon payment of damages to affected landowners:** The attacked use is found to be a nuisance but is permitted to continue so long as the nuisance maker pays damages to the plaintiff landowner. The plaintiff landowner's use is protected by a liability rule. Courts employ this remedy when they think that the nuisance use is the more valuable but believe that the transaction costs of shifting the right to the nuisance user would prove to be insuperable.

    d. **Alleged nuisance enjoined upon payment of damages to the enjoined user:** Whether or not the attacked use is found to be a nuisance it is enjoined if the complaining landowner pays damages to compensate the attacked user for the discontinuance of the use. The attacked use is protected by a liability rule. Courts employ this remedy when they think that the plaintiff's use is the more valuable, but it is not clear that the attacked use is a nuisance, and transaction costs appear to be an insuperable obstacle to shifting the right from the attacked user to the plaintiff.

III. SUPPORT RIGHTS

A. Generally: Every landowner has the right to both *lateral support* and *subjacent support* of his land. A landowner may not modify his own land in such a way as to deprive his neighbor of either support right.

B. Lateral support: The extent of the duty to maintain lateral support differs with respect to the land itself and structures upon the land.

1. **Land:** A landowner is strictly liable for removal of lateral support from the land itself.
2. **Structures:** A landowner is strictly liable for damage to structures resulting from the removal of lateral support if the collapse would have occurred even without the structures. But if the collapse would not have occurred but for the added weight of the structure, a landowner is liable for removal of lateral support only if he was negligent in doing so.

C. Subjacent support: This right becomes an issue only if the surface is owned by one person and the right to mine underground is owned by another. The underground miner is strictly liable for damages caused to land or structures resulting from withdrawal of subjacent support.

CHAPTER 8
PUBLIC CONTROL OF LAND USE: ZONING

I. ZONING BASICS

A. **Definition and purpose:** Zoning is the use of governmental power to regulate land use. Its purpose is usually to prevent incompatible uses (rather than relying upon nuisance to abate them), to increase property values by minimizing conflicting uses, and to channel development into patterns that are thought to serve larger social goals.

B. **Validity:** In general, zoning is constitutionally valid. Specific applications may, however, offend a variety of constitutional limits on governmental power.

C. **Statutory schemes:** Zoning can be accomplished by either *cumulative* or *mutually exclusive* zoning.

1. **Cumulative zoning:** Land uses are identified and arranged in a spectrum from "highest" to "lowest." Cumulative zoning permits all uses at the zoned level or higher.

2. **Mutually exclusive zoning:** By contrast, mutually exclusive zoning permits only the uses designated by the particular zoning classification.

D. **Density zoning:** Zoning laws do not stop with use regulation. Most zoning laws also seek to control the density of occupation within any given use classification.

II. ZONING AUTHORIZATION

A. **Enabling legislation:** Most states reserve to the state government the power to adopt zoning laws. But since almost all zoning is done at the local level, the state must first give municipalities power to zone, through an enabling law. In most states, local government power to zone is derived entirely from the enabling act and must be exercised in conformity with it.

1. *Ultra vires* **action:** Local action beyond the authority granted by the enabling act is *ultra vires* and thus void. This can only be determined by examining the enabling act but some issues have been frequently litigated.

    a. **Aesthetics:** The traditional rule was that a state has no power to regulate to achieve purely aesthetic objectives, because aesthetic judgments are entirely subjective and standardless. Today, most states permit regulation for aesthetic purposes, either solely or in conjunction with some other objective. This does not, however, remove the claim that aesthetic regulation is so inherently vague and capricious as to amount to a denial of due process.

    b. **Exclusionary zoning:** Zoning that has the effect of excluding unwanted users may violate state or federal laws. Most such cases revolve around effective exclusion of poor people. While these practices do not offend the federal Constitution (unless they are intended to produce racial exclusion) they may violate state constitutional provisions.

    c. **Growth controls:** These zoning laws, which seek to exclude everybody, have generally been found to be within the authority conferred by the various enabling acts.

2. **Defective enabling act:** An enabling act might be defective if it grants state legislative power to a locality without tying the exercise of that power to some clear standard set forth in the enabling act. This amounts to an unconstitutional delegation of legislative authority.

B. **Comprehensive plan:** Enabling acts require zoning to be done consistent with a "comprehensive plan" of development. The plan itself is not law but, in the absence of any implementing law, local action that violates a comprehensive plan is probably void.

III. STATUTORY DISCRETION AND RESTRAINT

A. **The idea and the problems it creates:** To accommodate change, zoning laws (1) tolerate continuation of non-conforming land uses existing prior to adoption of the zoning law, (2) permit amendment of the law, and (3) confer discretion on public officials in applying the law. These mechanisms invite claims of lawlessness in their administration.

B. **Nonconforming uses:** Even though zoning laws permit continuation of nonconforming uses, most zoning laws confine such uses or force their gradual elimination. Zoning laws typically do so by forbidding any expansion or rebuilding of the nonconforming use. The validity of a forced phase-out of a nonconforming use generally depends on the length of the amortization period. If it is long enough to be reasonable a forced phase-out is valid. But some states hold that all forced phase-outs are void.

C. **Amendments:** The power of amendment may be abused.
   1. **Spot zoning:** An amendment that does not conform to the comprehensive plan is spot zoning and is invalid. But if the comprehensive plan is also amended the alterations are valid if they bear a *substantial relationship to the general welfare of the affected community*.
   2. **Abusive amendments:** Amendments may comply to the letter of a comprehensive plan but arguably violate its spirit. Zoning amendments are generally presumed to be valid and so the challenger has the burden of proving that the amendment is illegal spot zoning. But a few states have reversed the burden of proof as to zoning amendments. There are two approaches. One is to require the state to prove a *demonstrable public need* for the amendment. The other is to require the state to prove either (1) the amendment *corrects a mistake* in the original law or (2) is needed to *adapt to a substantial change in conditions affecting land use*.

D. **Administrative discretion:** There are lots of ways to exercise discretion. Here are the principal methods.
   1. **Variances:** Almost all zoning laws invest a zoning appeals board with the power to vary the law to alleviate practical difficulty or undue hardship on an owner. But the problems must not be of the owner's creation. Undue hardship means, in practice, that the land cannot be used effectively without the variance.
   2. **Conditional uses:** A "variance" to permit use in a fashion not otherwise permitted is called a conditional use. Conditional uses are granted when the proposed use is compatible with existing uses or in "furtherance of public health, safety, and general welfare." But if there is no standard for granting conditional uses, the granting of a conditional use is an invalid delegation of legislative authority.
   3. **Floating zones:** Some zoning laws create "floating zones," a use classification that does not attach to any particular land until application is made and a particular parcel is so designated. Floating zones my violate the comprehensive plan unless the criteria for attachment to land is very specifically drafted.
   4. **Conditional zoning:** When land is rezoned to permit development upon the condition that the developer create new servitudes burdening the land, a number of objections may be raised. It is said that conditional zoning is (1) spot zoning, (2) an invalid disposal of the police power, (3) *ultra vires,* and (4) a waiver of governmental power to restrict land use. These objections are usually found to be insufficient.
   5. **Cluster zoning:** Cluster zoning zones land areas for particular uses and densities but leaves to public officials to determine how those uses and densities will be actually achieved. So long as cluster zoning conforms to the comprehensive plan it is not problematic.

E. **Voter discretion:** The public may exercise discretion through the initiative (by which legislation is proposed and adopted directly by the people) or the referendum (by which legislation does not become effective until approved by the people). Some states do not permit the initiative or referendum to be used to alter zoning laws.

IV. CONSTITUTIONAL LIMITS ON ZONING

A. **Generally:** Zoning laws, as applied, may violate either the federal Constitution or the state constitution. Some of the common constitutional problems are discussed here.

B. **Equal protection:** Generally, a zoning law is valid unless the challenger can prove that it is not rationally related to a legitimate state interest. However, if the zoning law classifies on the basis of some suspect trait (like race) or substantially infringes upon a fundamental right (like the right of privacy), it is presumed invalid and is valid only if the state can prove that it is necessary to accomplish a compelling state objective. State constitutions often contain an equal protection clause as well, which may be interpreted to restrain more government action than does the federal clause.

C. **Due process:** The due process guarantee has a procedural and substantive component.

1. **Procedural due process:** A government may not take a person's life, liberty, or property without at least giving him *notice* of the reason for doing so, and an *opportunity to be heard* before action is taken. While this does not apply to legislation it does apply to individual applications of zoning laws.

2. **Substantive due process:** Laws that infringe constitutionally fundamental rights are void unless the state proves that they are necessary to achieve a compelling state interest.

    a. **Incorporation:** Substantive due process incorporates most of the provisions of the Bill of Rights, making them applicable to the states. Thus, a zoning law violates due process if it infringes such constitutionally fundamental rights as free speech, free press, or free exercise of religion.

    i. **Free speech:** Zoning laws that classify on the basis of speech content are void unless the state can prove that they are necessary to achieve a compelling interest. Zoning laws that regulate speech in a content-neutral fashion are void only if they are either (1) broader than reasonably necessary to achieve a significant government purpose other than speech regulation, or (2) so restrictive they fail to leave open ample alternative channels of communication.

    ii. **Free press:** Zoning laws that single out the press for unfavorable treatment are void unless the state can prove that they are necessary to achieve a compelling objective.

    iii. **Free exercise of religion:** Zoning laws that prohibit acts only when engaged in for religious reasons, or because of the religious belief they display, are invalid restrictions on freedom of religion.

    b. **Economic substantive due process:** Zoning laws that regulate economic activity are valid unless they are not rationally related to any legitimate state objective. A zoning law is valid if (1) there is a public problem the law is intended to address, (2) the law actually tends to alleviate the problem, and (3) the public benefits are not so slight in comparison to the burdens imposed that the law is unduly oppressive.

    c. **Privacy or autonomy rights:** Zoning laws that substantially interfere with constitutionally fundamental "privacy" or "autonomy" rights (such as the right to live with family members) are void unless the state can prove that they are necessary to achieve some compelling state interest.

D. **The takings clause:** The government may not take private property for public use except upon payment of just compensation. Some regulations so restrict the use of property that they are claimed to constitute a *de facto* taking. This topic is discussed in Chapter 11. Two important zoning applications are dealt with here.

1. **Historical preservation:** A zoning law that is designed to preserve an entire historical district is generally not a taking because landowners are (1) left with a wide variety of permitted uses and (2) the restrictions are generally of mutual advantage to all affected landowners. A zoning law that mandates preservation of an isolated historic site is not a taking if it can be shown that the owner is left with a reasonable and viable economic use of the property.

2. **Environmental preservation:** Zoning laws that seek to preserve open space or other environmental values are takings if they deprive the owner of (1) possession, or (2) all economically viable use of the property, or (3) leave the owner with an unreasonably low rate of return on his investment in the property.

V. PLANNED DEVELOPMENTS

A. **Subdivisions:** Laws regulating creation of new subdivisions seek to limit approval of new subdivisions to those likely to advance public welfare. Approval of new subdivisions is often conditioned upon certain acts of the developer, such as the creation of basic infrastructure (e.g., streets and sidewalks) or dedication of land for parks or schools. Some of these forced extractions may violate the takings clause.

1. **Essential nexus:** A condition to development is void unless it is substantially related to the reason for imposing the development regulations without regard to the condition.

2. **Rough proportionality:** Even if the condition meets the "essential nexus" test, it must be roughly proportional to the problem caused by the development.

3. **State constitutional limits:** States are free to impose even tighter controls upon forced extractions. Some states hold that forced extractions are void unless the need addressed by the condition is "specifically and uniquely attributable" to the new development.

B. **Planned unit developments:** Planned unit developments involve a mix of uses within a single development. So long as the PUD uses and densities are consistent with the comprehensive plan, a PUD is not an unlawful waiver of the zoning law.

CHAPTER 9
TRANSFERS OF REAL PROPERTY

I. CONTRACTS FOR SALE

A. **Introduction:** Virtually all non-gratuitous transfers of real property involve contracts for sale.

1. **Brokers:** Most sales involve a broker. The seller hires a broker (the listing agent) to sell the property on the terms and conditions in the listing agreement. A commission is due when the broker procures a buyer ready, willing, and able to perform on those conditions or others acceptable to the seller.

2. **Lawyers:** Lawyers are always valuable — to draft the contract, provide advice concerning the legal effect of the transaction, and to examine title — but are often ignored, particularly in residential sales.

3. **Mortgage lenders:** Most of the purchase price of most transactions is supplied by a mortgage lender, who lends a large portion of the purchase price to the buyer and secures repayment of the loan by taking a mortgage of the property.

4. **Closing:** Real estate sales are a two-step transaction. First, a contract is entered into. Second, a closing occurs, at which the purchase price is exchanged for title. This closing occurs

through a third party, an escrow agent, who holds the money and documents and disburses them in accordance with the parties' instructions.

- **B. Statute of frauds:** The Statute of Frauds requires that a contract for sale of real property must be in writing and signed by the party against whom it is sought to be enforced. In practice, this means both parties must sign. A formal contract is not necessary, so long as the key terms are present in the writing, which need not consist of a single document. Contracts for sale are usually subject to conditions and, if the conditions are not carefully spelled out, the entire contract may fail for want of an essential term.
  1. **Exceptions:** There are two major exceptions to the Statute of Frauds: *part performance* and *equitable estoppel.* Since each is an equitable doctrine they are generally available only in a suit seeking specific performance of an otherwise unenforceable contract.
     a. **Part performance:** Every state requires proof of an oral contract. Some states insist that the acts making up part performance be of the sort that would not occur but for the existence of a contract — partial or total payment, taking possession, or making improvements. Many states are content with reasonable reliance on the oral contract. Both buyers and sellers may invoke the doctrine.
     b. **Equitable estoppel:** This familiar doctrine is closely related to the reasonable reliance branch of part performance.
  2. **Revocation of contracts:** Most (but not all) states do not apply the Statute of Frauds to revocations of a contract for sale of real property.
- **C. Implied obligations:** Here are the principal obligations implied in any contract for the sale of realty.
  1. **Good faith:** Each party is required to act with good faith in discharging the express duties of the contract.
  2. **Time of closing:** Performance tendered within a reasonable time after the specified closing date is adequate *unless* the contract specifies that *time is of the essence* of the bargain.
  3. **Marketable title:** The seller has an implied duty to deliver *marketable title* to the buyer — title that a prudent buyer would accept, reasonably free of doubt that there are any rival claimants to title. Marketable title can be delivered by *good record title* or *proof of title through adverse possession.*
     a. **Defective title:** Defects in title must be substantial and likely to injure the buyer to render title unmarketable. A defective link in the chain of title makes title unmarketable. Encumbrances make title unmarketable unless the encumbrance is (1) a beneficial easement known to the buyer or (2) a restrictive use covenant that does not limit the particular use specified in the sale contract. Zoning restrictions are not encumbrances.
- **D. Default and remedies:** Default occurs when one party has tendered timely performance, demanded timely performance from the other party, and reciprocal performance is not forthcoming. Available remedies include specific performance, damages, or rescission.
  1. **Specific performance:** Since land is unique damages are inadequate compensation. The equitable remedy of specific performance is available, subject to equitable defenses.
  2. **Rescission:** This is the polar opposite of specific performance. If the seller breaches, the buyer may rescind, recover any payments made, and depart. If the buyer breaches the seller may rescind and sell to another party.
  3. **Damages:** The measure of damages is usually the benefit of the bargain, but may sometimes be limited to out of pocket losses or defined by contractual liquidated damage provisions.

E. **Duties of disclosure and implied warranties:** Sellers are obligated by law to disclose known defects and builders impliedly warrant the quality of their construction.

  1. **Disclosure:** The common law rule was that a seller's duty was to refrain from intentional misrepresentation or active concealment of a known defect, unless the seller (1) has a fiduciary duty to the buyer, in which case the seller must reveal all known defects, or (2) has created hidden conditions that materially impair property value. The majority rule today is that a *seller must reveal all latent material defects* — defects known to the seller, not easily discoverable by the buyer, that materially affect the value or desirability of the property. Some states, by statute, impose specific disclosure obligations on sellers and brokers.

  2. **Implied warranty of quality:** Traditionally, builders were liable only to those with whom they contracted for breaches of an express warranty of quality. But courts today frequently imply a warranty of quality that runs to benefit subsequent purchasers for some reasonable time — a period long enough for the latent defects of original construction to become apparent.

F. **Risk of loss and equitable title:** Between the making of a sale contract and the closing, the property may be damaged or parties may die.

  1. **Equitable title:** The doctrine of *equitable title* (or *equitable conversion*) was the common law's method of dealing with these problems. Equitable title held that equitable ownership of property passed to the buyer at the moment the contract of sale was made. The seller's legal title was a form of security for the buyer's performance at closing.

    a. **Death of a party:** One consequence of equitable title is that, for purposes of death of a contracting party, title is treated as having passed at the moment the contract was made. The decedent thus has an interest in real property rather than personal property, which can have consequences under wills or in intestacy.

    b. **Risk of loss:** The traditional and still widely prevailing rule is that equitable title places on the buyer the risk of loss prior to closing. English law gave the seller the proceeds of any insurance, on the theory that rights under an insurance contract were personal. Most American states reject this rule and require that insurance proceeds be credited to the buyer. A few American states place risk of loss on the seller. And some states have enacted statutes that make the risk of loss go with possession.

II. DEEDS

A. **Formalities:** The Statute of Frauds requires that a deed be in writing. In order to be recorded, almost all states require that the grantor's signature be acknowledged by a notary. Any words that express an intent to transfer realty will suffice to make the grant, but the grantee must be identified and the property must be clearly and precisely described.

B. **Delivery:** A deed must be delivered in order to be effective. Delivery means action demonstrating the grantor's intent to transfer immediately an interest in land to the grantee. Courts presume delivery if there has been (1) physical transfer, (2) notarial acknowledgment, or (3) recordation of the deed.

  1. **Delivery at death:** Attempts to deliver a deed at death are usually ineffective. Exceptions include (1) delivery to an escrow agent under irrevocable instructions to hold until the grantor's death, or (2) where the words of the grant create a springing executory interest upon the grantor's death.

  2. **Commercial escrows:** Delivery of a deed to a commercial escrow agent under instruction to release it upon payment from the buyer constitutes delivery.

  3. **Delivery by estoppel:** A grantor who lacks intent to deliver a deed will nevertheless be estopped from denying delivery where the deed is either (1) entrusted to a deceitful grantee, who uses it to transfer title to a innocent third party, or (2) entrusted to an escrow agent who negligently gives it to the grantee.

C. **Warranties of title:** A seller's warranties concerning the state of title are expressed in the deed, and depend upon the deed used.

1. **General warranty deed:** A general warranty deed contains six covenants of title, each of which is a promise that title is free of the warranted defect, regardless of when the defect arose. By the covenant of *seisin* the grantor promises that he owns what he is conveying. By the covenant of *right to convey* the grantor promises that he has authority to convey the property. By the covenant *against encumbrances* the grantor promises that there are no liens or encumbrances upon title other than those excepted in the deed. By the covenant of *general warranty* the grantor promises that he will defend against lawful claims of superior title in the property. By the covenant of *quiet enjoyment* the grantor promises the grantee will not be disturbed in possession or enjoyment by someone with better title. By the covenant of *further assurances* the grantor promises to do whatever is reasonably necessary to perfect the conveyed title.

2. **Special warranty deed:** This deed contains the same six covenants of title but the grantor makes these promises only with respect to *defects of title that arose during the grantor's time of holding title.*

3. **Quitclaim deed:** A quitclaim deed contains no warranties of title whatever. It simply conveys whatever the grantor owns.

4. **Merger:** The traditional rule is that any promises in the contract of sale with respect to title are merged into the deed once the buyer accepts the deed. Promises that are collateral to transfer of title are not merged.

5. **Breach of covenants of title:** The covenants of title are either *present covenants* and *future covenants.* A present covenant — seisin, right to convey, and encumbrances — is breached, if at all, at the moment the deed is delivered. A future covenant — general warranty, quiet enjoyment, and further assurances — is breached when the grantee is actually or constructively evicted at some time in the future.

    a. **Present covenants:** The benefit of present covenants is generally assignable, though this was not true at common law. The statute of limitations with respect to present covenants begins to run at the moment the deed is delivered.

    b. **Future covenants:** These covenants are breached only when the grantee is actually or constructively evicted. Actual eviction is actual dispossession from title or possession. Constructive eviction occurs whenever the grantee's possession is interfered with in any way by someone holding a superior title. The benefit of future covenants runs to later grantees if there is privity of estate between the original grantee and the remote grantee. Privity of estate is satisfied if whatever the original grantor conveyed is conveyed to the remote grantee. Damages for breach of a future covenant is generally limited by the rule that the grantee may not recover more than what the grantor-in-breach received for the property.

6. **After-acquired title:** If a grantor conveys property he does not own and later acquires it, this doctrine (also called *estoppel by deed*) holds that the after-acquired title is sent immediately and directly to the original grantee.

III. FINANCING DEVICES

A. **Mortgages:** A mortgage is a device to secure repayment of a loan, often made to enable a person to acquire real property. The mortgage vests in a lender the power to take the mortgaged property in partial or total satisfaction of the loan debt. In form, the lender makes the loan and the borrower executes a promissory note (the promise to repay with interest) and a mortgage to secure repayment of the loan. The mortgage gives the lender the power to sell the property and apply the proceeds to the loan, if the borrower defaults. But the mortgagor has an equitable right to redeem the property (the *equity of redemption*). The equity of redemption can be eliminated by *foreclosure* but many states have created a separate, independent ***statutory right of redemption*** which gives the borrower a specific period of time after foreclosure sale to redeem the property.

1. **Types of mortgages:** There are a variety of mortgages. The same property can be used to secure more than one loan, so the most senior mortgage is the first mortgage. A fully amortized mortgage is one that is paid off in equal payments over a fixed term. A balloon mortgage is one that requires a lump-sum payment of principal at maturity. A purchase money mortgage is one made for a portion of the purchase price.

2. **Title or lien:** States differ as to whether a mortgage creates a ***lien*** on the property or transfers ***title*** to the property, subject to a condition subsequent requiring retransfer upon payment of the loan. Title theory states, however, commonly conclude that the title is transferred for the limited purpose of securing repayment of the loan.

3. **Sale or transfer by the mortgagor:** A mortgagor may transfer his interest in the mortgaged property. The buyer may ***assume the mortgage*** or may take ***subject to the mortgage.*** A buyer who takes subject to a mortgage incurs no personal liability on the mortgage. A buyer who assumes the mortgage becomes personally liable on the mortgage loan. Lenders often impede these transfers by inserting a ***"due-on-sale"*** clause in the mortgage, which makes the loan immediately due and payable upon any transfer.

4. **Default:** In most states the lender has the option of a suit to collect the debt or to foreclose and sell the mortgaged property to satisfy the debt. If the foreclosure sale proceeds are inadequate to extinguish the debt the borrower is personally liable for the deficiency. Some states have "anti-deficiency" statutes that prohibit deficiency judgments, typically with respect to purchase money mortgage loans for residences.

B. **Deeds of trust:** Some states use a deed of trust in lieu of a mortgage. The borrower conveys the property to a third party as trustee for the lender, for the limited purpose of securing repayment of the loan. The trustee has a power of sale of the property upon default, with an obligation to use the proceeds to pay the debt and return any excess to the borrower. The chief difference from the mortgage is that no judicial foreclosure is required to sell the property, but even this difference has begun to disappear.

C. **Installment sale contracts:** An installment sale contract is, in form, a contract for sale of real property that obligates the purchaser to pay the purchase price in installments and obligates the seller to convey title to the buyer after the purchase price has been fully paid. But since the installment sale contract is economically indistinguishable from a transfer of title followed by a note and purchase money mortgage, most states treat the installment sale contract as a security device.

Chapter 10
ASSURING GOOD TITLE TO LAND

I. THE PROBLEM

People sometimes convey the same property more than once. The problem that results is to decide which innocent purchaser should prevail.

A. **Common law:** The common law awarded title to the grantee who took ***first in time***.

B. **Modern answers:** Today, the common law approach is the last resort. American states rely primarily on the following methods of resolving conflicting claims to title.

1. **Recording:** A public record of conveyances enables priority to be given to recorded conveyances but still requires some mechanism for sorting out priority between recorded conveyances to the same property.

2. **Registration:** An official registry of land titles makes the registered title dispositive title. By contrast, a recording system merely contains evidence of title.

3. **Title insurance:** Title insurers agree to defend the title they insure and compensate for any defects in title. Title insurance is based upon the recorded title and provides an added measure of security, but does not establish title.

II. RECORDING ACTS AND CHAIN OF TITLE

A. **The recording system:** A public official, the recorder, maintains a record of real estate transactions presented for recording and indexes those transactions by grantor and grantee, and sometimes by tract. A title searcher is then able to search backward in time through an alphabetical index of grantees to find the transaction by which the present owner received title, and to repeat that process until an adequate root of title is found. Then the searcher looks forward in time through an alphabetical index of grantors to find out if there were any title transactions made by each owner other than the grant to the next owner. If a tract index is maintained, all of this information is collected in one location.

B. **Types of recording acts:** There are three types of recording acts: a *race* act, a *race-notice* act, and a *notice* act.

1. **Race acts:** A race act provides that, as between two grantees to the same property, the *earliest to record* prevails. There is a race to record.

2. **Notice acts:** A notice act provides that a *later bona fide purchaser without notice of a prior unrecorded grant prevails over the prior grantee, whether or not the later grant is recorded.*

3. **Race-notice acts:** A race-notice act provides that *only those later bona fide purchasers who (1) lack notice of a prior unrecorded grant and (2) record first* prevail over the first grantee.

C. **The consequences of recordation:** Recording provides constructive notice to the world of the grant. In a race or race-notice state, recording cuts off the possibility that either a prior unrecorded purchaser or a later purchaser could prevail. In a notice state, recording prevents a later purchaser from prevailing.

1. **The consequences of *not* recording:** If nobody has recorded the common law first-in-time rule applies, except in a notice state where the later grantee lacked notice. More importantly, without recording the grantor is left with a power to convey good title in someone else.

D. **When recording occurs:** An instrument is recorded when (1) it is eligible to be recorded and (2) is actually entered in the public records in a manner that complies with the jurisdiction's requirements.

1. **Ineligible instruments:** These are usually instruments that lack a notarial acknowledgment. If the defect is apparent on the face of the instrument, most states treat it as *not* recorded, and it does not give constructive notice. If the defect is hidden most states treat it as providing constructive notice.

2. **Unindexed instrument:** The older rule is that an improperly indexed instrument provides constructive notice, on the view that the grantee has done all he can to provide record notice. But the newer view is that it does not provide constructive notice because even the most diligent searcher will not find it.

3. **Omnibus clauses:** These clauses, inserted in a deed to one clearly described parcel, purport to cover "all other property" of the grantor. Since there is no way a diligent searcher of title to the "other property" will ever find such a clause, tucked away in an apparently unrelated deed, they are usually held to be inadequate to provide notice.

E. **Scope of protection:** The protection provided by recording acts is defined by the act. Recording does not make valid an invalid grant. Recording acts only apply to conveyances and not to interests created by operation of law (e.g., adverse possession or prescriptive or implied easements).

   1. **Bona fide purchasers:** Notice and race-notice acts are intended to protect only bona fide purchasers. A bona fide purchaser gives valuable consideration and lacks notice of any prior unrecorded conveyance. Race acts protect BFPs only to the extent they are first to record. A donee cannot be a BFP because she gives no consideration.

      a. **Shelter rule:** The protection given a BFP extends to all takers from the BFP, even if that taker knows of a prior unrecorded conveyance. The later taker receives the "shelter" of the BFP's status.

      b. **Mortgagees:** Mortgagees are generally treated as bona fide purchasers, though some states deny BFP status to a mortgagee who takes the mortgage to secure a pre-existing debt.

      c. **Creditors:** Some recording acts only protect purchasers, a term that excludes creditors unless they purchase at an execution sale. Other recording acts specifically protect creditors or "all persons."

F. **Notice:** Notice (which the BFP must lack) may be actual or constructive. Actual notice is real knowledge. Constructive notice may be derived from the record or may be the result of an obligation to make reasonable inquiry. A person obliged to inquire is constructively notified of facts that would reasonably be revealed by the inquiry. Common circumstances triggering inquiry notice include (1) possession of the property by somebody else, (2) record reference to an unrecorded instrument, (3) deeds from a common grantor, and (4) the character of the neighborhood (at least with respect to the possibility of an implied reciprocal covenant).

G. **Chain of title problems:** Some chain of title problems are fairly common and are considered here.

   1. **Instrument made by a stranger to the chain of title:** An instrument made by a total stranger to the record chain of title does not give notice. It is not within the chain of title.

   2. **After acquired title:** Most jurisdictions say that an instrument made and recorded before the grantor acquires title is inadequate to impart constructive notice, even if the grantor later acquires title. A few hold to the opposite view, thus expanding the concept of the chain of title.

   3. **Deed recorded after grantor has parted with record title:** States are about evenly divided. A slight majority hold that the chain of title includes all instruments recorded up to the point the later purchaser acquires title, which means that a title searcher must search the grantor index up to the present for every grantor. The minority reject this rule as too burdensome.

   4. **Deeds from a common grantor:** States divide over whether a deed from a common grantor to other property, but which imposes a restrictive covenant on the grantor's remaining property, is in the chain of title of the remaining property. States that say "yes" impose an enlarged search burden, since title searchers must locate and read all the deeds ever made by every owner of the subject property. States that say "no" permit title searchers to confine their efforts to the immediate chain of title.

H. **Marketable title acts:** These acts, adopted by about 20 states, bar all claims of title that predate a specified point in the past — anywhere from at least 22 to 50 years ago. Claims that are based on an instrument older than a ***root of title*** that is itself before the statutory time period are forever barred. The effectiveness of marketable title acts is diluted by provisions that either exempt some pre-root interests from the act or permit them to be kept alive by re-recording during the marketable title act period.

III. TITLE REGISTRATION

A. **The concept:** Title registration is a substitute for recording. The certificate of title is *the title,* not just evidence of title. The certificate of title is absolutely binding and definitive ownership.

B. **How it works:** To register title initially it is necessary to join in one judicial proceeding everybody who conceivably claims a title interest in the property. Once that proceeding results in a final determination of title, the title is registered and a certificate issued. All interests in title, such as mortgages or easements, are noted as "memorials" on the registered title. The only way thereafter to acquire title is to obtain a new registered title by cancellation of the old certificate and issuance of a new one in the new owner's name. But registered title acts often exempt some claims of title from this rule, thus diminishing the effectiveness of the concept. Typical exceptions include claims of governments, claims of persons in actual possession, mineral claims, visible easements, and railroad or utility easements. Also, if a title claimant is not joined in the original proceeding leading to issuance of registered title, her claim is not cut off. Fraud in the procurement of registered title also vitiates it. Title registration is not used much in the United States.

IV. TITLE INSURANCE

This is the most common form of title assurance. Title insurance involves the issuance of an insurance policy by which the insurer warrants that title is as stated in the policy. Title insurance policies contain a number of exclusions, typically such things as off-record liens or interests asserted by persons in possession, boundary disputes, off-record easements or servitudes, and government land use regulations. The insurer is liable for the difference in value of the property with and without the insured-against defect, up to the maximum limit specified in the policy.

CHAPTER 11
TAKINGS: THE POWER OF EMINENT DOMAIN AND REGULATORY TAKINGS

I. INTRODUCTION

A. **Eminent domain power:** All governments have the power to take private property for public use. The Constitution's "takings" clause requires that "just compensation" be paid for any such taking by any government. All types of property are protected. The takings clause was intended to prevent forcible redistributions (by requiring payment of compensation) and to limit takings to those for some public benefit. The principal issues that arise under the takings clause are (1) whether a taking has occurred, (2) whether a taking is for public use, and (3) whether just compensation has been paid.

B. **Compensation:** The property owner is entitled to the *fair market value* of the property taken. When only a portion is taken, the owner is entitled to *severance damages* — the difference between the value of the entire parcel before the taking and the value of the parcel the owner is left with after the taking. Fair market value is computed without regard to other collateral effects on the value of the property or on businesses conducted on the property.

II. THE PUBLIC USE REQUIREMENT

The takings clause is interpreted to mean that no taking can occur except for a public use, although the text of the clause does not dispositively say so. The public use requirement is easily met. So long as a taking is *rationally related to any conceivable public purpose* the public use requirement is met.

III. REGULATORY TAKINGS

A. **The problem:** At some point government regulation of property becomes so extensive or burdensome that a *de facto* taking occurs, even though the government may deny that a taking has occurred. Finding the point at which regulation ceases to be mere regulation and becomes a taking (requiring just compensation) is not easy.

B. **The *per se* rules:** There are three *"per se"* rules: one identifies when a taking has **not occurred;** the other two identify certain takings.

   1. **Nuisance abatement:** When governments regulate to abate what would be a private or public nuisance under the then current common law of nuisance, **no taking has occurred,** even if facts are present that would otherwise invoke either of the remaining *per se* rules.

   2. **Permanent dispossession:** If the property owner is permanently dispossessed from his property, or any part of it, the regulation is a taking.

   3. **Loss of all economically viable use:** If the regulation leaves the owner with absolutely no economically viable use, a taking has occurred. Problems with this rule include (1) determining when *no economically viable use* is left to the owner, and (2) determining whether the property that has been stripped of all economically viable use is a discrete, separate piece of property or simply a piece of a larger parcel that, considered as a whole, still may be used in some economically viable manner.

C. **Balancing public benefits and private costs:** If the *per se* rules do not dispose of the issue, courts will balance the public benefits and private costs. A regulation is a legitimate regulation, and not a taking, if it substantially advances a legitimate state objective. This means that three factors must be present: (1) the public benefits from the regulation must outweigh the private costs imposed, (2) the regulation must not be arbitrary, and (3) the property owner must be left with a reasonable return on her investment.

   1. **Conditional exemptions from regulations:** When governments impose conditions to permits that exempt the owner from a regulation (e.g., a building permit) the condition attached must clear two hurdles. First, the condition must be *substantially related to the legitimate objective underlying the original regulation* — the condition must have this *"essential nexus"* with the regulation. Second, the *nature and scope* of the condition must be *roughly proportional* to the impact of the proposed development.

D. **Remedies:** Once a regulation is found to be a taking the affected property owner may either (1) obtain an injunction preventing enforcement of the regulation, until and unless the government provides just compensation for its imposition, or (2) seek damages for the taking effected by the regulation. If the government imposes a regulation later found to be a taking, and the government then rescinds the regulation, the property owner is entitled to damages for the period the regulation was in effect.

CHAPTER 1
CONCEPTUAL BASICS, POSSESSION, AND PERSONAL PROPERTY

I. WHAT IS PROPERTY?

A. Introduction: There is no absolute, immutable principle that defines "property." Property is *socially contingent* — its definition will vary from culture to culture and, within cultures, over time. An obvious example is the immoral practice of human slavery. To paraphrase Felix Cohen, if property is what the state does to enforce the private citizen's declaration to the world to keep off without consent, property depends on who the "world" is, or who counts as a "private citizen," or even the identity of the state. "[P]roperty merges by imperceptible degrees into government, contract, force, and value." Cohen, 9 RUT. L. REV. 357, 374 (1954). Property is whatever interest in a thing — whether tangible or intangible — that is protected against invasion by others by the legal system of the society. But this definition is too general to be useful. Another way is to look at the theory and doctrine of property.

B. Theory: There are as many theories about property as there are theoreticians. Here are a few of the more important ones:

1. **Locke's labor theory:** John Locke, the 17th century political philosopher, started from the natural law premise that every person owns himself. Since you own your own labor, when you mix that labor with something unowned, you own the resulting mixture. See John Locke, *Two Treatises on Government*, Book II, Ch. V (1690).

    Example: Rob Crusoe arrives on a previously unknown island, unclaimed by any political jurisdiction, and proceeds to excavate a colorful rock partially buried in the beach sand. The rock turns out to be a valuable meteorite. Locke's labor theory explains Crusoe's property right in the meteorite by his labor in finding and excavating it.

2. **Other natural law theories:** Some theoreticians explain property as a pre-political entitlement, something "natural" and eternally existing. The problem with this view is that conceptions of "natural" property rights vary greatly. Its strength lies in the fact that it is a near-universal human trait to link possession of an object with ownership. But this linkage can also be explained by lass mystic utilitarian theories.

3. **Utilitarian theories:** David Hume, the 18th century Scottish philosopher, contended that property was nothing more than self-inter-

ested acquiescence in social and legal rules. We accept legal protection for other's property because we desire the same protection for our own. In a world without scarcity, there would be no need for property. You could always get more of whatever was lost or taken from you. But in our real world of scarcity it is important to protect what we possess. Jeremy Bentham popularized Hume's utilitarian explanation, rooting property in the protection of expectations. Note that both Hume's and Bentham's theories rest on the unarticulated premise that the initial possession (which is what is being protected) is legitimate. Locke explained why that was so. Hume and Bentham did not. But there is a utility-based expectation.

4. **Utility and efficiency:** Economists explain property as an efficient response to scarcity. Efficiency is utilitarian; why waste things? The economic explanation is that *externalities* — costs that are produced by an activity not borne by the person reaping the benefits of the activity — are *internalized* — borne by their maker. This makes the production of goods needed for human life more efficient.

Example 1: Suppose the Centurions, a society of 100 people, exists by fishing for enormous trout in a lake open to all Centurions. Centurions recognize a captured fish as property but not the free-swimming fish in the lake. The Centurions don't know it, but there are about 1000 fish in the lake. (Each Centurion has a theoretical 1/100th interest in the free swimming fish, or 10 fish.) If Sam, a Centurion, catches one fish he has acquired a property right to one fish, and continues to have the inchoate, theoretical interest of a 1/100th share in 999 fish. Sam's loss of a theoretical common interest (from 10.0 to 9.99) is more than offset by his acquisition of property in one whole fish, which he can eat. Most of the cost of losing one fish from the lake is borne by others, not Sam. The cost is external to Sam. So long as the subsistence needs of the Centurions and the reproduction rate of the fish remain in balance there is no need to create a property right to the free swimming fish, despite the external costs associated with fishing.

Example 2: But now imagine that Lewis Clark, an explorer and trader, arrives. He offers $5 per fish, a fabulous sum eagerly desired by Centurions. Each Centurion now has the incentive to catch as many fish as possible, for the costs of the loss will be borne mostly by other Centurions. If Centurions are skillful fishers the trout will soon be extinct. This does not do the Centurions any good. In the pursuit of self-interest, the common interest of everyone is destroyed because nobody is bearing that cost. To see why, imagine that the real value of each fish is $20. Although a Centurion loses 20 cents every time he catches a fish (1/100th of $20), he earns $5, for a net increase to his wealth of $4.80. But Centurion society as a whole is poorer by $15 (loss of $20 true value less $5 received).

Even if Centurions see the problem nobody will quit fishing because there is no assurance that others will cease if they do. Centurions probably can't simply agree to stop because it is probably too difficult to obtain unanimity. Unanimity takes time, and some people will hold out in the hopes of freeloading off of others' forbearance from fishing.

Example 3: Now suppose the Centurions divide the fish into 100 units of ownership of 10 fish each. A Centurion who captures and sells one of his own fish will reap the benefit of Clark's $5 but will also suffer the full loss of the $20 true value of the fish. More importantly, by not fishing the individual Centurion keeps the full value of the fish, rather than seeing it disappear into his competitor's nets.

5. **Custom:** Some observers point out that property rights often occur by custom, and note that the customs are intended to maximize aggregate wealth of the customary participants. Whalers, for example, had many customs designed to deal with the uncertain business of capturing giant sea mammals and maximizing the possibility of profit in the enterprise. See generally Robert Ellickson, *Order Without Law: How Neighbors Settle Disputes* (1991).

C. **Doctrine:** The simplest doctrinal answer to the question of what is property is to say that property is whatever the legal system protects as property. Simple, but useless. Courts tend to break property down into three core elements: the right to exclusive ***possession***, the right to exclusive ***use***, and the right to ***dispose or transfer***. But there is no formula by which you can assemble these elements into property. Two atoms of hydrogen and one of oxygen make water, but it is not at all clear that a use right coupled with a disposition right make property. Nevertheless, these are the doctrinal elements of property and these concepts will pop in and out of your study of property, like the Banks children and their chalked pictures in *Mary Poppins*.

II. POSSESSION

A. **Introduction:** Whatever the best theoretical explanation of property, all rely on the presumption that possession of an object implies a property right in it. Possession may be "nine points of the law," as the old saying has it, but it isn't all of it. Some people (*e.g.*, thieves) are wrongful possessors. Others (*e.g.*, a finder) have property claims that are only ***relative*** to the claims of others. Sorting these issues out is the objective of this section.

B. Two meanings of possession: The term "possession" means two different things. It describes a physical act — by falling down dead drunk at the dinner party you take possession of the floor under you. It also describes a legal conclusion — the host of the dinner party is in possession of his home when he tosses you out, for purposes of a law that immunizes self-help by "possessors" of property in ousting unwanted visitors. But sometimes physical possession is the fact that produces the legal possession that flows from ownership of property. People, including judges, are careless in their usage of this term. Be precise; it clarifies your arguments.

C. Of "unowned" things — wild animals, discovery and creation: Many property courses begin with these issues because they provide an opportunity to use real cases grappling with the thorny question of initial acquisition of property rights.

　1. Wild animals: Wild animals may be one of the few things that are unowned. Indeed, that is why they capture our imagination. In an earlier age, when our ancestors relied on game, the acquisition of property rights in wild animals was more relevant.

　　a. Actual possession: The usual method of acquiring a property right in a wild animal is actually to possess it — dead or alive.

　　　Example: Post chases a fox on common land (a wild beach). Before Post has wounded or captured the fox, Pierson intervenes and kills and takes the fox, though he knows of Post's chase. Did Pierson interfere with any property right of Post? Did Post own the fox?

　　　　Not until he has actual physical possession, said a New York appellate court in 1805. Mere pursuit is not enough. Perhaps pursuit was the labor, but until pursuit produced capture it wasn't mixed enough with the fox to create property. The result was defended on the ground that a rule of actual possession would promote certainty and peace. Justice Livingston dissented on the ground that it was better to adopt the customs of sportsmen, or, failing that, to announce a rule that would best rid the world of predatory foxes. Livingston urged recognition of property rights in wild animals when there was a reasonable likelihood of capture. *Pierson v. Post*, 3 Cai. R. 175 (N.Y. 1805).

　　b. Relative title: Actual possession isn't everything. One person's claimed property right is almost always good (or not good) only in ***relation*** to others. In *Pierson* the fox was on common —

unowned — land. What if the hunt occurred on Post's land and Pierson was a trespasser? Pierson's actual possession of the fox would give him a property right in it but only until that right was trumped by Post, invoking his right to exclude others from his real estate. Note that this is a conflict between two different property rules: **first possession** and the landowner's **right to exclude** others. Post, the landowner, would have a better claim to the fox, not because he was a **prior possessor** of the fox, but because he was entitled to deprive trespassers of their game taken from his estate. And it would be Pierson's fox if Post had bagged it on Pierson's farm. The law rarely encourages trespassing. Cf. *Keeble v. Hickeringill*, 103 Eng. Rep. 1127 (Q.B. 1707) (finding that Hickeringill's act of scaring the ducks off his neighbor Keeble's pond was tortious interference with trade, but treated by later courts as resting on the fact that the ducks were on Keeble's land).

Example: Suppose that Post had clobbered the fox, picked up its limp carcass, and slung it across his saddle. If Pierson yanked it off as he cantered by, Post would get it back because he was a **prior possessor** of the single object in dispute. It is first possession that counts. To see this, suppose Post trespassed on Morton's land, took the fox, and Pierson came upon Post's land and took it. As between Post and Pierson, who has title? Post wins, since even among wrongdoers the prior possessor prevails. See *Anderson v. Gouldberg*, 51 Minn. 294 (1892).

   c. **Escapees and domesticated animals:** When the wild animal escapes it is unowned. It belongs to the next first possessor. *Stephens & Co. v. Albers*, 256 P. 15 (Colo. 1927) (person who captured escaped silver fox owned it). Domesticated animals aren't wild, so they continue to belong to their prior possessor when they wander off. A wild animal becomes domesticated when, as a matter of fact, it demonstrates a propensity to return "home" (*animus revertendi*).

2. **Discovery:** Not much is undiscovered today. But the idea that property could be acquired by discovery has some modern implications. In *Johnson v. M'Intosh*, 21 U.S. 543 (1823), the U.S. Supreme Court confronted rival claims for ownership of land in Illinois. Johnson's claim was the last link in a **chain of title** going back to the Piankeshaw, the aboriginal inhabitants of the land. M'Intosh said his title was better because it came from the United States, although after the Piankeshaw conveyance to Johnson's predecessor. The Court held for M'Intosh. Why? The Piankeshaw, as Indians, only held aboriginal title, a right of occupancy that could be cut off

at any moment by the United States, as the successor to the European discoverers of the land. This Eurocentric approach to discovery was supplemented by the idea that the U.S. also derived its ownership by **conquest** of the Piankeshaw. There may not be much land left to discover but there is still the same amount around to conquer. Consider Bosnia. The fact of conquest as a source of property rights is a reminder of the socially contingent nature of property.

3. **Creation:** Many intangible property rights are created. A novel is the creation of an inventive and communicative mind. Its property right is the **copyright** of the creator — the right to own the reproduction of the creation. Some creations are also discoveries — Edison and the incandescent lamp — and the law protects them by **patent** and the law of **trade secrets**. Courses in **intellectual property** deal with these subjects in fascinating detail.

   a. **Exclusivity:** A key issue is the degree of exclusivity the property owner has in exploiting the intangible right. Some argue that since information can be used by many people at once (unlike an ear of corn, where the value is in personal consumption to the exclusion of others) the owner ought not be able to insist on exclusive use. Free availability of information (whether novels or computer software) may make "the public as a whole ... better off, as long as this freedom to imitate does not destroy the incentive for people to come up with new ideas." Baird, 50 U. CHI. L. REV. 411, 414 (1983). The contrast may be seen in the law of misappropriation — the branch of unfair competition law that protects new ideas.

   Example: In *International News Service v. Associated Press*, 248 U.S. 215 (1918), the U.S. Supreme Court held it was misappropriation for INS to copy AP's news and release it before AP could. But later courts have held that skilled imitation of Chanel No. 5 perfume and seasonal fabric designs is not misappropriation. See *Cheney Brothers v. Doris Silk Corp.*, 35 F.2d 279 (2d Cir. 1929); *Smith v. Chanel, Inc.*, 402 F.2d 562 (9th Cir. 1968). The law is well-headed in Professor Baird's direction.

   b. **Creation vs. first possession:** A famous conflict pitting the property right of first possession against that asserted by a creator occurred in *Moore v. Regents of the University of California*, 793 P.2d 479 (Cal. 1990). Moore's cancerous spleen was removed and, without either his knowledge or consent, a valuable patented cell line was developed using Moore's unique "hairy leukemia" cells. The California Supreme Court ruled that there was no cause of action for conversion, a tort that is the wrongful exercise of ownership rights over the personal property of another.

The majority said Moore had no ownership because he never expected to retain possession of the spleen. The court's reasons for refusing to extend conversion to the human waste tissue from surgery were that it would chill medical research, the moral issues involved ought to be left to the politically accountable branch — the Legislature, and Moore still had available to him claims based on asserted breach of fiduciary duty by his caregivers.

    i. Significance of *Moore*: *Moore* poses a conflict between Moore's right of first possession of his body parts (recall Locke's premise that we own ourselves) and the scientist's right to own the unique cells developed from Moore's discarded spleen. In concluding that Moore's spleen was not his property the court was saying only that Moore didn't own it in the limited sense of having the right to profit from it after he had discarded it. So long as the spleen was in him, it was Moore's exclusively to possess and use. But did he ever have the right to transfer it by sale, as opposed to giving it away? We tolerate a great many limitations on transfer rights by sale — you can give away your baby but you can't sell it. *Moore* reflects the view that body parts ought not be for sale. It is not the last word. Resolution of the precise issue is for philosophers, not property lawyers, but a property lawyer must make the philosopher's arguments. *Moore* illustrates the malleability of the concept of property and the fact that the decision to call something property has enough consequence to cause courts to weigh social and juridical factors heavily in deciding whether to call it property. *Moore* does not stand for the proposition that in order to have property it is necessary to have all of the sticks in the property bundle: use, possession, and disposition.

D. Finders keepers: A property owner continues to own his property even after he loses or misplaces it. But lost property often ends up in the finder's pocket. The finder's claim to the property depends on who the rival claimant is and whether the property was lost, mislaid, or abandoned by the true owner. A finder has relative title. The policy objectives in finder's law are to

- Restore property to the true owner;
- Reward honest finders;
- Deliver the reasonable expectations of landowners;
- Discourage trespassers and other wrongdoers; and
- Encourage the productive use of found property.

1. **Abandoned property — general rule:** Abandoned property is property to which the true owner has voluntarily given up any claim of ownership. Except for trespassing finders, and unless the rule is modified by statute, a *finder of abandoned property acquires title*.

   Example: True Owner places his old computer on the sidewalk in front of his house, with a placard that says "Free — Take Me." True Owner has abandoned his ownership. The first possessor becomes the next True Owner.

   a. **How to determine if abandoned:** Property is not usually labeled as abandoned. The conclusion of abandonment usually has to be made from circumstantial facts.

      Example: True Owner places a bundle of newspapers outside his house for curbside recycling. Absent any relevant statutes, has True Owner abandoned the papers? Almost certainly. His action indicates intent to renounce ownership. If Scavenger takes the papers he has acquired ownership.

   b. **Intent to relinquish ownership:** Intention to relinquish ownership is critical. A true owner may be prevented from possessing his property but, so long as he never intends to give up his claim of ownership it remains his.

      Example: In 1857 the steamship *Central America* sank in a storm off Cape Hatteras, carrying a large cargo of California gold to the bottom. The insurers paid off, and thus acquired ownership of the insured cargo. In 1988 the wreck of the *Central America* was discovered and part of the cargo recovered. Though 131 years had elapsed, the Fourth circuit ruled that the mere elapse of time was not enough to prove abandonment. *Columbus-America Discovery Group v. Atlantic Mutual Insurance Co.*, 974 F.2d 450 (4th Cir. 1992).

   c. **Trespassers:** Trespassing finders of abandoned property are denied title unless the trespass is "trivial or merely technical." *Favorite v. Miller*, 407 A.2d 974 (Conn. 1978), in which a trespasser found the severed head to an equestrian statue of George III, buried in a Connecticut pasture by Loyalists during the American Revolution. (The true owner of the statue — the British Crown — presumably abandoned its claim by recognizing American independence.)

2. **Lost and mislaid property — general rule:** *A finder's title is good against the whole world except the true owner, prior finders, and (generally) the owner of land where an object is*

found. Lost property is just that — it slid out of the hole in your pocket. Mislaid property is property that the true owner placed somewhere with the intention of returning for it, but which cannot now be located — the wallet left on the grocer's counter.

Example: A chimney sweep found a gem in a setting and took it to a jeweler for appraisal. The jeweler's apprentice removed the gem and refused to return it. The sweep was awarded damages, measured by the value of the finest stone that would fit the setting, unless the master produced the stone. *Armory v. Delamirie*, 1 Strange 505 (K.B. 1722). If the jeweler had been the true owner of the gem, the chimney sweep would have lost. Remember, a finder has only relative title.

- **a. Prior finders:** Prior finders prevail over later finders. If logic dictates that the True Owner's title prevails over the title of First Finder, then the same logic dictates that Prior Finder prevails over later finders.

    Example: True Owner loses his watch, which is found by First Finder. First Finder then loses the watch, which is found by Second Finder. In this case, First Finder would prevail over Second Finder on the basis of his prior possession. True Owner would, of course, prevail over First Finder. See *Clark v. Maloney*, 3 Harr. 68 (Del. 1840).

    The prior possession principle applies even if First Finder had stolen the watch from True Owner. See *Anderson v. Gouldberg*, 51 Minn. 294 (1892). This is efficient, by avoiding litigation over the circumstances of the finding, and the contrary rule would neither deter thievery nor increase the likelihood of restoring the object to the true owner. The rationales for protecting prior possession, especially when we know there is some unknown true owner, are (1) to encourage finders to make productive use of their finds rather than hide them, and (2) to provide a cheap, easy means of establishing presumptive title.

- **b. Finder vs. landowner:** Conflicts frequently arise between a finder and the owner of the land upon which the property was found (often called the owner of the *locus in quo*). Of course, there is no conflict if the landowner also owns the found object. If the hostess exclaims "I've lost my wedding ring!" and you find it in your salad the ring is not yours. But if the true owner is neither the finder nor the landowner, conflict erupts.

    - **i. Trespassing finders:** As is true of abandoned property, trespassing finders of lost or mislaid property lose. See *Favorite v. Miller, supra*.

ii. **Employee finders:** Older cases tend to find that employee finders must surrender the find to their employer if the employee has a contractual duty to report finds.

Example: A carpenter employed by a hotel was allowed to keep property he found in a hotel guest room he was redecorating because his carpentry duties did not include reporting found property. The court said the outcome would be reversed if he had been a chambermaid, because "[c]hambermaids frequently find [property] guests have forgotten." *Erickson v. Sinykin*, 26 N.W.2d 172 (Minn. 1947).

(1) **Poor rationale:** Putting aside the (perhaps) sexist subtext of *Erickson* the rationale is poor. The duty to report makes sense as a way to facilitate restoration of found property to the true owner, but if the true owner is never found, it makes little sense to deprive the honest chambermaid of her find. If reporting the find causes its loss to the finder, diamond rings left on the hotel dresser are likely to disappear silently. The objectives of restoring lost property to the owner and of rewarding honest finders can be achieved by combining a duty to report with award to the finder when the true owner never materializes. For this reason, other cases tend to award found property to the employee finder. *Hamaker v. Blanchard*, 90 Pa. 377 (1879); *Danielson v. Roberts*, 74 P. 913 (Or. 1904); *Toledo Trust Co. v. Simmons*, 3 N.E.2d 661 (Ohio Ct. App. 1935).

iii. **Invitee finders:** Landowners often invite workmen and others on to their property for specific and limited purposes. Finding property is almost never one of those purposes. An invitee who finds property in the course of doing what he was invited to do must ***surrender it to the landowner***. But why? Leaving the property with the landowner may slightly improve the odds of returning the property to the true owner, and landowners do have expectations of ownership of immobile things on their land. But awarding the find to the landowner undermines the goal of rewarding honest finders. Some argue that the value of the find should be split between finder and landowner.

Example: Landowner employed Sharman to clean out the Minster Pool. In doing so, Sharman found two gold rings. The rings went to Landowner, who concededly was unaware of their existence until the find. Landowner was treated as the ***constructive possessor*** of the rings — a legal conclusion that the Landowner should prevail. *South Staffordshire Water Co. v. Sharman*, [1896] 2 Q.B. 44.

- iv. **Embedded objects and treasure trove:** When property is embedded in or under the soil it is awarded to the landowner, on the rationale that the landowner's expectations of owning things in the dirt itself are especially strong.

    Example: A meteorite slammed into Goddard's land and was dug up by Hoagland, an invitee of Elickson, Goddard's tenant in possession. Hoagland sold the meteorite to Winchell. Goddard sued for its return and won, mostly because the meteorite became a part of Earth upon its arrival. *Goddard v. Winchell*, 52 N.W. 1124 (Iowa 1892).

    - (1) **Treasure trove:** But when the embedded property is ***treasure trove*** — gold, silver, or money buried with the intent of return and recovery — different rules may apply. In England, treasure trove belongs to the Crown — the government. American states have largely rejected the doctrine but are split as to whether the find should go to the finder or landowner. Compare *Danielson v. Roberts*, supra, awarding treasure trove to the finder, and *Schley v. Couch*, 284 S.W.2d 333 (Tex. 1955), awarding treasure trove to the landowner. Logic suggests that rejection of the treasure trove doctrine means that the normal rules apply.

- v. **Private homes:** Homeowners are awarded objects found in their homes. A homeowner has an especially strong expectation of ownership of objects found inside her home and, to the extent the property was mislaid, the odds of its recovery by the true owner are increased by leaving it with the homeowner. When the homeowner is an absentee owner — not in possession of the home — resolution of the question turns on whether the homeowner was in constructive possession of the home. If the homeowner is briefly absent — a mere sojourner away from home — she is in constructive possession of objects found in her absence. But what if she never moved in?

    Example: Major Peel purchased Gwernhaylod House, a country estate in Shropshire, but never moved in. When World War II broke out, the Crown requisitioned Gwernhaylod House to quarter soldiers. Corporal Hannah found a valuable brooch while adjusting his blackout curtain. He reported the find. Two years later, the owner not having appeared, the brooch was turned over to Peel, who then sold it. Hannah demanded the sale proceeds and won. Since Peel had never moved in, he never had constructive possession of Gwernhaylod House's unknown lost contents. *Hannah v. Peel*, [1945] 1 K.B. 509.

Hannah is a case where the "all-or-nothing" approach to ownership seems poorly fitted to the goals of finder's law. Ownership in Peel punishes the honest finder. Ownership in Hannah defeats Peel's reasonable expectation that he owns everything that came with Gwernhaylod House. Perhaps the value of the find should have been split between Hannah and Peel.

vi. **Public places:** Lost property found in public places goes to the finder. Mislaid property found in public places goes to the landowner. The rationale for this distinction is that the odds of restoring lost property to the true owner are slim, while the true owner of mislaid property may well return to the place where it was mislaid. But true owners often retrace their steps when they lose items, so this rationale is not airtight. For instance, if a wallet is found on a barber shop counter, it was probably placed there by a customer and then forgotten. As mislaid property, it goes to the barbershop owner. *McAvoy v. Medina*, 93 Mass. 548 (1866). But if the wallet is found on the barber's floor it was probably dropped there unintentionally by a customer. As lost property, it goes to the finder. *Bridges v. Hawksworth*, 21 L.J. (N.S.) 75 (K.B. 1851). But is it so clear that the wallet on the counter was mislaid? Maybe it fell out as the customer leaned over. And perhaps the wallet on the floor was carefully placed there, or accidentally knocked to the floor from some more secure locale. The lost-mislaid distinction requires courts to surmise from circumstantial evidence. Again, critics argue that the policies of finder's law might be better served by a sharing rule, or giving temporary custody to the landowner and, if no true ower emerges, title to the finder.

3. **Statutory modification:** Some states have enacted statutes modifying these common law rules. A typical approach is to call all found property lost property and award it to the finder after a reasonable search for the true owner has proved unsuccessful. *Hurley v. City of Niagara Falls*, 289 N.Y.S.2d 889 (N.Y. Sup. Ct. 1968), applied New York's statute to award a plumber $4900 in cash found by him while working in a customer's house.

E. Adverse possession: Virtually all legal causes of action must be brought within the period of time set out in a statute of limitations. If the true owner of land fails to start legal proceedings to remove a person who adversely possesses his land within the period of the statute of limitations, the true owner is forever barred from removing the adverse possessor. Since there is no other owner, the adverse possessor has taken title to the land and can obtain a judgment to that effect. The adverse possessor acquires whatever title to the property the owner had. This is the doctrine of ***adverse possession***. It combines two broad requirements: (1) expiration of the relevant statute of limitations, and (2) adverse possession during the limitations period. The first requirement is statutory and its elements are determined by the statute. The second requirement consists of a series of common law elements concerning the nature of the possession that must be proven.

1. **Rationales for adverse possession:** There are three major justifications for adverse possession:

    a. **Sleeping theory:** Slothful owners, who ignore people using their land in brazen violation of legal right, deserve to be penalized. By failing to bring a timely action for ejectment they create a problem: adjudicating stale claims is very difficult — witnesses die and disappear, memories fade, documents are lost. The slothful owner ought to bear the risk of losing his property if he does not care enough to assert his ownership. Some argue that stripping the slothful owner of title comports with his reasonable expectations. In a sense, use it or lose it.

    b. **Earning theory:** People who use land productively and beneficially for a long time ought to be rewarded. Even though the land is owned by someone else, the actual possessor has invested time and effort in making it productive. After a long enough period, the adverse possessor has earned some interest in the land. When coupled with the sleeping theory, the justice of cutting off the true owner's claim seems even stronger. Psychologically if not legally the adverse possessor develops expectations of continued possession, which expectations are met by the doctrine of adverse possession.

    c. **Stability theory:** Adverse possession enables disputes or doubts about land titles to be cleared expeditiously by delivering title to the person who has occupied the land as if she were the owner for a long time without objection.

    Example: O, the true owner of Blackacre, conveys it to A by deed in 1965. A fails to record the deed so the public land records indicate O as the owner. In 1990 A sells Blackacre to B, who records his deed from A. In 1997 B agrees to sell Blackacre to C, who balks because the public land records fail to show any deed to A. From the records O is still the owner. The relevant limitations statute is 20 years. Adverse possession cures the problem. B will be able (at some cost) to establish his ownership and thus convey good title to C.

2. **Elements of adverse possession:** To acquire title by adverse possession the adverse possessor must prove four elements. The possessor must (1) actually enter and take exclusive possession that is (2) open and notorious, (3) adverse or hostile to the true owner's interest and under a claim of right, and (4) continuous for the limitations period. In some places the possessor must also prove she has paid the property taxes for the limitations period.

   a. **Actual and exclusive possession:** Actual entry means just that — the possessor must actually, physically, take possession of the owner's land. The owner's cause of action accrues at that moment, and the clock on the limitations period starts to run at the moment of actual entry. Exclusive possession means that the possessor has excluded the public and the owner. It does not mean that only one adverse possessor can occupy. A group of people adversely occupying may acquire a shared title — concurrent ownership — by adverse possession.

   b. **Open and notorious possession:** Occupation must be open and notorious. This means that the adverse possession must be readily visible to any inspector of the property. The idea is that the true owner would know of the occupation if he visited his property. Open and notorious occupation constitutes notice to the owner that his rights are being violated. Occupation is open and notorious if it is the type of occupation a true owner would make.

   Example: An adverse possessor of a fenced pasture would possess openly and notoriously if he kept horses or cattle in the pasture. An adverse possessor of an urban home would possess openly and notoriously by moving in and coming and going without concealment. An adverse possessor of undeveloped land must do something to leave a visible mark of his control, such as building a cabin, or fencing, or posting a sign announcing his occupancy.

   i. **Underground occupation:** It is difficult to occupy subsurface locations openly and notoriously. To satisfy the open and notorious element in such cases it is probably necessary to prove that the owner knew of the occupation, or at least knew of the underground space and that it was accessible by outsiders. See *Marengo Cave Co. v. Ross*, 10 N.E.2d 917 (Ind. 1937).

ii. **Adverse possession of subsurface minerals:** Because an adverse possessor takes whatever title the true owner had, an adverse possessor of the surface acquires title to subsurface minerals if the true owner had title to them. But if the mineral rights were owned by someone other than the surface owner when the adverse possessor occupied the surface, the adverse possessor acquires title only to the surface. To acquire mineral rights by adverse possession the possessor would have to remove minerals in a manner that meets each of the elements of adverse possession.

iii. **Minor encroachments:** Some jurisdictions hold that encroachments by one neighbor onto the land of another are not open and notorious if the encroachment is of a small area and is not "clearly and self-evidently" an encroachment. In such situations the limitations statute does not begin to run until and unless the owner has actual knowledge of the encroachment. See *Mannillo v. Gorski*, 255 A.2d 258 (N.J. 1969).

iv. **Statutory modifications:** Some states impose special rules on open and notorious occupation. A typical scheme is the New York law at issue in *Van Valkenburgh v. Lutz*, 304 N.Y. 95 (1952), which required adverse possessors occupying without color of title (see p. 12 *supra*) to prove that they had "substantially enclosed" or "usually cultivated or improved" the property. These statutes simply make the open and notorious element more specific.

c. **"Hostility" or adverse claim of right:** An adverse possessor must occupy the land without the consent of the owner and with an intention to remain. This element is often called "hostility" but it does not mean "with malice" or ill will. It simply means that the adverse possessor has no permission to be there and also claims the right to stay there. "Consent" or "permission" means that the possessor has occupied in some capacity subordinate to the owner's title.

Example: Owen, owner of Blackacre, leases it to Charlene. Charlene's entry is consensual; her occupancy is subordinate to Owen's title.

i. **Claiming a right to stay:** It is relatively easy to decide whether or not the owner has consented to the occupation;

but it is difficult to decide whether the possessor claims a right to stay. Courts apply three different tests to this problem. Two are subjective — what was the possessor's state of mind? — and the third is objective — what did the possessor do?

ii. Subjective — good faith occupation: Under this test, the adverse possessor must have a genuine, good faith belief that she owns the occupied property. Possessors who know that the property they are occupying is not their own can never acquire title by adverse possession in a jurisdiction applying this version of hostility.

Example: True Owner tells Friend that the farm is Friend's. Friend occupies for the limitations period. Friend is not the record owner because land cannot validly be transferred by oral conveyance (see Chapter 9, p. 292, *infra*), but Friend has acquired title by adverse possession. He genuinely believed the farm was his own. His entry was not consensual because it was not subordinate to the owner's continued claim of title. Rather, True Owner intended to pass title to Friend. See *Newells v. Carter*, 119 A. 62 (Me. 1922).

(1) Test criticized: This test is roundly criticized by professors as a perversion of the policy objectives and justifications for adverse possession. It rewards the slothful owner, penalizes the productive occupier who lacks a good faith belief of ownership, and does little to promote settlement of clouded land titles. This test is often claimed to be the minority test but a respected property scholar claims that, in fact, it is the majority view. Squatters and other deliberate trespassers rarely win without a strong equitable case. Helmholz, 61 Wash. U.L.Q. 331 (1983). The good faith view probably persists out of the belief that rewarding deliberate trespassers permits acquisition of title by "larceny."

iii. Subjective — aggressive trespass: There are a few old cases that appear to require that the occupier know the property is ***not his own but that he intend to claim it nevertheless***.

Example: Reigle and Shingledecker moved onto a parcel they knew wasn't theirs. They said they "intended to leave when the real owner, ... the old soldier, should come for it, but not till then." The court awarded title to them: they intended to claim it as against everyone but the old soldier and the old soldier's claim was time-barred. *Patterson v. Reigle*, 4 Pa. 201 (1846).

- **(1) Not followed today:** Almost nobody adheres to this view today. It rewards only the most determined of deliberate trespassers. A better reason why nobody clings to this view is that it is merely a way station on the road to the objective test.

iv. **Objective state of mind irrelevant:** Under this test, which is often claimed to be the majority view, the state of mind of the occupier is essentially not relevant. Instead, courts focus on two things: (1) lack of permission (in the sense that the occupation is not subordinate to the owner's title) and (2) whether the occupier's acts and statements objectively appear to be claims of ownership. In short, we don't care what you secretly believe, but have you acted like a true owner should?

Example: Refer to the last example, concerning Reigle and Shingledecker. R & S were not occupying with the permission of the old soldier, the true owner, but they conducted themselves as the true owners. "We settled it to hold it until a better owner came for it." No one but the old soldier could be a better owner and he never came. To the world's objective eye, R & S appeared to be the true owners. *Patterson v. Reigle, supra.*

v. **Disclaimers of ownership:** If an adverse possessor disclaims ownership in order to persuade the owner not to sue, the possessor has stopped being adverse. The adversity element is destroyed and the limitations clock stops. The conclusion that adversity has ended is a bit fictional — actually it's just not fair to let the adverse possessor lull the owner into a loss of his rights.

Example 1: Squatter occupies Blackacre and satisfies all the elements of adverse possession for nine years. The limitations period is ten years. Then Owner discovers Squatter's presence and confronts him. Squatter says "I'll leave as soon as I can arrange a new place. Just don't sue me." If Squatter stays for another two years, has he acquired title by adverse possession? No. He disclaimed ownership.

Example 2: But suppose Squatter had said, "Look, I'll buy the place," and offers a price. If negotiations drag on for more than a year has Squatter acquired title? Not necessarily. It depends on how the trier of fact sees the offer. If it was an implicit disclaimer of ownership, Squatter doesn't own Blackacre. But if it was an implicit statement to the effect, "I own Blackacre, but I'm willing to buy off your spurious claim to avoid litigation," Squatter does indeed now own Blackacre. Delay is risky for true owners.

vi. Boundary disputes: Often one landowner mistakenly occupies a strip of her neighbor's land in the belief that it is her own. Most courts apply an objective test of hostility to these cases. If the encroaching owner's actions appear to the world to be those of a true owner (*e.g.*, she built a fence) she occupies adversely to her neighbor. A minority applies a variant subjective test, often called the ***Maine doctrine*** after a Maine case, *Preble v. Maine Central Railroad*, 27 A. 149 (Me. 1893). Under the Maine doctrine the occupier is not possessing adversely if she occupied under a good faith but mistaken belief that the land is hers, but she would not have occupied if she knew the true facts. This is not quite the same thing as the subjective good faith test.

Example: If Joe occupies his neighbor Bill's land without concern whether he is occupying his own or Bill's land, Joe can acquire title by adverse possession under the Maine doctrine. But Joe lacks the subjective good faith belief to establish adversity in those jurisdictions applying subjective good faith.

(1) *Maine* doctrine criticized: The Maine doctrine is frequently criticized as perverse. It encourages perjury ("Sure, I would have stayed anyway"), rewards the intentional trespasser but not the honest one, and requires a difficult and contested judgment about what somebody might have done if their state of knowledge had been different. No wonder it's the minority rule.

vii. Color of title, *not* claim of right: Claim of right is the term often used to describe the element of hostility or adversity. It is sometimes confused with color of title. Don't make this error! A possessor who enters under color of title is one who has a defective deed or other writing that purports to deliver title to the possessor, but which the possessor does not know to be invalid. The deed might be improperly executed, or forged, or signed by somebody who doesn't own the land. But note: Possessors who enter under color of title satisfy the adversity element. On the other hand, only a few states require color of title to satisfy hostility, or adversity. Color of title has other implications concerning how much land the occupier is deemed to have adversely possessed. See p. 21, *infra*.

d. **Continuous possession:** An adverse possessor must occupy continuously — without interruption — during the limitations period. But this does not mean that the adverse possessor must stay on the land for every moment of the 10 or 20 years of the limitations period. Rather, it means that the adverse possessor must occupy the property as continually as would a reasonable and average true owner of the property. If the possessor ever abandons the property — intentionally gives up possession with no intent of returning — continuity is destroyed. A later return by the possessor triggers a new cause of action in the owner and the start of a fresh limitations period. This element combines the subjectivity of the possessor's state of mind (When he left the property was it always his intention to return?) with objective appraisal of what the possessor actually did. If the possessor always intended to return, treated absences as sojourns, and actually occupied the property for as much time as an average true owner would, this element is satisfied. The key here is to decide what the normal use of the property is. If the adverse possessor makes that use, she has likely occupied continuously. But intermittent use that is not sufficient to satisfy continuity may be enough to create a prescriptive easement — a right to use another's property for a limited purpose. See p. 210, *infra*.

Example: Kunto occupied a summer residence under color of title (a defective deed). When Howard, the record owner, sought to eject him, Kunto countered that the limitations period had expired. Not if you failed to occupy continuously, retorted Howard. But I was here every summer, replied Kunto. That was good enough. The property was intended for summer occupancy, as were the surrounding properties. A reasonable owner would use the property during the summer and not at other times. *Howard v. Kunto*, 477 P.2d 210 (Wash. Ct. App. 1970).

  i. **Tacking — adverse possessors:** A common problem with continuity is whether one possessor can add — **tack** — the possession of a prior possessor to his own. If ***privity of estate*** exists between the prior possessor and the present possessor, tacking is permitted. ***Privity of estate*** means the ***voluntary transfer*** from the first possessor to the second possessor of ***either*** an ***estate*** in the land (see Chapter 2, p. 40, *infra*) or ***actual possession*** of it. (**Caution:** In the context of servitudes, privity of estate has a different meaning. See p. 230, *infra*.)

Example: Able adversely entered Blackacre in 1970. The limitations period is 20 years. In 1980 Able gave Baker a deed to Blackacre and Baker took possession. In 1991 Charles, owner of Blackacre, sues Baker for ejectment. Who wins and why? Baker will win, assuming all the other elements of adverse possession have been met by Able and Baker over the 20 year period. The limitations period started to run in 1970. By the deed to Baker, Able did not transfer an estate in Blackacre (because he had no estate to transfer) but the deed is excellent evidence of a voluntary transfer of actual possession. Privity of estate is present and Baker is permitted to tack his possession of 11 years onto Able's prior possession of 10 years. The statute of limitations has run. Charles is too late.

- **(1) English courts:** English courts don't require privity for tacking to occur. In the U.K. the sleeping theory alone is sufficient justification for this result. U.S. courts prefer to penalize the slothful owner only when the victor is a deserving possessor.

ii. **Tacking — owner:** Tacking follows automatically on the owner's side. Once the statute of limitations has started to run, the cause of action for ejectment (together with its expiring limitations period) goes along with ownership.

Example: In 1970, Bebe entered Blackacre adversely. In 1975 Jojo, owner of Blackacre, sells it to Hojo. In 1980 Hojo dies and leaves Blackacre by will to Zaza. In 1985 Zaza gives Blackacre to Dada. In 1991 Dada sues to eject Bebe. The limitations period is 20 years. Bebe wins, assuming she meets all the elements of adverse possession. The statute of limitations was triggered in 1970 and the expiring cause of action traveled from Jojo to Hojo to Zaza to Dada.

iii. **Ouster:** If an adverse possessor is ousted from possession by a third party, the third party may not tack the ousted possessor's period of possession onto his own. Privity is lacking because the transfer was not voluntary. But courts take three different views of what happens if the ousted possessor returns.

- **(1) Least preferred view:** The *least preferred view* is that the limitations period starts anew with the re-entry. This view treats ousted possessors harshly, ignoring their determined (and successful) effort to regain possession.

(2) Most preferred view: The *most preferred view* is that the ousted possessor can tack her new possession onto her old possession but cannot take credit for occupation by the third party. For the duration of that third party's occupation the limitations period is tolled, or suspended. The effect is that for the possessor to acquire title she must occupy for the limitations period plus the period of third party occupation.

(3) Logically confused view: A *logically confused view* (but one adopted by some courts) is that the ouster does not interrupt the continual running of the limitations period. The problem with this view is that it permits the ousted possessor to tack her possession after re-entry onto the third party's possession, but there is no privity to support this conclusion. Courts paper over this flaw by calling the ousting third party a trespasser rather than a possessor, and treating the ousted possessor as being in constructive possession during the third party's occupation.

e. **Payment of taxes:** Some states (mostly in the West) require adverse possessors to prove that they have paid the property taxes on the occupied property for the duration of the limitations period. Because tax collectors will usually make the owner aware of a stranger's attempt to tender taxes, this element makes it extremely unlikely that a person can adversely possess without uncommon negligence on the part of the owner or a mutual mistake as to ownership of the property.

3. **Property acquired by adverse possession:** Once the adverse possessor has satisfied the elements of adverse possession for the limitations period she acquires title to the occupied property. But what is the physical extent of the occupied property? The answer depends on whether the adverse possessor entered with or without color of title. Recall that color of title, in essence, means entry under a defective deed, but without knowledge of the defect. See p. 18, *supra*.

   a. **Entry without color of title:** An adverse possessor without color of title acquires *only the property she has actually physically possessed* for the limitations period.

   b. **Entry under color of title:** Adverse possessors who enter under color of title are deemed to possess *all the property described in the defective deed*, so long as it consists of a *single parcel* and the possessor has occupied a *significant por-*

tion of the parcel. Remember: a possessor lacks color of title if he does not believe, in good faith, that his defective deed is valid.

Example: Echo enters Blackacre, a 100 acre farm, under color of title to Blackacre but actually possesses only 50 acres for the limitations period. Echo is deemed to have ***constructively possessed*** the remaining 50 acres and will acquire title to all of Blackacre.

   i. **Rationale:** The "single parcel" rule is designed to make sure that the owner of each parcel has a chance to protect his interest. If there has never been an actual entry against the owner, she has no way of knowing of any adverse claim.

      Example: Hal gives Barbara a deed to Blackacre, a 100 acre farm, and Whiteacre, an adjacent but separate 70 acre farm. Barbara does not know that Tom owns Blackacre and Mabel owns Whiteacre, but thinks Hal owns both. Barbara enters and actually occupies 50 acres of Blackacre for the limitations period. Barbara will acquire title to all of Blackacre but not to any portion of Whiteacre. Barbara's occupation gave ample notice to Tom of her adverse possession but Mabel could not reasonably have ever known that Barbara thought she owned Whiteacre.

   ii. **Actual possession better than constructive possession:** Constructive possession is never as good as actual possession, so an adverse possessor entering under color of title does not acquire title to land that, while described in the defective deed, is actually occupied by somebody else. The same principle applies when the owner is in possession and an adverse possessor enters a portion of the property under color of title.

      Example 1: John enters Blackacre, a 100 acre farm owned by Phil, under color of title to Blackacre and actually occupies 60 acres. He would have occupied the remainder but for the fact that Max, a squatter, had already taken possession of those 40 acres. John can only acquire title to the 60 acres he actually occupies.

      Example 2: Jane, a reclusive artist, owns Mountaintop, a 100 acre tract on which she has built a studio and cabin, occupying one acre. Harry enters Mountaintop under color of title to the entirety of Mountaintop and occupies two acres, building a cabin and woodshed. Harry will eventually acquire title to the two acres he has actually occupied, but nothing more. Harry's actual possession of the two acres is better than Jane's constructive possession of it, but Jane's constructive possession (and actual ownership) of the 97 acres not actually occupied by either Jane or Harry is better than Harry's constructive possession of it.

4. **Statutory issues:** Adverse possession law is a blend of statutory and common law. Some of the common statutory issues are discussed here, but each statute is different. Read your applicable statute carefully!

   a. **Length of the limitations period:** Limitations periods vary from statute to statute, from 5 years to 21 years. States with the shorter periods often require payment of taxes to establish adverse possession.

   b. **When the cause of action accrues:** The owner's cause of action to recover possession accrues (begins) when there is an adverse entry of the land. Once that happens the clock on the limitations period starts running.

      i. **Disabled owner:** Statutes of limitation typically provide for *tolling* (suspension) of the limitations time clock if the owner is disabled from bringing an action to recover possession *at the time the cause of action accrues*. Statutory disabilities vary but typically include (1) *insanity* or other *unsound mind*, (2) *imprisonment*, or (3) *the condition of being a minor*. Read your statute carefully! A typical statute provides that if the owner is disabled *at the time the cause of action accrues* the owner may bring suit for some specified period *after the disability ceases*, even though the normal limitations period has expired.

      Example 1: A statute of limitations on actions to recover possession of land provides that such actions must begin "within 21 years after the cause of action accrues, but if the person entitled to bring such action is imprisoned, of unsound mind, or a minor at the time the cause of action accrues, such person may bring such action after the expiration of 21 years from accrual of the cause of action, so long as the action is commenced within ten years after the end of the disability." If Owner is imprisoned when Possessor enters in 1970, and is released from prison in 1995, Owner has until 2005 to file suit to recover possession.

      (1) Disabilities in existence when cause of action accrues: The only disabilities that matter are those that *exist at the time the cause of action accrues*.

Example: Assume the limitations statute presented in the last example. Bob enters Blackacre, owned by Jill, in 1970. In 1971 Jill is imprisoned for 25 years. Jill's right to bring suit expires in 1991. She was not disabled when the cause of action accrued.

(2) **Cause of action accompanies title:** The cause of action *goes along with title* when title is transferred.

Example: Assume the limitations statute previously presented. Alan enters Blackacre, owned by Hazel, in 1970. Hazel is a free adult of sound mind. In 1982 Hazel dies, leaving Blackacre by will to her granddaughter Beth, age two. Beth succeeds to Hazel's cause of action. That cause of action will be time-barred in 1991. But Beth will only be 11 years old in 1991. No matter. Hazel was not disabled at the time the cause of action accrued. Beth's adult guardian is responsible for protecting Beth's interests. The guardian should bring suit in Beth's name.

ii. **Lienholders and future interest owners:** Some people are not entitled to file suit to recover possession so the limitations statute simply doesn't apply to them. No cause of action has accrued. Lienholders (like mortgage lenders) have a claim on the property but no right to possession until and unless there has been a default and foreclosure, so their claims are not destroyed by expiration of the limitations period. Holders of *future interests* — present ownership interests in property of a right to possession at some future time (see Chapter 4, p. 122, *infra*) — are also not entitled to possession now. Adverse possession does not cut off their future claim to possession. When the future interest holder becomes entitled to possession, his cause of action accrues and the limitations period starts running.

Example: Assume the prior limitations statute. Wilma owns a life estate in Blackacre. Jane owns the *remainder* — the right to take possession as soon as Wilma dies. Sam enters and adversely occupies Blackacre in 1970. Wilma does nothing. In 1991 Sam acquires title by adverse possession (consisting of Wilma's life estate). In 1995 Wilma dies. Jane's cause of action now accrues. Jane has until 2016 to bring suit to eject Sam. If she does nothing Sam will acquire yet another title by adverse possession in 2016, consisting of Jane's interest in Blackacre.

5. **Adverse possession by tenants and co-owners:**

    a. **Tenants:** Tenants are not usually capable of adverse possession against their landlords because their entry was permissive — subordinate to the owner's claim of title. They lack hostility, or adversity. Rarely, a tenant will so clearly repudiate the leasehold that she will become an adverse possessor. It takes extraordinarily explicit and clear action on the tenant's part to do this.

    b. **Co-owners:** One co-owner may not usually adversely possess against her co-owner because every co-owner has an equal right to possession. A co-owner's possession is not adverse to the claim of ownership of her fellow co-owners. In order to possess adversely against another co-owner, the adverse co-owner must *oust* the other co-owner by *excluding the co-owner from possession and claiming sole ownership*.

6. **Adverse possession of personal property:** The law of adverse possession was created to deal with real property, not personal property, but title to personal property can be acquired by adverse possession. A different (often shorter) statute of limitations usually applies. The principal reason that adverse possession is not well suited to personal property is the fact that possession of personal property in the manner of a true owner is often neither very open nor notorious. The traditional answer is that open and notorious possession is satisfied so long as the possessor uses the object in the way the average owner would.

    Example: Georgia, an artist, had a painting stolen. Years later it appeared for sale in an art gallery. Snyder, the gallery owner, argued that his predecessor in interest had acquired title by adverse possession. The answer hinges on whether the possessor's exhibition of the painting in his own home was sufficiently open and notorious. But the New Jersey Supreme Court, in *O'Keeffe v. Snyder*, 416 A.2d 862 (N.J. 1980), ruled that the law of adverse possession ought not apply. Instead, the court ruled that the limitations period for recovery of personal property starts to run at the earlier of (1) when the loss occurs (except where there is fraud or concealment) or (2) when the owner first *discovers, or through reasonable effort should have discovered, the cause of action (including the identity of the possessor)*. This turns the focus onto the owner's conduct, rather than the possessor's conduct, and encourages owners to report their losses and undertake reasonable investigation.

7. **Title acquired by adverse possessor:** When adverse possessors acquire title they acquire a new title. The former owner hasn't transferred his interest; rather, the law has stripped him of his title

and created a new one in the adverse possessor. But the new title cannot be any better or greater in scope than the former owner's title. The adverse possessor gets only what the old owner had.

Example: Oboe owned a life estate in Blackacre, meaning he owned it only for the rest of his life. (See Chapter 2, p. 40 *infra*.) Flute acquired Oboe's title by adverse possession. Though Flute got a new title it was a title to only a life estate in Blackacre. When Oboe dies, Flute's title to Blackacre dies too. If Oboe had owned Blackacre in fee simple absolute (essentially forever; see Chapter 2) but subject to a mortgage lien, Flute would acquire a new title in fee simple absolute but subject to the mortgage lien.

   a. **Must bring suit to quiet title:** The adverse possessor must bring a suit against the former owner to quiet title in the adverse possessor. This is because the adverse possessor's new title cannot be recorded in the public land records because there is no written record of it. While an adverse possessor can transfer his title by deed (the Statute of Frauds requires a writing to transfer a land title), and that deed can be recorded, there will be no evidence in the record of title by adverse possession until an action is brought and a judgment is entered and recorded. The transferee from the adverse possessor receives the adverse possessor's title and still must act to quiet title if the transferor has not already done so.

8. **Alternatives to adverse possession in boundary disputes:** Boundary disputes between neighbors comprise a fair amount of adverse possession cases and, as seen in pp. 15 and 18 *supra*, some courts have modified adverse possession doctrine to deal with such disputes. But there are other ways to solve these problems.

   a. **Agreed boundaries:** Neighbors can always agree on a new boundary, reduce the agreement to writing, and record a conveyance to carry it out. If neighbors *orally agree* on a new boundary when there is *genuine uncertainty about the boundary*, the oral agreement is a binding method of locating the boundary. The law splits hairs here. The oral agreement is not a conveyance, for that would violate the Statute of Frauds, but it has all the effect of a conveyance.

   b. **Acquiescence:** If one owner acquiesces in a known encroachment for an indefinite but long time the acquiescence is evidence of an agreed boundary.

   c. **Equitable estoppel:** If one neighbor does or says things that cause the other neighbor substantially to rely to his detriment on the first neighbor's actions, the first neighbor is estopped from denying his statements or actions.

Example: Matilda moves into her new house and has a backyard conversation with Lulu, her neighbor, in which Lulu points out a sagging fence as the boundary. "Trust me," she says, "You don't need to do a survey. I know it for a fact." In fact, the fence encroaches on Lulu's property by ten feet. Matilda dispenses with her intended survey and proceeds to rebuild the fence and construct a workshop that partially encroaches on Lulu's property. Lulu then sues for ejectment of the encroachments. Lulu will lose. She will be estopped from denying her statements on which Matilda relied to her substantial detriment.

F. Accession: Accession occurs when a person in *good faith* adds his labor to the property of another, or when a person in *good faith* mixes his labor and his property with the property of another. The problem is who owns the resulting product.

1. **General rules:** When only labor is added the owner of the original property owns the resulting product, unless the value added by the labor is substantial. In that case, the laborer owns the resulting product but must compensate the owner of the original property for the trespass. When labor and new material is mixed with another's original property the resulting product goes to whichever person supplied the more significant and valuable material. If that is the good faith improver, she must pay for her trespass.

2. **Mistaken improver of real property:** The mistaken improver doctrine is a variation of accession that is applied to real property. A person who *in good faith* constructs an improvement on the land of another (usually a neighbor) creates in the neighbor an *option* to either (1) sell the land to the improver at its fair market value (net of the improvement) or (2) paying to the improver the fair value of the improvement itself.

III. PERSONAL PROPERTY

A. Introduction: Issues concerning personal property are present in many areas of law: *e.g.*, contracts (particularly sales of goods), commercial transactions, and intellectual property. This section deals with some of the personal property issues that are frequently encountered in your course on Property, but is not intended to be a comprehensive treatment of legal issues pertaining to personal property.

B. Bailments: A bailment is a *legitimate possession* of personal property by someone who is *not the owner* of the property. The person who owns the property is called the bailor and the non-owner in possession is called the bailee. Bailments can be created voluntarily or involuntarily.

Example: You leave your watch with the jeweler to be repaired. A voluntary bailment is created. But if you forgetfully leave your car keys on the jeweler's counter when you leave, and the jeweler pockets them, an involuntary bailment is created.

1. **Elements of bailment:** In order for a bailment to exist the bailee must have *actual control* of the property *together with intent to possess* the property.

   a. **Actual control:** Actual control can prove problematic when one person merely provides space for accommodation of personal property.

   Example: Ace Parking owns an unattended paved lot with marked parking spaces. Customers park and lock their cars, deposit the fee in a locked box, and leave. No bailment is created. Ace does not have actual control. But if Ace provided an attendant who parked the cars and kept the keys until the owner's return and presentment of receipt, a bailment would be created. Now Ace has actual control.

   b. **Custody and intent to possess:** People sometimes have temporary physical custody of property but lack any intention of possession.

   Example: The jeweler hands you an expensive ring to try on in his shop. No bailment is created while you are admiring the ring on your finger. You have custody but lack any intent to possess.

   c. **Mistakes in identity or composition:** Problems with the putative bailee's intent to possess the property usually arise when there is some mistake concerning the identity or composition of the property.

   Example: Mary Ann asks her landlady to keep a wooden box for her while she is on vacation. Upon Mary Ann's return she recovers her box, opens it, and discovers her pet cobra has died. A bailment was created with respect to the box but was a bailment created with respect to the cobra? No doubt the landlady never intended to possess a cobra. The better answer is no bailment.

2. **Rights and obligations:** Bailees have some rights and lots of obligations. Bailors have many rights and few obligations.

   a. **Bailee's rights as to third parties:** A bailee has a better claim to the property than any third party and is thus entitled to damages from any third party who wrongfully injures the property. Third parties are not permitted to assert the defense that the property really belongs to the bailor. The corollary to this rule is that the bailee must turn over the damage proceeds to the bailor.

b. **Bailor's rights as to third parties:** Bailors may recover from a third party for injury to the property if the third party has not already paid the bailee. A bailor of a voluntary bailment may not proceed against a third party who has already paid the bailee. The bailor's remedy is to recover from the bailee, his chosen agent. This rule is sometimes called the ***Winkfield doctrine*** after a case so holding. *The Winkfield*, [1902] P. 42 (1901). But the Winkfield doctrine does not apply to an ***involuntary*** bailment. The ***involuntary bailor may recover from a third party who has already paid the bailee***. The rationale is that the bailor had no opportunity to select his bailee and thus ought not be bound by whatever settlement or judgment the bailee obtained.

c. **Bailee's duty of care:** Bailees have a duty to care for the property in their possession. It is often said that the degree of care required varies with the benefit received by the bailee, but the preferred rule today (though not universally adopted) is to make all bailees liable for ***negligence — ordinary care under the circumstances***. See Note, 61 S. Cal. L. Rev. 2117 (1988). Because the variable standards of care are still applied in some jurisdictions, that taxonomy is discussed below.

   i. **Variable duty of care:** A bailment created for the ***exclusive benefit of the bailee*** ("Sure, you can borrow my laptop computer") obligates the bailee to exercise the ***utmost care***. A bailment created for the ***mutual benefit of bailor and bailee*** (*e.g.*, you leave your laundry with the cleaner and he charges you for his services upon its return) obligates the bailee to use ***ordinary care***. The bailee is liable for his ***negligence***. A bailment created for the ***exclusive benefit of the bailor*** ("Please take care of my cat while I'm gone for the weekend") obligates the bailee to exercise only ***minimal care***. The bailee is liable only for his ***recklessness or gross negligence***. An involuntary bailment does not obligate the bailee to take any ***affirmative action*** to care for the property, but if the bailee does so he is held to a standard of ***minimal care***. Older cases require the bailor to prove the bailee's lack of due care. The modern trend is to require the bailee to prove he exercised due care.

d. **Bailee's duty to return property:** Voluntary bailees are *strictly liable* for the return of the property because they are contractually obligated to return the goods. Involuntary bailees are liable only for their *negligence* in failing to return property because they have no such contractual obligation.

3. **Contractual changes to bailment rules:** Bailees frequently attempt to alter these legal rules by contract. So long as the bailor consents to the contract courts enforce such contracts except to the extent they purport to exonerate the bailee from his gross negligence or willful misconduct. The issue of bailor consent is sometimes difficult. Disclaimers of liability printed on the back of a receipt establish bailor consent *only if the bailee can prove that the bailor was (or should have been) aware of the disclaimer* at the time the bailment was created. This is fertile soil for later dispute.

C. **Gifts:** A gift is a *voluntary transfer* of property for *no consideration*. To accomplish a gift of personal property the donor must *intend to make a gift*, the property must be *delivered to the donee* (the recipient of the gift), and the donee must *accept* the property. Gifts are commonly divided into gifts *inter vivos* (during life) and gifts *causa mortis* (in contemplation of impending death). A gift is *inter vivos* if it is made with no knowledge or threat of impending death. *Inter vivos* gifts are irrevocable. A gift is *causa mortis* if it is made with knowledge or under threat of immediate death. Gifts *causa mortis* are revocable if the donor recovers from the illness or threat causing the donor to make the gift in contemplation of death, or if the donor dies of some other cause which did not prompt the gift. Courts view gifts *causa mortis* with some skepticism since the donor is likely to be dead and the completed gift is a substitute for a will, a form of giving at death that is laden with formalities to be sure that the dead person's wishes are accurately carried out.

1. **Intent:** For a gift to occur the donor must intend to transfer *title*. If the donor's intent is *merely to transfer possession*, no gift has been accomplished. Evidence on this element is usually circumstantial, unless the donor executes a deed or some other written expression of donative intent.

    a. **Gifts *causa mortis*:** Recall that gifts *causa mortis* are revocable if the donor recovers from the threat of death that motivated the gift. The donor's intention is presumed to be to make the gift *only because of impending death*. But if a donor intends the gift to be irrevocable regardless of her impending death, it is not a gift *causa mortis* (revocable) but is an irrevocable *inter vivos* gift.

2. **Delivery:** The general rule is that the subject of the gift must be *delivered* to the recipient in order for the gift to be complete. The best form of delivery is *actual physical possession*, but that is not always required. When physical delivery is *impractical* or *impossible*, delivery may be accomplished by *symbolic delivery* or *constructive delivery*.

   a. **Rationale:** Delivery is thought to perform three valuable functions:

   - *Making abstraction a reality:* When a donor must part with a cherished possession, the idea of giving becomes real. A donor will part with possession of an object only if she truly wishes to give. As the ancient bromide has it: "Actions speak louder than words."

   - *Objective evidence of intent:* Intent is subjective, but delivery is objective. Delivery acts as a secondary check on intent.

   - *Objective evidence of acceptance:* Delivery of property is presumptive evidence of acceptance by the donee.

   b. **Relationship of delivery to intent:** To the extent that the element of delivery is easily satisfied by something other than delivery of *actual physical possession* — either *symbolic delivery* or *constructive delivery* — the element of delivery becomes virtually the same as intent. In both cases the issue becomes, "What did the donor intend by her acts?"

   c. **Delivery by deed:** Delivery can be accomplished by a *deed of gift* or some other *writing under seal*. Although the law no longer makes much of the distinction between sealed instruments (those that bore a ritual indication of authenticity, as a notarial seal) and unsealed instruments (merely signed by the maker), this distinction persists here. Some courts only recognize sealed instruments as adequate to deliver by writing. But unsealed instruments may accomplish the work of delivery if they are adequate to constitute symbolic or constructive delivery.

   d. **Symbolic delivery:** When actual physical delivery is *impossible* or *impractical*, delivery can be accomplished by delivering some object that is *symbolic of possession*.

   Example: Tom, author of a series of hugely successful adventure novels, decides to give to his daughter the copyright in his latest novel, *Last Clear Chance*. He writes the following on his letter paper: "I hereby give my daughter Jane my copyright in *Last Clear Chance*. [signed] Tom." Tom physically gives the paper to his daughter. Jane owns the copyright. It is impossible to physically deliver intangible personal property like a copyright. Tom's writing is symbolic of possession of the intangible right. Cf. *In re Cohn*, 176 N.Y.S. 225 (N.Y. Supp. 1919) (gift of corporate stock); *Gruen v. Gruen*, 496 N.E.2d 869 (N.Y. 1986) (gift of future interest).

    i. Adequacy: Symbolic delivery is adequate when physical delivery is simply not practical.

    Example: Tom decides to give his daughter Jane his concert grand piano, even though she has no room for it in her apartment. He gives to Jane a signed letter: "Dear Jane, I hereby give you my concert grand piano. Come play it whenever you wish and take it away whenever you can. Love, Tom." The letter constitutes symbolic delivery of the piano.

e. Constructive delivery: When actual physical delivery is ***possible but impractical***, delivery of some object that is the ***means of obtaining possession*** of the property constitutes ***constructive delivery***.

Example: On his deathbed, Jack gives to Julia all the keys to the household furniture, saying that he intends for her to have everything in the house. Delivery of the keys constitutes constructive delivery of the furniture, since it is impractical to make physical delivery under the circumstances. But delivery of the keys does not constitute constructive delivery of a life insurance policy locked in a bureau drawer, because it was not impractical to deliver the tangible evidence of the life insurance right — the policy itself. *Newman v. Bost*, 29 S.E. 848 (N.C. 1898).

    i. Delivery as an independent contrat: Constructive delivery cases often raise the problem of whether delivery is an independent element or merely a double check on donative intent.

    Example: Phyllis has two keys to her safe deposit box, which is stuffed with valuable stocks, bonds, and jewels. She gives one key to Maude, saying "Everything in this safe deposit box is yours." Is the gift complete? Cases split on this. Some say that retention of the second key negates constructive delivery because Phyllis did not surrender her control over the box. In essence, this view focuses on doubts about Phyllis's intent. The contrary view — holding that delivery of one of two keys constitutes constructive delivery — focus more on the fact that the key is, literally, the key to possession. Most often, courts look to other factors to decide whether the donor really intended to make a gift. Compare *Hocks v. Jeremiah*, 759 P. 2d 312 (Ore. 1988) and *Estate of Abramowitz*, 329 N.Y.S.2d 932 (N.Y. Supp. 1972) (no delivery; no gift) with *Gilkinson v. Third Ave. RR Co.*, 47 App. Div. 472 (N.Y. 1900) and *In re Parkhurst's Estate*, 167 A.2d 476 (Pa. 1961) (constructive delivery; valid gift).

f. **Special problems:** Some delivery problems warrant special mention.

- *Agents:* When donors deliver the property to an agent of the donee, delivery is complete. But sometimes it's not clear whether the third person is an agent of the donor or the donee. If the delivery is to the **donor's agent there is no delivery** because it is as if the donor had "delivered" the gift to himself. This problem usually comes up when the donor delivers property to his own attorney for the benefit of a donee. The lawyer's client is the donor, but can she also be the agent of the donee? Yes, but courts split on this. This form of delivery is risky at best, and involves courts in the debate over whether delivery is of independent significance or just a redundant test of donative intent.

- *Delivery on death:* If a donor delivers property to a third party (even a conceded agent of the donee) under instructions to deliver the property to the donee on the death of the donor, there may be **no gift**. The condition attached (death) to ultimate delivery is sometimes seen as an impermissible attempt to avoid the formal requirements for a will, and thus invalid. The preferred (and more modern) view is that the gift is complete upon delivery to the donee's agent, regardless of the condition attached. There are two reasons for this view. First, delivery has been made to the donee through his agent. Second, the attached condition amounts to little more than the creation of a valid oral trust, with the donee's agent as trustee. See p. 34, *infra*.

- *Choses in action:* The delivery requirements of a **chose in action** (an inchoate legal right) depend on whether the chose in action has assumed tangible form by a writing. Choses in action reduced to a writing (*e.g.*, a promissory note, or an insurance policy) must be delivered in the same way as tangible personal property. To deliver by written assignment it is necessary to show that the assignment is a valid symbolic delivery. Those not reduced to a writing (*e.g.*, a personal injury claim) may always be delivered by a written assignment without the necessity of proving symbolic delivery.

- ***Donee in possession:*** When a donee already has possession there is no need to perform the useless act of shifting the property back and forth to prove "delivery." It has been delivered. Once is enough.

3. **Acceptance:** A gift is not complete until it has been accepted by the donee. Delivery triggers a presumption of a completed gift, which presumption can be rebutted by the donee's rejection of the gift. The presumption of acceptance is strongest when the gift benefits the donee and virtually non-existent when the gift is (rarely) of no benefit. A donee's delay in rejecting known unwanted gifts also endangers the donee's ability to claim that there was no acceptance.

4. **Trusts:** A trust involves a split of ***legal ownership*** of property (in a trustee) and ***beneficial or equitable ownership*** (in a beneficiary). The creator of a trust supplies the assets owned by the trust and is called the ***trustor*** or ***settlor***. Real property may only be held in trust pursuant to a written trust, but personal property may be put in trust on the strength of an oral agreement.

   a. **Oral trusts:** Two types of oral trusts of personal property may be created. The trustee may be a third party or the trustee may be the same person who created the trust (the trustor or settlor). If a ***third party is trustee*** the property must be delivered to the trustee in accord with the usual delivery rules. If the ***trustee is also the settlor, delivery is not required*** because the property has already been "delivered."

   b. **Revocable trusts:** Trusts may be revocable. It is up to the settlor, when establishing the trust, to decide what she wants. This fact clashes with the long established law on gifts. Generally, a gift may not be ***revocable***. The donor's retention of the right to revoke is said to be inconsistent with donative intent — the intent to part with ownership and control. But note that a donor may give property to a trust that is itself revocable at the option of the settlor-donor.

      Example: John delivers a brooch to his good friend Ethel, together with a letter in which he declares "I intend to give this brooch to you; but if I should decide that I would prefer my daughter Liz to have it, I retain the right to take it back and give it to Liz." No gift. But John could validly create a revocable trust, even with himself as trustee, under terms that would obligate the trustee to deliver possession of the brooch to Ethel "until such time as the settlor (John) should revoke the trust."

      i. **How long does power to revoke last?:** Some argue that donors should be permitted to retain the power to revoke the gift so long as the revocation power is in writing at the time of the gift (to avoid fraud and litigation) and the donee still has the property at the time of revocation (to avoid inequity to transferees from the donee, who probably lack knowledge of the revocable nature of the donee's title).

5. **Bank accounts:** Special rules have grown up around gifts of bank accounts. The problem occurs where two or more people have an interest in the same bank account and one of them dies. There are four patterns.

   a. **Power of attorney:** Depositor may give another person power of attorney to withdraw money from her account. The power expires upon Depositor's death or prior revocation, but Bank may not know this until the power holder has wrongly withdrawn money, thus rendering Bank liable to Depositor's statutory heirs or devisees (takers under a will). For this reason, most banks refuse to open such accounts or recognize such powers of attorney unless they are adequately protected from the liability risks.

   b. **"Pay on Death" (POD) accounts:** Depositor opens an account in the name of Depositor but payable on Depositor's death to B. The majority rule at common law was that there was no gift from Depositor to B because (1) there had not been any delivery of a present property right to B and (2) the entire arrangement was an invalid will substitute since it lacked the formalities required for a will. See, *e.g.*, *Northwestern Nat'l Bank v. Daniel*, 127 N.W.2d 714 (S.D. 1964). This rule has been gradually eliminated by statute in many states and is eliminated by the Uniform Probate Code. Other states hold that, even without a statute, POD accounts are valid because there is little practical risk of fraud and the donor's testamentary intent is quite clear. See, *e.g.*, *Logan v. Citizens Nat'l Bank*, 460 So. 2d 1239 (Ala. 1984).

   c. **Totten trusts:** A Totten trust is a POD account in the form of a trust. When POD accounts were generally void, somebody had the bright idea to create an account in the form of "Depositor as trustee for B, but with the right of Depositor to withdraw any and all amounts." This accomplished a completed gift to the trust of a present interest in the bank account. Of course, it was nothing more than a POD account in trust. But its validity was upheld in *Matter of Totten*, 179 N.Y. 112 (1904). It makes little sense to invalidate POD accounts while upholding Totten trusts. p. 34 *supra*.

d. Joint tenancy with right of survivorship: Two persons — A and B — establish a bank account that is owned jointly during their lives and exclusively by the survivor. During the joint life of A and B each person may withdraw the account, although some states (and the Uniform Probate Code) hold that each person is entitled only to the proportion of the account they contributed. The death of one — either A or B — vests ownership solely in the survivor. This is the usual form of joint tenancy bank account. Problems arise when A deposits the money intending to make a gift to B. Generally, it is valid as a gift of a present interest in the account. But if there is adequate evidence to prove that A intended to create a POD account it is an invalid gift in those states that do not recognize POD accounts. If there is adequate evidence that A intended to create only a power of attorney account, B takes nothing at A's death because the power of attorney expires at A's death.

D. Transfers for value: It is simply not practical to create a registry of ownership of all the vast amount of personal property in existence. It is practical to do so for real property because it is not portable and there is less of it. When a registry exists (as it does for real property) we can rely upon the records of the registry as evidence of ownership. Without a registry (as for personal property) we are forced to rely on possession as evidence of ownership. But some possessors (*e.g.*, thieves or finders) have less than true ownership. What happens when a third party pays good value to acquire personal property from somebody without true ownership of the property?

   1. General rule: The general rule is that the seller of property can *only transfer the title he has*.

   Example: The chimney sweep in *Armory v. Delamirie*, *supra* p. 8, had the rights of a finder in the gem he found. Under the general rule, a purchaser of the gem from the sweep would have to surrender it to the true owner because the purchaser acquired only the sweep's title to the gem.

   a. Exception: But this general rule is riddled with exceptions, all of which are designed to protect **bona fide purchasers for value**. But the exceptions do **not protect all bona fide purchasers**. It is **necessary** to be a bona fide purchaser to get a **better title** than the seller, but it is **not sufficient** by itself that one is a bona fide purchaser.

   2. Who is a bona fide purchaser?: A bona fide purchaser (BFP) is somebody who (1) pays **good value** for property, (2) **does not know**

that the seller is either a wrongful possessor or not the true owner, and (3) has a *good faith belief* that the seller is the true owner.

   a. **Good value:** Any valuable consideration suffices. Some common law courts held that transfers in exchange for cancellation of a pre-existing debt were not for valuable consideration. This rule has been reversed by Uniform Commercial Code § 1-201(44). Note that donees have not paid good value.

   b. **Good faith:** If the purchaser *actually knows* that the seller lacks title he is, of course, not a bona fide purchaser. If the purchaser does *not actually know* that the seller lacks title, but has *inquiry notice*, he is not a bona fide purchaser. Inquiry notice means that, under the circumstances of the transaction, a reasonable person would ask questions of the seller, which questions would likely either expose the seller's lack of title or raise serious doubts on that score.

   Example: If a homeless person, dressed shabbily and otherwise bearing the ill effects of poor sanitation and nutrition, were to appear in a jeweler's shop carrying a rope of exquisite pearls, the jeweler is on inquiry notice.

3. **Exceptions to the general rule:** Exceptions to the general rule permit bona fide purchasers to acquire clear title — a better title than the seller had. These exceptions are designed to facilitate commerce or to place the loss on the more culpable party — the one who had the better opportunity of avoiding the loss.

   a. **Negotiable instruments:** Writings that function as a medium of exchange (*e.g.*, currency, promissory notes, checks) are negotiable instruments. Because their free exchange is indispensable to a large and complex economy, BFPs acquire title free of prior claims. Any other rule would cause commercial chaos. Imagine trying to prove your ownership of the $20 bill you tender the grocery clerk. Imagine the resentment of the people in the line behind you.

   b. **Equitable estoppel:** This universal principle — that a person who induces another to rely detrimentally upon his words or actions will be estopped from denying his words or acts — prevents a true owner from asserting his paramount claim against a BFP when the true owner has induced the BFP's reliance. This will not happen very often.

   Example: Municipality imposes a personal property tax on every computer in excess of five that any one person owns. Bill, who owns six computers and employs Louise as a salesperson, attempts to avoid the tax by telling Sam, Municipality's tax collector, that the laptop computer in Louise's possession is hers. If Louise then sells "her" laptop to Sam for good value Bill will be estopped from denying his representation to Sam.

  c. **Entrustment to a merchant for sale:** At common law, the mere entrusting of goods to a merchant for sale did not operate to estop the owner from denying the merchant's authority to deliver good title. The owner would have to give the merchant actual or apparent authority to sell the goods (*e.g.*, by giving express written authority or by permitting the merchant to hold the goods out as his own) in order to be estopped. The Uniform Commercial Code changes this rule by creating a statutory estoppel that operates *in addition to the common law rule*. Under the statutory rule (section 2-403) the bare entrusting of goods by an owner to a merchant who ordinarily deals in such goods gives the merchant power to deliver the owner's title to purchasers in the ordinary course of business.

  Example: Owner entrusts his midnight blue Corvette to Honest Al, a used car dealer, for sale. Honest Al lends the Corvette to Slim Jim, an acquaintance who is a pharmaceutical salesman. Slim Jim sells the Corvette to Ed, after telling Ed that he owns the Corvette. Ed does not acquire Owner's title from Slim Jim because Owner did not entrust the auto to him, Slim Jim was not a dealer in autos, and the sale was not in the ordinary course of Slim Jim's business. But Ed would have obtained Owner's title had he bought the car from Honest Al.

    i. **UCC rule is in addition to common law rule:** Remember: The UCC rule is in *addition* to the common law of equitable estoppel. If the UCC statutory estoppel rule does not apply, but the purchaser can prove common law equitable estoppel, the purchaser prevails.

  d. **Voidable title:** Another exception created by UCC § 2-403 is the concept of *voidable title*. A *person with voidable title can transfer good title to a bona fide purchaser*. Voidable title results when an owner intends to transfer title, but the other party is guilty of fraud or duress that permits the owner to void the transaction.

  Example: Tim agrees to sell his beloved wooden sailboat to Rob in exchange for what Rob represents is a genuine Picasso. After the swap, Tim learns that the painting is a forgery and that Rob knew it was a fake. Tim delays taking any legal action and, during the delay, Rob sells the sailboat to Old Salt for good value.

Old Salt has a good title since Rob held voidable title. Rob's title was voidable since Tim intended to give him title but Rob induced that intention by fraud.

i. **Voidable title is not void title:** Don't confuse *voidable title* with *void title* Title is void when the owner never intended to transfer title or lacked the capacity to do so.

Example: Sally, age fourteen, takes her mother's diamond earrings to a flea market and sells them to Lucy for good value. Sally represents that she owns the earrings. Lucy has void title because Sally's mother never intended to transfer title. Sally is a thief, and a thief has void title. Even if the earrings were owned by Sally (her mother gave them to her as a present) Lucy would have void title because Sally lacks capacity to transfer title. Sally is a minor.

Chapter 2
FREEHOLD ESTATES

I. ORIGINS AND TAXONOMY OF FREEHOLD ESTATES

A. **Estates generally:** A legitimate possessor of land — *real property* — has an *estate in land* rather than the land itself. A *possessory estate* is a legal right to occupy the land immediately. By contrast, a *future interest* is the right (and sometimes only the possibility) to possess the land at some time in the future. A future interest is a presently existing estate but the estate does not include the right of possession until some future event or events have occurred. See Chapter 4, p. 122, *infra*. Possessory estates are further divided into *freehold estates* (essentially the various types of *ownership*) and *non-freehold* or *leasehold estates* (possession subordinate to the owner's rights of ownership). At early common law the distinction between freehold and non-freehold estates was that the freeholder had *seisin* and the non-freeholder had *possession but not seisin.* See p. 40, *infra*. Possessory estates may be of perpetual duration or for some shorter period. The various forms of possessory estates are discussed in this chapter. Our system of estates is derived from the feudal origins of land ownership. While we are long removed from feudal society and, hopefully, your professor is not anxious to test you on your knowledge of feudal law, a brief understanding of the origins will help you to make sense of the contemporary concepts.

B. **Feudal tenures:** When William of Normandy — William the Conqueror — seized the English crown in 1066 he claimed ownership of all the land in England. Then he handed out possession of separate parcels to his henchmen, but with a catch. This possession-with-a-catch was called *seisin.* Each possessor was a tenant of the King, and his continued possession (his *tenure*) depended on his performance of services for the King. The tenant was *seised of the land*, which meant he held possession from the King, his lord, and owed *services to his lord.* These services could be almost anything from the important (*e.g.*, 50 mounted knights to do combat for the King, 100 bushels of corn each year) to the frivolous (*e.g.*, a sprig of holly at the winter solstice). The first tenant (the one holding directly from the King) was the *tenant-in-chief.* The tenant-in-chief could and often did transfer all or a part of his possession rights to some lesser chief, who was known as a *tenant in demesne* (pronounced "demean"), and who was obligated to provide services (*e.g.*, 10 knights) to the tenant-in-chief, also known as a *mesne lord* (pronounced "mean"), because he was intermediate in the feudal chain of obligation, having a lord above and a tenant below him in the feudal pecking order. This process was called **subinfeudation** and it could produce a lengthy chain of possession and obligation. Everyone but the King owed duties to some lord. Everyone in the feudal chain also was owed services by his tenants. Those at the bottom only owed services to their lord. Holders of non-freehold estates (lessees for a term of years) were not seised and owed no feudal duties to the lord from whom their landlord held. (This was because leaseholders were regarded as a bit low and untrustworthy, not because there was something special about leaseholds). Think of the feudal services as a fixed tax — set at the time the tenant was *seised in possession* and constant thereafter.

1. **Feudal incidents:** As you can imagine, the value of possession rose as population increased but the annual services remained constant. This fact made the imposition of *feudal incidents* (essentially death taxes) important, because the lord acquired the tenant's rights (usually possession of the land) — whenever incidents came due. The lord could then either use the property himself or *subinfeudate* — transfer — it anew in exchange for a new package of annual services. The principal incidents were *escheat, forfeiture,* and *wardship and marriage.*

    a. **Escheat:** If a tenant in possession died without heirs, his tenure ended and possession returned to the next lord up the feudal ladder.

    b. **Forfeiture:** If a tenant in possession committed treason against the King or violated his obligations to the lord from whom he held possession, his tenure was forfeited and the next lord up the chain took possession.

    c. **Wardship and Marriage:** If a tenant in possession died leaving an heir who was a minor, the next lord up the chain was entitled to the profits from the land until the heir reached adulthood, and was also entitled to arrange the minor's marriage and receive payment from the family of the minor's prospective spouse for the marriage. (This was before the age of romantic love; marriage was a cold-blooded calculation of financial and social gain.)

2. **Feudal death tax avoidance and *statute quia emptores*:** To avoid the imposition of incidents, tenants in possession would subinfeudate to their children for nominal services.

    Example: Lord gave possession of Blackacre to Tenant in return for 50 hogs each year. If Tenant dies while his Son is a minor, Lord has possession of Blackacre until Son reaches maturity. But if Tenant had subinfeudated Blackacre to Son for a sprig of mistletoe in midwinter, Lord's incident on Tenant's death would consist of the receipt of a sprig of mistletoe each midwinter.

    a. Statute Quia Emptores: Statute Quia Emptores (1290) destroyed this tax avoidance scheme by forbidding any further subinfeudation in fee simple (in essence, for perpetuity; see p. 43, *infra*). But the political price for this was recognition of the right of free tenants to transfer, or alienate, their land. A tenant could convey his interest to another in substitution for himself in the feudal chain. This was the beginning of free alienability of land in English law, a critical component of modern property law. Over time, Quia Emptores eliminated most mesne lords, leaving the right of incidents largely held by the King. This fact produced some new tax avoidance devices by lawyers and freeholders of the 15th and 16th centuries, another statutory response by the King (in 1536), and the development of new estates, all considered in Chapter 4, p. 122, *infra*. By then, however, the feudal economy was all but dead and the feudal system of tenure, marked by personal obligations, was essentially replaced by the modern view of ownership — private rights of use, possession, and alienability coupled with mostly financial obligations to the state in the form of taxes.

C. A taxonomy of freehold estates: Feudal holdings were determined by status and obligation. The King held by divine right; the Duke of Winchester held his land of the King; the Squire of Winchester held of the Duke of Winchester; a knight in the Squire's service held of the Squire. But when these holdings became alienable by free tenants ("free holders") the modern *freehold estate* began to evolve. There are four basic types of freehold estates: the *fee simple,* the *fee tail,* the *defeasible fees,* and the *life estate.* Each of these has its variations and all are considered in the rest of this chapter. *Leaseholds* — the *non-freehold estates* — are considered in Chapter 3, p. 69, *infra*. The principal difference between each freehold estate is the *duration of the estate.* Some freehold estates are of finite duration; some may last forever (or at least as long as the legal system that created them). Remember: an estate in land is *not the same thing as the land itself.* An estate in land is a legal abstraction — a fictional, imaginary thing that is connected to the land but existing apart from it. An estate in land consists of an important bundle of legal rights and obligations toward others with respect to a particular parcel of Earth. It can move from one person to another, be subdivided in various ways and put back together again, all while the land itself remains unchanged.

II. FEE SIMPLE

A. Introduction: The fee simple is the most common freehold estate. There are two types of fees simple: the ***fee simple absolute*** and the two forms of ***defeasible fees.*** The difference between the two types is that the fee simple absolute can endure forever and the defeasible fees can be terminated upon the happening of some specified future event. The fee simple absolute is considered here. The defeasible fees are discussed in p. 50, *infra*.

B. Fee simple absolute: The fee simple absolute is a bit of a misnomer. It is absolute ownership in the sense that its **duration is perpetual.** It may last forever (or at least as long as the legal system). It is what you thought of as land ownership before you started law school. It is **not absolute** in the sense that nobody can restrict the owner's use, possession, or alienability of the estate. The state can and does impose such restrictions for perceived public objectives. The question of when such restrictions amount to a taking of the estate is considered in Chapter 11, p. 345, *infra*. People (including professors) often speak of a "fee simple" as a shorthand form of the fee simple absolute. But since there are defeasible forms of fee simple, be precise and speak of a fee simple absolute.

  1. Creation of the fee simple absolute:

  a. Common law: At common law the fee simple absolute was created by a grant ***"to A and his heirs."*** The words "to A" are ***"words of purchase"*** — words describing the person or persons who are the takers of the fee simple absolute. The words "and his heirs" are ***"words of limitation"*** — words ***limiting the duration of the estate.*** In the early common law, "to A and his heirs" meant that A was granted an estate that was **capable** of inheritance and, therefore, of ***potentially infinite duration.*** It did not mean that A's heirs (who would not be known because A, being alive, had no heirs) had an interest in the estate.

  Example 1: O grants Blackacre to "A and her heirs." Fee simple absolute in A is created. If O grants Blackacre to "the heirs of A" no fee simple absolute is created. Until A dies the "heirs of A" — the takers of the interest created — are unknown. A contingent future interest is created (see Chapter 4, p. 122, *infra*) in a set of unknown people — the "heirs of A." Since no words of limitation were used in the second grant, the "heirs of A" would acquire a life estate — a freehold estate that ends with the life (or lives) of the heirs of A. See p. 58, *infra*.

   i. Words of limitation: The words of limitation — "and her heirs" simply meant that since the estate could be inherited the estate could endure forever. The words "to A and his heirs" created a perpetual estate, presently held by A. That is a fee simple absolute. Of course, A will not live forever, but his fee simple absolute might. During A's life A might convey it to someone else and, if not, after A's death his fee simple absolute will be held by his *devisees* under his *will* or, in the absence of a will, by his *heirs*. Old owners of fees simple absolute wither and die, but their fees go on and on. If the grant did not include the words of limitation, only a life estate was created, even though the grantor's intentions might be clear.

Example 2: William Shakespeare, owner of Blackacre-on-Avon in fee simple absolute, conveys Blackacre-on-Avon in 1610 "to A for eternity." A does not have fee simple absolute. A has a life estate. If William Shakespeare wishes to convey his fee simple absolute to A — as his original conveyance plainly suggests — he must convey it "to A and his heirs."

b. **Modern view:** In virtually every American jurisdiction today it is not necessary to use the magic words of limitation — "and his heirs" — to create fee simple absolute. Either by statutory change or judicial decision the ***usual rule*** is that a grantor ***conveys his entire estate unless the grant is to the contrary.***

Example: Will Shakespeare, an American contemporary descendant of the bard, owns Blackacre-on-the-Hudson in fee simple absolute. He conveys Blackacre "to A." Fee simple absolute in A is created. Since there is nothing to the contrary in the grant Will is presumed to have conveyed his entire estate in Blackacre — fee simple absolute — to A.

C. **Alienability and inheritance of the fee simple absolute:** A fee simple absolute is freely alienable, devisable by will, or inheritable in intestacy (the state of dying without a will).

1. **Alienation:** An owner of fee simple absolute can convey the entire fee simple absolute to another person. If O conveys his fee simple absolute to A the fee simple absolute continues without interruption. It just has a new owner. An owner can also split his fee simple absolute into lesser estates, but the sum of the estates will add up to a fee simple absolute.

Example: Blackacre is owned by O in fee simple absolute. O conveys Blackacre "to A for her life." By this transaction O has split his fee simple absolute into two parts: a ***life estate*** in A (see p. 58, *infra*) and a ***reversion,*** an estate retained by O. The reversion is a ***future interest,*** a presently existing estate that entitles its holder,

O, to future possession (when A dies and her life estate expires). The sum of the two parts adds up to fee simple absolute. If O later conveys his reversion to A, the reversion and the life estate will be ***merged*** and their sum is fee simple absolute in A.

2. **Devise:** In England, an estate in land could not be devised (transferred by will) until the Statute of Wills in 1540. Until then, an estate could pass at death only to one's heirs. The difference is that one's heirs are prescribed by law (usually children, then the next closely related persons) and devisees can be anybody the testator specifies in his will. Today, an owner of fee simple absolute can send it under his will to whomever he pleases, or split it up into pieces that when added together equal fee simple absolute.

3. **Inheritance:** Lay persons (and many lawyers) often use the term inheritance to describe all testamentary transfers, but the strict meaning of the term is limited to transfers of property owned by a person dying ***without a will.*** This condition, called ***intestacy,*** is dealt with by statutes that specify the ***heirs.*** Strictly speaking, a person dying with a will does ***not have heirs***; he has ***devisees.*** Only a person dying intestate has heirs. At early common law the heirs were the decedent's ***issue,*** and the rule of ***primogeniture*** applied: estates in land went to the decedent's first born son; daughters inherited only in the absence of sons. The usual statutory scheme today sets aside some portion of the intestate decedent's property for the surviving spouse, and distributes the remainder to the decedent's children. In the absence of a spouse or children, the decedent's parents are heirs. If the decedent leaves no surviving children, spouse, or parents, the heirs are his ***collateral kin*** — brothers, sisters, nieces, nephews, aunts, uncles, and cousins. At some point these people become so collateral they are not treated as heirs. If an intestate decedent has ***absolutely no heirs*** the decedent's property will ***escheat*** to the state.

III. FEE TAIL

A. **Introduction:** The fee tail is virtually extinct but its vestigial implications continue to pop up like an unexpected and unwanted guest. Fee tail problems mostly occur, if at all, in connection with the various modern methods of destroying this estate.

B. **Origin and operation of the fee tail:** To understand the fee tail we must briefly return to medieval law.

1. **The fee simple conditional:** The aristocracy of medieval England were very anxious to keep their wealth, represented by

their land tenures, in the family for generation after generation. They attempted to do so by conveying their estates to the scion of the next generation "and the heirs of his body," hoping that this would have the desired effect of making the estate non-transferable outside of the family. Unhappily for the gentry, the medieval courts construed this language to mean that it created a ***fee simple conditional*** — the estate holder was empowered to convey fee simple absolute if and when he should have a child.

Example: Duke, holder of Blackacre from the King, conveys it to his son, Clarence "and the heirs of his body." Prior to 1285, this created a fee simple conditional in Clarence. Upon the birth of Lester, Clarence's son, Clarence could convey fee simple absolute to a third party. If he had a trusted confederate, Clarence could convey fee simple absolute to Buddy, who would then convey fee simple absolute back to Clarence.

2. **The rise of the fee tail:** In 1285 the English Parliament bowed to the demands of the powerful medieval tenants of the King and enacted Statute de Donis, which created the ***fee tail.*** The purpose of the fee tail was to permit the landed nobility to keep their power over land centralized in their families. Statute de Donis accomplished this by creating an estate, the fee tail, that automatically passed from one generation to the next, expiring only when the lineal bloodline runs out. Upon expiration, the estate reverts to the original grantor and through inheritance or devise (since the grantor is then very likely to be an ancient skeleton) to the grantor's presently living remote heirs or devisees. The magic words necessary to create a fee tail were "to A ***and the heirs of his body***" — meaning his lineal descendants. Note: The "h" is silent in "heirs;" don't speak of the "hairs" of the body — you will look foolish.

   Example: O conveys Blackacre "to A and the heirs of his body." A has a fee tail in Blackacre. If A conveys Blackacre "to B and his heirs" B does not have a fee simple absolute. Rather, B has possession of Blackacre only until A's death, at which point A1, A's son, gets possession and the fee tail.

   a. **Must be followed by a reversion or a remainder:** Since a fee tail *might expire* — the lineal bloodline might die out — every fee tail was followed by either a ***reversion*** in the grantor or a ***remainder*** in a third party.

      Example 1 (Reversion): Oscar owns Blackacre in fee simple absolute. Oscar conveys Blackacre "to my daughter Alma and the heirs of her body." A fee tail in Alma is created, as is a reversion in Oscar. If Alma dies childless, Oscar's reversion becomes possessory. Since the fee tail would have expired the reversion, once possessory, would be a fee simple absolute. Oscar's reversion might well survive him: it could pass by transfer during his life, by will, or through intestate succession. Whoever owns it, though, would acquire possession when Alma died childless. The same would be true if Alma had one child, Peter, who had one child, Gordon, who then died without ever having begotten a child. At the point of Gordon's death the **lineal bloodline would expire** and that would terminate the fee tail. The holder of Oscar's reversion would be entitled to possession and would own Blackacre in fee simple absolute.

Example 2 (Remainder): Oscar owns Blackacre in fee simple absolute. Oscar conveys Blackacre "to my daughter Alma and the heirs of her body, but if Alma dies without issue, then to my son Benjamin and his heirs." A fee tail in Alma is created and Benjamin has a **remainder** in Blackacre. The phrase "if Alma dies without issue" means **general** or **indefinite failure of issue** — the expiration of Alma's bloodline at any point in the future. It does **not** mean **definite failure of issue** — the possibility of Alma individually dying without children. If Alma has one child, Peter, and Peter has one child, Gordon, who dies childless, Benjamin's remainder will become possessory upon Gordon's death. Benjamin will then own Blackacre in fee simple absolute.

C. **Elimination of the fee tail:** Two hundred years after Statute de Donis the royal judges ruled in *Taltarum's Case*, Y.B. 12 Edw. 4th 19 (1472), that a collusive suit called a common recovery could **bar the entail,** or terminate the fee tail.

Example: In 1475, Able owns Blackacre in fee tail and wishes to convey fee simple absolute to Baker. Able and Baker agree on a price and place the purchase price in a secure escrow, pending a successful common recovery. Baker then sues Able, making plausible but wholly fictional allegations that he, Baker, owns fee simple absolute in Blackacre. Able would answer that he derived title from Fallguy, that if what Baker said was true it was all due to Fallguy, and implead Fallguy as a defendant. Fallguy, chosen because he was impecunious, would appear, admit that Baker was correct and that he had no defense. Judgment would be rendered for Baker, giving him fee simple absolute in Blackacre. Able would be given judgment against Fallguy for the value of the lost estate, which judgment was deemed by *Taltarum's Case* to be an adequate substitute for the estate. Then the purchase price would be disbursed from escrow to Able. Fallguy would drink up his fee and remain broke. Able's lineal descendants were out of luck. See Bigelow, Introduction to the Law of Real Property 27 (1945); Simpson, A History of the Land Law 125-138 (2d ed. 1986); Plucknett, A Concise History of the Common Law 620-621 (5th ed. 1956).

1. **Largely abolished:** In the United States today, the fee tail has been largely abolished. An attempt to create a fee tail will result in one of the following: (1) a fee tail that can be ended by a simple conveyance, (2) a fee simple absolute, (3) a fee simple subject to an executory limitation, (4) a life estate followed by a remainder in the issue of the life tenant, or (5) a fee simple conditional. Each is discussed below.

2. **Fee tail and disentailing conveyance:** Perhaps four states permit creation of the common law fee tail, but all provide that the fee tail is destroyed by a *disentailing conveyance* — an ordinary conveyance of fee simple absolute. This is an exception to the usual rule that a grantor cannot convey more than he owns.

   Example: Harold conveys Blackacre to William and the heirs of his body. William has a fee tail. William conveys Blackacre to George and his heirs. George has fee simple absolute. If William wants to keep possession of Blackacre but wishes to own it in fee simple absolute, he must use a *straw conveyance.* William would convey Blackacre to his lawyer in fee simple absolute and the lawyer would immediately reconvey it to William, thus giving William both possession of and a fee simple absolute in Blackacre.

3. **Statutory conversion to fee simple absolute:** Many states have, by statute or state constitutional provision, converted the fee tail into a fee simple absolute. There are two versions of this, each leading to the same end.

   a. **Fee simple absolute in the first taker:** The first holder of the purported fee tail receives fee simple absolute.

      Example: Bill conveys Blackacre to June and the heirs of her body. June has fee simple absolute.

   b. **Non-recognition of the fee tail:** Some states declare that the fee tail shall not be recognized. See, *e.g.*, Texas Const. Art. I, § 26. In these states, a purported fee tail is a nullity. By applying the presumption that a grantor intends to convey the largest estate he owns, the result is a fee simple absolute in the first taker.

      Example: Glen owns Blackacre in fee simple absolute and conveys it to Margaret and the heirs of her body. The purported fee tail is not recognized, but since Glen owned fee simple absolute it will be presumed that he intended to convey fee simple absolute. The presumption cannot be rebutted because Glen's evident intent to create a fee tail will not be recognized.

4. **Statutory conversion to fee simple subject to executory limitation:** Some states provide that an attempt to create a fee tail will create a fee simple in the first taker under the grant, but if the purported fee tail contains a *remainder* the purported remainder will be given effect *if and only if* the *first taker dies without surviving issue.* See, *e.g.*, Cal. Civ. Code §§ 763-764. This statutory method of eliminating a fee tail creates in the first taker a *fee simple subject to an executory limitation.* An executory limitation, or *executory interest,* is a future interest in a transferee from the grantor that becomes possessory by either cutting off another transferee's estate or cutting off the grantor's estate at some future time. See Chapter 4, p. 122, *infra*.

Example: Fred, owner of Blackacre in fee simple absolute, conveys Blackacre to "Emma and the heirs of her body, then to Jane and her heirs." At common law Emma would have a fee tail and Jane would have a remainder (which would become possessory when Emma's bloodline expires — indefinite or general failure of issue). But under this statutory scheme Emma receives a fee simple subject to an executory limitation — the executory interest in Jane. If Emma is survived by Caleb, her son, Emma's estate will own Blackacre in fee simple absolute. Jane will get nothing. If Emma dies without surviving issue — definite failure of issue — Jane's executory interest will become possessory and she will own Blackacre in fee simple absolute. Jane's interest is an executory interest because she is a transferee from Fred and her interest becomes possessory (if at all) by cutting off the fee simple held by Emma. Emma's fee simple doesn't die with her; it either becomes absolute (if she is survived by Caleb) or shifts over to Jane (if Emma dies without surviving issue) and becomes absolute in Jane.

5. **Life estate and remainder in life tenant's issue:** A few states essentially permit a fee tail to persist for one generation, then convert it into a fee simple absolute. They do this by treating the first holder of the purported fee tail as the owner of a life estate, and recognizing a remainder interest in the issue of the life tenant.

Example: David conveys Blackacre to Alice and the heirs of her body. Alice has a life estate. Her issue own a remainder in fee simple absolute. But this remainder is contingent upon Alice having issue. If Alice has a child, Mary, upon Alice's death Mary will own Blackacre in fee simple absolute. If Alice dies childless, the contingent remainder in Alice's issue will fail and David's reversion will become possessory. David or his successors will own Blackacre in fee simple absolute. See, e.g, *Morris v. Ulbright,* 558 S.W.2d 660 (Mo. 1977).

6. Fee simple conditional created: Perhaps three states — South Carolina, Iowa, and Tennessee — treat an attempted fee tail as creating a fee simple conditional. These states do not recognize Statute de Donis as part of the common law received from England. The holder of a fee simple conditional has a life estate, but if a child is born to the holder she may convey fee simple absolute.

Example: Ernie conveys Blackacre to Susanna "and the heirs of her body." Susanna has a fee simple conditional and Ernie retains a reversion. If Susanna never has a child her estate will expire on her death and Ernie's reversion will become possessory, creating a fee simple absolute in Ernie (or his successor to the reversion). But if Susanna gives birth to Bert, Susanna now has the power to convey a fee simple absolute (destroying Ernie's reversion).

IV. DEFEASIBLE FEES

A. **Introduction:** Any estate may be made *defeasible* — subject to termination — upon the happening of some future event. This section considers defeasible fees simple, but the principles discussed here may be used in connection with other estates. The distinction between a fee simple absolute and a defeasible fee simple is that **no future event can terminate or divest a fee simple absolute,** while a defeasible fee simple is **subject to termination or divestment upon the occurrence of a future event.** Of course, the future event may never happen, in which case a defeasible fee endures as long as a fee simple absolute, but all the while the threat of termination hangs, like the sword of Damocles, over the defeasible fee. There are two types of defeasible fees simple: (1) the *fee simple determinable* and (2) the *fee simple subject to condition subsequent.* The fundamental difference between the two is that the fee simple determinable *terminates automatically* upon the occurrence of the future event and the fee simple subject to condition subsequent *terminates only when proper action is taken to terminate the estate* following the occurrence of the future event.

B. **Fee simple determinable:** A fee simple determinable is created when the grantor intends to grant a fee simple *only until a specified future events happens* and uses language in the grant that manifests that intent.

Example: Rick, owner of Blackacre in fee simple absolute, conveys Blackacre to "the Town Library Association for only so long a time as Blackacre is used as a free lending library." Rick has created a fee simple determinable in the Town Library Association. His intent, and the words of his grant are clear: Town Library's estate will last only until the moment Blackacre ceases to be used as a free lending library. If the grant had merely said "to the Town Library Association for the purpose of use as a free lending library" a fee simple determinable *would not* be created. The Town Library Association would have fee simple absolute. Mere expressions of purpose are legally inconsequential surplusage.

1. **Possibility of reverter.** Because a fee simple determinable is less than a fee simple absolute, a grantor of a determinable fee (who owned fee simple absolute before the grant) necessarily retained an interest. That retained interest is called a *possibility of reverter*. Note: the retained interest is *not* a reversion, and it is *not* a reverter; it is a *possibility of reverter*. The possibility of reverter is discussed in detail in Chapter 4, p. 122, *infra*.

    Example: In the last example, Rick would retain a possibility of reverter in Blackacre. Rick did not have to mention expressly its creation because it was created by operation of law — the fact that he conveyed a fee simple determinable, a estate of less duration than his fee absolute requires that he be deemed to retain something. The algebra of estates is simple but inexorable. Of course, in the grant Rick could expressly retain his possibility of reverter, but he does not need to.

2. **Words evidencing intent to create fee simple determinable:** Some "magic words" still matter when courts decide whether or not a fee simple determinable has been created. Usages like *"so long as," "until," "during,"* or *"while"* are indicative of a grant for a limited duration, and thus are likely to be construed as creating a fee simple determinable. This conclusion will be bolstered if the grantor also expressly retains a possibility of reverter or uses other words indicating an intention to create an automatic return of possession and fee simple absolute.

    Example: Tom, owner of Blackacre in fee simple absolute, conveys Blackacre "to Swank Yacht Club only for so long as Blackacre is used as the SWC clubhouse and, if not so used, the estate granted hereby shall automatically terminate and all right, title and interest in Blackacre shall revert to grantor." A grant for a limited duration is clear and the nature of the grant is equally clear even though Tom never described the granted estate as a fee simple determinable or the retained interest as a possibility of reverter. See, *e.g.*, *Mahrenholz v. County Board of School Trustees,* 417 N.E.2d 138 (Ill. App. Ct. 1981).

3. **Transferability:** A fee simple determinable is a freely transferable estate but the nature of the estate stays the same. The transferee takes the estate subject to the limitation that makes it defeasible.

4. **Abolished in some states:** At least two states, California and Kentucky, have abolished the fee simple determinable. An estate that would be a fee simple determinable is, instead, a fee simple subject to condition subsequent.

C. **Fee simple subject to condition subsequent:** A fee simple subject to condition subsequent is created when the words of a grant support the conclusion that the grantor intends to convey a fee simple "absolute," but has attached a string to the grant so that if a specified future event happens (the ***condition subsequent*** to the grant) the grantor may pull the string and get his fee simple absolute back. Conceptually, the grantor has conveyed his fee simple forever, but has added (almost as an afterthought) a condition that will enable him to get it back. By contrast, the theory of the fee simple determinable is that the grantor has conveyed his fee simple only for a limited period. It is somewhat like the difference between a loan (fee simple determinable) and a revocable gift (fee simple subject to condition subsequent).

Example: Orville, owner of Blackacre in fee simple absolute, conveys Blackacre "to Battered Women's Shelter; provided, however, that if Blackacre should ever be used for any purpose other than sheltering abused women, grantor may enter and retake possession of and title to Blackacre." Orville has indicated an intent to part with his entire estate in Blackacre ("to Battered Women's Shelter"). By itself, that would give BWS fee simple absolute. But Orville added a proviso ("if Blackacre should ever be used ...") and appended to that proviso a retained power ("grantor may enter and retake possession of and title to Blackacre") that is utterly inconsistent with the preliminary conclusion that Orville conveyed fee simple absolute. Orville has conveyed a fee simple subject to condition subsequent.

1. **Right of entry or power of termination:** As with the fee simple determinable, since the grantor has parted with less than fee simple absolute the grantor necessarily retains an interest. The interest retained by the grantor when a fee simple subject to condition subsequent is created is called a ***right of entry*** or ***power of termination.*** Unlike the possibility of reverter, which automatically becomes a possessory interest upon occurrence of the future event, a

holder of a right of entry (power of termination) must ***actually exercise the power to terminate*** the fee simple subject to condition subsequent in order for that defeasible fee to come to an end. The holder of a right of entry has the ***option to terminate*** the fee simple subject to condition subsequent.

Example: In the last example, if the Battered Women's Shelter started to use Blackacre as an amusement park instead of a shelter for abused women the condition subsequent would have occurred. But the Shelter's estate in Blackacre would not end ***until and unless*** Orville takes affirmative action to retake possession and thus terminate the Shelter's estate.

2. **Words evidencing intent to create fee simple subject to condition subsequent:** If the words used in the grant indicate an intention to convey the grantor's entire estate and but then express a conditional right to take it back, courts will construe the grant as creating a fee simple subject to condition subsequent. Phrases suggesting this intent include ***"provided, however," "but if," "on condition that."*** The key is whether the grant evidences intent to pass title completely, save only for a right to take it back.

3. **Action necessary to assert right of entry:** To exercise a right of entry the holder must take substantial steps to recover possession and title. The right of entry holder need not actually physically enter and retake possession, but must do more than merely proclaim his intentions to retake possession. Filing suit to recover possession is surely good enough. A letter demanding possession is debatable; whether it is enough to constitute exercise of the right of entry may depend on other added facts.

Example: Bruce conveys fee simple in Blackacre to Ian, subject to the condition subsequent that "no hunting shall ever occur on Blackacre." Bruce writes Ian as follows: "I hear you have been shooting deer on Blackacre. If true, this is to let you know I hereby exercise my right of entry." If Bruce does nothing further for 5 years, this is probably not enough to constitute exercise of the right of entry. But if Bruce followed up that letter with an investigation that proved conclusively that Ian had shot 40 deer on Blackacre, turned over these facts to the relevant government authorities, posted signs at the edge of Blackacre stating "No Hunting; signed Bruce, Owner" and retained a lawyer to advise him, his efforts probably amount to exercise of the right of entry.

4. **Transferability:** Like the fee simple determinable, the fee simple subject to condition subsequent is freely transferable during life, inheritable, and may be devised by will. Of course, once the limiting

condition has occurred and the right of entry exercised there is no estate left to be transferred.

5. Preference for fee simple subject to condition subsequent: It is often difficult to determine which defeasible fee has been created. In ambiguous cases courts prefer to find fee simple subject to condition subsequent. The reason for this preference is that a fee simple determinable produces *automatic forfeiture* of title and possession, while the fee simple subject to condition subsequent makes *forfeiture an option* of the holder of the right of entry. In general, courts try to avoid forfeiture of title because it is harsh, depriving a fee holder of the considerable reliance interest she has developed by possession of the land.

Example: Simon, owner of fee simple absolute in Blackacre, conveys Blackacre "to Alicia and her heirs so long as Blackacre is left forever wild, but if it is not, then grantor has the right to enter and retake possession and title." This confused grant suggests that the grantor intended to pass title for only a limited time ("so long as") but also indicates reservation of the future interest connected to a condition subsequent ("but if ... then ... right to enter and retake possession and title"). Courts will resolve this mess in favor of the condition subsequent in order to avoid the harsh consequence of automatic forfeiture of Alicia's estate.

   a. Use of extrinsic evidence: Sometimes courts will rely on extrinsic evidence — evidence wholly apart from the grant itself — to decide which defeasible fee has been created. This usually occurs where the consequences of automatic forfeiture are especially severe.

   Example: Larry, who holds fee simple absolute in Blackacre, a large but idle wheat ranch, conveys it "to Lynn so long as within one year from today she places Blackacre into agricultural production and harvests a crop of wheat in an amount of not less than 50 bushels per acre." Lynn invests a very large sum to bring Blackacre back into cultivation (buying machinery, seed, and other tools of the farming trade; hiring people; making contractual commitments) and she is about to harvest her wheat crop 10 months later when a freak hailstorm wipes out the crop. A sympathetic Larry writes Lynn that she has another year to fulfill the terms of the original deed. Larry then dies and his heir, Madeline, sues to eject Lynn, contending that Lynn owned fee simple determinable in Blackacre, that the limitation had occurred and, consequently, title had automatically reverted to Larry and descended to Madeline as Larry's heir. What result?

Although the grant seems clearly to create a fee simple determinable many courts will look to the extrinsic evidence (the freak hailstorm, Larry's extension of time, the substantial expenditures of Lynn) to conclude that Lynn had a fee simple subject to condition subsequent and that Larry, holding a right of entry, could and did waive his right for the extended period. Lynn will prevail.

D. Fee simple subject to executory limitation: A fee simple subject to executory limitation is a fee simple that is ***divested***, or ***shifted,*** from one transferee to another transferee upon the occurrence of some future event. Both the fee simple determinable and the fee simple subject to condition subsequent involve the creation of a defeasible fee with a future interest retained by the grantor (either a possibility of reverter or right of entry). But the same defeasible fee estates can be created with the future interests transferred to a third party instead of retained by the grantor. When this happens, a fee simple subject to executory limitation is created.

1. **Automatic termination:** If a grantor uses the words necessary to create a fee simple determinable but, ***instead of retaining the possibility of reverter the grantor transfers that interest to a third party,*** the interest created in the third party is called an ***executory interest*** and the interest created in the immediate transferee is a ***fee simple subject to executory limitation,*** but the legal effect of the interests created is identical to the fee simple determinable and its corollary future interest, the possibility of reverter.

    Example: Joe, owner of Blackacre in fee simple absolute, conveys Blackacre "to Emily and her heirs for so long as Blackacre is cultivated annually and, if not, to Paula and her heirs." Joe has used words indicating his intent to convey Blackacre for a limited time — "so long as Blackacre is cultivated annually." If the grant had stopped there, Joe would have created a fee simple determinable and retained a possibility of reverter. But the grant sends what would have been Joe's possibility of reverter to Paula. Emily has a fee simple subject to executory limitation and Paula has an executory interest. The ***limitation*** on Emily's fee simple is ***identical to what it would have been had a fee simple determinable been created.*** The nature of Paula's executory interest is ***identical to the possibility of reverter that would have existed had a fee simple determinable been created.*** Emily's fee simple ***automatically terminates*** if Blackacre is not cultivated in any year and Paula's executory interest ***automatically becomes possessory*** if that event occurs. Only the names have changed.

2. **Optional termination:** If a grantor uses the words necessary to create a fee simple subject to condition subsequent but, *instead of retaining the corollary right of entry the grantor transfers that interest to a third party,* the interest created in the third party is called an *executory interest* and the interest created in the immediate transferee is a *fee simple subject to executory limitation.* The legal effect of the interests created is identical to the fee simple subject to condition subsequent and its corollary future interest, the right of entry.

   Example: Phil, who holds fee simple absolute in Blackacre, conveys it "to Michelle and her heirs; provided that no banana trees shall ever be planted on Blackacre, and if so, to Bob and his heirs." Without the last clause this would have created fee simple subject to condition subsequent in Michelle and a right of entry retained by Phil. But the added clause turns Michelle's estate into a fee simple subject to executory limitation and creates an executory interest in Bob. Michelle's estate has the same quality, though; it can be terminated only if Bob acts affirmatively to exercise his executory interest.

   a. **Two types of fee simple, one name:** Somewhat inexplicably, the law does not give different names to these two examples of a fee simple subject to an executory limitation. Remember: the two types of defeasible fees can be found under the same name when the corollary future interest is created in a third party. Pay attention to the language of the grant in order to understand the legal rights and obligations of the defeasible fee holder and the executory interest holder.

E. **Some consequences of classification of defeasible fees:** Classification of a defeasible estate as a fee simple determinable or as a fee simple subject to condition subsequent can have significant legal consequences. Some of these are introduced here.

   1. **Transferability of the interest retained by the grantor:** At early common law, neither a possibility of reverter nor a right of entry could be alienated or devised. They could only be inherited. This was because they were not regarded as estates — a presently existing property right — but something more gossamer — a mere possibility. Today, most states permit a possibility of reverter and a right of entry to be alienated, devised, or inherited. But some states only permit possibilities of reverter to be freely transferable. And other states extinguish possibilities of reverter if the holder attempts to transfer them. See 2A Powell, The Law of Real Property ¶¶ 275[2]-275[3] (Rev. ed. 1992).

2. Accrual of a cause of action for recovery of possession: Since a possibility of reverter is automatic, once the limitation has occurred the holder of the possibility of reverter has a right to possession. A cause of action accrues at that moment against the person in possession of the property. The possessor, who used to occupy under a fee simple determinable, is now an adverse possessor. If suit is not timely instituted a new title by adverse possession may result.

Example: Ron holds a possibility of reverter in Blackacre and Caroline holds a fee simple determinable in Blackacre. In 1980 the limitation occurs. Ron does nothing about it until 1991, when he files suit to eject Caroline, who has remained continuously in possession. The state has a 10 year statute of limitations for actions to recover possession of real property. Assuming Caroline can prove the elements of her adverse possession, she now has fee simple absolute in Blackacre, via adverse possession.

- **a. Accrual when title is fee simple subject to condition subsequent:** But the cause of action for recovery of possession does not accrue the moment the limitation occurs if the title is fee simple subject to condition subsequent. Since the holder of the right of entry must take affirmative action to exercise the right of entry, the cause of action accrues when the right of entry is exercised.

    Example: Refer to the last example. If Ron held a right of entry and Caroline a fee simple subject to condition subsequent, Ron's cause of action for recovery of possession accrued in 1991, when he first took action to recover Blackacre, thus exercising his right of entry. Ron's suit would be timely and Caroline would likely be ejected.

- **b. Doctrine of laches:** This stark difference in result has been softened somewhat by various doctrines. Some states apply the equitable doctrine of *laches* — undue delay in asserting one's rights — to bar the assertion of stale claims.

    Example: Refer to the last example. Even though Ron's cause of action for recovery of possession accrued in 1991 (for purposes of the statute of limitations), a court applying the laches doctrine might well conclude that Ron's delay in exercising his right of entry was undue, producing inequitable consequences to Caroline. The equitable doctrine of laches — not the limitations statute — might bar Ron's recovery of Blackacre.

- **c. Statutory and judicial rules regarding accrual:** Some states have statutorily or judicially altered their rules concerning accrual of causes of action to recover possession of real property to remove this anomaly. In such states the cause of action would accrue the moment the limitation occurs, regardless of whether the retained future interest is a possibility of reverter or right of entry.

3. **Effect under the Rule Against Perpetuities:** The Rule Against Perpetuities (see p. 148, *infra*) is a tricky doctrine designed to further free alienability and marketability of property. Under the Rule, when uncertainty concerning ownership of a future interest persists too long the future interest will be destroyed. The details are best left for Chapter 4. However, a possibility of reverter and a right of entry are each exempt from the Rule. But if the very same interest is created in a third party (not the grantor), and thus called an executory interest, it is subject to the Rule and will most likely be invalid. Moreover, the consequences of a destroyed executory interest are quite different, depending on whether the void executory interest was akin to a possibility of reverter or a right of entry. In general, a void executory interest akin to a right of entry will leave the holder of the defeasible fee with fee simple absolute, and a void executory interest akin to a possibility of reverter will leave the holder of the defeasible fee with a fee simple determinable and the original grantor (or his heirs) with a possibility of reverter. The details of this bizarre result are examined in Chapter 4, p. 122, *infra*.

V. LIFE ESTATES

A. **The nature of a life estate:** A life estate is, as its name implies, a possessory estate that expires upon the death of a specified person. Usually, the life estate expires upon the death of the life estate holder.

Example: John, owner of Blackacre in fee simple absolute, grants Blackacre "to Bonnie for life." Bonnie has a life estate that expires on her death. John has a reversion, which will become possessory upon Bonnie's death.

1. **Always followed by a future interest:** A life estate is always followed by some future interest — either a ***reversion*** in the grantor or a ***remainder*** in a third party. A reversion may only be created in a grantor. A remainder may only be created in a transferee.

Example: Liz owns Blackacre in fee simple absolute. She conveys Blackacre "to Guy for life." Liz has retained a reversion. If Liz conveyed Blackacre "to Guy for life, then to John and his heirs," Liz would no longer have any interest in Blackacre. Guy would own a life estate and John would own a remainder.

2. **Life estate *pur autre vie*:** When the duration of a life estate is measured by the life of a person other than the estate holder, it is a ***life estate pur autre vie*** — for the life of another.

   Example: Alison, owner of Tribune Lodge in fee simple absolute, conveys it to Gordon for life. If Gordon then conveys his life estate to Eric, Eric will own a life estate **measured by Gordon's life** — a life estate ***pur autre vie***. Similarly, if Alison had granted Tribune Lodge to Gordon for "the life of Vincent" Gordon would own a life estate *pur autre vie* — lasting as long as Vincent remains alive.

3. **Defeasible life estates:** Life estates may be defeasible, and the same rules apply to defeasible life estates as to defeasible fees. See p. 139, *supra*.

   Example 1: Lady Catherine grants Rosary Park "to Rev. Collins for life, so long as he never preaches a sermon." Collins has a determinable life estate and Lady Catherine has both a possibility of reverter (which would become possessory if Collins preaches a sermon) and a reversion (which will become possessory on Collins's death if he refrains from ever preaching a sermon).

   Example 2: Lady Catherine grants Rosary Park "to Rev. Collins for life, but if he ever preaches a sermon, Lady Catherine retains the right to enter and retake possession." Collins has a life estate subject to condition subsequent and Lady Catherine has both a right of entry and a reversion.

   Example 3: Mrs. Blackett grants Beckfoot to Nancy for life, but if she ever commits an act of piracy, to Peggy. Nancy has a life estate subject to an executory limitation in favor of Peggy.

4. **Life estates in a group or class of people:** A life estate may be created in a group of people. The problem with such class interests is that some of the life tenants will die before others, and there is some uncertainty whether the surviving life tenants take the deceased life tenant's share or whether the remainderman or reversion holder is entitled to possession.

   Example: Suppose Elizabeth Taylor were to convey her royalty interest in the film "National Velvet" to "all of my former husbands for their lives, and then to the ASPCA." Assume there are six former husbands, and Eddie, one of them, dies. Most courts rule that Eddie's life interest is absorbed by the remaining five life tenants, rather than permitting ASPCA to take Eddie's interest. The

ASPCA's remainder would not become possessory until all of the former husbands are dead. But if the original grant specified the opposite outcome — "to all of my former husbands for their lives, and upon the death of each one, to the ASPCA" — the ASPCA would be entitled to possession upon Eddie's death.

5. **Ambiguous grants:** A recurring problem is the ambiguous grant. Courts try to follow the ***grantor's intent,*** but that is itself often indeterminate. Other factors are often relied upon to decide whether a life estate or some other interest is created.

Example 1: Jessie Lide's handwritten will stated: "I wish Evelyn White to have my home to live in and *not* to be *sold.*" The Tennessee Supreme Court relied on a Tennessee statute to presume that Jessie meant to give Evelyn fee simple absolute, there being no "clear evidence" to the contrary. The court treated the "no sale" restriction as an invalid attempt to restrain alienation of a fee simple absolute rather than clear evidence of a life estate. *White v. Brown,* 559 S.W.2d 938 (Tenn. 1977).

Example 2: Father devises Hollyhock Farm "to Son, so long as he refrains from imbibing any intoxicating liquors." Courts are split on whether this creates a fee simple determinable or a determinable life estate. Most courts hold that a fee simple determinable is created, on the theory that Father intended to pass his entire estate save for the limitation. See, *e.g. Lewis v. Searles,* 452 S.W.2d 153 (Mo. 1970) (construing a grant "to Hattie so long as she remains single and unmarried" to be fee simple determinable). The theory of a determinable life estate is that, since the condition can only be satisfied or broken during Son's life, Father must have intended to give him only a life estate. The problem with this is that it is equally probable (if not more so) that Father wanted to give Son an incentive to stay sober.

6. **Transferability and valuation:** A life estate is freely alienable during life, but the transferee receives the transferor's life estate. The market value of a life estate is thus a fraction of the value of a fee simple absolute. The fraction is determined by multiplying the life expectancy (in years) of the person whose life measures the duration of the estate by the annual value of possession and discounting the product to reflect the fact that payment must be made now to receive value over time.

Example: If the market value of fee simple absolute in Runymede is $100,000 and the life tenant has a life expectancy of 5 years, the value of the life estate can be computed by determining the annual value of possession (say 5% of $100,000, or $5,000) and multiplying that annual value for the remaining expected duration of the life estate ($5,000 x 5 = $25,000). But that product overstates the "present" value of the life estate — its value today — because the receipt of $5,000 every year for the next five years is worth less than $25,000 today. If the $25,000 were invested at 6%, compounded annually, it would be worth about $32,400 in five years. By inverse reckoning, the right to receive $5,000 per year for the next five years (the value of the life estate) is about $21,000.

- **a. Valuation when life estate and remainder are sold together:** This valuation procedure is also used whenever a life estate and the remainder are sold in a single package — fee simple absolute — and the sale proceeds must be divided between the life tenant and the remainderman.

    Example: In the prior example, if Runymede were sold for $100,000, 21% of that sum ($21,000) would go to the life tenant and 89% ($89,000) to the remainderman. The percentages would be more-or-less reversed if the life tenant had a long life expectancy instead of only five years.

B. Relationship to fee tail: The life estate supplanted the fee tail. By granting a life estate in one generation and a remainder in the next generation the feudal gentry were able to keep their land in the family.

Example: Darcy owns Pemberly in fee simple absolute. He leaves it by will "to Earl, my son, for life, then to the heirs of Earl's body and their heirs." Earl has a life estate and his heirs, who will not be known until Earl's death, have a ***contingent remainder*** in fee simple absolute. The remainder is not in fee tail because the words "heirs of Earl's body" are words of purchase, describing the owner of the interest created. It is contingent because we don't know who owns it and can't know that until Earl dies.

1. **Comparison:** Compare this with a fee tail.

    Example: If Darcy left Pemberly by will "to Earl, my son, and the heirs of his body," Earl would have a fee tail. Earl could destroy the fee tail by a common recovery (in 15th century England) or, later, by the disentailing conveyance. Today, it would be destroyed by statute or through the disentailing conveyance. See p. 47, *supra*. However destroyed, Earl or his transferee would end up with fee simple absolute in Pemberly. But the devise in the prior example would validly create an property interest in Earl's heirs — the contingent remainder — that could not be destroyed by Earl.

C. The modern life estate: The ***equitable*** life estate is a common and important modern estate, but the ***legal*** life estate is uncommon and a bad idea. An equitable life estate is a property interest, owned for life, in the assets of a trust. A legal life estate is an estate for life in the assets themselves.

Example: Arnie devises Deer Park "to my brother Jack, as trustee, to hold for the benefit of my wife, Elka, for life, then to Lucia and Paul, outright and free of trust." Jack has ***legal title*** to Deer Park in fee simple absolute. Elka has an ***equitable life estate*** and Lucia and Paul concurrently own a remainder. If Arnie had left Deer Park "to Elka for life, then to Lucia and Paul in fee simple absolute" Elka would have a ***legal life estate*** and Lucia and Paul would own the remainder.

1. **Duties of trustee:** A trustee has fiduciary duties to the equitable owners of the trust but, within the limits of those duties, is free to convey the assets in exchange for other assets in order to benefit the equitable owners.

    Example: Refer to the prior example. If Elka moves from Deer Park to Palm Beach, making Deer Park useless to her, Jack has the power to sell Deer Park and add the proceeds of sale to the trust *corpus*. A purchaser of Deer Park will receive fee simple absolute in Deer Park.

2. **Owner can only convey life estate:** But the owner of a legal life estate can only convey her life estate, which may not be very marketable. A purchaser will likely want fee simple absolute, and that can only be delivered by conveying both the life estate and the remainder (or reversion).

    Example: If Elka had a legal life estate in Deer Park, she would need the consent of ***every remainderman*** to convey fee simple absolute in Deer Park. Suppose Paul thinks it is a bad idea for his mother, age 80, to move to Palm Beach. His refusal to sell his remainder would effectively frustrate Elka's plan to substitute Palm Beach for Deer Park since nobody would pay very much for Elka's life estate alone, or even for the combination of Elka's life estate and Lucia's remainder.

3. **Flexibility:** Much more flexibility is possible with the equitable life estate than the legal life estate.

    Example: Arnie could have made Elka both trustee and holder of an equitable life estate. She could then sell Deer Park as trustee (without having to convince her brother-in-law, Jack, to do so) and use the proceeds to purchase Palm Beach.

4. **Judicial responses to inflexibility of the legal life estate:** There are two principal devices courts use (sparingly) to avoid the effects of the legal life estate.

a. **Construction:** Courts try to implement the grantor's intent, but if a grant is sufficiently ambiguous courts may interpret it to create a more flexible estate, such as fee simple absolute. See p. 60, *supra*.

b. **Judicial sale:** Courts sometimes order the sale of the life estate and the remainder and either divide the sale proceeds between the life tenant and the remainderman (see p. 60, *supra*) or order the sale proceeds held in trust with the income payable to the life tenant and the trust *corpus* preserved for the remainderman. This is rarely done. The life tenant and the remainderman can always agree to sell their interests as a package. If they fail to agree courts are reluctant to impose agreement. Even so, there are two situations where courts might order sale.

   i. **Equitable necessity:** Where it can be proved that *sale is in the best interests of all parties* and is the only practical method to effectuate the grantor's intention to provide material comfort for the life tenant and preservation of asset value for the remainderman, a court may invoke its equity powers and order sale of all or part of the property.

      Example: John Weedon devised Oakland Farm to his wife, Anna, for life, remainder to his grandchildren. Over time, Oakland Farm became valuable for development but produced almost no income to the elderly and impoverished Anna. Anna and the remaindermen could not agree on a sale. The Mississippi Supreme Court ruled that a portion of the property could be sold, since sale was in the best interest of all parties. But "equity does not warrant ... sale of all the property since this would unjustly impinge upon the vested rights of the remaindermen" to receive Oakland Farm. *Baker v. Weedon,* 262 So. 2d 641 (Miss. 1972). Courts may also order a sale when the remaindermen are incompetent (*e.g.*, minors, insane) but only when sale is in the best interests of the parties.

   ii. **Waste avoidance:** Courts may also order sale when it is necessary to avoid *waste* — the deterioration or destruction or the underlying property. Again, the idea is that it is in the best interest of all parties to sell the asset before its value is dissipated or destroyed. See *Kelly v. Neville,* 101 So. 565 (Miss. 1924).

D. **Waste:** Inherent in a life estate is the idea that the life tenant gets to *use* property for life, thus deriving the economic value of possession (*e.g.*, rents, farm income). This use must be consistent with the fact that the property will be handed over to the remainderman on the life tenant's death. ***Waste*** is the term used to describe actions of the life tenant that ***permanently impair*** the property's value or the interest of the future interest holders. Older cases tend to conceptualize waste as derived from the grantor's desire to give the life tenant reasonable use of the land, consistent with its preservation in the same character as when received. Newer cases tend to regard waste as a device to prevent one person from unfairly reaping benefits from land possession and imposing economic losses on another person who shares an interest in the land. Waste may be categorized as follows.

1. **Affirmative waste:** When a life tenant acts affirmatively to damage land permanently the life tenant has voluntarily committed waste. This is sometimes called ***voluntary waste.***

   Example: Erma, life tenant in Woodacre, burns the barn, cuts down all the standing mature timber, and removes a large deposit of gravel from Woodacre. Each of these acts is affirmative waste.

2. **Permissive waste:** When a life tenant fails to act reasonably to protect deterioration of the land, permissive or ***involuntary waste*** has occurred.

   Example: Ivan, life tenant in Homestead, fails to repair a chronic leaking roof (which permits dry rot to set in) and fails to pay the property taxes on Homestead. Each omission is unreasonable. Each constitutes permissive waste. See, *e.g.*, *Moore v. Phillips,* 627 P.2d 831 (Kan. Ct. App. 1981) (failure to repair); *Hausmann v. Hausmann,* 596 N.E.2d (Ill. App. Ct. 1992) (failure to pay taxes).

   a. **Determining which omissions are unreasonable:** The question of which omissions are unreasonable is dependent on the particular circumstances. The life tenant must "exercise the ordinary care of a prudent man for the preservation and protection" of the property.

3. **Ameliorative waste:** When the life tenant acts affirmatively to change the principal use of the land, and thereby ***increases the value of the land,*** waste has occurred. This is ***ameliorative waste.*** Ameliorative waste is actionable, however, only when it is clear that (1) the grantor intended for there to be no change in use, and (2) the property may still reasonably be used in the fashion the grantor intended.

   Example: Adam, owner of Waterside, builds an elaborate complex of tanks, ponds, and buildings comprising a profitable fish farm and hatchery. He devises Waterside "to my partner in the fish farm and my son, Abel, for life, then to the University of Eden for use as a fish hatchery and marine biology research facility." Waterside is well-suited to these piscine purposes. Abel replaces the fish farm and hatchery complex with a factory, which doubles the value of Waterside. Abel has committed ameliorative waste. It is actionable by the remainderman, University of Eden, because Adam made it clear that he intended Waterside to be preserved as a fish hatchery and Waterside may still reasonably be used for that purpose.

- a. **Owner does not intend property to be preserved:** If the grantor makes clear that he does not intend for the property to be preserved in its original use, ameliorative waste is not actionable.

    Example: Suppose Adam had devised Waterside "to my son Abel for life, in order to provide Abel with an opportunity to use Waterside to maximize income, and then to my alma mater, University of Eden." Abel's ameliorative waste would not be actionable because it is clear that Abel didn't care about preserving its original character.

- b. **Owner intends property to be preserved:** If the grantor intends that the property be preserved in its original character, but it may no longer reasonably be used in that fashion, ameliorative waste is not actionable.

    Example: Otto, founder of a brewery, devises his residence (adjacent to the brewery) to his son, Wilhelm, for life, remainder to his grandchildren. Time passes, and the residence becomes isolated in a sea of industrial facilities. Wilhelm destroys the residence to incorporate the site into the brewery, thereby making the residence site much more valuable. This ameliorative waste is not actionable, because the ***changed conditions*** render continued use as a residence unreasonable. See *Melms v. Pabst Brewing Co.,* 179 N.W. 738 (Wis. 1899).

VI. RESTRAINTS ON ALIENATION OF FREEHOLD ESTATES

- A. **Types of restraints:** Attempts to prevent alienation of a freehold estate are generally void. These restraints are of three types:

  - **Forfeiture:** A forfeiture restraint purports to cause forfeiture of the estate if alienation is attempted, as when Will conveys The Farm "to Margy, but if she should ever attempt to transfer it in any fashion, to the Modern Language Ass'n."

- **Disabling:** A disabling restraint purports to disable the owner by depriving him of any power to transfer the estate, as when Will conveys The Farm "to Margy, but no further transfer by Margy of any interest in The Farm shall be valid."

- **Promissory:** A promissory restraint purports to extract a promise from the transferee that she will not alienate the property, as when Will conveys The Farm "to Margy, and Margy promises that neither she nor any of her successors in interest will ever transfer any interest in The Farm."

B. **Total restraints on a fee interest:** No matter what type of restraint is used, a *total restraint on alienation* of a fee interest is *void*. The reason for this rule is mostly economic efficiency. Restraints on alienation prevent property from moving into the hands of the person who would use it most productively.

C. **Partial restraints on a fee interest:** Some partial restrictions on alienation of a fee interest are valid, but most are void. The general rule is that a restraint on alienation that is *for a reasonable purpose* and *limited in duration* is *valid*.

   1. **Consent required:** Restraints that permit alienation only upon the *totally discretionary* consent of another person are *void*. But when there is *very good reason* for the consent and the consent is *not wholly discretionary* it is *valid*.

      Example: Cooperative apartments involve ownership of an undivided interest in the apartment building and the exclusive right to occupy a particular apartment. Because each owner is liable for a portion of the building's expenses (particularly the mortgage encumbering the entire building) a restraint conditioning transfer upon the consent of the cooperative's directors is valid, especially if the directors' discretion is confined to determining whether the buyer is financially sufficient. A similar rule applies to condominiums, where each condominium owner is liable for common expenses and her own mortgage.

   2. **Use restrictions:** Some use restrictions are so onerous that they amount to a restraint on alienation, but because these restrictions take the form of a *use restriction* they are usually valid.

      Example: Toscano gave to the Odd Fellows Lodge certain property, and by the deed restricted its use to the Odd Fellows Lodge only. A California appellate court upheld the restriction, on the theory that Toscano meant to convey a determinable fee to the Odd Fellows ("to the Odd Fellows Lodge so long as used only for Lodge purposes").

Mountain Brow Lodge No. 82, Ind. Order of Odd Fellows v. Toscano, 64 Cal. Rptr. 816 (Ct. App. 1967).

3. **Agreements among co-owners:** Concurrent owners of real property have a right at any time to demand *partition* of the property into separate estates. If co-owners have a reasonable purpose for an agreement not to transfer or demand partition, limited to a reasonable time, courts will uphold it.

   Example: Carol and Tony, business partners, are co-owners of Rose Garden, a rose nursery. Tony is the gardener and Carol is the businesswoman. Realizing they need each other's skills for a successful business, they agree not to transfer or seek partition until either (1) they agree to sell the Rose Garden nursery business or (2) one of them dies. The agreement is valid. Its purpose is reasonable — to preserve mutual dependency in a business — and it can last no longer than the life of the first to die.

4. **Unconstitutional restraints:** Some partial restraints may not be enforced by courts because enforcement by an arm of the state violates constitutional limits on government action. The principal example is racial restraints on alienation.

   Example: Fitzgerald owned fee simple in a St. Louis residence burdened by a restraint that forbade transfer to "any persons not of the Caucasian race." Fitzgerald conveyed his interest to Shelley, a person of African ancestry. Kraemer, a "beneficiary" of the restraint, sued to enforce it by enjoining Shelley from taking possession and obtaining an order returning title to Fitzgerald. The U.S. Supreme Court ruled that the Missouri courts could not constitutionally take action to enforce the restraint, because such action would violate the 14th Amendment's command that no state may deny a person the equal protection of the law. *Shelley v. Kraemer,* 334 U.S. 1 (1948).

   a. **State action:** A racial restraint, by itself, does not offend the Constitution since the Constitution controls ***government action,*** not the acts of private parties. But when the machinery of government is invoked to enforce a privately negotiated racial restraint the Constitution is implicated because it is ***government action*** — enforcement of the covenant — that would prevent two willing citizens from transferring an estate for reasons that are generally impermissible to governments. This complex state action doctrine is considered in detail in courses on Constitutional Law. Statutes, whether federal or state, control private actions, and many such laws prohibit private discrimination in housing on the basis of race.

D. Restraints on life estates: Restraints on alienability of life estates are more readily upheld, but validity depends on the type of restraint and the type of life estate to which it is applied.

1. **Legal life estates:** A life estate is theoretically alienable, but not readily marketable by itself. Thus, the practical effect of a restraint on alienation of a life estate is to prevent gift of the estate or creditor seizure of it. These are considerable impediments to economic efficiency and, in the form of a disabling restraint, operate totally to bar alienability, so courts almost always void disabling restraints on alienation. Forfeiture or promissory restraints pose no less a roadblock to economic efficiency but courts sometimes uphold them on the ground that, unlike the disabling restraint, these restraints can be released.

2. **Equitable life estates:** Disabling restraints on equitable life estates are freely permitted. Such a restraint is called a ***spendthrift trust,*** because it is usually created in a trust designed to provide a spendthrift relative with an income but prevent him from his folly by denying him power to pledge the trust assets as security for a loan or otherwise use it to tempt creditors to extend credit to the spendthrift beneficiary.

   Example: Decedent devises $75,000 in trust and instructs the trustees to pay the income from the fund "to my brother Charles W. Adams during his natural life, … free from the interference or control of his creditors, my intention being that the use of said income shall not be anticipated by assignment." This is a valid spendthrift trust. No payments may be made to Charles's creditors to discharge his debts. Of course, once payments are made directly to Charles, creditors may seize the funds disbursed. *Broadway National Bank v. Adams,* 133 Mass. 170 (1882).

   a. **Defense of spendthrift trusts:** The validity of spendthrift trusts is defended on the ground that the property itself — the trust *corpus,* legally owned by the trustee — is freely alienable, so the spendthrift trust poses no danger to economic efficiency. Moreover, creditors are not defrauded since they can determine before extending credit whether the borrower's source of wealth is available to repay the debt. Objection to spendthrift trusts is mostly moral: "[I]t is not the function of the law to join the futile effort to save the foolish and the vicious from the consequences of their own vice and folly. … [S]pendthrift trusts … form a privileged class, … an aristocracy, though certainly the most contemptible aristocracy with which a country was ever cursed." John Chipman Gray, Restraints on the Alienation of Property 247 (2d ed. 1895).

CHAPTER 3
LEASEHOLD ESTATES

I. THE NATURE OF LEASES

A. Origins and development: Common law treated the leasehold as a non-freehold estate. Some say that this was due to the lease's origin as a device to avoid canon law — church law — restrictions against charging interest.

Example: In 1350, Rodrigo, needing money, might borrow a sum of money from Walter, a money lender. But Walter could not charge interest, since church law (backed by the Crown) forbade interest. Walter would receive in exchange for the loan Rodrigo's promise to repay the principal on a future date and possession of some of Rodrigo's land for a term of years. The length of the term would be set to permit Walter to earn enough profits and rents from the land to produce a satisfactory interest rate on the loan.

1. Background: Since money lenders were thought to be unscrupulous and untrustworthy (cf. William Shakespeare, Merchant of Venice) the money lender was not a fit person to perform feudal obligations, and was not permitted to hold seisin. Thus, the estate acquired by the money lender (a term of years) was treated as a non-freehold estate. The termor only had possession; the owner never parted with title. The possessory interest of the termor was treated as a "chattel real" — a form of personal property, not real property. That distinction is still observed. A leasehold interest is classified as personal property.

B. Dual nature — estate and contract: The leasehold is an evolving hybrid. It started out as a personal contract, then sometime in the 16th century courts began to treat it as an estate in land. In this century, courts have come to regard the lease (especially the residential lease) as mostly a contract. A lease has both aspects: it is a conveyance of an estate in land and it is a contract. This duality affects the way courts decide the rights and obligations of landlords and tenants.

1. The traditional view — estate: In this view, a lease is a conveyance of an estate in land. The tenant has purchased possession of an estate for a term. The responsibility for maintaining the property and the risk of its destruction is upon the tenant. The landlord's obligation is to deliver possession. The tenant has the obligation to pay rent no matter what, since rent is the price for possession and nothing more. The landlord has the right to retake possession only if the tenant defaults in paying the rent. This view is not entirely a relic of the past, but almost no jurisdiction construes a lease exclusively in this manner.

2. **The contemporary view — contract:** In this view a lease is just another package of bilateral promises that are mutually dependent. If the landlord fails to perform a promise (*e.g.*, to provide access to tennis courts and a swimming pool) the tenant may refuse to perform his promises (*e.g.*, pay rent). The estate view treats these promises as completely independent; the tenant must pay the rent no matter how many promises the landlord breaks. The tenant's remedy is to sue the landlord for damages. Today, courts are apt to treat residential leases as a contract in most respects, but are less quick to do so with respect to commercial leases. And even in residential leases the leasehold has a property aspect as well as a contractual one. Leases are legal hybrids — they are **estates and contracts**.

C. **The general requirement of a written lease:** The original Statute of Frauds (enacted in 1677, during Charles II's reign) required all leases for a period of more than three years to be in writing in order to be valid. By statute, most American states have made the requirement of a writing apply to all leases except "short-term" ones, usually defined as those for a year or less. An oral lease for longer than the short-term period is void and unenforceable, but if the tenant takes possession anyway a **tenancy at will** is created. See p. 75, *infra*. Once the tenant pays rent and it is accepted a **periodic tenancy** is created, though jurisdictions differ as to the length of the period. See p. 74, *infra*.

D. **What makes it a lease?** Sometimes it is difficult to tell whether a transaction has created a leasehold or some other interest, like an **easement,** license, or **profit a prendre.** Easements and licenses are rights to use the land of another, although they differ in some important respects. See p. 198, *infra*. A profit a prendre is the right to take away something fixed to the land of another, such as the right to cut and remove timber, or the right to gather wild blackberries. None of these interests is **possessory,** in the sense that they give the holder the right to exclusive possession of the property. The lease, by contrast, gives the leaseholder the right to exclusive possession for the duration of the term, so long as the tenant performs the lease obligations. A lessee has all the legal rights of a possessor and may sue others for invasion of his possessory interest, via **ejectment** (to oust the wrongful possessor), **trespass** (to recover damages for physical invasion of the property), or **nuisance** (to recover damages or to abate non-physical interference with a possessor's use and enjoyment of property). The easement holder, licensee, or profit holder lacks these powers since they do not have a possessory interest in property.

Example 1: Landowner executes a "lease" giving Oil Corp. the "right to drill for oil within two years and, if oil is discovered, to remove it from the property via pipeline or trucks passing across the property." Though called a lease this is either a fee simple determinable (terminated when either drilling is not timely commenced or oil production ceases) or a profit a prendre (the right to pump oil) coupled with an easement (the right of access to remove oil). States differ on this point but none consider this a leasehold, no matter what the parties call it.

Example 2: Helen, tired after a day's travel, checks into a hotel and rents a room. No lease is created; Helen holds a license to occupy the room overnight. The hotel does not even give Helen exclusive possession. Maids can and do enter her room. But if Helen rented the room on a weekly or monthly basis, a lease might well be created, given the longer duration and the consequent heightened expectation of possession.

II. THE TYPES OF LEASEHOLDS

There are four types of leasehold estates.

A. Term of years: The ***term of years*** is a lease for a ***single, fixed term*** of any length. The term must either be set out clearly in the lease (*e.g.*, "for five years, ending on July 1, 2002") or by reference to a formula that will produce a fixed calendar date for the beginning and ending of the leasehold. Though called a "term of years," it can be of any length — a month, six months, ten years — so long as the period is fixed.

Example: On July 1 Rosemary leases Salmon House to Don "from today until the end of the current salmon fishing season." If local law provides that the salmon season ends on October 31, a term of years has been created, beginning 12:01 a.m., July 1 and ending at midnight on October 30.

1. May be defeasible: A term of years may be defeasible, either ***determinable or subject to condition subsequent.***

Example: If Rosemary added to the lease with Don the phrase "so long as Don uses Salmon House as a salmon smokehouse" a ***determinable term of years*** would be created. If the added phrase was "but if Don shall stop using Salmon House as a salmon smokehouse, Rosemary may terminate the lease and retake possession," a ***term of years subject to condition subsequent*** would be created.

2. **Indeterminate term:** Sometimes a lease is for an indeterminate term, as "for the duration of the war." These leases are puzzlers, because at the time nobody knows when the war will end. Courts adhering to the letter of the common law find these leases to create a tenancy at will (terminable by either party), since the ending date cannot be precisely determined. See, *e.g.*, *National Bellas Hess, Inc. v. Kalis,* 191 F.2d 739 (8th Cir. 1951) (applying Missouri law). But other courts reason that the parties intended to create a term of years since they used an event that neither of them could influence, thus indicating that they wished the leasehold to endure until that future date. See, *e.g.*, *Smith's Transfer & Storage Co. v. Hawkins,* 50 A.2d 267 (D.C. 1946).

Example: Bob leases Fairhaven to Kathy "from today until Halley's Comet next appears visible to the human eye on Earth." Is this a tenancy for years? There might be some dispute about the exact termination date — when is the first moment that Halley's Comet will become visible? — but we can reliably predict that Halley's Comet will appear about 2062. The better conclusion is to call this a term of years, since it seems clear that the parties intended to create a single, fixed term ending around 2062.

3. **Length of the term:** Common law permitted a term of years of any length, but some states have enacted statutes restricting the length of a leasehold term.

B. **Periodic tenancy:** A *periodic tenancy* is a leasehold for a *recurring period of time*, such as month-to-month or year-to-year. A periodic tenancy continues in existence until either the landlord or tenant give *advance notice* to the other party of termination of the lease. Common law required at least six months advance notice to terminate a year-to-year tenancy, and notice equal to the length of the period (but not more than 6 months) for periods of less than a year (*e.g.*, a month's advance notice to terminate a month-to-month tenancy). A periodic tenancy is created by the *parties' intentions* or by *operation of law.*

Example 1: Otis leases Blackacre to Terry "from year to year, beginning on January 1, 1990." A periodic tenancy — from year-to-year — is created by the clearly expressed intentions of the parties.

Example 2: Otis leases Blackacre to Terry "for an annual rent of $12,000, payable in monthly installments of $1,000." This creates a periodic tenancy but the period — month-to-month or year-to-year — is none too clear. Common law treated this as year-to-year, reasoning that a statement of "annual rent" set the period of the tenancy as a year and that monthly payments were a mere "convenience." Without any more evidence as to the parties' intentions, most contemporary courts would treat this as a year-to-year tenancy, especially in a non-residential lease.

Example 3: On January 1, 1996, Otis leases Blackacre to Terry from year-to-year. Terry gives Otis timely notice of termination as of December 31, 1996, but Terry remains in possession on January 1, 1997. Terry is a "holdover," or a tenant at sufferance, and Otis may elect to treat Terry as having renewed his tenancy for another year. This is a new periodic tenancy created by operation of law. See p. 76, *infra*.

Example 4: Otis leases Blackacre to Terry for 100 years, rent payable in monthly installments of $1,000. State law invalidates leases for a term of more than 60 years. Terry takes possession and pays the rent monthly for five years, when Otis decides he made a bad deal and notifies Terry that the lease is terminated in 60 days. All courts will treat this as a periodic tenancy, but they will differ as to whether it is year-to-year or month-to-month. See p. 74, *infra*. By operation of law, Terry's occupancy under a void lease created at least a tenancy at will and, also by operation of law, the tender and acceptance of rental payments transformed the leasehold into a periodic tenancy.

1. **Notice necessary to terminate:**

    a. **Common law:** Six months advance notice is necessary to terminate a year-to-year tenancy, and notice equal to the length of the period (but not more than 6 months) is necessary for periods of less than a year. Notice is only effective as of the *end of the period.*

    Example: Olivia leases Blackacre to Tom "from year to year, beginning on January 1, 1995, for an annual rent of $12,000." Tom takes possession and, on July 10, 1995, notifies Olivia that he is terminating the lease "at the end of the year." Tom moves out on December 31, 1995. On January 15, 1996 Olivia notifies Tom that his notice was defective, the periodic tenancy has been renewed, and that he is liable for $12,000 rent for 1996. What are Tom's obligations to Olivia, if any? The notice was defective in order to terminate on December 31, 1995. To do so, Tom must have notified Olivia no later than July 1. Tom is liable for another $12,000 in rent. But some jurisdictions (and the Restatement 2d of Property, § 1.5, comment f) treat Tom's notice as effective six months after it was given, or January 10, 1996. In that case, Tom is liable for about $330 in rent. A few states treat a defective notice as no notice at all, so the periodic tenancy will continue until and unless Tom gives proper notice.

    b. **Statutory changes:** Many states have legislated on this subject, typically by reducing the notice period to a single month. A few states (notably California Civ. Code § 1946) stipulate that notice is effective one month after it is given, regardless of whether that date happens to coincide with the end of a period.

c. **Modification by agreement:** The parties may shorten or eliminate notice times, but they cannot agree to make them longer than allowed by law.

2. **Fixing the period of periodic tenancies created by operation of law:** The problem here is deciding what the period is when a tenant has taken possession under a void lease, usually an oral long-term lease that is void under the Statute of Frauds, but has paid rent which has been accepted. All courts agree that a periodic tenancy results but there are three different views on the period.

   a. **Year-to-year:** Most courts conclude that a year-to-year tenancy results, reasoning that this is closest to what the parties intended.

   Example: Josie orally agrees to lease Seaside to David for a five year period, rent to be $1,000 per month. David takes possession and pays the rent for six months, then decides that he doesn't like Seaside. He tells Josie he is moving out, does so, and immediately stops paying rent. Assume that the state in which Seaside is located regards year-to-year tenancies as terminated six months after notice is given. The parties intended a term of years for five years, so it is the closest approximation of their intent to treat this as a year-to-year tenancy. David is liable for six months rent.

   b. **Period measured by the rent calculation in the void lease:** Some courts measure the period by the way the rent is calculated, or stated, in the void lease.

   Example: Refer to the prior example. Suppose David and Josie agree that the oral agreement provided simply that the rent was "to be $1,000 per month." Since the rent is stated in monthly terms, a month-to-month tenancy was created. David is liable, at most, for a month's rent.

   c. **Period measured by the way rent is paid:** Finally, some courts measure the period by the way the rent is *actually paid*.

   Example: Suppose Josie and David had signed a written lease, under which Josie leased Seaside to David "for a term of 70 years for a rent of $840,000, payable (solely for the convenience of the parties) in monthly installments of $1,000 each." The state in which Seaside is located prohibits leases of longer than 60 years. David takes possession and pays the rent for two years.

On June 15th, Josie notifies him that she is terminating the lease "effective as soon as the law allows." When must David move out? In jurisdictions that measure the period of the periodic tenancy resulting from operation of law by the way rent is actually paid, a month-to-month tenancy has resulted. David must vacate Seaside no later than July 31st, unless Seaside's state follows the California rule (see p. 73, *supra*), in which case David must vacate no later than July 15th.

C. **Tenancy at will:** A *tenancy at will* is a leasehold for no fixed time or period. It lasts as long as **both** parties desire. Termination is bilateral — **either** party may terminate it at any time — or by operation of law. It may arise by agreement, though this is uncommon because of the lack of security of the tenure, or by operation of law, usually upon the failure of some other leasehold or intended leasehold.

1. **Distinguished from leaseholds unilaterally terminable:** A unilaterally terminable leasehold — only one party has the right to terminate — *cannot be a tenancy at will*. It is a determinable tenancy.

    Example: Jim leases Acorn Farm to Pam "for two years, but Pam may terminate sooner if she wishes." A determinable term of years is created. If Jim had leased Acorn Farm to Pam "from year-to-year, but Pam may terminate whenever she wishes," a determinable periodic tenancy is created. Pam need not give *advance* notice to terminate, but Jim must.

    a. **When lease is both determinable and for uncertain duration:** The problem that occurs is when a lease is both determinable and for an *uncertain duration.*

    Example: Patrick leases a barn to Kathy "for so long as Kathy desires." What tenancy is created?

    b. **Determinable leasehold life estate:** There are two answers to the question posed in the example. The older one is that a tenancy-at-will is created; the more modern (and better) answer is that a determinable leasehold life estate is created.

    Example 1: Robert leased a house to Lou for $100 per month from May 1, 1977 until Lou decides to terminate. Robert then died and David, Robert's executor, notified Lou that he was terminating the lease. In order to carry out the parties' intentions the New York Court of Appeals construed this to create a determinable leasehold life estate. Lou alone held the power to terminate the lease before his death. *Garner v. Gerrish,* 473 N.E.2d

223 (N.Y. 1984). See also *Thompson v. Baxter,* 119 N.W. 797 (Minn. 1909) (finding a determinable life estate on similar facts).

Example 2: Frye leased a house to O'Reilly for "so long as you please for $40 per month." After several years Frye notified O'Reilly that the lease was terminated. Because the lease term was of indefinite duration and tenancies-at-will are of indefinite duration, the Massachusetts Supreme Judicial Court reasoned that it must be a tenancy at will and so implied a power to terminate on the part of Frye. Little attention was paid to the intentions or expectations of the parties. *O'Reilly v. Frye,* 160 N.E. 829 (Mass. 1928).

2. **Termination:**

   a. **By the parties:** Since a principal feature of the tenancy at will is that it can be terminated by either party, the question here is whether a party has so acted. A landlord terminates by giving notice. A tenant terminates either by giving notice or by abandoning the property. Advance notice was not necessary at common law but many states today require some notice (usually a month) and some require only the landlord to give notice.

   b. **By operation of law:** If either party dies, if the tenant attempts to assign his tenancy, or if the landlord conveys his interest in the property, a tenancy at will is terminated by operation of law. Most states require notice of termination to be given under these circumstances, so the tenancy may continue if both parties desire and, in any case, will last until the end of the required notice period.

D. **Holdovers — the tenancy at sufferance:** Tenants sometimes "hold over" — remain in possession after their right to do so has expired. When this happens a ***tenancy at sufferance*** is created. A tenancy at sufferance is a legal limbo — the tenant has no right to be there but he is not treated as a trespasser (mostly to avoid triggering adverse possession). For this reason a tenancy at sufferance is not a true tenancy. The landlord has not consented to the tenant's occupation. A tenancy at sufferance only lasts until the landlord exercises one of two options the law makes available: (1) ***eviction*** and recovery of damages for the lost possession or (2) ***binding the tenant to a new term.*** The landlord must exercise one of these options within a reasonable time.

1. **What constitutes holding over?** At common law a tenant held over if she stayed for the merest tick of the clock past the old term. Excuses, however compelling, were simply not accepted.

Example: Two days before Halloween Meg, age 89, breaks her hip while moving her household goods out of The Lawn, a cottage she has rented for a year's term, ending October 31. Her son, Ron, continues to move her goods out and care for the old lady. But the result is that Meg has not fully vacated The Lawn until noon on November 1. At common law Meg is a holdover tenant. The landlord may elect to bind Meg to another one year term.

- **a. Common law:** The common law ameliorated this harsh rule by grafting onto it the principle that a holdover must be ***voluntary.***

    Example: Tenant stays on because her physician advised her that she is too ill to move. She vacates as soon as she is sufficiently recovered to move. No holdover tenancy resulted because her continued occupancy was involuntary. *Herter v. Mullen*, 53 N.E. 700 (N.Y. 1899).

- **b. Modern doctrine:** From this principle the prevailing modern doctrine has evolved: There is **no holdover** so long as the ***tenant's continued possession is the product of circumstances beyond the tenant's control.*** On this view, the holdover tenancy is created when the tenant fails to vacate as soon as possible under the exigent circumstances. Modern doctrine would not treat Meg, in the first example, as a holdover tenant. A few courts go even further and find no holdover tenancy even without extenuating circumstances, so long as the tenant's action causes no hardship to the landlord.

    Example: Hirschfield's leasehold to his Chicago apartment expired on September 30. He started moving on September 27. By the night of September 30 the only items remaining were the beds and some carpets. Hirschfield's family slept in the apartment that night and removed these last items the following morning. By 10 a.m. the landlord had elected to renew the lease for another year. The Illinois Appellate Court found no tenancy at sufferance, reasoning that Hirschfield's acts could not have caused a reasonable landlord to assume Hirschfield intended to stay for another term, nor did his acts significantly damage landlord. In this connection the court relied on the fact that the lease stipulated that Hirschfield would be liable for double rent for "the actual time of his occupancy" after midnight on September 30. The landlord got a few hours of double rent, not the right to renew for another year. *Commonwealth Building Corp. v. Hirschfield*, 30 N.E.2d 790 (Ill. Ct. App. 1940).

2. **Eviction and damages:** A landlord may evict the holdover tenant and recover damages, measured by the reasonable value of the use of the property for the holdover period.

   a. **Eviction:** Every state provides an expeditious (usually summary) procedure for eviction and recovery of possession. Some states permit the landlord to use *reasonable self-help* to evict holdovers and recover possession.

   b. **Damages for wrongful possession:** A landlord who opts for eviction may also recover damages for the period of wrongful occupancy. The common law measure of these damages is the fair market value of the occupied premises, plus any special damages (*e.g.*, physical injury to the premises). The original rent is presumptive evidence of the fair market value but that presumption may be rebutted if there is convincing evidence that the fair market value is greater or lesser than the original rent.

3. **Election of a new term:** If a landlord elects to bind the holdover tenant to a new term, a number of issues occur, dealt with in the succeeding subsections. Although permitting the landlord to bind the tenant to a new term may seem harsh, the usual rationale for this rule is that it deters holdovers, and deterrence of holdovers is for the benefit of tenants generally, since a new tenant places a great deal of reliance on the old tenant's timely departure. Nobody wants to sleep in the moving van while waiting for the old tenant to move out.

   a. **Nature of the new leasehold:** Most states treat the new tenancy as a periodic tenancy. Some treat the new tenancy as a term of years for a maximum of one year. A very few regard the new tenancy as a tenancy at will, with the tenant liable only for the fair market value of the premises. See, *e.g.*, *Townsend v. Singleton*, 183 S.E.2d 893 (S.C. 1971) (interpreting a statute abrogating the common law of holdover tenancies).

   b. **Length of the new term:** Whether a periodic tenancy or a term of years results, courts divide over how to determine the length of the new term. Some states determine the new term's length by the *way the rent is stated (reserved) in the old lease.*

   Example: Allan holds over and Max, his landlord, elects to renew. The old lease was a term of years for three years, with rent stated as $10,000 per year. In a jurisdiction using the old stated rent as the measuring rod for the new term, Allan's new term is one year. The nature of the tenancy may be a term of years for one year or a periodic tenancy from year-to-year, depending on the state.

> **i. Original term:** Other states use the *original term* as the measure of the new term, except that no state will permit the term to be longer than one year.
>
> **Example:** Allan's new term, by this measure, is one year. Again, it may be a periodic tenancy or a term of years, depending on the state's view of this issue.

c. Provisions of the new leasehold: The provisions of the old lease (except for length or anything else inconsistent with the new relationship) apply to the new leasehold. But if the landlord notifies the tenant of his election to renew at a higher rent and the tenant makes no objection, the tenant is liable for the higher rent.

> **Example:** Selk remained in possession after expiration of a term of years for 70 days at a rent of $1.00. Forty seven days later the landlord notified Selk that his continued occupancy would cost $300 per month rent. Selk never replied to this letter or to a later, similar one, but remained in possession for 23 months after his original term ended. A Florida appellate court ruled that the rent for the new periodic tenancy was $300 per month. Selk's failure to object to the new rent constituted his implicit agreement to pay the higher rent. *David Properties, Inc. v. Selk*, 151 So. 2d 334 (Fla. Dist. Ct. App. 1963).

d. What constitutes election? The easy case is when a landlord clearly states his election of a remedy. But once the landlord has done so, the *election is irrevocable* — the landlord **cannot change his mind.**

> **Example:** Crechalle leased certain premises to Smith for a five year term, ending February 7, 1969. Before expiration of that term, Crechalle and Smith discussed a short-term extension of the term to accommodate Smith's relocation. Smith wrote a letter to Crechalle confirming his understanding of an oral extension. On Feb. 6, Crechalle replied by letter, denying any such extension and demanding that Smith vacate on schedule. Smith stayed on, tendered rent for one month (accepted by Crechalle), and then vacated. Crechalle then declared that he was electing to renew the tenancy. The Mississippi Supreme Court ruled that Crechalle's Feb. 6 letter constituted his election "to terminate the lease and to treat [Smith] as [a] trespasser." *Crechalle & Polles, Inc. v. Smith,* 295 So. 2d 275 (Miss. 1974).

i. **When election must be inferred:** More often, the landlord never clearly states his intentions and election must be inferred from his acts.

Example: Forester leased an apartment to Kilbourne for a term of years. After expiration of the term Kilbourne held over for two more years. During that time Kilbourne tendered rent on a monthly basis but Forester never accepted it. Forester sent Kilbourne many letters demanding that she vacate but never did anything more to enforce the demand. Finally, Forester brought suit to recover possession. A Missouri appellate court rejected Kilbourne's contention that, by laches and acquiescence, Forester had elected to treat her as a tenant for a new term. However dilatory Forester had been, he had at least been consistent in never accepting Kilbourne's tendered rent, and had never otherwise manifested an intention to recognize Kilbourne as a tenant for a new term. It is the landlord's intention that counts. *Kilbourne v. Forester*, 464 S.W.2d 770 (Mo. Ct. App. 1970).

e. **When must the landlord elect the remedy?** The landlord must make his election within a ***reasonable time,*** but there are not many decided cases on the question of what period is reasonable. *Kilbourne v. Forester, supra*, implicitly found two years to be a reasonable time, but that is surely at the outer edges of reasonableness. If the landlord fails to act within a reasonable time, whatever it is, the tenant's status is unclear. Some of the few cases addressing the issue treat the tenant as a periodic tenant, others treat the tenant as a trespasser, and still others conclude that a tenancy at will is created. The periodic tenancy conclusion punishes the landlord for his sloth; the trespasser conclusion gives no reward to the wrongful occupier but starts the adverse possession clock; and the tenancy at will is a pragmatic compromise. See 1 American Law of Property § 3.33.

4. **Statutory alterations:** The common law of holdovers has been altered by statutes, mostly designed to limit the landlord's common law remedies. These statutes take a variety of forms. Some states require that holdover tenants of farm land must be permitted to remain for six months to even a year, in order to enable the tenant to harvest crops. See, *e.g.*, *Estate of Thompson v. O'Tool*, 175 N.W.2d 598 (Iowa 1970). Some statutes prescribe the nature of the new tenancy resulting from landlord election to bind the tenant to a new term. And some statutes provide for penalties for the ***willful holdover.*** The Uniform Residential Landlord & Tenant Act (URLTA), § 4.301(c), provides that a willful holdover may be liable for treble

damages or three months' rent, whichever is greater, plus the landlord's reasonable attorney's fees. Some states have statutes that subject holdover tenants to liability for double or triple rent. These statutes are usually expressly or impliedly limited to the willful holdover tenant, but some states have adopted the double damage remedy as the exclusive remedy for any holdover. See, *e.g.*, *Mississippi State Dep't of Public Welfare v. Howie*, 449 So. 2d 772 (Miss. 1984), which held that Mississippi's double rent statute was the sole remedy for "a tenant's holdover. The common law rule has been abrogated ... and may no longer be used to impose the renewal of an expired lease."

III. DELIVERY OF POSSESSION

A. **Introduction:** Delivery of possession is the essence of a leasehold. All agree that the landlord has an implied-in-law obligation to deliver to the tenant the ***legal right to possession,*** but states are divided on the subsidiary question of whether a landlord has an implied obligation to deliver ***actual physical possession*** at the beginning of the lease term. Everyone agrees that there is no implied-in-law obligation of the tenant actually to take possession or to use the premises for any particular purpose. These matters are discussed below.

B. **Implied obligation to deliver legal right of possession:** A landlord is obligated to deliver to the tenant the ***legal right*** to possess the leased premises. If a third party has a better claim to possession than the landlord, the landlord will not be able to deliver to the tenant the legal right to possess.

Example: Buck, in adverse possession of Blackacre for five years (the limitations statute is ten years), leases Blackacre to Buster. Soon after Buster takes possession of Blackacre, Sophie, the true owner, sues Buster for ejectment and evicts him. Buck has breached his implied obligation to deliver to Buster the legal right to possession.

1. **Consists of two promises:** The obligation to deliver the legal right to possession consists of two promises, implied in law, by the landlord:

    - The landlord has the ***power to demise*** — the power to grant to the lessee the interest he purportedly grants under the lease. In the prior example, Buck would have violated this promise the moment the lease was made, since he had no legal right to possession.

    - The landlord promises that the tenant will have the ***quiet enjoyment*** of possession — meaning that the landlord promises that the tenant will not be evicted by somebody with a legally better title to the property than the landlord. In the prior example, Buck breached this promise when Sophie, the true owner, evicted Buster.

2. **Continuing obligation:** The obligation to deliver legal right to possession is a continuing one, as the quiet enjoyment promise makes clear. If at any time during the tenant's possession, someone with ***paramount title*** — a better legal claim to the property than the landlord — interferes with the tenant's possession, the landlord has failed to deliver his promise of legal right to possession.

    Example: Richard owns and leases Charter House to Serena. Prior to the lease, Richard had borrowed money from OmniBank, giving OmniBank a mortgage on Charter House to secure repayment. OmniBank has paramount title, but so long as Richard is not in default on the loan, there will be no interference with Serena's right of possession. But if Richard defaults, OmniBank forecloses on the mortgage and evicts Serena, Richard has breached his continuing obligation to deliver legal right of possession. See *Ganz v. Clark,* 252 N.Y. 92 (1929); *Standard Livestock Co. v. Pentz,* 269 P. 645 (Cal. 1928).

3. **Waiver by tenant:** This obligation may be ***waived*** by the tenant, either ***expressly*** or by the ***tenant's knowledge,*** at the time he enters into the lease, that there is a paramount title. If the tenant is ignorant of the paramount title and takes possession, he has not waived the landlord's obligation but he has no remedy until and unless the holder of paramount title interferes with his actual possession. By contrast, if the tenant does not know of the paramount title when he signs the lease, but learns of it before he takes possession, the tenant is entitled to repudiate the lease without penalty.

C. **Obligation to deliver actual possession:** The problem here is another facet of a tenant holdover. Does the landlord have an obligation implied in law to deliver ***actual possession*** to the tenant at the beginning of the term? If he does, the burden of removing the holdover tenant is borne entirely by the landlord and the landlord is liable to the new tenant for damages resulting from delay in placing him in possession. If he does not, the burden of ousting the holdover falls on the new tenant. There are two opposing views.

1. **The English Rule:** Under this view (said to be the majority view of American states) the landlord has an implied-in-law obligation to deliver actual possession to the tenant on the first day of the lease term. See *Coe v. Clay,* 130 Eng. Rep. 113 (1829); *Jinks v. Edwards,* 11 Exch. 775 (1856); *Adrian v. Rabinowitz,* 186 A. 29 (N.J. 1936);

Herpolsheimer v. Christopher, 111 N.W. 359 (Neb. 1907); *King v. Reynolds,* 67 Ala. 229 (1880). The rationale for the English Rule is that the lessee "expects to enjoy the property, not a mere chance of a lawsuit." Also, the landlord (especially a large one) is probably more efficient at ousting the holdover because he is likely to be more familiar with eviction procedures. Finally, a landlord is more apt to know when a holdover problem is likely to occur and can thus avoid the problem by refraining from a lease in advance of vacation.

    a. **Tenant remedies:** The tenant may either: (1) ***terminate the lease,*** find other premises, and recover ***damages*** pertinent to this exercise in musical chairs, or (2) ***adhere to the lease, withhold rent*** for the period he is out of possession, and ***recover damages*** related to the lost possession. If the tenant affirms the lease, the measure of damages is the excess of fair market value over the agreed rental for the period of lost possession, plus special damages (*e.g.,* storage costs, temporary quarters). Special damages may, but usually do not, include lost profits. Lost profit claims must be supported by especially clear proof. If the tenant terminates the lease, his damages are measured by the excess of the replacement rent over the agreed rent (assuming equivalent premises) for the lease term, plus special damages (*e.g.,* storage costs, transaction costs associated with the replacement leasehold).

    b. **Partial possession:** If the tenant is deprived of only part of the leased premises, the tenant is entitled only to abate a proportionate share of the rent for the period of lost possession. Do not confuse this with the independent phenomena of a landlord's partial eviction of a tenant in possession, which may give the tenant the right to suspend rent entirely, depending on the jurisdiction. See p. 100, *infra.*

    c. **Waiver:** Some jurisdictions applying the English Rule permit the parties to waive this obligation in the lease. The Restatement (2d) of Property, § 6.2, adopts this position. But other English Rule jurisdictions do not permit waiver. See URLTA § 1.403. Since leases are also contracts, some jurisdictions that otherwise permit waiver might find a particular purported waiver to be unenforceable as unconscionable (*e.g.,* the waiver is in microscopic type on page 10 of a 15 page lease).

2. **The American Rule:** Under this approach, which is the minority rule in the United States, the landlord has no implied obligation to deliver actual possession. The tenant has the legal right to possession; obtaining actual possession is up to the tenant. See *Hannan v. Dusch,* 153 S.E. 824 (Va. 1930); *Snider v. Deban,* 144 N.E. 69 (Mass.

1924); *Gazzolo v. Chambers,* 73 Ill. 75. Justifications offered for this rule are: (1) the landlord is not responsible for wrongful possessors after the tenant takes possession so he should not be responsible for those existing at the dawn of the lease term, (2) the lease delivers to the tenant the landlord's possessory rights, so the wrongful possession interferes only with the tenant's rights, and (3) the tenant could have bargained for an express promise of the landlord to deliver actual possession.

    a. Tenant's remedies: The tenant has the same rights against the holdover tenant that the landlord would have had, absent the new lease. The incoming tenant can treat the holdover as a trespasser, evict and recover damages, or the incoming tenant can renew the holdover for a new term, receiving the rent from the holdover. See p. 76, *supra*. These may not be satisfactory remedies to most incoming tenants, especially in residential leases.

    b. Landlord's remedies: The logic of the American Rule suggests that the landlord should have no remedies against the holdover tenant, but American Rule jurisdictions frequently ignore logic and permit the landlord to elect one of the customary remedies. There is some practical sense in this, since an incoming tenant in an American Rule jurisdiction, disgusted with what law serves up to him, is simply apt to disappear.

    c. Modification by agreement: In American Rule jurisdictions the parties are free to create an express obligation on the landlord's part to deliver actual possession. Indeed, one of the rationales for the American Rule is that parties may do so. It is obviously a good idea for tenants in American Rule jurisdictions to insist on such an express promise from the landlord.

D. Tenant obligation to take possession: Tenants have no obligation to take possession or to use the leasehold for a particular purpose, *unless the lease obligates them to do so.* Absent such an express promise, the tenant is free to leave the leased space vacant, although he is still obliged to pay the rent. Sometimes this situation may constitute an abandonment of the leasehold by the tenant, with the consequences discussed in p. 96, *infra*. This issue, as distinguished from abandonment, usually arises where the lease stipulates that the rent is some percentage of the tenant's sales at the leased premises.

Example: Byron, owner of a parcel located next to an exit from an interstate highway, leases it to Major Brand Gas, a national refiner and retailer of gasoline for a term of 15 years. The rent consists entirely of 3 cents per gallon of gasoline sold at the premises. If Major Brand Gas never occupies the parcel, Byron is an enormous loser. Byron would be extremely foolish to sign such a lease without explicit promises from Major Brand to build a first class gasoline station, occupy it, and use its best efforts to sell as much gasoline as possible. Cf. *Mercury Investment Co. v. F.W. Woolworth Co.,* 706 P.2d 523 (Okla. 1985).

IV. SUBLEASES AND ASSIGNMENTS

A. Introduction: An ***assignment*** of a leasehold places the assignee in ***privity of estate*** with the landlord, meaning that the assignee and landlord are liable to each other for performance of the lease obligations that "run" with the leasehold estate — carry over from one estate holder to the next. See p. 86, *infra.* An assignment of the landlord's reversion similarly places the assignee and the tenant in privity of estate. Assignment does not destroy ***privity of contract,*** which means that the contractual duties created by a lease continue to be personal obligations of the original parties to the lease even after assignment. By contrast, a ***sublease*** by the tenant does ***not*** create privity of estate between the landlord and the subtenant. The subtenant is liable only to the tenant for the sublease obligations, and the subtenant has no claim against the landlord for failure to perform his lease obligations. There is generally no privity of contract, either, since only the tenant and subtenant have a contractual relationship. Consequently, the critical issue here usually is to decide whether any given transfer of a leasehold is an assignment or a sublease.

B. Assignment: An assignment is the ***transfer of the party's entire interest under the lease.*** If a tenant retains any interest it is a sublease. See p. 90, *infra.* The methods of deciding whether any given transfer is an assignment or sublease are discussed in p. 91, *infra.* Unless the lease prohibits or conditions assignment, either the landlord or the tenant may freely assign the reversion or leasehold, respectively, that they hold. Most leases either prohibit assignment by the tenant, or require the tenant to obtain the landlord's consent.

1. **Privity of estate:** An assignment places the assignee in privity of estate with the other original party. Privity of estate is rooted in the conception of a leasehold as an estate in land.

    Example: Lord leases Blackacre to Tenant, who assigns the leasehold to Newcomer. Lord and Newcomer are now in privity of estate with respect to Blackacre. Lord and Newcomer have the relationship of landlord and tenant.

    a. **Obligations of assignee:** The consequence of being in privity of estate is that the assignee is obligated to perform all the lease covenants that "run with the estate." See Chapter 6, p. 227, *infra*. For the moment, accept the assertion that the most important lease promise that definitely runs with the estate is the promise to pay rent.

Example: The lease between Lord and Tenant provided that Tenant would pay $1,000 per month rent. This promise runs with the estate. Since Newcomer is in privity of estate with respect to Blackacre, Newcomer must perform it.

b. Promises that run with the leasehold estate: For a promise to run with the leasehold estate, and thus be enforceable against assignees, the following elements must be present:

- **Intent:** The original parties to the lease must intend that the promise bind assignees.

- **Privity:** The assignee must be in *either* privity of estate or privity of contract with the party enforcing the promise or against whom the promise is sought to be enforced.

- **"Touch and Concern":** The promise must "touch and concern" the assigned estate — either the leasehold (when the tenant assigns) or the reversion (when the landlord assigns). A promise "touches and concerns" an estate when its performance (or non-performance) is integrally connected with the *use or enjoyment* of the estate. Any promise has both a *benefit* and a *burden*. For an assignee to enforce a promise or to have a promise enforced against her, it must be shown that the benefit of the promise, or the burden of the promise, respectively, touches and concerns the assignee's estate.

Example: L1 leases Blackacre to T1, who promises to keep the fences mended. If L1 assigns her reversion to L2, L2 must prove that the benefit of this promise touches and concerns L2's reversion in order to enforce it against T1. If T1 assigns his leasehold to T2, L1 must show that the burden of the promise touches and concerns T2's leasehold in order to enforce it against T2. If L2 seeks to enforce it against T2, L2 must demonstrate that both burden and benefit touch and concern the leasehold and reversion, respectively.

- **Notice:** The assignee must have either actual or inquiry notice of the promise. Recall that inquiry notice means that notice will be implied when the circumstances are such that the assignee should have inquired, and inquiry would have revealed the promise.

i. Contentious issues: Most of the contentious issues revolve around "touch and concern." Usually, both the benefit and burden of a promise will either touch or concern the relevant estates, or neither will. But sometimes a landlord (or tenant) will extract a promise that benefits other property of the landlord (or tenant), and not the reversion (or leasehold).

Example: Landlord leases Blackacre to Tenant, and Tenant promises not to build a fast food restaurant on Blackacre. Landlord operates Quik Fat, a fast food restaurant located on Whiteacre, a neighboring property. Tenant's leasehold is burdened but Landlord's reversion is not benefited. Rather, the benefit resides in Whiteacre, Landlord's neighboring property.

c. Personal promises don't run: A personal promise does not run with the estate, but the promisor remains obligated to perform it even after assignment, unless he is released from the obligation. See p. 87, *infra*.

Example: Landlord leases Blackacre to Tenant and Tenant promises to walk Landlord's dog daily. Tenant then assigns her leasehold to Katt, who refuses to walk the dog. The promise is personal to Tenant, does not burden the leasehold (because it does not "touch or concern" the leasehold) and so cannot be enforced against Katt. But Landlord can enforce the promise against Tenant, even after the assignment.

2. Privity of contract: Remember that a lease is also a contract. An assignment does not, by itself, destroy the binding effect of contractual promises as personal obligations.

Example: Lord leases Blackacre to Tenant, who assigns the leasehold to Newcomer, who fails to pay the rent. Lord may sue Newcomer because Newcomer is in ***privity of estate*** with Lord, but Lord ***may also*** sue Tenant, since Tenant and Lord remain in ***privity of contract*** with each other. Of course, Lord can only recover once, but Lord has two pockets out of which to satisfy his judgment.

a. Release and novation: To destroy privity of contract it is necessary for the landlord and original tenant to agree to release each other from their contractual promises. A landlord's consent to an assignment and acceptance of rent from the tenant's assignee ***does not constitute a release.*** There must be clear evidence of a landlord's intent to release, usually found in some explicit agreement. This ***express release,*** when coupled with a promise by the assignee to ***assume performance*** of the lease obligations, is called a ***novation.***

Example: If Newcomer had expressly agreed to assume the obligations of Tenant in the lease, and Lord had expressly agreed to release Tenant from his obligation to perform those promises, a novation would have occurred. Tenant would no longer be in privity of contract with Lord. And, since the assignment placed Newcomer in privity of estate with Lord (in substitution of Tenant), Tenant would have no liability to Lord.

  b. Assumption: Assumption of performance of the lease obligations can occur without release, a condition that places both the original tenant and the assignee in privity of contract.

  Example: Suppose the instrument of assignment between Tenant and Newcomer contained an explicit consent by Lord to the assignment and an express assumption of the lease obligations by Newcomer. Now both Tenant and Newcomer would be in privity of contract. Tenant remains in privity under the original lease because there has been no release. Newcomer and Lord forged a new contractual relationship, the terms of which are embodied in the lease, by their bilateral promises — Lord's consent to the assignment and Newcomer's promise of assumption.

    i. Express assumption of lease: In states that recognize the contract notion of ***third party beneficiary,*** an assignee can acquire privity of contract with the landlord by an ***express assumption*** of the lease obligations. Once privity of contract is created by assumption it remains until and unless the contractual obligations are released.

    Example 1: Suppose that the instrument of assignment by which Tenant assigned his leasehold to Newcomer recited that "Newcomer assumes the obligation to perform all of Tenant's duties under the lease." Lord is the third party beneficiary of this promise and thus Lord and Newcomer are in privity of contract.

    Example 2: Newcomer assumes Tenant's lease obligations to Lord and performs them diligently. Then Newcomer assigns the lease to Thrifty, who is now in privity of estate (but not privity of contract) with Lord, since Thrifty does not assume the lease obligations. Thrifty performs, then assigns the lease to Deadbeat, who defaults. Absent any releases, Newcomer and Tenant are both liable for Deadbeat's default, since they are in privity of contract with Lord. Thrifty has no liability: his privity of estate ended with the assignment to Deadbeat and he was never in privity of contract. See, *e.g.,*

First American Nat'l Bank of Nashville v. Chicken System of America, Inc., 616 S.W.2d 156 (Tenn. Ct. App. 1980).

   ii. **No implied assumption:** Assumption will *not be implied* from the mere fact of assignment, or from the fact that the instrument of assignment recites that the assignment is "subject to the lease" or "subject to the obligations and covenants of the lease." See 1 American Law of Property § 3.61. An express assumption is needed. Once in privity of contract, the assuming tenant remains in privity until released.

3. **Assignor tenant as surety:** When a tenant assigns his leasehold and *is not released from the contract* he becomes a *surety* — a guarantor of the assignee's performance. Upon default, the landlord is free to sue either or both of the original tenant and assignee. The original tenant's status as surety simply means that he is entitled to recover from the assignee any amount he pays to landlord on behalf of the assignee's default.

   Example: Tenant assigns his leasehold in Blackacre to Newcomer. Newcomer fails to pay rent for six months. Lord sues Tenant and recovers $6,000. Tenant is *subrogated* to Lord's status as a creditor of Newcomer, which means that Tenant can now pursue Lord's claim against Newcomer and recover the $6,000.

   a. **Material alteration of lease:** But if the assignee and the landlord materially alter the lease to the detriment of the surety, the surety is excused from his suretyship.

      Example: Suppose that, after assignment, Newcomer and Lord agreed to raise the rent to $2,000 per month in exchange for Lord's granting to Newcomer a purchase option on Blackacre. This modification is materially disadvantageous to Tenant (who gets no benefit from the purchase option in Newcomer) so Tenant is no longer a surety. If Newcomer now defaults, Lord's remedies are only against Newcomer.

4. **Multiple assignments:** When a leasehold is assigned several times things may appear more complicated but the general rules outlined still apply. Keep in mind the following:

   - An assignee in *privity of contract* with the landlord remains liable for the default of subsequent assignees, however remote, unless there has been a release.

   - An assignee in *privity of estate* with the landlord is liable only for the default that occurs *during the period in which there is privity of estate.*

Example: Tenant assigns to Newcomer, who assigns to Thrifty, who assigns to Deadbeat. Newcomer commits no default, Thrifty defaults one month's rent of $1,000, and Deadbeat defaults on five months' rent. Tenant is liable to Lord for all the defaults ($6,000) since he is in privity of contract and has not been released, but Tenant is entitled by subrogation to recover $1,000 from Thrifty and $5,000 from Deadbeat. Newcomer has no liability, since he was never in privity of contract and no default occurred during his period of privity of estate. Thrifty is liable to Lord for $1,000 since he was only in privity of estate and $1,000 is the measure of his default during that period of privity. For the same reasons, Deadbeat is liable to Lord for $5,000.

C. **Subleases:** A *sublease* occurs when the lessee transfers ***anything less than his entire interest in the leasehold,*** thereby retaining a ***reversion.*** A minority of states treat the retention of a ***right of entry*** as sufficient to create a sublease. See p. 91, *infra*. Absent a prohibition in the principal lease, a tenant is free to sublease at will. Many leases prohibit subletting or condition a sublease upon the landlord's approval.

Example: Owner leases Blackacre to Lessee for a term of four years under a lease that says nothing about subletting. A year later, Lessee transfers possession to Subb for a year. A sublease between Lessee and Subb is created, with Lessee as the sublessor and Subb as the sublessee.

1. **No privity:** A sublessee has ***neither privity of contract nor privity of estate*** with the principal lessor. A sublessor remains in both privity of contract and privity of estate with his landlord. The sublessor and sublessee are in privity of contract with respect to their new contract — the sublease.

   Example: Owner leased Blackacre to Lessee for a rent of $1,000 per month. Lessee subleased Blackacre to Subb for a rent of $1,500 per month. Lessee remains in privity of estate and privity of contract with Owner. Subb is in neither relationship with Owner, but Subb is in privity of contract with Lessee, with respect to the separate sublease contract. The result is that Owner is entitled to receive $1,000 per month from Lessee and, under the sublease, Lessee is entitled to receive $1,500 per month from Subb.

2. **Tenant default under the principal lease:** The fact that the subtenant has no personal liability to the landlord under the principal lease has its negative qualities from the subtenant's perspective. If the principal tenant/sublessor defaults on the principal lease the landlord is entitled to terminate the principal lease. Since the sub-

lease is merely a lease of whatever leasehold the principal tenant had, and that leasehold is now over, the subtenant has no further right of possession.

Example: Suppose that Lessee subleases Blackacre to Subb for one year for a rent of $18,000, payable in advance. Lessee collects the $18,000, Subb takes possession, and Lessee fails to pay any rent to Owner under the principal lease. Two months later Owner exercises his right under the principal lease to terminate that lease. Subb has no further right of possession, despite having paid Lessee the year's rental in advance. Subb's remedy is a lawsuit against Lessee for breach of the sublease.

   a. Avoiding this outcome: To prevent such disastrous outcomes, subtenants often insist on paying the tenant/sublessor's rental obligation directly to the landlord of the principal lease, and remitting any excess between the principal lease obligation and the sublease rental to the sublessor.

D. Distinguishing an assignment from a sublease: Courts claim to use two methods to determine whether any given transfer is a sublease or assignment: (1) examining the ***substance*** of the transaction to determine if the tenant has transferred her entire interest in the leasehold, and (2) examining the ***intentions of the parties.***

   1. Parties' intentions: The problem with intentions is that the parties often do not appreciate the legal significance of the two modes — assignment and sublease — and so lack any real intention. Sometimes courts rely on the words the parties use to characterize the transfer, but the words are insignificant if the parties don't understand the legal consequences. And if they do appreciate the legal significance the substance will probably support their intentions, making reliance on labels unnecessary.

   Example: Jaber transferred his leasehold under an instrument entitled "assignment" but which expressly reserved in Jaber the right to re-enter if the "assignee" defaulted. Rent payments were made by the assignee, Miller, to Jaber. The Arkansas Supreme Court mostly ignored the substance of the parties' dealings in professing to ascertain their intentions, but found those intentions exclusively in their chosen nomenclature: "assignment." *Jaber v. Miller,* 239 S.W.2d 760 (Ark. 1951).

   a. Interpretation by the courts: Courts relying on intentions do look beyond labels, though. If the transfer is for an increased rent, a sublease is usually indicated. If the transfer is for a lump sum, assignment is the usual inference. See *Jaber v. Miller, supra.* If the transferee expressly assumes the lease obligations an assignment is the inferred intention. See *Ernst v. Conditt,* 54 390 S.W.2d 703 (Tenn. Ct. App. 1964).

2. **Substance of the transfer:** Courts that examine the substance of the transfer may well parse the labels the parties place on the transfer but are more likely to examine whether the transferring tenant has reserved a sufficient interest in the leasehold.

   a. **Reversion:** The common law rule was that the transfer was an assignment ***unless*** the tenant retained a reversion, no matter how brief its duration.

      Example: Tenant transfers the "remainder of the term of my leasehold, 40 years, except for the very last second of the term." This is enough of a reversion at common law — one second! — to qualify as a sublease.

   b. **Right of re-entry:** A right of re-entry is simply the right to retake possession if the transferee defaults. At common law, this right, which was not a reversion and lacked any certain duration, was not an estate and so not enough to create a sublease.

      Example: Tenant transfers the "remainder of the term of my leasehold, 40 years, but reserves the right to re-enter and retake possession in the event of any default by transferee." The common law view was that Tenant had transferred her entire interest in the leasehold and so an assignment had occurred.

      i. **Minority rule:** A significant minority of American states treat the retention by the tenant of a right of re-entry, when coupled with a transfer of the remainder of the term, as sufficient to create a sublease. See, *e.g., Dunlap v. Bullard,* 131 Mass. 161 (1881); *Davis v. Vidal,* 151 S.W. 290 (Tex. 1912); *Hartman Ranch Co. v. Associated Oil Co.,* 73 P.2d 1163 (Cal. 1937). This view is also endorsed by the Restatement (2d) of Property, § 15.1, comment i.

3. **Pitfalls of error:** Two common misadventures result from erroneously thinking an assignment is a sublease.

   a. **Double rent:** A transferee who thinks he has a sublease (but actually has an assignment) and pays the rent to the tenant/sublessor will find that he is liable for the same rent to the landlord (assuming the tenant/sublessor pockets the rent). The transferee may recover the sums paid to the tenant if he is solvent. Fortunately, this condition will not persist for long, as the landlord will not likely let too many months go by with unpaid rent.

b. Merger: A tenant who "subleases" for the entire remainder of his term (at a handsome profit) will find that he is denied that profit if he fails to retain a reversion or, where permitted, a right of re-entry. The transfer is an assignment and the "subtenant's" occupation places him in privity of estate with the landlord, thus extinguishing the intervening purported subleasehold through merger. See *Webb v. Russell,* 3 Term Rep. 393, 100 Eng. Rep. 639 (1789); *Smiley v. Van Winkle,* 6 Cal. 605 (1856).

E. Lease provisions restricting assignment or sublease: Unless a lease expressly limits or prohibits assignment or sublease, a tenant is free to transfer the leasehold by either method. But many leases do contain such restrictions.

1. **Strict construction of restrictive covenants:** Because restrictions on assignment or sublease inhibit alienability, they are narrowly construed by courts, but are generally valid.

    Example: L leases Blackacre to T, under a lease prohibiting "any assignment by T." T is free to sublease. If L leases to T under a lease prohibiting "any sublease by T." T is free to assign the leasehold.

    a. **Only apply to voluntary *inter vivos* transfers:** Express restrictions only apply to ***voluntary inter vivos*** transfers.

        Example: L leases Blackacre to T, under a lease prohibiting "any transfer, whether by assignment or sublease." If T dies, devising the unexpired leasehold to his daughter, D, the covenant has no effect. The result is the same if T dies intestate and D takes the leasehold by intestate succession. If T declares bankruptcy and the leasehold is transferred by the bankruptcy estate, the transfer is deemed to be involuntary and the covenant does not apply.

        Of course, when an express restriction does apply the landlord may consent to a transfer.

2. **Limits on landlord power to deny consent:** Common law permitted a landlord to deny consent to a transfer ***for any reason, or for no reason at all.*** That view is under attack.

    a. **Anti-discrimination laws:** Anti-discrimination statutes (see p. 119, *infra*) limit landlord ability to reject prospective tenants, including assignees or sublessees.

    b. **Implied obligation of reasonableness:** A number of states have implied a landlord obligation to ***act reasonably when denying consent to a transfer,*** a position endorsed by the Restatement (2d) of Property, § 15.2, and adopted by statute in some states. This obligation is typically limited to ***commercial*** *leases only.* See, *e.g., Kendall v. Ernest Pestana, Inc.,* 709 P.2d 837 (Cal. 1985); *Newman v. Hinky-Dinky Omaha Lincoln, Inc.,* 427 N.W.2d 50 (Neb. 1988). However, these jurisdictions typically uphold flat bans on transfers, and some even uphold lease provisions that explicitly give the landlord the right to deny consent arbitrarily. See, *e.g., Julian v. Christopher,* 575 A.2d 735 (Md. Ct. App. 1990). Despite this trend toward an implied obligation of reasonableness, some states have recently rejected it and reaffirmed the traditional common law doctrine. See, *e.g., 21 Merchants Row Corp. v. Merchants Row, Inc.,* 587 N.E.2d 788 (Mass. 1992); *First Federal Sav. Bank v. Key Markets, Inc.,* 559 N.E.2d 600 (Ind. 1990). The rationale for the emerging view is the perception that increased alienability is a practical necessity in our restless society. The rationale for judicial rejection of an implied obligation of reasonableness is that legislatures ought to make this essentially social judgment, and that commercial lessees particularly are usually able to protect themselves in lease negotiations.

c. **What's reasonable?** Courts apply an *objective* test to this question. Landlords may reject transferees of doubtful financial strength or if the transferee's proposed use is not suitable in light of other commercial uses of this or similar property. But landlords may not reject transferees to secure a commercial advantage or because the transferee's proposed use is ethically offensive to the landlord though otherwise reasonable.

Example 1: Harry, an enormous landlord, rejects Ted, a transferee, because Ted was a tenant in another building owned by Harry, and Harry desired to retain Ted as a tenant. Harry and Ted were at a stalemate in negotiations over a new lease, and Harry's rejection of Ted as a transferee was designed to pressure Ted into accepting Harry's terms. Harry's rejection was not reasonable. See *Krieger v. Helmsley-Spear, Inc.,* 302 A.2d 129 (N.J. 1973).

Example 2: Landlord, a religious organization that abhors abortion as a tenet of the faith, refuses to consent to a transfer to a birth control and abortion counseling center, although the center was financially responsible and its use was otherwise suitable. Landlord's rejection was not *commercially* reasonable. See *American Book Co. v. Yeshiva Univ. Dev. Found.,* 297 N.Y.S.2d 156 (Sup. Ct. 1969).

3. **Landlord waiver:** A landlord may waive lease restrictions on transfer, either expressly or by implication, usually as a result of

knowing acceptance of rent from an assignee. An old common law rule, originating in *Dumpor's Case,* 4 Coke 119b, 76 Eng. Rep. 1110 (1578), holds that **once the landlord has expressly waived a transfer restriction the restriction is destroyed.** Though heavily criticized as nonsensical, and rejected by the Restatement (2d) of Property, § 16.1, this rule is still followed by most American jurisdictions. The Rule in *Dumpor's Case* is easily avoided, though, by either (1) an express declaration by the landlord, at the time of transfer, that waiver is **limited to this transfer only,** or (2) an express statement in the lease that transfer restrictions bind the **tenant's assignees,** thus preserving the transfer restrictions as to future assignees.

V. TENANT'S OBLIGATIONS

A. **Introduction:** A tenant's obligations are defined by the lease, but in the absence of an express lease provision the law presumes the existence of certain duties. The nature of these duties reflects the hybrid nature of leaseholds — both an estate and a contract.

B. **Pay the rent:** This is the principal obligation. At common law it was an **independent obligation,** meaning that the tenant had to pay rent regardless of the landlord's breach of any of his obligations. This view reflected the conception of a leasehold as an estate and the rent as the payment for the estate. In most American jurisdictions today, the rent obligation is **dependent** on the landlord's performance of his lease obligations, reflecting the modern conception of the lease as a contract. Upon landlord breach in these jurisdictions, a tenant may terminate and vacate, withhold rent, or abate a portion of the rent. See p. 105, *infra*. The right to receive the rent is normally part of the landlord's reversion, but can be separately assigned or retained upon any transfer of the reversion.

1. **Amount of rent:** The rent amount is virtually always stipulated in the lease but, if not, the tenant must pay the **reasonable rental value** for the occupied property. This same rule applies if the lease is void for some reason, such as non-compliance with applicable housing and building codes.

2. **Accrual:** Unless the lease says otherwise, rent is due on the last day of the term (*e.g.*, at the end of the month in a periodic tenancy from month-to-month; on the last day of the term in a tenancy for a term of years). Many states have, by statute, changed this rule to provide for apportionment of rent when a lease is terminated in mid-term. A handful of states hold that, for any purpose, rent is

apportioned daily throughout the term. The Restatement (2d) of Property, § 12.1, endorses this view.

C. **Waste avoidance:** Given the limited duration of a leasehold estate, the common law imposed on tenants the duty to avoid waste. The duty to avoid permissive, or involuntary, waste (see p. 64, *supra*) is addressed in the ***duty to repair.*** The duty to avoid affirmative, or voluntary, waste (see p. 64, *supra*) is addressed in the ***duty to avoid damage.***

   1. **The duty to repair:** Common law required a tenant to keep the premises in good repair, ***ordinary wear and tear excepted,*** but imposed no obligation to make extraordinary or substantial repairs. The common law duty may be altered by agreement in the lease, and many states have modified it by imposing a duty to repair on the landlord, either by statute or an implied-in-law warranty of habitability on the part of the landlord. See p. 109, *infra*.

      a. **Alteration by agreement:** The common law rule allows ordinary deterioration of the premises since the landlord has no repair obligation and the tenant's duty is limited. Thus, leases typically address responsibility for repairing ordinary wear and tear. Except when the result is unconscionable or where prohibited by law (see p. 109, *infra*) the parties may agree to impose the repair obligation however they wish. A typical lease might impose on the landlord the duty to make exterior or structural repairs, with the tenant obligated to make all remaining repairs.

         i. **"General Repair" clauses:** A "general repair" clause obligates either tenant or landlord to make all repairs necessary to preserve the property in the same condition as it was at the outset of the lease term. A tenant who is bound by an unqualified general repair clause is traditionally obligated to make ***any and all repairs,*** even including the ***duty to rebuild*** after complete destruction of the premises by acts not of the tenant's fault (*e.g.*, flood, earthquake, hurricane, war, riot). See, *e.g.*, *Chambers v. North River Line,* 102 S.E. 198 (N.C. 1920); *Armstrong v. Maybee,* 48 P. 737 (Wash. 1897). The same rule applies to a landlord bound by an unqualified general repair clause. But this rule is eroding: by statute, some states have eliminated the tenant duty to rebuild and judicial decisions are undermining its vitality. See, *e.g.*, *Washington Hydroculture, Inc. v. Payne,* 635 P.2d 138 (Wash. 1981).

   2. **The duty to avoid damage:** Affirmative acts of the tenant that ***substantially damage*** the premises constitute affirmative (volun-

tary) waste, and are breaches of this duty. To constitute waste the damage must change the appearance, function, or utility of the property, and be "extraordinary in scope and effect, or unusual in expenditure." *Pross v. Excelsior Cleaning & Dyeing Co.*, 179 N.Y.S. 176 (Mun. Ct. 1919).

Example: Tenant replaced a defective ceiling, added a light fixture and switch, a closet, and a window frame. These changes were not waste, even though the ceiling replacement was substandard. *Rumiche Corp. v. Eisenreich,* 352 N.E.2d 125 (N.Y. 1976).

Although common law courts found ameliorative waste to violate the duty to avoid damage most courts today find the opposite, so long as there is no long-term economic loss inflicted on the landlord.

D. Refrain from illegal uses: Tenants may not devote the leasehold premises to illegal uses. At common law, the landlord's remedy and the tenant's continued right to occupation depended on whether the landlord knew of the intended illegal use at the time the leasehold was created.

1. **Landlord knowledge of intended illegal use:** If the landlord actually intends the tenant to make illegal use, or if the landlord simply knows of the tenant's intention to make illegal use, the lease was ***unenforceable at common law.*** While the landlord could not recover rent, he could recover possession since there was no valid leasehold created. This is still good law, with the added wrinkle that the landlord may not even recover possession if eviction constitutes unlawful retaliation. See p. 113, *infra.* See, *e.g., Brown v. Southall Realty Co.,* 237 A.2d 834 (D.C. 1968); Rest. (2d) of Property, § 9.1.

2. **Landlord ignorance of illegal use:** At common law, if the landlord was ignorant of the tenant's illegal use, the lease remained ***enforceable.*** Absent an express provision in the lease, the landlord could not terminate, but could only enjoin the illegal use and obtain damages. The preferred view today is to permit the landlord to terminate the lease if she acts while the illegal use is ongoing or within a short time of its cessation. See Rest. (2d) of Property, sec. 12.5. Termination is an effective device to deter and stop illegal activity centered at a given location, such as "drug houses" or houses of prostitution.

E. Honesty as to intended purpose: As with all transactions, a tenant has a duty not to misrepresent his intentions. Even if the tenant's use is completely legal, but is utterly inconsistent with his representations, the landlord may terminate the lease because of the misrepresentation.

Example: Landlord leases space to Tenant, on the strength of Tenant's representation that no toxic chemicals will be used on the property. After occupation, Tenant uses the property for stripping chrome plating from metal parts. To do so, Tenant uses a variety of legal, but toxic, chemicals and takes care to employ and dispose of them in compliance with all applicable laws. Landlord may terminate the lease because of the misrepresentation.

F. **Duty not to commit nuisance:** Any possessor of land, including a tenant, has the obligation not to commit a nuisance — a non-trespassory interference with the use and enjoyment by others of their property. Reasonable noise or other activity that is bothersome to other tenants in an apartment building does not constitute nuisance. Landlords often insert express covenants against noise or other disturbance, but these covenants are construed to prohibit only ***unreasonable noise or disturbance,*** so they add little to the common law duty not to commit nuisance. On nuisance generally, see Chapter 7, p. 255, *infra*.

G. **Duties from express lease provisions:** The lease may impose just about any duty imaginable on a tenant, so long as the duty is not illegal, unconscionable, or otherwise violative of public policy. Read the lease carefully!

H. **Common law — no excusing tenant of obligations:** The common law did not admit of any such excuses. The tenant had purchased a leasehold estate, and any act of a third party preventing the tenant from enjoying the estate was his problem. The tenant still had to perform all of his leasehold obligations, including rent payment.

Example: Tenant leases Blackacre, a large country home, for a term of years. Civil war breaks out during the term and one side destroys Blackacre. Tough luck; the tenant still must pay rent. See, *e.g.*, *Paradine v. Jane,* 82 Eng. Rep. 897 (1647).

I. **Modern circumstances excusing tenant of obligations:** Modern law has softened this harsh doctrine by recognizing a number of such excuses, summarized here.

1. **Sole use becomes illegal:** If the tenant has bargained for one specific use, which later becomes illegal, the tenant is excused.

   Example: Landlord and Tenant agree that the leasehold property will be used solely for a brewery. Prohibition arrives. The unintended use is now illegal. Tenant is excused from the lease. *Brunswick-Balke Collender Co. v. Seattle Brewing & Malting Co.,* 167 P. 58 (Wash. 1917).

2. **Primary use illegal but other uses permitted:** If the tenant has not bargained for a specific use, now illegal, but the premises

may *reasonably* be used for another purpose by the tenant, the tenant is *not excused.* Rest. (2d), § 9.2.

3. **Conditional legality of use:** If the *sole intended use* may be continued only by *obtaining a governmental permit* (typically a conditional use permit or zoning variance) jurisdictions split on whether the tenant or the landlord is obliged to apply for the permit, though most place the burden on the tenant. See, *e.g., Warshawsky v. American Automotive Products Co.,* 138 N.E.2d 816 (Ill. Ct. App. 1956). All jurisdictions excuse the tenant if the permit is denied.

4. **Destruction of the leasehold property:** Destruction of the property, even by causes outside the tenant's control, was no excuse at common law. This is not true today, unless a tenant foolishly undertakes such an obligation pursuant to an express lease provision. See p. 102, *supra.* By statute, most states permit a tenant to terminate if the premises are destroyed or rendered unusable for their intended purpose, unless the destruction is due to tenant negligence or intentional misconduct. See, *e.g., Albert M. Greenfield & Co., Inc. v. Kolea,* 380 A.2d 758 (Pa. 1977); Rest. (2d) of Property, § 5.4.; URLTA § 4.106.

5. **Loss by eminent domain:** When governments take leased property by exercising their power of eminent domain the leasehold is automatically terminated. The very idea of a government taking is to seize all private interests in the property. The government must fairly compensate owners of the interests taken, though, so the tenant is entitled to just compensation for the value of the remainder of the leasehold. For eminent domain generally, see Chapter 11, p. 345, *infra*.

   a. **Amount of compensation:** Governments provide a lump sum payment for *all* the interests taken, so there must be an apportionment of the award between the landlord and the tenant. The tenant is entitled to the fair market value of the remainder of the leasehold minus the rent obligation for that period. A tenant will receive nothing unless he holds an advantageous lease — the fair market value exceeds the rental obligation. A tenant may sometime receive damages reflecting the cost of relocation or of damage to items, like fixtures, that are not taken by the government but must be severed from the taken leasehold ("severance damages").

6. **Frustration of intended purpose:** In a *commercial lease only* a tenant may be excused if (1) *extreme hardship* would result from (2) some third party's *unforeseeable* action (usually a government)

that (3) makes the *mutually intended purpose of the leasehold* (4) *virtually impossible* to accomplish. This is *very difficult to prove.* This concept is *not* the same thing as the contract doctrine of impossibility of performance — performance is possible, but accomplishment of the intended purpose is not.

VI. LANDLORD'S REMEDIES

A. **Introduction:** There are a variety of remedies available to a landlord to deal with a tenant's default under the lease. Some are the product of a lease term, others are provided by statute, and still others are old common law remedies.

B. **Remedies typically derived from lease provisions:** As the remedies discussed in this section illustrate, a landlord can augment his remedies by a well-drafted lease.

   1. **Rent acceleration:** A rent acceleration clause makes the rent for the entire balance of the term immediately payable (if the landlord so elects) upon a tenant default under the lease. Since the parties were free to prepay rent for the entire term at the outset, courts find nothing infirm about a rent acceleration clause. See, *e.g.*, Rest. (2d) of Property, § 12.1. If a landlord elects to accelerate rent she may not terminate the lease. By accelerating rent the landlord has chosen to enforce an immediate sale of the balance of the lease term. A landlord may not sell the remainder of the term and then take it away from the tenant. For the same reason, a landlord who retakes possession after tenant abandonment may not then elect to accelerate rent.

      a. **Prepaid rent:** If a tenant prepays rent (*e.g.*, pays the last month's rent at inception of the lease, the landlord is entitled to retain the prepaid rent if the tenant terminates without justification before expiration of the lease term. The rationale for this rule is the same as that justifying rent acceleration.

   2. **Security deposits:** Almost every lease contains a security deposit clause, under which the tenant deposits a sum of money as security for her performance of the tenant's lease obligations. The landlord is indebted to the tenant and must return the deposit at expiration of the leasehold, less any charges attributable to tenant default, and provide an accounting of the deposit amount. Some states require, by statute, that security deposits bear interest, or be placed in trust or escrow accounts. Other statutes penalize landlords for failure to provide an accounting. Some states make tenants a preferred class of creditor in the event of landlord insolvency.

3. **Liquidated damages:** A lease may provide for liquidated damages but such clauses are not always valid. Generally, the amount of liquidated damages must be reasonably related to the probable amount of damages suffered by the landlord upon tenant default, but those damages must not be capable of easy determination. This validity rule is, of course, a bit of a "Catch 22." A security deposit may be retained as *liquidated damages* only if this test can be met. Lease clauses that provide for increased rent (*e.g.*, double rent) upon default (as well as acceleration) are of doubtful validity. The increased rent is, in effect, a liquidated damage clause and it is unlikely that the probable damages (even if not readily ascertainable) are reasonably related to the increased amount of accelerated rent.

4. **Confession of judgment:** Leases sometimes provide that, upon default, the tenant agrees to waive personal service of process and authorizes someone (perhaps anybody, perhaps a landlord nominee) to confess judgment against him. This permits the landlord to reduce his claim to judgment quickly, cheaply, and *without notice to the tenant,* who may well have some defense since lease covenants are mostly dependent today. Confession of judgment clauses have been widely prohibited by statute and are of doubtful validity even where apparently permitted. See, *e.g.*, URLTA § 1.403.

C. **Remedies derived from statute and common law:** Most common law remedies have been codified by statute and altered in that codification. Accordingly, this section treats them as a package.

1. **Eviction:** Because lease covenants were regarded as independent, the common law did not permit a landlord to terminate the lease and evict the tenant upon default, even for non-payment of rent. The landlord could only sue for the unpaid rent. Today, because lease covenants are generally regarded as dependent, statutes permit a landlord to terminate the lease and evict the tenant for non-payment of rent, but usually not for breach of most other lease covenants. As a result, most leases contain express provisions permitting the landlord to terminate the lease upon tenant *default of any lease obligation.* Of course, even at early common law the landlord had the power to evict the holdover tenant — the tenant who remained unlawfully after expiration of the term.

   a. **Procedural prerequisites for eviction after tenant default:** If the lease provides only that the landlord *may terminate* upon tenant default, the landlord has retained a *right of re-entry* which must be properly exercised before the landlord becomes entitled to possession and may evict. If, instead, the lease provides that the lease terminates automatically after the landlord notifies the tenant of termination following tenant default, the lease is ***determinable*** and the landlord is entitled to immediate possession, thus hastening eviction. As explained below, this distinction has been partially eroded by statute.

   i. **Right of re-entry:** To perfect the right to eviction, the landlord must notify the tenant of the default and permit the tenant a ***reasonable time to cure the default.*** See Rest. (2d) of Property, § 13.1. In some states, the landlord may not be entitled to proceed judicially by a summary proceeding, where the only issue is entitlement to possession. See p. 102, *infra*. But many states have, by statute, made summary proceedings available to landlords regardless of whether the forfeiture provision in the lease is determinable or confers a right of re-entry.

   ii. **Determinable:** If the lease is determinable the landlord is immediately entitled to possession and may proceed judicially by a summary proceeding.

b. **Summary proceedings: unlawful detainer:** The most expeditious judicial eviction remedy is the summary proceeding known variously as ***unlawful detainer*** or forcibly entry and detainer. This remedy is created by statute, and every American state has enacted such a statute.

   i. **Notice to quit:** Under a typical statute the landlord is required to give the tenant minimal notice before filing suit (called ***notice to quit,*** and often no more than 3 days). The substance of a notice to quit is that the landlord will terminate the lease and file suit for unlawful detainer if the default (usually non-payment of rent) is not cured within three days.

   ii. **Unlawful detainer procedures:** Unlawful detainer suits are entitled to a calendar preference on the court's docket and so are speedily concluded. The only issue that is permitted to be contested is ***entitlement to possession.*** Thus, the landlord must prove that the lease has been validly terminated and he is now entitled to possession. This means that the landlord will usually have to prove the fact of tenant default and proper notice to quit. Tenants may defend only on grounds that, if proven, would give the tenant a continued right to possession.

   Example: A residential tenant in an unlawful detainer action may defend on the ground that the landlord has violated his implied-in-law obligation to provide habitable premises, on the theory that breach of this obligation abates the rent obligation and that, since no rent is due, the landlord is not entitled to possession. *Jack Spring, Inc. v. Little,* 280 N.E.2d 208 (Ill. 1972). On the landlord's implied warranty of habitability, see p. 109, *infra.*

Depending on the state, a jury trial may be available and sometimes may be constitutionally required. See *Pernell v. Southall Realty,* 416 U.S. 363 (1974). Appeals are usually allowed, although a stay of execution of judgment is conditioned upon the appellant's posting of adequate security.

c. Ejectment: Ejectment was the traditional common law remedy and is still available. It is not used much because it is not a summary proceeding and so not entitled to any calendar preference. Moreover, a tenant in an ejectment action is entitled to plead and prove any affirmative defense or counterclaim she may have, and can implead third parties.

d. Landlord self-help: At common law a landlord was entitled to use ***reasonable force*** to oust the tenant himself, but after 1381 a landlord's forcible ouster of a tenant was criminal. American jurisdictions are badly splintered on this remedy.

   i. No self-help: Some states absolutely forbid self-help. A tenant may recover personal and property damages if ousted non-judicially by the landlord. See, *e.g., Kassan v. Stout,* 507 P.2d 87 (Cal. 1973); *Berg v. Wiley,* 264 N.W.2d 145 (Minn. 1978). In these jurisdictions, lease provisions giving the landlord the right to use self-help upon tenant default and termination are void. See, *e.g., Jordan v. Talbot,* 361 P.2d 20 (Cal. 1961).

   ii. Reasonably forceful self-help: At the opposite end of the spectrum are those states that permit landlords to use reasonable force to oust the tenant. See, *e.g., Shorter v. Shelton,* 33 S.E.2d 643 (Va. 1945); *Gower v. Waters,* 125 Me. 223 (1926).

   iii. Peaceable self-help: Some jurisdictions limit self-help to peaceful ouster, but then go on to define force so broadly that practically no ouster will be considered peaceful. In practice, these jurisdictions are virtually indistinguishable from those that prohibit self-help.

2. Tenant abandonment: If a tenant abandons the leasehold premises in the midst of a valid lease term the tenant is regarded as having offered to ***surrender*** the lease. Traditionally, the landlord has one of three options: (1) accept the offered surrender and ***termi-***

nate the lease, (2) ***retake possession and relet the premises*** for the benefit of the tenant, or (3) reject the surrender by ***leaving the premises untouched,*** thus preserving the landlord's entitlement to rent as it comes due for the remainder of the term. But the neatness of these options has broken down. Today, some jurisdictions prohibit the third option (at least for residential leases), and some regard the second option (under some circumstances) as effecting a surrender.

- a. **Termination:** If the landlord elects to terminate the lease after tenant abandonment the tenant is treated as having surrendered the lease. Tenant obligations cease at the moment of termination and surrender, not the moment of abandonment. Similarly, if the landlord elects to terminate, termination is the exclusive remedy available to the landlord. The tenant's liability is for unpaid rent accrued to the moment of termination plus damages created by the abandonment.

    - i. **Damages:** Most of the damage caused by abandonment consists of the transactional costs of finding a new tenant, plus whatever shortfall exists between the lease rentals for the remainder of the surrendered lease and the fair market value of that remainder. At common law the landlord was not entitled to damages resulting from abandonment because the common law regarded the rent obligation as non-existent until it came due under the lease. This rule is still followed in some jurisdictions. See, *e.g., Jordon v. Nickell,* 253 S.W.2d 237 (Ky. Ct. App. 1952). Other states apply the contract doctrine of anticipatory repudiation to leases (since leases are contracts as well as estates) and permit the landlord to recover damages when the tenant has made it clear that he is not only abandoning but denies any further lease obligations. See, *e.g., Kanter v. Safran,* 68 So. 2d 553 (Fla. 1953). Damages recoverable from anticipatory repudiation are limited to a period in which such damages can be "reasonably forecast." See, *e.g., Hawkinson v. Johnston,* 122 F.2d 724 (8th Cir. 1941), in which such damages were limited to a ten year period even though there were 67 years left in the lease term.

- b. **Retake and relet for the tenant:** A landlord may retake possession and relet the premises for the tenant's account. If he does so, a landlord must be careful to avoid action that implies acceptance of the offered surrender. In some states, acceptance of surrender is implied by reletting unless the tenant has consented to the reletting. Other states conclude that reletting without notice to the tenant constitutes acceptance of surrender. Still other states regard acceptance of surrender as determined by the landlord's intent, and treat the landlord's acts simply as evidence bearing upon his intent. Virtually all states regard reletting for a term longer than the abandoned term as acceptance of surrender. The importance to the landlord of avoiding acceptance of surrender is that the landlord is able to recover from the abandoning tenant any shortfall between the original lease rentals and the relet rentals, even in states that do not permit recovery of damages for anticipatory repudiation of the lease.

- c. **Leave the premises untouched:** Since a lease is also an estate, the traditional and still prevailing view is that the tenant is free to abandon his unpaid-for property but is still liable for the payments. See, *e.g.*, Rest. (2d) of Property, § 12.1(3). The contrary, and minority, view is that the landlord ought not have this option, but should be held to a duty to mitigate damages caused by the tenant's abandonment. See. *e.g.*, *Sommer v. Kridel,* 378 A.2d 767 (N.J. 1977); *United States National Bank of Oregon v. Homeland, Inc.,* 631 P.2d 761 (Or. 1981). These minority jurisdictions further divide on the question of whether this landlord option should be abolished for *all leases* or only for *residential leases*. Most of the minority jurisdictions limit abolition to residential leases. But see *McGuire v. City of Jersey City,* 593 A.2d 309 (N.J. 1991).

3. **Seizure of the tenant's personal property:** If a tenant failed to pay the rent, the landlord was entitled by the common law to seize the tenant's personal property in the leased premises and to hold it until the tenant cured the default. This was called **distress,** or **distraint.** Some states have abolished distress completely. Others have substituted a more limited right, usually requiring the landlord not to breach the peace and sometimes forbidding landlord self-help altogether. See Rest. (2d) of Property, § 12.1, statutory note.

- a. **Liens on personal property:** A related remedy, provided by statute, is a lien in favor of the landlord against the tenant's personal property on the leased premises, in order to secure performance of the tenant's obligations. The landlord has no right to seize these goods, and must file suit to enforce the lien.

VII. LANDLORD'S OBLIGATIONS AND TENANT'S REMEDIES

A. **Introduction:** The landlord's obligations considered here are either implied or imposed by operation of law. These and other obligations can be imposed by agreement in the lease. The tenant's remedies for breach of these obligations are considered in the context of each obligation.

B. Quiet enjoyment: Every tenant has the right to *quiet enjoyment* of the leased premises. A landlord may explicitly promise the tenant quiet enjoyment but it doesn't matter much, since this obligation is also implied-in-law. One aspect of this obligation — the landlord's obligation to deliver to the tenant the legal right to possession of the premises — was considered in p. 81, *supra*. Another aspect of this obligation is considered here: the ***duty of the landlord to refrain from wrongful actual or constructive eviction*** of the tenant. Unlike other lease obligations, common law made the tenant's duty to pay rent conditional upon the landlord's performance of this obligation.

1. **Actual total eviction:** A tenant who has been ***totally ousted from physical possession*** of the leased premises — whether by the landlord or by someone with better title than the landlord — no longer is obligated to pay rent and may elect to terminate the lease.

2. **Actual partial eviction:** The traditional rule is that actual physical ouster of the tenant from ***any part of the premises*** relieves the tenant of the obligation to pay ***any rent at all*** until and unless the tenant is restored to possession of the entire leasehold property. This is true even if the tenant remains in possession of the rest of the property.

    Example: Landlord permits a brick wall to encroach upon Tenant's leased property, ousting Tenant of a small strip of land. Tenant's rent obligation is suspended until the wall is removed, restoring him to full possession. *Smith v. McEnany,* 48 N.E. 781 (Mass. 1897).

    a. **Partial abatement of rent:** The preferred view of academics is to permit only ***partial abatement*** of rent in cases of actual partial eviction and to give the tenant the further option of termination or suit for damages. Rest. (2d) of Property, § 6.1. In any case, if actual partial eviction occurs by a third party holding paramount title, the tenant's rent obligation is only ***partially abated.*** This makes sense only because of recording acts (see Chapter 9, p. 292, *infra*) that effectively define paramount title as a claim of which the tenant has actual or constructive knowledge. If the tenant knew about the better title, or with reasonable diligence should have known about it, the landlord ought not be punished for the tenant's assumption of a known risk.

3. **Constructive eviction:** If the landlord ***substantially interferes*** with the tenant's use and enjoyment of the leased property — so much so that the intended purposes of the tenant's occupation is frustrated — a ***constructive eviction*** has occurred. Eviction is con-

structive, rather than actual, because the tenant has **not been physically ousted;** instead, the utility of physical possession has been virtually destroyed. The tenant may terminate the lease, move out, and thereafter will be excused from any further lease obligations.

Example: If the owner of a high-rise office building promises but fails to provide heat, air conditioning, or elevator service after normal working hours a constructive eviction has occurred, not a partial actual eviction. See, *e.g.*, *Charles E. Burt, Inc. v. Seven Grand Corp.*, 163 N.E.2d 4 (Mass. 1959); *Barash v. Penn. Terminal Real Estate Corp.*, 256 N.E.2d 707 (N.Y. 1970).

a. **Three elements:** There are three elements to constructive eviction:

- *Wrongful act or failure of the landlord* that
- *Substantially and materially deprives the tenant of beneficial use and enjoyment of the premises*, and
- *Complete vacation of the premises* by the tenant.

i. **Landlord's wrongful action:** The *landlord* must act wrongfully, *not a third party.* If the alleged wrongful act is the landlord's failure to act, the landlord must be under a duty to act.

Example: Landlord refuses to provide heat on weekends, even though the lease expressly obligates the Landlord to provide heat "at all times." Landlord is under a duty to act; his failure to act is wrongful.

(1) **Interference by third party:** If a third party causes the interference it is usually not constructive eviction. This is normally true even if the third party is another tenant. "The general, but not universal, rule ... is that a landlord is not chargeable because one tenant is causing annoyance to another, even where the annoying conduct would be a breach of the landlord's covenant of quiet enjoyment if the landlord were the miscreant." *Blackett v. Olanoff*, 358 N.E.2d 817 (Mass. 1977). But a landlord is responsible for tenant actions that constitute a **nuisance** or which occur in **common areas** under the control of the landlord. Some courts have held that actions of a tenant may be attributable to the landlord if the landlord could control them and the "disturbing condition was the natural and probable consequence" of landlord action.

Example 1: Landlord maintained a residential apartment building and then leased adjacent space to a nightclub, under a lease that obligated the nightclub to conduct operations so as not to disturb the residential tenants. Nightclub's entertainment was so loud and prolonged that residential tenants could not sleep and even had difficulty conversing within their apartments. Because Landlord retained the power to control Nightclub's conduct, introduced the problem, and the result was a natural and probable consequence of Landlord's action, Nightclub's action was deemed to be Landlord's. *Blackett v. Olanoff,* 358 N.E.2d 817 (Mass. 1977).

Example 2: Tenant leased space in a shopping mall to sell patio furniture. Landlord promised Tenant that it would take action to abate the "[l]oud music, screams, shouts and yells" from Body Electric, an adjacent workout salon. The interference "caused walls to vibrate" and prevented normal business operations. Landlord's failure to act on his promise was wrongful, and it was no defense that Tenant had agreed in the lease that Landlord would neither be liable for its failure to perform its obligations nor for actions of other tenants. *Barton v. Mitchell Co.,* 507 So. 2d 148 (Fla. Dist. Ct. App. 1987).

ii. **Substantial interference with tenant use and enjoyment:** The rule is easy to state: The tenant must be so "essentially deprived of the beneficial enjoyment of the leased premises [that] they are rendered unsuitable for occupancy for the purposes for which they are leased." *Barton v. Mitchell Co., supra.* But application is more difficult. Courts try to be objective, taking into account the duration and severity of the interference, its foreseeability, and the ease or difficulty of abatement.

Example: Cooper leased office space on the bottom floor of a building. Landlord maintained an adjacent driveway in such a manner that after every rainstorm Cooper's space would be inundated with water running off the driveway. The problem waxed and waned, but eventually became so repeated and severe that she could not conduct normal business at the premises and had to rent space in a hotel for a sales meeting. Cooper was sufficiently deprived of her use and enjoyment of the premises as to constitute constructive eviction. A single flooding would probably not have been sufficient. *Reste Realty Corp. v. Cooper,* 251 A.2d 268 (N.J. 1969).

(1) Ripeness of claim: For a constructive eviction claim to ripen, the tenant must notify the landlord of the interference and give the landlord a reasonable opportunity to fix it. If the tenant knows of the problem before signing the lease, the tenant is deemed to have waived any constructive eviction claim arising from that problem.

iii. **Complete vacation of the premises:** A tenant may not remain in possession and still press a constructive eviction claim. The tenant must completely vacate the premises within a reasonable time after the interference. But if the tenant moves out and a court later determines that there was no constructive eviction, the tenant has abandoned the leasehold and is very likely liable for unpaid rent or damages from anticipatory repudiation. See p. 103 *supra*. One solution is to permit the tenant to bring an action for declaratory relief, prior to vacating the premises, to establish whether it would be constructive eviction if the tenant actually vacates. Cf. *Charles E. Burt, Inc. v. Seven Grand Corp.*, 163 N.E.2d 4 (Mass. 1959) (dicta). Another is the Restatement position that a tenant ought to have the option of vacation and termination (at the tenant's risk that there is no constructive eviction) or remain in possession and receive damages and/or rent abatement. Rest. (2d) of Property, § 6.1.

b. **Tenant remedies after vacation:** The tenant's rent liability stops and the lease is terminated upon justified vacation of the premises. The tenant is also entitled to recover damages caused by the constructive eviction.

C. **Warranty of habitability:** The traditional rule is that a landlord has no implied obligation to warrant that property is suitable for the intended purposes of the tenant, so long as the tenant "has a reasonable opportunity of examining the property and judging for himself as to its qualities." *Anderson Drive-In Theatre v. Kirkpatrick,* 110 N.E.2d 506 (Ind. Ct. App. 1953). Under the traditional view a landlord has such an obligation only if he expressly makes such a warranty. Otherwise, "the rule of caveat emptor applies." *Id.* This rule has partially broken down.

1. **Implied warranty of habitability — general:** The modern trend is to imply into every residential lease a warranty of habitability. But this is a minority view; only twenty or so American states have adopted this rule. The majority rule is typified by *Miles v. Shauntee,* 664 S.W.2d 512 (Ky. 1983), in which the Kentucky Supreme Court rejected the idea that a warranty could be implied by the existence of housing codes: "It is for the legislature to create

rights and duties nonexistent under the common law. ... No implied warranty of habitability exists under Kentucky law." The Restatement phrases this emerging duty as a warranty of suitability for residential use. Rest. (2d) of Property, § 5.1. Under either label it is really an implied-in-law obligation of the landlord to provide premises that are fit for human inhabitation, both at the inception of the lease and continuing throughout the lease term. This obligation consists of ***two separate obligations:*** (1) An "implied warranty of habitability" that properly refers to the warranty implied at ***inception of the lease*** and (2) an implied ***continuing duty of repair.*** Neither courts nor commentators make this distinction with any regularity; in practice, both are lumped together as the implied warranty of habitability. The differences between the two are not significant, although a lease of premises that the landlord knows is not habitable and in violation of local housing codes is an illegal, unenforceable lease, while a lease of property that degenerates during the term into an uninhabitable condition is valid. See *Brown v. Southall Realty Co.*, 237 A.2d 834 (D.C. 1968).

2. **Implied warranty of habitability — rationale:** The implied warranty of habitability is defended on several grounds: (1) implied warranties of quality and fitness are a commonplace feature of contract law and, since leases are contracts, should be a feature of landlord-tenant law; (2) urban tenants lack the skills necessary to repair uninhabitable premises and the judgment necessary to detect such premises; (3) an implied warranty of habitability is necessary to redress the unequal bargaining power of rich landlords and poor tenants, and (4) an implied warranty will encourage compliance with local housing codes. See, *e.g.*, *Javins v. First National Realty Corp.*, 428 F.2d 1071 (D.C. Cir. 1970).

3. **Implied warranty of habitability — criticism:** The implied warranty is effectively criticized on economic grounds. If implied warranties achieve their intended effect by forcing compliance with housing codes the result will be to reduce the supply of low-income housing and raise its price. See Richard Posner, Economic Analysis of the Law, § 16.6 (4th ed. 1992), for a complete demonstration of this conclusion. The standard remedy for breach of the implied warranty of habitability is to abate the rent obligation, but "[f]rom the standpoint of protecting poor people [this] is particularly pernicious." *Id.* It raises landlords' costs (thus increasing rental rates in times of low vacancy) and reduces the supply of rental housing since landlords have an additional incentive either to withdraw from the market by converting their property to some other use (*e.g.* commercial or conversion to condominiums), or to improve the housing to the point that it is no longer affordable by the poor. The entire

movement towards implied warranties of habitability has been marked by a belief that it aids the poor, but perhaps this may be another example of the road to Hell being paved with good intentions.

4. **Scope of the implied warranty of habitability:** The implied warranty is generally limited to residential leases, but there are a few cases applying it to small-scale commercial tenants. See, *e.g.*, *Davidow v. Inwood North Professional Group*, 747 S.W.2d 373 (Tex. 1988). The measure of "habitability" is usually the standards set by the local housing code, since the acknowledged objective of proponents of the implied warranty is to spur compliance with such codes. However, minor violations of housing codes that do not immediately affect habitability do not trigger the landlord's implied duty to repair the premises. Nor is the landlord in breach until he has been *notified of the uninhabitable condition and given a reasonable opportunity to correct the problem.* See, *e.g.*, *King v. Moorehead*, 495 S.W.2d 65 (Mo. Ct. App. 1973).

5. **Tenant's remedies for landlord breach of the implied warranty of habitability:** Upon breach, and after notice to the landlord, the tenant's rent obligation is suspended and the tenant has the following remedies.

    a. **Terminate and leave:** The tenant may terminate the lease, vacate the premises, and recover damages (usually relocation costs plus the excess of fair market value over the lease rentals for the balance of the term).

    b. **Stay and withhold rent:** The tenant may remain in possession and withhold rent, pending landlord correction of the defects. Rest. (2d) of Property, § 11.3, provides that a tenant must notify the landlord of exercise of this remedy and deposit rent into an escrow account.

    c. **Stay and repair:** The tenant may remain in possession and use a reasonable amount of the rent to make repairs sufficient to bring the premises into habitable condition. *Marini v. Ireland*, 265 A.2d 526 (N.J. 1970). Some states have codified this remedy in statutory "repair and deduct" provisions that specify how much rent may be used for repair purposes and how frequently this remedy may be invoked. See, *e.g.*, Cal. Civ. Code § 1942.

    d. **Stay and recover damages:** The tenant may remain in possession and recover *damages in the form of a rent abatement or deduction* plus, in some jurisdictions, damages for *discomfort and annoyance.* See, *e.g.*, *Hilder v. St. Peter,* 478

A.2d 202 (Vt. 1984). There are three different measures of the amount of damages in the form of a rent deduction.

i. **Value as warranted:** The tenant is entitled to the difference between the value of the premises *as warranted* (*i.e.*, in habitable condition) and the value of the premises *as is* (*i.e.*, in uninhabitable condition), up to the amount of the stated rent. The stated rent is rebuttably presumed to be the value as warranted. In essence, this method causes the stated rent to be reduced to actual value, which may be zero. This seems to be the prevailing method. See, *e.g.*, *Hilder v. St. Peter, supra*; *Berzito v. Gambino,* 308 A.2d 17 (N.J. 1973).

Example: George leases an uninhabitable apartment to Amy for $150/month. Amy proves that the value of the apartment if it were habitable is $200/month, rebutting the presumption that stated rent equals value as warranted. The apartment's value "as is" is $100/month. Amy is entitled to the difference between the last two values, or $100/month, deducted from the stated rent of $150/month, leaving Amy with a rent obligation of $50/month. If the value "as warranted" had been $275/month, Amy's damages would have been $175/month, or more than the stated rent, but Amy would be entitled only to a complete abatement of rent.

ii. **Value as-is:** The tenant is entitled to the difference between the *stated rent* and the *actual fair value* of the premises in their uninhabitable condition. If the stated rent accurately reflects the fair value of the premises in their dilapidated state damages are nil. Of course, in that situation the tenant is not paying for more than he receives.

Example: George leases the same dilapidated apartment to Amy for $150/month, and its actual value is $100/month. Amy is entitled to damages in the form of a rent reduction of $50/month, leaving her with a rent obligation of $100/month. If the actual value of the apartment in its sorry state was $150/month, Amy would not have been damaged.

iii. **Proportionate reduction:** The tenant's rent obligation is reduced to a percentage of the stated rent. The percentage is determined as follows: (1) compute the fair market value of the premises *as warranted* (habitable); (2) compute the value *as is* (uninhabitable); (3) compute the percentage relationship of actual value to warranted value; and (4) apply that percentage to the stated rent. Rest. (2d) of Property, § 11.1 adopts this method.

Example: George leases the same substandard apartment to Amy for $150/month. Its value as warranted (habitable) is $200/month and its value as is (uninhabitable) is $100/month, or 50% of the habitable value. Amy is entitled to damages in the form of a rent reduction of 50% of the stated rent, or $75/month, leaving her with a rent obligation of $75/month.

e. **Stay and defend:** The tenant can remain in possession and plead and prove the landlord's breach of the implied warranty as a *complete defense* to an eviction action *based on the tenant's failure to pay rent.* This is a complete defense because, after breach and notice to the landlord of the breach, there is *no further rent obligation.* Note: If the landlord is seeking to evict the tenant because the term has expired and the tenant is a holdover, this is *not a defense.* It is a defense only to a landlord's claim of possession founded on failure to pay rent.

f. **Punitive damages:** In circumstances involving willful, wanton, and fraudulent conduct on the part of the landlord a tenant may be entitled to recover punitive damages. "When a landlord, after receiving notice of a defect, fails to repair the facility that is essential to the health and safety of his or her tenant, an award of punitive damages is proper." *Hilder v. St. Peter, supra.*

6. **Waiver by tenant:** Courts uniformly hold that a tenant may not waive the landlord's obligation to provide habitable premises. This position is adopted by the Rest. (2d) of Property, § 5.6, which provides for waiver of the landlord's obligations only to the extent such waiver is neither unconscionable or against public policy. The URLTA, § 2.104, permits a limited imposition of a duty to repair on the tenant, but not elimination of the landlord's implied obligation to comply with housing codes.

7. **Statutory codification:** A number of states have enacted statutes that codify these rules, usually with some modifications that increase the breadth of tenant remedies. See, *e.g.*, URLTA § 2.104 (imposing specific landlord duties), § 4.103 (repair and deduct remedy), § 4.104 (permitting the tenant to obtain emergency services, such as heat, light, and even substitute housing by deducting its cost from rent), and § 4.105 (permitting the tenant to offset her expenses incurred against landlord rent claims in summary eviction proceedings).

8. **The retaliatory eviction doctrine:** The usual rule is that, so long as a landlord is entitled to possession, the landlord's *motivation* for evicting the tenant is *irrelevant.* But some jurisdictions

hold that a landlord may not evict a tenant, even if he is otherwise entitled to do so, if the landlord seeks to evict the tenant in ***retaliation*** for the tenant's reporting of housing code violations to government authorities. See, *e.g.*, *Dickhut v. Norton,* 173 N.W.2d (Wis. 1970); *Edwards v. Habib,* 397 F.2d 687 (D.C. Cir. 1968). This position is often codified by statute. See, *e.g.*, URLTA § 5.101; Rest. (2d) of Property, § 14.8, § 14.9 and commentary thereto. The URLTA extends the retaliatory eviction doctrine to instances of tenant invocation of the implied warranty of habitability and it is likely that this position will be adopted by courts even in non-URLTA jurisdictions.

- **a. Rationale:** The rationale for this doctrine is that, without it, landlords will simply refuse to renew periodic tenancies (usually month-to-month) of tenants who have been so bold as to report substandard conditions to government enforcement officials. To insure the effective operation of housing codes, it is argued, landlords must be prevented from retaliating against tenants who report these violations of law. Some courts have hinted that the retaliatory eviction doctrine is required by the U.S. Constitution's free speech guarantee (see, *e.g.*, *Edwards v. Habib, supra*) but that position is probably wrong because there is likely no state action involved in a landlord's assertion of his right to possession.

- **b. Proof of retaliatory motive:** The tenant has the burden of proving retaliatory motivation. By statute, some jurisdictions provide that retaliatory motive is presumed if the landlord terminates the tenancy, raises rent, or decreases services within some period (typically 90 to 180 days) after the tenant has complained of housing code violations. In those states, the landlord has the burden of proving that his motive is not retaliatory.

- **c. Available only to tenant not in default:** The retaliatory eviction defense is available only to a tenant ***not in default.*** But, of course, a tenant who is withholding rent after landlord breach is not in default.

- **d. Eviction after retaliatory motive found:** A landlord who has been determined to have sought a retaliatory eviction is not forever barred from eviction. If the landlord can later prove that there are good business reasons for eviction he is entitled to evict.

- **e. Indirect eviction:** A landlord may not seek to evict a tenant ***indirectly*** in retaliation for the tenant's reporting of housing code violations. Indirect eviction can take a variety of forms, but typically consists of draconian reductions in service (*e.g.*, a utility cutoff) or dramatic increases in rent that are designed to drive the tenant away.

D. Tort liability of landlords: This issue is merely a specialized application of the ordinary tort doctrine of negligence. Negligence is conduct that deviates from the standard of care — what a reasonable person would do in similar circumstances. Every person has a duty to use ordinary care to avoid foreseeable harm to others. Except for a few exceptions, the common law provided that landlords had no duty to make the leased premises safe for tenants or their guests. The tenant took the property as it was. If there were dangerous aspects to the premises that could foreseeably injure others (*e.g.*, a beam protruding into a dark doorway at head height) the tenant had the duty of correcting the condition and was liable to others for injury caused by his failure to do so. Today, the duty of landlords to maintain leased premises in a fashion that avoids foreseeable injury to others is increasing. This section deals with this phenomenon, but does not attempt to deal with all facets of the law of negligence. Your Torts course is the place for that.

1. **An aside on tort theory:** The law of torts developed on the principle of *fault* — people ought to be held responsible for their individual failures but nothing more. In the last half of the 20th century American courts began to reconceive tort law as a device to *share the cost of personal injury.* Accordingly, the fault principle has been eroded (*e.g.*, strict liability torts). In this area, a minority of courts seem willing to impose greater duties (and ultimately tort liabilities) on landlords because they believe that the (sometimes) extremely high cost of personal injury judgments will be borne by all tenants as a class through higher liability insurance premiums paid by landlords and passed on in higher rents. This rests on two assumptions: (1) liability insurance is endlessly available in sufficient amounts to share the costs of accidents widely, and (2) personal injury awards will fairly reflect the fault of tortfeasors and the true value of the injuries suffered. These assumptions may not be accurate in a world where tort law is no longer based entirely on fault. Nevertheless, expansion of duties and consequent tort liability continues.

2. **Pre-existing dangerous conditions:** The common law recognized the following exceptions to the general rule that a landlord had no tort liability to the tenant or his guests for dangerous conditions existing on the leased premises at the inception of the lease.

    a. **Latent defects:** Because only the landlord would know (if anyone did) of a concealed defect, common law imposed on the landlord a duty to warn the tenant of their existence and apprise him of the specifics of the defects. If the landlord did so and the tenant occupied anyway, the landlord had no liability to either the tenant or his guests. The tenant assumed the risk and acquired a duty to correct the condition.

    b. Public use: A landlord is liable to the public for injuries occasioned by a defect *existing at inception of the lease* which is *known to the landlord,* if the premises are *intended for use by members of the public,* the landlord *knows or should know that the tenant will probably not correct the defect* before admitting the public, and the landlord has *failed to use ordinary care to correct the defect.* The term "pubic use" usually means use by any members of the public, though some courts interpret this more narrowly, confining it to cases where a great many members of the public are invited (*e.g.*, a theater).

3. **Conditions occurring during the lease term:** A landlord generally has no liability for dangerous conditions that occur after the tenant has taken possession. A landlord can voluntarily assume such a duty, though, by undertaking repairs. If the repairs do not comport with the duty of ordinary care and skill, the landlord will be liable for resulting injuries.

4. **Common areas:** A landlord has a duty to exercise reasonable care over common areas that remain under his control. This duty extends to taking reasonable precautions to prevent criminal activity by third parties that injures tenants. See, *e.g., Kline v. 1500 Mass. Ave. Apt. Corp.,* 439 F.2d 477 (D.C. Cir. 1970).

5. **Landlord covenant to repair:** The common law rule was that a landlord assumed no tort duty of care by agreeing to repair leased premises. This view is rejected by most American jurisdictions today, as well as the Rest. (2d) of Torts, § 357, and the Rest. (2d) of Property, § 17.5.

6. **Statutory or judicially created duty of landlord to repair:** Landlords may be under a duty to repair that flows from a statute, like a housing code or a codified version of the implied warranty of habitability. Or they may simply have that duty by virtue of a judicially created implied warranty of habitability. Failure to conform to a *statutory duty* may be treated as *negligence per se* or merely as *evidence of negligence.* Failure to make repairs sufficient to cure breach of the implied warranty of habitability may result in tort liability if the landlord was negligent in correcting the defect — he knew or should have known of the problem and failed to correct it within a reasonable time. See, *e.g., Dwyer v. Skyline Apartments, Inc.,* 301 A.2d 463 (N.J. Super.), *aff'd,* 311 A.2d 1 (N.J. 1973). Cali-

fornia adopted and then rejected a rule of strict liability for failure to cure breach of the implied warranty of habitability. See *Becker v. IRM Corp.,* 698 P.2d 116 (Cal. 1985), overturned by *Peterson v. Superior Court,* 899 P.2d 905 (Cal. 1995). No other jurisdiction seems to have followed California's experiment, although Louisiana has a statutory rule of strict liability for defects in existence at inception of the lease term.

7. **No special rules for landlords:** Perhaps less than ten American jurisdictions have rejected the categorical rules summarized above in favor of a rule that treats landlords like everybody else. In this approach, a landlord is liable to the tenant or third parties for injuries occurring on the leased premises if the landlord failed to "act as a reasonable person under all the circumstances." *Sargent v. Ross,* 308 A.2d 528 (N.H. 1973). The categories are treated as factors to be taken into consideration, but not used as rigid rules to define liability. See also *Pagelsdorf v. Safeco Insurance Co.,* 284 N.W.2d 55 (Wis. 1979).

8. **Exculpatory clauses:** An exculpatory clause in a lease is an attempt to relieve the landlord of any liability he might otherwise have to the tenant for personal injuries or property damage caused by defective conditions in the leased premises or common areas. Exculpatory clauses are generally ***valid,*** but some courts refuse to enforce them in ***residential leases,*** either because of supposed unequal bargaining power or because they are thought to increase the risk of personal injury. See, *e.g., Cappaert v. Junker,* 413 So.2d 378 (Miss. 1982); *McCutcheon v. United Homes Corp.,* 486 P.2d 1093 (Wash. 1971). Some states have voided such clauses by statute, usually with respect to residential leases but sometimes including commercial leases, too. See Rest. (2d) of Property, § 17.3, statutory note. URLTA § 1.403 voids exculpatory clauses in residential eases only. Except where voided by statute, exculpatory clauses are virtually always valid in commercial leases.

VIII. FIXTURES

A. **Introduction:** Tenants often attach personal property — ***chattels*** — to the leasehold premises. Who owns the chattels upon termination of the lease — landlord or tenant?

B. **Fixtures:** Fixtures belong to the landlord. Common law defined a fixture as any chattel ***permanently affixed*** to the leased property, a definition that merely shifted the focus to defining "permanent" and "affixed." The modern approach is to define "fixture" by examining the ***tenant's intent*** through such objective measures as how it is attached, what sort of chattel it is, and the damage that removal would cause. The last factor — ***removal damage*** — is often dispositive. Courts tend to conclude "no fixture" if the removal damage is not substantial.

Example: Tenant removed a large pipe organ at the end of the lease term. To do so, tenant removed and restored part of a brick wall to the building. The damage was ***not irreparable,*** and after restoration (at tenant expense) the premises were in substantially their original condition. The Washington Supreme Court ruled that the pipe organ was not a fixture. *Ballard v. Alaska Theater Co.,* 161 P. 478 (Wash. 1916).

1. **Trade fixtures:** Despite the general rule, a tenant is permitted to remove and retain ownership of trade fixtures — attached items of personal property used in carrying on a trade or business, broadly defined.

    Example: Tenant, a bookseller, bolts bookshelves to the wall and floor for display of the inventory. Though the shelves are as "permanently affixed" as is practical, courts regard them as trade fixtures and permit their removal at the end of the lease term.

C. **Attached chattels, but not fixtures:** If a tenant attaches a chattel to the property, but it is ***not a fixture*** (*e.g.*, a bookcase secured to the wall to prevent earthquake damage) it belongs to the tenant ***unless the tenant leaves it behind at the end of the lease term.*** Such chattels belong to the landlord, since the tenant has effectively abandoned them.

IX. SOCIAL REGULATIONS OF LEASEHOLDS

A. **Introduction:** Many of the issues discussed so far in this chapter involve "social regulation" of leaseholds, but this section deals with two particular areas of regulation that are avowedly for the accomplishment of social objectives larger than either landlord or tenant.

B. **Rent control:** Rent control laws have been adopted in many places, usually at the local level. Rent control consists of price controls (set below market rates), usually augmented by limitations on a landlord's ability to evict tenants at the end of the lease term (to prevent the landlord from leasing to a new tenant at market rates). Some argue that rent control amounts to a governmental seizure of the landlord's reversion followed by its transfer to the tenant in place, coupled with an obligation delegated to the tenant to compensate the landlord for the seizure at a below-market rate. See Richard Epstein, Takings (1985). By this reasoning, rent control laws ought to be violations of the constitutional requirement that private property may not be taken for public use without payment of just compensation. But the Supreme Court has rejected that argument. See *Pennell v. City of San Jose,* 485 U.S. 1 (1988). But if the permitted rents are set so low that the landlord is deprived of a ***reasonable rate of return on his investment*** a taking has occurred. See generally Chapter 11, p. 345, *infra*. Rent controls are often criticized on the economic ground that they benefit in-place tenants at the expense of would-be tenants, provide an incentive for landlords to skimp on maintenance, deter the construction of new rental housing, benefit landlords in neighboring jurisdictions that lack rent controls, and produce an inefficient allocation of residential living space.

C. **Anti-discrimination statutes:** The common law gave unlimited freedom to a property owner to decide to whom he wished to sell or lease his property. Today, that freedom is circumscribed by federal, state, and local statutes that prohibit discrimination in the ***sale*** or ***rental*** of real property on the basis of race, sex, ethnicity, national origin, age, religion, and under some state and local laws, sexual orientation. The major federal statutes are considered here.

1. **42 U.S.C. § 1982 — The 1866 Civil Rights Act:** During Reconstruction the 1866 Civil Rights Act was enacted, providing in part that "All citizens of the United States shall have the same right ... as is enjoyed by white citizens ... to inherit, purchase, lease, sell, hold, and convey real and personal property." This provision is now codified at 42 U.S.C. § 1982. Its intent was to place newly emancipated black Americans on the same footing as white Americans with respect to property rights. In *Jones v. Alfred H. Mayer Co.,* 392 U.S. 409 (1968), the Supreme Court held that this provision applied to private conduct as well as state action, and that Congress had power under section 2 of the 13th Amendment to regulate this private behavior. Thus, 42 U.S.C. § 1982 ***prohibits private discrimination on the basis of race or ethnicity with respect to sales or rentals of real property.*** Violators are subject to injunction and liable for damages.

2. **Fair Housing Act:** Title VIII of the 1968 Civil Rights Act is the Fair Housing Act. In its original form it prohibited private discrimination in the sale of rental of residential housing on the basis of race, color, religion, or national origin. It has since been amended to forbid discrimination against people with handicaps, people with children (except in "seniors only" developments), and on the basis of sex. The definition of handicap includes physical or mental impairments that "substantially limit" at least one major life activit[y]," but specifically excludes drug addiction or cross-dressing. This handicap definition is not as broad as that under the Americans with Disabilities Act of 1991.

a. **Exemptions:** There are several important exemptions to the discrimination ban of the Fair Housing Act.

   i. **Sale or lease by owner of a single-family dwelling:** A person who does not own more than three single-family residences may discriminate on otherwise forbidden grounds in the sale or lease of his single-family residence so long as he neither uses a broker nor advertises in a manner that reveals his discriminatory intent. See 42 U.S.C. § 3603(b)(1).

   ii. **Owner-occupied rental housing of four units or less:** In the debates concerning adoption of the Fair Housing Act, certain members of Congress worried about the application of the law to "Mrs. Murphy's boardinghouse" — small owner-occupied rental housing. Out of concern that these situations might be sufficiently intimate to implicate free association rights, Congress adopted this exemption, which permits a landlord to discriminate on otherwise forbidden grounds in the rental of residential housing so long as the landlord is an owner and occupant of the house or apartment building and it consists of four units or less. See 42 U.S.C. § 3603(b)(2).

b. **Remedies:** Violators are subject to injunction, compensatory, and punitive damages. Jurisdiction over Fair Housing Act claims is vested in the federal courts.

3. **Comparison of 42 U.S.C. § 1982 and Fair Housing Act:** The Fair Housing Act forbids discrimination on more grounds, but it only applies to residential housing, and admits of some exemptions. 42 U.S.C. § 1982 applies to all types of property but only forbids private racial or ethnic discrimination, and has no exemptions to the transactions to which it applies.

4. **Proof of forbidden discrimination:** Under either 42 U.S.C. § 1982 or the Fair Housing Act a presumptive case of forbidden discrimination is made out if the landlord's or seller's practices produce a forbidden *discriminatory effect.* The burden then shifts to the landlord or seller to prove that he was not, in fact, motivated by forbidden grounds. This is mostly a matter of offering convincing alternative reasons for rejection and benign explanations for the discriminatory effect. But if a forbidden ground is even one of many motivations, prohibited discrimination is proven.

5. **State and local laws:** There are a variety of state and local laws that address discrimination in the sale or rental of real property. Most apply to residential property. The forbidden grounds of discrimination vary. Almost all forbid discrimination on the basis of race, ethnicity, or national origin; most include religion and sex;

some add age, marital status, having children, or physical handicap to the forbidden categories. A few include sexual orientation. These statutes differ widely in their enforcement mechanisms (some involve administrative complaint and investigation; others permit private lawsuits directly against alleged violators) and available remedies.

Chapter 4
FUTURE INTERESTS

I. INTRODUCTION

A. Definition: Future interests are legal interests in property that are ***not possesory*** but which ***are capable of becoming possessory*** at some time in the future. A future interest is a ***presently existing*** property interest but it confers only a ***future right to possession.***

Example: Philip, owner of Drippy Trees in fee simple absolute, conveys Drippy Trees to Ethel for her life, then to Muriel and her heirs. Ethel has a life estate — a presently possessory interest — and Muriel owns a ***remainder*** — a future interest. Muriel's remainder is in existence now but it will not become possessory until the expiration of Ethel's life estate.

B. Five types: There are five types of future interests. Three of these — the ***reversion,*** the ***possibility of reverter***, and the ***right of entry*** (or ***power of termination***) — are the future interests ***retained by the grantor.*** The remaining two — the ***remainder*** and the ***executory interest*** — are future interests ***created in a transferee.*** Remainders are either ***contingent*** or ***vested.*** A contingent interest is subject to one or both of two uncertainties: it is either granted to an ***unknown person*** or there is some ***condition precedent*** to the future right to possession (other than the natural expiration of the preceding possessory estate). Contingent and vested remainders are fully explored on p. 128, *infra.* Executory interests are future interests that ***divest*** (cut off) either (1) another transferee's possessory or future interest (a ***shifting executory interest***) or (2) the grantor's interest at some future time (a ***springing executory interest***). Executory interests are discussed on p. 136, *infra.*

II. FUTURE INTERESTS RETAINED BY THE GRANTOR

A. Reversion: The reversion is the future interest that is created when the grantor conveys a ***lesser estate*** than that he originally owned. A reversion is freely alienable *inter vivos* and may be devised or inherited.

Example 1: Barry, owner of Blackacre in fee simple absolute, conveys Blackacre to Scott for life. Barry has conveyed a life estate, which is less than a fee simple absolute. When Scott dies, the life estate will end and somebody will then be entitled to possession. That "somebody" is the owner of the *reversion* which Barry necessarily retained (even without mentioning it in the grant) because he conveyed less than his own estate, fee simple absolute. Barry might still own the reversion when Scott dies, or he might have conveyed it, or it might have passed via Barry's will (if he predeceases Scott), or through intestate succession.

1. **Created automatically:** A reversion is created automatically, by operation of law, whenever the grantor conveys less than his entire interest in the property. It need not be expressly retained. A person need not own fee simple absolute to convey a lesser estate and create a reversion. The conveyance of *any estate that is less than the original estate* will create a reversion.

    Example 1: Suppose Scott leases Blackacre to Elmer for 1 year. Scott retains a reversion in Blackacre. Scott's reversion will become possessory upon expiration of the lease.

    Example 2: Suppose Scott conveys Blackacre to Elmer for life. Scott has retained a reversion. Elmer has a life estate *pur autre vie* — measured by Scott's life. Of course, Elmer's life estate might be even shorter, if he dies before Scott. But if he outlives Scott, his life estate will expire with Scott. Since Scott's life estate is greater than Elmer's, Scott has retained a reversion.

2. **Does not necessarily become possessory:** A reversion is *not necessarily* certain to become possessory in the future.

    Example 1: In the last example, Scott's reversion would never become possessory if he died before Elmer. Scott's death would terminate his own life estate and also that of Elmer, leaving the reversion in Barry as the possessory estate. But Scott's reversion **could become possessory** — Elmer might die before Scott. In the next to last example, Scott's reversion would never become possessory if he died during the term of the 1 year lease to Elmer but would become possessory if Scott was alive at the end of the term.

    Example 2: Lewis, owner of Blackacre in fee simple absolute, conveys Blackacre to Mary for life, then to Alice and her heirs if she survives Mary. Lewis has retained a reversion, but it will never become posessory if Alice does, in fact, survive Mary. Alice has a *contingent remainder.* It is contingent on her surviving Mary. If she does, her remainder becomes a possessory estate — fee simple absolute. Lewis's reversion is then destroyed, since Alice at that point would own Lewis's entire original estate in Blackacre. Similarly, if Alice does not survive Mary, her remainder will be destroyed because the contingency never occurred and Lewis's reversion will become possessory.

3. **When a reversion is not created:** A reversion is ***not created*** when the grantor conveys to one person part of his estate and simultaneously conveys the rest of his estate to another person.

    Example: Jonathan, owner of fee simple absolute in Blackacre, conveys Blackacre to Eleanor for life, then to Roberta and her heirs. Jonathan has ***not*** retained a reversion. Eleanor has a presently possessory life estate (which is, of course, a lesser estate than Jonathan's fee simple absolute) but Roberta has a ***vested remainder in fee simple absolute.*** Roberta is a known person and there is no condition precedent to her ultimate possession upon the natural expiration of Eleanor's life estate. Roberta's vested remainder is in fee simple absolute because the grant makes clear that it is to "Roberta and her heirs." Jonathan has conveyed his entire interest in Blackacre — part of it in the form of a presently possessory estate and the rest of it in the form of a future interest.

4. **Conveyance of a lesser estate:** Note that a person has ***not conveyed their entire interest*** when they convey a lesser present possessory estate followed by a ***contingent remainder*** in fee simple absolute.

    Example: Suppose Jonathan, in the last example, had conveyed Blackacre to Eleanor for life, then to Roberta and her heirs if she should survive Eleanor. Now Roberta has a ***contingent remainder in fee simple absolute.*** While Roberta is a known person, we do not know whether the express condition precedent to her possession — survival of Eleanor — will or will not occur. Jonathan has retained a reversion.

5. **Reversions are always vested:** Even though not all reversions will certainly become possessory all reversions are ***vested interests.*** Normally, for a future interest to be a vested interest it must be created in a known person and must not be subject to a condition precedent. The law regards reversions as vested because they are created in the person who owned the entire estate at the moment of creation. The retention of this interest by the grantor, even when ultimate possession is uncertain, causes the law to treat the reversion as a vested interest. This is important because, being vested at creation, it is ***not subject to destruction by the Rule Against Perpetuities.***

6. **Distinguished from remainder and possibility of reverter:** A remainder looks very much like a reversion but is created in a ***transferee,*** not retained by the grantor. A possibility of reverter is

retained by the grantor, but is the future interest created when the grantor conveys a *determinable* version of the *same estate he owns.*

Example: John, owner of Blackacre in fee simple absolute, conveys Blackacre to Judy so long as she refrains from growing marijuana on Blackacre. John has retained a *possibility of reverter,* not a reversion, because the estate conveyed to Judy is the same quantum — fee simple — as held by John. It is, however, determinable.

B. Possibility of reverter: A possibility of reverter is created whenever the grantor conveys the same *quantity* of estate that he originally had, but conveys it with a *determinable limitation* attached.

Example: Bill conveys Blackacre to Pete so long as it is used as a warehouse. Pete has fee simple determinable. Bill has retained a possibility of reverter.

1. **Conveyance of a determinable estates:** Though the possibility of reverter is usually created when the grantor conveys fee simple determinable it can be created by the conveyance of any determinable estate.

   Example: Orca, owner of a life estate in Blackacre, conveys Blackacre to Sal so long as Blackacre is devoted to agricultural use. Orca has conveyed her life estate to Sal — an estate of the same quantity she originally had — but with an attached determinable limitation. If during Orca's life Sal uses Blackacre for any purpose other than agricultural, Orca's possibility of reverter will become immediately possessory. If Sal farms Blackacre until Orca's death, Orca's life estate will come to its natural end and the holder of the reversion or remainder (whichever was created simultaneously with Orca's life estate) will be entitled to possession. In that event Orca's possibility of reverter will expire with her life estate.

2. **Helpful hint — Link the possibility of reverter and determinable estate:** Another way to remember this is to link together the possibility of reverter and determinable estates. Whenever a determinable estate is created the grantor retains a possibility of reverter, *unless the grantor simultaneously creates in a third party what would be a possibility of reverter if retained by the grantor.*

   Example: April, owner of Rose Park in fee simple absolute, conveys Rose Park to May so long as Rose Park is used solely as a single-family residence and, if not, to June and her heirs. April has conveyed fee simple determinable to May and has created in June a future interest that would be a possibility of reverter if April had retained it. But since it is created in a transferee — June — it is an ***executory interest.***

3. **Never created in a grantee:** Put another way, a possibility of reverter can ***never*** be created in a grantee.

4. **Transferability:** Common law did not permit transfer of a possibility of reverter *inter vivos* or by will, but only by inheritance. Today, most states permit a possibility of reverter to be alienated *inter vivos,* devised, or inherited.

5. **Termination:** Both the possibility of reverter and the right of entry (see p. 127, *infra*) can endure forever, because (1) the triggering limitation may never occur, and (2) both future interests are vested at creation and so immune from destruction under the Rule Against Perpetuities. Some jurisdictions have enacted statutes that terminate the possibility of reverter and right of entry after some fixed period, typically 30 years. Other statutes provide for termination after 30 years unless the interest is re-recorded within that period (thus evidencing a fresh desire to maintain the limitation). See, *e.g.*, Cal. Civ. Code § 885.010 *et seq.* This type of statute permits a possibility of reverter to remain in existence in perpetuity, so long as it is re-recorded every 30 years. A third approach is Britain's, which has by statute made these interests subject to destruction under the Rule Against Perpetuities.

6. **Eminent domain:** When property is taken by eminent domain and its ownership is divided between a possessory defeasible fee and a possibility of reverter or right of entry, the question arises of whether the owner of the possessory defeasible fee should receive the entire compensation award or whether it should be shared with the future interest holder. Most states give the entire award to the owner of the possessory interest, but a minority hold that the future interest holder is entitled to the difference between the value of a fee simple absolute in the property the defeasible fee. See, *e.g.*, *Ink v. City of Canton,* 212 N.E.2d 574 (Ohio 1965); *Leeco Gas & Oil Co. v. County of Nueces,* 736 S.W.2d 629 (Tex. 1987). The problem with this rule is that it is often very difficult to determine the value of a defeasible fee, especially when the limitation confines use to some public or charitable purpose.

Example: Harry Ink conveyed land to Canton, Ohio so long as it was used as a public park. When the State of Ohio condemned a portion of the park for construction of a highway, Ink sought to recover a portion of the eminent domain award and succeeded. But how does one value a public park as a park, since parks are generally not sold as parks? *Ink v. City of Canton, supra.*

7. **Statutory abolition:** In those few states that have abolished determinable estates by statute (see Chapter 2, p. 126, *supra*) the possibility of reverter, its corollary future interest, has also been abolished.

C. **Power of termination or right of entry:** A power of termination (or right of entry) is created whenever the grantee retains the power to cut short the conveyed estate before its natural termination.

   Example: Hilda conveys Driftwood Farm "to Olga and her heirs, but if Driftwood Farm should cease to be used for pasturing horses, Hilda may terminate the conveyed estate and retake possession." Olga has a fee simple subject to condition subsequent and Hilda has retained a power of termination (right of entry).

   1. **Only created in the grantor:** Like the possibility of reverter, a power of termination (or right of entry) may only be created in the grantor. The analogous interest created in a grantor is an executory interest.

      Example: Hilda conveys Driftwood Farm "to Olga and her heirs, but if Driftwood Farm should cease to be used for pasturing horses, to Gertrude and her heirs, who may terminate the conveyed estate and retake possession." Olga has a fee simple subject to condition subsequent; Gertrude has an executory interest, and Hilda has retained nothing.

   2. **Transferability:** Like the possibility of reverter, at common law a power of termination (right of entry) was neither alienable *inter vivos* nor devisable by will. It could only be inherited. Jurisdictions today split over whether to follow the common law rule or to permit free alienability. A very few jurisdictions follow the common law and stipulate that the mere ***attempt*** to alienate a power of termination (right of entry) destroys it, freeing the possessory estate of the condition subsequent.

   3. **Termination:** This issue is discussed on p. 126, *supra*.

   4. **Eminent Domain:** This issue is discussed on p. 126, *supra*.

   5. **Effect of abolition of determinable estates:** In those few jurisdictions that have abolished determinable estates (and, thus, the corresponding future interest — a possibility of reverter) what would have been a possibility of reverter is converted by operation of law into a power of termination (right of entry).

III. FUTURE INTERESTS CREATED IN GRANTEES

A. Remainders:

1. **Definition:** A remainder is a future interest created in a *grantee* that will become possessory (if it ever becomes possessory) upon the *natural expiration of the preceding possessory estate.* The parenthetical clause is in the prior sentence because some remainders are *certain to become possessory* and others have *only the possibility of becoming possessory.* But all remainders *never divest* another estate. The *only* way a remainder becomes possessory is the natural expiration of the prior estate.

   Example 1: Olga conveys Blackacre to Nicholas for life, then to Alexandra and her heirs. Alexandra has a remainder. It is certain to become possessory upon Nicholas's death, which is the *natural expiration* of Nicholas's life estate.

   Example 2: Olga conveys Blackacre to Nicholas for life, then to Alexandra and her heirs if Alexandra survives Nicholas. Alexandra has a remainder. It is not certain of becoming possessory (Alexandra must outlive Nicholas) but it is capable of becoming possessory and the only way it can become possessory is to succeed the natural expiration of Nicholas's life estate.

   Example 3: Olga conveys Blackacre to Nicholas for life, but if Alexandra should win the Nobel Prize for Literature, to Alexandra and her heirs. Alexandra does *not* have a remainder. Her future interest will become possessory, if at all, by *divesting* Nicholas of his life estate, or Olga of her fee simple (if Alexandra wins a Nobel Prize after Nicholas's death, since then Olga's reversion would become possessory). Alexandra has an *executory interest.*

2. **Nature of the estate held in remainder:** The term remainder simply identifies the type of *future interest* it is. A remainder is a future interest in some estate — fee simple, fee tail, life estate, or a term of years. It can be any estate.

   Example: Heinrich conveys Blackacre to Dieter for life, then to Erwin for 5 years, then to Helmut for life, then to Wilhelm and the heirs of his body, then to Olga and her heirs. Erwin has a remainder for a term of years. Helmut has a remainder for life. Wilhelm has a remainder in fee tail (if fee tail is permitted). Olga has a remainder in fee simple absolute.

3. **Classification of remainders:** Remainders are classified as *vested* or *contingent.* The purpose of distinguishing between the two is to identify those remainders that are of uncertain ownership

or ultimate possession. Persistent uncertainties of these sorts make property difficult or impossible to alienate. Common law devised a number of "marketability rules" designed to destroy contingent remainders (and other contingent future interests) if the contingency persisted for too long. See p. 139, *infra*.

   a. **Classification method:** To classify future interests, you must classify each interest created by a grant *in the order of creation.* Examine the first interest created. Is it presently possessory or a future interest? If it is a future interest, what kind is it? If it is a remainder, is the interest created in a known person? If so, is ultimate possession subject to any condition precedent? If not, you have a vested remainder. Do this again for each subsequent interest in the grant.

   Example: Roger conveys Holly Farm to Susan for life, then to Dorothea and her heirs if she has published a novel, but if not, to Nancy's then living children and their heirs. The first interest created is a presently possessory life estate, held by Susan. The next interest, Dorothea's, is a future interest. It is a future interest because it is not now possessory. It is a remainder because it will become possessory, if at all, upon the natural expiration of Susan's life estate. It is a contingent remainder because, although Susan is a known person, there is no certainty that Dorothea will have satisified the condition precedent to possession — publication of a novel. The last interest, in Nancy's then living children, is also a remainder because it will become possessory, if at all, upon the natural expiration of Susan's life estate. It is a contingent remainder for two reasons: (1) the class of grantees — Nancy's then living children — is unknown and cannot possibly be known until Susan's death, and (2) there is a condition precedent to possession — that Nancy's children survive Susan.

   b. **Vested remainders:** A remainder is vested if it is created in a known person and possession is not subject to any condition subsequent. As a result, a vested remainder *must necessarily become possessory* whenever the prior possessory estate expires.

   Example: Oscar conveys Arrowsmith to Margot for life, then to Connie and her heirs. Connie's remainder is vested because she is a known person and there is no condition precedent to her possession. Whenever Margot dies, Connie (or her legal successor) is ready to take possession of Arrowsmith.

i. **Natural expiration of preceding estate:** The natural expiration of the preceding estate is ***not*** a condition precedent.

   Example: In the prior example, Connie will not receive possession of Arrowsmith until Margot dies, but Margot's death is not a condition precedent to possession because her death simply marks the natural expiration of her life estate. By contrast, if Oscar had conveyed Arrowsmith "to Margot for life, then to Connie and her heirs if Connie survives Margot," there would be a condition precedent to Connie's possession — surviving Margot. Connie would hold a contingent remainder. These look like the same thing but they are not: In the first example, if Connie dies before Margot, Connie's vested remainder passes to her devisee or heir (call him Hector); but in the second example if Connie dies before Margot, Connie's contingent remainder is destroyed and Hector receives nothing. Since Connie can never satisfy the condition precedent, it dies with her. It has ***lapsed.***

ii. **Not uniform:** Vested remainders are not uniform. There are three types of vested remainders: ***indefeasibly vested remainders,*** vested remainders subject to complete divestment, and vested remainders subject to open (or partial divestment).

iii. **Indefeasibly vested remainders:** An indefeasibly vested remainder is ***certain to become and remain possessory.*** Nothing will prevent possession from happening eventually, and once possession occurs, it will last forever.

   Example: Dahlia conveys Laurel Hill to Pietro for life, then to Arturo and his heirs. Arturo has an indefeasibly vested remainder in fee simple absolute. Arturo (or his legal successor) is certain to obtain possession following expiration of Pietro's life estate and. once he has possession, Arturo cannot be divested of his possession (except, of course, by operation of law, as by eminent domain). He has a fee simple absolute.

iv. **Vested remainders subject to complete divestment:** A vested remainder subject to complete divestment is a remainder created in a known person and not subject to any condition precedent, but which is either (1) ***subject to a condition subsequent*** that, if it occurs, will ***completely divest*** the remainderman of his interest, or (2) ***subject to destruction because of an inherent limit in the estate held in remainder.***

Example 1 — condition subsequent: Keith conveys Blackacre to Edgar for life, then to Eve and her heirs, but if Adam should ever return from Vietnam, to Adam and his heirs. Eve has a vested remainder subject to complete divestment. Adam has an executory interest. Eve is a known person and there is no condition *precedent* to her possession. If Edgar dies today Eve will be entitled to possession. But both Eve's remainder and her possession, should it occur, may be taken away from her if Adam ever returns from Vietnam.

Example 2 — inherent limit: Ivan conveys Peach Orchard to Boris for life, then to Nikita for life, then to Leonid and his heirs. Nikita has a vested remainder subject to complete divestment because his remainder is in a life estate. If Nikita should die before Boris, his remainder will be destroyed. An inherent limit of Nikita's remainder for life is that he must be alive to enjoy possession of Peach Orchard. Leonid's indefeasibly vested remainder in fee simple absolute will become entitled to possession as soon as Boris dies. If Nikita survives Boris, Nikita's vested remainder will become possessory but his estate will still expire, due to its natural limit, and ultimately Leonid will move into possession.

(1) **May not be passed at death:** Vested remainders subject to complete divestment are still *vested* and they may be transferred *inter vivos,* devised, or inherited. Note, however, that a vested remainder subject to complete divestment can be created in such a way that it cannot be passed on at death.

Example: Frieda conveys Round Top to Dan for life, then to James and his heirs, but if James does not survive Dan, to Robert and his heirs. James's vested remainder is subject to complete divestment by Robert's executory interest. Since the divesting conditon subsequent is James's failure to survive Dan, James could never pass his remainder at his death. If James dies before Dan his remainder dies with him. If Dan dies before James, James acquires possession and the divesting condition subsequent can never occur. In that event, James will pass his fee simple absolute at death, not a remainder.

v. **Vested remainders subject to open (or partial divestment):** A vested remainder subject to open (or partial divestment) is a remainder created in a *class* (or group) of grantees, at least one of whom is presently existing and entitled to possession as soon as the preceding estate expires, but which is capable of expansion to include as yet unknown people. It is called "subject to open" because the class is left open for the entry of new members.

Example 1: Robin devises Orange Hall "to my husband, Harold, for life, then to such of my children who have graduated from law school." Robin has created a remainder in a class — her children who have graduated from law school. If, at the moment of creation, Robin has three children — Tom, Dick, and Harry — but none have graduated from law school the remainder is contingent. At the moment that Tom graduates from law school Tom has acquired a vested remainder, but it is subject to open (or partial divestment) because it is possible that Dick or Harry, or both, will graduate from law school. If Dick does graduate from law school, Tom's vested remainder will be partially divested in favor of Dick. Tom and Dick must share possession of Orange Hall. If Harry also graduates from law school, the remainder held by Tom and Dick is further diluted. But then the remainder shared by Tom, Dick, and Harry is indefeasibly vested because Robin is dead and can have no more children, and all of her children have satisified the condition precedent. The class is closed.

(1) **Are vested:** Remember: vested remainders subject to open are *vested.* Even though they are subject to dilution, the interest will survive its holder.

> **Example:** In the prior example, if Tom had graduated from law school, thus acquiring a vested remainder subject to open, and then died from the stress, his vested remainder would pass under his will or by intestate succession.

(2) **Subject to partial and complete divestment:** A vested remainder can be subject to *both partial and complete divestment.*

> **Example:** Peter devises Blackacre "to William for life, then to Catherine's children and their heirs, but if Ivan returns from Turkey, to Ivan and his heirs." At Peter's death Catherine is living and has two children, Anna and Russell. The class of Catherine's children has a vested remainder subject to partial and complete divestment. Catherine may have another child before William's death and, if so, that child would enter the class, partially divesting Anna and Russell. And Ivan, holder of an execu-

tory interest, may return from Turkey at any time, thus completely divesting Anna, Russell and any new members of the class of Catherine's children.

    vi. Class gifts: Whenever a grant creates an interest in a group of people, it is a ***class gift.*** The group can be any ascertainable body of people, but is most often a family group; *e.g.*, "to my children," or "to my surviving nieces and nephews," or "to my grandchildren who have reached age 21." A class is ***open*** if it is possible for new people to enter it, and is closed if new entrants are ***not possible.***

    vii. Class-closing rules: A class closes when either of two events occurs: (1) it is ***no longer physiologically possible to have new entrants,*** or (2) under the "rule of ***convenience***" any ***member of the class is entitled to immediate possession.***

        Example 1 — physiologically closed: Arthur devises Hilltop "to Maggie for life, then to my children and their heirs." Arthur is survived by two children, Mordred and Cedric. Arthur has created an indefeasibly vested remainder in the class of his children. It is indefeasibly vested because the class of Arthur's children is physiologically closed — Arthur is dead and can have no more children. Mordred and Cedric compose the entire class; nobody else can enter.

        Example 2 — Rule of Convenience: George devises Blackacre "to my wife, Liz, for life, then to my grandchildren and their heirs." George is survived by Liz and one child, Betty. Betty has two children, Charles and Diana. Charles and Diana, George's grandchildren, hold a vested remainder subject to open. But when Liz dies they will be entitled to immediate possession. Under the rule of convenience, the class of George's grandchidren then closes. If Betty later gives birth to Anne, this third grandchild of George's is born too late to share in the class gift.

c. Contingent remainders: A contingent remainder is a remainder created in an ***unknown person*** or that has a ***condition precedent*** to ultimate possession.

    Example 1 — unknown persons: Martha conveys Blackacre to Kevin for life, then to Ellen's children. Ellen is 12 years old and has no children. Ellen's nonexistent children have a contingent remainder. Martha has retained a reversion.

Example 2 — unknown persons: Martha conveys Blackacre to Kevin for life, then to Kevin's heirs. Kevin's heirs are not known until Kevin dies, so the class of Kevin's heirs have a contingent remainder. Recall that the term "heirs" refers to those people who inherit by intestate succession. Again, Martha has retained a reversion.

Example 3 — condition precedent: Martha conveys Blackacre to Kevin for life, then to Ellen if she graduates from Princeton. Ellen is 12 years old. Ellen has a contingent remainder. Martha has retained a reversion.

i. **Not certain to become possessory:** Contingent remainders have no certainty of becoming possessory, but that is also true of vested remainders subject to complete divestment. Don't make the error of thinking that certainty of ultimate possession is the dividing line between vested and contingent remainders. Note also that a contingent remainder in fee simple will *always* leave a reversion in the grantor.

ii. **Conditions precedent:** A condition precedent must be expressed in the grant. Neither the natural expiration of the prior estate nor precatory language in the grant constitutes a condition precedent.

   Example 1 — condition precedent: Harry conveys Elderfield to Annie for life, then to Eileen if she graduates from Harvard. The condition of graduation from Harvard is expressed in the grant and is a condition precedent to Eileen's possession.

   Example 2 — condition precedent: Jose conveys Salal to Rose for life, then to William if he survives Rose. The condition of survival is expressed in the grant as a condition precedent to William's possession.

   Example 3 — not a condition precedent: Jose conveys Salal to Rose for life, then to William. William (or his legal successor) has no right to possession until the natural expiration of Rose's life estate, but that is inherent in the estates conveyed by Jose. William has a vested remainder.

   Example 4 — not a condition precedent: Jose conveys Salal to Rose for life, and in the event of Rose's death, to William. Though couched as a condition, the language "and in the event of Rose's death" is wholly precatory. It adds nothing. It merely describes the natural expiration of Rose's life estate.

iii. **Recognizing the difference between a condition *precedent* and a condition *subsequent*:** The difference is often subtle between a vested remainder subject to complete divestment upon the occurrence of some condition subsequent and a contingent remainder subject to a condition precedent. You must pay careful attention to the language of the grant. If the condition is made an integral part of the grant in remainder, it is a contingent remainder. But if the grant uses words to create a vested interest, and then proceeds to add a divesting condition, it is a vested remainder subject to partial or complete divestment.

Example 1 — vested remainder: Phil conveys Seabreeze to Jane for life, then to Emily, but if Emily ever goes to Canada, to Evan. Emily has a vested remainder subject to complete divestment upon the occurrence of the condition subsequent of Emily going to Canada. Evan has an executory interest. Because Phil has created a vested remainder in fee simple, he has not retained a reversion.

Example 2 — alternative contingent remainders: Phil conveys Seabreeze to Jane for life, then to Emily if she has never gone to Canada, but if she has ever gone to Canada, to Evan. Now Emily has a contingent remainder because the condition — never going to Canada — is expressed as an integral part of the grant in remainder to her. Evan also has a contingent remainder because the same condition is repeated as an integral part of the grant to Evan. These are ***alternative contingent remainders.*** Because contingent remainders are created, Phil has retained a reversion. Phil's reversion will only become possessory in the unlikely event that Jane's life estate will terminate prior to her death, perhaps by conveyance of her life estate to Phil, holder of the next vested estate (the reversion), thus resulting in a merger of the two estates and elimination of the contingent remainders in between. Phil's intentions are identical in both examples, but quite different consequences flow from the choice of language.

(1) **Vested remainders are preferred:** In cases of hopeless ambiguity, the law prefers a vested remainder to a contingent remainder.

iv. Alienability: With a few exceptions, common law did not permit alienability of contingent interests. Today, nearly every jurisdiction permits alienability of contingent interests. Of course, if the contingency is survival, the interest cannot pass by will or intestate succession. And if the contigency results from the fact that the holder is unknown (perhaps not born) there is no owner to convey it, so as a practical matter it is not alienable.

B. Executory interests: Executory interests are future interests in a grantee that divest either (1) another grantee's possessory or future interest (a *shifting executory interest*) or (2) the grantor's interest at some future time (a *springing executory interest*).

1. A note on history: Executory interests resulted from Henry VIII's desire to eliminate the *use,* an early form of the trust, in order to stop death tax avoidance by means of the use. In order to provide the economic benefits of land to another, a feudal grantor might enfeoff (convey possession of a freehold estate) to another person, to hold "for the use and benefit" of a third party. The law courts did not recognize the use, but the equity courts (with power only to act upon a person) would command the feofee to administer the land in accordance with the instructions in the use.

Example: John, a sea captain, enfeoffs Blackacre to his brother, Robert, for the use and benefit of John's wife, Elizabeth, and her children. The chancellor in equity would force Robert, on pain of imprisonment, to administer Blackacre for the benefit of Elizabeth and her children.

a. Advantages of the use: The use began to be recognized as providing a number of advantages.

Example: Common law required conveyances of realty to occur by *livery of seisin,* a formality in which the seller physically handed the buyer a clod of earth or a twig from the property, while both were on the property. No doubt this was annoying. So lawyers began to convey property by *deed,* in which the buyer would pay valuable consideration for the property. The law courts refused to recognize a deed because there had been no transfer of seisin, but the chancellor in equity would order the seller to hold seisin for the use of the buyer. Equitable title was every bit as good as legal title.

i. Creation of springing and shifting sue: Lawyers and landowners quickly recognized other advantages of flexibility provided by the use. Common law forbade the creation of interests springing out of the grantor at some future time, because the ritual of livery of seisin could not be performed in advance. For equally rigid reasons the common law also forbade creation of interests shifting ownership of freehold estates from one grantee to another. But both of these arrangements could be accomplished through the use.

Example 1 — springing use: Basil conveys Blackacre "to Orlando for the use of Basil, and upon the marriage of my daughter, Sybil, to Norbert, for the use of Sybil." This enabled Basil to provide a dowry to Sybil, but only upon her marriage, and simultaneously to satisfy Norbert's family that the dowry would really be there when the marriage vows were pledged.

Example 2 — shifting use: Basil conveys Oak Park "to Orlando for the use of my son, John, but if my son Roger, who went off with John Cabot should ever return from the Western Ocean, for the use of Roger." This enabled Basil to provide for the contingency of Roger's return while still providing for his other son.

ii. **Avoidance of death taxes:** But perhaps the most exciting advantage of the use to wealthy landowners was that it afforded a method to avoid the feudal incidents, or death taxes. Recall that these death taxes fell due whenever a freeholder died and seisin descended to his heirs. The use enabled seisin to stay frozen in the hands of the trustee (the feoffee to use) forever.

Example: Basil conveys Blackacre to Alvin, Bertrand, Charles, and David, jointly, to hold for the use of Basil's first son, then to the first son's first son, then to the first son's first son's first son, then ... and so forth. Seisin stays in the hands of the four feoffees, so no death taxes ever become due. If Alvin and Bertrand die, it would be prudent for Charles and David to convey, jointly, to themselves and some younger persons, say Edward and Frank. This process could go on forever.

b. **The Statute of Uses:** The corpulent, self-indulgent, and profligate Henry VIII resolved to end this tax avoidance. He forced the ***Statute of Uses*** (1535, effective 1536) upon an unwilling Parliament. The Statute of Uses simply converted the beneficial interests in uses to legal interests. Because the Statute of Uses "executed" the use, the term executory interest eventually was bestowed on those future interests that would have been beneficial interests in a springing use or a shifting use prior to its adoption.

Example 1: After 1536, Sybil, in the earlier example of a springing use, would have a legal interest in Blackacre — an executory interest before her marriage to Norbert and a fee simple afterwards.

Example 2: After 1536, Roger, in the earlier example of a shifting use, would have a legal interest in Oak Park — an executory interest before his return from the Western Ocean, and a fee simple afterwards.

    i. **No longer necessary to "raise a use":** For a time after enactment of the Statute of Uses it was necessary to "raise a use" in order for the Statute to execute it into a legal interest. This is no longer necessary. Any conveyance — deed or will — can create an executory interest.

    ii. **How the trust survived the statute of uses:** The Statute of Uses was held by the courts not to apply to so-called active trusts, where the trustee was charged with a duty to manage the property for the beneficiary. Thus, it was a simple matter to create an active trust. Also, the courts held that a "use-on-a-use" was not affected by the Statute. Thus, after 1536, a conveyance "to X for the use of A for the use of B" resulted in the creation of a legal estate in A (because the first use was executed by the Statute of Uses) for the benefit of B. Again, by this device it was simple to create a trust. Finally, the Statute of Uses did not apply to personal property, so conveyances of money or securities in trust could continue to be created.

2. **Springing executory interests:** A springing executory interest is a future interest created in a grantee that ***divests the grantor*** at some future time after the conveyance. Thus, it "springs" out of the grantor.

Example 1: Professor Dweeb, a teacher of Property law, conveys Blackacre to the first student in his Property class who becomes a judge. This unknown student has a springing executory interest.

Example 2: Alice conveys Carter Hall to Ben for life, then to Stephen if he shall give Ben a proper funeral. Stephen has a springing executory interest, not a contingent remainder. It is not possible for Stephen to give Ben a proper funeral (or any funeral, for that matter) until at least some time has elapsed following the expiration of Ben's life estate. During that interval, possession has reverted to Alice (or her legal successor to her reversion). Thus, when Stephen delivers the proper funeral for Ben, possession will spring out of Alice.

3. **Shifting executory interests:** A shifting executory interest is a future interest in a grantee that ***divests another grantee*** upon the occurrence of some condition. By such divestiture, the shifting executory interest ***cuts short*** the preceding estate prior to its natural expiration.

   Example 1: Ron conveys Waterfront to Alex, but if Sarah should ever be released from prison, to Sarah. Sarah has a shifting executory interest. It will divest Alex, another grantee, by cutting short his fee simple if and when Sarah is released from prison.

   Example 2: Woody conveys Rose Arbor to Tammy for life, then to Esther, but if Esther does not survive Tammy, then to Arlo. Arlo has a shifting executory interest. It will divest Esther, another grantee, of her vested remainder in fee simple if Esther does not survive Tammy.

4. **The executory interest following a fee simple determinable:** All executory interests, ***except for this one,*** are either a springing or shifting executory interest.

   Example: Oscar conveys Clef House to Richard so long as Andrew Lloyd Webber's music is never played in Clef House, then to Lorenz. Richard has a fee simple determinable, which naturally expires upon the occurrence of the limiting condition. It is followed by Lorenz's interest. This looks like a remainder but the common law insisted that a remainder only followed upon an estate of ***less than a fee simple.*** So, we call this an executory interest. Though it does not, strictly speaking, ***divest*** the preceding estate, it is the possessory successor to a fee simple brought to its end by a condition subsequent, so it does bear some functional similarity to a shifting executory interest. In any case, remember that an interest in a grantee following a fee simple determinable is an executory interest.

IV. THE MARKETABILITY RULES

A. **Introduction:** Common law judges devised a number of rules to increase the marketability of land by eliminating uncertainties of title that inhibited alienability. These rules are considered here. Three doctrines — ***destructibility of contingent remainders,*** the **Rule in Shelley's Case,** and the ***doctrine of worthier title*** — are mostly abandoned today, although enough jurisdictions cling to them to make it worthwhile to study them briefly. The principal modern marketability rule is the **Rule Against Perpetuities.**

B. **Destructibility of contingent remainders:** At common law, a ***contingent remainder in land was destroyed if, at the expiration of the preceding freehold estate, it was still contingent.*** To become possessory, a contingent remainder had to vest at or prior to the termination of the prior freehold estate.

Example: Roger conveys Baskerville Hall to Arthur for life, then to Holmes if he should be knighted. Holmes has a contingent remainder, subject to the condition precedent that he receive a knighthood. If Holmes is knighted by the King before Arthur dies, his remainder will become vested, since the condition precedent will have been satisfied. Upon Arthur's death, Sir Holmes would take Baskerville Hall in fee simple absolute. But if Holmes has not been knighted before Arthur's death, his contingent remainder would be destroyed, leaving Roger's reversion as the possessory interest in Baskerville Hall in fee simple absolute.

1. **Rule is virtually non-existent today:** The rule was created when seisin was still important. The holder of seisin was responsible for the feudal obligations. Since seisin could not be passed from an expiring freehold estate to a contingent remainderman the contingent remainder must be eliminated, because seisin must go somewhere. There could be no gaps in seisin. Since seisin is irrelevant to the modern world, this rationale is utterly useless today. The amazing thing is that about a quarter of American states have not explicitly abolished this rule. The issue is rarely litigated and when it is courts appear to use good judgment and eliminate the rule as part of the common law. See, *e.g.*, *Abo Petroleum Corp. v. Amstutz*, 600 P.2d 278 (N.M. 1979).

2. **Preceding freehold estate:** The rule only applied to remainders following a ***freehold estate*** — which meant either a fee tail or a life estate — and did not apply to leaseholds, since the leaseholder did not have seisin. Thus, an easy way to avoid the destructibility rule was to convey a leasehold followed by a contingent remainder, rather than a life estate followed by a contingent remainder.

Example: Suppose Roger, in the prior example, had conveyed Baskerville Hall to Arthur for a term of 100 years so long as he remains alive, then to Holmes if he should be knighted. Arthur now has a determinable term of years in Baskerville Hall, rather than a life estate, but Arthur's tenure of possession will be identical. Roger holds seisin, not Arthur. If Holmes has not been knighted when

Arthur dies, the rule does not apply. After the Statute of Uses, Holmes's interest was given effect as a springing executory interest.

3. **Life estates:** The rule had a significant impact on contingent remainders following a life estate because it applied at the ***natural termination*** and at the ***artificial termination*** of a life estate.

   Example — natural termination: Paul conveys Pembroke to Peter for life, then to "the heirs of Peter's wife, Mary." Peter dies, survived by Mary. The remainder in Mary's heirs is contingent because we won't know their identity until Mary dies. It is destroyed.

   a. **Artificial termination:** A life estate could terminate early — before the death of the life tenant — by forfeiture or merger. Forfeiture occurred if the life tenant committed treason or tortiously attempted to convey a fee simple. Merger occurred if the same person held the present possessory freehold estate (the life estate) and ***the next vested estate,*** which would be a reversion if the following remainder was contingent. Forfeiture is irrelevant today, but not merger. The merger doctrine enabled conspiracies by the life tenant and the holder of the reversion to destroy the intervening contingent remainder.

      Example: William conveys Bayberry Hall to Alfred for life, then to Hortense if she survives Alfred. Hortense has a contingent remainder. If she survived Alfred it would become both vested and possessory at the same instant and would, of course, not be destroyed. But suppose that William dies before Alfred and his reversion is inherited by his greedy son Cecil. If Cecil can persuade Alfred to convey his life estate to him, Cecil will own both the possessory freehold estate and the ***next vested estate*** (the reversion). The merger doctrine extinguishes the life estate prematurely and, since Hortense has not yet satisfied the contingency of surviving Alfred, her remainder is destroyed. Cecil owns Bayberry Hall in fee simple absolute.

4. **Limited effectiveness of the rule:** The destructibility rule had lots of loopholes so it wasn't very effective.

   a. **Vested remainders:** By definition, vested remainders were exempt. But the inclusion of a vested remainder before a contingent remainder would block the merger doctrine.

      Example: Suppose William, in the prior example, had conveyed Bayberry Hall to Alfred for life, then to Mortimer for life, so long as he remains Vicar of Bayberry Parish, then to Hortense if she survives Alfred. Now, if William dies and the greedy Cecil inherits his reversion, a conveyance to Cecil of Alfred's life estate will not destroy Hortense's contingent remainder because Mortimer holds a vested remainder subject to divestment in a life estate. Cecil would own the present possessory freehold but his reversion would **not** be the **next vested estate.** Mortimer owns that, and his intervening vested estate prevents the merger doctrine from destroying Hortense's contingent remainder.

b. **Executory interests:** Executory interests are not remainders and so the rule did not apply to them, despite the fact that they are contingent interests. This was logical in the world of seisin, since an executory interest posed no possibility of any gap in seisin. Seisin would either spring from the grantor to the holder of the executory interest or shift from one seised freeholder to another.

Example 1: Ovid conveys Maytree to Abby for life, and if Beatrice wears proper mourning clothing for a year after Abby's death, to Beatrice. Beatrice has a springing executory interest. For the year following Abby's death possession (and seisin) is in Ovid (or the legal successor to his reversion), springing from him to Beatrice if the mourning condition is satisfied. Beatrice's executory interest is unaffected by the destructibility rule.

Example 2: Orville conveys Lakehead Inn to April for so long as Lakehead remains an inn, then to Bertrand. April has a fee simple subject to an executory limitation and Bertrand holds a shifting executory interest. Though the limiting condition may not happen for a very long time, if ever, there will never be any gap in seisin. Possession (and seisin) will pass from April to her successors in interest, with Bertrand (and his successors in interest) always ready to grab seisin. Bertrand's executory interest is unaffected by the destructibility rule.

c. **Leaseholds:** Because a leasehold is considered personal property, a leaseholder could not hold seisin. Thus, a contingent interest following a term of years was treated as an executory interest, not a remainder (since it does not follow a freehold estate) and was exempt from the destructibility rule.

Example: Owen conveys Blackacre to Jennifer for 100 years so long as she remains alive, then to Jennifer's children who survive her. Jennifer's children are unknown (Jennifer may have more, if she already has some) and there is a condition precedent to possession, but this is not a contingent remainder because it does not follow the natural expiration of a freehold estate; it follows a determinable term of years. Jennifer's children hold a shifting executory interest, exempt from the destructibility rule.

    d. Trusts: Contingent equitable remainders were unaffected by the rule, because the trustee held legal title and was thus seised for the duration of the trust. Thus, real property could be placed in trust, held there until the contingency was satisfied, and then distributed. Of the two examples that follow, the first is the device used by skilled lawyers in the heyday of the destructibility rule; the second example is a modern trust.

    Example 1: James conveys Blackacre "to my wife, Maria, for life, then to my lawyers, Harum, Scarum, and Suave, as trustees for the life of Maria and to preserve contingent remainders, then to such of Maria's children as shall survive her." This device prevented the possibility of early termination of the life estate by merger with the reversion, thus extinguishing the contingent remainder. If Maria's life estate terminated early for any reason, possession of Blackacre (and seisin) passed to Harum, Scarum, and Suave, who held it (paying the income to Maria for life) until Maria's death, when possession (and seisin) of Blackacre would pass to Maria's surviving children.

    Example 2: James conveys Blackacre "to Harum & Scarum, as trustees, to hold for the benefit of Maria for her life, then to convey outright and free of trust to such of Maria's children who reach the age of 21." Suppose Maria later dies, leaving two children, Alex (age 24) and Lizzie (age 18). If the destructibility rule existed in the jurisdiction, it would have no effect on Lizzie's contingent remainder, because it is an equitable remainder. When and if Lizzie reaches age 21 her portion of Blackacre will be distributed to her.

  5. Modern Replacement of the Rule: All the work performed by the destructibility rule can be and is performed by the Rule Against Perpetuities. See p. 148, *infra*.

C. The Rule in Shelley's Case: This rule, which takes its name from *Wolfe v. Shelley (Shelley's Case)*, 1 Co. Rep. 93b, 76 Eng. Rep. 206 (1581), was originally intended to prevent avoidance of the feudal incidents (death taxes). After the abolition of feudal incidents in the mid 17th century the rule survived because it improved marketability of land. That function, however, is fully performed by the Rule Against Perpetuities. While most of the states have eliminated this rule of law, it survives in three or four and applies in other states to grants made prior to elimination of the rule.

1. **The Rule:** If (1) *one instrument* (2) creates a *freehold in real property* and (3) a *remainder in the freeholder's heirs (or heirs of the freeholder's body),* and (4) the freehold estate and the remainder are *both* equitable *or both legal,* then (5) the *remainder becomes a remainder in the freeholder.*

   Example 1: Warren conveys Blackacre to Smith for life, then to Smith's heirs. In this *single instrument* Warren has created a life estate in Smith and a purported contingent remainder in Smith's heirs. The Rule in Shelley's Case converts the remainder in Smith's heirs into a remainder in Smith. That is all the Rule in Shelley's Case does. The *merger doctrine* operates independently but inexorably to give Smith a fee simple absolute in Blackacre, thus making Blackacre easily alienable by Smith rather than only after his death.

   Example 2: Suppose Warren had conveyed Blackacre to Smith for life, then to the heirs of Smith's body. The Rule in Shelley's Case would operate as before, but since the purported remainder refers to Smith's lineal descendants ("heirs of Smith's body") the remainder in Smith would be in fee tail. Merger would create a possessory fee tail in Smith. At common law Smith could convert the fee tail to fee simple absolute by the disentailing conveyance. Today, Smith's fee tail would be converted by law into a fee simple absolute in almost every American jurisdiction.

   a. **Freehold estate:** Given the virtual extinction of the fee tail, the only freehold estate which can be followed by a remainder is a life estate. As a practical matter, a Rule in Shelley's Case problem will only occur if the freehold estate is a life estate. It *does not matter* that the life estate is *determinable*, or *pur autre vie*, or *not possessory,* so long as the remainder that follows is in the heirs of the life tenant. However, if the life estate is *subject to some condition precedent that is not attached to the remainder,* the Rule in Shelley's Case does *not* apply.

      Example 1: Omar conveys Hickory Hill "to Alf for life, then, if Bob has never joined the Army, to Bob for the life of Chuck so long as Bob remains a bachelor, then to Bob's heirs if Bob hasn't joined the Army." Bob has a contingent remainder in a determinable life estate *pur autre vie*. The purported remainder in Bob's heirs is subject to the same condition precedent (Bob's not joining the Army) so the Rule applies, converting this remainder into one held by Bob. Since Bob holds the life estate following Alf's life estate and the remainder, he would have a contingent remainder in fee simple absolute, subject to the condition precedent of not joining the Army. If the phrase following "Bob's heirs" had read "no matter what" the Rule in Shelley's Case would *not* apply.

    i. Condition precedent not attached to a life estate: It is a quirk that the Rule in Shelley's Case *does apply* when the ***remainder is subject to a condition precedent that is not*** attached to the life estate.

    Example: Tom conveys Blackacre to Rick for life, then to Rick's heirs if Rick stops practicing law. The condition of Rick ceasing to practice law makes the putative remainder in Rick's heirs a contingent remainder and no such contingency is attached to Rick's life estate. The Rule in Shelley's Case operates to convert the putative remainder in Rick's heirs into a contingent remainder in Rick. But because it is contingent, rather than vested, the merger doctrine does not operate. Rick has a life estate and contingent remainder in fee simple in Blackacre. If he never stops practicing law, his contingent remainder will lapse at his death and the reversion retained by Tom will become possessory. If he does stop practicing law, the remainder will vest and the merger doctrine will give Rick fee simple absolute in Blackacre.

b. Remainder only: The Rule in Shelley's Case only applies to remainders, not to executory interests, but the rule does apply to the rare case of a life estate and a remainder combined within an executory interest.

    Example: Amy conveys Blackacre to Hazel so long as motor vehicles never enter Blackacre and, if so, to Florette for life, then to Florette's heirs. The shifting executory interest is split into a life estate in Florette and a remainder in Florette's heirs. The Rule in Shelley's Case applies, giving Florette the entire shifting executory interest.

c. Heirs: The common law judges who created the Rule had in mind a special meaning of the term "heirs." They did *not* mean the ***specific persons who would inherit,*** for in their time that was usually only one person, the decedent's eldest son. Rather they meant the term to describe an ***indefinite line of succession*** of heirs: the class of people, ***over time***, who would be heirs in each successive generation. This means that if the remainder is phrased to describe ***only the specific immediate heirs of the freeholder***, the Rule does ***not*** apply.

    Example: Eric conveys Blackacre to Rich for life, then to "Rich's heirs, his children." Though the grant reads to "Rich's heirs" it adds language — "his children" — that makes it plain that the term heirs does **not** refer to an **indefinite** line of succession but only to Rich's **immediate heirs.** The Rule in Shelley's Case does not apply. Even so, some confused American courts have applied the Rule in similar circumstances.

    d. Both estates legal, or both equitable: Remember that the Rule does **not** apply if one of the two estates is equitable and the other is legal. The usual situation in which this occurs is an equitable life estate followed by a legal remainder.

    Example: David conveys Tribune Hall to Harry in trust, for the possession and benefit of Lucille for life, then outright and free of trust to Lucille's heirs. Lucille has an equitable life estate (Harry has a legal fee simple subject to his trust obligations). Lucille's heirs have a contingent legal remainder in fee simple. The Rule does not operate.

2. Avoidance techniques: In those few jurisdictions still clinging to this anachronism, it is easy to avoid the Rule. One device is to use the trust. See p. 146, *supra*. Another is to convey the real property to A for a lengthy term of years "if he should live so long," then to A's heirs. Since A holds a term of years (a leasehold, not a freehold) the Rule does not apply.

D. The Doctrine of Worthier Title:

1. Statement of the Doctrine: If an *inter vivos* conveyance creates **any future interest** in the **heirs of the grantor** the future interest is **void.** Instead, the **grantor** retains a **reversion.**

Example: Lewis conveys Tucker Hall to "my son Scott for life, then to my heirs." Lewis has purportedly created a future interest — a vested remainder — in Lewis's heirs. The doctrine of worthier title voids this interest. Lewis is necessarily left with a reversion, which may be conveyed by him during his life, devised, or inherited by his heirs.

    a. A rule of construction: A very few courts have applied this doctrine to testamentary gifts, but mostly it applies to *inter vivos* conveyances. In its modern form the doctrine is a **rule of construction** — it raises a **rebuttable presumption** that the grantor did not intend to create a future interest in her heirs. The rationale for this presumption is that a **living grantor** is not likely deliberately to create a future interest in his **heirs,** but is far more likely to make that decision as part of his will. Worthier title preserves that option **unless the grantor clearly intended otherwise.** Note, by contrast, that the Rule in Shelley's Case and the rule of destructibility of contingent remainders are *rules of law*. This old common law rule was originally formulated to curb avoidance of feudal death taxes (by causing real property to descend by inheritance rather than pass inter vivos), but persisted because it also improved alienability of land. Worthier title is still observed in a scant majority of American states.

2. **Operation of worthier title:** The scope of the worthier title doctrine is very broad. It applies to both *real and personal property*. It applies to *any kind of future interest* — remainder or executory interest. It applies *regardless of the nature of the preceding estate* — fee tail, defeasible fee, life estate, or term of years. It applies *regardless of intervening future interests* in people who are not the grantor's heirs.

   a. **Heirs of the grantor:** Worthier title applies to future interests in the "heirs" of the grantor, so long as it appears that the term "heirs" is used to mean *indefinite succession* rather than specific people (who are likely to be the prospective immediate heirs of the grantor). See p. 145, *supra*.

   Example: James conveyed 37 Acres to Nate for life, and if Nate "should die leaving no lawful heir from his body, then the land ... shall revert back to James ... or to his lawful heirs." The Virginia Supreme Court ruled that worthier title applied to create a reversion in James rather than a remainder in his heirs, since this language did not "signify anything other than its normal and technical meaning of indefinite succession as determined at the death of the grantor." But if James had said "the land shall pass to my children," or "to my issue," or even "to my heirs as determined when Nate dies," worthier title would not apply because of these references to *immediate and specific heirs*. *Braswell v. Braswell,* 81 S.E.2d 560 (Va. 1954).

   b. **Trust revocation:** Worthier title commonly crops up when a person establishes an irrevocable trust for the benefit of himself and his heirs, but has a change of heart and seeks to revoke it.

   Example: Maude conveys property irrevocably to Opus in trust for the benefit of Maude for life, then to Maude's heirs. An irrevocable trust can be terminated only if all the beneficial interest holders consent. Maude owns all those interests (and so can terminate this trust) if worthier title applies, since the remainder in Maude's heirs is void, leaving instead a reversion in Maude. But if Maude left persuasive evidence that she *intended* to create a remainder in her heirs, she is out of luck. Remember that the modern version of worthier title is a rebuttable presumption that Maude retained the reversion instead of creating the remainder in her heirs. See, *e.g.*, *Hatch v. Riggs National Bank*, 361 F.2d 559 (D.C. Cir. 1966).

   i. **Modern treatment:** This problem is common enough that some states that have abolished worthier title have, by statute, retained the principle that the settlor of a trust may terminate it if she owns all the interests except for a remainder in her heirs. See, *e.g.*, N.Y. Estates, Powers & Trusts Law § 6-5.9.

3. **Distinguished from Shelley's Case:** The Rule in Shelley's Case involves grant of a future interest to the heirs of the life tenant, while worthier title involves a grant of a future iinterest to the *grantor's heirs.* The Rule in Shelley's Case is completely independent of worthier title. Abolition of the Rule in Shelley's Case has no effect on worthier title.

   Example: John Paul conveys Wolfwood to Terry for life, then to Terry's heirs if they are Roman Catholic, otherwise to John Paul's heirs. If both Shelley's Case and worthier title apply the contingent remainder in Terry's heirs is converted by Shelley's Case into a contingent remainder in Terry, and the alternative contingent remainder in John Paul's heirs is converted by worthier title into a reversion in John Paul. If Shelley's Case is abolished, but not worthier title, Terry's heirs hold a contingent remainder and John Paul has a reversion.

4. **Criticisms of worthier title:** It is charged that the doctrine breeds litigation since the presumption can be overcome by sufficient evidence that the grantor really meant what he apparently said. It is also claimed that worthier title is a death tax trap since the grantor may think he has parted with all interest in property during his life, but in fact has retained a reversion that is part of his taxable estate. Finally, some critics doubt the assumption that a person is unlikely to wish to give his heirs a future interest in his property. The legendary Professor Richard Powell's rejoinder was to note that stability was more important than either outcome, but worthier title's presumptive reversion "would be less likely to run counter to the real desires of settlors and would help to keep trusts readily revocable and property more easily alienable." 3 R.B. Powell, Real Property ¶ 269 (1952).

E. **The Rule Against Perpetuities:** After the Statute of Uses lawyers began to employ shifting executory interests to tie up ownership of property for very long periods into the future. The marketability rules considered so far mostly applied to remainders and not to executory interests. A rule was needed that would apply to **all contingent future interests** to prevent uncertainty about future ownership and not allow possession to drag on so far into the future that land would become inalienable but would be controlled by the dessicated dead hand of a past owner. Beginning with the *Duke of Norfolk's Case,* 3 Ch. Cas. 1, 22 Eng. Rep. 931 (1681), that rule is the Rule Against Perpetuities.

1. **Brief summary of the rule:** The classic statement is that by John Chipman Gray: *"**No interest is good unless it must vest, if at all, not later than twenty-one years after some life in being at the creation of the interest.**"* J.C. Gray, The Rule Against Perpetuities 191 (4th ed. 1942).

    a. **Vesting:** The Rule is designed to eliminate **uncertainty about ownership** that persists too long. If an interest is **certain to vest or certain not to vest** within the permitted period it is good. But if there exists **any possibility, no matter how unlikely,** that vesting could occur after expiration of the permitted period the interest is void. See p. 151, *infra.*

    b. **Permitted period of uncertainty:** An interest is good under the Rule if it will **certainly vest or certainly fail to vest** within (1) 21 years from its creation, or (2) during the life of some person **alive at its creation,** or (3) upon the death of some person **alive at its creation,** or (4) within 21 years after the death of some person **alive at its creation.** Thus, the Rule requires you to identify some person, **living on the effective date of the grant,** whose life can serve as the **measuring life** (or **validating life**) for the interest in question. That person, which may consist of a class or group of persons, is always a person whose life is germane to the grant — a person who can affect vesting of the interest. If an effective measuring (or validating) life cannot be identified the interest is void. See p. 152, *infra.*

    c. **Future interests to which the rule applies:** The Rule applies to all **contingent** future interests (**executory interests** and **contingent remainders**) except for interests **created in the grantor** (reversions, possibilities of reverter, and rights of entry). These latter interests are regarded as vested at the moment of creation, because they represent a **retained portion** of the grantor's estate. The contingency concerning future possession is thus permitted to persist forever. Note that when these latter interests are created in a grantee (and so are executory interests) they are subject to the Rule. See p154, *infra.*

d. Validity tested at creation: The validity of future interests under the Rule is tested *when they are created*. This means that, in order to prove validity (or invalidity), you must conjure up *what might happen* in the future. The Rule boils down to proof. If you can prove that the future interest in question is *certain* to vest or fail to vest within the permitted period the interest is valid. If you can prove *any single scenario, now matter how improbable of actual occurrence,* in which uncertainty of vesting will continue until after expiration of the permitted period, the interest is void.

Example: On July 15, 1997 Alice dies and devises Blackacre "to Barry's first child to graduate from college." Barry's only child, Ted, is a senior at Columbia. The validity of this springing executory interest is tested at the moment of its creation — July 15, 1997. It is void. It is *possible* (though unlikely) that (1) Ted will die tomorrow, before graduating from college, (2) Barry will have another child, Mary, born in 1998, (3) Barry will die immediately after Mary is born, and (4) Mary will graduate from Yale 23 years later. The only conceivable validating lives are Barry and Ted. The hypothetical Mary's hypothetical graduation *could occur* more than 21 years after the expiration of all conceivable measuring (or validating) lives.

i. **Must vest within permitted period:** For an interest to be valid, it must be proven that the interest will *necessarily vest or fail to vest* within the permitted period.

   Example: Martha devises Blackacre "to my husband William for life, then to my children for their lives, then to my grandchildren then living." At Martha's death she has two children, Thomas and Louise. The life estate in William is presently possessory. The remainder to Martha's children is vested at its creation (since there is no condition precedent and the class of Martha's children closes at her death around Thomas and Louise) so the Rule does not apply to it. The remainder in Martha's grandchildren who survive both Thomas and Louise is contingent, but that contingency will be eliminated the instant that both Thomas and Louise are dead. At that moment, the remainder will *certainly vest* (there will be surviving grandchildren) *or certainly fail to vest* (there will be no surviving grandchildren). Since both Thomas and Louise are lives in being at the creation of the interest, this interest will *certainly vest or fail to vest* at the expiration of the second of two lives in being. The interest is valid.

2. **Vesting:** With one major exception (see p. 151, *infra*) an interest is vested for perpetuities purposes when it has ***either*** become ***possessory*** (sometimes referred to as vesting in possession) or has ***vested in interest*** (the owners are known, existing people and there are no unsatisfied conditions precedent). Some interests (*e.g.*, an executory interest following or divesting a defeasible fee) can only vest in interest at the same time that they vest in possession. But many interests can and do vest in interest well before vesting in possession. An interest that is vested for classification purposes is vested for perpetuities purposes ***except for vested remainders subject to open (or partial divestment).***

   a. **Class gifts:** For purposes of the Rule Against Perpetuities, a gift to a ***class*** of people is ***not vested in any member of the class until it is vested in every member of the class.*** For this to happen, two things must be true: (1) the ***class must be closed*** and (2) ***any conditions precedent must be satisfied by every member of the closed class.***

      Example: In 1997, Olga devises Blackacre "to my son Martin for life, then to Martin's children for their lives, then to Martin's grandchildren." Olga is survived by Martin's two children, Victor and Alexa, and Martin's sole grandchild, Natalie. Martin's life estate is possessory and the remainder in Martin's children is vested, so neither interest is subject to the Rule. For ***classification purposes,*** Natalie has a vested remainder subject to open. But for ***perpetuities purposes*** the remainder in Martin's grandchildren is contingent, since the class of Martin's grandchildren is open. That contingency will be removed when the class of Martin's grandchildren is finally closed, which will not occur until the death of ***all of Martin's children.*** The ***class*** of Martin's children is not a "life in being" since that class is not closed (there could be another child born to Martin, a child not a life in being when Olga died). None of the lives of Martin, Victor, or Alexa provide sufficient certainty to serve as validating lives. The remainder in Martin's grandchildren is void in its entirety. The following scenario ***might happen:*** (1) Martin has another child, Tony, in 1999; (2) Martin, Victor, Alexa, and Natalie all die in a plane crash in 2000; (3) Tony has a child, Ava, in 2026. At that point — 2026, or 26 years after the death of all the relevant lives who could have served as measuring (or validating) lives — Ava would have a vested remainder subject to open (Tony could have more chidren). It is too late. Note, of course, that Natalie's remainder interest is destroyed in 1997 simply because of this chain of unlikely possibilities.

3. **Measuring or validating lives:** The concept of the measuring or validating life is crucial to the Rule Against Perpetuities. To validate future interests under the Rule you must prove that the interest is ***certain to vest or fail to vest*** within the lifetime of one or more people alive when the grant becomes effective, or within 21 years after the death of that person or persons. This person serves as the measuring or validating life. This person will be found among the relatively small number of people whose lives are relevant to the interest in question — they ***can affect vesting of the interest in question.***

   Example: Orville devises Cliff House to Tina for life, then to Tina's children who reach age 21. The contingent remainder in Tina's adult children is valid because (1) the uncertainty as to the identity of "Tina's children" will be resolved at Tina's death, and (2) the uncertainty as to which, if any, of Tina' children will reach age 21 will be resolved no later than 21 years after Tina's death (Tina might die in childbirth). Tina, a life in being when Orville died, is clearly relevant (she can affect the vesting of the remainder) and her life will serve to prove the validity of the remainder.

   a. **Measuring life not always mentioned in grant:** The measuring or validating life is not always mentioned in the grant.

      Example: Erwin, an orphan, devises Holmescroft "to my nieces and nephews who reach age 21." Erwin is survived by two sisters, three nieces and two nephews, ranging in age from 3 to 15. The springing executory interest is good because the unmentioned class of Erwin's siblings can serve as validating or measuring lives. Since Erwin's parents are dead the class of Erwin's siblings is closed; all possible members of that class are lives in being. The contingency in the executory interest will be resolved no later than 21 years after the death of both of Erwin's sisters.

   b. **Use of different lives:** Different lives may be used to validate different interests.

      Example: Al conveys to Bill for life, then to Bill's widow for life, then to Connie if she is then alive and, if not, to Connie's heirs. The remainder in Bill's widow is good because we will know her identity when Bill dies (Bill is the validating life). The remainder in Connie is good since it will vest or fail during (or at the end of) Connie's life (Connie is the validating life). The alternative contingent remainder in Connie's heirs is good because it will vest or fail no later than upon the death of Connie (Connie is the validating life).

c. **Person *in utero*:** A person is a life in being if *in utero* at the effective date of the grant. Common law considered (and still does) a person born within nine or ten months of the effective date of the grant to be a life in being at the effective date.

d. **Class of persons as measuring lives:** It is possible to use a group or class of people as measuring or validating lives, but ***every possible member of the class must be alive at the effective date of the grant.*** In other words, the ***class must be closed at the effective date of the grant*** for a class of persons to be effective as validating lives.

   Example: Suppose Erwin, in the prior example, had been survived by his parents as well as his two sisters and five nephews and nieces. Now the springing executory interest is void. The class of Erwin's siblings is ***not closed*** (Erwin's parents may have another child) and may not be used to validate the executory interest in the nephews and nieces. Here's what ***might*** happen: (1) Erwin's parents have another child, Zelda; (2) Erwin's parents, both of his older sisters, and all five nieces and nephews are killed by a mass murderer; (3) Zelda, the sole survivor, has a child, Zoe, who reaches age 21. At this point Zoe has vested, having satisfied the condition. But it is surely well over 21 years since Erwin's death, or that of his parents, the two most relevant lives in being at Erwin's death.

   i. **Artificially relevant people:** Occasionally, lawyers make a large number of people artificially relevant to the grant for purposes of creating a large class of lives of being. This works only if the class is sufficiently small that it will be practical to know when the perpetuities period has expired.

   Example 1: Rocco conveys Sweetbrier to Maribelle for life, then to Maribelle's children after the last person now alive in the City of Los Angeles has died. The springing executory interest in Maribelle's children is void because it is simply not possible to know when this event will occur.

   Example 2: Viscount Leverhulme devises gobs of property in trust to be distributed to a class of beneficiaries when all descendants of Queen Victoria living at the time of his death have died. An English chancery court upheld this artificial class of lives in being, though there were "at least 134" members of the class and the court admitted that there were "certain difficulties in ascertaining exactly how many of Queen Victoria's descendants were living" on the date of the Viscount's death, to say nothing of the problem of determining when this class would expire. *Cooper v. Leverhulme*, 2 All.E.R. 274 (Ch. 1943).

4. **The curious problem of defeasible fees:** Recall that a defeasible fee is followed by either a possibility of reverter or right of entry (if retained by the grantor) or by an executory interest (if transferred to a grantee). Executory interests are subject to the Rule but neither a possibility of reverter nor a right of entry is subject to the Rule. Thus, the ***identical contingency*** can last forever (if preserved by a possibility of reverter or right of entry) but may well be destroyed by the Rule if created in a grantee (executory interest). That is curious enough, but even more curious is the fact that, due to the differing grammatical construction of a fee simple determinable as opposed to a fee simple subject to condition subsequent, the estate left after destruction of the executory interest will differ.

   Example 1 — executory interest following determinable fee: Thomas conveys Thimbleberry to Edward and his heirs so long as Thimbleberry is never fenced, then to Paul and his heirs. The executory interest in Paul is void because you cannot prove that it will necessarily vest or fail to vest within 21 years after any life in being at the time of Thomas's conveyance. The condition of "no fences" may not be broken for generations, if ever. Paul's executory interest is erased. It is as if the grant stopped at "fenced," with the final clause expunged. The effect of this removal is to leave Edward with a fee simple determinable. The law then operates to create a possibility of reverter in Thomas. To avoid this result, Thomas would first have to convey a determinable fee to Edward, then separately convey his possibility of reverter (if permitted) to Paul.

   Example 2 — executory interest following a fee simple subject to a subsequent executory limitation: Thomas conveys Thimbleberry to Edward and his heirs, but if Thimbleberry is ever fenced, then to Paul and his heirs. The executory interest in Paul is void because you cannot prove that it will necessarily vest or fail to vest within 21 years after any life in being at the time of Thomas's conveyance. The condition of "no fences" may not be broken for generations, if ever. Paul's executory interest is erased. It is as if the grant stopped at "Edward and his heirs," with the final clauses expunged. The effect of this removal is to leave Edward with a fee simple absolute. To avoid this result, Thomas would first have to convey a fee simple subject to condition subsequent to Edward, then separately convey his right of entry (if permitted) to Paul.

   a. **Difference is hard to justify:** This dramatic difference in result is hard to justify, as is the difference in result between a possibility of reverter or right of entry, on the one hand, and the analogous executory interest on the other. This common law result has been modified in some jurisdictions, but modification schemes differ.

b. **Apply the Rule Against Perpetuities to possibilities of reverter or rights of entry:** By statute, this change has been adopted in the United Kingdom but has not been widely adopted in the United States. This approach eliminates the preferential treatment under the Rule accorded possibilities of reverter and rights of entry but does nothing to alter the different estates that result from destruction of the future interest following a defeasible fee.

c. **Statutory destruction of possibilities of reverter and rights of entry:** A number of American states have enacted statutes that automatically destroy possibilities of reverter and rights of entry a specific number of years after creation, usually 30 years. See, *e.g.*, Mass. Ann. Laws Ch. 184A, § 7. Some of these statutes permit a possibility of reverter or right of entry to be preserved for an additional period if notice of that intention is recorded prior to expiration of the initial period. These interests continue to be exempt from the Rule Against Perpetuities. The statutory destruction rule performs the work of the Rule and, in practice, can be more harsh than the Rule Against Perpetuities.

d. **Statutory destruction of all future interests following defeasible fees:** Some states have enacted statutes that automatically destroy possibilities of reverter, rights of entry, ***and*** executory interests ***following a defeasible fee*** a specific number of years after creation, usually 30 years. These statutes typically permit a possibility of reverter, right of entry, or analogous executory interest to be preserved for an additional period if notice of that intention is recorded prior to expiration of the initial period. This process of preservation can go on forever, so long as somebody cares enough to record the notice of intent to preserve every 30 years. See, *e.g.*, Cal. Civ. Code §§ 885.010-.030. In this scheme, all of these interests are exempt from the Rule Against Perpetuities but the statutory destruction rule will accomplish that job once the holder of the interest fails to keep it alive. Though conceivable, no jurisdiction exempts possibilities of reverter, rights of entry, and the analogous executory interests from the Rule Against Perpetuities ***without subjecting them to some statutory rule of destruction.***

e. **Charity-to-charity exemption:** By statute, and sometimes by judicial decision, an executory interest following a defeasible fee is exempt from the Rule Against Perpetuities *if the defeasible fee and the following executory interest are both owned by charities.* The justification for this rule is to foster and preserve charitable giving.

Example: Ellen conveys Thornhedge to Whitman College so long as it is used for educational purposes, and if not, to the National Trust for Historic Preservation. Whitman College has a determinable fee and the National Trust has an executory interest. This executory interest would normally be destroyed by the Rule Against Perpetuities, but since **both** Whitman College and the National Trust are charities, the executory interest in the National Trust is exempt from the Rule.

    f. **Testamentary creation of fee simple determinable:** Creation of a fee simple determinable by will means that the resulting possibility of reverter is retained by the grantor's **heirs** and does not pass via the will. The contrary conclusion, though adopted by the Massachusetts Supreme Judicial Court in *Brown v. Independent Baptist Church of Woburn,* 91 N.E.2d 922 (Mass. 1950), a case featured in some Property casebooks, is simply in error. The possibility of reverter is not created until the will becomes effective, and the will becomes effective *upon the testator's death.* The will disposes of the testator's property owned at death, but that does not include the as-yet-uncreated possibility of reverter. Being dead, the testator cannot retain the possibility of reverter created at death. Thus, the retained interest goes to the testator's **heirs**.

5. **Classic traps for the unwary:** This section discusses two of the classic traps of the Rule Against Perpetuities. Each results from the Rule's insistence on considering *future possibilities,* no matter how outlandish, rather than *probabilities.*

    a. **The fertile octogenarian:** The Rule presumes that a person of any age, whether male or female, can produce a child. This presumption can lead to some harsh results, as the classic case of *Jee v. Audley,* 1 Cox 324, 29 Eng. Rep. 1186 (Ch. 1787), demonstrates.

        i. *Jee v. Audley*: **The rule in a nutshell:** Edward Audley devised property "to my niece Mary Hall and the issue of her body lawfully begotten, and to be begotten, and in default of such issue ... to ... the daughters then living of my kinsman John Jee and his wife Elizabeth Jee." John and Elizabeth Jee "were of a very advanced age" when Audley died. Mary Hall was unmarried and age 40. The Jees had four adult daughters and no sons. The Chancery Court construed the will to mean that Mary Hall had a fee simple subject to an executory limitation — her death without lawful issue — in the Jee daughters. But the Chancellor made two additional interpretations. First, he construed the phrase "issue of her body lawfully begotten" to refer to **indefinite failure of issue** — the extinction of Mary Hall's lineal bloodline, whenever occurring. By this construction Mary Hall is "dead without issue" when (1) she is dead *and* (2) all her lineal descendants are dead. Under indefinite failure of issue, President Theodore Roosevelt is not dead without issue. Second, he construed the reference to the Jee daughters to mean **all possible daughters** of John and Elizabeth Jee, including those which might not yet be born at the time Audley died, meaning that the executory interest was a **class gift** and that the class — the Jee daughters — is not closed. The "indefinite failure of issue" construction requires assuming the possibility that Mary Hall, a 40-year old 18th century spinster, will marry and bear a child. Not impossible, but unlikely. Call this fictional child Zoe Hall. The "all possible daughters" construction requires assuming that Elizabeth Hall is a **fertile octogenerian,** able to bear another child, and that she and John will produce such a child in their dotage. Call this as-yet-unborn Jee daughter Miracle Jee. It is now easy to see that the interest in the Jee daughters *could* vest too remotely: (1) Mary Hall dies right after bearing Zoe Hall; (2) John and Elizabeth Jee die right after producing Miracle Jee; (3) the four adult Jee daughters contract pneumonia at their parents' burial and promptly die; (4) Zoe Hall lives a full life, dying childless at age 80 (at that moment, Mary Hall has died without issue); and (5) Zoe is survived by Miracle Jee, also age 80. At that moment Miracle Jee has vested in interest and possession. But this moment is too remote: there is no life (or class of lives) in being at Audley's death that will validate the executory interest. Neither Audley, Mary Hall, nor John and Elizabeth Jee will suffice. The class of the Jee daughters won't work because that class is open at Audley's death, meaning that not every possible member of the class was alive at Audley's death. If you understand *Jee v. Audley* thoroughly, you have a good grasp of the Rule Against Perpetuities in its full common law glory.

b. **The unborn widow:** This is another classic. Without more, a bare reference to "A's widow" is construed to refer to the unknown person who answers that description on A's death, not necessarily the person who is A's wife when the instrument is drafted. The Rule presumes the possibility that aged men and women might substitute fresh youngsters for their elderly mates — so young that they were not even born at the time of the grant.

Example: William devises Mosswood to "my son, Charles, for life, then to his widow for life, then to his children then living." At William's death, Charles is 40, married to Diana, age 35. Charles has a possessory life estate. The remainder to "his widow" is contingent since we cannot know the identity of this person until Charles's death. But this contingent remainder is valid under the Rule Against Perpetuities because the uncertainty concerning her identity will be removed at Charles's death. Charles can serve as a validating or measuring life. The contingent remainder in Charles's children is void, however, because the uncertainty as to which, if any, of Charles's children will survive Charles's widow will not be removed until the death of that person. It may be Diana, a life in being, but *it is possible that it may be someone not alive when William died.* Diana may die, or Charles may divorce her, and as an 80 year old man might marry Lolita, age 16, a person born 24 years after William's death. The "class" of "Charles's widow" is open at William's death and, even though it is a class of one, it may be composed of a person not alive when the executory interest is created. So "Charles's widow" is ineffective as a validating life.

6. **Reform doctrines:** The common law Rule Against Perpetuities has been reformed in about half the American states by adoption of *"wait-and-see"* statutes. Most jurisdictions also attempt to save interests by *construction of the grant*, if possible, and some are willing to engage in *reformation of the grant* in order to save interests created by it from destruction.

   a. **Wait-and-see:** As the name implies, this statutory reform evaluates the validity of future interests under the Rule Against Perpetuities *as events unfold,* not at the time of creation of the interests. The focus under "wait-and-see" is on *what actually happens,* not on *what might happen.* The common law Rule has the virtue of supplying a quick answer to the question of validity of future interests, albeit sometimes at the expense of common sense. Wait-and-see avoids that expense, but at the cost of years of uncertainty while we wait to see what actually happens. Wait-and-see comes in two essential forms, with a few permutations on each.

b. **Wait-and-see for the permitted period:** Around half of the wait-and-see states wait for the period permitted by the common law Rule Against Perpetuities. This means that you must still determine the appropriate measuring or validating life for the interest in question, *even if it won't work to validate the interest under the common law Rule,* and then wait for that life to expire plus 21 years.

Example: Chuck devises Converse Hall to Taylor for life, then to Taylor's children for their lives, then to Taylor's grandchildren. At Chuck's death, Taylor has two children, Agnes and Ethel, and one grandchild, Sean. Under the common law Rule, the contingent remainder in Taylor's children is good because their identities will be fully known upon Taylor's death (the class will close) and Taylor is a life in being. But the contingent remainder in Taylor's grandchildren is void because their identity will not be known until all of Taylor's children are dead, and the class of Taylor's children, being open at Chuck's death, cannot serve as a validating life since the *class* is not a life in being. Under wait-and-see, we wait for the following lives to end: Taylor, Agnes, Ethel, and, if necessary, Sean. All of these people were lives in being at Chuck's death. If Taylor never has any more children, the remainder in Taylor's grandchildren will be completely vested when both Agnes and Ethel are dead, and will be good. If Chuck has an after-born child, Cedric, the remainder in Taylor's grandchildren will not vest when both Agnes and Ethel are dead, since the class of Taylor's grandchildren is not yet closed. We would continue to wait for Sean's death. If Sean dies before Cedric, we will wait for 21 years more. If Cedric is still alive at that point the class of Taylor's grandchildren is still open and the contingent remainder in the grandchildren is void. If Cedric predeceases Sean or dies within 21 years after Sean's death, the class of Taylor's grandchildren closes and the contingent remainder is vested within the permitted perpetuities period.

   i. **Wait-and-see for 90 years:** The Uniform Statutory Rule Against Perpetuities (USRAP) provides for waiting for a maximum of 90 years after the creation of the interest to see if it has vested. This avoids the necessity of locating the lives that measure the common law perpetuities period, but may (in some cases) permit uncertainty to persist for a longer period than under wait-and-see for the common law period.

      Example: In the prior example, we would simply wait for 90 years after Chuck's death to see if all of Taylor's children had died, thus closing the class of Taylor's grandchildren and causing the remainder in Taylor's grandchildren to vest (or fail, in the absence of any grandchildren).

Under USRAP, an interest is good if it is valid **either** under the common law Rule Against Perpetuities **or** under the wait-and-see for 90 years approach.

c. Construction of the instrument: Most modern courts will construe an instrument to save future interests from destruction by the Rule, if possible to do so without plainly violating the grantor's intent. By contrast, Baron Kenyon, the author of *Jee v. Audley*, opined that he "would not strain to serve an intention at the expense of removing the landmarks of the law." Most modern judges regard Kenyon's "landmarks" as pitfalls, and are only too happy to supply a saving construction.

Example: Recall the bequest in *Jee v. Audley*, discussed in p. 156, *supra*. A "reform by construction' approach would treat the limitation on Edward Audley's bequest to Mary Hall ("upon default of ... issue") as referring to **definite failure of issue** — the possibility that Mary Hall might die childless, not that some imaginary bloodline would expire years hence. This alone would have saved the executory interest in the Jee daughters since the executory interest was to the Jee daughters "then living" — at the death of Mary Hall, childless. But a modern approach might also go further and **construe the gift to "the daughters" of John and Elizabeth Jee to refer to the four living persons who answered that description when Audley's will was written and when it became effective** — not to a class composed of those four plus a miraculous afterborn child conceived by a pair of octogenarians with a foot apiece in the grave. This closing of the class of Jee daughters by construction would also, by itself, have saved the executory interest in the Jee daughters. Even if "Mary Hall's death without issue" refers to the extinction of her imaginary bloodline sometime in the future, that event would either occur or not within the lifetime of the four living Jee daughters. Thus, the condition precedent would be satisfied (and the interest would vest) or it would not (and the interest could never vest) within the joint lives of the four Jee daughters, lives in being.

d. Reformation of the instrument: Some modern courts apply the *cy pres* doctrine to reform a grant to make it comply with the Rule Against Perpetuities. *Cy pres* is a doctrine of wills and trusts that permits courts to revise the grantor's instrument to get as close as possible to the grantor's intentions when the grantor's actual intentions are impossible to accomplish.

Example: Harry conveys Woodlot to Angela for life, then to Angela's children who reach age 30. The contingent remainder is void under the Rule because Harry and Angela's presently living children might all die, Angela might have another after-born child, and die in childbirth. The afterborn child could satisfy the contingency 30 years after the expiration of Angela's life and Angela is the only conceivable measuring or validating life. Reform by *cy pres* would rewrite Harry's conveyance to read "to Angela's children who reach age 21." Now the remainder is good since even the hypothetical afterborn born at Angela's death would necessarily satisfy (or fail to satisfy) the contingency no later than 21 years after Angela's death.

7. **Drafting issues:** In drafting trusts, Rule Against Perpetuities problems can often be avoided by inserting a "savings clause" in the trust, providing for termination of the trust no later than 21 years after the end of all relevant lives in being at the creation of the trust. Because many trusts are created for tax avoidance purposes the U.S. Treasury's Internal Revenue Service has ruled that trust settlors in USRAP jurisdictions must choose at the outset whether to use the common law Rule or wait-and-see for 90 years. If you use the common law Rule you better be sure the interests created are valid, because if they are not and you must later rely on USRAP's wait-and-see rule you will have lost whatever tax advantages inhered in the trust. Truly this is a modern estate planner's version of sailing betwixt the rock of Scylla and the whirlpool of Charybdis.

8. **Applicability of the Rule Against Perpetuities to commercial transactions:** The Rule applies to option agreements with respect to real property. The optionee has an equitable interest in the property, consisting of a specifically enforceable right to purchase on the terms of the agreement.

   Example: For valuable consideration, Railroad Co. agrees with Smith that Smith may purchase Railroad Co.'s right-of-way bisecting Smith's farm "whenever Railroad ceases to operate daily train service on the right of way." The option in Smith is void under the Rule because there is no certainty that the triggering condition will ever occur, much less within some life in being plus 21 years.

   a. **Justification and criticism:** The justification for application of the Rule Against Perpetuities to commercial options is that options of indefinite duration will act as a disincentive to improve the land and inhibit or foreclose sale to someone other than the optionee who might make a better use of the land. But application of the Rule to these situations is also criticized on the ground that the perpetuities period is ill-suited to commercial transactions, and that the general principle against unreasonable restraints on alienation is sufficient to deal with the marketability clog posed by options of indefinite duration. Some courts avoid applying the Rule to options by implying into the option agreement a proviso that the option must be exercised, if at all, within 21 years of its creation. See, *e.g.*, *Robroy Land Co. v. Prather,* 622 P.2d 367 (Wash. 1980).

Chapter 5
CONCURRENT OWNERSHIP AND MARITAL INTERESTS

I. FORMS OF CONCURRENT OWNERSHIP

A. Introduction: When the same interest in property is owned by more than one person at the same time there is *concurrent ownership.* There are at least five forms of concurrent ownership recognized by the common law, only three of which are studied in the typical Property course: *tenancy in common, joint tenancy,* and *tenancy by the entirety.* Of the remaining two, *coparceny* is extinct in the United States and *tenancy in partnership* is usually covered in courses on Business Associations. This chapter also covers marital interests, only some of which are forms of concurrent ownership.

B. Tenancy in common:

1. **Nature of tenancy in common:** Tenants in common own *separate but undivided* interests in the same interest in property. Conceptually, each tenant in common owns the entire property, but must necessarily share that ownership with the other tenants in common. Two people who own a sailboat as tenants in common each own the entire boat, and they are each entitled to sail it, but they cannot prevent the other from doing so. Much of the law of concurrent ownership is designed to mediate the friction that can arise from co-ownership of the same article. A tenancy in common interest may be alienated, devised, or inherited separately from the other tenancy in common interests. Unlike the joint tenancy, there are *no survivorship rights* among tenants in common.

   Example: Tim conveys Roundhouse to Ezra and Geraldo, as tenants in common. If Ezra conveys his interest in Roundhouse to Newt, Geraldo and Newt are tenants in common. If Geraldo dies, devising his interest in Roundhouse to Maxine, Newt and Maxine are tenants in common.

2. **Presumption of tenancy in common:** By statute or judicial decision, a conveyance of real property to two or more persons who are not married to each other is *presumed to convey a tenancy in common.* That presumption is rebuttable. The best evidence rebutting it is a clear statement in the conveyance of the alternative form of co-ownership (*e.g.*, joint tenancy). Property that passes by intestate succession to two or more heirs is *always* taken as tenants in common.

3. **Rights to possession:** Each tenant in common is entitled to possess the entire property. In practice, this means that a tenant in common can possess the entire property if **no other co-tenant objects.** Tenants in common may, and often do, regulate their rights to the property by agreement among themselves. But if they do not, and disagreement erupts, their rights and obligations are governed by "default" rules of law. See p. 183, *infra*.

4. **Uneven shares and different estates:** Tenants in common may own *unequal shares* and *different estates.*

   Example: Able, Baker and Cassie own Blackacre, in equal shares, as tenants in common. Able conveys his interest to Baker. Baker and Cassie are still tenants in common, but Baker has a 2/3 share and Cassie a 1/3 share. Cassie conveys her interest in Blackacre to Sophie for life, then to Andrea and her heirs. Baker is now a tenant in common with Sophie (as to possession) and with Andrea (as to her remainder).

   a. **Rebuttable presumption of equal shares:** There is a rebuttable presumption that tenants in common have equal shares in the property. The best evidence rebutting this presumption is a clear statement in the conveyance creating the tenancy in common (*e.g.*, "O conveys a 2/3 share to A, and 1/3 share to B, as tenants in common"), but evidence extrinsic to the conveyance (*e.g.*, relative contributions of purchase cost or carrying costs) is germane to this issue.

C. **Joint tenancy:**

1. **Nature of joint tenancy:** Joint tenants own an undivided share in the same interest in either real or personal property, but the surviving joint tenant owns the entire estate. This *right of survivorship* is the hallmark of joint tenancy, setting it apart from tenancy in common. Any number of people may be joint tenants. Upon the death of one joint tenant, the share held by the remaining joint tenants increases proportionately.

   Example: Alan, Betty, and Charles own equal undivided interests in Blackacre as joint tenants. Alan dies, leaving all his property by will to David. Betty and Charles now own equal undivided interests in Blackacre. Alan's will is ineffective to transfer his interest in Blackacre because the nature of joint tenancy is that his interest expires at his death. Charles then dies intestate, leaving Emmy as his heir. Betty now owns the entirety of Blackacre by herself. Charles's estate has no interest in Blackacre. When a joint tenant dies, his *entire interest* dies with him.

a. **Creation:** A joint tenancy may only be created by an *inter vivos* conveyance or a will. Property acquired by multiple heirs through intestate succession is taken as tenants in common.

b. **The theory of joint tenancy:** Common law conceived of joint tenants as bound together as a single owner. The common law's expression for this unwieldy concept was to say that each joint tenant owned the property *per my et per tout* — by the moiety (the half) and the whole. This summed up the inherent duality of the joint tenancy — multiple people owned an equal interest in the entirety of the property. Each joint tenant owned it all. Thus, when a joint tenant died, his interest died because he was a mere participant with others in a single ownership entity. The dead joint tenant simply dropped out of the ownership unit. No interest in property passed to the survivors, because they already owned the entire property. There was just one less member of the ownership consortium. There are two **significant consequences** to this basic concept: (1) since no interest passes at death, a *joint tenancy is not subject to probate,* and (2) joint tenancy interests are *not subject to inheritance taxes imposed on property that "passes" at death,* since no property passes at death.

2. **The four unities of joint tenancy:** From the theory of the joint tenancy, common law judges derived the principle that the *interests of joint tenants must be equal in every respect.* Hence, the *four unities* of joint tenancy: *all joint tenants* must take their interests: (1) at the *same time,* (2) under the *same instrument,* (3) with the *same interests* and (4) with the *same right to possession of the entire property.* At common law a joint tenancy *could not be created without the four unities being satisfied.* If the four unities were not satisfied, a tenancy in common resulted. This is still the law in many states, though some have relaxed the rule to permit creation of a joint tenancy whenever there is sufficiently clear intention that a joint tenancy was intended.

   a. **Time:** The joint tenants must receive their interests at the same moment in time.

   Example: Oliver conveys Blackacre to "my son, Michael, and to my daughter, Eliza, if and when they marry, as joint tenants." This springing executory interest vests in interest and possession as each of Michael and Eliza marry. Obviously, they cannot marry each other and, unless they happen to marry in an exquisitely timed double ceremony their respective interests in Blackacre will vest at different times. When Michael marries

Jane and, a year later, Eliza marries Roger, Eliza and Michael will own Blackacre as tenants in common, not as joint tenants.

b. Title: All joint tenants must receive their interests under the same instrument: a deed, a will, or a decree quieting title by joint adverse possession.

Example: Edward was the sole owner of Bower Cottage prior to his marriage to Andrea. As a marriage present, Edward conveyed Bower Cottage "to Andrea and Edward, as joint tenants." At common law this did ***not*** create a joint tenancy, because Edward's interest in Bower Cottage was created by a prior instrument. The deed from Edward to Edward and Andrea was construed as a nullity insofar as it purported to transfer Edward's interest, but did operate to convey 1/2 of Edward's interest to Andrea. Common law did not recognize transfers from oneself to oneself. Thus, Edward and Andrea would be tenants in common.

i. "Straw man" conveyances: This example, which occurred with some frequency, proved to be a bothersome annoyance. The solution at common law was for Edward to convey to his lawyer (or some other trusted friend) who would promptly convey back to Edward and Andrea, as joint tenants. This second conveyance met the four unities requirement. But this "straw man" conveyance was cumbersome and, in essence, an empty formality. As a result, many states today have, by statute, provided that a person may create a joint tenancy by a conveyance from himself to himself and another, as joint tenants. Under such a statute Edward, in the example, would have created a joint tenancy between himself and Andrea.

c. Interest: Each joint tenant must have the identical interest in the property. This means two things: (1) each joint tenant must have the same share of the undivided whole, and (2) each joint tenant must have the same durational estate.

Example 1 — same share: George conveys "a two-thirds interest in Whitewall to Andrew, and a one-third interest in Whitewall to Bruce, as joint tenants." Andrew and Bruce take as tenants in common since the unity of equal interest is not present.

Example 2 — same durational estate: George conveys Whitewall to Andrew and his heirs, and to Bruce and his heirs so long as Whitewall's library remains intact, as joint tenants. Bruce and Andrew are tenants in common since Andrew has fee simple absolute and Bruce has fee simple determinable (George retaining a possibility of reverter as to 1/2 of Whitewall).

   i. **Tenancies may differ:** But this requirement does ***not*** preclude holding a portion of an estate in joint tenancy and another portion in tenancy in common.

      Example: Olivia conveys "a 1/2 interest in Tinderbox to Amy and Ben, as joint tenants, and a 1/4 interest in Tinderbox to Cameron, as a tenant in common." After this conveyance, Amy and Ben own an undivided interest as to 1/2 of Tinderbox in joint tenancy; Cameron owns a 1/4 undivided interest as a tenant in common, and Olivia continues to own a 1/4 undivided interest as a tenant in common. If Ben dies, Amy will be the sole owner of an undivided 1/2 interest in Tinderbox, as a tenant in common with Cameron and Olivia. Remember: the joint tenancy is considered a single ownership entity, so throughout this scenario the joint tenancy owned an undivided 1/2 interest in Tinderbox as a tenant in common with Cameron and Olivia. When Ben dies, Amy simply owns the entire interest formerly held by the joint tenancy, but the relationship of tenancy in common with respect to the other interests is not altered.

   d. **Possession:** At creation of the joint tenancy, each joint tenant must have the right to possession of the whole property. After creation, joint tenants may agree among themselves to divide possession, or to deliver exclusive possession to one joint tenant. So long as the arrangement is consensual, it amounts to a voluntary waiver of a joint tenant's legal right to possess the whole. Generally, the law is willing to enforce the voluntary agreements of co-owners concerning their co-ownership.

3. **Creation of joint tenancy:** Common law presumed that any conveyance or devise to two or more persons (other than husband and wife) was in joint tenancy. This simplified the performance of feudal obligations, since only one entity — the joint tenancy — owed those obligations. Since we don't live in a world of feudal obligations, every American jurisdiction has reversed the presumption. Today, a tenancy in common is presumed, unless there is clear evidence of joint tenancy. At common law, husbands and wives were presumed to take as tenants by the entirety. Today, husbands and wives are presumed to take either as tenants by the entirety or as joint tenants.

   a. **Evidence sufficient to create joint tenancy:** The modern presumption of tenancy in common can be overcome only by a clearly expressed intention in the grant itself. The best expression is "to A and B, as joint tenants with right of survivorship," although Michigan and Kentucky regard this clear expression as creating a joint life estate in A and B, with a contingent remainder in the survivor. See *Albro v. Allen,* 454 N.W.2d 85 (Mich. 1990); *Sanderson v. Saxon,* 834 S.W.2d 676 (Ky. 1992). The significance of this view is that the survivorship right cannot be destroyed by a joint tenant through a conveyance to a third party that severs the joint tenancy. See p. 168, *infra*.

b. Evidence insufficient to create joint tenancy: The following common expressions are dangerous. Some courts regard them as adequate to create a joint tenancy; others do not.

Example 1: "To A and B as joint tenants." This is ordinarily adequate to create a joint tenancy but some states hold that failure to include the phrase "with right of survivorship" renders this usage inadequate to create a joint tenancy. But note that inclusion of that phrase in Michigan and Kentucky creates a joint life estate with contingent remainder in the survivor.

Example 2: "To A and B jointly." This is problematic, since the term "jointly" is often used colloquially to refer to any form of co-ownership.

Example 3: "To A and B, joined together." This probably produces a tenancy in common, since the term "joined together" is not a term of art, and is probably a lay reference to co-ownership.

Example 4: "To A and B as joint tenants, then to the survivor and her heirs." This is hopelessly ambiguous; a mixed message. The phrase "joint tenants" is clear enough, but when followed by the express conveyance of an interest "to the survivor and her heirs" the inference is reasonable that the grantor intended to create a remainder in the survivor. On the other hand, the "survivor and her heirs" language could be taken to mean nothing more than an empty restatement of the legal effect of a joint tenancy. This usage may result in a joint tenancy but is probably more apt to create a joint life estate or tenancy in common in A and B, followed by a remainder in the survivor. The latter result prevents either A or B from destroying the survivorship right by an *inter vivos* conveyance.

4. **Severance of joint tenancy:** A joint tenant may destroy the joint tenancy at any time by severing the joint tenancy, usually by conveyance. A tenancy in common results. Since the "four unities" were

necessary to create a joint tenancy at common law, the destruction of any one of those unities would operate to sever the joint tenancy. While that rule is still followed, many courts prefer to rely more on evidence of the intention of the conveying party.

- a. **Conveyance:** If a joint tenant conveys his interest to a third party or to another joint tenancy, the joint tenancy is severed *as to that interest.*

    Example: Tom, Dick, and Newt are joint tenants. If Tom conveys his interest to Bill, the joint tenancy is severed *as to that interest.* Bill owns a 1/3 undivided interest as a tenant in common with Dick and Newt. Dick and Newt continue as joint tenants with respect to their interests. If Dick then conveys his interest to Newt, Bill and Newt will be tenants in common, with Newt holding 2/3 and Bill 1/3. Same result if Dick died, since Newt would then own the entirety of the 2/3 interest formerly held by Dick and Newt as joint tenants. If Tom had conveyed his interest to Newt, instead of to Bill, Newt would own a 1/3 interest (the interest acquired from Tom) as a tenant in common with Dick and a 1/3 interest in joint tenancy with Dick. If Newt then died, Dick would own a 2/3 interest as a tenant in common with Newt's heirs or devisees.

    - i. **Contract to convey:** A conveyance includes a contract to convey that is specifically enforceable, since the buyer under such a contract has equitable title to the property. Severance occurs at the moment such a contract is made.

    - ii. **Unilateral severance: conveyance to self:** Common law regarded a conveyance of an interest held by a person to himself as an empty act, devoid of legal effect. Thus, to convert a joint tenancy into a tenancy in common, the joint tenant would have to employ a straw man, to whom the severing conveyance would be made and from whom a reconveyance would be made. Some courts have dispensed this requirement, particularly where the jurisdiction has by statute permitted creation of a joint tenancy by a conveyance from "A to A and B, as joint tenants." See, *e.g.*, *Riddle v. Harmon*, 162 Cal. Rptr. 530 (Ct. App. 1980).

- b. **Mortgage:** Jurisdictions differ as to whether a joint tenancy is severed by the act of one joint tenant mortgaging his interest. Resolution of this issue traditionally depended upon whether the jurisdiction adhered to the *lien theory* or the *title theory* of mortgages, but that distinction has partially broken down for this purpose.

i. **Title theory of mortgages:** The title theory holds that a mortgage effects a transfer of legal title, subject to an equitable right of the mortgagor (the borrower) to reclaim title by paying off the loan secured by the mortgage (***equity of redemption***). This was the common law theory of mortgages. As a result, a mortgage by one joint tenant had the effect of severing a joint tenancy because the unity of interest is destroyed. The joint tenancy could not be restored by redemption because the unities of time and title would not be present. After the mortgage, the former joint tenants would become tenants in common and there would be, of course, no right of survivorship. See, *e.g.*, *Stewart v. AmSouth Mortgage Co., Inc.*, 679 So. 2d 247 (Ala. Ct. App. 1995). This result has often been criticized as inconsistent with the mortgagor's intentions (who likely never considered, or even knew of, the magic four unities of the common law). Many (but by no means all) jurisdictions today modify the title theory to treat the title held by the mortgagee (the lender) as one held only for purposes of securing the loan, a view that effectively makes a title theory state into a lien theory state for purposes of resolving this issue of severance. See, *e.g.*, *Brant v. Hargrove*, 129 Ariz. 475 (1981); *Hamel v. Gootkin*, 20 Cal. Rptr. 372 (Ct. App. 1962).

ii. **Lien theory of mortgages:** The lien theory of mortgages holds that the mortgagee (lender) only has a lien against the property (an inchoate right to seize title if the loan is not paid). On this view, a mortgage by one joint tenant makes no alteration to title and thus does ***not*** sever the joint tenancy. But another problem crops up, one that divides lien theory states (and title theory states that treat mortgages as liens for this purpose): Upon death of the mortgaging joint tenant while the loan is unpaid, does the surviving joint tenant have an interest that is ***wholly unencumbered by mortgage,*** or an interest that is ***burdened by the mortgage?*** The prevailing answer is that the surviving joint tenant takes free and clear of the mortgage.

Example: John and William owned Bottomland as joint tenants. John mortgaged his interest to Carl and Mary in order to secure a loan made by them to John's friend, Charles. Later, John died while the loan was unpaid. The Illinois Supreme Court held that (1) there was no severance, and (2) William owned Bottomland entirely free of the mortgage to Carl and Mary. The court reasoned that the mortgage burdened only John's interest and that since John's interest died with him, leaving only the previously unencumbered interest of William as the surviving title, the mortgage had died with John. See *Harms v. Sprague,* 473 N.E.2d 930 (Ill. 1974). Accord: *People v. Nogarr,* 330 P.2d 858 (Cal. Ct. App. 1958); *Ogilvie v. Idaho Bank & Trust Co.,* 582 P.2d 215 (Idaho 1978); *Irvin L. Young Foundation, Inc. v. Damrell,* 511 A.2d 1069 (Me. 1986).

(1) Criticism of majority view: The majority, or *Harms v. Sprague* view, is criticized on the ground that it penalizes the unsophisticated lender (since a savvy lender will never lend to just one joint tenant) and delivers a windfall to the surviving joint tenant. Consider the opposite result.

Example: Suppose that William took John's interest in Bottomland subject to the mortgage to Carl and Mary. This result would fully preserve William's survivorship rights and still preserve Carl and Mary's expectations that a half interest in Bottomland could be reached by them as security for their loan to Charles. After all, John always had the right to mortgage his interest, or even convey it outright (which would destroy William's survivorship right), so it does not seem unfair to William to allow him to take John's interest subject to the burden John placed upon it. Cf. Wis. Stat. § 700.24.

c. **Lease:** At common law, if one joint tenant leased his interest the joint tenancy was severed. The unity of interest was destroyed, since the leasing joint tenant retained only a reversion in the property. The lease, however, was valid. Cf. *Swartzbaugh v. Sampson,* 54 P.2d 73 (Cal. Ct. App. 1936). Most jurisdictions today do ***not*** regard a joint tenancy as severed by one joint tenant's lease of his interest. The survivorship right continues but, as with mortgages, the problem is presented of whether the lease survives the death of the leasing joint tenant. Most jurisdictions say "No."

Example: Johnson and Tenhet were joint tenants. Without Tenhet's knowledge or consent, Johnson leased the entire parcel to Boswell for ten years, then died three months later. Tenhet demanded that Boswell vacate. He refused, relying on his lease. The California Supreme Court held that (1) the lease did not sever the joint tenancy, and (2) the lease expired on the death of

Johnson, the lessor. See *Tenhet v. Boswell,* 554 P.2d 330 (Cal. 1976).

    i. Prospective lessee: As a practical matter, the *Tenhet v. Boswell* view requires a prospective lessee either (1) to examine title to be sure that the lessor is not a joint tenant, or (2) to insist that all joint tenants join in the lease. The opposite view, which rejects the idea that the lease expires with the lessor, allows the surviving joint tenant to take subject to the possessory interest of the lessee.

d. Agreement: A joint tenancy can be severed by agreement, so long as the intention is clearly manifested. This usually occurs in the context of marital dissolution.

Example: Betty and Aaron owned their residence as joint tenants. When they divorced they agreed that the house would be sold and the proceeds evenly divided between Betty and Aaron when (1) Betty remarried, or (2) their youngest child reached age 21, or (3) they agreed to sell. Before any of those events occurred, Betty died and Aaron claimed to own the entire house by virtue of the right of survivorship. The Colorado Supreme Court ruled that the agreement severed the joint tenancy because it clearly "evince[d] the intent to no longer hold the property in joint tenancy." Thus, because Betty was a tenant in common her 1/2 interest in the property passed to her children instead of to her ex-husband. See *Mann v. Bradley,* 535 P.2d 213 (Colo. 1975).

    i. Can be inferred: An agreement to sever can be inferred from the manner in which the parties deal with the property. See, *e.g., Thomas v. Johnson,* 297 N.E.2d 712 (Ill. Ct. App. 1973); *Mamalis v. Bornovas,* 297 A.2d 660 (N.H. 1972); *Wardlow v. Pozzi,* 338 P.2d 564 (Cal. Ct. App. 1959).

    However, an agreement to permit one joint tenant to have exclusive possession of the property does not destroy a joint tenancy, absent additional and specific evidence of intent to sever. See *Tindall v. Yeats,* 64 N.E.2d 903 (Ill. 1946).

e. Operation of law: Most severance issues begin with some voluntary act of a joint tenant that immediately implicates the four unities and thus, joint tenancy. But there are two recognized instances in which the law operates to sever a joint tenancy even in the absence of these voluntary acts.

    i. Murder: If one joint tenant murders another joint tenant, the usual result is severance of the joint tenancy by operation of law, thus turning the interests into tenancy in common. This sometimes occurs by statute, or by interpretation of a statute, but mostly results from judicial conclusion that murder is "inconsistent with the continued existence of the joint tenancy." *Duncan v. Vassaur,* 550 P.2d 929 (Okla. 1976). Accord: *Bradley v. Fox,* 129 N.E.2d 699 (Ill. 1955); *Grose v. Holland,* 211 S.W.2d 464 (Mo. 1948); Uniform Probate Code § 2-803.

  ii. **Simultaneous death:** Under section 3 of the Uniform Simultaneous Death Act, applicable in most states, the simultaneous death of joint tenants (*e.g.*, a plane crash) results in a division of the joint tenancy into separate shares.

D. Tenancy by the entirety:

1. **Nature of tenancy by the entirety:** A tenancy by the entirety is a *form of joint ownership available only to a husband and wife.* Like the joint tenancy, each tenant by the entirety has a right of survivorship. In essence, this is the common law's special joint tenancy for marital partners. The usual four unities of joint tenancy are required for its creation, plus the requirement of marriage between the tenants. There are, however, significant differences from the joint tenancy. About half the states recognize tenancy by the entirety.

   a. **One person:** The common law presumed that upon marriage, a husband and wife merged into *one legal person.* The woman lost her legal identity and became the legal ward of her husband. Before marriage she was a *femme sole;* after marriage she was a *femme covert.* Marriage produced one person, perhaps, but all male insofar as the law was concerned. Of course, we do not observe this disabling condition of married women today, but states that recognize tenancy by the entirety still observe the fiction that the tenancy by the entirety is owned by one person, with consequences that are discussed in the remainder of this section.

   b. **No severance:** A key attribute of the tenancy by the entirety is that it *may not be severed.* Unlike the joint tenancy, neither tenant acting alone can destroy the tenancy by the entirety. Thus, neither tenant may obtain partition (see p. 163, *supra*) nor can either spouse, acting alone, convey the entire estate. The right of survivorship is indestructible and continues despite such attempts.

2. **Creation:** At common law a conveyance to a husband and wife necessarily created a tenancy by the entirety. Since they were one person, legally speaking, they could not share a tenancy in common or joint tenancy. It was all or nothing, and the "all" was tenancy by the

entirety. No American jurisdiction observes this rule today. A husband and wife may own property as joint tenants, tenants in common, or as tenants by the entirety. Some states recognize the civil law institution of the "marital community" as the owner of property, and in these ***community property*** states a husband and wife compose a marital community that owns most property acquired by them during marriage. See p. 183, *infra*. Tenancies by the entirety are not recognized in the community property states.

  a. **Presumptions concerning creation:** Most states that recognize tenancies by the entirety observe a ***rebuttable presumption*** that a conveyance to a husband and wife creates a tenancy by the entirety. A minority of states recognizing the tenancy by the entirety presume (unless rebutted) that the ambiguous grant to a husband and wife creates a tenancy in common. Another minority of states recognizing tenancy by the entirety employ a rebuttable presumption that the ambiguous grant to a husband and wife creates a joint tenancy.

  b. **Failed attempts:** An attempt to create a tenancy by the entirety in unmarried persons will fail everywhere. Most states treat this failed attempt as creating a tenancy in common, though a few hold that it creates a joint tenancy since a joint tenancy is closer to a tenancy by the entirety than a tenancy in common.

3. **Operation of the tenancy by the entirety:** The modern tenancy by the entirety functions differently from its common law predecessor.

  a. **Common law:** The common law fiction that marriage produced one person, embodied by the husband, made the husband the controlling master of the tenancy by the entirety. The husband had the right to exclusive possession as well as his survivorship right. Both of those rights could be alienated by the husband *inter vivos*, and so could be seized by the husband's creditors. The wife had only her survivorship right, which could not be alienated by her without her husband's consent (and thus could not be seized by her creditors).

     Example: Harry and Wanda own Blackacre as tenants by the entirety. If Bank, Harry's creditor, seizes and acquires Harry's interest in Blackacre, Bank is entitled to exclusive possession of Blackacre during Harry's life. Wanda must move out. If Wanda predeceases Harry, Blackacre is owned solely by Bank. If Harry predeceases Wanda, Blackacre is owned solely by Wanda and

Bank has no further interest. Wanda's creditors, however, may then seize her possessory interest in Blackacre.

   i. **No longer exists:** The pure common law tenancy by the entirety no longer exists in the United States, except for such tenancies created in Massachusetts prior to 1980 (and, perhaps, a few very old tenancies in other jurisdictions). The male-biased common law tenancy by the entirety has been upheld against constitutional attack on equal protection grounds, on the theory that the estate is voluntarily chosen. See *D'Ercole v. D'Ercole,* 407 F. Supp. 1377 (D. Mass. 1976).

b. **Modern operation of the tenancy by the entirety:** The modern tenancy by the entirety treats both spouses as equals. The principal source of this change has been the Married Women's Property Acts. These acts were adopted by every state in the mid-19th century in order to eliminate the legal disabilities placed on married women by the common law. They did so by restoring to a married woman her separate legal identity which the common law took away from her on the occasion of her marriage. Courts then interpreted these acts, as applied to a tenancy by the entirety, to equalize the interests of husband and wife in the tenancy. But this could be done in one of two ways: Either (1) the ***woman acquired equal rights with the man to alienate her possession and survivorship rights,*** or (2) ***neither spouse was permitted to alienate their possession and survivorship rights.***

   i. **Equal right to alienate:** Perhaps a half dozen states (including Alaska, Oregon, New York, and New Jersey) provide that either spouse may alienate their possession or survivorship rights in a tenancy by the entirety. The principal effect of this version of equality, which gives the wife the same rights the husband had at common law, is to ***enable her creditors to seize her possessory interest*** in the tenancy but not the survivorship right. The husband's possessory interest, of course, was always subject to seizure by his creditors.

   ii. **Neither spouse may alienate:** The majority of states recognizing tenancy by the entirety provide that neither spouse may alienate their possession or survivorship rights in a tenancy by the entirety. The principal effect of this version of equality, which places the husband on the same footing as the wife at common law with respect to a tenancy by the entirety, is that it ***prevents the creditors of either spouse from seizure of their interest*** in the tenancy. See, *e.g.*,

Sawada v. Endo, 561 P.2d 1291 (Hawaii 1977). The rationale for this view is partly the fiction of one person (the estate is owned by the marital couple, not the constituent partners), partly the view that contract creditors have ample opportunity to insist on both spouses pledging the property as security for extensions of credit, and partly the view that tort creditors of a single spouse ought not be permitted to seize a portion of the family residence with dangerous consequences to the innocent spouse.

    iii. Variations on the theme: A few states recognizing tenancy by the entirety hold that creditors can seize the ***survivorship right*** of a spouse but ***not the possessory rights*** of either spouse. See, *e.g.*, *Fischre v. United States*, 852 F. Supp. 628 (W.D. Mich. 1994) (applying Michigan law).

    Example: Creditor obtains a judgment lien against Henry, owner with Willa of Blackacre in tenancy by the entirety. If Willa predeceases Henry, Creditor may enforce the lien on Blackacre, owned now entirely by Henry. If Henry predeceases Willa, Creditor's lien is extinguished with respect to Blackacre. If Henry and Willa divorce, or Henry and Willa join together to convey Blackacre, Creditor can enforce the lien against Henry's share of Blackacre, since the tenancy by the entirety would have terminated.

4. Termination: A tenancy by the entirety is terminated (1) by death of a spouse, (2) divorce, or (3) joint action of both spouses to convey the property held in tenancy by the entirety. Upon divorce, most states convert a tenancy by the entirety into a tenancy in common, but a few inexplicably convert it into a joint tenancy.

5. Personal property: Common law did not recognize a tenancy by the entirety in personal property because the husband, upon marriage, became the sole owner of his wife's personal property. Most states today permit tenancies by the entirety in most forms of personal property. Some forms of personal property (*e.g.*, deposit accounts) are not susceptible to tenancy by the entirety because it is impossible to maintain inviolate survivorship rights when either spouse can withdraw the deposited property at any time.

E. Partnerships and coparceny:

1. Nature of partnership tenancy: Tenancy in partnership is inextricably connected to the rights and obligations of business partners. The property is owned by the partnership and each partner has an interest in the property via their partnership interest. The details of partnership are covered in courses in Business Associations, not usually in Property courses.

2. **Nature of coparceny:** Coparceny is extinct. The English common law system of primogeniture made the first born son the sole heir. If a decedent had no sons, his daughters inherited as coparcenors, an estate that was a bit like tenancy in common. Since primogeniture never took root in America, coparceny never had occasion to develop. Good riddance.

II. RIGHTS AND OBLIGATIONS OF CONCURRENT OWNERS

A. **Introduction:** In general, the rights and obligations of co-owners are the same regardless of the type of concurrent ownership. The exceptions, of course, are the rights and duties ***inherent in the type of concurrent ownership,*** *e.g.*, the right of survivorship that forms part of the joint tenancy and tenancy by the entirety, or the inseverable nature of the tenancy by the entirety. Those exceptional issues have been discussed on p. 163, *supra*.

B. **Partition:** A joint tenant or a tenant in common may demand ***partition*** of the property at any time and for any reason, or no reason at all. A tenant by the entirety may not demand partition — the effective remedy is divorce. Absent agreement among the parties, partition is accomplished by a suit in equity. The court will order ***either*** (1) ***physical division*** of the property, or (2) ***sale and division of the sale proceeds.*** Any other claims among the parties (*e.g.*, for an accounting or for rent — see pp. 179 and 181, *infra*) will also be resolved in the same proceeding.

1. **Partition in kind:** Physical division of the property (called ***partition in kind***) is the preferred method. Courts will order partition in kind unless a party can prove either (1) that physical partition is ***impossible*** or ***extremely impractical***, or (2) that physical partition is ***not in the best interest of all parties.*** See, *e.g.*, *Delfino v. Vealencis*, 436 A.2d 27 (Conn. 1980). Evidence germane to the "best interest" prong includes the economic costs (or gain) involved in physical partition, as well as the more subjective costs imposed on a tenant in possession by ordering partition by sale. Compare the following examples.

Example 1: Helen owned Twenty acres as a tenant in common with Angelo. Helen lived on a portion of the property and operated a garbage hauling business from there. Angelo wished to develop the property into single family residences and so demanded partition by sale. Although the evidence suggested that the total value of the property would be maximized by sale and development, the Connecticut Supreme Court held that it was not in the best interest of ***all parties*** (including Helen) to sell the entire property. Helen's value of continued possession (secured by physical partition) was sufficient to convince the court that partition in kind should be ordered. *Delfino v. Vealencis,* 436 A.2d 27 (Conn. 1980).

Example 2: Karl and his twin sons lived on and farmed a 160 acre farm, in which they owned a 1/3 interest as tenants in common with the Baumans, a group of relatives who owned fractional shares ranging from 1/12 to 2/9. The Baumans sought and obtained partition by sale under a statute authorizing partition by sale if physical partition could not be accomplished without "great prejudice to the owners."

The South Dakota Supreme Court gave little weight to the value of continued possession to Karl and his sons, relying almost entirely on the conclusion that division of the farm into parcels ranging in size from 13.33 acres to 53.33 acres would "materially depreciate its value, both as to salability and ... use for agricultural purposes." The court did not even consider the possibility that the Baumans could unite to sell their 106.67 acre block after physical partition. *Johnson v. Hendrickson,* 24 N.W.2d 914 (S.D. 1946).

    a. Division in equal shares: Courts strive to divide property so that the value of each divided parcel (as a fraction of the value of the entire property) is equal to the ownership share of the recipient. If not, the recipient of the disproportionately valuable parcel is obligated to pay enough cash to the other tenant(s) to equalize values.

    Example: Ed and Louise own Blackacre as tenants in common. Louise has a 2/3 interest, Ed owns a 1/3 interest. The value of Blackacre is $120,000. If, after partition in kind, Ed's parcel is worth $50,000 and Louise's is worth $70,000, Ed will owe Louise $10,000 cash to equalize their proportionate shares.

2. Partition by sale: Even though partition by sale is not favored by courts it is probably the most common method of partition. This is because it is impractical or impossible physically to divide most real property in America. Houses, condominiums, office buildings, warehouses, retail stores are all ill-suited to physical division. Rural undeveloped land is the most likely candidate for physical division. After a partition by sale, the net proceeds are divided among the co-owners in proportion to their ownership interests. In the absence of express evidence in title of unequal shares, courts employ a rebuttable presumption that each co-owner is entitled to an equal share of the proceeds.

3. **Agreement not to partition:** Though courts often say that "partition between cotenants is an absolute right," an agreement between cotenants not to partition is *enforceable* if (1) it *clearly manifests the parties' intent not to partition,* and (2) its *duration is limited to a reasonable period of time.*

   Example 1: Marion and Alexandra, husband and wife, separated and entered into an agreement by which they promised not to "do or permit anything [to be done] to defeat the common tenancy" of Marion and Alexandra in certain properties for the remainder of their joint lives. A New Jersey appellate court found this to be a sufficiently clear expression of their intent not to partition. Its duration was reasonably limited because it would expire upon the death of either party, and both Marion and Alexandra were of "advanced age" (apparently about 60 when they entered into the agreement). *Michalski v. Michalski,* 142 A.2d 645 (N.J. Super. 1958).

   Because partition is inherently equitable, a non-partition agreement (even if otherwise enforceable) will be enforced only if it is "fair and equitable." Changed circumstances are especially relevant to this inquiry.

   Example 2: In their 1949 non-partition agreement, Marion and Alexandra promised to treat each other "with kindness and respect" and agreed that they would continue to reside together in their home. By 1951 they were not living together in the home and had embarked on a continuous bout of civil and criminal litigation against each other that was merrily bubbling along in 1958, when a New Jersey appellate court ruled that "the circumstances have so changed that it would be inequitable to deny partition. The intent of the parties has been entirely destroyed." *Michalski v. Michalski,* 142 A.2d 645 (N.J. Super. (1958).

C. **Rents, profits, and possession:** Each co-owner has the right to possess the entire property and no co-owner may exclude his fellow co-owners. If co-owners cannot agree on how they share possession, the "default" rules discussed here apply.

   1. **Exclusive possession by one co-owner:** This possession is presumptively legitimate. If it is pursuant to agreement of all co-owners it is conclusively valid. If not by agreement, the co-tenant in exclusive possession has the following obligations to his co-tenants.

      a. **Rental value of exclusive possession:** Jurisdictions split on the question of whether the co-tenant in exclusive possession is liable to his co-tenants for their share of the fair rental value of his exclusive possession.

Example: Vicki and Beth are equal co-tenants in Blackacre. If Vicki goes into exclusive possession does she owe Beth 1/2 the fair rental value of Blackacre as a whole? Here are the two views on this question.

  i. **No liability absent ouster or special duty:** The *majority rule* is that a co-tenant in exclusive possession has no liability for her share of the rental value of possession unless: (1) the other co-tenants have been *ousted,* or (2) the co-tenant in possession owes a *fiduciary duty* to the other co-tenants, or (3) the co-tenant in possession has *agreed to pay rent.* This rule makes sense because the co-tenant in possession is entitled to be there. The exceptions reflect instances in which the co-tenant in possession has voluntarily assumed a duty to his co-tenants (by agreement to pay rent or by acting as a fiduciary) or has prevented his co-tenants from exercising their equal right to possession (*ouster*). The corollary to this rule is that the co-tenant validly in exclusive possession is obligated to pay the "carrying costs" of the property (*e.g.*, mortgage payments, taxes, utilities, maintenance) up to the fair rental value of the property. Any excess costs must be shared ratably by all co-tenants. *Ouster* occurs if the tenant in exclusive possession *either:* (1) actually *prevents or bars physical entry by a co-tenant,* or (2) *denies the co-tenant's claim to title.* The former can occur by such things as changing the locks; the latter can occur by express statements denying that the co-tenant out of possession has any valid claim of ownership of the property, but can also be implied from ignoring or refusal of a non-possessory co-tenant's demand for reasonable rental. Finding ouster by implication from refusal to pay rent that is not owed, absent ouster, seems virtually to eliminate the ouster requirement as a precondition for the obligation to pay rent.

  ii. **Liability for rent:** The *minority rule* is that the co-tenant in exclusive possession is liable to co-tenants out of possession for their share of the fair rental value of the occupied premises, *unless there has been an agreement among the parties to excuse the tenant in possession from this obligation.* On this view, there is no need to show ouster, or agreement to pay rent, or the presence of a fiduciary obligation to the co-tenants out of possession. Indeed, the burden is on the co-tenant in possession to prove the existence of an agreement excusing him from the obligation to pay rent. This rule is designed to induce agreements among the parties by placing the burden on the tenant in possession (the one is gaining the economic value of occupancy) to pay or prove an agreement not to pay. But this rule also undercuts the general principle that a co-tenant is entitled to possess the whole.

2. **Rents from third parties:** A co-tenant who receives rents on the property from a third party is obligated to account to his co-tenants for those rents. If the rents or other income received by a co-tenant are greater than the co-tenant's share, he is obligated to pay the excess to the other co-tenants.

    Example: Anne and Clarke own Blackacre as equal co-tenants. A portion of Blackacre is rented to Ajax for $500/month and the remainder is rented to Hector for $700/month. If Clarke receives Hector's rent and Anne receives the rent from Ajax, both must account to each other for the rents they received, and Clarke must pay $100 to Anne.

    a. **Duty to account is continuing one:** This duty to account is a continuing one and may be enforced at any time during the co-tenancy, upon partition, or within the period of the statute of limitations following expiration of the co-tenancy.

3. **Profits from the land:** The normal rules regarding possession (see p. 179, *supra*) apply to exclusive possession for farming, animal husbandry, or other agricultural uses. But if a co-tenant permanently removes an asset from the land, thus reducing its value, he must account to co-tenants. If minerals are removed, the co-tenant must pay to the other co-tenants their proportionate share of the value of the removed minerals. Other natural resources, like standing timber, may be removed by a co-tenant without payment to other co-tenants so long as the co-tenant does not cut more than her share of the total timber. Some states require the consent of all co-tenants to the cutting of timber.

D. **Accounting for the costs of ownership:** Subject to the exceptions set forth on p. 179, *supra*, and others discussed here, each co-tenant is liable for his proportionate share of the costs of ownership — mostly mortgage payments, taxes, repairs, and maintenance.

1. **Mortgage payments:** Mortgage payments consist of ***principal*** and ***interest.*** A co-tenant's payment of a disproportionate share of these items is treated differently.

a. Interest: Each co-tenant is obligated to pay his proportionate share of mortgage interest. A co-tenant who pays more than his share can force the other co-tenants to reimburse him for their share immediately, upon partition, or within the limitations period following the end of the co-tenancy.

   b. Principal: Each co-tenant is obligated to pay his proportionate share of the mortgage principal, but the co-tenant who pays more than his share of the mortgage principal has additional remedies. The paying co-tenant succeeds to the mortgagee's (lender's) rights. This is called ***subrogation.*** The paying co-tenant can enforce all the rights and powers of the mortgagee against his co-tenants who fail to pay their share of the principal, including foreclosure sale.

2. **Taxes:** Each co-tenant is obligated to pay his proportionate share of the taxes, and a co-tenant who pays more than his share can recover the excess from his fellow co-tenants at any time during the tenancy, upon partition, or within the limitations period after cessation of co-tenancy.

3. **Repairs:** A co-tenant has no obligation to repair his property. If he wishes to let it fall into ruin, that is his choice. The law will not generally compel prudent and responsible behavior towards one's own affairs. Accordingly, a co-tenant who voluntarily repairs the property may not force his co-tenants to reimburse him for their share of the repairs. But the repairing co-tenant can recover those excess repair costs in two situations.

   a. Accounting for rents: If a repairing co-tenant is under a duty to account to his fellow co-tenants for rent (whether received from third parties or for the reasonable rental value of exclusive occupancy) the repairing co-tenant may deduct from the rents due the other co-tenants their share of the repair costs incurred by the repairing co-tenant.

   b. Partition: Upon partition, a repairing co-tenant is entitled to be reimbursed for the repair costs in excess of her share. If partition is by sale, this will occur by a cash reimbursement from the sale proceeds before pro rata distribution to all co-tenants. If partition is in kind, the repairing co-tenant will either receive cash reimbursement from the other co-tenants before physical division or the repairing co-tenant will receive a larger parcel, representing reimbursement in kind.

4. **Improvements:** No co-tenant has a duty to improve property. Indeed, co-tenants may disagree about what constitutes an improvement, or what improvement is optimal. Accordingly, an

improving co-tenant may not recover from her fellow co-tenants their pro rata share of the cost of the improvements. Upon partition, or if the improving co-tenant is under a duty to account to co-tenants for rent, the improving co-tenant is entitled to ***recover only the value added by the improvements, not the cost of the improvement***. If the improvements add no value, there is no recovery. If the value added is less than the cost of the improvement, the improver is only entitled to her fellow co-tenants' share of the added value.

E. Adverse possession: Co-tenants can occupy adversely to their fellow co-tenants, but it takes more than mere possession to do so, since every co-tenant is entitled to be in possession. A co-tenant must give his co-tenants ***absolutely clear and unequivocal notice that he claims exclusive and sole title*** in order for adverse possession to begin. Nothing less will do.

F. Implied fiduciaries: In general, co-tenants have no fiduciary duties to each other. A co-tenant can, of course, voluntarily assume such a duty. Law will imply that duty, however, when one co-tenant acts to gain an advantage of title over his fellow co-tenants.

Example: Bert and Ernie own Blackacre as co-tenants. They fail to pay the property taxes and Blackacre is sold by the government at a tax foreclosure sale. Bert buys Blackacre at that sale for a fraction of its fair market value. Bert is not the sole owner of Blackacre. He will be held to a fiduciary obligation toward Ernie, and Ernie has the right to pay his share of the purchase price to Bert in order to redeem his co-tenancy. See, *e.g., Massey v. Prothero,* 664 P.2d 1176 (Utah 1983). The same principle applies to mortgage foreclosure sales. See, *e.g., Barr v. Eason,* 728 S.W.2d 183 (Ark. 1987).

III. MARITAL INTERESTS

A. Introduction: Many of the property issues involved in the law governing the property of married people are covered in other courses dealing with marital dissolution, family, and related issues. These issues are discussed here only to the depth commonly reached in many survey courses of Property.

B. The common law system: The pure common law system of marital property no longer exists in any relevant jurisdiction, but knowledge of its structure will help you in understanding the many current versions of marital property.

1. **Femme sole and femme covert:** A single woman (a ***femme sole***) had power to use, dispose, and possess her own property. While that

sounds axiomatic, a married woman (a *femme covert*) had almost none of those rights. One of my students summed this up with the quip, "Life's a bitch, and then you get married." Common law said husband and wife were one, but the husband was the One. The severity of these rules was evaded by the very wealthy through the creation of elaborate marriage settlements, usually involving trusts, that were designed to place a friendly and compliant trustee in nominal control over a married woman's property.

2. **Husband *uber alles*:** With the marriage vow the common law bestowed *jure uxoris* on the husband: the right to possess, use or convey all of his wife's property except her clothes and jewelry for the duration of the marriage. Even her earnings were his. In the hands of an honorable and capable husband in a happy marriage, *jure uxoris* preserved or increased the value of the wife's property. In the hands of a rogue, *jure uxoris* was license to steal. Like the dodo, *jure uxoris* is extinct.

3. **Wife's rights:** A wife had no legal control of her property, but had some inchoate property rights

    a. **Support:** A wife had the right of *support* from her husband. Thus, in the event of divorce, the husband was obliged to continue support by paying *alimony* to her.

    b. **Dower:** On death of her husband, a wife had the ***right of dower.*** Dower was the right to a ***life estate*** in ***1/3*** of each and every ***possessory freehold estate*** the husband enjoyed at ***any point during the marriage*** which was ***capable of inheritance by children born of the marriage.*** This was a valuable right for a widow of a wealthy landowner or freeholding tradesman in 17th or 18th century England, but was useless to those without land ownership.

        i. **Each freehold ever possessed:** The dower right attached to every freehold the husband possessed that was capable of inheritance by children of the marriage. Thus dower did ***not*** attach to the husband's life estates, leaseholds, personal property, equitable interests, future interests, or any possessory freehold held in tenancy by the entirety with the wife or in joint tenancy, whether with the wife or a third party. The common law's gift to the bride was a dower right in all the inheritable freeholds her husband possessed at the moment of the ceremony, ***and*** to every additional such freehold he possessed in the future during their marriage. But, as seen from the list of property to which dower did not attach, it was an easy matter for a husband to acquire property in a manner that avoided dower.

ii. **Scope and release of dower:** The inchoate dower right, once attached, could only be removed by divorce or with the wife's consent.

Example 1: Harry owns Blackacre in fee simple while married to Molly. Harry mortgages Blackacre, then defaults on the mortgage, and Bank buys it at foreclosure sale. Bank conveys Blackacre to Zelmo. Harry dies. Molly is entitled to a life estate in 1/3 of Blackacre. Zelmo must turn over to Molly possession of 1/3 of Blackacre or 1/3 of the rents and profits from Blackacre.

Example 2: Suppose Harry paid off the mortgage, then conveyed Blackacre to Arnie without Molly signing anything. Upon Harry's death Molly is entitled to dower in Blackacre, since she never released her dower.

Example 3: Molly and Harry divorce. Molly's inchoate dower rights are irrevocably extinguished. But if Molly and Harry simply separate and remain legally married, Molly's inchoate dower rights are unaffected.

iii. **Operation of dower:** A physical third of all properties subject to dower that were capable of physical division was set aside for the wife's life estate. If a property was not susceptible to division the wife received 1/3 of the rents or profits from the land for the remainder of her life.

iv. **Defeasible fees:** Most jurisdictions hold that a dower interest in a defeasible fee ends if the limiting condition occurs, reasoning that the dower interest is derived from the husband's title, which was defeasible. A few reject this logic and hold that dower is indefeasible, a conclusion permitting a widow to flout limiting conditions during her lifetime.

Example: By dower, Georgia acquired a life estate in Thirdacre, a property her husband had acquired "so long as Thirdacre is used for agricultural purposes." A jurisdiction treating dower as indestructible would permit Georgia to erect a factory on Thirdacre and retain possession. Of course, the property would revert to the grantor as soon as Georgia died, since the limiting condition would be broken. But if Georgia is a hale and hearty 30 year old, and decides it is economically advantageous to construct a factory on Thirdacre, the frustration of the grantor's pastoral land use intention is irrevocable. This might lead to some courts treating the limiting condition as a land use servitude, enforceable by an injunction preventing the factory construction or by recovery of damages resulting from its construction. See Chapter 6, p. 197, *infra*.

    v. **Abolition:** Less than ten states continue to observe dower. In most dower has been abolished by statute, usually replaced by an analogous right usually known as the ***elective share***. See p. 193, *infra*. Some states that observe dower have made the widow's share more generous: a fee simple interest in 1/3 or even 1/2 of dower lands.

4. **Curtesy:** Common law gave a husband who survived his wife a right similar to dower, called ***curtesy***. Curtesy attached to ***all possessory interests in land*** of the wife, ***including equitable possessory interests***. Thus, while the marriage settlement trust avoided *jure uxoris*, it did not evade curtesy. But curtesy only attached if ***issue were born to the marriage***. Once a child was born, even if it later died, curtesy attached. Curtesy no longer exists in the United States. Where dower has been abolished so has curtesy. Where dower exists, the curtesy right is congruent with dower.

C. **The modern (mostly statutory) "common law" system:** Every common law marital property jurisdiction (as distinguished from community property states, see p. 188, *infra*) has altered the common law system substantially. Statutes vary considerably, but set forth below are the major themes of these statutory alterations.

1. **Rights on divorce:** Almost every jurisdiction has adopted some form of an ***equitable distribution*** statute. These statutes are designed to produce an equitable (usually equal) division of the marital property subject to the statute. Thus, differences occur in the way the states define what marital property is subject to equitable distribution. Some say all property owned by either spouse, whenever and however acquired. Others limit equitable distribution to property acquired during marriage, no matter how. Still others limit equitable distribution to property acquired by the earnings of the marital partners. Some kinds of personal property, like clothing and jewelry, are often exempted.

    a. **Professional skills and credentials:** A major issue is whether professional degrees and skills acquired during marriage are subject to equitable distribution. What happens when one spouse supports another while he or she obtains a professional degree or some similar enhancement of earnings power? Courts divide three ways.

    i. **Not property:** Some states hold that professional degrees and skills are not property, but simply personal accomplishments that may or may not produce property, and thus not subject to equitable distribution. See, *e.g.*, *In re Marriage of Graham*, 574 P.2d 75 (Colo. 1978).

    ii. **Property subject to equitable distribution:** New York treats professional degrees and enhanced professional skills as property subject to equitable distribution. See *O'Brien v. O'Brien*, 489 N.E.2d 712 (N.Y. 1985) (professional degree); *Elkus v. Elkus,* 572 N.Y.S.2d 901 (Sup. Ct. 1991) (enhanced skill as opera mezzo-soprano). Because professional degrees and skills cannot be divided and conveyed, this position requires the degree holder to pay a lump sum now or a portion of future earnings to satisfy equitable distribution.

    iii. **Restitution:** Some states take the middling course of requiring the degree-enhanced spouse to reimburse the supporting spouse for the financial support (***"reimbursement alimony"***). See, *e.g.*, *Mahoney v. Mahoney,* 453 A.2d 527 (N.J. 1982).

2. **Rights on death:** In place of dower, most states give the surviving spouse the right to receive in fee simple a fraction (usually 1/2) of all property owned by the deceased spouse at his or her death. This is called an ***elective share*** because a surviving spouse may elect this share or to take under the deceased spouse's will, ***but can't have both***. Some states recognizing dower give a surviving spouse the further election of whether to take dower or a statutory elective share.

    a. **Difference between dower and elective share:** The elective share applies to ***all property of the deceased spouse*** but ***only with respect to property owned at the spouse's death.*** Thus the elective share is broader than dower ("***all*** property" and fee simple instead of a life estate) and narrower ("only property owned at spouse's death").

    b. **Avoidance of the elective share:** A spouse sometimes tries to avoid the elective share by omitting his spouse from the will, and transferring all his property to a trust, retaining an income interest for life, remainder in someone other than the spouse.

    Example: Oscar, married to Hilda, conveys all his property to his brother Sam, as trustee, under directions to pay to Oscar for life the income and such principal as necessary to support Oscar, then to distribute the principal outright and free of trust to Minnie, Oscar's paramour. (Oscar's will, which disposes of only the incidental property of Oscar that was not placed in trust, leaves everything to Minnie.)

   i. **Nature of the trust:** This works to defeat the elective share if the trust is irrevocable (since the spouse owns no property at death) but is more problematic if the trust is revocable. Some states treat a revocable trust just like an irrevocable one, so long as the assets are conveyed to the trust prior to death. Others refuse to recognize a revocable trust if the settlor's intent was to defeat the elective share. Still other states focus on how much real control the settlor retained over the trust assets — the more control retained, the more likely that the surviving spouse's elective share will reach the trust assets.

3. **Antenuptial agreements and spousal contracts:**

   - **Antenuptial agreements:** Agreements made between prospective spouses prior to marriage purporting to govern property division upon divorce were not generally enforceable at common law. Jurisdictions today split on their enforceability. The emerging standard is that such agreements are enforceable if (1) the parties' assets and earnings power have been fully revealed to each other, and (2) the substantive terms of the agreement are not unconscionable. See, *e.g.*, Uniform Marital Property Act § 10(g); Uniform Premarital Agreement Act § 6.

   - **Spousal contracts:** In community property states, spouses may agree to transmute separate property into community property and to divide community property into separate property. It is an open question, however, whether agreements between spouses in a common law jurisdiction to hold their property as community property will be enforced. Generally, a contract between spouses by which one spouse agrees to care for another in return for property to be received at the death of the invalid spouse is not enforceable for want of consideration, since spouses are obliged to care for one another. See, *e.g.*, *Borelli v. Brusseau,* 16 Cal. Rptr. 2d 16 (Ct. App. 1993).

D. **Community property:**

1. **Origins and concept:** The civil law of Spain and France recognizes marriage as creating a "marital community" of husband and wife, and treats that community, rather than its constituent members, as the owner of most property acquired during marriage. The

fundamental premise of community property is that each spouse is an equal partner in marriage, and that each spouse has an equal claim to the material possessions that are derived from the efforts of either spouse during marriage. By contrast, the pure common law system subjugated a wife to her husband. The modern common law system is, of course, far more equitable and produces results that often are not dramatically different from community property. Community property came to America through French and Spanish colonization and was absorbed into the United States along with formerly French or Spanish territory. Arizona, California, Idaho, Louisiana, Nevada, New Mexico, Texas, and Washington are the only states recognizing community property. This discussion of community property is cursory, adequate for the survey course in Property but not detailed enough for a separate course in Community Property.

    a. Uniform Marital Property Act: The Uniform Marital Property Act, proposed in 1983, is based on community law principles and, for all practical purposes, is a community property regime. Wisconsin is the only state to have adopted the UMPA. The UMPA defines *marital property* to include all property acquired during marriage except through gift, devise, or inheritance. Everything else is *individual property.*

2. **Definition of community property;** American community property systems define community property as the *earnings during marriage* of either spouse and *all property acquired from such earnings.* This definition *excludes* property acquired *before marriage* or acquired during marriage *by gift, devise, or inheritance.* Such property is *separate property* and is owned solely by that spouse. The character of property — separate or community — may *not be changed except by agreement of both spouses.* When it is difficult to determine the character of property, courts apply a *rebuttable presumption that the property is community property.*

    a. Tracing, not title: Once property becomes community character, it retains that character even if it is exchanged for other property and *regardless of its title.* If its original source can be *traced to community property* it is community property, absent agreement of both spouses to change its character.

    Example: Irene, married to Al, lives in a community property state. She deposits one of her paychecks in a deposit account owned solely by Irene. She then uses the money in the deposit account to purchase a painting, which she trades for a vacation home, taking title in her name alone. Since the source of this chain of assets — deposit account to painting to second home — was Irene's earnings during marriage, each of these assets are community property. Title in Irene's name doesn't matter if the property's source can be traced to community funds. The vacation home is community property and Al has an equal interest in it.

b. Commingling of separate and community property: The tracing rule applies to commingled property as well. If the sources of commingled property can be identified accurately as separate or community funds, the commingled property will be divided into separate and community portions. But if it is ***impossible to trace*** the sources of commingled funds, the entire property will be ***presumed to be community property.*** In the absence of accurate records, commingled property will, in practice, become community property. A variation on this principle occurs when a partially paid-for asset is brought to a marriage and the remainder of the purchase price is paid with community funds. There are three approaches to this problem.

   i. Inception of right: This approach (followed by Texas) holds that the character of the property is determined at the inception of the legal right to the property.

   ii. Time of vesting: This approach (followed by Idaho and New Mexico) holds that the character of the property is determined when title passes.

   iii. Pro-rata apportionment: This approach (followed by California and Washington) holds that the percentage of the purchase price paid prior to marriage establishes the portion of the property that is separate, and the percentage of the purchase price paid with community funds establishes the community interest in the property.

   Example: Al enters into an installment sale contract to purchase a building lot for $45,000. He pays a total of $15,000 under the contract, then marries Jane. The remaining $30,000 is paid with the combined earnings of Al and Jane. Then Al and Jane divorce. The lot is worth $120,000. Who owns the lot?

   - In Texas, an ***inception of right*** state, the lot is Al's separate property (because Al acquired a contract right in the property before marriage), but the community is entitled to return of $30,000 plus interest (but Al is entitled to half this sum). Ignoring interest, Jane gets $15,000; Al gets

$105,000. See *McCurdy v. McCurdy.* 372 S.W.2d 381 (Tex. Civ. App. 1963).

- In Idaho or New Mexico, ***time of vesting*** states, the lot is community property because title did not pass until the payments were completely made. Al and Jane each get $60,000 out of the lot.

- In California or Washington, ***pro-rata apportionment*** states, 1/3 of the lot is Al's separate property, and 2/3 is community property. Al's share is $80,000 (consisting of $40,000 separate property and his equal $40,000 share of the community property). Jane's share is $40,000, one-half of the community's 2/3 interest in the lot. See, *e.g.*, *Estate of Gulstine,* 6 P.2d 628 (Wash. 1932).

c. **Agreement transmuting the character of property:** So long as both spouses are fully informed about the consequences of their actions, an agreement to transmute community property into separate property or separate property into community property will be enforced.

d. **Income from separate property:** The general rule is that income earned from separate property retains its character as separate property. Three states (Texas, Louisiana, and Idaho) hold that income earned from separate property is community property.

e. **Pensions:** Vested pension rights are community property because they are the fruits of earnings. The status of non-vested pension rights is less clear. California and Nevada treat such rights as community property. See *In re Marriage of Brown*, 544 P.2d 561 (Cal. 1976); *Gemma v. Gemma*, 778 P.2d 429 (Nev. 1989).

f. **Personal injury damages:** The portion of personal injury damage awards that is compensation for ***pain and suffering*** is ***separate property,*** but the portion that is compensation for ***lost earnings*** is ***community property.*** See, *e.g.*, *Rogers v. Yellowstone Park Co.,* 539 P.2d 566 (Idaho 1975).

g. **Increased value of separate property from community efforts:** A spouse may devote time and energy to the management of his or her separate property. The community is entitled to share in the value added to the separate property by those efforts. The amount of the community's share depends on whether the increased value of the separate property is primarily attributable to the ***spouse's personal effort*** or to the ***capital investment.*** If the spouse's personal effort produced the increased value, the increment is community property (after deduction of a fair rate return on the separate capital investment.

Example: Hugo owned an art gallery and then married Alice. Hugo's capital investment in the gallery at the time of marriage was $100,000. During the marriage the art gallery prospered because of Hugo's unerring eye for art that would be highly in demand. As a result, when Hugo and Alice divorced after 10 years of marriage, the gallery was worth $500,000. The increment ($400,000) is due primarily to Hugo's personal efforts. But first Hugo must receive a reasonable rate of return on his separate capital investment of $100,000. Assume 6% annually is a reasonable rate of return. Ignoring compounding, Hugo would be entitled to receive, as his separate property, 6% of $100,000 (or $6,000) multiplied by 10 years ($60,000). The remainder of the increment ($340,000) is community property (of which Hugo and Alice are each entitled to half).

i. **Capital investments:** If the increased value is due to the capital investment, the community's share is simply the value of the spouse's services; the remainder is separate property.

Example: Suppose when Hugo married Alice he also had a $100,000 portfolio of stocks and bonds. Hugo hired Lou to manage the portfolio, paying Lou from his separate property. Hugo took no active role in managing the portfolio. Ten years later, when Hugo and Alice divorce, the portfolio is worth $500,000. The community's share of this increase is the value of Hugo's services, which appears to be practically nil. Call it $10,000, of which half belongs to Hugo. The remainder of the increment ($390,000) is Hugo's separate property.

ii. **Inflation:** Some courts hold that the community is entitled to share in the increased value of separate property attributable to inflation in the proportion that the community has contributed to acquisition cost. See, *e.g.*, *In re Marriage of Elam*, 650 P.2d 213 (Wash. 1982).

3. **Management of community property:** Husband and wife have equal management powers. Either spouse, acting alone, may sell, lease, or otherwise deal with community property. Of course, neither spouse acting alone may convey their ***interest in the community*** to a stranger. And, as a practical matter, both spouses will be required to join in a conveyance of real property held as community property. But the equal management rule permits either spouse to

invest or otherwise deal with deposit or investment accounts. Each spouse has a fiduciary duty towards the other spouse in the management of community affairs. States differ with respect to gifts: some hold that gifts of community property may not be made by a single spouse, others hold that only gifts defrauding a spouse may be set aside, and still others hold that either spouse may make "reasonable" gifts from community funds. The exception to the equal management rule is that each spouse is the sole manager of any business carried on by the spouse, even if the business itself is a community asset.

4. **Rights upon divorce:** At divorce, each spouse is entitled to half of the community property and, of course, all of their separate property.

5. **Rights upon death:** Upon death of one spouse, the one-half interest of the decedent spouse in the community property is disposed of according to the decedent spouse's will. In the absence of a will, it descends by intestate succession.

   Example: Donald, married to Marla and residing in a community property state dies, devising all his property to Babette. Babette takes a half interest, as a tenant in common with Marla, in all the former community property. If Donald died intestate, survived by Marla and Zoe, their child, Zoe would take Donald's half interest in the former community property, as a tenant in common with Marla.

6. **Creditors' rights:** In general, debts incurred during marriage are presumed to be community obligations and the community's assets are liable for their satisfaction. Debts incurred by a spouse prior to marriage are separate obligations and only that spouse's separate property is exposed to the creditor. The extent to which separate creditors may reach community property is in disarray.

E. **"Quasi-marital" property — unmarried cohabitants:**

1. **Common law marriage:** Common law recognized a de facto marriage between a man and woman if they were cohabitants, agreed between themselves to be husband and wife, and thereafter represented to the public that they were husband and wife. The status thus acquired was indistinguishable from ceremonial marriage. Common law marriage is still recognized in many states, although a number have abolished the doctrine.

2. **Contracts:** Unmarried cohabitants may create *express contracts* to govern their property upon death or termination of the relationship in a fashion similar to that delivered by law to married couples. Such agreements are generally enforceable. See, *e.g.*, *Cook v. Cook*,

691 P.2d 664 (Ariz. 1984). This extends to contracts *implied from the parties' conduct.* See, *e.g., Marvin v. Marvin,* 557 P.2d 106 (Cal. 1976). But see *Hewitt v. Hewitt,* 394 N.E.2d 1204 (Ill. 1979), in which Illinois refused to enforce such contracts (whether express or implied) on the ground that they were an attempt to create by contract the doctrine of common law marriage, which had been eliminated by statute. "The policy of the Act gives the State a strong continuing interest in the institution of marriage and prevents the marriage relation from becoming in effect a private contract terminable at will. … [P]ublic policy disfavors private contractual alternatives to marriage." Even where enforceable, a contract cannot create rights entirely dependent on legislation, such as the right to spousal benefits under social security, or the right to file a joint tax return, or the right to take the marital deduction for federal estate tax purposes.

IV. CONDOMINIUMS AND COOPERATIVES

A. Introduction: Strictly speaking, neither condominiums nor cooperatives are true forms of concurrent ownership, but they combine sole ownership with concurrent ownership in unique ways.

B. Condominiums: The condominium consists of (1) fee ownership (or long term leasehold) of an individual unit (usually defined to include the interior perimeter surfaces of the unit) and related auxiliary space (*e.g.*, parking or storage spaces), and (2) a fractional or percentage tenancy in common interest with all other condominium owners of the common areas (walls, roof, foundation, grounds, stairs, elevators, etc.).

1. **Creatures of statutes:** Every state has enacted legislation governing the creation and administration of condominiums. These statutes vary. The description here is a typical composite.

2. **Creation:** The owner wishing to establish a condominium development usually does so by recording a master deed or declaration stating that intent.

3. **Owner's association:** Once the condominium units are sold the owners are members of an association that is empowered to elect a board of directors to run the association, usually by hiring a manager or making important decisions about repair, maintenance or improvement of common areas, and promulgating rules for the use of owners' units and common areas. These rules can be very restrictive (*e.g.*, no pets, no laundry lines, no loud noise, no prickly plants) but are generally enforceable if they are reasonable. See, *e.g., Nahr-*

stedt v. Lakeside Village Condominium Association, 878 P.2d 1275 (Cal. 1994).

4. **Conveyance and financing of units:** Because each condominium unit is a separate freehold estate, each unit is conveyed by deed (like any other real property). Purchase of condominiums is conducted like any other realty transaction, in that the buyer is likely to obtain a loan secured by a mortgage on the borrower's individual unit.

5. **Responsibility for common areas:** Pursuant to condominium by-laws, each condominium owner is responsible for his or her proportionate share of the cost of maintaining or improving common areas. Owners are also jointly and severally liable for injuries resulting from failure adequately to maintain the common areas.

6. **No right to partition:** Even though each owner is a tenant in common with respect to the common areas, the governing statutes deny to owners any right to partition this tenancy in common.

7. **Restrictions on condominium conversion:** Many municipalities have legislated to limit the ability of owners of rental housing to convert such units to condominiums. These laws are designed to preserve rental housing, but probably serve more to drive up the price of condominiums. Nonetheless, such ordinances are usually valid exercises of municipal authority.

C. **Cooperatives:** A cooperative apartment building is owned by a corporation. To acquire an apartment one must purchase the capital shares of the corporation that represent the value of the apartment and enter into a lease with the corporation for occupancy of the apartment. Each cooperative apartment owner is part owner (by virtue of owning shares in the corporate building owner) and tenant (by virtue of the lease).

1. **Financial operation:** The corporation will, of course, have a board of directors elected by the tenant-shareholders. Lease rentals are set to reflect the operational costs of the building. Since the corporation is the sole owner of the freehold, any mortgage loan will be the corporation's obligation, but a proportionate share of the mortgage expenses will be passed on to each tenant under the leases. Mortgage lenders insist on clauses in each lease subordinating the tenant's interest to that of the mortgage lender. The effect of these clauses is that, in the event of default and foreclosure, the mortgage lender is entitled to occupancy of the entire building and the tenants have no further occupancy right or ownership interest.

2. **Transfer restrictions:** Given the high interdependence of tenant-shareholders, restrictions are typically placed on transfer of both stock and lease in order to be sure that any transferee is financially

and otherwise capable of discharging the obligations of ownership and tenancy. These restrictions are typically valid. New York goes so far as to hold that consent to transfer may be withheld for any reason, though most jurisdictions hold that consent may not be withheld unreasonably.

3. **Limited liability:** Since the corporation is the sole owner of the building, any tort liability accruing from ownership is the corporation's responsibility. The liability of tenant-shareholders is limited to their capital investment in the corporation.

CHAPTER 6

SERVITUDES: LAND USE LIMITS CREATED BY PRIVATE BARGAIN

I. INTRODUCTION

A. **The concept:** Neighbors often desire to make private agreements concerning use of their land. These agreements come in two varieties. First, one landowner may grant to another person the right to use his land for some specific purpose or in some manner. This type of agreement creates either an *easement* or *profit.* Both will be discussed under the heading of "easements." Second, one landowner may promise another landowner that she will use (or refrain from using) her land in a specified way. Depending on what remedy is sought for enforcement, these agreements create either a *real covenant* or an *equitable servitude.*

B. **Easements:** The principal issues surrounding easements are *creation,* scope of the permitted use, and *termination.* Easements are created by express grant, by equitable estoppel, by implication from prior use of an owner who divides land into separate parcels, by necessity resulting from an owner's division of land into separate parcels leaving one or more without access, and by prescription (the analogue to adverse possession). Issues of scope involve identifying what landowner (or person) is entitled to use the easement and deciding the proper intensity of use. Easements may be terminated by abandonment, merger, release, actions inconsistent with the granted right and prejudicial to the burdened landowner, accidental destruction, prescription, or markedly changed circumstances.

C. **Covenants running with the land:** These promises concerning land use consist of *real covenants* (enforceable at law to recover damages for breach) and *equitable servitudes* (enforceable in equity by an injunction).

   1. **Real covenants: enforceable at law:** The principal issue concerning these covenants (created only by express agreement) is whether they may be enforced by or against subsequent owners of the land burdened or benefited by the promise. Often the sticking point in this inquiry is whether or not *privity of estate* exists. Privity *must exist* for a real covenant to be enforceable by or against successors to the estate. The reason for seeking to enforce a real covenant is to obtain damages resulting from its breach.

2. **Equitable servitudes — enforceable in equity:** These promises may be created by implication from a development scheme as well as by agreement. Privity is *not* required for these promises to be enforceable by or against successors to the estate, but the promise must be *intended to bind successors*, the successor *must have notice* of the promise, the nature of the promise must *touch and concern* use of the burdened land, and the promise must benefit adjacent land. Equitable servitudes are enforceable by an injunction and, in some cases, a lien.

II. EASEMENTS

A. Introduction:

1. **Defined and distinguished from fee simple:** An easement is an interest in land that entitles the holder to use land owned or possessed by another person. It is not a freehold estate. An *easement* almost always gives its owner the right to *use another person's* land; a freehold (*e.g.*, fee simple) gives its owner the right to *exclusive possession of one's own land.* In rare circumstances an easement may give its owner the right to prevent another person from using their land in a certain way.

    a. **Ambiguous grants:** Some grants are none too clear about whether an easement or fee simple was intended, but if the interest conveyed is a limited area for a limited purpose, especially if there are no defined boundaries, an easement is the likely intention. Most courts employ a *rebuttable presumption* that an ambiguous grant conveys an *easement*. See, *e.g.*, *Northpark Associates No. 2, Ltd. v. Homart Development Co.*, 414 S.E.2d 214 (Ga. 1992); *Homan v. Hutchison*, 817 S.W.2d 944 (Mo. App. 1991); *Boucher v. Boyer*, 484 A.2d 630 (Md. 1984); 2 Thompson on Real Property, § 381, at 505 (1980 ed.). This presumption is supported by economic reasoning — it minimizes the transaction costs of uniting ownership of efficiently usable parcels. See Richard Posner, Economic Analysis of the Law 76 (4th ed., 1992). But some courts presume that an ambiguous grant conveys the largest estate the grantor could convey — usually fee simple absolute. See, *e.g.*, *Midland Valley R.R. Co. v. Arrow Industrial Mfg. Co.*, 297 P.2d 410 (Okla. 1956).

    Example: Many old grants to railways conveyed a ribbon of land for a "right of way." As railways atrophied and rail tracks were abandoned, litigation developed over whether these ambiguous grants conveyed fee simple (with the consequence that the abandoned rail corridor remains property of the railway) or an easement (with the consequence that the abandoned rail corridor reverts to the owner of the fee). Courts have divided on this issue though the better resolution is generally to rule that the corridors were easements.

2. **Types of easements:** There are two ways to classify easements — (1) *affirmative* or *negative* and (2) *appurtenant* or *in gross* — with the result that there are four basic types of easements: *affirmative appurtenant, negative appurtenant, affirmative in gross, negative in gross.* To simplify, this discussion deals first with the distinction between easements appurtenant and in gross, then with the distinction between affirmative and negative easements.

   a. **Appurtenant and in gross:** Every easement must be either appurtenant or in gross.

      i. **Easement appurtenant:** An easement *appurtenant* is one that *benefits the owner of another parcel of land.* The benefited parcel is called the *dominant estate* (or dominant tenement) and the burdened parcel is called the *servient estate* (or servient tenement). An easement appurtenant passes along with the dominant estate whenever the dominant estate is transferred to a new owner. The easement right is incidental to, or appurtenant to, the dominant estate.

         Example: Randall owns Blackacre and Guy owns Whiteacre, an adjacent parcel. Guy grants an easement across Whiteacre from Blackacre for foot passage to and from the beach. The easement benefits whoever possesses Blackacre and is therefore appurtenant to Blackacre. If Randall sells Blackacre to Rodney, the easement passes along and Rodney may enjoy the easement so long as he owns Blackacre.

      ii. **Easement in gross:** An easement that is designed to deliver a *personal benefit* rather than to benefit a landowner is an easement in gross. Easements in gross are not attached to, or appurtenant to, any parcel of land. They create a personal right to use the servient estate, but that personal right may be assigned if the parties so intended.

         Example 1: Refer to the prior example. Guy, owner of Whiteacre, grants "to Randall and his assigns the personal right to enter upon and cross Whiteacre for purposes of reaching the beach." An easement in gross is created in favor of Randall. If Randall sells Blackacre to Rodney without any assignment of this personal right, Rodney has no right to enter upon and cross Whiteacre. If Randall assigns his easement in gross to

Sally, she will have the right to cross Whiteacre. If Guy sells Whiteacre to Moira, Whiteacre continues to be burdened with the easement in gross in favor of Randall and his assigns.

Example 2: Roscoe, owner of Broadmeadow, grants to Power Corp. the right to string electrical transmission cables over a portion of Broadmeadow. Since Power Corp. does not own any property benefited by this grant, the easement must be in gross.

iii. **Ambiguous grants:** Courts prefer to construe ambiguous grants as creating easements appurtenant. This preference is partly historical, since England did not (and does not) recognize easements in gross, but mostly rooted in policy preferences. Easements appurtenant are easier to eliminate when their utility ceases because the easement owner is easier to locate. Easements appurtenant are more likely to create value. And easements appurtenant are more likely to be intended than an easement in gross.

Example: Suppose Guy, in the earlier example, conveyed "to Randall and his assigns the right to enter upon and cross Whiteacre for purposes of reaching the beach." This grant is ambiguous because it lacks the specific qualifier of the previous grant ("the *personal* right"). It will be construed as an easement appurtenant for three reasons. (1) Randall owns Blackacre and the easement benefits the owner of Blackacre, raising a presumption that an easement appurtenant was intended. (2) If beach access across Whiteacre becomes useless it is easier to eliminate the easement if the owner of Whiteacre can negotiate with the owner of Blackacre than if the owner of Whiteacre must locate Randall or some assignee (who may have no interest in asserting the easement and therefore is not easily located). (3) An easement appurtenant creates value in Blackacre that probably more than offsets the burdens on Whiteacre, or the easement would not be created. If the burden on Whiteacre is $50 and the value to Blackacre is $100, Randall will pay more than $50 but less than $100 to obtain the easement. No matter how the difference between damage ($50) and added value ($100) is split between Guy and Randall, the easement will add $50 to the total value of Whiteacre and Blackacre. If the easement is Randall's in gross, the only effect on land values will be to lower them by $50, the damage to Whiteacre produced by the easement.

b. **Affirmative and negative easements:** The overwhelming majority of easements are affirmative. Only a few types of negative easements may be created.

   i. **Affirmative easements:** As the name implies, an affirmative easement *permits a person to use the servient estate* in a specified manner.

   Example: Leroy owns Rockbottom, a farm situated between Hardscrabble, a farm owned by Lester, and a riverside dock used to ship farm produce. If Leroy grants Lester the right to cross Rockbottom for purposes of moving his farm produce to the riverside dock, an *affirmative easement appurtenant* has been created. Lester (or his successors in Hardscrabble, the dominant estate) have the affirmative right to use Rockbottom (whether owned by Leroy or his successors) in the specified fashion. If Leroy had granted to Cyril, fly fisherman who owns no real property, the right to cross Rockbottom to fish in the river, an *affirmative easement in gross* would be created.

   ii. **Negative easements:** A negative easement confers only the right to *prevent specified uses of the servient estate;* it confers *no right to use* the servient estate.

   Example: Jonah, owner of Laurel Hollow, grants to Deborah, owner of Hillside, the right to prevent diversion of the flow from the irrigation ditch that crosses Laurel Hollow on its way to Hillside. This is a *negative easement appurtenant.* Hillside, the dominant estate, has no right to use Laurel Hollow, the servient estate, but does have a right to prevent Laurel Hollow from being used in a way that would divert the flow of water in the irrigation ditch.

   (1) Four negative easements recognized by common law: Common law recognized only four negative easements, all appurtenant: (1) for light, (2) for air, (3) for subjacent or lateral support, and (4) for the continuing flow of artificial streams. By these easements, the owner of the servient estate could not block off his neighbor's light or air, or excavate to undermine his neighbor's structure or surface ground, or stop or divert irrigation ditches or aqueducts. Modern courts have analogized to these four by permitting negative easements for view (analogous to light and air) and for solar collection (a variation on light). It is sometimes claimed that negative easements are always appurtenant and that they may not be in gross. This was true at common law but is no longer correct. By statute, many jurisdictions have permitted creation of negative conservation easements, which do not benefit any dominant estate but are for the benefit of conservation organizations.

Example: Lydia, owner of Flora Island, a nesting ground for the Caspian Tern, grants to the Audubon Society, a non-profit charitable corporation, an easement of protection of the nesting habitat of the Caspian Terns. This is a ***negative easement in gross,*** and is permitted by statute. It would not be recognized by common law.

  (2) **Restrictive covenant:** Even if a negative easement is not recognized as valid, the same promise restricting land use may be enforced as a restrictive real covenant or equitable servitude. See pp. 227 and 239, *infra*.

3. ***Profits a prendre*:** A profit (as it is normally shortened) is the right to take a natural resource or crop from the land of another. Typical profits include the right to take minerals (*e.g.*, sand, gravel, ore), timber, fish, game, or crops. Common law courts preferred to construe profits as in gross rather than appurtenant, perhaps because in their origin many of these profits were vested in the landless. It makes economic sense to treat profits as in gross because the right conferred (*e.g.*, to mine for copper ore) has substantial economic value by itself and thus is most efficiently utilized if it is easily transferable by itself, rather than as an adjunct to some unrelated property. For that reason, profits are freely assignable.

4. **Licenses:** A license is simply ***permission*** to enter the licensor's land. Licenses are ubiquitous (*e.g.*, dinner guests, repairmen, shoppers all have licenses), may be oral or written, and are ***revocable*** at any time unless the licensor makes the license irrevocable, either expressly or by his conduct.

Example: Aldo tells his neighbor Fred that he may leave his canoe on Aldo's beach. Fred has a license to do so, but Aldo may revoke the license whenever he wishes.

  a. **License or easement in gross?:** The same language may be construed as either a license or easement in gross. The consequential difference is that an easement may not be revoked and continues to bind successors to the servient estate who have notice of it, while a license is revocable and binds only the licensor so long as it remains alive.

Example: If, in the prior example, Aldo's act was construed as creating an easement in gross in Fred, the easement would continue to inure to Fred's benefit if Aldo sold his beach front to Winnie after telling Winnie about Fred's right. Not so if it is a license.

    i. **Ambiguous cases:** *Courts prefer to construe ambiguous cases as creating a license,* because easements in gross are often difficult to eliminate (*e.g.*, Fred moves, leaving no forwarding address) and thus depress land values and make land less easily alienable.

b. **Assignment:** Licenses are generally not assignable, but this rule is not invariable. Licenses are assignable if the parties so intend, and also if a license becomes irrevocable through operation of equitable estoppel, thus effectively becoming an easement appurtenant. See p. 203, *infra*.

c. **Irrevocable licenses:** Licenses may become irrevocable in three different ways.

    i. **Intention:** A license is irrevocable if the licensor expressly makes the license irrevocable.

    ii. **Equitable estoppel:** A license is irrevocable if equitable estoppel operates to make it so. If a licensor grants a license on which the licensee reasonably relies to make substantial improvements to property, equity requires that the licensor be estopped from revoking the license.

    Example: Holbrook permitted Taylor to use a roadway across his property in order for Taylor to reach his own property. With Holbrook's knowledge, and without any objection, Taylor used the access road to construct a substantial single-family residence. Holbrook later blocked the road with a steel cable strung taut across it. The Kentucky Supreme Court held that Holbrook was equitably estopped from revoking the license. See *Holbrook v. Taylor*, 532 S.W.2d 763 (Ky. 1976). Accord, *Camp v. Milam*, 277 So. 2d 95 (Ala. 1973).

    • **Duration:** A license made irrevocable through equitable estoppel continues to exist until the value of the improvements made in reliance on the license has been fully realized. This period is at least as long as the useful life of the improvements, and some courts have hinted that such a license might last forever: "[T]he license will continue for so long a time as the nature of it calls for." *Stoner v. Zucker*, 83 P. 808 (Cal. 1906).

- **Easement compared:** An easement is of indefinite duration, and can continue forever. An irrevocable license that expires when the value of the improvements has been fully recouped lasts for a shorter period. But an irrevocable license that endures "for so long a time as the nature of it calls for" may last forever (*e.g.*, an easement for access, as in *Holbrook v. Taylor, supra*), thus causing some courts to characterize an irrevocable license as "similar in its essentials to an easement, ... irrevocable to prevent the licensor from perpetrating a fraud upon the licensee." *Cooke v. Ramponi*, 239 P.2d 638 (Cal. 1952).

- **Minority view — no estoppel:** A minority of jurisdictions reject application of equitable estoppel to oral licenses. The rationale for their view is that an irrevocable license is indistinguishable from an easement, and so the Statute of Frauds ought to apply to bar creation of irrevocable oral licenses. "The right ... is essentially an easement and should be the subject of a [written] grant ... . It is no hardship ... to secure an easement in perpetuity ... or, such being refused, to [assess] the uncertainty implicit in the making of expenditures on the basis of a revocable license." *Henry v. Dalton*, 98 R.I. 150 (1959). Accord, *Crosdale v. Lanigan*, 29 N.E. 824 (N.Y. 1892).

- **Policy arguments:** The argument in *favor of irrevocability* based on estoppel is that it is unfair for the licensor to stand by and watch the licensee expend considerable money and effort in reliance on the license, then to rescind the license. By this theory, the fair licensor would revoke as soon as the improvements started. The licensor is in the best position to avert these reliance expenditures. The argument *against irrevocability* is that estoppel penalizes the "good neighbor" who fails to say no until the improvement is completed. The landowner who freely gives permission and is loathe to be a "bad guy" is the one who bears the cost of an irrevocable license imposed on his land. At the least, the licensee should pay to the licensor the value of the irrevocable license (measured by the damage to the licensor's land resulting from irrevocability).

iii. **License "coupled with an interest:"** When a license is tied together with some other legally recognized interest the license is irrevocable until that other interest is vindicated.

Example: Dieter agrees to purchase from Parker a truckload of fertilizer, payment to be made only after Parker has delivered the fertilizer and spread it on Dieter's oat field. By virtue of the contract, Dieter has granted a license to Parker to enter upon Dieter's land, and that license is coupled with Parker's interest in performance of the contract, so it may not be revoked until Parker has had a reasonable opportunity to perform.

B. Creation of easements: Easements may be created by *grant,* by *estoppel* (though usually called an irrevocable license), by *implication* (in two different ways), and by *prescription* (the close cousin to adverse possession).

1. **Easements by grant:** Most easements are created expressly by a deed or other grant. Since an easement is an interest in land its creation is subject to the Statute of Frauds, which requires a *writing signed by the grantor.* Of course, there are exceptions to the Statute of Frauds, which permit the creation of easements by estoppel, implication, and prescription.

   a. **By reservation:** Grantors sometimes convey land and, in the same deed, purport to "reserve" an easement in favor of the grantor or a third party. This creates problems.

      i. **In favor of grantor:** For archaic feudal reasons, early common law did not recognize easements reserved in favor of the grantor. Then common law judges invented the fiction that the grantee, by accepting the deed, had granted an easement back to the grantor. The modern upshot is that a reservation of an easement in favor of the grantor is valid. Common law distinguished between such a reservation (which created a *new easement*) and an *exception* (which passed title subject to a *preexisting easement*). The distinction was important when easements could not be created in the grantor by reservation, but is of no importance now.

      ii. **In favor of a third party:** Common law did not recognize the validity of easements purportedly reserved in favor of a third party because the fiction of a grant back to the grantor could not be extended to a third party, who was a stranger to the deed. The reasons for this refusal no longer exist but the majority of modern courts continue to treat reserved easements in favor of a third party as void. See, *e.g., Estate of Thomson v. Wade,* 509 N.E.2d 309 (N.Y. 1987). This is especially peculiar because a real covenant (which burdens land in much the same way as an easement) can be created in favor of a third party. A minority of modern courts have done the sensible thing and ruled that easements reserved in favor of a third party are valid. See, e.g, *Willard v. First Church of Christ, Scientist,* 498 P.2d 987 (Cal. 1972). In most states, though, it is still necessary to use two conveyances instead of one to create an easement in favor of a third party.

Example: Carolyn, owner of Blackacre, wishes to convey Blackacre to Jake but reserve an easement for parking in favor of her neighbor, Liza. In California, Carolyn can simply convey to Jake under a deed that expressly reserves the parking easement in favor of Liza. But in New York (and in most states) Carolyn must first convey Blackacre to Liza, who would then convey to Jake, reserving an easement in favor of herself. This two-step shuffle does not make such sense.

2. **Easements by estoppel:** An irrevocable license, the functional equivalent of an easement, can be created by estoppel. See p. 203, *supra.*

3. **Easements by implication:** Easements may be implied in law under two circumstances: (1) where property has been divided and, prior to the division, one portion of the property has been used in an easement-like fashion for the benefit of another part of the property (implied from ***prior use***), and (2) where property has been divided in such a manner that an easement for access is necessary (implied from ***necessity***).

    a. **Easements implied from prior use:** The following elements must be proven to establish an easement implied from prior use.

    - **Common owner:** Prior to division, the ***"quasi-servient estate"*** and the ***"quasi-dominant estate"*** must be owned by the same person.

    - **Reasonable necessity:** The prior use must be ***reasonably necessary*** for the use and enjoyment of the "quasi-dominant estate."

    - **Continuous use:** The prior use must be ***continuous,*** not sporadic.

    - **Intended continuation:** The parties must ***intend,*** at the time of division, to continue the prior use.

    - **Existing use at division:** The prior use must be ***existing*** at the time of division, a requirement implied by the element of intended continuation.

    - **Apparent use:** The prior use must be ***apparent,*** which does ***not*** necessarily mean that it is visible.

i. **Common owner:** A person may devote part of her property to a use that benefits another part. There is no easement created while the property is owned by one person, but this prior use creates a so-called *quasi-easement,* an inchoate easement-in-waiting. When the common owner divides the property by selling one part to another person an easement from prior use may be created. If the owner/grantor retains the quasi-servient estate (the burdened part) the implied easement is by *implied grant.* If the owner/grantor retains the quasi-dominant estate (the benefited part) the implied easement is by *implied reservation.*

    Example: Brenda owns two lots, adjacent to each other. She constructs a driveway over lot 1 to her house on lot 2. No easement is created since Brenda cannot have an easement in her own property. She owns it all. An inchoate quasi-easement exists. If Brenda sells lot 2 to Richard, an easement by implied grant may be created. Brenda owns lot 1, the servient estate, and Richard owns lot 2, the dominant estate. If, instead, Brenda sells lot 1 to Richard, an easement by implied reservation may be created. Richard owns lot 1, the servient estate, and Brenda owns lot 2, the dominant estate.

ii. **Reasonable necessity:** The easement must be *reasonably necessary for the owner of the dominant estate to use and enjoy her property.* Reasonable necessity assures that the easement was likely intended to continue after division. A corollary implication is that an easement implied from prior use can *only be appurtenant.* The term "reasonable" is capacious. Courts tend to find reasonable necessity if it would be costly or difficult to use the dominant estate without the easement, or if the price paid for either the dominant or servient estate reflects the existence of the easement. Most courts today require reasonable necessity for easements implied by grant and for easements implied by reservation. See, *e.g., Otero v. Pacheco,* 612 P.2d 1335 (N.M. Ct. App. 1980); *Jack v. Hunt,* 265 P.2d 251 (Or. 1954); *Van Sandt v. Royster,* 83 P.2d 698 (Kan. 1938). But some states cling to the older view that when an easement implied from prior use is created by implied reservation, *strict necessity* — absolute, indispensable necessity — is required. See, *e.g., Abbott v. Herring,* 469 N.Y.S.2d 268 (Sup. Ct. 1983); *Mitchell v. Castellaw,* 246 S.W.2d 163 (Tex. 1952); *Winthrop v. Wadsworth,* 42 So. 2d 541 (Fla. 1949). The justification for this latter view is that the grantor ought not be permitted impliedly to derogate from her grant, but if the other elements — especially intention and apparent existing use — are present, it is hard to see why there should be a difference between reservation and grant.

iii. **Continuous use:** The use must be continuous, not sporadic. This element buttresses the fundamental concept that the use must be such that both parties *intended for it to continue.* Continuous use does not mean that it must be used constantly; rather, it means that the easement must be embodied in some ***permanent physical alteration.***

Example: An outdoor concrete staircase serving Parcel A, but located entirely on Parcel B, is permanent (and thus continuous) even though it is not in constant use.

iv. **Intended continuation:** This is the fundamental element, but the parties rarely provide express evidence of their intentions, or they would have memorialized the easement by express grant. Accordingly, many of the other elements — reasonable necessity, continuity, and apparent use — are proxies for this element. The price paid (which is also considered in deciding whether the claimed easement is reasonably necessary) is helpful to this issue, since parties who intend for a quasi-easement to continue are likely to settle on a price that reflects the value (and detriment) of the easement.

v. **Existing use at division:** The prior use must actually exist at the time of division. If it does not, there is surely no reason to think that the parties intended the continuation of a non-existing use.

vi. **Apparent use:** The use must be apparent. This does ***not*** mean that the use must be visible. A prior use is apparent if it could be detected, or even inferred, from a reasonable inspection of the premises.

Example: Laura owns Lot 1 and Lot 2. She constructs an underground sewer across Lot 1 to service her home on Lot 2. She then builds a house on Lot 1, connecting it to the same sewer, and sells Lot 1 to Vaughan. The easement thus created is apparent because Vaughan could have inferred the existence of some sewer by noting the existence and operation of plumbing fixtures, and he could have employed a skilled plumber to detect the actual location of the sewer. See, *e.g., Van Sandt v. Royster, supra*; *Romanchuk v, Plotkin,* 9 N.W.2d 421 (Minn. 1943). But see *Campbell v. Great Miami Aerie No. 2309,* 472 N.E.2d 711 (Ohio 1984).

vii. **Easements implied from a subdivision map:** When a common owner divides property under a deed that incorporates or refers to a map on which proposed streets or other rights of way are platted on the common owner's property, an easement in favor of the grantee with respect to the platted streets is implied even though there has been no prior use. The rationale for this deviation from the elements of easements implied from prior use is that the purchaser has relied on the future creation of the streets and paid accordingly. See 3 Powell, The Law of Real Property ¶ 409 (1992 ed.).

b. **Easements implied from necessity:** An easement is implied from necessity only when one owner divides his property in such a way that one of the resulting parcels is left without access to a public roadway. An easement for right of way between the landlocked parcel and the public road across the owner's remaining parcel is then implied, either because the parties must have intended this result or because it is economically efficient and socially beneficial to create an easement for access. Easements by necessity are permitted only for right of way — ingress and egress between the landlocked parcel and a public road.

Example: Eunice, owner of Black Heart Ranch, divides it into two parcels, Sweetwater and Bitterroot. Sweetwater is bounded by a public road on the west, two ranches owned by neighbors on its north and south sides, and Bitterroot on the east. Bitterroot is bounded by Sweetwater on the west and National Forest wilderness land on the remaining sides. An easement implied from necessity will burden Sweetwater for the benefit of Bitterroot, enabling the occupier of Bitterroot to cross Sweetwater to gain access to the public road.

i. **Common owner:** An easement by necessity can be created *only* over property owned by the person who also owned the landlocked parcel and who divided the property to create the access problem. In cases of multiple division, an easement by necessity is created at the moment a parcel is landlocked, and thus the easement burdens the *last parcel* split off by the common owner — the parcel that completed the landlocking. See, *e.g.*, *Othen v. Rosier*, 226 S.W.2d 622 (Tex. 1950). It cannot burden property never owned by the common grantor who created the problem.

ii. **Necessity at severance — not prior use:** Necessity must exist at the moment the property is divided. No prior use is needed to establish an easement by necessity. The necessity of access is there the moment the parcel is landlocked, though the practical need may lie dormant for years.

    iii. Duration: An easement by necessity lasts as long as the necessity exists. If the necessity is removed (perhaps by creation of a new public road that provides access) the easement is terminated.

    iv. Location: Once the servient estate is identified the owner of the servient estate is permitted to select a *reasonably convenient location* for the easement, on the theory that the servient estate owner can best minimize the damage to the servient estate.

4. Easements by prescription: Prescription is analogous to adverse possession. Easements are *not possessory interests* so an easement cannot be acquired by adverse *possession.* But *adverse use* for a sufficient period of time can ripen into an *easement by prescription.* American courts ground prescription in the same policies that justify adverse possession. The archaic English fiction that a prescriptive use was pursuant to a grant, now lost, has been largely discarded by American courts. The English view pretended that prescription was really use by right; the American view frankly recognizes the adverse nature of prescriptive use. Easements by prescription may be appurtenant (as when one homeowner acquires a driveway easement over his neighbor's land) or in gross (as when repeated hunting or fishing create a prescriptive easement in gross in favor of the hunter or fisher).

    a. Elements of prescriptive use: Virtually the same elements are needed to establish prescriptive use that are needed to establish adverse possession: (1) *adverse use under a claim of right* that is (2) *open and notorious* and (3) *continuous* for the prescriptive period. Note, however, that *exclusive use is so altered that it is effectively not required.*

        i. Prescriptive period: The required prescriptive period is the same as the limitations period applicable for adverse possession. If the jurisdiction has a 20 year limitations period for adverse possession, the adverse use of another's land must continue for 20 years in order for an easement by prescription to be created.

        ii. Adverse use under a claim of right: The use of another's land must be *adverse* and *not with permission of the owner.* As with adverse possession, there is an *objective* and *subjective* version of this test. The objective version focuses on whether a neutral observer would think the use is under a claim of right and not permissive. The subjective version requires the adverse user to prove that she had a good faith belief that she had a right to use the land, and not just permission to do so.

Example: A frequent problem is the common driveway. Suppose Mary and Al, neighbors, agree to split the cost of a driveway which both will use and which is located exactly on the property line. Under the objective version of adverse use, Mary and Al are each using their neighbors' property in a fashion that is not permissive, since they are asserting their right to use a driveway for which they have each paid half the cost. The result is the same under the subjective test — both Mary and Al are likely have a good faith belief that they are entitled to use the driveway. See, *e.g.*, *Shanks v. Floom*, 124 N.E.2d 416 (Ohio 1955). Contra: *Banach v. Lawera*, 47 N.W.2d 679 (Mich. 1951).

- (1) **Permissive use never becomes prescriptive:** If a use is permissive, it can never ripen into a prescriptive right, no matter how long the use goes on. But a permissive use can become adverse if the user does things that are inconsistent with mere permission and which give the owner notice of the user's claim of right.

    Example: Janet gives Bob permission to use a footpath through her rural wood for beach access. Bob then proceeds to widen the path, pave it with stones, and digs drainage ditches to prevent erosion. These acts are inconsistent with permission to use a rural footpath and ought to put Janet on notice that Bob claims a right to use the path that is independent of her permission. See, *e.g.*, *Hester v. Sawyers*, 71 P.2d 646 (N.M. 1937).

- (2) **Use of easement after termination:** Use of an easement by necessity ***after it has terminated*** is likely adverse and may ripen into an easement by prescription. Use of an easement by necessity is by right, and thus not prescriptive, but if the necessity ends the easement by necessity terminates. Further use of the terminated easement is adverse, unless permission for the continued use is granted.

iii. **Open and notorious use:** To be open and notorious the adverse use must be conducted so that the use may be discovered by any reasonable inspection. It may not be carried on in secret or carefully concealed.

- iv. **Continuous use:** The element of continuous use is satisfied if the adverse user continually asserts her claim of right by making whatever use is consistent with the nature of the claimed easement, even if that use is periodic or episodic. It does ***not*** mean that the adverse user must use the property constantly.

  Example: Adam and Eve own adjacent waterfront lots in a summer home community. Each summer Adam crosses Eve's lot whenever he wishes to go to the beach, sometimes several times a day, but sometimes only a few times a week. Adam beats down a clear footpath by his crossings and goes so far as to construct steps to the beach. Adam makes no use of the footpath during the fall, winter, and spring, when neither he nor Eve is there. This use involves a continual claim of right and adverse use that is consistent with the nature of the claimed easement — a footpath beach access during the summer period. It satisfies the continuous use element.

  - (1) **Occasional adverse use:** But occasional adverse use does not satisfy the continuous element.

    Example: If Adam crossed Eve's lot only a few times each summer, made no alterations to the lot, and otherwise used a public beach access, his use would be so occasional that it would not satisfy the continuous element.

  - (2) **Tacking:** As with adverse possession, tacking is permitted.

- v. **Interrupted use:** If the adverse use is interrupted, the prescriptive period starts over. Jurisdictions differ as to what constitutes interruption. Most states follow the adverse possession rule that only the owner's action of filing a lawsuit to stop the adverse use or physical prevention of the adverse use constitutes interruption. A minority hold that mere notice (a sign or letter) that tells the adverse user to stop is sufficient to interrupt the use. The minority view is a vestige of the "lost grant" theory of prescription: If prescription is founded on a fictional "lost grant," the owner's statement that there is no grant is sufficient to rebut the existence of the fictional lost grant.

- vi. **Exclusive use not required:** Many courts say that exclusive use must be shown to establish a prescriptive easement, but the meaning of exclusivity is so altered that, in effect, it is not required. For prescription purposes, exclusive use does not mean that the adverse user was the only user; rather, it means that the adverse user's claim "does not depend on a like right in others." *Page v. Bloom,* 584 N.E.2d 813 (Ill. App. Ct. 1991). In other words, exclusive use is shown simply by claiming an easement from *one's own use,* and not in common with the public or somebody else. Thus, even in the case of the common driveway, each neighbor's use is "exclusive" in this sense. See, *e.g., Causey v. Lanigan,* 159 S.E.2d 655 (Va. 1968).

b. Public prescriptive easements: Many jurisdictions permit the public at large to acquire prescriptive easements in private lands, so long as all the elements of prescription are satisfied. Other jurisdictions achieve the same result through *implied dedication, custom,* or the *public trust doctrine.* Some states reject all these theories.

  i. Prescriptive easements in favor of the general public: The general rule is that the public at large can obtain a prescriptive easement in private property so long as the elements of prescriptive use are established. See, *e.g., Sellentin v. Terkildsen,* 343 N.W.2d 895 (Neb. 1984); *Buttolph v. Erikkson,* 648 A.2d 824 (Vt. 1993); *Concerned Citizens of Brunswick County Taxpayers Ass'n v. Holden Beach Enterprises, Inc.,* 404 S.E.2d 677 (N.C. 1991). However, most courts apply a rebuttable presumption that public use is permissive. And the use must be sufficiently widespread to be truly public. Use by the neighborhood alone may not be sufficiently public to create a public prescriptive easement. See, *e.g., Gore v. Blanchard,* 118 A. 888 (Vt. 1922) (neighbors' use of a road to reach a pond for ice cutting was a mere "neighborly concession" and not "used for public purposes as a public way").

  ii. No public prescriptive easements: States that reject public prescriptive easements rely on one of two rationales. The older reason is rooted in the fictional "lost grant" — since the "public citizenry" could not receive a grant there could not possibly have been such a grant, now lost. Hence, no prescriptive easements in the public. See, *e.g., Ivons-Nispel, Inc. v. Lowe,* 200 N.E.2d 282 (Mass. 1964). The more modern objection is that the owner's cause of action (barred by elapse of the prescriptive period) can only run against specific persons, so the owner's cause of action to stop adverse use can never expire as against the entire public at large. See, *e.g., State ex rel. Haman v. Fox,* 594 P.2d 1093 (Idaho 1979). Some states have enacted statutes that permit owners to record and post notices that public use is by permission, thus negating any possible claim of public prescriptive right. See, *e.g.*, Cal. Civ. Code § 1009.

iii. **Implied dedication:** This theory is simply a pseudonym for a public prescriptive easement. The idea is that the owner ***intends to dedicate*** his property to ***public use,*** but the evidence of such intent is entirely inferred from (1) long-standing public use and (2) the owner's failure to halt the use. See, *e.g., Gion v. City of Santa Cruz,* 465 P.2d 50 (Cal. 1970). The California legislature subsequently overturned *Gion* by statute.

iv. **Custom:** Beach front property owners own the "dry sand" portion of the beach, since their title extends to the mean high tide mark. Ancient common law held that the public acquired a customary right to use the dry sand portion of a beach if such public use had gone on so long that "the memory of man runneth not to the contrary." 1 W. Blackstone, Commentaries *67. That doctrine has been revived in at least four states: Florida, Hawaii, Oregon and Texas. To establish this customary right, the public must prove ***immemorial usage without interruption*** that is ***peaceable, reasonable, certain,*** and consistent with other customs. See, *e.g., Public Access Shoreline Hawaii v. Hawaii County Planning Comm.,* 903 P.2d 1246 (Hawaii 1995); *City of Daytona Beach v. Tona-Rama, Inc.,* 294 So. 2d 73 (Fla. 1974); *State ex rel. Thornton v. Hay,* 462 P.2d 671 (Or. 1969); *Matcha v. Mattox,* 711 S.W.2d 95 (Tex. App. 1986). Idaho has embraced the doctrine in dicta but has not had occasion to apply it. See *State ex rel. Haman v. Fox, supra*. Claims of customary rights to private beaches have been considered and rejected elsewhere. See, e.g, *Bell v. Town of Wells,* 557 A.2d 168 (Me. 1989).

v. **Public trust doctrine:** New Jersey's approach to the issue of public beach access is to invoke the public trust doctrine. The water and beach front below the mean high tide mark is held by the state in ***public trust,*** to enable the public to use these tidal waters and lands for swimming, boating, fishing, and other common pursuits. But to vindicate this right, New Jersey has created a rule that requires private beach front owners to give the general public "access to and use of privately-owned dry sand areas as reasonably necessary." *Matthews v. Bay Head Improvement Ass'n,* 471 A.2d 355 (N.J 1984). But *Matthews* involved dry sand beaches that were owned by a "quasi-public" entity. It is quite possible that this rule, as applied to purely private dry sand beaches, amounts to a taking of private property for which the Constitution requires just compensation. See Chapter 11, p. 345, *infra*.

c. **Prescriptive easements not permitted:** There are two types of easements that may not be acquired by prescription.

   i. **Negative easements:** A negative easement may not be acquired by prescription because there is no cause of action that is cut off by elapse of the prescriptive period.

   Example: Otto builds a solar collector on the roof of his home. Twenty years later his neighbor, Patricia, builds a tall addition to her home which completely blocks sunlight from falling on Otto's solar collector for nine months of each year. Otto has no prescriptive easement for sunlight. During the 20 year period when Otto's collector was soaking up sunshine Patricia had no cause to action to stop him from doing so. There is no right of Patricia's that is extinguished by elapse of time. Put another way, if Otto received a prescriptive negative easement for sunlight there is nothing Patricia could do (short of blocking Otto's sunlight immediately) that would stop Otto from acquiring an interest in her property. It is not thought to be sound public policy to encourage neighbors to cut off each other's light and air simply to avoid the possibility that a prescriptive easement might otherwise result. See, *e.g.*, *Cohan v. Fleuroma, Inc.*, 346 N.Y.S.2d 157 (Sup. Ct. 1973); *Parker & Edgarton v. Foote,* 19 Wend. 309 (N.Y. 1838).

   ii. **Easements upon public land:** As with adverse possession, it is not generally possible to obtain a prescriptive easement in public land. This rule is, at bottom, another manifestation of the sovereign's prerogative.

C. **Scope of easements:** The scope of an easement involves two separate questions.

- How *extensively* and *intensively* may the *easement holder use the easement?*

- To what degree may the *owner of the servient estate use or interfere with the easement?*

1. **Parties' intentions control:** The overriding principle in determining scope of an easement is to identify and uphold the parties' intentions. But this is not always so easy. Intentions frequently must be at least partly inferred. To do so, courts examine the following factors.

- *How easement was created* (*i.e.*, whether by grant, implication, or prescription).

- *How conditions have changed to affect the originally intended use.*

- *What changes in use were reasonably foreseeable by the parties.*

- *What changes are necessary to achieve the intended purpose of the easement.*

- *Whether a changed use imposes an unreasonable burden on the servient estate.*

2. How easement was created:

    a. **Easements by grant:** The express language of the grant controls insofar as it may be dispositive, but extrinsic circumstances often must be consulted.

    Example 1: An easement granted in 1870 in upper Michigan for "winter access to Horseshoe Pond for ice fishing" implied access by ski, sleigh, sled, or snowshoe in 1870, but it would not be unreasonable to interpret it today as including access by snow machine.

    Example 2: In 1876 the owner of Blackacre conveyed an easement for right of way over Blackacre for the benefit of Whiteacre. The easement was used to transport animals to Whiteacre for slaughter and removal of their carcasses for sale. Around 1916 the slaughterhouse burned and Whiteacre was converted to farming. The easement was then used for farm machinery and crop removal. By the 1950s Whiteacre was used by the Kentucky Highway Department to store vehicles and equipment, which it moved in and out via the easement. The Kentucky Court of Appeals held that the easement "may be used in such a manner as is necessary in the proper and reasonable occupation and enjoyment of the dominant estate. As the passage of time creates new needs and the uses of property change, a normal change in the manner of using [an easement] does not constitute a deviation from the original grant, and modern transportation uses are not restricted to ancient modes of travel." *Cameron v. Barton*, 272 S.W.2d 40 (Ky. 1954).

    b. **Easements by implication:** The scope of implied easements depends on the reason for the implication.

        i. **By prior use:** Easements implied from prior use are construed the same way as easements by grant.

Example: An agribusiness company constructed a roadway on its property to serve its lemon and avocado groves, then divided the property creating a roadway easement implied from prior use. The dominant estate was later acquired by a person who constructed a residence on the property. The California Supreme Court ruled that even though the prior use that created the easement was agricultural it was "within the reasonable contemplation of the parties" at the time of division that the easement could be used for residential purposes. *Fristoe v. Drapeau,* 215 P.2d 729 (Cal. 1950).

    ii. By necessity: The scope of an easement implied by necessity is exactly congruent with the necessity. No more, no less.

  c. Easements by prescription: Since prescriptive easements come about by a particular long-standing adverse use by *one party alone,* there is no reason to assume that any greater or different use was intended by the parties. Accordingly, courts are most reluctant to permit any expansion of the scope of prescriptive easements to accommodate changed future needs of the dominant estate. See, e.g, *Wright v. Horse Creek Ranches, Inc.,* 697 P.2d 384 (Colo. 1985), where a prescriptive roadway easement for ranching and hunting was not permitted to be used for providing access to a residential subdivision. Accord: *Aztec Ltd., Inc. v. Creekside Investment Co.,* 602 P.2d 64 (Idaho). But despite this general rule, some courts do permit some modest alteration of the scope of a prescriptive easement where the *burden on the servient estate is moderate* and the *alteration is consistent with the general pattern formed by the adverse use.* See, *e.g. Glenn v. Poole,* 423 N.E.2d 1030 (Mass. Ct. App. 1981) (permitting a prescriptive roadway easement for hauling wood and gravel to be used for vehicle access to and from a garage and repair shop); *Farmer v. Kentucky Utilities Co.,* 642 S.W.2d 579 (Ky. 1982) (permitting the holder of a prescriptive easement for overhead passage of utility cables to clear brush and trees underneath).

3. Change in location of easement: If an easement specifies a specific location, or one has been agreed to by the parties' conduct, the location is permanently fixed unless the parties agree to a change.

Example 1: Harold, owner of a tract of ground including Long Lake and Whitechapel Pond, grants to Edgar an easement in gross "to fish in Whitechapel Pond." Edgar may not thereafter unilaterally change the easement to one permitting him to fish in Long Lake.

Example 2: Rosemary, owner of Blackacre (bounded on the west by a public forest, on the east by Big River, on the north by a public road, and to the south by Whiteacre) grants an easement appurtenant to Whiteacre for "passage across Blackacre to Big River." Over time, a well-beaten path is created across Blackacre from Whiteacre to Big River. The location of this easement is fixed by conduct. Moreover, there is no easement across Blackacre for passage to the public road.

- a. **Modifications with no additional burden allowed:** This rule does not prevent some modifications to the easement that impose no additional burden on the servient estate.

    Example: Landowner granted Public Irrigation District an easement across his property for an irrigation ditch. District permitted a public school, at its expense, to place the ditch entirely underground in a concrete pipe, but in the identical location as the surface ditch. The Idaho Supreme Court held that, since no additional burden was imposed, District and the public school could place the ditch underground. *Abbott v. Nampa School District No. 131*, 808 P.2d 1289 (Idaho 1991).

4. **Enlargement of the dominant estate:** An easement, however created, cannot be used for the benefit of land that is not the dominant estate.

    Example: Laura purchases Valleystream, which has appurtenant to it an easement for right of way over Blackacre, an adjoining parcel. Laura then acquires Ridgetop, a parcel bordering on Valleystream, and uses the access roadway across Blackacre to reach her new residence, constructed partly on Ridgetop and partly on Valleystream. She may not use the roadway easement to benefit Ridgetop, a non-dominant estate. See, *e.g., Brown v. Voss,* 715 P.2d 514 (Wash. 1986). Accord: *S.S. Kresge Co. of Michigan v. Winkelman Realty Co.,* 50 N.W.2d 920 (Wis. 1952); *Kanefsky v. Dratch Construction Co.,* 101 A.2d 923 (Pa. 1954); *Penn Bowling Recreation Center, Inc. v. Hot Shoppes, Inc.,* 179 F.2d 64 (D.C. Cir. 1949).

    - a. **Remedies:** he usual remedy for using an easement for the benefit of a non-dominant estate is an ***injunction*** to prevent the use. See, *e.g., Penn Bowling Recreation Center, Inc. v. Hot Shoppes, Inc., supra.* The parties are then left to reverse this outcome, if they wish, by private bargain. But some courts have denied injunctions and granted damages instead. See, *e.g., Brown v. Voss, supra.* This approach drags into court the private bargaining that would otherwise occur post-injunction, in the form of argument over the amount of damages and also over the relative equities of an injunction. Moreover, if damages only are awarded the litigation may not be over forever, since the use of the non-dominant estate now benefited by the easement might change, leading to further dispute. When the usual rule — injunctive relief — is ineffective to prevent use of the easement by a non-dominant estate, courts sometimes rule that the easement is extinguished. The same result can be achieved by foresight in drafting of an easement — by providing that the easement expires automatically if the dominant estate owner uses it for the benefit of a non-dominant estate.

5. **Division of an easement's benefit:** Different rules apply to division of the benefit of an appurtenant easement and an easement in gross, but both have the same objective — ***preventing an unintended increase in the burden on the servient estate.***

   a. **Division of a dominant estate:** The general rule is that a dominant estate may be divided and that each part of the divided estate is entitled to enjoy the easement, but this rule is subject to the important limit that the resulting increased burden on the servient estate must be within the original contemplation of the parties. This original state of mind is often necessarily inferred. Courts consider whether the division of the dominant estate is a "normal development," whether the division is foreseeable, and whether the burden on the servient estate is substantially increased.

   b. **Easements and profits in gross:**

      i. **Non-exclusive easements:** The holder of a ***non-exclusive*** profit or easement in gross (one shared with the servient estate) may ***not*** divide it, since division would likely result in decreased utility of the use to the servient estate.

         Example: George, owner of Blackpond Estate, grants Alexa the non-exclusive right to fish in Blackpond. If Alexa were permitted to subdivide the right, increased fishing pressure on Blackpond would result. This bright line prevents that result and does not consider the relative burden of Alexa's division of her non-exclusive right into two or 1,000 users. The assumption embedded in the bright line rule is that the more users, the higher the likelihood that each user will seek to catch as many fish as possible, since the cost of fewer fish will be borne by the other users. See, *e.g.*, *Hinds v. Phillips Petroleum Co.*, 591 P.2d 697 (Okla. 1979); *Stanton v. T.L. Herbert & Sons*, 141 Tenn. 440 (1919).

ii. **Exclusive easements in one person:** If a profit or easement in gross is *exclusive and vested in one person* that person has the right to divide it, unless the easement or profit stipulates to the contrary. The rationale is that the risk of excessive use is borne by the easement or profit holder alone, and that person has it within their power to limit the risk by refraining entirely from division, so division is legally not objectionable.

iii. **Exclusive easements in multiple persons: "One Stock" Rule.** If a profit or easement in gross is *exclusive and vested in two or more persons* the traditional rule is that division is permitted *but the easement or profit must be used as a single unit* (the *"one-stock"* rule). This rule, derived from *Mountjoy's Case*, 1 Godbolt 17, 4 Leonard 147, Coke on Littleton 164b, 78 Eng. Rep. 11 (1583), holds that joint users may divide their easement or profit but that the entire use must be conducted as a single unit. This rule prevents undue exploitation of resources by one user at the expense of his fellow users. A solo user has the incentive to take as much fish, or timber, or coal, as he can, since the cost of exhaustion of the resource is borne by everyone else. By contrast, if the easement or profit must be worked together there is no incentive to overexploit, since the cost of exhaustion of the resource is borne entirely by the easement or profit holders. See, *e.g.*, *Miller v. Lutheran Conference & Camp Ass'n*, 200 A.646 (Pa. 1938).

iv. **Exclusive easements in multiple persons: the "no increased burden" rule:** The "one stock" rule, while still predominant, has been discarded by some courts in favor of a rule that permits division (or "apportionment" as it is sometimes called) if the *burden on the servient estate is not increased beyond what was initially contemplated.* See, *e.g.*, *Centel Cable TV Co. of Ohio v. Cook*, 567 N.E.2d 1010 (Ohio 1991); *Jolliff v. Hardin Cable Television Co.*, 269 N.E.2d 588 (Ohio 1971); *Cousins v. Alabama Power Co.*, 597 So. 2d 683 (1992); *Witteman v. Jack Barry Cable TV*, 727 P.2d 753 (Cal. 1986). And some courts have avoided this forthright holding by finding that utility easements in gross are exclusive and, therefore, divisible. See, *e.g.*, *Hoffman v. Capitol Cablevision System, Inc.*, 383 N.Y.S.2d 674 (Sup. Ct. 1976).

6. **Use or interference by servient estate owner:**

   a. **Use by servient estate owner:** Unless the easement grants an *exclusive* use right to the easement holder, the servient estate may use the easement to the extent that the use is *reasonable* and does not substantially interfere with the easement holder's use.

Example: Landowner granted a non-exclusive easement to the city of Pasadena for the installation and maintenance of underground water mains along a five foot wide corridor, then granted California-Michigan Land & Water a similar easement along the same corridor. The California Supreme Court ruled that, since Landowner could use the easement so long as its use constituted no unreasonable interference with Pasadena's use, it was entitled to grant a competing easement to California-Michigan that was no more of an interference. *Pasadena v. California-Michigan Land & Water Co.,* 110 P.2d 983 (Cal. 1941).

  b. Interference by servient estate owner: The servient estate owner may not *unreasonably interfere* with the easement holder's use of the easement. What constitutes an unreasonable interference is highly fact specific.

Example 1: Sakansky owned property on Main Street in Laconia, N.H. that included an appurtenant easement for right of way, 18 feet wide, over Wein's property. Wein proposed to build a structure over the easement, leaving a passage way 18 feet wide and 8 feet high. To accommodate overheight vehicles Wein proposed a new and more circuitous way over his property to Sakansky's dominant estate. The New Hampshire Supreme Court concluded that a "rule of reason" applied, that it was not reasonable to limit the headroom of the easement to 8 feet (even with the proposed alternative access), but that Sakansky was free to erect a structure over the easement so long as the headroom was reasonable. *Sakansky v. Wein,* 169 A.1 (N.H. 1933).

Example 2: Servient estate owner constructs speed bumps in an easement for right of way to slow down the traffic. If the speed of the traffic before the speed bumps was excessive, this is a reasonable interference. See, *e.g., Marsh v. Pullen,* 623 P.2d 1078 (Or. Ct. App. 1981). But if the prior traffic was already slow, or if the speed bumps are exceedingly large, hazardous, or numerous, the interference might be unreasonable. See, *e.g., Beiser v. Hensic,* 655 S.W.2d 660 (Mo. Ct. App. 1983).

D. Transfer of easements: The transferability of easements depends on the type of easement.

  1. Easements appurtenant: By their nature, easements appurtenant are transferable as an incident to transfer of title to the dominant estate.

Example: Ingrid, owner of Blackacre, the dominant estate with respect to an easement for passage across Whiteacre, conveys her fee simple to Hendrik. The easement for passage that is appurtenant to Blackacre goes with the title. Similarly, if Hortense, owner of Whiteacre, conveys her fee simple to Emily, the burden of the easement passes along with title to Whiteacre.

2. **Easements in gross:** Since the owner of an easement in gross is not nearly so easy to locate as the owner of an easement appurtenant, and thus a burden on land may persist long after its practical utility has ceased, courts tend to restrict transferability of easements in gross. The general rule today is that ***commercial easements in gross are assignable*** and ***non-commercial easements in gross are not assignable unless the parties intend to permit assignment.*** See, *e.g., Miller v. Lutheran Conference & Camp Ass'n, supra*. A commercial easement primarily produces economic benefits. A non-commercial easement primarily produces personal pleasure.

   Example: An easement in gross for underground utilities produces economic benefits. An easement in gross for the right to meditate atop Mount Zen produces personal pleasure (and maybe enlightenment).

   a. **Rationale:** The rationale for the commercial assignability rule is that the public convenience is advanced by the rule. Without it, commercial easement holders would purchase fee simple corridors, which would cause fee titles, after a long period of time, to look like a bowl of spaghetti. Moreover, the holders of these easements are mostly corporations, entities with perpetual existence, and thus are easily located. Also, corporations alter their existence by merger or acquisition and it would be most inconvenient to wipe out, *e.g.*, utility easements simply because one utility company acquired another.

3. **Profits:** Profits have always been assignable. This might be due to the fact that, in their heyday, profits were valuable rights to the non-landowning laboring class of England, and common law courts recognized the exchange value of rights to take timber or game. But if profits may be freely assigned, why not easements in gross? Courts are probably headed in this direction.

E. **Termination of easements:** Easements are extinguished in five principal ways: (1) ***expiration,*** (2) ***merger,*** (3) some ***act of the easement holder,*** (4) ***complete cessation of purpose,*** or (5) some ***act of the servient estate owner.*** Once an easement is extinguished it ***cannot***

be revived — it must be created anew in one of the ways easements are formed. See p. 205, *supra*.

1. **Expiration:** An easement created by grant may expire by its terms.

    Example: Fred grants Wilma an easement appurtenant for right of way for 25 years. The easement expires automatically at the end of 25 years. If Fred had granted Wilma the easement appurtenant "only until the city constructs a dedicated street that abuts Wilma's property" the easement would automatically expire on that event.

2. **Merger:** If the easement holder also acquires title to the servient estate the easement is extinguished because an easement exists only in land owned by somebody else.

    Example 1: Winnie owns Blackacre, to which an easement for right of way over Whiteacre is appurtenant. Later Winnie acquires fee simple title to Whiteacre. At that moment the easement is extinguished forever.

    Example 2: Frieda owns an easement in gross to fish in Shire Pond, located on Shingleshire. Later, Frieda buys Shingleshire. The easement in gross is extinguished forever.

    The easement holder must acquire the ***entire servient estate*** for merger to extinguish the easement. If only part of the servient estate is acquired, and use of the easement still burdens the other part, the easement is not extinguished. See *Castle Associates v. Schwartz*, 407 N.Y.S.2d 717 (Sup. Ct. 1976). Note that these principles work in reverse, too. If the servient estate owner acquires the dominant estate, the easement is also extinguished forever.

3. **Actions of the easement holder:** The easement holder may do a number of things that will extinguish the easement.

    a. **Release:** The easement holder may release the easement, either unilaterally or as part of an agreement with the servient estate owner. Generally, a release must be written, because it affects an interest in real property and so is within the scope of the Statute of Frauds. An oral release is valid, through equitable estoppel, when it is relied on by the servient estate owner to his substantial detriment.

    b. **Abandonment:** An easement may be extinguished by abandonment if the easement holder manifests a ***clear and unequivocal intention to abandon*** the easement. Mere nonuse ***will not suffice*** to prove abandonment. Even if the easement is never used it is not extinguished by lack of use and nothing more. See, *e.g. Lindsey v. Clark*, 69 S.E.2d 342 (Va.

1952). But if nonuse is combined with other acts of the easement holder that clearly establish intent to abandon, the easement is terminated. Those actions must be clearly inconsistent with an intention to continue the easement's use. The easement holder's conduct can be affirmative or negative.

Example 1: Railway owned an easement over Norton's land. Railway removed its rail tracks and did not use the easement for 10 years. The affirmative act of removal, coupled with nonuse, proved abandonment. *Norton v. Duluth Transfer Ry.,* 151 N.W. 907 (Minn. 1915).

Example 2: In 1955 Fagan granted an easement for access to Gull Lake over Lot 20 in favor of property owned by Hickerson's predecessor. In 1958 Fagan conveyed Lot 20 to Bender, who lacked knowledge of the easement. Bender built a house and other improvements that blocked the easement. Thirty years later Hickerson sought to enforce the easement, which Bender claimed had been abandoned. The Minnesota Court of Appeals agreed with Bender, ruling that the failure of the easement holders to object was "conduct clearly inconsistent" with continued use of the easement. *Hickerson v. Bender,* 500 N.W.2d 169 (Minn. Ct. App. 1993).

   i. **Difficult to prove:** But don't assume it's easy to prove abandonment. "Far more decisions contain dictum about abandonment" than actually find abandonment. Mostly, courts "find that while the easement holder ceased to use the easement, he had no intention to abandon." R. Cunningham, et al., The Law of Property 465 (2d ed. 1993).

c. **Alteration of dominant estate:** If the ***dominant estate owner alters the dominant estate so that the easement may no longer be used*** the easement is extinguished.

Example: The owner of Adirondack, a three story office building, grants an easement appurtenant to Catskill, an abutting three story office building, "for access from Catskill, the presently existing office building, in case of fire or other emergency across the roof of Adirondack and down the existing fire escape." The owner of Catskill demolishes it and builds a ten story replacement. The easement is extinguished because its ***particular purpose,*** providing emergency access from the then-existing building, has been eliminated by the dominant estate owner's act of demolition. See, *e.g. Cotting v. Boston,* 87 N.E. 205 (Mass 1909). But if the easement was not limited to this particular purpose — if, instead, it was "for access from any structure ever erected on the ground presently occupied by Catskill ..." — the destruction of Catskill would not affect the easement. Unless the easement's limited purpose is very explicit, courts tend to place a general construction upon the purpose of easements. See, *e.g.*, *First Nat'l Trust & Savings Bank v. Raphael,* 113 S.E.2d 683 (Va. 1960).

4. **Cessation of purpose:** If the ***purpose of an easement*** has ***completely ceased*** the easement is extinguished.

    a. **Easements by necessity:** An easement created by implication from necessity terminates when the necessity is eliminated, because its purpose has ceased.

    b. **Easements by estoppel:** An easement by estoppel (an irrevocable license) terminates in most jurisdictions when the licensee has reaped the full value of the expenditures made in reliance upon the license. At that point its purpose has ceased to exist. See p. 203, *supra*.

    c. **Extrinsic changes that vitiate purpose:** If acts of third parties completely vitiate the easement's purpose the easement is extinguished.

        Example: Leaman's property benefited from a right of way easement appurtenant (created by grant, not implied from necessity) across American Oil's property for access to a public road. When the public road was abandoned and another created, making the easement pointless (it turned into a dead-end), its purpose ceased. Though this change was entirely brought about by third parties (public authorities) and was not of the dominant estate owner's volition, nonetheless the easement terminated. *American Oil Co. v. Leaman,* 101 S.E.2d 540 (Va. 1958).

    d. **Accidental destruction of the servient estate:** If the servient estate is ***accidentally destroyed*** (*i.e.*, not through the servient owner's intent) the easement is extinguished. This usually requires that the easement be ***limited to use of a specific building.*** If the easement extends to the ground itself, the destruction of a building will have no effect on the easement, but if the easement is just in the building (and not the land also) the easement terminates if the building is accidentally destroyed. See, *e.g.*, *Cohen v. Adolph Kutner Co.,* 171 P. 424 (Cal. 1918). Intentional destruction of the servient estate normally renders the servient owner liable for damages and does not extinguish the easement. See, *e.g.*, *Rothschild v. Wolf,* 123 P.2d 483 (Cal. 1942). But if a building is so obsolete and shabby that its continuation is uneconomic, its condition may be deemed "tantamount to [accidental] destruction," thus extinguishing the easement. See, *e.g. Walner v. City of Turlock,* 41 Cal. Rptr. 29 (Ct. App. 1964).

5. **Actions of the servient estate holder:** There are two principal ways the owner of the servient estate can extinguish an easement.

   a. **Intentional destruction of servient estate:** A minority of states hold that a servient owner's intentional destruction of a building burdened by an easement in the building alone (not the land) extinguishes the easement if continued operation of the servient building is economically disadvantageous. See, *e.g., Union Nat'l Bank of Lowell v. Nesmith,* 130 N.E. 251 (Mass. 1921). Most states reject this rule. See p. 225, *supra.*

   b. **Prescription:** A servient owner can extinguish an easement burdening the servient estate by adverse use sufficient to constitute prescription. The elements of adverse use are the same as for creation of an easement by prescription. See p. 210, *supra.*

   Example: Bender built a house and other improvements that blocked an easement for passage across his property to a lake. Thirty years later Hickerson sought to enforce the easement. The easement had been extinguished by Bender's adverse use. *Hickerson v. Bender, supra.*

6. **Changed circumstances in the surrounding area:** The doctrine of *changed circumstances in the surrounding area,* which may extinguish a real covenant or equitable servitude, does *not generally apply to easements.*

   Example: The Town of Brevard acquired an easement by grant for a garbage dump. The surrounding area changed and the garbage dump became disagreeable. Nevertheless, the mere change in *surrounding circumstances,* while perhaps sufficient to extinguish a real covenant or equitable servitude, was not a valid reason to extinguish an easement by grant. *Waldrop v. Town of Brevard,* 62 S.E.2d 512 (N.C. 1950).

   a. **Confusion among rules:** Don't confuse this rule — which deals with changed circumstances in the *surrounding area—* with changed circumstances in the *dominant estate* or *servient estate.* Some changes in circumstances in the dominant estate or servient estate do in fact extinguish an easement (*e.g.,* cessation of purpose or destruction of the servient estate). See, *e.g.,* pp. 225 and 226, *supra.*

III. REAL COVENANTS

A. Introduction:

1. **Real covenants defined:** A covenant is a promise and is generally the province of the law of contracts. A *real covenant* is a promise about land usage that *runs with an estate in land* so that it *binds subsequent owners.* A real covenant may be *affirmative* or *negative.* A promise to *use land in a specified fashion* (*e.g.*, to maintain a boxwood hedge) is affirmative; a promise *not to use land in a specified fashion* (*e.g.*, no industrial use) is negative. Both types are enforceable.

2. **Benefit and burden:** A promise about land usage burdens some land and normally benefits other land.

    Example: Barbara, owner of Blackacre, promises Thomas, owner of Monteverdi, that she and her assigns will maintain forever a boxwood hedge on Blackacre that forms a border with Monteverdi. Blackacre bears the *burden* of this promise and Monteverdi enjoys its *benefit.* (The nomenclature of dominant and servient estates is confined to easements).

3. **"Runs with the land:"** If one party breaches a covenant made with another person — even if it concerns land usage — the issues presented are purely a matter of contract law. Property law becomes involved only when a covenant about land use is sought to be enforced either by or against a *successor to the estate in the land* benefited or burdened by the covenant.

    Example: Refer to the prior example. If Barbara sells Blackacre to James and James rips out the hedge, Thomas may sue James for this breach of the covenant only if the burden of the covenant runs with the estate in Blackacre that James acquired from Barbara. Similarly, if Thomas sells Monteverdi to John and Barbara destroys the hedge, John may sue Barbara only if the benefit of the covenant runs with the estate in Monteverdi that John acquired from Thomas. Finally, if both Barbara and Thomas have sold to James and John, respectively, John may sue James for breach of the covenant only if both the burden and the benefit of the covenant run with their respective estates in land.

    a. **When the benefit or burden runs:** The question of exactly when the burden or benefit runs is a complicated, technical subject addressed on pp. 229, 230 and 231, *infra*. When you recall that a *real covenant* is defined as a covenant about land use that *runs with an estate in land,* you will realize that almost all the substance of this subject lies in the issue of when burdens or benefits, or both, run with estates in land. Although lawyers commonly speak of covenants "running with the land" that usage is mildly misleading. A real covenant runs with the *estate in land,* not the land itself. This distinction is important when considering whether *privity of estate* is present. See p. 230, *infra.*

4. **Remedy available — damages:** There are two principal remedies for breach of a promise — *money damages* or an *injunction* to compel performance of the promise. For historical reasons, an award of damages is a *legal remedy* and an injunction is an *equitable remedy.* Although virtually all American courts are combined courts of *law* and *equity,* it is still necessary to establish your client's entitlement to the remedy she seeks. If your client wants *damages* for breach of a covenant about land usage, she must prove that the covenant is a *real covenant.* If she cannot do that, the same promise might still be enforceable as an *equitable servitude,* but the only remedy then available for breach will be an injunction. See p. 239, *infra.* When you think *damages,* think *real covenant.* When you think *real covenant,* think *damages.*

5. **Development of the real covenant:** English judges invented the *real* covenant to make bargains about land use last. Before real covenants were invented, only the immediate parties to a covenant were able to sue to enforce the covenant or liable for its breach. But this rule frustrated the efficient allocation of interests in land.

   Example: Morton leases Blackacre to Selwyn for a term of 15 years. Morton promises to build a new barn if the existing one ever burns down, and Selwyn promises to pay an annual rent. Now suppose Morton conveys his reversion in Blackacre to Algernon. Then the barn burns. Before real covenants, only Morton was liable for failure to rebuild the barn. Similarly, if Selwyn conveyed his leasehold to Edward, Edward would not be liable for rent.

   a. **Restrictions of the real covenant:** Since these rules inhibited the formation and transferability of leaseholds, English judges decided that covenants about land use attached themselves to the estates in land benefited or burdened by the covenant. Thus, successors to those estates could enforce the covenant or be liable for its breach. This rule developed from *Spencer's Case,* 5 Co. 16a, 77 Eng. Rep. 72 (K.B. 1583) in which the requirements for "running covenants" first began to be stated. By the 19th century, though, English judges confined real covenants to leaseholds and have kept it there. See *Keppell v. Bailey,* 39 Eng. Rep. 1042 (Ch. 1834). In America, real covenants may be created when a fee simple is transferred or even between neighbors with no transfer of title. The rule governing this point is called *horizontal privity of estate.* See p. 231, *infra.*

6. **Covenant, not condition:** A real covenant is a *promise* concerning land use. It is *not* a *condition* of continued land use. Breach of a real covenant renders the violator liable for damages; breach of a condition causes forfeiture of the estate. Conditions concerning land use are the meat of defeasible fees. See p. 50, *supra.*

7. **Compared to easements:** Affirmative easements confer rights to use another's land. Real covenants do not. Real covenants are promises that land will be used, or not used, in specified ways. Negative easements, however, are very much like real covenants. A *right* to an unobstructed view over your neighbor's land (a negative easement) is functionally identical to a *promise* by your neighbor not to obstruct your view (a real covenant). While courts are reluctant to create negative easements (see p. 201, *supra*) they may well enforce the promise as a real covenant. Mostly, an interest claimed in another person's land that requires that person to refrain from some use will be construed as a covenant, enforceable against successors if the elements of a running real covenant or equitable servitude are established.

8. **Compared to equitable servitudes:** An equitable servitude is a covenant about land use that is enforceable in equity against successors to the benefited or burdened estates in land. The rules concerning the running of equitable servitudes differ from the rules concerning the running of real covenants. See p. 239, *infra.*

B. **Creation of real covenants:** A real covenant can only be created by a written instrument. A deed signed only by the grantor suffices to create a real covenant on the part of the grantee, because the grantee is held to have made the deed his own by accepting it. Real covenants may *not be created by implication or prescription.*

C. **Enforceability by or against successors:** The elements necessary to enforce the *burden* of a real covenant against a successor to the burdened estate are more difficult to establish than the elements needed to claim the *benefit* of a real covenant by a successor to the benefited estate. The rationale is that, since the burden of a real covenant exposes the successor to liability that is potentially unlimited, this burden ought to be imposed only on those people who acquire the *identical estate* that was initially burdened.

1. **Burden running with the estate in land:** The elements necessary for the burden of a real covenant to run with the estate in land are as follows.

a. **Intent:** The original parties must have *intended the burden to run.* Almost always this is satisfied by an explicit statement in the covenant that it binds "successors, heirs, and assigns." See p. 230, *infra.*

b. **Horizontal privity:** Most courts insist upon *horizontal privity — privity of estate* between the *original parties.* Only a few relationships satisfy this technical term and concept, which is discussed fully at p. 231, *infra.* Some courts have dispensed with this requirement altogether.

c. **Vertical privity:** Virtually all courts require *vertical privity — privity of estate* between the *original promisor and the successor to the burdened estate.* This technical concept is discussed fully at p. 233, *infra.*

d. **Touch and concern:** The substance of the promise must *touch and concern* the burdened land and, in most states, the benefited land as well. It is commonly said of real covenants that if the benefit is in gross, the burden will not run. See p. 235 *infra.*

e. **Notice:** The successor to the burdened estate must have *notice of the real covenant* when he acquires the estate. Notice may be *actual* or *constructive* (*e.g.*, the covenant is recorded in the chain of title).

2. **Benefit running with the estate in land:** For the *benefit* of a real covenant to run with an estate in land, the following elements must be present.

a. **Intent:** The original parties to the covenant must intend that the benefit of the covenant run. See p. 230, *infra.*

b. **Vertical privity:** There must be privity of estate between the original promisee and the successor to the estate benefited. By contrast, *horizontal privity is not usually required.* See p. 233, *infra.*

c. **Touch and concern:** The substance of the benefit conferred by the covenant must touch and concern use of the land. See p. 235, *infra.*

D. **"Running elements" — intent:** The original parties to the covenant must intend for its burdens or benefits, or both, to run to successors to their respective estates in land. Courts look first to the covenant itself. Covenants typically state that they are intended to run or, what is the same thing, the parties promise on behalf of themselves, "their heirs, successors, or assigns." But if the covenant is silent on this point, courts will examine all the surrounding circumstances (*e.g.*, covenant's purpose, conduct of the parties) to decide whether the parties intended to create a running covenant. Old English law required that covenants dealing with things not yet in existence (*e.g.*, a promise to build a structure) could not run unless the promisor had explicitly obligated his successors to perform the promise. See *Spencer's Case, supra*. This rule has been abandoned nearly everywhere.

E. "Running elements" — privity of estate: Privity of estate exists in two dimensions. *Horizontal privity* refers to a relationship between the *original parties* to the covenant. *Vertical privity* refers to a relationship between one of the original parties and her successor to the estate in land owned by the original party. Both horizontal and vertical privity are traditionally required for the burden of a real covenant to run. Most states require only vertical privity for the benefit of a real covenant to run.

   1. Horizontal privity: Horizontal privity exists when the law deems the relationship between the estates in land owned by the original contracting parties to be sufficiently connected to permit the burden of the covenant to run. But what connection is sufficient? There are three views, which can be combined. Each developed from a different reading of *Spencer's Case, supra*, where Elizabethan judges ruled that an original leasehold tenant's promise to build a wall on the premises could be enforced against a successor tenant because the original parties were in privity of estate. The court, however, didn't explain why.

      a. Landlord-tenant view: In 1834, two and one-half centuries after *Spencer's Case,* English judges finally held that horizontal privity was met *only if the original parties were landlord and tenant.* In the U.K., horizontal privity remains limited to covenants in leases. The burden of other covenants about land use are enforceable against successors, if at all, only as equitable servitudes. This view is no longer recognized in America, though some old cases did take this tight approach.

      b. Mutual interests in the burdened estate: Another view of *Spencer's Case* is that the parties there had *mutual interests* in the burdened estate. The lessee had a leasehold and the lessor had a reversion. On this view, *any mutual interest that exists at the time the covenant is created* would be sufficient to create horizontal privity. The requisite mutual interest could include a preexisting easement or profit, or possessory and future interests in the same land, as well as a landlord-tenant relationship.

Example 1: Adam owns Blackacre in fee simple and has a possibility of reverter in Whiteacre, which Eleanor owns in fee simple determinable ("so long as Whiteacre is used for animal husbandry"). Eleanor promises Adam, for herself and her assigns, that she will never again raise emus on Whiteacre. Horizontal privity is established, because both Adam and Eleanor have mutual interests in Whiteacre which preceded the covenant. If Eleanor should transfer her determinable fee to Mary Jane, who knows of the covenant, its burden will run with the estate Mary Jane acquired.

Example 2: Oilco has the right to remove oil from Blackacre, owned by Isaac. Isaac then promises Oilco that he will not graze his sheep within 100 yards of each oil well drilled by Oilco on Blackacre. Horizontal privity is established. Both Oilco and Isaac had interests in Blackacre prior to execution of the covenant. See, *e.g., Flying Diamond Oil Corp. v. Newton Sheep Co.,* 776 P.2d 618 (Utah. 1989).

    i. **American rule:** Every American state that requires horizontal privity recognizes at least this form of horizontal privity. Some recognize ***only*** this form of horizontal privity. See, *e.g., Morse v. Aldrich,* 36 Mass. 449 (1837).

c. **Conveyances, or "instantaneous privity:"** A third view of *Spencer's Case* is that the fact the promise was contained in a conveyance was what created horizontal privity. On this view, **any "connection of interest"** between the original contracting parties will do, whether or not that interest was mutual or in existence prior to the creation of the covenant. The most common such interest that suffices to create horizontal privity is a conveyance.

Example: Elmer divides Blackacre into two lots, retaining one and conveying the other to Juanita under a deed by which Juanita promises never to use the lot for commercial purposes. Horizontal privity is present. For that single, instantaneous moment when title passed from Elmer to Juanita there was a "connection of interest" between their estates. It's like the passing of the baton in a relay race — privity exists at the moment of exchange. See, *e.g., Runyon v. Paley,* 416 S.E.2d 177 (N.CX. 1992).

    i. **Cumulative interests:** The conveyance view is cumulative — mutual interests (including, of course, landlord-tenant) will suffice to create horizontal privity, but so will conveyances. This view is adopted by the original (1944) Restatement of Property, § 534.

- d. **Applies to *burdens,* not *benefits:*** In virtually every jurisdiction that requires horizontal privity, the requirement is applicable ***only for the burden of a covenant to run,*** and is ***not necessary*** for the benefit of a covenant to run. See, *e.g., City of Reno v. Matley,* 378 P.2d 256 (Nev. 1963); *165 Broadway Building v. City Investing Co.,* 120 F.2d 813 (2d Cir. 1941). But there is the inevitable exception. See, *e.g., Albright v. Fish,* 394 A.2d 1117 (Vt. 1978).

- e. **Horizontal privity abolished:** About eight states have abolished horizontal privity altogether and the pending Restatement (3d) of Property (Servitudes), § 2.4 also abolishes it. See *Orange & Rockland Util. v. Philwood Estates,* 418 N.E.2d 1310 (N.Y. 1981); *Gallagher v. Bell,* 516 A.2d 1028 (Md. Ct. Spec. App. 1986). Other states that have abolished horizontal privity include Illinois, Minnesota, Montana, New Mexico, and Pennsylvania. Still more have given broad hints that horizontal privity is on the way out. A moment's reflection will reveal that there is ***no logical connection*** between the relationship of the original parties' estates and the wholly separate question of whether the burden of a promise about land use ought to run with the estate in that land. Horizontal privity is simply a crude device to restrict the burdens of covenants from persisting into the future. If there are good reasons for doing so, they ought to be articulated and formulated into rules of law that restrict running covenants for those reasons.

2. **Vertical privity:** Vertical privity exists when the successor has acquired the burdened or benefited estate in land held by the original party to the covenant. But it is ***harder to establish vertical privity for the burden of a covenant than it is for the benefit of that covenant.***

    - a. **Burden of a covenant:** To establish vertical privity to enforce the burden of a covenant against a successor, it is necessary to prove that the successor acquired ***the exact same estate in land*** owned by the original contracting party. See Rest. Prop. § 535 (1944). If something less than the original promisor's estate is conveyed the burden does not run.

        Example: Paul purchases fee simple absolute in Blackthorn from Phyllis, owner of adjacent Tumbleweed. In the deed Paul promises for himself and his assigns that he will not use Blackthorn for industrial purposes. Later he leases Blackthorn to Ace

Industrial Corp. for use as a factory. Phyllis may not enforce the burden of the covenant against Ace since Ace did not succeed to the *identical estate* held by Paul. But Phyllis will of course have a contract claim against Paul. See, *e.g.*, *Old Dominion Iron & Steel Corp. v. Virginia Electric & Power Co.*, 212 S.E.2d 715 (Va. 1975).

b. **Benefit of a covenant:** The benefit of a covenant will run to a successor of *some interest* in the benefited estate. See Rest. Property, § 547 (1944). Just about any interest will do.

Example: Refer to the prior example. Suppose Paul had sold his fee simple absolute in Blackthorn to Ace, thus satisfying vertical privity for the burden. If Phyllis leased Tumbleweed to Jack for a 10 year term, Jack could sue Ace to enforce the real covenant and obtain damages. Jack succeeded to *some interest* of Phyllis in Tumbleweed. He need not acquire Phyllis's entire estate in order to reap the benefit of the original covenant. See, *e.g.*, *Old Dominion Iron & Steel Corp. v. Virginia Electric & Power Co.*, *supra*.

c. **The problem of adverse possessors:** Land burdened or benefited by a covenant may later be acquired by adverse possession. Is the adverse possessor in vertical privity? Rest. Prop. § 547 (Illus. 3) (1944) took the position that an adverse possessor lacked vertical privity with respect to both the burden and benefit of a covenant. There are no cases on point, probably because the preferred remedy for breach of a covenant is an injunction (thus taking the issue over to the realm of equitable servitudes and outside real covenants).

d. **The problem of third party beneficiaries:** Two parties may enter into a covenant about land use that imposes mutual benefits and burdens but also explicitly benefits a third party's estate. Is the third party beneficiary able to sue to enforce the benefit of the covenant? Probably not.

Example: Oboe purchases Lot 1 from Flute, under a deed that stipulates that Oboe, for himself and his assigns, agrees to use Lot 1 for residential purposes only, and which further states that the promise is for the benefit of Lot 2 (owned by Flute) and Lot 3 (owned by Cello, who purchased it from Flute prior to this transaction). Oboe builds a gas station on Lot 1. May Cello enforce the covenant at law? There is no vertical privity since Cello has not succeeded to any interest of Oboe *after the benefit was created.* See, *e.g.*, *Runyon v. Paley, supra*. But Rest. Property, § 541 (1944) provides that a covenant may be enforced by "such third persons as are also beneficiaries of the promise." The only cases recognizing the ability of third party beneficiaries to enforce covenants are suits in equity, thus involving equitable servitudes, not real covenants.

> **i. Homeowners' association:** Note, however, that a homeowners' association that does not succeed to any estate of the benefited promisee has been held able to enforce the benefit of such covenants on the theory that it is the corporate agent of the owners of benefited estates. See *Neponsit Property Owners Ass'n v. Emigrant Industrial Savings Bank,* 278 N.Y. 248 (1938).

F. "Running elements" — touch and concern the land: In order for either the benefit or burden of a real covenant to run to successors in interest the substance of the covenant must *touch and concern* the benefited or burdened land. The same is true for equitable servitudes. The meaning of touch and concern is the same for equitable servitudes and real covenants.

> **1. Essential meaning of touch and concern:** Judicial understanding of touch and concern has evolved. Early cases focused on whether the substance of the covenant delivered burdens and benefits that necessarily involved the *tangible use and enjoyment* of the land. More recent cases and commentators have focused on whether the substance of the covenant "affect[s] the legal relations — the advantages and the burdens — of the parties to the covenant, as owners of particular parcels of land and not merely as members of the community in general." *Neponsit Property Owners' Ass'n v. Emigrant Industrial Savings Bank,* 278 N.Y. 248 (1938). To do this courts have looked to the *effect of the covenant* — does it depress the value of the burdened land and increase the value of the benefited land? This approach uses *marketplace values* to determine what touches and concerns land. These two approaches are cruder versions of the third — an attempt to determine which covenants are *sufficiently economically beneficial that they would be imposed by the present owners if they had the opportunity to negotiate between themselves free of transaction costs.*
>
> > **a. The economic theory:** The law of servitudes is built on an implicit general presumption that servitudes reflect an efficient allocation of external costs associated with land use. Thus, they ought to be enforced by and against the original promisors (and successors, if the other elements of running covenants are present).

Example: Quikfat, a fast food chain, proposes to build a store in a residential neighborhood. The presence of the store will damage surrounding residential values and will provide economic benefits to Quikfat. To simplify, say that the total benefit to Quikfat is $100,000 and that 100 neighbors will each suffer damage of $2,500. If each neighbor contributes $1,500 to purchase from Quikfat its promise not to build a fast food store on the property, Quikfat will be better off (it will receive $150,000 to forego a benefit of $100,000) and each neighbor will be better off (by paying $1500 to avoid a loss of $2500). A servitude is efficient. See, *e.g.* Ronald Coase, The Problem of Social Cost, 3 J. Law & Econ. 1 (1960). But neighbors won't pay unless they can be assured that the promise will endure. It is the threat of damage, now or in the future, that they wish to forestall.

    i. Function of running covenants: Hence, a function of "touch and concern" is to limit running covenants to those promises that are the *type of promise about land use future owners might agree to.* From the above illustration it should be clear that these promises are those that *deliver net benefits.* In the above example, the servitude produces net benefits of $150,000 ($250,000 of avoided costs minus $100,000 of foregone gain). See. Rest. Property, § 537 (comment h) (1944) (relationship between benefit and burden must have a "reasonable prospect of promoting land utilization as a whole").

2. Negative covenants: Negative covenants almost always touch and concern the burdened land, because their nature is to restrict land use. In nearly every case they also deliver correlative benefits to other land.

Example: A promise given to neighbors not to use Greaseacre for a fast food restaurant imposes burdens on Greaseacre and also generates correlative benefits to the surrounding land, The burden of the promise touches and concerns Greaseacre. The benefit of the promise touches and concerns the neighbors' land.

    a. Covenants against competition: The burden of covenants against competition generally touch and concern land, so long as they are reasonable in scope and duration. See, *e.g., Newcomb v. Congdon,* 160 App. Div.2d 1192 (1990. The benefit of such covenants surely enhances the value of the benefited land, at least for the use insulated from competition, and so also touches and concerns the benefited land. See, *e.g., Whitinsville Plaza, Inc. v. Kotseas,* 390 N.E.2d 243 (Mass. 1979). In *Davidson Bros., Inc. v. D. Katz & Sons, Inc.,* 643 A.2d 642 (N.J. Super. Ct. 1994), a New

Jersey appellate court invalidated a covenant that a building not be used as a grocery on the ground that it violated a vague judicial sense of "public policy" that it would be a good idea for a grocery to be located there.

3. **Affirmative covenants:** Affirmative covenants are generally held to touch and concern land. See, *e.g.*, *Moseley v. Bishop,* 470 N.E.2d 773 (Ind. Ct. App. 1984). Nevertheless, an affirmative covenant that fails to address the economic external costs of land use is almost certainly one that does not touch and concern land.

   Example: Kendall owned an ironworks and, in concert with other ironmongers, formed a corporation to operate a railroad and a lime quarry. On behalf of himself and his assigns Kendall promised the corporation that his ironworks would purchase its requirements of lime from the quarry. Kendall sold the ironworks to Bailey, who refused to purchase lime from the quarry. The English Chancery court ruled that the burden of the covenant did not touch and concern the ironworks. Though it did not say so, it is evident that the covenant's purpose had nothing whatever to do with any external costs of using the land as an ironworks. It was a purely personal promise. *Keppell v. Bailey,* 39 Eng. Rep. 1042 (Ch. 1834). See also *Bremmeyer Excavating, Inc. v. McKenna,* 721 P.2d 567 (Wash. Ct. App. 1986) (burden of promise to use Bremmeyer to fill and excavate property did not run since it imposed a purely personal burden).

   a. **Covenants to provide utilities:** These covenants generally touch and concern. See, *e.g.*, *Choisser v. Eyman,* 529 P.2d 741 (Ariz. Ct. App. 1974) (benefit of covenant to provide water); *Nicholson v. 300 Broadway Realty Corp.,* 164 N.E.2d 832 (N.Y. 1959) (burden of covenant, to provide steam heat). But if such covenants lose their utility their burden may be seen as not touching or concerning the burdened land.

      Example: Orchard Hill developed a tract of rural land for use as summer homes, and sold lots subject to a covenant that the purchaser and his successors would take and pay for water provided by Orchard Hill for six months of the year. Orchard Hill conveyed its interest to Eagle, and Gross acquired a lot from an original purchaser. Gross drilled a well and then refused to take and pay for water. The burden of the "take and pay" covenant was held not to touch and concern Gross's property, mostly because it had lost its utility to Gross and its invalidation would not harm other lot owners who relied on seasonal water. *Eagle Enterprises, Inc. v. Gross,* 349 N.E.2d 816 (N.Y. 1976).

b. Covenants to pay money: The most common such covenant is one requiring payment of fees to a homeowners association to pay for the maintenance of common areas and facilities. These covenants are generally held to touch and concern land so long as the services produced by the payment enhance the value of the burdened land. This is virtually always the case when the payments maintain common streets, sidewalks, elevators or other "essential" attributes of the development. There is some disagreement over whether covenants to pay for common recreational facilities touch and concern the burdened property. While the test is the same — does it enhance value? —courts examine the following factors to determine this:

- Is the facility part of a ***common plan of development?***
- Is the facility in ***close proximity*** to the burdened land?
- Is the facility ***open to common use of all burdened property owners?***

   i. Majority view: Most courts considering this issue have found that such covenants do touch and concern land. See, *e.g., Regency Homes Ass'n v. Egermayer,* 498 N.W.2d 783 (Neb. 1993); *Streams Sports Club, Ltd. v. Richmond,* 457 N.E.2d 1226 (Ill. 1983); *Anthony v. Brea Glenbrook Club,* 130 Cal. Rptr. 32 (Ct. App. 1976). But see *Chesapeake Ranch Club v. CRC Members,* 483 A.2d 1334 (Md. Ct. Spec. App. 1984) (recreational facility benefited community as a whole and did not enhance value of burdened lots).

4. Benefit in gross: The majority rule is summed up by an old saying, "if the benefit is in gross, the burden will not run." The rule comes from England, where easements in gross are not recognized. It was thus sensible for English courts to refuse to enforce the burden of a covenant against successors where the benefit was held in gross, since such a covenant is functionally identical to an easement in gross (particularly when the covenant is negative). See, *e.g., London County Council v. Allen,* [1914] 3 K.B. 642. American courts recognize easements in gross but still cling to the rule that "if the benefit is in gross, the burden won't run." See, *e.g., Chandler v. Smith,* 338 P.2d 522 (Cal. Ct. App. 1959); *Johnson v. State,* 556 P.2d 724 (Or. Ct. App. 1976). Rest. Prop. §§ 537(a) (comment c), 543 (comment c) (1944). Contra: *Van Sant v. Rose,* 103 N.E. 194 (Ill. 1913). The pending Rest. (3d) Prop., Servitudes, § 2.6 (Tentative Draft No. 1, 1989), squarely rejects the majority rule. This is probably destined to be the majority rule in another generation.

a. **Policy considerations:** Covenants with the benefit held in gross can be useful, as when landowners burden their property for historic preservation or environmental conservation purposes, and make a non-landowning enterprise (*e.g.*, the National Trust for Historic Preservation or the Audubon Society) the beneficiary of the covenant. But the current majority rule is justified on the ground that the lack of benefited land raises a presumption that (1) the covenant was not designed to deal with externalities and (2) there was no net benefit to land as a whole by the covenant. Even so, it is difficult to justify a blanket prohibition against the running of the burden of a covenant whose benefit is held in gross.

5. **Burden in gross:** Though rarely encountered, it is possible for the benefit of a covenant to run with land and the burden of the covenant to be in gross. Courts have not hesitated to permit such benefits to run. See, *e.g. Mueller v. Bankers' Trust Co.*, 247 N.W. 103 (Mich. 1933) (seller of land promised to build a bridge over a creek on the land; subsequent purchaser was permitted to enforce the covenant which touched and concerned the benefited land).

IV. EQUITABLE SERVITUDES

A. **Introduction:** An equitable servitude is a ***covenant about land use*** that will be enforced in equity (by an ***injunction***) against a successor to the burdened estate who acquired it with ***notice*** of the covenant. A covenant need ***not*** meet all the criteria of a real covenant to be enforceable as an equitable servitude. Equitable servitudes are probably more common than real covenants because they are easier to enforce by or against successors and most people prefer enforcement of a covenant by injunction than damages for its breach.

1. **Differences between real covenants and equitable servitudes:** A covenant about land use may be a real covenant, an equitable servitude, or both. There are three major differences between real covenants and equitable servitudes.

    a. **Remedy:** A real covenant is enforceable ***at law by an award of money damages.*** An equitable servitude is enforceable in ***equity by an injunction.*** Most people prefer to enforce a covenant by an injunction than receive damages for breach because an injunction is more valuable.

    Example: Otto owns Blackacre, which is benefited by a covenant burdening Whiteacre, a neighboring parcel, limiting its use to single family residential houses. Suppose Buildmore Corp., owner of Whiteacre, starts to build an apartment building that will produce total economic benefits to Buildmore of $500,000 and damage to Otto of $30,000. Suppose that Otto can enforce the covenant as either a real covenant or an equitable servitude. If Otto sues for damages on the real covenant he will receive $30,000. But if Otto seeks an injunction on the equitable servitude he has stopped Buildmore's project and deprived Buildmore of its $500,000 gain. Suppose the cost to Buildmore of abandoning the project and finding another site that will produce the same gain is $150,000. Buildmore will likely seek to purchase the injunction from Otto by paying him to extinguish the covenant. Buildmore would be economically better off to pay anything up to $150,000 to Otto. Depending on the negotiating skill of Otto and Buildmore (and assuming that Otto is an "economic man") the injunction will be sold for a price between $30,000 and $150,000. From Otto's perspective the injunction is far more valuable. From Buildmore's perspective, the injunction is more expensive.

b. **No privity needed:** Neither horizontal nor vertical privity is needed for either the benefit or burden of an equitable servitude to run to successors in the burdened or benefited estates.

c. **Creation:** Equitable servitudes may be created by ***implication*** in many jurisdictions. A real covenant can only be created expressly.

d. **Interest in land:** An equitable servitude is an interest in land, which entitles the holder of the benefit of the equitable servitude to an injunction without proof of any damage to the benefit holder. A real covenant is a promise binding on a successor to a burdened estate, or a promise enforceable at law by the successor to a benefited estate.

2. **Origins of the equitable servitude:** The equitable servitude originated in *Tulk v. Moxhay,* 41 Eng. Rep. 1143 (Ch. 1848). Tulk sold Leicester Square to Elms who promised for himself and his assigns not to build on Leicester Square. With knowledge of the covenant, Moxhay purchased Leicester Square from Elms and then proposed to build on the Square. Under English law the burden of the covenant would not run because horizontal privity was lacking. See p. 231, *supra.* So Tulk sought and obtained an injunction. The Chancellor reasoned that it was highly unfair for Moxhay to purchase Leicester Square knowing of the covenant (and probably paying less because of its existence) only to ignore it with impunity. The covenant was intended to bind successors, its substance touched and concerned the land, and Moxhay had notice of it.

B. **Creation:** Because equitable servitudes are interests in land the Statute of Frauds requires that they be created in a writing signed by the promisor. Acceptance of a deed containing the promise suffices. There is a *major exception* to this rule. Many states permit *negative equitable servitudes* (a promise to refrain from using one's land in a specified fashion) to be created by implication when there is a common scheme of residential development.

1. **By implication from a common development scheme:** Many states will imply a *negative equitable servitude* where a real estate developer sells lots in a subdivision on the promise that all the lots will be burdened with the same use restriction (typically, single family residences only) and later fails to carry through on the promise to burden all lots.

    Example: Majestic Homes, a developer, subdivides a tract of land into building lots and starts to sell them under deeds that restrict use to single family residences. Majestic also tells each purchaser that all the lots in the subdivision will be similarly restricted. Mikhyla purchases a burdened lot in reliance on this promise and builds a residence on it. Later, as sales slow down, Majestic stops imposing the covenant restricting use, and sells an unburdened lot to Quikfat, although Quikfat is aware of the covenants on most of the remaining lots. Quikfat then builds a fast food restaurant on the lot. A covenant burdening Quikfat's lot and restricting use to single family residences may be implied on the theory of *equitable estoppel* — Majestic misrepresented its intentions, Mikhyla relied to her detriment on the representation, and thus both Majestic and its assignees with notice of the scheme will be estopped from asserting the Statute of Frauds. See, *e.g., Sanborn v. McLean,* 206 N.W. 496 (Mich. 1925); *Mid-State Equip. Co., Inc. v. Bell,* 225 S.E.2d 877 (Va. 1976).

    a. **Reciprocal negative easement:** Courts sometimes call the covenant so implied a *reciprocal negative easement,* although the term *implied reciprocal covenant* makes more sense. Whatever the label, it is (1) *reciprocal* (the common scheme contemplates covenants burdening all lots for reciprocal benefit) and (2) *negative* (restricts land use rather than requiring affirmative acts or use). Although *not* an easement it is in the nature of an easement since an equitable servitude is an interest in land. For an implied reciprocal covenant to be implied the following elements must be present.

    b. **Common scheme of development:** The development must be of uniform character and recognizable as such by purchasers. Otherwise, there is no basis for concluding that purchasers were relying on reciprocal covenants burdening everyone's use in order to produce a development of uniform character.

i. When does the scheme begin? Courts vary considerably in their answers to this question. In general, the following factors are often used to determine the existence of a common scheme:

- *Advertisements* mentioning the reciprocal covenants

- Use of a *map showing the entire development* as a sales aid in conjunction with sales of burdened lots

- *Representations* to buyers that all lots will be similarly burdened

- Sale of a significant number of lots with a common use restriction.

(1) Courts vary: See, *e.g.*, *Miniat v. McGinnis*, 762 S.W.2d 390 (Ark. Ct. App. 1988). At one extreme are courts that hold that the common scheme must exist at the very beginning of the project, before any sales have occurred. See, *e.g.*, *Johnson v. Mt. Baker Park Presbyterian Church*, 194 P. 536 (Wash. 1920). Many jurisdictions are more lenient. In *Sanborn v. McLean, supra*, a leading case, 21 lots (out of a total of 98) were sold with residential-only use restrictions before the lot at issue in the case was sold without such a restriction, yet the court ruled that a common scheme had been created, notwithstanding the fact that, by the time the "common scheme" was completed, less than 60% of the total lots in the subdivision were burdened by reciprocal covenants. But restricting 12 lots out of 23 has been held insufficient to create a common scheme. *Tindolph v. Schoenfeld Bros., Inc.*, 289 P. 530 (Wash. 1930). See also *3 W Partners v. Bridges*, 651 A.2d 387 (Me. 1994) (no common plan when only 3 out of 67 lots burdened).

ii. No covenants on lots conveyed before the common scheme begins: If a developer conveys land without use covenants *before the common scheme begins* no reciprocal covenant will be implied. The land is simply not part of the common scheme and so there is no basis for finding an implied reciprocal covenant.

Example: Developer buys Flatland, a 160 acre farm. Developer sells Homestead, a 10 acre portion consisting of the house, barns, and adjacent pasture, without covenants restricting use. Later, Developer subdivides the remaining 150 acres into 300 lots, selling them as "residential-only lots — no farm animals permitted." MacDonald, the owner of Homestead, maintains a wide variety of farm animals on Homestead. While a common scheme may exist with respect to this 150 acre development, sufficient to create implied reciprocal covenants if necessary, no such covenant applies to Homestead. MacDonald can keep his farm animals so far as the law of servitudes is concerned.

    c. **Negative covenant:** Courts will imply reciprocal covenants *only* when the substance of the covenant is *negative* — limiting the use that may be made of the property rather than requiring some positive act on the part of the owner of the burdened land.

  2. **No implied covenants:** Some jurisdictions, notably California and Massachusetts, completely reject creation of equitable servitudes by implication. See, *e.g.*, *Werner v. Graham,* 183 P. 945 (Cal. 1919); *Sprague v. Kimball,* 100 N.E. 622 (Mass. 1913). In California, even if use restrictions are recorded in the public records (*e.g.*, in a subdivision map) they do not burden the lots described unless the deed specifically refers to the recorded restriction. *Riley v. Bear Creek Planning Comm.,* 551 P.2d 1213 (Cal. 1976).

C. **Enforceability by or against successors:** As with real covenants, certain requirements must be met in order for the benefit or burden of an equitable servitude to run to successors to the original estate. These requirements are *not the same as for real covenants.* Some are the same but there are also significant differences

  1. **Intent:** This requirement is essentially the same as for real covenants. If the parties expressly or impliedly intended for the covenant to run to benefit or burden successors the equitable servitude created by the covenant will run.

  2. **Privity not required:** Unlike real covenants, *neither horizontal nor vertical privity of estate is required* for either the burden or benefit of an equitable servitude to run.

  3. **Notice:** As with real covenants, a purchaser who pays real value for an estate and *has no notice* of the servitude at the time is *not bound* by the servitude. Notice can be *actual* or *constructive.* Constructive notice most often comes through the *record* — the public records of real estate titles — but can also be the product of circumstances that should trigger *inquiry* on the part of the buyer, inquiry that would reveal the servitude.

    a. **Actual notice:** Actual knowledge of the servitude is actual notice. This can happen by design (*e.g.*, the seller tells the buyer, perhaps in person, by letter, or in the sale contract) or by accident (*e.g.*, an otherwise ignorant buyer mentions his prospective use plans to a neighbor who reveals a copy of an unrecorded servitude on the property).

b. Record notice: Every American jurisdiction (usually each county) maintains a public record of all transactions affecting title to real property. If a servitude is anywhere in the ***chain of title*** — the series of records that trace ownership back to some original title or before a specified point in history — the buyer has constructive notice of the servitude. Buyers are charged with knowledge of the contents of the chain of title because they ought to read it (or hire a professional to do so and report).

> **i. Deeds from a common grantor *not* in the direct chain of title:** States differ on whether a deed from a common grantor but not in the ***direct*** chain of ownership should be treated as in the ***chain of title.***
>
> **Example:** In Massachusetts, a state that does not recognize implied reciprocal covenants, Gilmore subdivided a tract and imposed single family residential use restrictions on several lots. In a deed to Guillette, Gilmore recited that the servitude created was thereby imposed on Gilmore's remaining lots. Later, Gilmore sold one of those lots to Daly without any servitude. Daly's direct chain of title went from himself to Gilmore to Gilmore's predecessor. No servitude was in any of those deeds. Nevertheless, the Massachusetts Supreme Judicial Court held that Gilmore's deed to Guillette was in Daly's chain of title. The effect of this rule is to require purchasers of property to search the records for all possible grants of ***other property*** owned by each grantor in the chain of title, on the possibility that there might be some servitude created in a deed outside the direct line of ownership. *Guillette v. Daly Dry Wall, Inc.*, 325 N.E.2d 572 (Mass. 1975). Accord: *Sanborn v. McLean,* 206 N.W. 496 (Mich. 1925).
>
>> **(1) Rejection of this view:** Most jurisdictions reject this latitudinarian view of the chain of title, on the ground that it imposes "intolerable" burdens on title searchers. *Mid-State Equip. Co. v. Bell, supra*, (Cochran, J., dissenting). See, *e.g., Buffalo Academy of the Sacred Heart v. Boehm Bros., Inc.,* 196 N.E. 42 (N.Y. 1935); *Land Developers, Inc. v. Maxwell,* 537 S.W.2d 904 (Tenn. 1976).

c. Inquiry notice: A few courts have ruled that a purchaser should inquire about the existence of servitudes if the neighborhood exhibits a common character.

Example: McLean buys a lot without any servitudes although it turns out his lot is part of a common scheme development where a reciprocal covenant for residential use will be implied. The Michigan Supreme Court thought that McLean should have inquired, and therefore had *inquiry notice,* because the neighborhood had a "strictly uniform residence character." *Sanborn v. McLean, supra.*

   i. Problems with the rule: This reasoning seems flimsy. Suppose that all the houses were two stories in height and had grass lawns. Should McLean have inquired about servitudes restricting use to two-story residences with grass lawns?

4. Touch and concern: In order for either the benefit or burden of an equitable servitude to run to successors in interest the substance of the covenant must *touch and concern* the benefited or burdened land. The same is true for real covenants. The meaning of touch and concern is the same for equitable servitudes and real covenants and was discussed in detail on p. 235, *supra.*

D. Identifying the benefited land: Courts identify the benefited land by (1) ascertaining the intentions of the parties and (2) determining whether the land intended to be benefited has actually received a benefit. This is easy if the covenant expressly states what land is intended to be benefited, but poses some problems when courts must infer those intentions.

1. Land retained by the promisee: If the party imposing the covenant owns land adjacent or near to the burdened land, courts presume that the covenant was intended to benefit the retained land. See, *e.g, Grady v. Schmitz,* 547 A.2d 563 (Conn. Ct. App. 1988). But that presumption is rebuttable by proof that the promisee had no such intention. See, *e.g., Haldeman v. Teicholz,* 611 N.Y.S.2d 669 (Sup. Ct. 1994). So long as the retained land is in the immediate vicinity of the burdened land, courts will usually employ the presumption that the benefit attaches to the retained land. See, *e.g., Malley v. Hanna,* 480 N.E.2d 1068 (N.Y. 1985) (benefited land three lots away from the burdened land).

   a. Promisee's assigns: The corollary to this principle is that if the promisee later conveys his retained and benefited land, the benefit runs to the assignee (assuming the other elements for a running benefit are present).

Example: Developer acquires St. John's Point and subdivides it into 10 lots. Developer sells Lot 1 to Carol under a deed restricting use to a single residence. The benefit of Carol's promise attaches to the 9 lots Developer retains. Developer then sells the remaining 9 lots, each burdened by the same covenant. Carol starts to construct a small hotel. Bret, owner of Lot 5, may enjoin Carol's hotel because he has succeeded to the benefit of Carol's promise. See, *e.g.*, *Grange v. Korff,* 79 N.W.2d 743 (Iowa 1956).

2. **Enforceability by third parties:** Sometimes the benefit of a covenant is sought to be enforced by a person who is neither a successor to the covenant nor a successor to land benefited by the covenant, but who was intended to be the beneficiary of the covenant. These situations are of two types: (1) the intended beneficiary is a ***prior purchaser*** of a lot in a subdivision developed by a common grantor, or (2) the intended beneficiary is a complete ***stranger to the chain of title*** — the beneficiary did not acquire his property from the person who imposed the covenant. Intended beneficiaries are generally able to enforce a covenant, but not always. Note the curiosity that most states refuse to permit creation of easements in third parties (see p. 205, *supra*) but will permit third party enforcement of real covenants and equitable servitudes.

   a. **Prior purchasers:** A prior purchaser of a subdivision lot burdened by covenants restricting use may enforce the benefit of the covenant, under one of three theories.

      i. **Through the title chain to the person imposing the covenant:** Some states insist that the prior purchaser and intended beneficiary have acquired title from the person imposing the covenant. In the case of a subdivision this requirement is easily met, since the developer is that person.

         Example: Refer to the prior example. Suppose that Bret, owner of Lot 5, starts to construct a convenience store on his lot, and Carol, owner of Lot 1, wishes to enjoin that use. Does Carol enjoy the benefit of Bret's ***later covenant?*** Carol is not the successor to land that enjoyed this benefit at the time she acquired it, since she is the first purchaser in the subdivision. Nevertheless, she can trace her title to Developer, the person who imposed the covenant, and she was pretty clearly an intended beneficiary of Bret's covenant, so she may enforce its benefit. See, *e.g.*, *Malley v. Hanna, supra*; *Brown v. Heirs of Fuller,* 347 A.2d 127 (Me. 1975).

(1) No enforcement of covenant by stranger: This insistence on a form of privity of estate prevents a covenant from being enforced by a stranger to the title chain descending from the person imposing the covenant.

Example: Suppose Developer, in the prior example, had inserted into Bret's covenant a statement that it was intended to benefit landowners in Cormorant Cove, an adjacent subdivision developed by somebody else. Evelyn, a Cormorant Cove landowner, would be unable to enforce the covenant since she could not trace her title to Developer, the party imposing the covenant.

ii. **Unrestricted third party beneficiary theory:** Some states follow the view, endorsed by Rest. Prop. § 541 (1944), that any intended third party beneficiary can enforce the benefit of a covenant. Thus, in the prior example, Evelyn (an intended beneficiary) could enforce the covenant burdening Bret's land.

iii. **By implication from a common scheme:** This is the mirror image of implied reciprocal covenants (see 241, *supra*). The doctrine of implied reciprocal covenants creates ***burdens by implication.*** This doctrine is quite separate — it uses a common scheme of development to ***identify the property benefited by covenants that are expressly created,*** not produced by implication. Thus, a state that does not permit the creation of implied reciprocal covenants might still use the existence of a common scheme to identify the land benefited from express covenants in a subdivision.

Example: Shackelford subdivided Brier Neck into about 100 lots and sold them over a 16 year period as summer residential lots. Each lot was sold under a deed restricting use to a single dwelling. Later, a corner lot across the road from the entrance to Brier Neck was sold by Shackelford to Clark under the same restriction. Clark constructed an ice cream stand and grocery on the corner lot. Owners of lots in Brier Neck sought to enjoin Clark's commercial use. The Massachusetts Supreme Judicial Court used the existence of a common scheme (including the corner lot) to identify the benefited property. The benefited land was held to consist of all the land within the common scheme. *Snow v. Van Dam,* 197 N.E. 224 (Mass. 1935). Note that Massachusetts does not permit the ***creation*** of servitudes by implication from a common scheme.

(1) More than two lots required: It may take more than two lots to create a common scheme sufficient to identify the benefited land.

Example: Lebold and Willett owned Lot 11 as co-owners. Lebold was the sole owner of a lot directly across the street from Lot 11 and Willett was the sole owner of the adjacent lot. Lebold sold his lot to Rodgers. Two years later Lebold and Willett conveyed Lot 11 to Reimann, subject to a covenant restricting the location of structures on Lot 11. Reimann began construction of a dwelling not in conformity with the covenant and Rodgers sought to enjoin the construction. The Oregon Supreme Court found the evidence insufficient to establish that the Lebold-Rodgers lot was the intended beneficiary of the covenant, whether via a common scheme or otherwise. *Rodgers v. Reimann,* 361 P.2d 101 (Or. 1961).

(2) Developer retains right to waive or modify use: If the developer retains the right to modify or waive the use restrictions imposed by covenant, that may negate any implication that the covenants were intended for the benefit of lot buyers.

Example: Dickason subdivided a tract of land, conveying lots under deeds containing use restrictions that could be eliminated at any time by agreement between Dickason and the owner of the burdened lot to be freed from the covenant. Consent of other owners in the subdivision was expressly unnecessary. This power retained by Dickason, even though unexercised, negated any inference that other lot owners were the beneficiaries of the covenants. The reservation made the covenant "a personal covenant between the grantor and his individual grantees." *Suttle v. Bailey,* 361 P.2d 325 (N.M. 1961). Other courts subject the exercise of a developer's reserved power to a rule of good faith, and thus inferentially hold that a developer's reservation does not necessarily negate intent to benefit lot buyers. See, *e.g., Moore v. Megginson,* 416 So. 2d 993 (Ala. 1982).

(3) Rejection of common scheme: Some states, notably California, reject the use of a common scheme altogether — either to create implied reciprocal covenants or to identify the property benefited by express covenants. In California, the scope of the benefit of a covenant is defined by its written text. See *Werner v. Graham, supra.*

b. Complete strangers to the title chain descending from the person imposing the covenant: A landowner who is *not part of a common scheme,* and who did *not acquire the land (immediately or remotely) from the person imposing the servitude*, may only enforce the benefit of a covenant if (1) the landowner is the *intended beneficiary,* and (2) the jurisdiction permits *any third party beneficiary* to enforce the benefit of a covenant.

V. INTERPRETATION OF COVENANTS

A. **General rule:** Courts try to implement the intentions of the parties in creating the covenant, but the very terms used in a covenant are often ambiguous.

B. **Building restriction or use restriction:** Covenants may restrict certain *uses* or they may restrict construction of certain types of *buildings*. The difference may be important.

Example: Aumiller purchased a lot under a covenant limiting "structures erected ... to residential purposes." Aumiller, a building contractor, built a "model home" in multiple senses of the term — it was "entirely residential in appearance" but was used as a site at which Aumiller's customers could inspect his work product and negotiate home building deals. A Pennsylvania appellate court applied a Pennsylvania policy disfavoring use restrictions and concluded that the covenant only limited the nature of the structure, not the use to which it was put. In Pennsylvania, use restrictions must "squarely address the use or manner of occupation of the property." *Groninger v. Aumiller,* 644 A.2d 1266 (Pa. Super. 1994), applying *Schulman v. Serrill,* 246 A.2d 643 (Pa. 1968). Accord: *Patton v. Madison County,* 877 P.2d 993 (Mont. 1994) (bed and breakfast use); *Jackson v. Williams,* 714 P.2d 1017 (Okla. 1985) (group home use). Contra: *Fox v. Smidt,* 869 S.W.2d 904 (Mo. App. 1994).

C. **Residential purposes:** Many covenants limit use to "residential purposes." The content of this term is not self-evident since people commonly use their residences for a variety of purposes.

1. **Combined business and residential use:** Some states take the view that any commercial or money-making enterprise, no matter how "domestic" it might be, is not residential.

Example: Wojdyla provided day care for six children (including two of her own) in her home, burdened with a "residential use only" covenant. The Washington Supreme Court restored a trial court's injunction of this activity, because it was commercial. *Metzner v. Wojdyla,* 886 P.2d 154 (Wash. 1994).

    a. Bed and breakfast: Use as a "bed and breakfast" has been found to violate a residential-only covenant. *Fick v. Weedon,* 613 N.E.2d 362 (Ill. App. Ct. 1993). But uses that are clearly not residential are often tolerated so long as no structures result. See, *e.g., Fitzwilliam v. Wesley United Methodist Church,* 882 S.W.2d 343 (Mo. App. 1994) (church parking lot); *Bagko Development Co. v. Damitz,* 640 N.E.2d 67 (Ind. App. 1994) (little league practice field).

2. Group homes: Most courts conclude that "group homes" for the handicapped, juvenile delinquents, or other groups do not constitute a violation of residential-only covenants because people do in fact live there. See, *e.g., Double D Manor, Inc. v. Evergreen Meadows Homeowners' Ass'n,* 773 P.2d 1046 (Colo. 1989). Some courts have ruled that use as a "group home" violates a residential-only covenant. See, *e.g., Mains Farm Homeowners Ass'n v. Worthington,* 854 P.2d 1072 (Wash. 1993). Enforceability of these covenants, as so construed, may be barred by the federal Fair Housing Act, 42 USC § 3604(f)(1), state statutes, or by judicial notions of public policy. See, *e.g., Broadmoor San Clemente Homeowners' Ass'n v. Nelson,* 30 Cal. Rptr.2d 316 (Ct. App. 1994) (Fair Housing Act and state statute); *Crane Neck Ass'n v. New York City/Long Island County Serv. Group,* 460 N.E.2d 1336 (N.Y. 1984) (public policy); *McMillan v. Iserman,* 327 N.W.2d 559 (Mich. Ct. App. 1983) (public policy, alternative holding).

3. What constitutes family? Many residential-only covenants are phrased to limit use to "single family residential use" or to a "single family residence." This sparks the problem of defining "single family." Courts often conclude that group residences, involving unrelated persons, are not single family residences. See, *e.g., Omega Corp. of Chesterfield v. Malloy,* 319 S.E.2d 728 (Va. 1984). Once again, enforceability of these covenants as so construed might be barred by federal or state statutes or public policy.

D. Architectural approval: Covenants forbidding erection of any structure without first obtaining the approval of a designated "architectural review committee" are generally upheld so long as the architectural reviewers act reasonably and in good faith. See, *e.g., Rhue v. Cheyenne Homes, Inc.,* 449 P.2d 361 (Colo. 1969).

VI. TERMINATION OF REAL COVENANTS AND EQUITABLE SERVITUDES

A. Merger: If the same person acquires title to the burdened land and all of the benefited land the covenant — whether a real covenant or equitable servitude — is extinguished by merger. It cannot be revived but must be created anew. See, *e.g.*, *Pollock v. Ramirez,* 870 P.2d 149 (N.M. Ct. App. 1994).

B. Eminent domain: Real covenants or equitable servitudes may be extinguished by eminent domain. This happens when the government takes the burdened land for a purpose inconsistent with the restrictive covenants. The majority of states require that the owner of benefited land be compensated for the loss of the benefit. The measure of that loss is the difference in value of the benefited land with the benefit and without the benefit. See, *e.g.*, *Southern California Edison Co. v. Bourgerie,* 507 P.2d 964 (Cal. 1973). A few courts cling to the view that the benefit of a servitude is not an interest in land, and so compensation for its destruction is not required. That view is poorly reasoned, since it ignores the fact that the constitutional requirement of compensation applies to governmental takings of **all forms of property,** whether tangible or intangible. See, *e.g.*, *Ruckelshaus v. Monsanto Co.,* 467 U.S. 986 (1984).

C. Express waiver or release: If all the holders of the benefit of a covenant expressly *release* the covenant it is extinguished. If all the benefit holders expressly waive the covenant to permit a specific non-conforming use the covenant remains alive to bar other non-conforming uses. See, *e.g.*, *Gibbs v. Kimbrell,* 428 S.E.2d 725 (S.C. Ct. App. 1993).

D. Expiration of the covenant: Covenants sometimes have a defined life span (*e.g.*, "until Jan. 1, 2000" or "for the next forty years"). When its defined life has expired the covenant is extinguished.

E. Doctrines terminating equitable servitudes: Since equitable servitudes are enforceable in equity, the following equitable defenses, if proven, will effectively extinguish an equitable servitude by blocking its enforcement.

  1. **Changed conditions within the affected area:** A covenant will no longer be enforced in equity if conditions have so radically and thoroughly changed *within the area affected by a covenant* (usually a subdivision) that the covenant can no longer achieve its purpose.

     Example: When Shippan Point was subdivided in the 1910s the lots were conveyed subject to a covenant limiting use to one single family dwelling per lot. By the 1990s twelve of the 25 lots in Shippan Point were in violation of the covenant. A Connecticut appellate court concluded that the covenant was no longer enforceable due to these changed circumstances. *Shippan Point Ass'n v. McManus,* 641 A.2d 144 (Conn. Ct. App. 1994).

    a. **Distinction between law and equity:** Courts split as to whether changed circumstances operate to extinguish the covenant entirely or merely bars its enforcement in equity. If the latter, a covenant unenforceable in equity might still be enforceable at law if the elements of a real covenant can be established. The modern trend is to extinguish covenants entirely when changed circumstances have been proven. See, *e.g., Hrisomalos v. Smith,* 600 N.E.2d 1363 (Ind. App. 1992). Some courts deal with widespread violations of covenants as evidence of abandonment, rather than as a subspecies of changed circumstances. See *infra.*

2. **Changed conditions in the surrounding area:** Another common claim is that the nature and character of the ***surrounding area*** has so changed that it would now be inequitable to enforce the servitude. To succeed with this claim it is necessary to establish that the extrinsic changes in the neighborhood have been so pervasive that ***all of the benefited lots*** have lost the benefit of the covenant at issue. Put another away, there is no point in enforcing the covenant any longer because its purpose can no longer be achieved.

Example: Land in New York City in the early 19th century was burdened by residential only covenants. As New York City grew northward an elevated railroad was constructed amidst this land, making it most unpleasant for residential use. The covenant was held unenforceable in equity. *Trustees of Columbia College v. Thatcher,* 87 N.Y. 311 (1882).

3. **Abandonment:** A servitude may be abandoned by widespread violation of the covenant without enforcement. If violations of a covenant are sufficiently numerous and there has been no enforcement action taken, the covenant may be seen as abandoned. There are two competing tests of when abandonment by widespread violation has occurred: (1) the average person would reasonably conclude that the use restriction has been abandoned, or (2) the covenant's purpose has been so frustrated that enforcement would seriously impair the value of burdened lots without producing any substantial benefit.

Example 1 — "average person" test: Lots in Maple Hills were burdened by a covenant requiring the use of wood shingles on the roofs of all structures, but the Homeowners' Development Committee, which was required by another covenant to approve all construction, inadvertently misled owners to believe that the roofing covenant had been amended to permit tile roofs. Of the first 29 homes, only 8 had wood roofs. Of the 81 houses ultimately built in Maple Hills, 23 had non-wood shingle roofs. A Utah appellate court concluded that the violations were so great that the average person would conclude that the covenant had been abandoned. *Fink v. Miller,* 896 P.2d 649 (Utah App. 1995).

Example 2 — "frustration of purpose" test: Landen Farms, a "planned development," consists of about 2000 residences. Among the many use restrictions burdening Landen Farm lots is one forbidding basketball hoops and backboards in the front driveway of any residence. Nevertheless, about 50 homes sported poles bearing a backboard and a hoop. An Ohio appellate court concluded that the covenant had been abandoned by non-enforcement, partly because the value lost by enforcement would be greater than any benefit produced and partly because the purpose of a uniform aesthetic had been lost by non-enforcement. *Landen Farms Community Services Ass'n v. Schube,* 604 N.E.2d 235 (Ohio Ct. App. 1992).

   a. Implied waiver or acquiescence: Some courts treat these factual patterns as simply another example of changed circumstances within the affected areas. See p. 251, *supra.* Other courts call these cases of ***implied waiver*** or ***acquiescence.***

4. **Equitable estoppel:** If the party seeking to enforce a covenant has made knowingly false representations to a defendant ignorant of the true facts, intending and inducing the defendant's reliance on the misrepresentation, he will be estopped from enforcing the covenant. See, *e.g., Hohman v. Bartel,* 865 P.2d 1301 (Or. Ct. App. 1993).

5. **Laches:** The doctrine of laches — the unreasonable failure to assert a known equitable right coupled with some prejudice to the defendant — will bar enforcement of an equitable servitude. The elapse of time necessary to establish laches as well as sufficiency of the prejudice suffered by the defendant from non-enforcement are matters within the reasonable discretion of the trial court.

6. **Unclean hands:** The equitable notion that a plaintiff must not be guilty of the conduct of which he complains may bar a person from enforcing a reciprocal servitude if guilty of the same violation.

   Example: Dick owns Blackacre and Jane owns Whiteacre. Each is burdened with a covenant limiting use to residential purposes, imposed for mutual benefit. Dick builds a self-storage warehouse on Blackacre. Then Jane builds a competing warehouse on Whiteacre. Dick will be barred by unclean hands from enforcing the covenant against Jane. And so will Jane. But if Dick merely rented out a room in his home on Blackacre, he would not be barred from enforcing the covenant against Jane. Trivial violations don't count for purposes of unclean hands. See, *e.g.*, *Grady v. Schmitz,* 547 A.2d 563 (Conn. Ct. App. 1988).

7. **Balance of hardships:** Even when injunctive relief is otherwise appropriate, a court may deny an injunction if the hardship imposed by the injunction is very large in relation to the benefits produced. But this principle is rarely invoked by courts in servitude cases, and may be more theoretical than actual. See, *e.g.*, *Rick v. West,* 228 N.Y.S.2d 195 (Sup. Ct. 1962).

Chapter 7
COMMON LAW CONTROL OF LAND USE: NUISANCE AND SUPPORT

I. THE SUBSTANCE OF NUISANCE

A. **The general principle:** An ancient common law maxim, *sic utere tuo ut alienum non laedas* (***one must use one's property so as not to injure another's property***) is the root of nuisance. Unfortunately, the maxim is not much help, since some injuries to another's land are permitted and others not. It is more helpful to say that a person may not use his own land in an ***unreasonable manner*** that ***substantially*** lessens another person's ***use and enjoyment*** of his land. A nuisance may be ***private*** or ***public.*** A private nuisance involves interference with purely private rights to the use and enjoyment of land — usually one or more nearby landowners. A public nuisance involves interference with public rights — those held in common by everybody — but a public nuisance can also be a private nuisance.

B. **Private nuisances:** A private nuisance occurs when there is ***substantial interference*** with private rights to use and enjoy land, produced by ***either*** of the following:

- ***Intentional and unreasonable*** conduct, or

- ***Unintentional*** conduct that is either ***negligent, reckless,*** or so ***inherently dangerous*** that ***strict liability is imposed.***

1. **Substantial interference:** The alleged nuisance, whether intentional or not, must be a substantial impediment to the use and enjoyment of land. The average person is the standard measurement for substantial interference. See, *e.g.*, *Morgan v. High Penn Oil Co.*, 77 S.E.2d 682 (N.C. 1953); *Rose v. Chaikin*, 453 A.2d 1378 (N.J. Supp. 1982).

    Example: Chemco operates a chemical fertilizer plant that sporadically emits odorless, colorless gases not toxic to humans, animals or most plants, but which are fatal to tropical orchids not native to the area. Judith purchases a tract that adjoins the Chemco plant, builds a large greenhouse, and begins the commercial cultivation of tropical orchids. Before long, the orchids die from the Chemco gas. Judith's use is unduly sensitive. Since the average person would experience no loss of use or enjoyment from the Chemco gas emissions, there is no nuisance. See, *e.g.*, *Amphitheaters, Inc. v. Portland Meadows*, 198 P.2d 847 (Or. 1948) (property use as a "drive-in movie" was unduly sensitive to artificial light from nearby property uses).

2. **Intentional conduct:** This is the most common form of nuisance. Intentional conduct is action that is known by the actor to interfere with another's use of land, but which is continued nevertheless. The focus here is upon whether the conduct is an ***unreasonable interference*** with another's land. A balancing test is used: If the ***gravity of the harm inflicted by the conduct outweighs its social utility*** the conduct is unreasonable. See Rest. (2d) Torts § 826(a) (1979). A minority of courts ignore this balancing test if ***substantial harm*** is inflicted. See, *e.g.*, *Jost v. Dairyland Power Cooperative*, 172 N.W.2d 647 (Wis. 1969) (To permit a socially useful public utility to "deprive others of the full use of their property without compensation ... would constitute the taking of property without due process of law."); *Dolata v. Berthelet Fuel & Supply*, 36 N.W.2d 97 (Wis. 1949)(an admittedly socially and economically useful coal yard abated because it caused substantial damage to adjoining landowner).

   a. **Gravity of the harm:** To measure the gravity of the harm, the Restatement (2d) of Torts suggests that courts should consider the ***extent*** of the harm, its ***character***, the ***social value*** of the use, the ***suitability of the use to the location***, and the ***burden of avoiding the harm***. See Rest. (2d) Torts § 827 (1979).

   b. **Utility of the conduct:** To measure the utility of the offending conduct, the Restatement (2d) of Torts suggests that courts should consider the ***social value*** of the conduct, its ***suitability to the location***, and the ***practical difficulty of preventing the harm***. See Rest. (2d) Torts § 828.

   c. **Practical effect:** In practice, this balancing test makes the issue of unreasonable use turn on the specific facts. "A nuisance may be merely the right thing in the wrong place — like a pig in the parlor instead of the barnyard." *Village of Euclid v. Ambler Realty Co.*, 272 U.S. 365 (1926). In theory fault is not an issue — the most careful and prudent use is a nuisance if its harm outweighs its utility. In essence, this test gives judges the opportunity to assess the worth of competing uses and to decide which user should shoulder the costs inherent in two incompatible uses.

3. **Unintentional conduct:** When an actor uses his land in a way that unintentionally injures another's use or enjoyment of land, the action is a nuisance if ***either*** the conduct is below the standard of care commonly required (*i.e.*, it is negligent or reckless) ***or*** the ***risk***

of harm is so great that the conduct ought not be tolerated (*i.e.*, it is inherently dangerous, like the unshielded storage of plutonium or large quantities of dynamite). Here the focus is entirely upon the actor's conduct — does it pose an unreasonable risk of harm either because it is careless or inherently dangerous?

C. Public nuisances: A public nuisance affects rights held in common by everybody — the public — rather than just private rights of land use held by landowners.

Example: A factory discharging pollutants into a publicly owned watershed, thereby contaminating the municipal water supply, is likely engaging in a public nuisance. Only the common right to potable water for the municipality is affected.

1. **Rarely occur:** A pure public nuisance is rare — more commonly, a public nuisance is also a private nuisance.

    Example: A factory discharging pollutants into a stream that supplies drinking water to downstream farmers as well as a municipality even further downstream, is likely engaging in both a public and private nuisance.

2. **Substantive test:** The substantive test for a public nuisance is the same as for a private nuisance: Is the conduct *intentional and unreasonable* or is it *negligent, reckless,* or *inherently dangerous?*

3. **Enforcement:** Public nuisances are normally abated by suits brought by public officials, but a *private citizen* may bring suit to abate a public nuisance if he has been *specially injured* by the nuisance. This means that the private plaintiff has suffered some particularized and personalized injury, but not necessarily in the use and enjoyment of land.

    Example: A factory discharges pollutants into the sea in a quantity sufficient to render the water unsafe for public bathing or fishing. A public nuisance results. Jill, who owns no land, cultivates oysters in the tidal waters. Her oyster farming is ruined by the pollution. Jill may maintain suit to abate the public nuisance. She has suffered a particularized injury, one different from the injury inflicted on the public at large.

    a. **Special injury rule minimized:** This rule of special injury has been relaxed by statute or judicial decision in some states to permit a private person to sue as the representative of affected persons to abate environmental nuisances.

D. **Relationship to trespass:** Nuisance and trespass are closely related. Trespass involves a physical invasion of a person's land — an interference with his ***exclusive right of possession.*** Once shown, the landowner is entitled to damages and an injunction regardless of his lack of any substantial injury. By contrast, nuisance involves an interference with another person's right to ***use and enjoy his land*** and does not necessarily involve interference with the exclusive right of possession. A landowner in a nuisance action must prove significant injury in order to recover, as well as unreasonable interference, and (usually) that equity is in his favor. The remedy available to a successful plaintiff in a nuisance action may be an injunction, damages, or even an obligation to pay damages to a defendant as the price for an injunction. See p. 263, *infra*.

II. REMEDIES — FOUR VIEWS OF NUISANCE

A. **Introduction — the economic theory of modern nuisance law:** The fundamental problem of nuisance law is that there are two incompatible uses of property. If Eve operates a dairy farm on Blackacre, necessarily producing odors that interfere with Adam's outdoor tanning salon on Whiteacre, the two uses are incompatible. Each use interferes with the other — Eve's dairy farm interferes with Adam's tanning salon (the odors inhibit the spa patrons from tanning) and Adam's tanning salon interferes with Eve's dairy farm (by preventing Eve from maintaining a dairy farm in order to accommodate the spa patrons). Each use produces *externalities* — costs that are not imposed on the person producing them. Eve's dairy farm produces the cost (external to Eve) of inhibiting Adam's use as a tanning salon. Adam's tanning salon produces the cost (external to Adam) of preventing Eve's use as a dairy farm in order to accommodate Adam's use. Economic theorists argue that decisions are more efficient if all of the costs of the decision are internalized — borne by the decision maker. If Adam and Eve were a single unit, the relative costs of these incompatible uses would be weighed by the single decision maker, and the more economically desirable use would prevail. But Adam and Eve are not a single unit. Never mind, said Ronald Coase in his famous Coase Theorem. In a perfect world free of transaction costs, it doesn't matter which of Adam and Eve are entitled to continue their use, because the use right will end up in the hands of the person whose use is the more valuable.

Example: Suppose the damage to Eve from ceasing to use Blackacre as a dairy farm is $100,000 and the damage to Adam from ceasing to use Whiteacre as a tanning salon is $40,000. If the law gives Eve the use right she will continue her dairy farming because Adam will pay her no more than $39,999.99 to stop and that sum is not enough to compensate her for the costs of stopping. But if the use right is given to Adam he will sell that right to Eve for some price greater than $40,000 and less than $100,000, since both Adam and Eve will be better off by such a bargain. If Adam suffered a greater damage from ceasing his activity then the use right would end up in Adam's hands no matter where it was initially assigned.

1. **Transaction costs — the gap between theory and reality:** We do not live in a perfect world free of transaction costs. The cost of moving the right from Adam to Eve or Eve to Adam is not zero; it is not even insignificant. Why? There are three standard answers.

   a. **Bilateral monopoly:** When there are only two persons involved in the transfer there is an inherent bilateral monopoly problem. There is only one seller and only one buyer — dueling monopolies. However, some empirical research suggests that bilateral monopoly situations frequently do result in efficient outcomes. See Hoffman & Spitzer, 25 J.L. & Econ. 73 (1982).

   Example: If Adam is given the use right and Eve values it more highly, Adam has only one potential buyer: Eve. And Eve has only source from which she can acquire the right she desires: Adam. They are forced to deal with only each other, if they are to deal at all. Adam is likely to want to extract as much of the potential gain of $60,000 ($100K – $40K) as he can, but Eve has the same objective. They will haggle; they will bluster; they will hire lawyers to threaten more litigation and thus spend gains before acquiring them. In short they will play negotiation games with each other, expending money and time as they do, thus making it harder to reach a deal and diminishing its value even if reached.

   b. **Free riders:** When there are numerous parties to the negotiation, different problems emerge. One of them is caused by the human impulse to get a free ride at somebody else's expense.

   Example: Suppose that in addition to Adam there were 99 other property owners all using their property for uses incompatible with Eve's dairy farm. Suppose that a cessation of each of those additional uses would damage each affected property owner by $40,000. The total cost imposed by giving the use right to Eve would thus be $4,000,000 ($40K x 100) but suppose that Eve's use is not a nuisance despite these disparate numbers. The rational response of Adam and his fellow landowners is to contribute something more than $1,000 apiece to amass a fund of more than $100,000 to purchase Eve's use right from her. But some landowners will not contribute because they hope to receive the benefit of Eve's cessation of use without paying for it. And this will inhibit other landowners from making their contributions because they dislike giving a free ride. Moreover, to complete the transfer the contributing landowners will have to contribute the share of the free riders. Many of them may balk at this. Since there is no effective way to compel contribution Eve's use right may not be purchased, even though it is clearly economically efficient to do so.

c. Holdouts: The mirror image to the free rider problem is the problem of holdouts.

Example: Suppose that the damage to Adam of ceasing his use is only $500 (he can use Whiteacre as an exotic vegetable farm) and there is also damage to 99 other property owners (each in the amount of $500), or total damages of $50,000 (100 x $500). Suppose also that Eve's use is found to be a nuisance and she is ordered to stop. Now it is efficient for Eve to purchase the use right vested in her 100 neighbors for some amount greater than $500 each and less than $1000 each. But it does Eve no good to purchase the use right from 99 owners if even one refuses to sell. And one is almost sure to hold out, because he will know that the marginal value of the last right is higher than $500 to $1000. To see this, imagine that Eve has purchased 99 use rights for $600 each, or a total of $59,400. The last holdout will realize that Eve will rationally pay as much as another $40,599 to obtain the holdout's right. This simple fact is likely to spur holdouts. Of course, Eve can make her purchases conditional upon obtaining all rights but that condition does not eliminate the incentive to hold out. Since Eve cannot compel everyone to sell on reasonable terms (*e.g.*, three people may each demand $40,000) she may never be able to complete the transaction and the right will stay with Adam and his cohorts, the inefficient outcome.

  i. Efficient results: However, some empirical studies suggest that efficient results may occur by private bargaining even when there as many as 40 parties involved. See Hoffman & Spitzer, 15 J. Legal Stud. 149 (1986). So the holdout problem may not be as large as it is often thought to be.

2. **Who gets the initial entitlement?** Economic theory supplies an answer to the obvious question of who should receive the initial entitlement of land use, but there are other rival answers, too.

  a. More valuable use: The most efficient and economically logical answer is that the *more valuable use* should receive the initial entitlement, since this is the outcome that (but for transaction costs) would ultimately result. The prevailing balancing test for intentional and unreasonable use partially addresses economic efficiency concerns by assessing the relative social utility of competing uses and other issues of practicality.

   b. **First user:** Some would give the initial entitlement to the *first user,* on the theory that later users should adapt themselves to existing conditions. This approach is embodied in the *"coming to the nuisance"* doctrine, by which courts hold that those who knowingly acquire and use land in a manner incompatible with existing uses have voluntarily assumed the burden of what might be a nuisance were it to have been the late arrival. The "coming to the nuisance" cases typically involve new residents in rural areas who object to preexisting rural uses. See, *e.g.*, *Dill v. Excel Packing Co.*, 331 P.2d 539 (Kan. 1958); *East St. John's Shingle Co. v. City of Portland,* 246 P.2d 554 (Or. 1952); *Gilbert v. Showerman,* 23 Mich. 448 (1871).

   c. **Disfavored uses:** Some would seek to identify uses that, however efficient or utile, are dangerous to public health or environmental preservation, and give the initial entitlement to the competing use. This approach suffers from the defect that it simply assumes that the dangers to public health or environmental preservation are always greater than the costs imposed by stopping the competing use, rather than relying on proof of that assertion. This approach is thus a simplistic version of the "more valuable user" approach.

   d. **Less valuable use:** Though inefficient and devoid of economic logic, some argue that the initial use entitlement should be given to the *less valuable use,* on the theory that this will accomplish a forced wealth transfer. The less valuable user will be spared the cost of cessation and may gain something more from selling the use right to the more valuable user. But this approach fails to explain why a wealth transfer should be forced. The less valuable user is not necessarily "deserving" of this gift, nor is the more valuable user necessarily "deserving" of this penalty.

3. **Economic and legal theory and remedies:** Economic theory tells us that either user — the "polluter" or the "receptor" of the pollution — can hold the initial entitlement. Another bit of legal theory holds that any property right can be protected by a *liability rule* or a *property rule.* A property interest protected by a property rule cannot be taken away from its owner involuntarily. A property interest protected by a liability rule can be taken away involuntarily but only upon payment of an award of damages. See Calabresi

& Melamed, 85 Harv. L. Rev. 1089 (1972). These two theoretical insights, taken together, suggest that there are four possible outcomes to a nuisance suit:

- *No nuisance:* The use continues without restraint.
- *Enjoin* the *nuisance* to stop it.
- *Award damages* to landowners affected by a *nuisance* but permit it to *continue.*
- *Enjoin* the use (though maybe not a nuisance) and *award damages to the enjoined user.*

   a. **Injunction vs. damages:** This pattern is in fact seen in the modern law of nuisance remedies. A court must both allocate the right and decide whether to protect the right as allocated by a property rule (injunction) or a liability rule (damages).

B. **No nuisance — continue the activity:** If a challenged activity is found not to be a nuisance the use right is allocated to the challenged user and is implicitly protected by a property rule. Since it is not a nuisance, the challenged user cannot be forced to stop the use without his consent. The use will continue unless the challenged use is the less valuable one and transaction costs do not inhibit its transfer.

Example: Eve's dairy farm is found not to be a nuisance. She receives the use right and cannot be made to stop unless she agrees to. But if the cost to Adam of ceasing his use is $200,000 and the cessation cost to Eve is $100,000, the use right should voluntarily shift to Adam upon his payment to Eve of something between $100,000 and $200,000 (assuming minimal or zero transaction costs).

C. **Nuisance — enjoin and abate the activity:** If a challenged activity is found to be a nuisance and the challenger's use is protected by a property rule, the challenged activity will be enjoined and it will thus stop. The challenger can continue his use at his pleasure. If the enjoined activity is the more valuable the use right will likely be shifted to the enjoined user unless transaction costs prevent the transfer.

Example: Eve's dairy farm is found to be a nuisance and she is enjoined from continuing her dairy farming. Adam's tanning use is protected by a property rule. But if the damage to Eve is $100,000 and the cost to Adam of ceasing to operate his tanning spa is $50,000, the use right should shift to Eve upon her payment to Adam of some price between $50,000 to $100,000 (assuming minimal or zero transaction costs). See, *e.g., Estancias Dallas Corp. v. Schultz,* 500 S.W.2d 217 (Tex. Civ. App. 1973).

D. Nuisance — pay damages and continue the activity: It is not possible to ignore the real world presence of transaction costs. Thus, in situations where there are a large number of landowners affected by a more valuable use that is, on balance, a nuisance, the presence of hold-out transaction costs (see p. 260, *supra*) may prompt a court to protect the use right of the numerous landowners by a liability rule instead of a property rule. In short, the court may award damages to the affected landowners instead of enjoining the nuisance. The damages awarded are ***permanent damages*** — an amount sufficient to compensate now for all past and future injury that may be inflicted by continuation of the nuisance.

Example: Atlantic Cement's factory produced dirt, smoke, noise, and vibration that substantially interfered with the use and enjoyment of land owned by a large number of neighbors. The New York Court of Appeals upheld a trial court's finding that the factory was a nuisance and award of damages instead of an injunction. The case was remanded for determination of the amount of permanent damages to be awarded for the "servitude" thus created over the affected land. The Court's rationale was partly the technological impossibility of abatement, coupled with recognition that the factory was the more valuable use but that the holdout possibility might well frustrate a market transfer of the right if the factory was enjoined from further operation. *Boomer v. Atlantic Cement Co.*, 257 N.E.2d 870 (N.Y. 1970).

   1. **Large possibility of error:** Note that since we are not clairvoyant there is the possibility of considerable error in ascertaining the present value of future injury that has not yet been inflicted. And if the damage award is not permanent, transaction costs (in the form of repeated litigation to determine future damages as incurred) will be high.

E. Nuisance or not — enjoin the activity but award damages to the enjoined actor: Under some conditions courts may enjoin an activity but require that the benefited landowners compensate the enjoined actor for the lost use. Typically, this may occur when (1) the plaintiff asserts that his activity is the more valuable, (2) it is not clear that the challenged activity is a nuisance, and (3) it is unlikely that the plaintiff is able or willing to acquire the use right in the market.

Example: Spur operated a cattle feed lot in a rural part of Arizona. The feedlot necessarily generated enormous quantities of manure, attracting clouds of insects and creating noxious odors. But nobody objected because there were no neighbors. Then the Del Webb Corporation created Sun City, a retirement city, and expanded Sun City until it was sufficiently close to Spur's feedlot to make the two uses incompatible. The Arizona Supreme Court enjoined Spur from further operation of the feedlot, but required Del Webb to pay Spur "a reasonable amount of the cost of moving or shutting down." *Spur Industries, Inc. v. Del E. Webb Development Co.*, 494 P.2d 700 (Ariz. 1972).

1. **Who should pay?** This remedy forces the complaining user to "put his money where his mouth is." Since the plaintiff claims to have the more valuable use he ought to be willing to shoulder some of the lesser cost of his adversary's cessation of use. For this remedy to be effective it is necessary to join all parties who are adversely affected by the use to be enjoined; otherwise, the free rider problem can become insuperable.

III. SUPPORT RIGHTS

A. **Introduction:** Every landowner has the right to continued physical support of his land by abutting land. In essence, the natural topography may be altered only insofar as a neighbor's land is left with sufficient support. There are two types of support. *Lateral support* is the right to support from adjacent land — like the support supplied by a bookend to a row of books. *Subjacent support* is the right to support from underneath one's land — like the support supplied by the bookshelf to a row of books.

B. **Lateral support:** The scope of the right of lateral support is different for *land itself* and *structures* placed on the land.

1. **Land itself:** A landowner who alters his land by removing the lateral support from his neighbor's land is strictly liable for any resulting damage to his neighbor's land. No matter how careful the alteration, if lateral support is removed, strict liability follows. The same principle applies to artificial supports, like retaining walls. Once an artificial support is substituted for natural support the landowner and any successor in interest is obligated to keep the artificial support in place and effective.

2. **Structures:** Most states hold that a landowner is liable for damage to structures from withdrawal of lateral support if either of two conditions is met: (1) the landowner was *negligent* and the *collapse would not have occurred but for the added weight of the structures,* or (2) the *collapse would have occurred whether or not the structures were there.* If the withdrawal of lateral support is so extensive that the natural contours would have collapsed, the excavating landowner is strictly liable for all resulting injury to land or structures. But if the withdrawal of lateral support was not enough to cause the natural contours to collapse (*i.e.*, the collapse

was due to the added weight of the structures) the excavating landowner is liable only if he is negligent.

   a. Minority rule: Some jurisdictions hold that a landowner is strictly liable for removal of lateral support to adjacent buildings. This rule makes sense in dense urban locales, but probably not in rural locations. It is also justified on the ground that the second landowner to build can more easily avoid the costs of collapse. But the minority rule does give a boon to the first to build.

C. Subjacent support: The right of subjacent support is never an issue unless ownership has been split into two parts: (1) ownership of the surface and (2) ownership of the right to mine under the surface. When this happens the owner of the underground mineral rights is ***strictly liable*** for any damage caused to land or structures on the surface resulting from withdrawal of subjacent support.

Chapter 8
PUBLIC CONTROL OF LAND USE: ZONING

I. ZONING BASICS

A. Introduction: Zoning is the use of governmental power to regulate land use. Zoning laws divide a political jurisdiction into specific separate geographic areas and impose limits on the permissible uses of land within each area. Zoning has several legitimate objectives: (1) to *prevent incompatible uses* from occurring (thus reducing the need for nuisance law), (2) to *increase property values* generally by minimizing use conflicts (thus increasing the property tax base), and (3) to *channel development into patterns that may serve larger social goals* (*e.g.*, reduce urban sprawl to conserve resources and reduce air pollution from auto commuting). Zoning is the use of public power to impose uniform results that might otherwise be accomplished in more piecemeal and selective fashion by private bargains (via servitudes) and nuisance law.

B. General constitutional validity: In general, zoning laws are constitutionally valid, even though they restrict the uses to which a landowner may devote his property (possibly to his economic detriment). In *Village of Euclid v. Ambler Realty Co.*, 272 U.S. 365 (1926), the Supreme Court upheld the validity of a comprehensive zoning ordinance against a due process and equal protection challenge. The law's objective — minimizing land use conflicts to prevent nuisances from ever occurring — was a legitimate exercise of the state's inherent police power since its content was neither unreasonable nor arbitrary. A valid law can, however, be applied to an individual in an unconstitutional manner. See *Nectow v. City of Cambridge,* 277 U.S. 183 (1928). So, for example, a zoning law that so severely restricts use that no economically viable use is permitted is an unconstitutional taking of property without compensation. See *Lucas v. South Carolina Coastal Council,* 505 U.S. 1003 (1992), discussed in pp. 279 and 345, *infra*. Zoning ordinances that openly infringe constitutionally fundamental rights (*e.g.*, free speech) or that employ suspect criteria (*e.g.*, race) are presumptively unconstitutional. Zoning laws that lack these damning characteristics, however, are presumptively valid. See p. 279, *infra*.

C. Statutory Schemes: The point of zoning is to separate land uses and regulate the density of use within use districts. This can be done by *cumulative* zoning or *mutually exclusive* zoning.

1. **Cumulative zoning:** This type of zoning law identifies land use in a spectrum from "higher" to "lower." The least dense single family residential use is the highest use, proceeding downward to more dense residential (*e.g.*, apartments and other multiple family dwellings), light commercial (*e.g.*, a corner bookstore), heavy commercial (*e.g.*, a supermarket or an office building), industrial (*e.g.*, a factory or power plant). The idea of cumulative zoning is that all uses at the level of the zoned district ***and higher*** will be permitted.

   Example: A cumulative zoning law divides a city into four districts, labeled Single Family Residential ("SFR"), Dense Residential ("DR"), Commercial ("C"), and Industrial ("I"). Only single family residences will be permitted in SFR. Single family residences and apartments will be permitted in DR. Those two uses plus commercial uses will be permitted in C, and all uses will be permitted in I.

2. **Mutually exclusive zoning:** This type of zoning law permits some uses and excludes all others within the zoned area.

   Example: A city's mutually exclusive zoning law divides the city into four districts: Industrial, Commercial, Dense Residential, and Single Family Residential. Only the defined uses are permitted within each district, and all others are excluded. The result will be a city that has four separate monolithic use districts.

   a. **Generally used in industrial or heavy commercial districts:** Mutually exclusive zoning is most often used with respect to industrial or heavy commercial districts. Residential use is often barred in such districts, partly to dampen use conflicts, partly out of public health concerns, and partly to preserve space for industrial users. Zoning laws may be partly mutually exclusive and partly cumulative.

      Example: A city's zoning law divides the city into four districts: Single Family Residential, Dense Residential, Commercial, and Industrial. Cumulative zoning applies to the first three classifications but not to Industrial. The result will be a monolithic industrial zone, mixed uses within the Commercial and Dense Residential classifications, and a monolithic single family residential zone.

3. **Density zoning:** In addition to use regulation, zoning laws often seek to control the density of occupation within any given use district. This is usually done through a wide variety of limits on the size or height of structures, their location upon their site, and the functional uses created within the structure (*e.g.*, limits on the number of bathrooms or bedrooms within a single family structure).

Density controls supplement use controls. They are not considered an alternative to use controls.

II. AUTHORIZATION FOR ZONING

A. Enabling legislation: Most zoning laws are adopted at the local level, although some states (*e.g.*, Oregon) have enacted laws regulating land use statewide. The powers of local governments in relation to the government of the state in which they are located is controlled by the state constitution and state statutes. Usually, the power to adopt zoning laws is reserved to the state government. When this is the case a state's legislature must enact legislation authorizing local governments to adopt zoning laws. Some state constitutions recognize a semi-autonomous status for certain cities and, in those states, a city with such status may have power to adopt zoning laws without express legislative authority from the state. In general, though, a local zoning law is void unless it is in conformity to the state's *enabling act* — the law authorizing localities to engage in zoning. Every state — even those with "home rule" cities — has enacted legislation authorizing localities to zone.

1. **Defective enabling act:** Every state has its own constitutional law concerning the proper scope of a legislature's *delegation of legislative authority.* In general, legislatures may not simply hand over to someone else (*e.g.*, the state's Governor, or a city, or a private entity) unbounded discretion to legislate. But legislatures are generally permitted to delegate to administrative agencies, cities, and other non-legislative bodies the power to make rules that look exactly like laws, so long as that law-making power is exercised in conformity with clear standards in the authorizing legislation.

   Example: The Standard State Zoning Enabling Act (which, with some modifications, is in effect in every state) empowers cities: (1) to "regulate and restrict the height, number of stories, and size of buildings and other structures, the percentage of lot that may be occupied, the size of yards, courts, and other open spaces, the density of population, and the location and use of buildings, structures, and land for trade, industry, residence, or other purposes;" (2) to create use zones with differing regulations, and (3) modify zoning laws and grant variances when in the public interest to do so. The Standard Act also requires cities to (1) create a comprehensive plan designed to accomplish various public objectives specified in the Standard Act, (2) create procedures to establish, enforce, and alter zoning regulations, and (3) establish a zoning commission and an appeal mechanism for affected landowners. The limits on local discretion are clearly expressed in the Standard Act; it is not an unconstitutional delegation of legislative authority.

2. ***Ultra vires* local action:** If a local zoning law violates some express provision of the enabling act, or if it deals with matters not authorized by the enabling act, the law is void to that extent. It is *ultra vires* — beyond the authority given the locality under the zoning act.

   Example: The state of Nirvana has enacted the Standard Act. The city of Saint Cecilia, located in Nirvana, enacts a zoning law that prohibits the ownership of more than one motor vehicle by any individual. The law is *ultra vires*. While nothing in the Standard Act expressly forbids such local legislation, the subject matter — regulation of motor vehicle ownership — is beyond the scope of the powers granted Saint Cecilia under the Standard Act. The "zoning" law is not a regulation of land use. By contrast, a Saint Cecilia law forbidding the parking of more than one motor vehicle on any lot zoned single-family residential would be within the scope of Saint Cecilia's authority under the Standard Act.

   a. **Zoning for aesthetic objectives:** The traditional rule, made by judges, was that a state's police power (including the power of zoning) may not be used to achieve aesthetic objectives. The traditional view embodied the idea that since beauty is subjective, entirely in the eye of the beholder, governments have no business imposing their aesthetic judgments on others. But this view has mostly broken down. A substantial number of courts have upheld aesthetic land use regulations banning activities that lower property values because they are offensive to the average person. The modern view seems to be that if enough beholders have the same notion of beauty, it is objective enough to be enforced by law.

      Example: The city of Rye, New York enacted an ordinance banning clotheslines in front or side yards abutting streets. The New York Court of Appeals concluded that it was a permissible exercise of the police power to legislate for aesthetic concerns and that the ordinance was reasonably related to those legitimate concerns, even though there was evidence that Rye might have been attempting to squelch the Stovers' practice of protesting high municipal taxes by the odd means of stringing old clothes on a line in their front yard. *People v. Stover,* 191 N.E.2d 272 (N.Y. 1963).

      i. **Jurisdictional breakdown:** About twenty states permit regulations solely for aesthetic reasons; another 15 or so permit regulation for aesthetic reasons if coupled with other objectives; less than 10 have never addressed the issue; and only a half-dozen cling to the rule that aesthetic regulation is outside the police power. See, *e.g., State v. Jones,* 290 S.E.2d 675 (N.C. 1982) (upholding a regulation restricting use of land as an auto junkyard).

    ii. **Architectural review:** One of the principal applications of aesthetic zoning is the proliferation of architectural review controls. Typically, such a scheme conditions a land use permit of some kind (*e.g.*, planning approval, building permit) on (1) the conformity of the proposed structure to the *existing character* of the neighborhood, and (2) the likelihood that the proposed structure will *not* cause *substantial depreciation* of neighboring property values.

    Example: The affluent St. Louis suburb of Ladue enacted an architectural review ordinance designed to preserve property values and maintain Ladue's conventional architectural aesthetic sensibilities. Stoyanoff proposed to build a pyramidal, flat-topped residence with triangular window and door openings arranged asymmetrically on the structure. The proposal was rejected and Stoyanoff attacked the validity of the entire scheme as unauthorized by the enabling act, outside the scope of the police power if so authorized, and a violation of due process if within the otherwise permissible scope of the police power. Ladue's law was upheld. Architectural review is for the general welfare and thus authorized by the enabling act. The rejection of Stoyanoff's "monstrosity of grotesque design," as Ladue termed it, was reasonably related to preserving land values and the prevailing (if dull) aesthetic sense. *State ex rel. Stoyanoff v. Berkeley,* 458 S.W.2d 305 (Mo. 1970).

    (1) Criticism of trend: It is hardly a foregone conclusion that this trend toward permitting exercise of the police power in furtherance of aesthetics is a good thing. Some of the nation's leading architects have expressed the view that architectural review promotes trite mediocrity, going so far as to suggest Frank Lloyd Wright would never have constructed anything if he had faced architectural review. Maybe beauty really is wholly subjective. If so, aesthetic zoning may be inherently vague and capricious.

  b. **Exclusionary zoning:** All zoning is exclusionary in that it seeks to exclude unwanted uses. But sometimes zoning is used to exclude unwanted people, though perhaps not for forbidden reasons. A typical example is a zoning law that, in the interest of preserving open space, aesthetics, and high property values (with its corollary, a high tax base), requires a minimum lot size of two acres. The result is a landscape of expensive homes occupied almost entirely by affluent owners. The poor (often disproportionately composed of a racial minority) are excluded. But excluding the poor, even if done intentionally, does not trigger any presumption of invalidity under the federal Constitution. See *James v. Valtierra,* 402 U.S. 137 (1971); p. 279, *infra.* The exclusion is rationally related to the legitimate objectives of preserving open space, aesthetics, and high property values and is thus valid under the federal constitution. But states are free to interpret their own constitutions and enabling acts to ban actions permitted under the federal Constitution.

Example: The New Jersey township of Mount Laurel developed rapidly from 1950 to 1970. The zoning law in effect excluded all multiple family residential dwellings (*e.g.*, apartments) and mobile homes. The required minimum lot sizes and dwelling sizes for single family residences were sufficiently large that low income persons were effectively excluded from Mount Laurel. The New Jersey Supreme Court ruled that the New Jersey Constitution and the state's zoning enabling act both required that local zoning further the "general welfare," and that Mount Laurel's failure to accommodate the housing needs of poor people was contrary to the general welfare. *Southern Burlington County NAACP v. Township of Mount Laurel,* 336 A.2d 713 (N.J. 1975); *Southern Burlington County NAACP v. Township of Mount Laurel,* 456 A.2d 390 (N.J. 1983).

i. **Minority view:** The *Mount Laurel* approach remains a minority view. Most states hold that so long as a zoning law does not exclude people on a suspect basis (*e.g.*, race) it need only be rationally related to a legitimate state interest to be valid. Some economists, notably Charles Tiebout, argue that it is more efficient to let communities specialize in land use, so that people will have a choice of various types of communities in which to live. The *Mount Laurel* approach "produces great diversity *within* neighborhoods, but no diversity *between* neighborhoods, and thus may limit the variety of residential choices available to households." Ellickson & Tarlock, Land Use Controls 812 (1981). See also Tiebout, 64 J. Pol. Econ. 416 (1956).

c. **Growth controls:** Growth controls are even more exclusionary in that they seek to exclude everybody. Almost no growth controls are absolute, in the sense that they exclude all new additions for all time henceforth. Rather, they are either temporary stoppages (*e.g.*, a building moratorium) or permanent limitations on the rate of new entrants (*e.g.*, annual quotas for building permits). These techniques have generally been upheld as within the authority conferred by the enabling act and as constitutionally valid exercises of that power. They are viewed as rationally related to the legitimate state interest of orderly growth. See, *e.g.*, *Associated Home Builders v. City of Livermore*, 557 P.2d 473 (Cal. 1976) (building moratorium upheld); *Golden v. Planning Board of Ramapo*, 30 N.Y.2d 359 (1972) (timing controls upheld); *Construction Industry Ass'n v. City of Petaluma*, 522 F.2d 897 (9th Cir. 1975) (annual building quota upheld).

B. **Comprehensive plan:** The Standard Act (the common enabling act) requires that zoning decisions be made "in accordance with" a comprehensive plan for land use in the locality. The comprehensive plan is intended to be a general guide for overall development of a locality. Zoning laws are the specific means of implementing the vision of the comprehensive plan. In the past, the requirement of a comprehensive plan has not been taken very seriously. Unwritten plans sufficed, or sometimes the zoning laws themselves were the plan. The comprehensive plan is treated more seriously today, hastened perhaps by enabling acts that require zoning to be consistent with a written and adopted comprehensive plan.

1. **Legal status of the comprehensive plan:** Generally, the plan itself is not binding. It must be implemented by actual zoning ordinances. But a few courts have held that, even without implementing law, local action violative of a comprehensive plan is void. See, *e.g.*, *Baker v. City of Milwaukie*, 533 P.2d 772 (Or. 1975). Even though a comprehensive plan may not, by itself, be binding law it is an important legal benchmark to assess the validity of ***discretionary action*** by zoning officials under a zoning law. See p. 272, *infra*.

III. STATUTORY DISCRETION AND RESTRAINT

A. **Introduction:** Communities are dynamic. Appropriate land usage should change as the underlying economic and social conditions dictate. Zoning responds to this fact in several ways:

- Tolerating the continued existence of land uses existing prior to adoption of the zoning law,

- Providing for amendment of the zoning law, and

- Conferring discretion on administrators in the application of the zoning statute. None of these mechanisms is without controversy.

B. **Nonconforming uses:** When zoning is introduced, some existing land uses will not be in conformity with the uses permitted under the new zoning law. These ***nonconforming uses*** are permitted to continue to exist because their immediate abatement would amount to either a taking of property without just compensation (see p. 287, *infra*, and Chapter 11, p. 345, *infra*) or a denial of substantive due process (see. p. 282, *infra*). But nonconforming uses may be, and often are, eliminated gradually.

1. **No expansion:** A typical zoning gambit is to stipulate that the nonconforming use may not be expanded beyond the precise boundaries of the existing use. Thus, a successful and growing business located as a nonconforming use will be forced to move to expand. A new occupant will be required to conform to the zoning law.

2. **No rebuilding:** Another common ploy is to stipulate that if the nonconforming use is destroyed (*e.g.*, fire, flood, earthquake, tornado) it may not be rebuilt. Any replacement structure and use must conform to the zoning law.

3. **Forced phase-out:** Yet another mechanism to abate the nonconforming use is the forced phase-out. The zoning law (or zoning administrators, exercising discretion under the law) may specify a period after which the nonconforming use must cease. This so-called ***"amortization period"*** will vary, depending on the investment in the nonconforming use. The amortization period must be long enough to avoid a successful charge that the forced phase-out amounts to an uncompensated taking or denial of substantive due process.

    a. **Majority rule — valid if reasonable period:** The majority view in American states is that forced phase-outs are valid so long as the amortization period is reasonable as to the affected nonconforming user. The general calculus of reasonableness "involves a process of weighing the public gain to be derived from a speedy removal of the nonconforming use against the private loss which removal of the use would entail." *Metromedia, Inc. v. City of San Diego,* 610 P.2d 407 (Cal. 1980). But every case will turn on its own facts. Factors courts use to make this determination include the ***nature of the use,*** the ***character of the structure,*** the ***location,*** what ***portion of the user's total business is affected,*** the ***salvage value,*** the ***extent of depreciation*** of the use, and ***any monopoly or other advantage conferred on the user by reason of the foreclosure of simi-***

lar and competing uses. See *Art Neon Co. v. City and County of Denver,* 488 F.2d 118 (10th Cir. 1973).

    b. Minority rule — invalid: A minority of states hold that forced phase-outs are invalid. Some states conclude that localities lack statutory authority to impose forced phase-outs. See, *e.g., James J.F. Loughlin Agency, Inc. v. Town of West Hartford,* 348 A.2d 675 (Conn. 1974). Other states conclude that forced phase-outs constitute an uncompensated taking of property and denial of substantive due process, no matter what the length of the amortization period may be. See, *e.g., Ailes v. Decatur County Area Planning Commission,* 448 N.E.2d 1057 (Ind. 1983) (unclear whether decision based on federal or state constitutional law).

C. Amendments — spot zoning and abusive amendments: While enabling acts provide for amendment of zoning laws, this power may be abused. The doctrines discussed here are the primary mechanisms for controlling abuse of the amendment power.

  1. Spot zoning: An amendment not in conformity with the comprehensive plan is called *spot zoning.* The usual form of spot zoning is to rezone one parcel (or a handful) for a use inconsistent with the comprehensive plan in order to confer a benefit not available to neighboring landowners (and often, as a collateral consequence, to impose external costs on those neighbors). Since spot zoning violates the comprehensive plan, it is *ultra vires* and therefore void. But when the comprehensive plan is also amended the issue becomes more muddled. The applicable standard then is whether the changes bear a **substantial relationship to the general welfare of the affected community.** See, *e.g., Save Our Rural Environment v. Snohomish County,* 662 P.2d 816 (Wash. 1983).

  2. Curbing abusive amendments: To avoid illegal spot zoning, amendments to a zoning law must conform to the comprehensive plan. But given the generality of comprehensive plans there are creative ways to feign compliance while delivering most of the benefits of spot zoning. At worst, this subversion is carried on via bribery; at best, it is the product of ignorant, misinformed, or supine lawmaking.

    a. General presumption of validity: The widely held rule is that a zoning amendment, like any other statute, is presumed to be valid. The burden of proving otherwise is on the challenger to the law. A challenger must show that the amendment is not in compliance with the comprehensive plan. This is a difficult hurdle; only the most unartful amendments will fail.

b. **Minority view — no presumption of validity:** A few jurisdictions, recognizing the tendency of lawmakers to delude themselves that they are acting in the public interest, have reversed the burden of proof on zoning amendments. There are two approaches to reversing the burden of proof.

   i. **Public need for the amendment:** Some states require the government to prove that there is a demonstrable ***public need*** for the changed land use, and that the property affected by the change is the ***most suitable property for the change.*** See, *e.g.*, *Fasano v. Board of County Commissioners of Washington County*, 507 P.2d 23 (Or. 1973).

   ii. **Correct original mistake or respond to changed conditions:** Some jurisdictions require the government to prove that the zoning amendment is necessary either to (1) correct a mistake in the existing law, or (2) adapt to a substantial change in conditions affecting land use. See, *e.g.*, *Greenblatt v. Toney Schloss Properties Corp.*, 235 Md. 9 (1964).

D. **Administrative discretion — variances, conditional uses, floating zones, conditional zoning, and cluster zoning:** Zoning laws, like all other exercises in central government planning, cannot deal with the incredible kaleidoscopic complexity of human nature. Accordingly, zoning laws attempt to respond to this by conferring discretion upon zoning administrators in the actual application of the law. The principal such devices are discussed in this section.

1. **Variances:** Virtually every zoning law establishes a ***zoning appeals board***, or board of adjustment, usually a group of people appointed by the local executive. This appeals board is empowered to grant variances from the zoning law in the interest of alleviating ***practical difficulties*** or ***unnecessary hardships.*** Usually the appeals board is assisted by zoning officials in discharging this power to dispense with the law. Variances are usually awarded to alleviate siting problems (*e.g.*, setback requirements, minimum yard area). Use variances (*e.g.*, multiple family residence in a single-family residential district) are properly treated as ***conditional uses,*** not variances. See p. 276, *infra*.

   a. **Standard for granting variances:** Almost every zoning law provides that a variance may be granted upon a showing that compliance with the zoning law would impose ***practical difficulties*** or ***unnecessary hardships*** on an ***individual owner.*** These difficulties or hardships must ***not*** be created by the owner.

Example 1: Aronson wished to add a porch on the back of his house to accommodate his invalid child. The porch would violate setback requirements but was well-screened by shrubs and thus posed no visual intrusion on neighbors' privacy, nor would it lower property values. There was no other spot for the porch. A variance was denied. The pitiful condition of Aronson's child was not a hardship! *Aronson v. Board of Appeals of Stoneham,* 211 N.E.2d 228 (Mass. 1965).

Example 2: Commons owned a residential lot that had been created before the current zoning law. The lot was 50 feet wide, with a total area of 5190 square feet. The zoning law required lots to be a minimum of 75 feet wide and with an area of 7500 square feet. Commons' builder proposed to construct a residence conforming to setback requirements that would be of the same value as existing homes. In the past Commons had attempted to sell the lot to a neighbor and to acquire additional land adjacent to his lot. Both attempts were unsuccessful. The New jersey Supreme Court reversed the denial of a variance. "Undue Hardship" means that, absent a variance, the property may not effectively be used. Commons had shown that to exist. *Commons v. Westwood Zoning Board of Adjustment,* 410 A.2d 1138 (N.J. 1980).

  i. **Limitation:** The comprehensive plan also limits variances; a variance may not substantially depart from the comprehensive plan.

2. **Conditional uses:** Zoning laws frequently specify conditions that warrant deviation from the law to permit an otherwise prohibited use. These ***conditional uses,*** or ***special uses,*** are in theory limited to uses that do not impose external costs on neighbors. But the standards set out in the zoning law for granting a conditional use are rarely phrased in this fashion. More commonly, the standard is something like "compatibility with existing uses," or "in furtherance of public health, safety, and general welfare." While these standards seem vague enough to raise concern about an impermissible delegation of legislative power (see p. 268, *supra*) most courts uphold the validity of these general standards. But an empty standard like "with the permission of the zoning appeals board" is almost surely void, even though it implicitly incorporates the enabling act's requirement that zoning be exercised to further public health, safety, and general welfare. This is because the determination of public health, safety, and general welfare is a legislative question that cannot be delegated. See, *e.g. Cope v. Inhabitants of the Town of Brunswick,* 464 A.2d 223 (Me. 1983). The municipal legislative body

must give more detailed instructions to the zoning appeals board as to what constitutes the public health, safety, or general welfare.

3. **Floating zones:** Some zoning laws provide for *floating zones,* a use designation not attached to any particular land until a landowner seeks to have his land designated as the recipient of the floating classification.

   Example: Because it desires to encourage the responsible disposal of toxic wastes (like motor oil, paints, or chemicals) the city of Ford Cove creates a floating zone dedicated to toxic waste collection and shipment to a disposal facility ("TWC"). The floating zone specifies the criteria that any land must meet to receive the TWC designation: a site of at least 1/2 acre, no residences, schools, office buildings, churches, or retail establishments within 1000 yards, drive-through vehicle access. The TWC designation does not attach to any land. Fred, owner of a one acre lot surrounded by heavy industrial uses for over 1000 yards in every direction, applies for the TWC designation. Fred's land is suitable and likely to be rezoned TWC.

   a. **Objections:** The objection to floating zones is that they violate the comprehensive plan. The comprehensive plan is supposed to inform people about the future direction of land use, but a floating zone can conceivably land anywhere, thus undermining the predictive value of the plan. This objection loses some of its force if the criteria for its attachment to land are drawn with great specificity. Moreover, the discretion created by floating zones is no more than that exercised by granting variances and conditional uses. See, *e.g., Rodgers v. Village of Tarrytown,* 96 N.E.2d 731 (N.Y. 1951) (upholding floating zones).

4. **Conditional zoning:** Sometimes a developer wishes to use land in a fashion not permitted by the zoning law, and requests rezoning in exchange for the creation of a servitude burdening the land that is intended to eliminate or dampen the negative externalities of the proposed use.

   Example: A developer wishes to build townhouses on land zoned for "fully detached single-family residences." The developer offers to cluster the townhouses in a portion of the site shielded from view from neighbors, and covenant that the undeveloped portion of the site will remain undeveloped forever. Upon execution of the servitude the land is rezoned. In essence, imposition of the servitude is the condition of rezoning.

   a. **Criticisms:** Conditional zoning is criticized on several grounds. A good review of the following criticisms is contained in *Collard* *v. Incorporated Village of Flower Hill,* 421 N.E.2d 818 (N.Y. 1981) (upholding conditional zoning).

  i. **Illegal spot zoning;** Some say it is illegal spot zoning, but if the rezoning is consistent with the comprehensive plan it is valid. Moreover, the servitude partially offsets the claim that an individual parcel is receiving a special benefit. Conditional zoning ought to be assessed by the same standards applicable to any zoning amendment. See p. 274, *supra*.

  ii. **Invalid disposal of the police power:** This claim is that governments may not bargain away their legislative power. But conditional zoning does not do this. The locality is not precluded from changing the zoning use at some time in the future if public welfare so requires.

  iii. ***Ultra vires*:** Enabling acts typically do not expressly authorize the attachment of conditions to zoning amendments, but neither do enabling acts forbid the practice. The better view is that the attachment of conditions is in furtherance of the public welfare.

  iv. **Waiver of restrictions:** Some object that conditional zoning amounts to a waiver of governmental ability to restrict use of the affected land any further. This argument rests on the assumption that conditional zoning amounts to a binding contract between the landowner and the city, but this construction has been repudiated by courts. The bargain is imposition of a servitude in exchange for an immediate rezoning, but the government has not waived its power to change the zoning classification in the future.

5. **Cluster zoning;** The idea of cluster zoning is to zone a particular area for a particular use at a specified level of density of occupation, but confer upon zoning administrators discretion to decide exactly how that use and density will achieved.

   Example: The city of Grassy Point designates a particular area as single-family residential with no more than 3 such residences per acre. The city is then free to permit division of this area into 3 lots per acre, each with a single family residence, or to permit the construction of 60 single-family townhouses on a 20 acre parcel, with the structures clustered on 8 acres and the remaining 12 acres devoted to common amenities, such as a swimming pool, tennis courts, park and gardens.

   a. **Generally acceptable:** Cluster zoning is usually not problematic, so long as it is in conformity with the comprehensive plan.

E. **Voter discretion — initiative and referendum:** Some zoning laws permit or require that some or all zoning amendments be subject to popular approval by referendum. And the initiative, by which the people propose and vote directly upon legislation, may be used to amend zoning laws. So long as the subject initiated by or referred to the people is in fact a legislative judgment, there is no impermissible delegation of legislative power since the people are the source of legislative power. See, *e.g. City of Eastlake v. Forest City Enterprises, Inc.,* 426 U.S. 668 (1976); *Arnel Development Co. v. City of Costa Mesa,* 620 P.2d 565 (Cal. 1980). But some states are of the view that piecemeal alterations of zoning laws are adjudicative acts, not legislative. See, *e.g., Leonard v. City of Bothell,* 557 P.2d 1306 (Wash. 1976); *West v. City of Portage,* 221 N.W.2d 303 (Mich. 1974); *Fasano v. Board of County Commissioners of Washington County,* 507 P.2d (Or. 1973). In these jurisdictions the initiative and referendum could not be used because the subject is deemed adjudicative, not legislative. Treating piecemeal alterations of zoning as adjudicative actions opens up many other questions: Are judges competent to second-guess zoning decisions? What standards of review apply? Can change occur only by trial-type hearings? These problems have caused some states to reconsider the wisdom of this view. See, *e.g., Neuberger v. City of Portland,* 603 P.2d 771 (Or. 1979).

IV. CONSTITUTIONAL LIMITS ON ZONING

A. **Introduction:** States possess an inherent *"police power"* — the power to act to achieve the people's vision of public welfare, as communicated through their governmental agents. That power is not unlimited. The United States Constitution and federal law limit a state's police power, as does the state's constitution. This discussion focuses upon constitutional challenges to zoning laws that might be made under the federal Constitution. Although zoning laws are presumptively valid they may be unconstitutional under some circumstances. This section briefly discusses the major areas in which zoning laws might be constitutionally vulnerable. The substance of the constitutional doctrines discussed here is covered in greater detail in your Constitutional Law course.

B. **Equal protection:** The equal protection clause of the 14th Amendment prohibits any state or locality from denying to any person "the equal protection of the laws." In applying this guarantee, courts look to see whether the challenged action has some indicator of presumptive invalidity. If not, the challenged statute is presumptively valid and is voided only if the challenger can prove that the action is *not rationally related to a legitimate state interest.* Very little government action is voided on this basis.

Example: The city of Cleburne's zoning law barred all group homes for the mentally retarded though it allowed group homes for many other purposes. The classification was treated as presumptively valid but the Court voided it anyway, on the ground that the ban embodied an irrational prejudice against the mentally retarded, and thus did not further any *legitimate* state objective. *City of Cleburne v. Cleburne Living Center, Inc.*, 473 U.S. 432 (1985).

1. **Presumption of invalidity:** If a zoning law *infringes upon a constitutionally fundamental right* or employs a *suspect classification* it will be presumed to be invalid and will be upheld only if the government can prove that the classification at issue is *necessary to achieve a compelling state interest.* This test for overcoming the presumption of invalidity is called *strict scrutiny.*

2. **Strict scrutiny:** Strict scrutiny is triggered by *either* an infringement of a constitutionally fundamental right or the use of a suspect criterion for classification.

    a. **Constitutionally fundamental rights:** Constitutionally fundamental rights (for purposes of equal protection) are limited to voting, access to the judicial process, and interstate migration. Since housing is *not* a constitutionally fundamental right (see *Lindsey v. Normet*, 405 U.S. 56 (1972)), zoning ordinances are rarely presumed to be invalid as infringing upon a constitutionally fundamental right. But it could happen.

    Example: The city of Saragossa, located in the state of Barmania, amends its zoning law to forbid any occupation of any dwelling by any person who has not lived in Barmania for at least one year. Saragossa acted because of a huge influx of new residents into Barmania, making housing scarce and expensive. This zoning classification infringes upon the constitutionally fundamental right of interstate migration and will be struck down unless Saragossa can overcome the very large burden of proving its necessity to achieve some compelling interest. Excluding new arrivals to keep housing available and cheap is not adequate justification. See, *e.g., Shapiro v. Thompson*, 394 U.S. 618 (1969).

    b. **Suspect classifications:** Suspect classifications are race and ethnicity. The mere fact that a zoning classification (*e.g.,* a two-acre minimum lot size) may be shown to have a *disparate impact* on a particular racial or ethnic group is *not enough to establish a suspect classification.* See *Washington v. Davis*, 426 U.S. 229 (1976). The suspect nature of the classification must be on the *face of the law* or, if not, proven to have been the *underlying intention* of the apparently neutral classification.

> **Example:** The suburban city of Greenleaf establishes a five acre minimum lot size for any residence. The zoning commission recommends that the City Council adopt this provision "because it will be effective to keep poor Haitian immigrants out of Greenleaf." The City Council approves the law after a short discussion in which each council member declares the importance of enacting the measure in order to exclude "poor Haitians." Although the law does not mention ethnicity it has the effect of excluding poor Haitians and that was surely its intent. Unless Greenleaf can prove that, despite this damning legislative history, it really had some benign intention, the law will be subjected to strict scrutiny and likely invalidated. See, *e.g.*, *Village of Arlington Heights v. Metropolitan Housing Development Corp.*, 429 U.S. 252 (1977).

3. **Intermediate scrutiny:** A few classifications (sex and illegitimate birth) are subjected to *intermediate scrutiny*. Intermediate scrutiny involves a presumption of invalidity that may be overcome if the government proves that the classification (sex or illegitimacy) is *substantially related to an important state interest*. It is highly unlikely that a zoning classification drawn on the basis of sex or illegitimacy could be successfully justified.

4. **State analogues:** Most state constitutions contain some version of an equal protection clause. A state's supreme court is free to interpret the substance of that clause more generously than the federal equal protection clause. A state might choose to recognize housing as a fundamental right for purposes of its state equal protection guarantee, and thus might scrutinize some or all zoning classifications more strictly than would be the case under the U.S. Constitution. Of course, if a state construes its equal protection clause to permit action that violates the federal equal protection clause, that permissive construction will be pre-empted by the paramount status of the federal Constitution.

C. **Due process:** The due process clause of the 14th Amendment forbids any state from depriving "any person of life, liberty, or property, without due process of law." There are two components to this guarantee: *procedural* and *substantive*.

1. **Procedural due process:** Government action that infringes upon a person's "life, liberty, or property" may only be taken in accordance with the procedural safeguards implied in the phrase "due process of law." That usually means that the affected person must be given

notice of the impending action and an *opportunity to be heard* before the action is taken. But this rule does *not apply to legislation,* such as a zoning law itself. It is impractical to give everyone affected by pending legislation notice and an opportunity to be heard. In essence, we treat the democratic nature of the legislative process as adequate notice and opportunity to be heard. See *Bi-Metallic Investment Co. v. State Board of Equalization,* 239 U.S. 441 (1915). But *individual applications* of a zoning law that affect property rights are subject to the requirements of notice and an opportunity to be heard.

Example: The Zoning Board of the city of Turingia changes the zoning of Mort's four-unit apartment building to single family residential, thus rendering his current use unlawful and depressing the value of his property. Mort learns of the alteration when he receives a "Notice of Violation" from the city. Turingia has denied Mort procedural due process; he is entitled to advance notice of the pending change and an opportunity to oppose the move.

- a. **Greater protection under state constitution:** As with equal protection, states may provide greater procedural due process protection under their state constitutions than is available under the federal Constitution.

2. **Substantive due process:** Though controversial in part, the Supreme Court recognizes a substantive component to the due process clause. If a law infringes a liberty that is "deeply rooted" in our shared history, traditions, or conscience, it will be subject to *strict scrutiny* — presumed void unless the government can prove that the infringement is *necessary to achieve a compelling state interest.* There are three aspects of substantive due process relevant to zoning laws.

   - a. **The incorporation doctrine:** This doctrine holds that certain of the liberties guaranteed by the Bill of Rights are "incorporated" into the substantive component of the 14th Amendment's due process clause, and thus apply to the states and their political subdivisions. Through this vehicle the states are required to conform to most of the Bill of Rights guarantees, including the 1st Amendment's guarantee of freedom of speech, assembly, press, association, and exercise of religion. Thus, if a zoning law substantially infringes any of these rights without adequate justification, it is void.

      - i. **Free speech:** In general, laws that regulate speech based on its content are subject to strict scrutiny, and laws that regulate speech in a content-neutral fashion (*e.g.*, the time, place, or manner of speaking) are subjected to more relaxed scrutiny. Zoning laws sometimes classify on the basis of the content of speech.

Example: The zoning law of the New Jersey borough of Mt. Ephraim prohibited "all live entertainment." The Court struck down the law as applied to an "adult bookstore" that permitted its customers to watch a live nude dancer through peepholes. The flat ban on live entertainment entirely suppressed whatever expression component there is to nude dancing so, as applied, it banned a form of expression — nude expression — because of its content. *Schad v. Borough of Mt. Ephraim,* 452 U.S. 61 (1981).

(1) Instance where zoning law upheld: But this rule is not ironclad. A ban on public nudity as applied to nude dancing was upheld in *Barnes v. Glen Theatre, Inc.,* 501 U.S. 560 (1991), on the ground that the purpose of the ban had nothing to do with suppression of speech, and the incidental restriction on expression via dancing in the nude was no more extensive than necessary to achieve the non-speech related goal of preserving a sense of decency. Further, if a zoning law discriminates on the basis of speech content but does so to regulate the ***secondary effects of speech*** — consequences that are not the product of the communicative impact of speech — the law is presumptively valid and will generally be upheld.

Example: Detroit adopted a zoning law that dispersed "adult theaters," cinemas displaying non-obscene pornography. The objective of the law was to eliminate the critical mass of seedy establishments that attracted "an undesirable quantity and quality of transients, adversely affect[ed] property values, cause[d] an increase in crime, ... and encourage[d] residents and businesses to move elsewhere." The Court upheld the law against a first amendment challenge, reasoning that it was not designed to suppress speech on account of its sexual content, or expression of any particular viewpoint, but was intended to disperse a "low value" form of speech in order to mitigate the secondary, non-speech effects empirically associated with it. *Young v. American Mini-Theatres,* 427 U.S. 50 (1976). Accord: *City of Renton v. Playtime Theatres,* 475 U.S. 41 (1986) (zoning law that consolidated adult theaters and bookstores into about 5% of the land area of the city upheld as a content neutral regulation of the secondary effects of such speech).

(2) **Invalid where unduly broad or restrictive:** But zoning laws that regulate speech in a content neutral fashion are invalid if they are *either* (1) broader than reasonably necessary to achieve a significant government purpose other than speech regulation, or (2) so restrictive that they fail to leave open ample alternative channels of communication.

Example: In order to minimize "visual clutter," the affluent St. Louis suburb of Ladue banned all signs except "for-sale" signs, business or home identification signs, and a few others. It did ban, however, Gilleo's 8 1/2 by 11 inch window sign declaring "For Peace in the Gulf." Even though Ladue's regulation was content-neutral (it was not attempting to regulate the message on signs) the Court unanimously voided it because its "near-total prohibition" on signs failed to leave open enough alternative means of communication. Ladue's law banned an entire medium of communication. *City of Ladue v. Gilleo,* 512 U.S. 43 (1994).

(3) **Valid prohibition:** A narrower prohibition of signs — one that leaves open ample alternative channels of communication — would be valid.

Example: Los Angeles prohibited the posting of signs on public property. Roland Vincent, a political candidate, attached signs advertising his candidacy to utility poles. The City removed them and Vincent's supporters attacked the validity of the ban. The Court upheld the law, reasoning that it was content-neutral and that the ban left Vincent free to attach his signs to private property (*e.g.,* distribute bumper stickers, rent space) and to use other low-cost substitute means to reach voters (*e.g.,* distribute handbills). *Members of the City Council of Los Angeles v. Taxpayers for Vincent,* 466 U.S. 789 (1984).

ii. **Free press:** Laws that single out the press for unfavorable treatment are subject to strict scrutiny. But the test of whether a law does so is often whether it "threatens to suppress the expression of particular ideas or viewpoints," or employs "content discrimination," or "targets a small group of speakers."

Example: The city of Zuni's zoning code requires printers of "newspapers, magazines, or newsletters with an average daily circulation of greater than 300,000" to be located in single story buildings with "at least 10 acres of off street parking." Only one entity, the *Zuni Daily Star,* was affected by the provision. The *Star's* printing plant was not in compliance with the zoning code and there was no land available for purchase or lease within Zuni which would enable it to comply. The law might be subject to strict scrutiny. Cf. *Minneapolis Star & Tribune Co. v. Minnesota Commissioner of Revenue,* 460 U.S. 575 (1983) (sales tax that applied to only 11 newspaper publishers in the state voided after strict scrutiny applied).

iii. **Free exercise of religion:** Laws that prohibit acts only when engaged in for religious reasons, or because of the religious belief that they display, are invalid attempts to suppress the free exercise of religion. A zoning law can run afoul of this rule.

Example: The city of Viola's zoning code prohibits the use of land anywhere within Viola for the "ritual slaughter" of animals, but exempts almost every such ritual killing except those engaged in for religious purposes. Viola is home to a large number of adherents to the Santeria religion, a sect that has as its central sacramental rite the ritual slaughter of an animal. Because the zoning code has been carefully drawn to apply only to ritual slaughter of animals for religious purposes, it is an invalid suppression of free exercise of religion. See *Church of the Lukumi Babalu Aye v. City of Hialeah,* 508 U.S. 520 (1993) (virtually the same facts).

b. **Economic substantive due process:** In the 19th century and early part of the 20th century courts often struck down economic regulation as violative of substantive due process. Indeed, *Euclid v. Ambler Realty Co., supra,* upheld a zoning law against just such a challenge. Today, a law regulating economic activity only is presumed to be valid unless the challenger can prove that it is ***not rationally related to any legitimate state interest.*** Thus, a zoning law is valid if (1) there is a ***public problem*** that the zoning law is ***intended to address,*** (2) the law ***actually tends to alleviate the problem,*** and (3) the ***public benefits*** are not so slight in comparison to the ***burdens imposed*** that the law is ***"unduly oppressive."*** See *Lawton v. Steele,* 152 U.S. 133 (1894). Consequently, there is little reason to challenge zoning laws on this ground because they will almost always be rationally connected to *some* legitimate governmental objective. There is probably some public problem that zoning tends to alleviate, and the benefits of zoning in any given case are rarely so meager in relation to the burdens imposed that the regulation is "unduly oppressive." Only the most bizarre, irrational, arbitrary zoning law would be voided under this standard. However, states remain free to use the due process clause of their state constitutions to impose more stringent standards on zoning laws.

c. **"Privacy" or "autonomy" rights:** Laws that substantially interfere with the exercise of certain constitutionally fundamental "privacy" or "autonomy" rights are subject to strict scrutiny. Among these constitutionally fundamental liberties are the right to terminate a pregnancy prior to fetal viability and the right to associate together in traditional family relationships. Zoning laws can easily interfere with these liberties.

   i. **Family rights:** Freedom of personal choice in matters of marriage and family life is a constitutionally fundamental liberty. Hence, governmental intrusion on "choices concerning family living arrangements" triggers strict scrutiny.

   Example: East Cleveland's zoning ordinance limited occupancy of dwellings to members of the same family, and defined "family" so narrowly that it excluded a family unit consisting of a woman, her son Dale, Dale's son Dale, Jr, and another grandson, John, who was a nephew of Dale and Dale, Jr.'s first cousin. The Court applied strict scrutiny because the zoning law substantially interfered with the right of members of the same extended family to arrange their living relationships. The law failed strict scrutiny. *Moore v. City of East Cleveland,* 431 U.S. 494 (1977).

   (1) **Unrelated persons:** But zoning laws that substantially interfere with the ability of unrelated persons to live together are presumed valid and subject only to minimal scrutiny.

   Example: The village of Belle Terre's zoning law prohibited occupancy of dwellings by more than two unrelated persons. Minimal scrutiny was applied since the law did not substantially burden the deeply rooted liberty of related family members to arrange their living patterns. The liberty of unrelated persons to live together in a group is simply not constitutionally fundamental. Since the law was rationally related to the legitimate governmental objectives of residential tranquility and low residential density it was upheld. *Village of Belle Terre v. Boraas,* 416 U.S. 1 (1974).

(2) **State constitutions:** State constitutions can produce a different result. The Supreme Courts of New Jersey, California and Michigan have construed their state constitutions to protect the right of unrelated people to live together. See *New Jersey v. Baker,* 405 A.2d 368 (N.J. 1979); *City of Santa Barbara v. Adamson,* 610 P.2d 436 (Cal. 1980); *Charter Township of Delta v. Dinolfo,* 351 N.W.2d 831 (Mich. 1984).

ii. **Abortion:** Prior to fetal viability, the right to terminate one's pregnancy is a constitutionally protected liberty interest. States may not regulate pre-viability abortions so that an "undue burden" is placed on a woman's decision to terminate her pregnancy.

Example: A city's zoning code completely bans the use of any structure within the city for purposes of performing an abortion. This is almost surely an undue burden, since abortions would be effectively eliminated within the city, whether before or after fetal viability.

D. **The takings clause:** The Fifth Amendment's taking clause (made applicable to the states via the Fourteenth Amendment's due process clause) prohibits the taking of private property except for public use and upon payment of just compensation. Government regulations of property, including zoning, can be so onerous that they amount to a *de facto* taking. One test of a ***regulatory taking*** is whether the landowner is left with some reasonable economic use of his property. If not, a taking has occurred. See Chapter 11, p. 345, *infra,* for a general discussion of takings. This discussion focuses on a few problematic applications of zoning.

1. **Historical preservation:** Zoning may be used to preserve entire historic districts or to preserve an isolated historic structure or site.

   a. **Historical districts:** Zoning laws that are designed to keep entire historic districts intact (*e.g.*, Old Town Alexandria, Virginia or Charleston, S.C.) are generally not takings because (1) landowners are left with a wide variety of economically valuable uses and (2) the mutual restrictions are to the advantage of all landowners within the district since the value of historic property within an historic district usually increases. See, *e.g., Smith v. Zoning Board of Appeals of the Town of Greenwich,* 629 A.2d

1089 (Conn. 1993); *Figarsky v. Historic District Comm.*, 368 A.2d 163 (Conn. 1976).

    b. Isolated historic sites: A zoning law that mandates preservation of an isolated historic site is more problematic. Such a law confers no reciprocal benefits on the landowner since his property is the only one affected. Analysis centers on whether the landowner is left with a sufficiently viable economic use. If not, the regulation is a taking.

    Example: New York City law required the preservation of a number of identified historic buildings, separated from each other. One of the buildings was Penn Central's Grand Central Station. The law, as applied to Grand Central, prevented Penn Central from building a high-rise office building over the terminal building. The law was upheld against a takings challenge on the ground that Penn Central was permitted to use the existing facility for transportation and office purposes, and was permitted to reap some of the economic benefit of the foregone development by sale of its "air rights" to adjoining properties. *Penn Central Transportation Co. v. City of New York*, 438 U.S. 104 (1978).

2. Environmental preservation: Zoning is often employed as a device to preserve open space and achieve other environmental objectives. While these public objectives are important they cannot be achieved by imposing their cost entirely on affected landowners.

    Example: In an attempt to mitigate destruction of the fragile barrier islands by the combination of development and severe storms, South Carolina enacted a law designed to curb development within a specified distance from the shore of the barrier islands. As applied to Lucas's land, the law made it impossible for him to use it in any economically viable manner. The public goal was achieved by a *de facto* taking of Lucas's land and South Carolina was required to compensate Lucas or permit him to develop his land. *Lucas v. South Carolina Coastal Council*, 505 U.S. 1003 (1992).

V. PLANNED DEVELOPMENTS: SUBDIVISIONS AND THEIR KIN

    A. Introduction: Much of the modern development of America is done in a wholesale fashion — large tracts of rural land are turned into entire communities by well-financed developers. Even smaller developers typically acquire 20 or 40 acres and subdivide it into residential lots. This process of transforming larger tracts into smaller ones used more intensively is typically governed by *subdivision regulations*. A related phenomenon is the *planned unit development (PUD),* by which a developer creates a variety of uses within a single planned development. Both types of planned development are discussed in this section.

B. Subdivisions: If given authority under an enabling act, political subdivisions of a state may enact laws regulating the creation of new subdivisions. These regulations focus on the layout of the subdivision — streets, sidewalks, lot sizes, attention to topography, and other relevant matters. The regulations assume that the proposed subdivision complies with separate land use laws. The point of subdivision regulations is to limit approval of new subdivisions to those that are likely to advance the general welfare. To that end, subdivision regulations often require developers to perform certain acts as a condition of approval of a subdivision.

  1. **Creation of infrastructure:** Subdivision approval is often conditioned upon the developer's creation of the basic infrastructure — streets, curbs, sidewalks, water and sewer mains — at the developer's expense. This necessarily involves a dedication of some of the property for public purposes (*e.g.*, streets).

  2. **Dedication of land for parks and schools:** Another fairly common condition for subdivision approval is the developer's dedication of property for parks and schools.

  3. **Validity of conditions:** Some of these forced extractions from developers are problematic.

      a. **Federal constitutional limits:** The United States Supreme Court has ruled that forced dedication of property for a public purpose as a condition for regulatory approval is an uncompensated taking if the government cannot demonstrate that the condition — forced dedication — is both *substantially related to the reason for imposing regulations in the first place* and *"roughly proportional" to the problem caused by the development.* See *Nollan v. California Coastal Commission,* 483 U.S. 825 (1987); *Dolan v. City of Tigard,* 512 U.S. 374 (1994); Chapter 11, *infra*. In the case of infrastructure, both criteria are surely met. But forced dedication of land for parks and schools is less clearly valid. Subdivision regulations are imposed in order to be sure that development will not occur without provision for appropriate pedestrian, vehicle and utility access. The purpose of subdivision regulation is not generally to create new parks or schools. The *"essential nexus"* required by *Nollan* may be missing. If that essential nexus is established, the rough proportionality test might remain at issue. Very large subdivisions might create enough new demand for schools or parks that the requirement is met, but imposing a forced dedication for schools or parks on a small subdivision almost surely fails *Dolan*'s rough proportionality test.

    b. State limits: States may impose even tighter limits on forced dedications as a condition of subdivision approval. The power to force dedications must be conferred by statute, but even if there is statutory authority, some states hold that a forced dedication is an uncompensated taking unless the need for the new park or school is *"specifically and uniquely attributable"* to the subdivision. See, *e.g.*, *Pioneer Trust & Savings Bank v. Village of Mt. Prospect,* 176 N.E.2d 799 (Ill. 1961) (forced dedication voided; unclear whether court relied on federal or state constitution); *Jordan v. Village of Menomonee Falls,* 137 N.W.2d 442 (Wis. 1965) (forced dedication upheld).

C. Planned unit developments (PUD): Planned Unit Developments involve a mix of uses within a single development. The idea is to permit a large tract to be developed in a fashion that is consistent with the comprehensive plan and pre-existing overall density requirements of the zoning law, but enable the developer to vary and mix uses and densities within the development in a fashion that would not conform to the zoning law if engaged in piecemeal by individual landowners. A PUD is typically created by a zoning amendment that designates a tract as a PUD, if it meets local statutory criteria for creating a PUD. Unlike a subdivision, a PUD contemplates mixed uses and densities. The problem with the PUD is said to be that planning officials are, in essence, permitted to waive the zoning law. But so long as the PUD is consistent with the comprehensive plan, the overall density of development is no more than permitted under the zoning law, and the mix of uses is not appreciably different than could be accomplished by conditional use permits, the PUD does not seem to be objectionable to courts. See, *e.g.*, *Cheney v. Village 2 at New Hope, Inc.,* 241 A.2d 81 (Pa. 1968).

VI. WHO NEEDS ZONING?

A. Theoretical objections to zoning: The theoretical justification for zoning is that it controls the imposition of externalities the private market cannot control. But servitudes (see Chapter 6, p. 197, *supra*) and nuisance law (see Chapter 7, p. 255, *supra*) are privately bargained-for or initiated devices to control externalities. Are they adequate? Some think so. It has been argued that zoning imposes enormous administrative costs (*e.g.*, the zoning bureaucracy and the huge costs of compliance) and, even worse, imposes new externalities. For example, zoning often produces use-segregated housing patterns that impose high commute costs and social costs of traffic, pollution, and resource depletion that could be avoided if more mixed use patterns were permitted. Reliance on private bargains to produce servitudes and litigation to control nuisances would accomplish most of what zoning sets out to do. See Ellickson, 40 U. CHI. L .REV. 681 (1973).

B. **Houston — the empirical example:** The only large scale empirical evidence for the lack of utility of zoning was Houston, a city that, until recently, had no zoning controls. The principal difference between the unzoned Houston and its zoned peer cities was (1) Houston had more apartments and, hence, lower rents, (2) Houston's major arterial streets were more intensively commercial, and (3) Houston's residential areas included more non-residential uses (*e.g.*, the corner grocery). See Siegan, 13 J.L. & Econ. 71 (1970). The necessity of zoning is surely oversold. The utility of zoning is fairly debatable. But the pervasive presence of zoning is beyond dispute.

Chapter 9
TRANSFERS OF REAL PROPERTY

I. CONTRACTS OF SALE

A. Introduction: All arm's length transfers for consideration will involve a contract for the sale of the land involved. Much of the law pertaining to that contract is the domain of your Contracts course. This discussion focuses on aspects of the contract for sale that are peculiar to the fact that land is the subject matter.

1. **Brokers:** Brokers are ubiquitous. Very few transfers of houses occur without the involvement of one or more brokers, and many transfers of commercial real estate involve a broker. In the typical arrangement, a seller hires a broker (the *listing agent*) to sell the property on terms and for a commission specified in the *listing agreement.* In most states the commission is earned when the broker has produced a buyer *ready, willing, and able* to purchase on the terms of the listing agreement or other terms acceptable to the seller. If the deal falls through because the *seller defaults* or the *seller refuses to sell on the terms of the listing agreement,* the broker is entitled to the commission anyway. But if the *buyer defaults,* no commission is earned. The listing broker is the seller's agent. Surprisingly, in many states the buyer's broker is a subagent of the seller's broker and so owes his or her duties to the seller, not the buyer he or she appears to be representing.

2. **Lawyers:** Most residential sale transactions are done via a standard, pre-printed contract, with critical terms (*e.g.*, price, financing, closing costs) to be supplied by the parties. Often brokers fill in these gaps and lawyers are not involved. Brokers must be careful not to do much more than "fill in the blanks" lest they be deemed to be practicing law. Of course, the choices made or advised by brokers have large legal consequences. Buyers and sellers are well-advised to consult lawyers in the making of the contract, but most don't. In some states, lawyers are engaged to prepare a *title abstract* — a history of the chain of title — and an opinion as to the state of title that would pass from seller to buyer. In other states, title insurance companies perform this chore and insure that the buyer receives good title. See Chapter 10, p. 325, *infra*. In more sophisticated transactions, lawyers will draft the sales contract, draft the deed, examine title or obtain title insurance, and oversee the closing.

3. **Mortgage lenders:** Very few people buy real property without borrowing a substantial portion of the purchase price. Key portions of

any sales contract deal with the seller's existing and the buyer's proposed mortgage. The mortgage lender is usually a third party but sometimes the seller will become a mortgage lender by agreeing to receive a portion of the purchase price in the form of the buyer's promissory note secured by a mortgage to the property. See p. 319, *infra*.

4. **Closing:** Real estate sales are two-step transactions. The nature of a real estate sales transaction is that some time will elapse between execution of the sales contract and the closing — the actual exchange of title and purchase price. Time is needed for the buyer to arrange financing, for a proper examination of title, and for various inspections and other acts to occur as called for under the sale contract or as required by law. Closings are usually conducted through an independent *escrow agent.* The critical items are deposited into escrow — the executed deed, the purchase price, the mortgage (if any) executed by the buyer. The escrow agent makes various adjustments of the purchase price to reflect pro rata apportionment of taxes and other prepaid expenses, and then disburses a portion of the purchase price to extinguish the seller's old mortgage, records the deed and buyer's new mortgage, and finally delivers the balance of the purchase price to the seller.

B. **Statute of Frauds:** The Statute of Frauds, adopted in some form by every state, requires that, unless there is some exception available, a contract for the sale of land ***must be in writing*** and ***must be signed by the party against whom it is sought to be enforced.*** Since both parties wish to enforce the agreement, if necessary, against the other, this means in practice that ***both parties must sign the contract for sale.***

1. **Formal contract not necessary:** A binding contract can be quite informal. So long as the key terms are present — price, description of the property, and the parties' signatures — an enforceable contract may exist. Parol evidence — evidence extrinsic to the document — is permissible to remove ambiguities.

    Example: George agrees to sell his beach house to Martha for $100,000. On a cocktail napkin, George writes "I will sell my Malibu beach house to Martha for $100,000 as soon as practical. [signed] George." Martha writes "OK. [signed] Martha." This contract is sufficient. As they part, George and Martha orally agree to close the transaction ninety days later. Parol evidence concerning this oral clarification of the closing date is admissible to clear up the contractual ambiguity of what is "as soon as practical."

2. **Single instrument not necessary:** The contract need not consist of a single document, so long as the multiple writings are consistent, embody the essential terms (price, parties, and property description), and are signed by the parties.

   Example: Martha sees her friend George in a bar and passes George a note, "George, will you sell me your Malibu beach house for $100,000 cash? Martha." George passes a separate note back to Martha: "Martha, I wouldn't sell my beach house to anybody but you and I'm happy to take $100,000 cash for it. George." The two notes, taken together, constitute an enforceable contract. See, *e.g.*, *Ward v. Mattuschek,* 330 P.2d 971 (Mont. 1958).

3. **Conditions:** Real estate sale contracts often make the buyer's obligation subject to financing conditions — that the buyer obtain loans in an amount sufficient to meet the purchase price and on terms acceptable to the buyer — or some other condition (*e.g.*, the property is acceptable to the buyer's structural expert, or the issuance of a building permit to enable the buyer to build an intended structure). Financing conditions are usually spelled out carefully and precisely. If not, two problems can occur. If the financing conditions are vague, and there is no parol evidence to clarify the ambiguity, the contract may be void for want of an essential term. Or, if the financing conditions are "to the buyer's satisfaction," an obligation is implied on the part of the buyer to use reasonable efforts to obtain the necessary financing on commercially reasonable terms. Failure to do so will result in buyer's default. The same obligation of good faith is implied with respect to other conditions that are "to the buyer's satisfaction."

4. **Exceptions to the Statute of Frauds:** There are two major exceptions to the Statute of Frauds — *part performance* and *equitable estoppel.* Each is an *equitable doctrine* and thus is generally available only when a buyer seeks *specific performance* of an otherwise unenforceable contract of sale.

   a. **Part performance:** The elements necessary to establish part performance vary among the states. Every state requires proof of an oral contract. The differences occur with respect to the additional elements.

      i. **Unequivocal evidence of contract:** Some states insist that the acts constituting part performance must be of the sort that would not occur but for the existence of a contract — often labeled as actions of *unequivocal reference to a contract.* These acts consist of *payment of all or a part of the purchase price,* taking *possession,* and making

improvements. None of these things are likely to be done if there were not a contract. Some states require all of these elements to establish part performance, but others are satisfied if possession alone is proven.

ii. **Reasonable reliance:** The modern trend is to require proof of (1) an ***oral contract*** and (2) ***reasonable reliance*** on the contract — enough reliance that it would be inequitable to deny specific performance.

   Example: Mrs. Green orally agreed to sell Hickey a building lot for $15,000 and accepted but did not deposit Hickey's check for part payment. Hickey then sold his house, expecting to build a new house on the lot. Mrs. Green refused to complete the sale. The Massachusetts Appeals Court held that Hickey's reliance was reasonable and that equity required specific performance of the oral sale contract. *Hickey v. Green,* 442 N.E.2d 37 (Mass. App. Ct. 1982).

iii. **Enforceable by seller:** The part performance doctrine is a two way street, available to both buyers and sellers. In most states a seller may invoke the part performance doctrine to compel specific performance by the buyer, if the buyer's acts are sufficient to constitute part performance and the buyer has acted to diminish the value of the property in the hands of the seller. A few states do not require any proof of diminished value. In those states the principle of mutuality reigns — if the buyer can compel specific performance, mutuality of remedies requires that the seller have the same opportunity.

b. **Equitable estoppel:** The familiar doctrine of equitable estoppel may be used to enforce an oral sale contract if the seller has caused the buyer reasonably to rely significantly to his detriment upon the seller's oral agreement to sell. This is not much different from the reasonable reliance branch of part performance.

   Example: Cities Service orally agreed to sell Newman two building lots and to convey title when "construction was well under way." Cities Service reaffirmed this promise to Newman's construction lender, inducing a $5,000 loan to Newman. After the foundation was constructed, Newman ran out of money and assigned his contract to Baliles. Cities Service refused to convey and the Tennessee Supreme Court ruled that Cities Service was equitably estopped from asserting the Statute of Frauds as a defense. *Baliles v. Cities Service Co.,* 578 S.W.2d 621 (Tenn. 1979).

5. **Revocation of contracts:** Most states do not apply the Statute of Frauds to revocation of a contract for sale of realty. Thus, if both parties agree orally to revoke a contract, the oral agreement is sufficient to do so. A few states reason that the original contract vested equitable title in the buyer and that a revocation amounts to a transfer of title back to the seller. In those states, the Statute of Frauds applies to revocations.

C. **Implied obligations:** There are a number of obligations implicit in every contract for the sale of realty. The principal ones are considered here.

1. **Good faith:** Each party is required to act with good faith in discharging the express duties of the contract. This has particular force when the obligation to complete the transaction is expressly conditioned upon future events that are subject to influence by the parties. These conditions often refer to buyer's obtaining financing, or public approval of an intended use, or buyer's satisfaction with some unknown aspect of the property. A party must exert reasonable efforts to discharge such conditions. Failure to do so will result in default. See, *e.g.*, *Bushmiller v. Schiller,* 368 A.2d 1044 (Md. Ct. Spec. App. 1977).

   Example: Buyer agrees to purchase Blackacre "if Blackacre yields a well for potable water of at least 10 gallons per minute." Buyer makes no effort to determine whether Blackacre has any ground water. Buyer will be in default if he fails to complete the purchase. By contrast, if Buyer drills a well in the location recommended by a professional well driller, but it only yields 3 gallons per minute, Buyer has used reasonable efforts. Buyer need not drill in another location. Buyer may refuse to close without incurring liability.

2. **Time of closing:** Most contracts state a date for the closing — the completion of the transaction. But if the closing does not occur on the specified date, it still may be enforced in equity if full performance is tendered within a reasonable time after the closing date. Courts reason that a particular closing date is not an essential term on the contract. To avoid this lingering uncertainty, a well-drafted contract will stipulate that *time is of the essence* of the agreement. By expressly making the time of performance an essential term of the agreement, a party able and willing to perform on the closing date is relieved of any future obligations under the sale contract if the other party fails to perform on the required closing date.

3. **Marketable title:** Every contract for sale of realty contains an implied duty of the seller to deliver *marketable title* to the buyer. This obligation can be expressly disclaimed by agreement between

buyer and seller. Marketable title is a title a prudent buyer would accept, one reasonably free of doubt that there is any other rival to title or any portion of it. Any defect in title must be **substantial** and likely to result in injury to the buyer.

- **a. Proof of marketable title:** A seller can deliver marketable title by either (1) producing **good record title** — a recorded chain of title, showing an unbroken transfer of title from some original root of title in the past to the seller, with no recorded encumbrances (*e.g.*, mortgages, easements, or servitudes) — or (2) proving **title by adverse possession** — either through a successful quiet title action or admissible evidence sufficient to enable the buyer to quiet title. See, *e.g.*, *Conklin v. Davi*, 388 A.2d 598 (N.J. 1978). A careful buyer may well insist on a contractual term obligating the seller to deliver **good record title,** thus depriving the seller of the ability to deliver marketable title by proof of adverse possession.

    - **i. Root of title:** To deliver good record title it is usually **not necessary** to trace the chain of title back to the original possessor of the property. About 20 states have **marketable title acts,** which provide that a deed at some distance in the past (typically, older than 20, 30, or 40 years) is a **root of title,** and cutting off any claims to title founded on earlier instruments. See p. 338, *infra*. Even in states without marketable title acts, good record title may be produced by a title search that goes back to the point that is deemed acceptable under local practice. The rationale is that a search of the records for the preceding 80 years, for example, is adequate to reveal virtually all present claims to title and, if there is any claim founded on some earlier instrument it is likely barred by the limitations statute. Even though this may not always be so, the risk of such claims is so low that the courts regard the record title thus produced as "marketable." This risk to the buyer may be even further reduced or eliminated by title insurance (see p. 343, *infra*) or reliance on the seller's warranties of title in the deed (see p. 312, *infra*).

- **b. Defective title:** To be unmarketable, the defect in title must be **substantial** and likely to injure the buyer. Defective title does not always prevent the transaction from taking place. Buyers can and often do waive certain defects (*e.g.*, easements, or a mortgage that can be assumed by the buyer) and other defects can be removed prior to or at the closing (*e.g.*, an existing mortgage may be paid off by the sale proceeds so that the buyer receives unencumbered marketable title). Common defects in title are discussed in this section.

> **i. Defective chain of title:** The chain of title may have a faulty or nonexistent link. If a deed describes the wrong land, for instance, it is a faulty link. Or, if there is no record evidence of a deed from B to C in a chain of title purportedly from A to B to C to D, the nonexistent link makes D's title unmarketable. Since a chain is only as good as its weakest link, such defects make title unmarketable unless there is adequate proof of adverse possession sufficient to create a new, valid, and marketable title. See, *e.g.*, *Conklin v. Davi, supra.*
>
> **ii. Encumbrances:** With two exceptions, encumbrances (*e.g.*, mortgages, liens, easements, or covenants) make title unmarketable. See, *e.g., Lohmeyer v. Bower,* 227 P.2d 102 (Kan 1951). An easement that ***benefits the property*** (*e.g.*, a utility easement) is regarded by some courts as ***not an encumbrance*** so long as the easement is ***known to the buyer*** before entry into the contract. Covenants restricting use are encumbrances, but some courts treat them as not making title unmarketable if the sale contract specifies a particular use that is permitted by the restrictive covenants. The rationale for this exception is that the buyer has bargained for a specific and limited use, not all possible lawful uses.
>
> **iii. Zoning restrictions:** Use limits imposed by public authority through zoning laws are not regarded as encumbrances upon title. The rationale is that all property is subject to the lawful regulation of public authority, and that all land titles implicitly incorporate such use limits. But if the existing use of the property violates a zoning ordinance the title will be held unmarketable on the theory that the buyer could not possibly have intended to purchase a violation of law and consequent liability. See, *e.g. Lohmeyer v. Bower, supra.*

D. Default and remedies: Default occurs when one party has tendered performance in time, demanded timely performance from the other party, and reciprocal performance is not forthcoming. Remedies for breach are ***damages, rescission,*** and ***specific performance.*** The plaintiff may choose the remedy.

> **1. Specific performance:** Since land is unique, damages are thought to be inadequate compensation for breach. But since specific performance is an equitable remedy the defendant may assert

the usual equitable defenses (*e.g.*, if specific performance would work an undue hardship upon the defendant it will be denied).

- a. **Sought by buyer:** Buyers are generally able to demand specific performance. If the seller's title is defective (*e.g.*, an easement) and the buyer still wants the property, the buyer is entitled to an abatement of the price to reflect the diminution in value attributable to the defect.

- b. **Sought by seller:** Sellers have traditionally been able to demand specific performance from the buyer, but the emerging trend is to deny sellers specific performance if they are still able to sell the property at a commercially reasonable price. A seller entitled to specific performance will be required to reduce the price if there is an ***insubstantial defect in title.*** Of course, if the title defect is substantial, the title is not marketable and the seller would not be entitled to specific performance.

2. **Rescission:** The polar opposite of specific performance is rescission. If the seller breaches, the buyer may elect to rescind, recover his partial payments already made, and "walk away" from the deal. If the buyer breaches, the seller may elect to rescind the contract and sell the property to another party. The rescission right does not ripen until the closing date, however, since either party has until then to tender performance. An attempted rescission prior to the closing date is not only ineffective but is a breach of the contract.

3. **Damages:** If the plaintiff does not want (or cannot obtain) specific performance she may obtain money damages. The measure of damages is usually the ***benefit of the bargain,*** but under some circumstances damages are limited to recovery of ***money out of pocket,*** or damages may be defined by the contract's ***liquidated damages*** provisions.

    - a. **Benefit of the bargain:** This measure of damages gives the aggrieved party the difference between the contract price and the value of which she is deprived by the other party's breach.

        Example 1 — seller's breach: Seller agrees to sell Blackacre for $50,000, but refuses to convey at the closing date because she is aware that in the interim the value of Blackacre has risen to $90,000. Buyer is entitled to $40,000 damages, since this represents the value of which she is deprived by Seller's breach. Buyer thus gets the benefit of the bargain as of the date of breach. It would not reduce the damages if Seller were to sell the property later to another party for $80,000. The value of the bargain to Buyer on the date Buyer was entitled to it was $40,000.

Example 2 — buyer's breach: Seller agrees to sell Blackacre for $50,000, but Buyer refuses to perform on the closing date. The value of Blackacre has now dropped to $30,000 (perhaps the town's major employer has announced it will cease operations). Seller is entitled to $20,000 damages. If the value of Blackacre had increased (or even remained constant) Seller would not be able to recover any damages since he lost nothing by Buyer's breach.

  b. **Out of pocket:** This rule is designed to limit the exposure of the seller who breaches innocently — whose breach is in good faith. Half the states limit damages awarded against a seller who has breached in good faith to the actual money that the buyer has expended in reliance on the contract. This means that the buyer is able to recover any part payments, expenditures on experts (*e.g.*, engineers, lawyers, title insurers) and interest and fees incurred with respect to loans obtained in connection with the prospective purchase. The other half of the states, of course, make the good faith seller in breach liable for the entire benefit of the bargain.

     Example: Seller agrees to sell Blackacre for $50,000 but cannot deliver marketable title due to a title defect previously unknown to Seller. At the closing date, Blackacre is worth $90,000. Buyer has paid $5,000 to Seller, and has incurred another $5,000 in lawyers' fees, appraisals, loan fees, and title examination costs. Seller's default is not the product of bad faith. In an ***out of pocket*** state, Buyer is entitled to $10,000 damages. In a full ***benefit of the bargain*** state, Buyer will be able to recover $40,000 damages.

  c. **Liquidated damages:** Sellers typically protect themselves against a buyer's breach by stipulating in the contract that the buyer's deposit may be retained as ***liquidated damages*** in the event of buyer's breach. Such provisions are enforceable so long as there is some ***reasonable relationship*** between the deposit amount and the actual damages suffered by the seller.

     Example 1: Seller and Buyer agree to transfer Blackacre for $50,000, and Buyer gives Seller a deposit of $5,000 which the contract recites may be retained by Seller as liquidated damages if Buyer should breach. Buyer breaches. Seller will assert that his actual damages consist of (1) the added cost of reselling the property (*e.g.*, advertising and promotion), (2) the delay in consummating another sale and consequent reduction in the present value of a later sale at the same price (or, phrased differently, the loss of interest on the sale proceeds until the later sale is completed), (3) the uncertainty that any replacement sale will actually be for that price or better, (4) the loss of other prospective buyers, and (5) any expenditures made in reasonable reliance on Buyer's performance. Seller will probably be able to keep the $5,000 deposit as liquidated damages.

Example 2: Seller and Buyer enter into an ***installment sale contract*** for Blackacre, under which Buyer takes possession and pays Seller monthly installments of the $50,000 purchase price. Seller promises to deliver title after the entire purchase price has been paid. The contract recites that Seller may keep all payments as liquidated damages in the event of Buyer's breach. Buyer pays a total of $49,000 and then breaches. Most states will not permit Seller to keep the $49,000 as liquidated damages. The installment sale contract will be treated as a mortgage (see p. 319, *infra*) or the Seller will be required to refund to Buyer all payments in excess of Seller's actual damages. Otherwise, Seller gets $49,000 from Buyer and continued ownership of Blackacre.

E. **Duties of disclosure and implied warranties:** This section deals with the duties imposed by law on sellers to disclose known defects and the warranty, implied by operation of law, of quality in the construction of buildings. Warranties of title, which may be contained in the deed, are covered in p. 306, *infra*.

   1. **Duties of disclosure:** The traditional common law rule is that, absent a fiduciary relationship, a seller has no duty to disclose known defects in the property. The seller's duty was to refrain from ***intentional misrepresentation*** — the outright lie about the property's condition (*e.g.*, the seller says "the roof is watertight" when he knows it leaks like a sieve) or ***active concealment*** of a known defect (*e.g.*, the construction of a fake ventilation system to conceal the building's lack of ventilation). This rule of *caveat emptor* was justified on the theory that buyers ought to use diligence and care to examine the property for themselves. *Caveat emptor* has been largely abandoned today.

      a. **Fiduciary relationships:** Even under *caveat emptor*, if the parties were in a fiduciary relationship — a relationship in which one party is dependent upon and reposes special trust in the other — the fiduciary was obligated to reveal all defects known to him. This duty was based on the special obligation of the fiduciary to prefer the interests of the other party to his own.

b. **Disclosure of seller-created conditions:** The narrowest departure from *caveat emptor* is the rule that a seller is obligated to disclose conditions that (1) are ***created by the seller,*** (2) ***materially impair property value,*** and (3) are ***not likely to be discovered by a reasonably prudent buyer using due care.*** See, *e.g.*, *Stambovsky v. Ackley*, 572 N.Y.S.2d 672 (Sup. Ct. 1991) (ruling that seller's promotion of the property's reputation as haunted by poltergeists was a condition warranting disclosure).

c. **Disclosure of latent material defects:** The emerging majority rule today is that a seller must reveal all ***latent material defects.*** A latent material defect is a defect that (1) ***materially affects the value or desirability*** of the property, (2) is ***known to the seller*** (or only accessible to the seller), and (3) is ***neither known to or "within the reach of the diligent attention and observations of the buyer."*** *Lingsch v. Savage,* 29 Cal. Rptr. 201 (Ct. App. 1963). Courts differ as to whether the test of materiality is ***objective*** (would the ***reasonable person*** think the defect was important?) or ***subjective*** (did the defect affect value or desirability to ***this particular buyer?***). In these jurisdictions a seller who fails to disclose all latent material defects has committed fraudulent concealment. See, *e.g.*, *Johnson v. Davis,* 480 So. 2d 625 (Fla. 1985); *Posner v. Davis,* 395 N.E.2d 133 (Ill. Ct. App. 1979). The range of such defects is quite broad. See, *e.g.*, *Reed v. King,* 193 Cal. Rptr. 130 (Ct. App. 1983), in which the court concluded that a seller's failure to reveal the fact that the house had been the site of a decade old multiple murder was actionable.

d. **Statutory disclosure obligations:** Some states have enacted statutes that require sellers to disclose a number of specified conditions. See, *e.g.*, Cal. Civil Code § 1102.6, which obligates sellers to reveal structural or soil defects, hazardous materials, underground tanks, alterations made without permits, encroachments, or neighborhood noise problems or other nuisances. This extensive disclosure obligation requires sellers to reveal the presence of annoying neighbors (see, *e.g., Alexander v. McKnight,* 9 Cal. Rptr.2d 453 (Ct. App. 1992)) and possibly even barking dogs or crying infants. California has gone from "buyer beware" to "seller tell all."

e. **Broker's disclosure obligations:** Some states impose upon the seller's broker the duty of conducting a reasonably diligent investigation of the property and disclosing to prospective buyers anything learned thereby that would have a material impact on the property's value or desirability. See, *e.g.*, *Easton v. Strassburger,* 199 Cal. Rptr. 383 (Ct. App. 1984); Cal. Civ. Code § 2079.16.

2. **Implied warranty of quality:** The traditional rule was that a builder had no liability to anyone for his poor workmanship unless he had given an ***express warranty*** of quality. In time, a builder's warranty of quality was implied into the contract between builder and owner but the builder's liability for economic loss resulting from breach of this warranty was limited to those with whom he was in ***privity of contract*** — the immediate purchaser of the structure from the builder or the owner with whom the builder contracted. Recovery in tort for the builder's negligence was generally unavailable because the loss was neither damage to property or person. See, *e.g.*, *Sensenbrenner v. Rust, Orling & Neale,* 374 S.E.2d 55 (Va. 1988). In recent years, most jurisdictions have abandoned the traditional rules and now imply a warranty of quality by the builder of a new home that may be enforced by subsequent purchasers of the structure. See, *e.g.*, *Lempke v. Dagenais,* 547 A.2d 290 (N.H. 1988).

   a. **Unsettled rationale:** Courts are confused about the rationale for a warranty of quality that runs to subsequent purchasers. Some say it is grounded in tort law's implementation of public policies — protecting innocent buyers of houses from shoddy work, imposing the risk of loss on the builder (the party most able to avoid the loss by building with care), and encouraging the creation of a sound housing stock. See, *e.g.*, *LaSara Grain v. First Nat'l Bank of Mercedes,* 673 S.W.2d 558 (Tex. 1984). Other courts contend that the warranty is based on contract, but because the builder has created a defective product that will inevitably harm others beyond the initial buyer they have ignored privity of contract as a barrier to its enforcement. See, *e.g.*, *Redarowicz v. Ohlendorf,* 441 N.E.2d 324 (Ill. 1982). And some, including Prosser, the legendary torts maven, think it is "a freak hybrid born of the illicit intercourse of tort and contract." Prosser, 69 Yale L.J. 1099, 1126. Its origin ought to make a difference. If rooted in tort the implied warranty should be incapable of disclaimer, but if founded upon contract its scope and existence ought to be limited by the bargain struck. Courts, however, pay no attention to theory here and generally are reluctant to permit its disclaimer. But see *G-W-L, Inc. v. Robichaux,* 643 S.W.2d 392 (Tex. 1982).

   b. **Limitations period:** Courts permit subsequent purchasers to bring suit against the original builder for a ***"reasonable time"*** — a period at least long enough for latent defects of the original construction to become apparent. Some states have enacted statutory limitations periods. See, *e.g.*, Cal. Code Civ. Proc. § 337.15 (10 years). The Uniform Land Transactions Act § 2-521, provides for a six year limitations period commencing with the initial sale.

    c. Subsequent owner's liability: The owner of a home who is not the builder has no liability based on the implied warranty of quality. Only the original builder is liable on that theory. But a seller may be liable for breach of a duty to disclose a known defect. See p. 301, *supra*.

F. Risk of loss and equitable title: During the time between making of the contract for sale and the closing, various bad things can happen — the property can be destroyed or damaged, or one or both of the parties may die. The common law reacted to these possibilities by creating the notion of ***equitable title*** (or ***equitable conversion,*** as it is often called).

  1. Equitable title: This doctrine holds that equitable ownership of the subject property passes to the buyer at the moment the contract of sale is made. Of course, the seller remains the legal owner until the closing, but for purposes of equity the buyer is treated as the owner. The seller's legal title is analogous to the legal title held by mortgage lenders in states that treat the mortgage as a transfer of legal title. It is retained as security for the buyer's payment of the purchase price. Since the doctrine is equitable, courts apply it in order to deliver fair results. The touchstone for its application is often whether it is necessary to carry out the parties' intentions or to avoid a palpable injustice. Note that only equitable title is passed to the buyer; unless the contract of sale permits the buyer to take possession prior to the closing the buyer, as equitable owner, has no right to possession. If the contract does permit the buyer to take possession the buyer is obligated to avoid waste of the property, for that would impair the value of the seller's retained legal title. Equitable title does not apply to contracts giving the buyer an option to purchase until and unless the option is exercised.

    a. Application to death of a party: An important effect of equitable title is that, for purposes of the seller's or buyer's death before closing, the parties are treated as having transferred the real property by entry into the contract. This means that a seller who dies after contracting but before closing leaves an estate that owns personal property — a contract right — and not real property. If the buyer dies before closing, the buyer's estate includes the real property.

Example: Opus, owner of Blackacre, enters into a valid contract to sell Blackacre to Baggins for $100,000. Before the closing, Opus dies. His will devises his real property to Bertha and his personal property to Camellia. At his death, Opus's interest in Blackacre is deemed to be personal property, which passes to Camellia. If Baggins performs, Camellia will receive the sale proceeds. If Baggins should default and equitable title should return to Opus's estate Camellia will still receive Blackacre. At Opus's death, his interest in Blackacre was personal property; the later conversion of that interest into real property occurred after Opus's death so Blackacre represents the proceeds of the personal property. The character of Opus's property at his death is what matters. Similarly, if Baggins died before the closing his interest in Blackacre passes under his will as real property. Of course, Baggins's estate must perform at the closing for that real property to become tangible.

b. **Application to risk of loss of the property:** English law used the doctrine of equitable title to place on the buyer the risk of loss of the property from causes not attributable to either buyer or seller (*e.g.*, fire, earthquake, storm damage). See *Paine v. Meller*, 6 Ves. 349, 31 Eng. Rep. 1088 (Ch. 1801). That rule is still followed by most American states. The buyer must still perform at the closing and is liable for either damages (measured by the diminution of value produced by the loss) or subject to specific performance. Of course, the seller must tender timely performance to perfect these remedies.

  i. **Entitlement to insurance proceeds:** The old English rule was that the seller was entitled to insurance proceeds, even though the buyer had the risk of loss, because the insurance policy was regarded as a personal contract right of the seller. If the buyer wanted insurance protection, he would have to secure his own. Most American states reject this rule and require the seller to credit the insurance proceeds against the purchase price in an action for specific performance or, in an action for damages, reduce the damage award by the insurance proceeds. The rationale is that the seller is maintaining insurance as much for the benefit of the buyer as himself, and thus holds the proceeds in ***constructive trust*** for the buyer. See, *e.g.*, *Heinzman v. Howard*, 366 N.W.2d 500 (S.D. 1985). It is always a good idea, however, for the buyer either to (1) procure his own insurance or (2) insert a provision in the sale contract requiring the seller to keep the property insured for the benefit of the buyer. A buyer who procures his own insurance keeps the proceeds even if risk of loss is on the seller, because it is quite clear that the buyer's insurance is obtained solely to protect the buyer's interest. No constructive trust is created.

    ii. Minority rule: The minority of American courts place the risk of loss on the seller, despite the doctrine of equitable title, on the theory that an intact structure was an essential part of the bargain. See, *e.g., Caulfield v. Improved Risk Mutuals, Inc.,* 488 N.E.2d 833 (N.Y. 1985). Thus, if the loss is substantial, it falls entirely on the seller and the buyer may not be forced to perform. If the loss is insignificant, the buyer may still be forced to perform but is entitled to an abatement of the purchase price to reflect the lost value, usually measured by the insurance proceeds received by the seller. The minority rule is thus effectively the same as the majority rule in cases of ***insubstantial insured loss.*** The minority rule is different only in cases of ***substantial loss.*** In minority jurisdictions the buyer may ***not be forced to perform;*** in the majority of states the buyer ***must perform or incur liability,*** though the buyer will receive ***credit for the seller's insurance proceeds.***

2. Risk of loss goes with possession: Many states have enacted statutes that make the risk of loss go with possession. See, *e.g.*, Cal. Civ. Code § 1662. Thus, despite equitable title, if the seller remains in possession he assumes risk of loss. Buyers in these jurisdictions acquire risk of loss prior to closing only if they take possession or assume that risk under the sale contract.

II. DEEDS

A. Formal requirements and component parts: A deed is the usual method by which title to realty is transferred. This section addresses the formal requirements for a valid deed and the elements of the instrument.

    1. Writing required: The Statute of Frauds requires a writing signed by the grantor in order to transfer an interest in land. A deed signed by the grantor is the usual method of compliance, but other writings will suffice. Since the grantor is the only party bound by the deed (as distinguished from the contract of sale) only the grantor needs to sign the deed.

    2. Notarial acknowledgement: A notarial acknowledgement is the act of a notary public attesting to the fact of the grantor's signature and to the identity of the grantor. A deed is valid without acknowledgement but virtually all deeds are acknowledged because notarial acknowledgement is almost universally required for recording of the deed in the public land records.

3. **The grant:** The first clause in a deed is the *granting clause,* which recites the parties, the words effecting the grant, the consideration, and the description of the property.

   a. **Words effecting the grant:** Any expression of an intent to effect a transfer of realty will accomplish the grant. No "magic words" are required.

   b. **Description of the grantee:** Ordinarily the grantee is described clearly and specifically. But a grantee can be described without reference to a specific person, so long as the description is sufficient to identify an actual person. Otherwise the deed may not be valid, either because of uncertainty as to ownership or inability to deliver the deed to a nonexistent grantee.

   Example: A deed to the "first born son of Diana, Princess of Wales" is sufficient to describe William. A deed to the "eldest daughter of Diana, Princess of Wales" is invalid because no such person exists or ever will exist.

   i. **No grantee named:** While the traditional rule has been that a deed that mentions no grantee is void, most American states today hold that the *intended grantee* has *implicit authority,* as the *agent of the grantor,* to fill in the intended grantee's name at *any later time.* Without a grantee the deed is a legal cipher, but once the intended grantee's name is inserted it becomes effective. See, *e.g., Board of Education v. Hughes,* 136 N.W. 1095 (Minn. 1912).

   c. **Consideration:** While consideration is *not necessary* to convey land, deeds often recite the *fact of consideration* rather than the actual amount of the consideration. Thus, the granting clause often states "for ten dollars and other good and valuable consideration" in order to establish that the buyer is a bona fide purchaser for value (which gives the grantee the protection of the recording acts; see Chapter 10, p. 325, *infra*) and simultaneously keep the actual purchase price out of the public records.

   d. **Description of the land:** The property conveyed may be described in any fashion that clearly and precisely identifies the parcel. Common forms of description include *metes and bounds* (a surveyor's description of the length and direction of the boundaries), reference to a *recorded survey map* or other survey, and *street and number.* So long as the description contains enough to identify the land, an ambiguous description will suffice if extrinsic evidence will clarify the ambiguity. But if there is no ambiguity in the description extrinsic evidence is not permitted to contradict the deed except to establish a mutual mistake in the description.

i. **Rules of construction:** If a property description is internally inconsistent, plainly mistaken, or incomplete, courts strive to ***determine the intentions of the parties.*** If there are no better clues to intent, courts employ a hierarchy of rules to sort out these problems. In descending order of preference and reliability, these are as follows: (1) ***original survey markers***, (2) ***natural monuments*** (*e.g.*, trees), (3) ***artificial monuments*** (*e.g.*, structures), (4) ***maps,*** (5) ***courses of direction*** (*e.g.*, "a line running ENE" or "a line 90 degrees to the left of the baseline"), (6) ***distances,*** (7) ***common names*** (*e.g.*, "McDonald's Farm"), and (8) ***quantity*** (*e.g.*, 140 acres).

Example: The deed description reads as follows: "Brigham's Farm, being that tract of 40 acres encompassed by a line beginning at an iron survey marker topped with a brass ball, located 10 feet due north of Highway 1, going east 1000 feet to an old fir tree with a circumference of 25 feet, turning northerly 82 degrees and running for 1220 feet to a wood rail fence marked on the USGS topographical map for the region, following the rail fence in a westerly direction for 1750 feet to Bishop's Creek, then southerly along the bank of Bishop's Creek for 1072 feet to the intersection with an undeveloped road platted on county survey map No. 872, as recorded in the county records, then southeasterly 420 feet to the point of origin." In trying to make sense of this description, we would first prefer the original iron survey marker even if it was not 10 feet due north of Highway 1, then we would prefer the old fir tree (even if it is more or less than 1000 feet from the survey stake), then we would prefer the 82 degree course change to the 1220 foot distance in order to reach the rail fence. If the fence is located in some place different from that marked on the USGS topographical map we would prefer its actual location to its mapped location. Again, we will prefer the meandering fence line to Bishop's Creek rather than the described distance and the natural course of the creek to the described distance along the creek. We will also prefer the mapped location of the undeveloped road to the asserted distance to it. Finally, as a last recourse, we would prefer

"Brigham's Farm" over the described quantity of 40 acres. See, *e.g.*, *Riley v. Griffin,* 16 Ga. 141 (1854).

B. Delivery: A deed must be delivered by the grantor in order to be effective to transfer an interest in land. ***Delivery*** means that the grantor has said or done things that demonstrate the ***grantor's intent to transfer immediately an interest in land to the grantee.*** Delivery does ***not necessarily require*** the physical act of handing over the paper deed to the grantee. The key is ***grantor's intent.*** If a grantor hands a deed to the purported grantee and says, "You are to hold on to this until I'm dead, and only then will it be effective," there has been no delivery. And if the grantor executes and records a deed to the grantee, vacates the property, tells others that he has "given the farm" to the grantee, but neither informs grantee nor physically hands the deed to grantee, delivery has nevertheless occurred.

1. **Presumed delivery:** Courts employ a ***rebuttable presumption*** that delivery has occurred under any of the following circumstances: (1) ***physical transfer to the grantee***, (2) ***notarial acknowledgement*** of the deed, or (3) ***recordation*** of the deed. Courts also employ a ***rebuttable presumption*** that no delivery has occurred if the grantor retains physical custody of the deed. But these presumptions may be rebutted by contrary evidence.

2. **Attempted delivery at death:** An attempt to deliver a deed at the death of the grantor is almost always ineffective. If the grantor intends that the deed become effective only upon his death, the deed is void unless it can be admitted as a will, and this is not usually the case since the formalities required for making a will are often lacking in the execution of a deed. But if the grantor intended the deed to be effective during his life, the grantor's death does not destroy the delivery already accomplished by that intent.

   Example: Aaron executes a deed granting Blackacre to Jacob. Aaron places the deed in a safe deposit box accessible only to Aaron, in an envelope marked "Give to Jacob only after my death. Aaron." No delivery has occurred because Aaron lacked the intent to make an immediate transfer. But if the same deed had been placed in a safe deposit box accessible by either Aaron or Jacob, in an envelope marked "For Jacob — Aaron," and Jacob only discovered the deed after Aaron's death, most courts would rule that delivery had occurred, especially if other circumstances support the inference of an intended gift during Aaron's life.

   a. **Exception — irrevocable escrow:** If a grantor executes a deed in favor of a grantor and hands it over to an escrow agent with ***irrevocable*** instructions (either ***written*** or ***oral***) to hold it until the grantor's death, delivery has occurred. The rationale is that the escrow agent is the agent of **both the grantor and the grantee.** Delivery to the grantee's agent is delivery to the grantee. But if the escrow is *revocable* the escrow agent is deemed to be only the grantor's agent, so no delivery has occurred. It is sometimes said that delivery has not occurred because the deed is not yet out of the grantor's control. This rule is often criticized on the ground that a grantor can validly accomplish the same end by simply transferring the property into a revocable trust, with the grantor as both trustee and beneficiary for life, and the grantee as beneficiary upon the grantor's death.

   b. Uncertain exception — express conditions: A deed may contain an express provision that makes transfer of possession conditional upon the grantor's death (*e.g.*, "to A, effective upon my death" or "to A if A survives me"). These conditional grants can be interpreted to mean either that the deed has passed a **springing executory interest** (see p. 138, *supra*) to the grantee or that **no delivery has occurred** — the deed is a nullity until the subsequent condition (the grantor's death) occurs. By the latter construction the deed would be of no effect unless it could qualify as a will. By the former construction the grantee received a valid springing executory interest which became possessory upon grantor's death. Courts are badly divided on this issue, and there is no safe answer. The academic answer is that the deed should be given effect as making a transfer of a springing executory interest, because the deed is adequate by itself to indicate the grantor's intentions at death. There is little reason to be worried that, by giving effect to the deed, the grantor's wishes concerning disposition of his property upon death are not being carried out. Presumably the grantor appreciated the significance of the deed when he signed it and there is no need to rely on evidence other than the deed itself to carry out the grantor's wishes.

      i. Grant of life estate distinguished: Of course, a grantor can convey by deed a life estate to himself and a remainder in another grantee. Such grants are valid and not problematic, so long as they are clear. The effect of a grant from O "to A, effective on my death" and a grant from O "to O for life, then to A" may be functionally identical, but only the latter clearly creates a life estate. The former style is uncertain — it may be valid as a springing executory interest but many courts will conclude that it is void for want of delivery — the present intention to transfer an interest in the subject land.

3. **Commercial escrows:** Most real estate transfers involve a commercial escrow. Usually, the seller gives the escrow holder specific written instructions that define the escrow agent's authority to hand over the deed to the buyer. The transfer of a deed into escrow along with written instructions is a completed delivery. Delivery is also completed when the deed is given to the escrow holder under oral instructions *if there is a written sale contract.* But without a written sales contract, an escrow agent holding a deed under oral instructions is deemed to be the seller's agent only, and the seller is empowered to revoke the escrow at any time. The power to revoke undermines the claim that the seller had an intention to pass title at the moment the deed was placed into the escrow agent's hands. Also, the oral instructions may well be silent on the essential issue of price. Despite these objections, a few states regard delivery as completed when the deed is placed in escrow under oral instructions.

   a. **Equitable title:** Although legal title passes only when the deed is handed over to the grantee out of escrow, equitable title passes to the grantee once delivery is completed to the escrow agent. This is more usually called the *relation-back doctrine* — the essential idea is that the buyer's title, once acquired out of the escrow, will "relate back" to the moment the deed was delivered into escrow. This fiction enables courts to ignore the effect of the grantor's death or incapacity after deposit into escrow, or a creditor's attempted seizure of the property after the deed is delivered into escrow. From that moment on, the buyer has equitable title.

      i. **Exception — bona fide purchasers:** If a seller double-crosses his buyer after depositing a deed into escrow, by conveying a deed to a *bona fide purchaser* (a person who pays real consideration and has no knowledge of the pending escrow), the bona fide purchaser (holder of legal title) prevails over the first grantee's equitable title. As between two innocents, the loser is the one who has yet to rely completely upon the seller's duplicity.

4. **Delivery by estoppel:** Even if a grantor does not intend to deliver a deed, he will be estopped from denying delivery in two principal circumstances.

   a. **Entrustment to a deceitful grantee:** If the grantor gives a deed to a grantee with no intent to transfer title, but the grantee uses the deed to convey to a third party bona fide purchaser, the grantor will be estopped from denying delivery.

Example: Damian gives Agnes a deed to Blackacre, telling her, "Look it over and think about it, for this is what I propose to do if you will marry my son, Mordred." Instead of marrying Mordred, Agnes records the deed and promptly sells Blackacre to Myrtle, who pays good value and is utterly ignorant of the circumstances under which Agnes obtained the deed from Damian. Damian will be estopped from denying delivery to Agnes. Damian had more opportunity than Myrtle to avoid the problem (he could have simply told Agnes of his planned marital gift), so the loss should fall on him. Of course, he may have recourse against Agnes.

    b. **Entrustment to a negligent escrow agent:** If the grantor gives a deed to an escrow agent but the grantee obtains it wrongfully, using it to sell the property to a bona fide purchaser, courts are split on whether the grantor is estopped from denying delivery.

        i. **Rationale for estoppel:** The grantor chose his escrow agent so he ought to shoulder the consequences of a poor choice. The grantor could have picked a more careful or honest agent. The grantor is more culpable than the bona fide purchaser so the grantor should lose.

        ii. **Rationale for no estoppel:** The grantor didn't intend delivery so he ought not be prevented from denying delivery. The problem with this view is that it does not really address the underlying issue — of two innocents, which should bear the loss? The usual answer to this question is that it should fall on the party who had the better ability to prevent the loss in the first place. To say that the grantor didn't intend delivery does not address this problem. However, courts holding to this view will estop the grantor if the grantor knew about the grantee's wrongful possession and did nothing about it. In a sense, these courts are saying that they will not hold the grantor's agent's conduct against him, but will hold the grantor responsible for his own conduct.

C. **Warranties of title:** A seller's warranties concerning the state of the title conveyed are expressly contained, if at all, in the deed. No warranties are implied. There are three types of deeds: the ***general warranty*** deed, the ***special warranty*** deed, and the ***quitclaim*** deed. The general and special warranty deeds contain covenants that warranty the state of title. The quitclaim deed does not.

    1. **General warranty deed:** The general warranty deed usually contains six covenants concerning title. Each covenant is a promise

that the title is absolutely free of the warranted defect, regardless of whether the defect arose before or during the time the grantor had title. Occasionally, a general warranty deed will contain less than these six covenants. Some states have enacted statutes that provide that use of terms of conveyance in a deed (*e.g.*, grant, sell, convey) carries with them the six general warranties of title. Such deeds are sometimes referred to as ***statutory warranty*** deeds. They are simply a statutory form of a general warranty deed.

- **a. Covenant of seisin:** The grantor promises that he owns what he is conveying by deed.

- **b. Covenant of right to convey:** The grantor warrants that he has the power or authority to convey the property.

- **c. Covenant against encumbrances:** The grantor warrants that there are no liens, mortgages, easements, covenants restricting use, or other encumbrances upon title to the property other than those specifically excepted in the deed.

- **d. Covenant of general warranty:** The grantor warrants that he will defend against ***lawful claims*** of a ***superior title*** and will compensate the grantee for any loss suffered by the successful assertion of a superior title.

- **e. Covenant of quiet enjoyment:** The grantor warrants that the grantee will not be disturbed in his possession or enjoyment of the property by someone's successful assertion of a superior title to the property. This covenant is functionally identical to the covenant of general warranty and, for that reason, is frequently omitted from general warranty deeds.

- **f. Covenant of further assurances:** The grantor promises to do whatever else is reasonably necessary to perfect the conveyed title, if it turns out to be imperfect. This covenant is also frequently dropped from general warranty deeds, perhaps because of the open-ended obligation imposed on the seller, or because it adds little to the first four covenants, or because the doctrine of after-acquired title (see p. 318, *infra*) has made this covenant redundant.

2. **Special warranty deed:** A special warranty deed contains the same six (or fewer) covenants of the general warranty deed. The only difference is that the grantor warrants against defects of title that arose ***during the grantor's time of holding title.*** Defects arising ***before the grantor's ownership*** are not covered. The grantor warrants, in essence, only that the grantor has not created or suffered a defect to occur during his ownership period.

3. **Quitclaim deed:** A quitclaim deed contains no warranties of title whatever. The quitclaim deed operates to convey to the grantee whatever interest in the property the grantor may own. If the grantor owns the Brooklyn Bridge, a quitclaim deed is sufficient to transfer ownership; but if the grantor owns no interest whatever in the Brooklyn Bridge, nothing is transferred by a quitclaim deed, nor is the grantor liable for breach of any covenants of title since none were made. The usual function of a quitclaim deed is to remove apparent and uncontested defects in title without resort to litigation.

4. **Merger doctrine:** The traditional rule is that any promises in the contract of sale *with respect to title* are "merged" into the deed once the buyer accepts the deed. This means that the buyer can only sue for breach of the deed covenants of title and may not rely on the contract of sale's provisions with respect to title. The justification for this rule is that buyer's acceptance of the deed is conclusive evidence that the buyer was satisfied that the deed fully conformed to the seller's obligations under the sale contract with respect to title. If the buyer was not satisfied that the deed conformed to the contract he should not have accepted the deed. The merger doctrine does not extinguish those portions of the sales contract that are *independent of or collateral to the transfer of title,* such as seller's promise to remove all rubbish from the premises. The merger doctrine is under attack and courts are apt to find a great many provisions of the sales contract to be independent of or collateral to transfer of title. The Uniform Land Transactions Act, § 1-309, eliminates the merger doctrine and permits all provisions of the sales contract to remain alive and enforceable by the buyer after acceptance of a deed.

5. **Breach of covenants of title:** Covenants of title may be divided into *present covenants* and *future covenants.* A present covenant is breached, if at all, at the moment the deed is delivered. A future covenant is breached when the grantee is actually or constructively evicted at some time in the future.

    a. **Present covenants — seisin, right to convey, and encumbrances:** These are representations of presently existing facts. Either the grantor owns the property or he does not; he has the right to convey or he does not; title is burdened by an encumbrance or it is not. The covenant is either breached when made (since it is not true) or can never be breached (since the facts were as promised at that moment in time).

    i. **Breach of covenant of seisin:** This covenant is broken if the grantor doesn't own what he purports to convey, regardless of whether he is aware of the defect or not. The covenant is broken even if the grantee knows that the grantor does not own the interest purportedly conveyed. If title is totally defective (or so defective that the grantee is left with good title only to an unusable parcel) the grantee is entitled to a return of his purchase price but must reconvey the right to possession to the grantor. If title partially fails the grantee is entitled to recover that portion of the purchase price that is equal to the value of the failed title and must reconvey his possessory right.

ii. **Breach of covenant of right to convey:** This covenant is broken if the grantor lacks the power or authority to convey the interest (*e.g.*, grantor is a trustee who is barred by the trust instrument from transferring title), whether or not he is aware of the limits on his authority to convey. Grantee's knowledge of the grantor's lack of authority to convey is not usually a defense to suit on this covenant. The measure of damages for breach is the same as for breach of the covenant of seisin.

iii. **Breach of covenant against encumbrances:** This covenant is breached if the title is encumbered (other than as expressly excepted in the deed) at the time of delivery of the deed, whether or not the grantor is aware of the encumbrance. In most states, the grantee's knowledge of the encumbrance does not excuse or obviate breach. But a minority of states hold that the grantee's knowledge (actual or constructive) of an ***open and visible*** encumbrance (such as an easement) prevents breach. See, *e.g.*, *Leach v. Gunnarson*, 619 P.2d 263 (Or. 1980). The measure of damages for breach depends on whether the encumbrance is removable by the grantee. If the ***grantee can remove the encumbrance*** (*e.g.*, by paying off a mortgage or lien) the grantee is entitled to recover what he expended to remove the encumbrance. If a grantee fails to remove a removable encumbrance he will not receive damages unless he proves actual damage by selling the property for less than its unencumbered market value. If the encumbrance is ***not removable unilaterally by the grantee*** (*e.g.*, an easement or use covenant) damages are measured by the difference between the unencumbered and encumbered fair market value at the time of the conveyance,

iv. **Statute of limitations:** Since breach of present covenants occurs, if at all, at the moment the covenant is given, the statute of limitations begins to run at that moment. The length of these statutes varies, but is usually three to six years. Of course, the buyer ought to know about breach almost immediately.

> v. **Assignment of present covenants:** The still-prevailing majority rule in America is that a present covenant is for the benefit of the immediate grantee and that, if breached when made, the grantee has a ***chose in action*** — the claim against the grantor — that is ***not impliedly assigned*** if the grantee conveys to a remote grantee. This rule is rooted in the now outmoded view that choses in action are not assignable. But we permit assignment of choses in action today, so there is no good reason to bar implicit assignment of the chose in action to the remote purchaser — the person who needs the benefit. Some states recognize this logic and hold, as do English courts, that a transfer to a remote grantee implicitly operates to assign the grantee's chose in action to the remote grantee.
>
> **Example:** Connelly acquired title to 80 acres at a foreclosure sale, then conveyed the property by general warranty deed to Dixon, who in turn conveyed by special warranty deed to Hansen & Gregerson. The foreclosure sale was invalid so Connelly never owned the 80 acres and thus breached the covenant of seisin given to Dixon. But since Dixon had conveyed by special warranty deed he had not breached the covenant of seisin he gave to Hansen & Gregerson. H&G sued Connelly on the covenant of seisin he had given Dixon, H&G's vendor. The Iowa Supreme Court ruled that Dixon's chose in action was impliedly assigned to H&G by the conveyance to H&G. *Rockafellor v. Gray*, 194 Iowa 1280 (1922).

b. **Future covenants — general warranty, quiet enjoyment, and further assurances:** These are representations as to future events, guaranteeing the grantee's security of title in the future. They are breached only when the grantee is actually or constructively evicted, which always occurs some time after the transfer. Actual eviction is, of course, actual dispossession from title or possession. Constructive eviction occurs whenever the grantee's possession is interfered with in any way by someone holding a superior title.

Example: Bost conveyed 80 acres to Brown under a general warranty deed containing no exceptions, even though Bost only owned 1/3 of the mineral rights. After the statute of limitations on the present covenants had expired, Brown agreed to sell the mineral rights to Consolidated Coal for $6,000, but was forced to accept only $2,000 once it was learned that Brown owned only 1/3 of the mineral rights. The Illinois Supreme Court ruled that Brown had not been constructively evicted because "the mere existence of a paramount title does not constitute a breach of the covenant" of quiet enjoyment. If the owner of the other 2/3 of the mineral rights were to start mining coal under Brown's land, Brown would be actually evicted. And if Brown purchased the other 2/3 of the mineral rights to prevent such coal mining Brown would be constructively evicted. *Brown v. Lober*, 389 N.E.2d 1188 (Ill. 1979).

i. **Breach of future covenants:** The future covenants are breached only when the grantee's possession has been disturbed by someone holding superior title. That can occur years after the original transfer and, as in *Brown v. Lober, supra,* after the statute of limitations has barred suit on the present covenants.

ii. **Benefit runs with the estate:** If there is ***privity of estate*** between the ***original grantor*** and the ***remote grantee*** the benefit of a future covenant given to the original grantee runs with the estate conveyed to the remote grantee. For this purpose, privity of estate means that the original grantor conveyed ***either title or possession*** and the same interest was conveyed to the remote grantee. If the original grantor had ***neither title nor possession*** (*e.g.*, the original grantor was a brazen fraud with no interest in the subject property) there is no estate created with which the covenant can run. This rule, though logical, insulates the most brazen wrongdoer from liability to remote grantees. It is not surprising that some courts have invented an "estate" held by the original grantor and passed on to the remote grantee, usually the mere possibility that the original grantor might later acquire an interest that would be passed on the remote grantee under the doctrine of after-acquired title (see p. 318, *infra*).

iii. **Extent of the obligation to defend:** The covenant of general warranty obliges the grantor to defend against ***lawful superior claims of title,*** but imposes no obligation to defend against the spurious claim of paramount title. Since it is impossible to know one from the other with certainty prior to litigation, the effect is to require the ***grantee*** to defend. In the event the third party's claim of paramount title is lawful, the grantee will be able to recover the costs of defense plus damages. But if the third party's claim is defeated, the costs of the victory are borne entirely by the grantee, since the claim was not lawful. If the grantor is notified of the claim and asked to defend, the grantor will be bound by the result whether or not he defends. Otherwise, the litigation between the grantee and the third party does not bind the grantor.

- c. **General limit on damages for breach:** The overwhelming majority rule is that the grantee may not recover more than what the grantor-in-breach received for the property. This is problematic under several circumstances.

    - i. **Suit by original grantee:** When the original grantee has expended considerable sums to improve the property, or the property value has increased markedly due to extrinsic factors, the grantee will not be able to obtain the benefit of the bargain, but is limited to a return of his purchase price. On the other hand, without the basic damage limitation, grantors would face the specter of potentially ruinous open-ended liability. Pre-judgment interest on the damages is often awarded but courts split over whether the interest should accrue from the date of the promise or the date of eviction. Courts holding to the former view argue that, since the grantee might be liable to the paramount owner for the grantee's wrongful occupation, interest is fair compensation for that potential liability. Courts holding to the latter view argue that, unless such a claim for rent is actually made, it would be a windfall to the grantee to award interest for the time the grantee is in possession. Some courts refuse to award damages to the grantee if the transfer was a gift.

    - ii. **Suit by remote grantee:** Nearly all courts agree that if the remote grantee has paid *more* for the property than the original grantor received, the remote grantee is subject to the general damage limit and will only recover what the original grantor received. But if the remote grantee paid *less* for the property, courts differ on whether the remote grantee should recover (1) what the original grantor received, (2) what the remote grantee paid, or (3) actual damages up to the amount received by the original grantor.

6. **After-acquired title (estoppel by deed):** If a grantor conveys an interest in property that he does not own, and later acquires the unowned interest, this doctrine operates to send that after-acquired title directly and immediately to the grantee or his successors in interest. The grantor is estopped from denying the scope of the original deed. Put another way, the grantor's original deed carries an implied promise that he will convey the missing pieces of title

should be later acquire them. Though originally limited to warranty deeds this doctrine now applies to quitclaim deeds conveying fee simple absolute, on the theory that the doctrine operates to effectuate the parties' probable intent.

Example: Schwenn gave her mineral rights to oil-producing property to her daughter. Then she conveyed the property (with no exception or reservation of the mineral rights) to Kaye. Once litigation threatened to develop Schwenn asked her daughter to reconvey the mineral rights to her and the daughter did so. At that moment, Schwenn's after-acquired title to the mineral rights was vested in Kaye. Schwenn was estopped from denying the validity and scope of her original deed to Kaye. *Schwenn v. Kaye*, 202 Cal. Rptr. 374 (Ct. App. 1984).

III. FINANCING DEVICES: MORTGAGES, DEEDS OF TRUST, AND INSTALLMENT CONTRACTS

A. **Mortgages:** Loans secured by mortgages are the principal device enabling people to acquire real property. Very few people are able or willing to pay the entire purchase price in cash. Instead, they borrow a significant portion of the purchase price from a lender on terms that require them to repay the loan with interest via monthly payments made over an extended period of time (frequently 30 years). To secure repayment of the loan, the lender will require the borrower to give the lender a mortgage on the property. The mortgage empowers the lender to sell the property in the event of the borrower's default on the loan, and to apply the sale proceeds to repayment of the loan. Any proceeds left over go to the borrower. Generally, if the sale proceeds do not eliminate the loan the borrower remains liable for the deficiency. This discussion of mortgages is only the tip of the mortgage law iceberg. There are a great many state variations on the general principles outlined here, but this outline will enable you to understand mortgages in the context of a first-year Property course.

1. **The mortgage transaction:** The term "mortgage" is often used loosely to refer to the entire transaction, which consists of two distinct elements: the ***loan*** and the ***mortgage.*** The loan is evidenced by a ***promissory note,*** a personal promise to repay the loan on the terms contained in the note The mortgage is evidenced by a document called a ***mortgage.*** It is a ***security agreement*** between the parties, by which the borrower gives the lender the right to sell the property if the borrower defaults on the loan and to apply the sale proceeds toward reduction of the loan. The mortgage is usually recorded in the public land records, thus giving notice of the lender's

security interest in the property. In some places the note and the mortgage are combined into a single instrument, but they still perform separate functions. The borrower is often called the **mortgagor;** the lender is the **mortgagee.**

a. **Development of the mortgage:** The mortgage began as a conveyance. Lenders would require the borrower to convey the property to the lender in fee simple subject to a condition subsequent (*e.g.*, "Borrower conveys Blackacre to Lender, but if Borrower pays 1000 pounds to Lender on Christmas Day, 1643, Lender will reconvey Blackacre to Borrower"). The law courts rigidly enforced this provision. If Borrower tendered 1000 pounds on Boxing Day (Dec. 26), 1643, it was too late; Blackacre was irrevocably Lender's.

   i. **Equity of redemption:** The equity courts, though, began to rule that the borrower had an equitable right to redeem the property at any time after the due date. This *equity of redemption,* unlimited in time, was a constant cloud on title that made the property effectively inalienable. To remove the blot, lenders then brought suit in the law courts to *foreclose equity of redemption* — by obtaining a court order to extinguish the equitable right of redemption and sell the property free of that cloud to a new purchaser. Today's mortgage foreclosure is similar — the equity of redemption is extinguished, the property is ordered sold, the sale proceeds are applied to the loan and any excess is given to the borrower. Note carefully that the foreclosure sale cuts off *only* this judicially created equity of redemption.

   ii. **Statutory right of redemption:** About twenty states have created a separate, independent *statutory right of redemption,* which gives the borrower a defined period of time (anywhere from a few months to a year or two) *after the foreclosure sale* in which the borrower can redeem the property from the purchaser at the foreclosure sale.

b. **Types of mortgages:** Although all mortgages have the same general characteristics there are some terms of art used to describe mortgages with different features. The principal types follow.

   i. **First and second mortgages:** The same property can be used to secure more than one loan. The first mortgage is the mortgage that is given first in time. The second mortgage is given next in time. Sometimes these are referred to as senior mortgages or junior mortgages. The second mortgage is taken subject to the rights of the senior mortgage. Upon foreclosure, the holder of a second mortgage is entitled to share in the sale proceeds only after the first mortgage has been fully satisfied.

   ii. **Fully amortized mortgage:** A fully amortized mortgage loan is one in which the principal is retired over the life of the loan so that the monthly payments are constant (if the interest rate is fixed for the life of the loan) or vary with interest rates (if the interest rate is adjustable by formula during the life of the loan). Most residential mortgage loans in the United States are fully amortized.

   iii. **Balloon payment mortgage:** Some mortgage loans provide for small payments of principal during the life of the loan (or none at all). While such loans reduce the monthly payment, they require payment of the entire principal balance on the due date. Since few borrowers are likely to have cash on hand to make that payment, a balloon payment mortgage has the practical effect of forcing the borrower to obtain a new mortgage loan to retire the old one.

   iv. **Purchase money mortgage:** A mortgage loan made for a portion of the purchase price is a purchase money mortgage.

2. **Title or lien?:** States take different views of whether the mortgagee (the lender) has *title* to the mortgaged property or only a *lien* upon that property. The title theory predominates in the east and the lien theory is favored by western states. But the difference is no longer of much practical consequence, since title theory states treat the lender's title as for security purposes only, thus making it virtually indistinguishable from a lien. The only difference lies in who is entitled to possession. In some title theory states the mortgagee is entitled to possession. In other title theory states the mortgagor is entitled to possession until default and the mortgagee is entitled to possession thereafter. In lien theory states the mortgagor is entitled to possession until foreclosure. In title theory states a lender has enhanced ability to recover possession after default fairly quickly (by suit for ejectment or judicial appointment of a receiver).

3. **Sale or transfer by the mortgagor:** A mortgagor is always free to transfer his *"equity"* — his interest in the property. "Equity" is the term used to describe the value of the borrower's interest in the property — the difference between market value and the loan secured by the mortgage. The term originated as a shorthand expression for the interest protected by the equity courts in the early days of mortgages. A buyer of the mortgagor's interest can

acquire the interest **subject to the mortgage** or can **assume the mortgage.**

    a. **Acquisition subject to the mortgage:** By taking title subject to the mortgage the buyer incurs **no personal liability on the mortgage.** In the event of default the mortgagee can foreclose and sell the property, but if the foreclosure sale proceeds do not extinguish the debt the lender has no further recourse against the owner who has acquired title subject to the mortgage. The lender can, however, obtain a personal judgment against the original mortgagor for the deficiency, except to the extent states prohibit deficiency judgments. See p. 322, *infra*.

    b. **Assumption of the mortgage:** If a new buyer assumes an existing mortgage he becomes **personally liable for the mortgage loan.** The lender can obtain a deficiency judgment against the assuming buyer as well as the original mortgagee (unless the lender has released the original mortgagee).

    c. **Due-on-sale clauses:** Lenders dislike transfer of the mortgagor's interest, whether by assumption or by taking subject to the mortgage, because it is against their financial interest. In periods of declining interest rates, buyers will not likely assume or take subject to an existing fixed-rate mortgage, because they can obtain a new mortgage at lower rates. But in periods of rising interest rates, buyers will be anxious to assume or take subject to an existing fixed-rate mortgage at a lower rate. Lenders, of course, would prefer that the buyer obtain a new mortgage at a higher rate. Lenders also say they are concerned that the new buyer might be less creditworthy, but that argument is mostly bogus since the original mortgagor remains personally liable and the property is the principal security for the loan. To prevent assumption of or a sale subject to a mortgage lenders insert a **due-on-sale clause** into the mortgage and loan. This provision permits the lender to demand immediate payment of the outstanding principal balance of the loan in the event the mortgagor sells his interest. In the 1970s some states, particularly California, invalidated due-on-sale clauses. Lenders reacted by obtaining federal law, which pre-empts state law, making due-on-sale clauses enforceable. See, *e.g.*, *Fidelity Fed. Sav. & Loan Ass'n v. De La Cuesta*, 458 U.S. 141 (1982).

4. **Default by mortgagor:** In most states the lender has the option of a suit to collect the debt or to foreclose and effect a sale of the property to satisfy the debt. A few states require the lender first to foreclose and sell before seeking to enforce the debt personally by

obtaining a deficiency judgment. The availability and utility of deficiency judgments are often limited by statute.

- a. **Anti-deficiency statutes:** Some states prohibit deficiency judgments on purchase money mortgage loans for residences. These statutes reflect a legislative bias in favor of homeowners. A variation is to permit a deficiency judgment only for the amount by which the debt exceeds a judicially determined fair market value for the property.

- b. **Statutory right of redemption:** The statutory right of redemption after foreclosure (see p. 320, *supra*) typically permits redemption by paying the *foreclosure sale price* rather than the *mortgage debt*. This is a strong inducement to the mortgagee, who is often the only bidder at a foreclosure sale, to bid the amount of the mortgage debt. Otherwise, the mortgagee might buy the property for a trifling fraction of the mortgage debt and seek to collect the remainder through a deficiency judgment. In some states the mortgagor in default may stay in possession until the expiration of the statutory redemption period.

B. **Deeds of trust:** The deed of trust is used in many states as the form of mortgage.

1. **How it works:** The borrower conveys the real property to a third party as *trustee* for the lender, for the limited purpose of securing repayment of the debt. The trustee is often a nominee of the lender (*e.g.*, the lender's lawyer, employee, or affiliated corporation). The deed of trust gives the trustee the power to sell the property upon default (the *power of sale*), to use the proceeds to pay off the debt, and return any excess to the borrower.

2. **Difference from the mortgage:** Traditionally, judicial foreclosure was required to enforce a mortgage. This meant bringing suit and conducting a judicially supervised sale. This is time consuming and costly. A power of sale vested in a trustee, by contrast, is relatively quick and cheap. In some states, the mortgagee may not be given a power of sale. In other states, a mortgagee may exercise the power of sale if the mortgage gives the mortgagee that power. Under a deed of trust the sale is conducted by the third party trustee at the lender's request. This is virtually identical to the procedure under a mortgage with power of sale vested in the mortgagee. Some states treat deficiency judgments or redemption differently, depending on whether a deed of trust or mortgage is the security instrument.

C. **Installment sale contracts:** The installment sale contract is, in form, merely a contract of sale for real property obligating the purchaser to pay the purchase price in installments and obligating the seller to deliver title to the buyer after the purchase price has been paid in full. Economically, the transaction is indistinguishable from delivery of a deed to the buyer in exchange for a note and purchase money mortgage to secure the purchase price.

Example: Vendor, owner of Blackacre, agrees to sell Blackacre to Vendee for $133,333, under an installment sale contract by which Vendee takes possession and agrees to pay the purchase price at the rate of $1,111 per month for 10 years, and Vendor agrees to deliver a deed to Vendee when the purchase price is fully paid. This is economically identical to a transaction by which Vendor deeds Blackacre to Vendee now, and receives from Vendee a note for $100,000, bearing interest at 6% per year, requiring Vendee to make monthly payments of $1,111 for 10 years (at which time the debt will be extinguished), secured by a mortgage.

1. **Treated as contract of sale:** The original reason for the installment sale contract was the seller's desire to avoid the procedural difficulties of extinguishing a mortgagor's equity of redemption. If a buyer under an installment sale contract defaulted, the seller could summarily evict the buyer upon default and, perhaps, keep all or a large part of the partially paid purchase price as damages. See, *e.g.*, *Jensen v. Schreck*, 275 N.W.2d 374 (Iowa 1979). Moreover, the seller retained legal title until the buyer had fully performed, so buyer's default served to excuse any further performance on the seller's part. This result was very much like the old **"strict foreclosure,"** by which the equity of redemption was irrevocably cut off. See, *e.g.*, *Harris v. Griffin*, 818 P.2d 1289 (Or. Ct. App. 1991).

2. **Treatment as a security device:** The modern trend of courts is to treat installment sale contracts as security devices. There are two good reasons for this view: (1) the installment sale contract is economically indistinguishable from a mortgage, and (2) it is inequitable to permit a buyer to lose his equity of redemption under circumstances where an identically situated mortgagor would not. Nowadays, a court is likely to require judicial foreclosure of an installment sale contract, permit the seller to retain payments only to the extent of the reasonable rental value of the property, and perhaps give the buyer an equitable right to cure his default and resume payments (analogous to the mortgagor's equity of redemption). See, *e.g.*, *Parise v. Citizens Nat'l Bank*, 438 So. 2d 1020 (Fla. Dist. Ct. App. 1983); *Skendzel v. Marshall*, 301 N.E.2d 641 (Ind. 1973); *Union Bond & Trust Co. v. Blue Creek Redwood Co.*, 128 F. Supp. 709 (N.D. Cal. 1955).

CHAPTER 10
ASSURING GOOD TITLE TO LAND

I. INTRODUCTION

A. The problem: To paraphrase James Madison, if men were angels there would be no need for methods to assure good title to land. But humans are often rogues, and sometimes they convey the same property more than once. The rogue grantor may be universally condemned, but the remaining problem is to decide which purchaser from the rogue is to prevail.

Example: Rogue, owner of Blackacre, conveys it to Angel on January 1 for $50,000. On January 10, before Angel has taken possession, Rogue conveys Blackacre to Beatrice for $50,000. Beatrice is ignorant of the prior conveyance to Angel. Rogue is, of course, a scoundrel, but let us suppose he has disappeared with his $100,000 and so cannot be forced to disgorge his ill-gotten gain. As to the innocents — Angel or Beatrice — who should prevail?

1. **The common law answer:** The common law used the *first-in-time* principle to award title to Angel. She was the first grantee and, at that moment, Rogue conveyed his interest in Blackacre. Rogue had no interest in Blackacre to convey to Beatrice, so she was the loser. To protect grantees, the common law relied heavily on the warranties of title contained in a general or special warranty deed. See p. 312, *supra*. But these were of little use if Rogue had skipped off with his loot.

2. **Modern answers:** Since the common law method was crude, uncertain, and harsh, Americans quickly devised better methods of assuring good title. A brief summary of these methods follows.

    a. **Recording:** The first innovation was *recording*. A recording act creates a system for placing conveyances in a public record, and then stipulates who has priority in the event of conflict. A deed is valid without recording, but an unrecorded deed is likely to lose out to a recorded deed if both deeds are from the same grantor to the same property. In the example, neither Angel nor Beatrice have recorded, so the recording act does not apply until one or both records. There are three different types of recording acts, and the answer may vary. See p. 326, *infra*.

    b. **Registration:** A later method, and one not much used in the United States, is to create an official registry of land titles. This system is different from recording of conveyances in that the

registry is the title, and the public records simply contain ***evidence of title.*** In a registry system, Rogue's registered title would be replaced by a new registration in Angel. Beatrice would probably never part with the purchase price because of the inability to register title in her name. See p. 340, *infra*.

c. **Title insurance:** A ubiquitous method for obtaining practical assurance of good title is to obtain ***title insurance.*** For a fee, a title insurer agrees to ***defend title*** and to ***compensate for the loss of the insured title to the claim of a paramount owner.*** So long as the title insurer remains solvent, this is good enough for most buyers. The title insurer, of course, carefully examines title before issuing its title insurance policy, and will refuse to insure if it finds any defects in title. But a title insurer will not generally insure title unless the purchaser's deed is recorded and the insurer is satisfied that no rival claimant can have a better title. In the example, since neither Angel nor Beatrice have recorded, it is not likely that either could find an insurer willing to provide title insurance without specifically excepting from its coverage any unrecorded prior conveyances.

II. RECORDING ACTS AND CHAIN OF TITLE PROBLEMS

A. **The recording system:** A public official in each county, usually called the county recorder, maintains a record of the transactions affecting real estate located in the county. But that record is only as complete as what is presented to the recorder for filing. Any instrument affecting realty may be filed and recorded so long as it meets the formal requirements for recording (usually notarial acknowledgment). The most common instruments that are recorded are deeds and mortgages, but such things as judgment liens, tax liens, installment sale contracts, and leases can and often are recorded.

1. **What the recorder does:** The recorder's job is mostly ministerial. The recorder accepts instruments for filing by stamping the date and time of filing on them, then photocopying them and placing the copy in an official record. The original is returned to the person who presented it for filing. Then the recorder ***indexes the instrument*** by noting a description of the instrument in an index maintained to facilitate location of the instrument. Just as a searcher for a library book must consult a catalog of books by author, or subject, or title, the searcher of title records must consult the recorder's index. There are two types of indexes.

a. **Grantor-grantee index:** By far the most common type of index is the grantor-grantee index. An alphabetical record of all grantors and all grantees, by surname, is maintained in separate volumes. The typical entry will contain the date, the name of the grantor (or grantee, as appropriate), the other party to the transaction, a brief description of the property and the instrument, and a citation to the precise location in the public records of a complete copy of the instrument.

Example: On July 2, 1988, Harry Simpson conveyed 123 Elm Street to Agnes Darby. Here is how that transaction might appear in the grantor index of the county:

> Simpson, Harry to Darby, Agnes. 7/2/88. General warranty deed to 123 Elm Street, recorded in Book 484, Page 1186.

And here is how that transaction might appear in the grantee index of the county:

> Darby, Agnes from Simpson, Harry. 7/2/88. General warranty deed to 123 Elm Street, recorded in Book 484, Page 1186.

b. **Tract index:** A few jurisdictions maintain a tract index, in which every transaction pertaining to particular parcel is entered in one location, instead of chronologically by grantor and grantee. Tract indexes are most common where property has been platted by map into various blocks and lots within blocks.

Example: Here is how the transaction in the last example might be indexed in a tract index:

> Tract: Block 39, Lot 2 (123 Elm Street). 7/2/88, General warranty deed from Harry Simpson to Agnes Darby, recorded in Book 484, Page 1106.

2. **What the title searcher does:** A title searcher's objective is to identify all the *past* title transactions pertinent to a particular parcel, in order to determine the *present* state of title. This is a simple job if the jurisdiction maintains a tract index; the title searcher finds the page describing all title transactions pertinent to the parcel. The process is more complicated if a grantor-grantee index is involved. The searcher begins by looking back in time through the grantee index to find the transaction by which the present owner acquired title, then searches the grantee index further back to find the transaction by which the present owner's grantor acquired title. This process continues until an adequate root of title has been found (usually a title transaction far enough back in time to cut off any prior claims by a statute of limitations). Then the searcher will turn to the grantor index and search forward in time, beginning with the initial grantor, to see if any owner ever conveyed her interest prior

to the grant that appears to make up the chain of title traced backward in time. In most jurisdictions the searcher need only search forward from the time the grantor acquired title to the point when the grantor transferred title to the next owner in the chain. But in a few jurisdictions it is necessary to search forward to the present for every grantor. See p. 335, *infra*.

Example: In 1890, Arthur conveyed Blackacre to Smith. In 1910, Smith granted Wilson an appurtenant easement for right of way over Blackacre. In 1920, Smith conveyed Blackacre to Rogers. Rogers conveyed Blackacre to Candiotti in 1950. Candiotti conveyed to Alvarez in 1980. In 1990 Alvarez granted Trustco a mortgage upon Blackacre. Your client, Barker, wishes to purchase Blackacre. To determine the state of title you would search the grantee index, under Alvarez, from the present time back to 1980, when you would find the deed from Candiotti to Alvarez. Then you would search the grantee index under Candiotti back to 1950, when you would find the deed from Rogers. Then you would search the grantee index under Rogers back to 1920, when you would find the Smith conveyance. Ditto back to 1890 when you would find the Arthur conveyance. Assume that a conveyance more than 80 years old is an adequate root of title. That makes the Arthur to Smith conveyance of 1890 the root of title. Then you search forward from 1890 in the grantor index under Smith. You will first find the 1910 easement grant to Wilson, then the 1920 conveyance to Rogers. You will search the grantor index under Rogers until you find the 1950 conveyance to Rogers. You will then search under Rogers from 1950 until 1980, when you find the conveyance to Alvarez. A final search forward under Alvarez from 1980 will reveal the mortgage to Trustco in 1990. You now know that Alvarez has good title to Blackacre, subject to an easement for right of way in favor of the present owner of Wilson's property and a mortgage to Trustco.

   a. **Legal obligations of the title searcher:** Any title searcher is obligated to exercise reasonable diligence in performing the search. A searcher is liable for a negligent search that results in damage to the buyer if the search results are provided to the buyer. This is true even if the search is performed for the seller, since the buyer is universally treated as the third party beneficiary of the search and it is obviously foreseeable that a buyer might rely on any such search.

B. **Race acts:** A race act provides that, as between two grantees to the same property, the ***earliest to record*** prevails. Hence there is a race to record first. Under a race act, it does not matter that the first person to record had notice of a prior unrecorded conveyance. The reason for ignoring such notice is that making the record dispositive obviates the need to rely on extrinsic evidence about notice, which may be controverted and unreliable. But most jurisdictions regard the equitable cost of the race statute as too high, since it permits a later grantee to prevail over a known earlier grantee so long as the later grantee is quicker to record.

Example: On January 15 Rogue, owner of Blackacre, conveys for value to Prof. Scatterbrain, who absent-mindedly leaves the deed on his desk for a month, before recording on February 15. Prof. Sly, Scatterbrain's colleague, sees the deed on Scatterbrain's desk, reads it, and observes that it is not recorded. On January 30, Prof. Sly pays value to Rogue for Blackacre and receives a deed from Rogue, which Prof. Sly records on February 1. As between Sly and Scatterbrain, Sly prevails because he recorded first. Sly's knowledge of Scatterbrain's prior purchase is irrelevant.

C. **Notice acts:** Notice acts address the inequity of permitting a later purchaser to prevail over an earlier purchaser when the later purchaser knows of the prior purchase. They do so by providing that a ***subsequent bona fide purchaser without notice of a prior unrecorded transfer*** prevails over the prior purchaser who has failed to record. And this is true ***even if the subsequent purchaser has not recorded.*** Here is a simplified example of a notice statute: "No conveyance is valid against a subsequent bona fide purchaser who has no notice of the conveyance, unless the conveyance is recorded." About half of American states have notice acts.

Example: On January 15, Able conveys Blackacre to Hector, who fails to record the deed. On February 15, Able conveys Blackacre to Artemis for $100,000. Artemis is ignorant of the January conveyance to Hector. Artemis prevails over Hector, regardless of who might first record their deed. The critical facts are that, at the moment Able conveyed to Artemis for value, (1) Artemis lacked notice of the prior conveyance to Hector, and (2) Hector had not recorded his deed (which would have given constructive notice to Artemis).

D. **Race-notice acts:** A race-notice act protects a more limited class of subsequent bona fide purchasers who lack notice of the prior conveyance. It protects only those subsequent bona fide purchasers who lack notice and who ***record before the prior purchaser.*** Here is a simplified example of a race-notice statute: "No conveyance is valid against a subsequent bona fide purchaser who has no notice of the conveyance and who has recorded his conveyance first." The supposed virtues of a race-notice act, as compared to a notice act, are (1) encouraging recording, and (2) eliminating disputes over which of two conveyances was first delivered. The first rationale is probably true but weak, and the second addresses a largely imaginary problem. But these arguments are persuasive enough to cause about half of American states to have enacted race-notice acts.

Example: On June 1, Bilbo convey Blackacre to Jane, who does not record. On July 1, Bilbo conveys Blackacre to Sally for $100,000. Sally is ignorant of the prior conveyance to Jane. On July 15 Jane records her deed. On July 20 Sally records her deed. Jane prevails over Sally because, even though Sally lacked notice of the conveyance to Jane, Jane recorded before Sally.

E. **The consequences of recordation:** Recordation provides constructive notice to the world of a conveyance. Even if a later purchaser fails to consult the record he is charged with knowledge of its contents. In a race or race-notice jurisdiction, recordation cuts off the possibility that either a prior unrecorded purchaser or a later purchaser could prevail. In a notice jurisdiction recordation provides constructive notice, thus preventing later purchasers from prevailing.

1. **The consequences of no recordation:** There are two important consequences to failure to record.

    a. **Common law rule applies:** If nobody has recorded, the common law principle of "first-in-time" continues to apply, except in a notice jurisdiction when the subsequent bona fide purchaser lacks notice.

    b. **Grantor can convey good title to a later purchaser:** More ominous to purchasers is the fact that, without recordation, the grantor is left with the power to convey good title to a later purchaser. Of course, the grantor who does this is often a scoundrel, and may well be liable to the losing first purchaser for the proceeds received from the second purchaser.

    Example: Olivia, the record owner of Blackacre, conveys Blackacre to Brewster, who fails to record. Then Olivia conveys Blackacre to Abigail for $100,000. Abigail, who is ignorant of the conveyance to Brewster, then records. In all three types of jurisdictions Abigail will prevail. Had Brewster recorded before the sale to Abigail, Brewster would have prevailed everywhere. Brewster may be able to recover from Olivia the $100,000 she received from Abigail, on the theory that Olivia holds those proceeds in a constructive trust for Brewster. But Brewster could have avoided the whole mess by prompt recordation. Moral: Always record.

F. When is an instrument recorded: To be recorded, an instrument must be eligible for recording and be entered in the records in a manner that complies with the jurisdiction's requirements. Virtually anything that affects title to or an interest in real property may be recorded. Most states require that an instrument may not be recorded without a notarial acknowledgement. To obtain a notarial acknowledgement, the grantor must prove his identity to a notary and sign the document with the notary as witness. Some states require or permit witnesses to perform the function of the notary. The problem is that recorders, being human, are not infallible. The following are the common instances of instruments appearing in the record that are wholly are partially unrecorded.

1. **Ineligible instrument:** The usual ineligible instrument is an unacknowledged instrument that nevertheless appears on the record through the recorder's oversight. Since such an instrument is not eligible for recordation, it is treated as unrecorded and thus does ***not give constructive notice*** of its contents. A subsequent purchaser will prevail unless she has ***actual notice*** of the prior conveyance or is under a duty to inquire and that inquiry would reveal the prior conveyance.

   a. **Defect not apparent on the face of the instrument:** Jurisdictions split on whether constructive notice is imparted by an apparently recorded instrument that is ineligible for recording due to some defect ***not apparent*** from the instrument itself. Since even the most diligent searcher of the records could not possibly have any inkling of the defect, it makes little sense to rule that the instrument is not recorded and thus imparts no constructive notice. But some states do just that, and at least one famous case in a race-notice state, *Messersmith v. Smith*, 60 N.W. 2d 276 (N.D.1953), holds that no subsequent instrument in the chain of title passing through the secretly defective instrument is validly recorded. The majority rule is that an instrument with a defect on its face does ***not*** give constructive notice but an instrument with a hidden defect ***does impart*** constructive notice. See, *e.g.*, *Metropolitan Nat'l Bank v. United States*, 901 F.2d 1297 (5th Cir. 1990); *Mills v. Damson Oil Co.*, 437 So. 2d 1005 (Miss. 1983).

2. **Instrument not indexed:** Another recorder's error is to fail to index an instrument or to index it so improperly that it cannot be found by a diligent searcher using the standard search methods. Jurisdictions split on the proper resolution of this problem. The older rule is that "a purchaser is charged with constructive notice of a record even though there is no official index which will direct him

to [the particular instrument]." 4 Amer. Law of Prop. § 17.25 (1952). On this theory, the purchaser has done all he can do by tendering an eligible instrument to the recorder for recording. See, *e.g.*, *Haner v. Bruce*, 146 Vt. 262 (1985). But the diligent searcher cannot find the unindexed instrument. Since constructive notice from the record is founded on the assumption that a searcher can find it if he looks, the newer rule is that the unindexed or improperly indexed instrument ought not provide constructive notice. See, *e.g.*, *Hochstein v. Romero*, 268 Cal. Rptr. 202 (Ct. App. 1990).

3. **"Omnibus" clauses:** A variation on the improperly indexed instrument is an instrument that accurately describes one parcel, Blackacre, and also includes "all other land owned by the grantor in the county." These omnibus clauses are sometimes called "Mother Hubbard" clauses, since they "sweep the cupboard bare." The recorder can only record this instrument by reference to Blackacre, since it is an unreasonable burden on the recorder to search the records to identify all the other property owned by the grantor. Omnibus clauses are void as against later purchasers of the grantor's property (other than Blackacre) because a diligent searcher of the index (with respect to a parcel other than Blackacre) will never locate any reference to the omnibus clause.

Example: Barton, owner of Blackacre, Redacre, and Whiteacre, all located in Churchill County, grants a mortgage to Bank encumbering Blackacre "and all other real property I own in Churchill County." Bank records the mortgage and it is indexed as "Barton, grantor, to Bank, grantee; mortgage of Blackacre." Later, Barton sells Redacre to Thomas for $100,000. Thomas takes Redacre free of Bank's mortgage because it is not reasonable to expect a title searcher of Redacre to locate and read every other conveyance ever made by every owner of Redacre with respect to other parcels located in Churchill County. That would be a monumental task, greatly increasing the time and expense of title searches. See, *e.g.*, *Luthi v. Evans*, 576 P.2d 1064 (Kan. 1978).

G. **Scope of protection afforded by recording acts:** The protection afforded by a recording act is defined by the statute, as interpreted by the courts of the jurisdiction. Read the recording act carefully!

1. **Invalid conveyance:** Although recordation creates a presumption of validity, if in fact the instrument was invalid (*e.g.*, it was forged or never delivered) recordation does not make it valid.

2. **Interests in land created by operation of law:** Recording acts only apply to *conveyances* — deeds, mortgages, grants, contracts, and the like. They do **not apply to interests created by operation**

of law — adverse possession, prescriptive easements, or implied easements. Even though such interests are not of record, they are still valid and enforceable against subsequent purchasers.

3. **Bona fide purchasers:** Notice and race-notice recording acts are intended to protect the ***bona fide purchaser*** of property. A bona fide purchaser is one who gives ***valuable consideration*** to purchase the property and is ***without notice*** of a prior unrecorded conveyance. Race acts protect bona fide purchasers only to the extent they are the first to record. Obviously, a ***donee does not receive protection*** because a donee has not given value.

    a. **Shelter rule:** The protection given a bona fide purchaser under a recording act extends to all takers from the bona fide purchaser, even if such a taker knows of a prior unrecorded conveyance. This "shelter rule" is necessary to give the bona fide purchaser the full value of his purchase in reliance on the records. Part of that value is the ability to transfer good title to others.

        Example: Ovid conveys to Alan, who does not record. Ovid then conveys to Barbara, a bona fide purchaser, who does record. Barbara then conveys to Charles, who knows all about the Ovid to Alan deed. Barbara will prevail over Alan in all three types of jurisdictions. In a notice or race-notice jurisdiction, Charles's knowledge of Alan's deed is irrelevant only because he is a taker from Barbara, a bona fide purchaser. Charles is "sheltered" by his vendor's status as a BFP.

4. **Mortgagees:** Mortgagees are generally treated as bona fide purchasers, either because the statute specifically includes them or because courts have interpreted the phrase "bona fide purchaser" to include them. But this only applies to the mortgagee who actually gives value (*e.g.*, the loan proceeds) in return for the mortgage. In most states a mortgagee who receives a mortgage to secure a ***preexisting debt*** without some detrimental change in its position (*e.g.*, a reduction in the interest rate) has not acquired the mortgage for value and so is not a bona fide purchaser. See, *e.g.*, *Gabel v. Drewrys Ltd., U.S.A., Inc.*, 68 So. 2d 372 (Fla. 1953). The contrary view is taken by the Uniform Simplification of Land Transfers Act, §§ 1-201(31) and 3-202.

5. **Creditors:** The status of creditors depends on the language of the act.

    a. **No protection:** If a recording act protects only "purchasers," a creditor is protected only if he should purchase the owner's interest at a judicial sale resulting from a successful lawsuit to collect the debt.

 b. **Specific protection:** If a recording act specifically protects "creditors" or "all persons," a creditor will receive protection without the necessity of a purchase at a judicial sale. But the scope of that protection is often limited by courts to *judgment creditors* or *lien creditors.* The rationale is that creditors do not generally rely on the state of the public land records in extending unsecured credit, but a creditor who has reduced a claim to judgment or lien intends to seize and sell the debtor's property. The judgment or lien creditor has an interest in the state of the record in order to know what his priority is with respect to the debtor's property.

H. Notice: To be protected under a notice or race-notice statute, a purchaser must be without *actual or constructive notice* of any prior unrecorded interests at the time the purchaser pays the consideration.

 1. **Actual notice:** Actual notice is real, actual knowledge of the prior unrecorded transaction. Evidence beyond the record is necessary to prove actual notice.

 2. **Constructive notice:** There are two forms of constructive notice: *record notice* and *inquiry notice.*

  a. **Record notice:** The entire world, specifically including a subsequent grantee, is charged with constructive notice of the contents of the record. If an instrument is validly recorded, every subsequent grantee has constructive notice of it, and so cannot be a bona fide purchaser.

  b. **Inquiry notice:** In most states a subsequent purchaser has an obligation to make reasonable inquiries, and is charged with knowledge of what those reasonable inquiries would reveal. The following subsections explore some of the circumstances that trigger a duty to inquire.

   i. **Possession:** Most states impose a duty to inquire of whoever is in possession of the subject property. See, *e.g., Waldorff Insurance & Bonding, Inc. v. Eglin Nat'l Bank,* 453 So. 2d 1383 (Fla. Dist. Ct. App. 1984). If such inquiry would reveal that the possessor occupies under an unrecorded conveyance from the record owner, the subsequent purchaser has constructive notice of the claim by virtue of this doctrine of inquiry notice. There are various permutations on this theme. Some states limit the obligation to inquire to instances where the possession is by a stranger to the record title. Others limit inquiry to instances where the later purchaser has actual knowledge of the existence of a possessor.

ii. **Record reference to an unrecorded instrument:** If a recorded instrument refers expressly to an unrecorded instrument, a purchaser is under an obligation in most states to inquire about the substance of the unrecorded instrument to which the record refers. See, *e.g.*, *Harper v. Paradise*, 210 S.E.2d 710 (Ga. 1974).

iii. **Deeds from common grantor:** As discussed on p. 227, *supra*, reciprocal implied covenants restricting land use may be implied by a developer's conveyance of property subject to express covenants burdening the developer's retained land. But such a covenant does not appear in the chain of title of the retained land, if it is conveyed without any express such covenant. Does a deed by a developer to Lot 1, which imposes a use restriction on Lot 1 and all other lots retained by the developer (including Lot 2), impart constructive notice of the covenant to a later purchaser of Lot 2 from the developer? Note that the use restriction does not appear in the developer's deed to Lot 2. Jurisdictions split on this issue. Most conclude that the burden on title searchers to locate and read all deeds out from a common grantor is unreasonable. See, *e.g.*, *Buffalo Academy of the Sacred Heart v. Boehm Bros., Inc.*, 196 N.E. 42 (N.Y. 1935). But a few states conclude that purchasers of property from a common grantor have constructive notice of the contents of all deeds out from a common grantor, thus imposing the practical burden of searching all deeds out from a common grantor. See, *e.g.*, *Guillette v. Daly Dry Wall, Inc.*, 325 N.E.2d 572 (Mass. 1975). In these latter jurisdictions a purchaser is obligated to inquire of other conveyances made by the common grantor.

iv. **Character of neighborhood:** As discussed on p. 227, *supra*, reciprocal implied covenants restricting land use may also be implied by the doctrine of implied reciprocal covenants, under which a uniform development scheme creates use restrictions by implication. In the jurisdictions that recognize implied reciprocal covenants from a common scheme, a purchaser is under a duty to inquire about the deeds out from a common grantor, deeds which may establish the common scheme, if the character of the neighborhood suggests such a common scheme. The leading case is *Sanborn v. McLean*, 206 N.W. 496 (Mich. 1925).

v. **Immediate grantee of a quit-claim deed:** A few jurisdictions hold that a conveyance by quit-claim deed is inherently suspicious because it raises doubts about the grantor's belief in the validity of his own title. Thus, the immediate grantee of a quit claim deed is obligated to inquire into the actual state of the grantor's title, and cannot simply rely on the public records. But this is ***not the majority rule.*** In most states, the mere fact that a conveyance is by quit claim deed does not trigger inquiry notice. See 6A Powell, The Law of Real Property ¶ 905[1][B] (rev. ed. 1992).

I. **Common chain of title problems:** Grantor-grantee indexes, which are by far the most common form of index to public land records in the United States, conduce a variety of problems with the chain of title. A recorded and indexed instrument might not always appear in the chain of title — the unbroken linkage stretching back from the present record owner through the grantee index to an adequate root of title and forward through the grantor index to the present record owner. Search of this chain will reveal all transactions made by every grantor from the root of title forward, from the moment each grantor acquires title until the moment that grantor parts with title by conveying it to the next party in the chain of title. Transactions outside of this chain are often said to be ***wild deeds.*** The common chain of title problems are discussed here. These problems will not occur with a tract index, but most jurisdictions do not maintain tract indexes, and it would be very expensive to find and index, by tract, all of the prior transactions presently indexed by grantor and grantee.

1. **Instrument made by a complete stranger to the chain of title:** If a complete stranger to the record chain of title records a conveyance to another person, the conveyance does not give constructive notice because it is not within the chain of title.

    Example: In Minnesota, a race-notice state, Hoerger conveyed a lot to Duryea & Wilson, who did not record. Then D&W conveyed the lot to Board of Education, who did record. Then Hoerger conveyed to Hughes, who lacked notice of the conveyance from Hoerger to D&W. Hughes recorded. Hughes prevailed over the Board of Education because the conveyance from D&W to Board of Education is outside the chain of title and does not impart constructive notice. The Hoerger to D&W link in the chain is not recorded, so a diligent searcher would never find the D&W to Board conveyance. See *Board of Education of Minneapolis v. Hughes,* 136 N.W. 1095 (Minn. 1912); *Zimmer v. Sundell,* 296 N.W. 589 (Wis. 1941).

2. **After-acquired title:** Suppose a grantor conveys title without having title, but then later acquires title. Under the after-acquired

title doctrine (see p. 318, *supra*) the title "shoots through" the grantor to the grantee. But suppose the grantor conveys title twice, once before acquiring it and once afterwards, and both conveyances are immediately recorded. Does the first conveyance, made at a time when the grantor has never been a grantee (and thus will not be found in the usual backwards-in-time search by grantees) impart constructive notice? Or, should a title searcher be obligated to search a period earlier in time than the grantor acquired title, on the possibility that the grantor conveyed away his title before he ever got it?

Example — majority rule: The U.S. owned Fiveacre when Lowery conveyed his interest in Fiveacre to Horvath, who recorded the deed. Later, after the U.S. had conveyed its title in Fiveacre to Lowery (and Lowery had recorded the deed from the U.S), Lowery conveyed Fiveacre to Sabo, who recorded his deed. Sabo prevailed over Horvath, because Horvath's deed was outside the chain of title. A diligent title searcher would go back in time until he found the conveyance from the U.S. to Lowery in the grantee index, and would then search the grantor index (under Lowery) forward in time to see if Lowery had made any other conveyances, but could not reasonably be expected to search the grantor index **before Lowery had title.** See *Sabo v. Horvath,* 559 P.2d 1038 (Alaska 1976).

   a. Minority rule: A few jurisdictions, notably New York and Massachusetts, hold that title searchers must examine the grantor index before the time each record owner acquired title in order to see whether the owner conveyed title before he acquired it. See *Tefft v. Munson,* 57 N.Y. 97 (1874); *Ayer v. Philadelphia & Boston Face Brick Co.,* 34 N.E. 177 (Mass. 1893). By requiring a more extensive search these jurisdictions expand the scope of the chain of title. Such expanded searches are expensive, especially if the chain of title is long.

3. **Deed recorded after grantor has parted with record title:** Must a title searcher search the grantor index forward past the point that the record discloses he has already parted with title? Generally, there is no need to do so, but if the first instrument of record conveying title is not to a BFP (perhaps it is to a donee or a purchaser with actual notice of a prior unrecorded conveyance) the question becomes more complicated. Jurisdictions split on this issue.

   Example: Ovoid, owner of Blackacre, conveys to Alice, who fails to record. Then Ovoid conveys Blackacre to Ben, who knows of the Ovoid-to-Alice conveyance. Ben records his deed. Alice then records her deed from Ovoid. As between Alice and Ben, Alice will prevail because Ben is not a BFP without notice. But then Ben conveys to Charles, who pays value and is ignorant of the Ovoid-to-Alice conveyance. Charles records. Who prevails, Alice or Charles? The answer depends on whether the Ovoid-to-Alice deed, although recorded later than the Ovoid-to-Ben deed, gives constructive notice to Charles, a later BFP.

> a. **Majority rule:** A slight majority of states rule in favor of Alice, holding that the chain of title includes all instruments of record up to the moment the subsequent purchaser acquires title, even though they may be recorded after a grantor has first parted with record title. In these jurisdictions, a title searcher is obligated to search the grantor index forward to the present for each person who ever owned the property. See, *e.g.*, *Woods v. Garnett*, 16 So. 390 (Miss. 1894); *Westbrook v. Gleason,* 79 N.Y. 23 (1879); *Mahoney v. Middleton,* 41 Cal. 41 (1871); *Angle v. Slayton,* 697 P.2d 940 (N.M. 1985). This is an enormous burden, so great that most title examiners in these states don't perform such an extended search, preferring to take the risk of such conveyances. See, *e.g.*, Philbrick, 93 U. PA. L. REV. 391, 415.
>
> b. **Minority rule:** A narrow minority of states rule in favor of Charles, reasoning that a title searcher should be excused from further search forward in time after he finds a recorded conveyance of title from the grantor to another person. Thus, once a searcher has found the Ovoid-to-Ben deed, he need not search any further forward in time. In these jurisdictions the Ovoid-to-Alice deed is outside the chain of title and provides no constructive notice. See *Morse v. Curtis,* 2 N.E. 929 (Mass. 1885); *Day v. Clark,* 25 Vt. 397 (1853).

4. **Deeds from a common grantor:** A developer of property may sell some lots under deeds that impose use restrictions on the lots and on the lots retained by the developer. But when the retained lots are later sold they may be sold under deeds that make no mention of the use restrictions. Are the deeds to **other lots** conveyed by a common grantor, deeds which contain the use restriction, within the chain of title? If so, they impart constructive notice. Jurisdictions split. Some say yes. See *Guillette v. Daly Dry Wall, Inc.,* 325 N.E.2d 572 (Mass. 1975). Some say no. See *Buffalo Academy of the Sacred Heart v. Boehm Bros., Inc.,* 196 N.E. 42 (N.Y. 1935).

J. **Marketable title acts:** Marketable title acts are the principal legislative response to the fact that, like all human systems, the recording system is imperfect. Eighteen states have adopted marketable title acts, which are designed to limit the relevant chain of title to some specified period of recent history — from 22 to 50 years in the past. If a chain of title can be traced back to a root of title older than the period prescribed by the marketable title act (say 40 years, the most common period) most claims based on some older instrument are barred by the statute.

Example: Blackacre is located in a state with a 40 year marketable title act. The present record owner is Lottie, who purchased from George, via a deed recorded in 1970. George purchased Blackacre from Elvis, via a deed recorded in 1955. In 1964 George conveyed and recorded an easement for cable television access to Cablecorp. In 1953 Elvis conveyed to Frank an easement for parking on Blackacre, which Frank recorded. The deed from Elvis to George is the root of title, since it is more than 40 years old. If the jurisdiction's act makes no exception for older claims, the easement in Frank is extinguished by the marketable title act but the easement in favor of Cablecorp is valid since it is of record within the past 40 years. Note that in 2010 the root of title will be updated to the George to Lottie deed in 1970, and that will eliminate the easement in favor of Cablecorp, which dates from 1964.

1. **Validity of pre-root interests:** Unless the act makes a specific exception for pre-root interests, pre-root interests are invalid unless (1) they are referred to in the root of title itself or some post-root recorded instrument, or (2) they are recorded anew during the marketable title act period. In the preceding example, Frank and Cablecorp could keep their easements alive by re-recording them every 40 years.

    a. **Statutory exceptions:** The interests excepted from marketable title acts vary. Most statutes except most easements, claims of the current possessor, restrictive covenants, and, sometimes, mineral rights. These exceptions undercut the utility of marketable title acts.

2. **Twin chains of title:** Because marketable title acts rely on an artificial root of title it is possible that two separate chains of title can coexist. This conflict cannot be resolved by applying the marketable title act so the act is ignored and the conflict resolved by applying common law principles.

    Example: Assume a forty year marketable title act. In 1956, the record owner of Blackacre, Estella, conveyed her title to Richard, thus providing a root of title for a chain of title leading from Richard to Marvin (in 1969) to Zeke (in 1983). But in 1954 Slick, a stranger to title, forged Estella's name to a deed to Blackacre conveying it to Larry, who in turn conveyed to Maria in 1971, and from Maria to Esther in 1990. The 1954 forged deed to Larry is another independent root of title. The two chains conflict, and the marketable title act is not helpful to resolution. As between the two, the forged root of title must lose to the authentic chain. Zeke will prevail over Esther.

III. TITLE REGISTRATION — THE TORRENS SYSTEM

A. **Introduction:** Title registration is a substitute for recording. Instead of recording evidence of title, which is what a recording system does, a registration system makes a certificate of title the exclusive and definitive title. Title registration was invented in Australia in 1858 by Sir Richard Torrens, whose name is commonly used to describe the system. For a registration system to work there must first be a final and conclusive determination of ownership, binding on all the world. This requires a court proceeding to cut off all rival claims. Then the definitive title is registered and indexed in a tract index. When ownership changes, the certificate of title is cancelled and a new one issued. The Torrens system is widely used in the United Kingdom, Canada, Australia, and New Zealand. Title registration is an option in eleven American states but is not much used. It is most common in Hennepin County, Minnesota (Minneapolis), Cook County, Illinois (Chicago), and Hawaii.

B. **Adjudication of title:** To implement title registration it is necessary to adjudicate title, in order to cut off all possible rival claims. The owner must bring an *in rem* action that is functionally identical to a quiet title action. Notice must be given to all persons who might have any conceivable claim to title or an interest in the property. At the conclusion of this proceeding, the court will issue a certificate of title that declares the definitive title to the property. It will state the owner and itemize as "memorials" all encumbrances upon the property (*e.g.*, mortgages, easements, covenants, liens, etc.).

   1. **Scope of the certificate of title:** The certificate of title *is title*. It is binding on the entire world and cuts off all interests not included as memorials on the certificate, except for those discussed in this section. Otherwise, the certificate as registered in the public records is conclusive title. It is thus not possible to acquire title by adverse possession against a registered title. But the exceptions, which follow, are significant, and undercut the utility of title registration.

      a. **Federal government claims:** States lack the power to adjudicate claims of the federal government unless the federal government consents to such adjudication. Thus, a certificate of title does not eliminate federal tax liens or any other interest that might be claimed by the federal government.

- b. **Statutory exceptions:** Most of the American Torrens statutes except from the certificate of title any interests or claims held by persons in actual possession, mineral claims, visible easements, utility or railroad easements, public thoroughfares or other claims of state or local governments. These exceptions make the certificate of title a lot less definitive and conclusive than it purports to be.

- c. **Defective notice in initial adjudication:** If a person with an interest in the property does not receive constitutionally acceptable notice of the initial title adjudication proceeding the certificate of title that results is not effective to bar the person's interest. The due process clause of the 14th Amendment requires that governments give people adequate notice and opportunity to be heard before taking their property away.

- d. **Fraud:** If fraud or deceit is employed to procure the initial certificate of title it can be set aside by the true owner or, alternatively, the registered owner will be held to hold in constructive trust for the true owner. It is not clear whether the true owner could obtain the same remedies against a bona fide purchaser of registered title from the initial and deceitful "owner." But if the initial certificate of title is validly obtained, subsequent fraud that results in a new certificate upon which a bona fide purchaser relies is not sufficient to cancel the title held by the BFP.

    Example: Arnold adjudicates title to Blackacre and obtains a certificate of title. Then Arnold gives his copy of his certificate to his brother, Bill, who forges Arnold's signature to obtain a new registered title in Bill's name. Then Bill sells Blackacre for value to Jane, who knows nothing of Bill's forgery. Jane has a valid registered title that cannot be upset by Arnold.

- e. **Not bona fide purchaser:** Courts in many Torrens jurisdictions have preserved the rule that a person who takes with notice of some off-record claim or interest takes subject to that claim. Thus, a purchaser of registered title who actually knows of some interest not included as a memorial on the registered title is often held to take subject to that interest. See, *e.g.*, *Butler v. Haley Greystone Corp.*, 347 Mass. 478 (1964).

C. **Public records and title transfers in the Torrens system:**

1. **Public records:** Once a registered title has been adjudicated the official certificate of title is given to the recorder for preservation

and a copy given to the owner. The recorder will then maintain a tract index of registered titles and will enter in the tract index the certificate of title. A title searcher simply finds the property in the tract index and reads the certificate of title. If any memorials are noted on the certificate (*e.g.*, mortgages) the searcher will then look up the mortgage instrument to read it fully.

2. **Title transfers:** The holder of registered title may transfer title by surrendering his certificate, together with a deed or other instrument conveying title, to the recorder. The recorder will then cancel the old registered title and issue a new one in the name of the purchaser. If a holder of registered title mortgages the property, the mortgage is simply added as a memorial. If the mortgage is then paid off, the memorial is removed.

3. **Errors by the recorder:** Since the registered title is title, errors by the recorder are especially significant. If, for example, the recorder fails to include a mortgage as a memorial on the certificate of title the mortgage is extinguished. Or, if the recorder means to register title to Blackacre in Jones but actually registers title to Blackacre in Smith, Blackacre is owned by Smith, not Jones. This is a serious flaw. Torrens systems deal with this by providing for compensation to those who lose their interests due to recorder error, but the funds provided for compensation "are often absurdly small in comparison to ... potential liability." Nelson, Stoebuck, and Whitman, Contemporary Property 1004 (1996). Moreover, governments use their sovereign immunity to avoid liability except to the extent of these meager compensation funds. This glaring flaw has been a strong inhibition to acceptance of Torrens registration.

D. **The practical realities of Torrens registration:** Torrens registration has not caught on in the United States for three good reasons: initial cost, lack of comprehensiveness, and the risk of uncompensated recorder error.

1. **Cost:** The initial cost of title adjudication is high and most of its benefits are reaped in the form of lower costs of transferring title. There is little incentive for the first owner to incur costs for the benefit of later owners. A developer, however, might find it advantageous to register title for an entire subdivision, in order to minimize the title transfer costs as the subdivided lots are sold, and because the initial cost can be spread over the entire subdivision.

2. **Lack of comprehensiveness:** The exceptions that riddle the purported global effect of a certificate of title further dampen the incentive to incur the cost of obtaining a certificate that is not as conclusive as it is supposed to be.

3. **Risk of uncompensated error:** This problem could be corrected by governmental assumption of liability for all recorder errors, but it is probably politically and practically impossible for financially hard-pressed state and local governments to do so.

E. **Possessory title registration:** An innovative variant on the Torrens system is to permit landowners to register their title for a nominal fee, but receive a certificate of title that is good only from that day forward. Any claims or interests affecting the property that predate the issuance of the certificate of title are fully preserved. The certificate is not initially of much value but, over time, old claims or interests might disappear. When coupled with a statute of limitations as to old claims (patterned after the marketable title acts) the certificate of title issued under a possessory title registration system would become conclusive after the elapse of the limitations period. This would eliminate the initial cost objection to Torrens registration but, by itself, does nothing to eliminate the problems of lack of comprehensiveness or risk of uncompensated recorder error. Minnesota is the only state to have adopted possessory title registration as a voluntary option.

IV. TITLE INSURANCE

A. **Introduction:** Title insurance is the most common form of title assurance in the United States. Title insurance involves the issuance of an insurance policy to a person — usually either a mortgage lender or a purchaser of property — by which the insurer warrants that title is as stated in the policy. The policy is a personal contract between the insurer and the person who buys the policy. Title insurers perform their own examination of the public land records in order to issue an insurance policy. They either employ lawyers to search the public records or they maintain their own duplicate set of records, identical to that found in the recorder's office, but often supplemented by a tract index of their own creation.

B. **Coverage:** The scope of coverage is determined by the contract of insurance. The usual policy insures only that the title stated in the policy is a good record title. The policy does not insure against claims or interests that are not part of the record. Essentially, the insured has a claim under the policy only if someone else asserts a claim based on the public records inconsistent with the record title as stated in the policy. But unlike most insurance policies, a title insurance policy obligates the insurer to disclose any particular blots on title it may find.

Example: Title insurer conducts a search of title to Blackacre and determines that Whiteacre encroaches upon Blackacre by six inches. Title insurer issues an insurance policy excluding "encroachments not of record." Title insurer has insured only good record title but still has an obligation to reveal the actual encroachment it has discovered.

1. **Exclusions:** Policies typically contain specific exclusions from coverage, including such items as ***liens not on the record*** (*e.g.*, mechanics' liens), ***off-record interests asserted by persons in possession*** (*e.g.*, adverse possession), ***boundary disputes*** (*e.g.*, encroachments or other boundary disputes not of record but which might be revealed by a survey), ***off-record easements or servitudes*** (*e.g.*, implied easements or covenants or prescriptive easements), and ***government land use regulations.***

2. **Insurer liability:** A title insurer is generally liable for the difference in value of the property with and without the insured-against defect, up to the maximum liability specified in the policy. This is true regardless of the amount paid for the property.

   Example: Jonah purchased Blackacre for $50,000 and obtained Titleco's insurance policy for $20,000 insuring good record title. It turns out that Watts, an adjacent landowner, has a record easement over Blackacre for access. If the value of Blackacre without the easement is $65,000 and the value of Blackacre with the easement is $40,000, Jonah has suffered $25,000 in damages, but can only recover $20,000 (the policy limits), even though the diminution in value from Jonah's purchase price is only $10,000. This rule makes sense because Jonah is entitled to the full benefits of his excellent bargain.

CHAPTER 11
TAKINGS: THE POWER OF EMINENT DOMAIN AND REGULATORY TAKINGS

I. INTRODUCTION

- **A. The eminent domain power:** All governments in the United States have the power to take private property for public purposes, but that power (the *eminent domain* power) is limited by the U.S. Constitution, state constitutions, statutory law, and judicial decisions. The U.S. Constitution's 5th Amendment provides that "private property [shall not] be taken for public use without just compensation." This is often called the "takings clause" or the "eminent domain" clause.

- **B. All property protected:** The Constitution's takings clause protects *all property,* no matter whether it is tangible or intangible. See *Ruckelshaus v. Monsanto Co.,* 467 U.S. 986 (1984).

- **C. Applies to all governments:** The takings clause applies to the states as well as the federal government. The substance of the takings clause is "incorporated" into the 14th Amendment's due process clause, which is applicable to the states. See *Chicago, Burlington & Quincy Ry. v. Chicago,* 166 U.S. 226 (1897). The takings clause also applies to all governmental action, whether *legislative, executive,* or *judicial.* See *Hughes v. Washington,* 389 U.S. 290 (1967).

- **D. The purposes of the takings clause:** The takings clause serves two important and related purposes.

    - **1. Prevent forcible redistribution of property:** The takings clause *prevents forcible redistribution of property* by stipulating, through the *just compensation* requirement, that when governmental power is used to take private property the public pays the property owner the value of the property taken.

    - **2. Takings permitted only for public benefit:** The *public use* requirement of the takings clause was designed to *prevent any taking, whether or not compensated,* that forces a transfer of property from one private person to another. Governmental power to take property may only be exercised for public benefit.

- **E. The principal issues under the takings clause:** There are three principal issues that arise under the takings clause.

    - **1. Public use:** Is a governmental taking of property for public use? Governments sometimes take private property and convey it to another private person in order to reap some alleged collateral public benefit. Is this for **public use?** See p. 347, *infra*.

2. **Regulatory takings:** At what point does a governmental regulation of property (restricting its use, possession, or disposition) become so burdensome that it is a *de facto* taking of property which triggers the constitutional requirement of just compensation? See. p. 348, *infra*.

3. **Compensation:** It is well-settled that the private property owner is entitled to the *fair market value* of the taken property — the price that a willing buyer and a willing seller would agree upon. Fair market value includes any *reasonable expectations* that a buyer may have about possible future uses (*e.g.*, a change from cattle grazing to vineyard cultivation). An owner is not entitled to any additional value that is subjective and peculiar to the owner (*e.g.*, the sentimental value of the family homestead). If there is no practical market for the property (*e.g.*, it is a Gothic cathedral) any fair valuation method may be used. Common alternatives are capitalization of earnings and replacement value.

   a. **Severance damages:** When only a portion of a private parcel is taken the owner is entitled to *severance damages* — compensation for the resulting damage to the remaining portion. Severance damages are measured by a *"before-and-after"* rule — the owner must be paid the difference between the value of the entire parcel (before taking) and the value of the parcel the owner is left with (after taking). It does not matter that the value of property actually taken is less than this sum.

   Example: Blackacre, a ten acre tract, is worth $500,000 prior to condemnation of five acres for use as a public park. The five acre piece, by itself, is worth $150,000. The remaining five acre piece is worth $200,000. Blackacre's owner is entitled to $300,000 in compensation ($500K - $200K), *not* $150,000 (the value of the condemned portion considered in isolation.

   b. **Effect of condemnation on value:** The fair market value due to a property owner is calculated without regard to the effect of condemnation itself on values. This can work to the advantage or disadvantage of property owners.

   Example 1 — advantage: The government announces that it will condemn all property in a defined area for a new highway, but that the condemnation will not occur for three years. The market value of affected property will drop, because few people will wish to purchase a property that must be surrendered to the government in a few years. The government must pay the fair market value that existed *before* its market depressing action.

Example 2 — disadvantage: The government announces that it will build a huge ground control center for space probes in a certain city marked by economic depression and low property values, and that it will shortly condemn property for that purpose. In the weeks that follow the announcement and before the actual condemnation, speculators bid up the value of Blackacre, from $100,000 to $200,000. If Blackacre is actually condemned, its owner is entitled to $100,000, not $200,000.

c. **Effect of condemnation on business located on the property:** Compensation is not generally required for damage to a business conducted on condemned property. The rationale for this rule is that damage to a business is merely incidental to the loss of the land itself. This rule also applies (absent specific statutory provision to the contrary) to the loss of business goodwill that results from condemnation.

F. **Constitutionally non-controversial takings:** Most governmental takings of property are not constitutionally controversial. When a government condemns private property for a new public road it is clearly doing so for public use and will admit that it is obligated to compensate the private landowners. The only issue is the amount of the compensation. Constitutional issues arise if the government denies that it has taken the property or if the taking is arguably not for public use.

II. THE PUBLIC USE REQUIREMENT

A. **Constitutional text:** The Constitution states "... nor shall private property be taken for *public use,* without just compensation."

1. **No takings except for "public use:"** The near-universally accepted reading of the "public use" phrase is that it means that no governmental seizure of private property may occur, *even if just compensation is paid*, unless it is for a public use. A few academicians contend that the phrase should mean that the only takings requiring compensation are those for public *use,* and that takings that serve some public benefit without subjecting the property to actual public use are not compensable. See Rubenfeld, 102 YALE L.J. 1077. But this reading is ignored by the courts.

2. **The meaning of "public use:"** A literal reading of the Constitution's text would limit governmental power to take private property to instances where the property will actually be used by the public (*e.g.*, as a park, school, road, or military base). On this reading, sei-

zures designed to produce some collateral public benefit are not permissible (*e.g.*, a seizure of private property to convey it to a private corporation in order to construct a factory that will provide economic benefits to the community). In fact, the public use limitation has virtually been eliminated by the Supreme Court's extreme deference to legislative judgments about what constitutes public use. So long as a taking is ***rationally related to any conceivable public purpose*** the public use requirement is satisfied. In essence, "public use" is whatever the legislature rationally thinks is conducive to "the public welfare."

Example: Hawaii law permitted the state to seize property from landlords and convey title to the tenants, upon payment of fair market value to the landlord by the tenant. This use of Hawaii's sovereign power to transfer property from one private person to another was upheld by the Supreme Court. The public use requirement was satisfied, said the Court, because the takings were "rationally related to a conceivable public purpose" — elimination of "the perceived social and economic evils of a land oligarchy traceable to [the Hawaiian] monarchs." *Hawaii Housing Authority v. Midkiff,* 465 U.S. 1097 (1984). See also *Berman v. Parker,* 348 U.S. 26 (1954).

III. REGULATORY TAKINGS: HOW MUCH REGULATION OF PROPERTY IS TOO MUCH?

A. Introduction: At some point government regulation of property becomes so extensive that it amounts to a *de facto* taking, even though the government denies that it is taking the property. But when? Everyone agrees that a seizure of title is a taking, but regulations may also interfere substantially with an owner's right to use, dispose, or possess property. In an early regulatory takings case, *Pennsylvania Coal Co. v. Mahon,* 260 U.S. 393 (1922), the Court declared that "while property may be regulated to a certain extent, if regulation goes too far it will be recognized as a taking." The Court has devised three "bright-line" or *per se* rules and several balancing tests to determine when a regulation goes "too far" and becomes a taking.

B. The *per se* rules: One of the Court's *per se* rules identifies a form of regulation that, *per se*, ***does not constitute a taking.*** The other two *per se* rules identify when a taking ***has occurred.***

1. **Nuisance abatement:** If a government regulates property to ***abate activities that are common law nuisances*** there is ***no taking,*** even though the regulations might bar all economically viable uses of the property. The theory is that ownership of the prop-

erty never included the right to inflict nuisances, so nothing has been taken by forbidding what was never lawful.

Example: South Carolina prohibited any development of Lucas's beachfront lots in order to protect its ecologically fragile barrier islands. The South Carolina Supreme Court ruled that the legislation was not a taking. The United States Supreme Court reversed, and remanded the case to determine whether the law simply abated a common law nuisance. Regulation of private property is no taking if the regulations "do no more than duplicate the result [obtainable by private parties] ... under the State's law of private nuisance, or by the State under its complementary power to abate [public] nuisances." Even if a regulation forbids the only economically viable use of the property, it does not "proscribe a productive use that was previously permissible under relevant property and nuisance principles." But a government desire to "prevent harm" is not, by itself, enough to trigger *per se* validity because "the distinction between 'harm-preventing' and 'benefit-conferring' is ... in the eye of the beholder." The only regulations that fall within this rule are those designed to stop common law nuisances. On remand, the South Carolina Supreme Court ruled that the uses prohibited by the law were not common law nuisances. *Lucas v. South Carolina Coastal Council,* 505 U.S. 1003 (1992).

    a. "Noxious" uses: Several older cases sought to distinguish between regulations designed to prevent harmful (or noxious) uses and those designed to reap a public benefit. Only the latter were said to be takings. This distinction is no longer viable. See, *e.g., Miller v. Schoene,* 276 U.S. 272 (1928), upholding the uncompensated forcible destruction of red cedar trees harboring cedar rust fungus, a killer of apple trees. See also *Hadachek v. Sebastian,* 239 U.S. 394 (1915), upholding a zoning law that forced a brickyard to cease operations. In these cases the Court thought that the cedar trees were harmful to apple trees and the brickyard was harmful to residential neighbors. But it is equally true to say that the cedar trees were destroyed to reap the public benefit of a continued apple industry, or that the brickyard was quashed to reap the public benefit of residential tranquility. This approach is no longer viable after *Lucas,* since the Court rejected "the distinction between 'harm-preventing' and 'benefit-conferring'" as useless. After *Lucas,* regulations that are supposedly designed to prevent harms that are not common law nuisances are evaluated under the balancing tests. There is no *per se* insulation of such regulations from the takings clause.

2. **Permanent dispossession:** When a government regulation *permanently dispossesses* an owner of her property, the regulation is a taking.

   a. **Real property:** As applied to real property, a taking has occurred if a regulation produces a *permanent physical occupation* of all or a part of the property. Temporary occupations are not a *per se* taking.

   Example: New York required landlords to permit cable television operators to install cable facilities on their property. Loretto, a landlord, claimed that the forced cable installation was a taking of her property. The Supreme Court agreed, ruling that a "permanent physical occupation authorized by government is a taking without regard to the public interests that it may serve." *Loretto v. Teleprompter Manhattan CATV Corp.,* 458 U.S. 419 (1982).

   b. **Personal property:** A taking has occurred when governments, by regulation, confiscate personal property.

   Example: Florida law provided that the interest earned on private funds deposited into court in interpleader cases must be turned over to the state. The Court ruled that a taking had occurred because the property owner had been permanently dispossessed. *Webb's Fabulous Pharmacies v. Beckwith,* 449 U.S. 155 (1980).

   c. **Constructive dispossession:** When government action strips all utility from an owner's possession the government may be treated as if had constructively dispossessed the owner. But the degree of interference necessary to support constructive dispossession is so great that the owner is also left with no economically viable use. See p. 350, *infra*.

   Example: Government aircraft continually flew over Causby's land at low altitude, thus making his property unusable for any purpose. The Supreme Court held that a taking had occurred, since Causby's loss was "as complete as if the United States had entered upon the surface of the land and taken exclusive possession of it." *United States v. Causby,* 328 U.S. 256 (1946).

3. **Loss of all economically viable use:** If a government regulation leaves the owner with *no economically viable use* of his property, and the regulation does *not abate a common law nuisance,* a taking has occurred. There are two rationales for this rule: (1) the severity of such regulations impeach the usual assumption that government regulation of property is for the advantage of everyone,

including affected property owners, and (2) the effect of these regulations is to achieve public benefits by imposing the costs of such benefits *entirely upon affected property owners.* See *Lucas v. South Carolina Coastal Council, supra.*

   a. **Partial destruction — "conceptual severance":** The "loss of all economically viable use" rule probably applies only to the case of a regulation that strips the owner of all economically viable use of any of his property. If a regulation operates to deprive the owner of all economically viable use of only part of his property, it is likely that the question of whether or not the regulation is a taking will be decided by the balancing tests discussed at p. 351, *infra*. The Supreme Court has not resolved this issue, but two cases provide hints as to the answer.

      i. *Pennsylvania Coal Co. v. Mahon,* **260 U.S. 393 (1922):** Pennsylvania's Kohler Act prohibited underground coal mining of coal that would cause surface subsidence, but only where the surface and the underground coal were owned by two different people. Mahon, owner of the surface, had expressly assumed the risk of subsidence when he purchased his property, but invoked the Kohler Act to restrain the owner of the underground coal, Pennsylvania Coal Company, from further underground mining. The Court voided the Kohler Act because it destroyed the economic viability of the Pennsylvania Coal's property — the underground coal. The law made "it commercially impracticable to mine ... coal," a result with "very nearly the same effect for constitutional purposes as appropriating or destroying" the right to mine coal. Justice Brandeis dissented on the ground that the Kohler Act merely prevented a public nuisance.

      ii. *Keystone Bituminous Coal Ass'n v. De Benedictis,* **480 U.S. 470 (1987):** A later Pennsylvania law, the Subsidence Act, required coal miners to leave sufficient coal in place to support the surface. The Supreme Court ruled that this law was not a taking, and distinguished the Subsidence Act from the Kohler Act on two grounds: (1) the coal forcibly left in place to support the surface did "not constitute a separate segment of property for takings law purposes," and (2) the miners had "not come close to ... proving that they have been denied the economically viable use of [their] property" because the coal left in place was only a small fraction of the entire coal deposit owned by them.

C. **Balancing public benefits and private costs:** If the *per se* rules do not resolve the issue of whether a regulation is a taking, courts weigh the public benefits achieved by the regulation against the private costs imposed. A regulation is not a taking if it **substantially advances a legitimate state objective.** To determine whether this test has been met the following conditions must exist: (1) **public benefits from the regulation must outweigh the private costs of the regulation,** (2) the regulation must **not be arbitrary,** and (3) the property owner must be permitted to **earn a reasonable return on investment** in the property. The principal case developing this balancing test is *Penn Central Transportation Co. v. City of New York*, 438 U.S. 104 (1978), in which the Supreme Court upheld New York City's Landmarks Preservation law. As applied to Penn Central the law prevented Penn Central from building an office tower over Grand Central Station but left Penn Central with the economic return from the terminal building and "transferable development rights" — the right to develop other properties in the vicinity owned by Penn Central more intensively than New York's zoning law would otherwise allow. The Court admitted that the balancing test was an "essentially ad hoc, factual inquir[y]" and concluded that, on these facts, Penn Central could still earn a "reasonable return" on its "investment-backed expectations."

1. **Conditional exemption from regulation:** Governments frequently attach conditions to the granting of a permit that enable a property owner to use her property in a manner otherwise prohibited. The usual problem is a building permit. Without a building permit a property owner is barred from constructing improvements on her property. Suppose the state may deny a building permit without effecting a taking. May the state condition the grant of a building permit on the property owner's consent to what would otherwise be an uncompensated taking? Of course, if the condition by itself is not a taking, the condition *cum* regulation is also not a taking. But a government may not require a person to surrender their property without compensation "in exchange for a discretionary benefit conferred by the government where the property sought has little or no relationship to the benefit." *Dolan v. City of Tigard,* 512 U.S. 374 (1994). If the condition is a taking by itself, the condition *cum* regulation is a taking unless the government can prove (1) the condition is **substantially related** to the **government's valid regulatory objective,** and (2) the nature and scope of the condition are **roughly proportional** to the impact of the proposed development. The first requirement is sometimes described as an **"essential nexus"** between the legitimate regulatory interest and the condition, so that the condition advances the state's reason for limiting development in the first place.

Example 1 — "essential nexus": The city of Esmerelda imposes a building permit system in order to limit development because Esmerelda's city-owned electrical utility is unable to increase substantially its power production and no other sources of electricity are available. Cassie applies for a building permit to enlarge her house and is told that a building permit will be issued only if she deeds a strip in front of her house to Esmerelda for a public path. The condition — donation of a portion of her property to the city — is clearly a taking, considered in isolation. And it is not saved because it is imposed as a condition to an otherwise valid building permit scheme. The condition — dedication of the bicycle path — is wholly unrelated to the reason for limiting development — conservation of scarce electrical power. See, *e.g.*, *Nollan v. California Coastal Commission*, 483 U.S. 825 (1987).

Example 2 — "rough proportionality": Now suppose that the city of Esmerelda offers Cassie a building permit on the condition that she install a windmill to generate electricity and that the electricity generated be sent into the city's power grid. The condition likely satisfies the "essential nexus" test because the condition is directly related to the reason for the development limit. Suppose that Cassie's proposed addition will add 100 kilowatts monthly to the demand on the city electrical utility and that the windmill will likely generate 120 kilowatts monthly. The condition is "roughly proportional" to the electrical energy impact of Cassie's proposed development. See, *e.g.*, *Dolan v. City of Tigard*, 512 U.S. 374 (1994).

D. Remedies: Once a regulation is found to be a taking the affected property owner has several remedies.

1. **Injunctive and declaratory relief:** Enforcement of a regulation that is a taking will be enjoined and the regulation will be declared to be a taking. If the government wishes to proceed with the regulation, it must pay just compensation.

2. **Damages:** A regulation may take effect immediately but it takes some time for it to be determined to be a taking. Since injunctive and declaratory relief provide no redress for an "interim taking," the affected property owner is entitled to damages for the loss of his property during the period a regulatory taking was in effect.

   Example: For an interim period following a flood, Los Angeles County regulations prohibited a church from reconstructing its camp structures. The U.S. Supreme Court held that, if the regulations were proven to be a taking, the church was entitled to compensation, no matter how temporary or interim the taking. Interim takings are no different from permanent takings, save in their duration. "[W]here the government's activities have already worked a taking of all use of property, no subsequent action by the government can relieve it of the duty to provide compensation for the period during which the taking was effective." See *First English Evangelical Lutheran Church of Glendale v. County of Los Angeles*, 482 U.S. 304 (1987).

ESSAY EXAM QUESTIONS AND ANSWERS

The following are sample essay exam questions dealing with various principles of Property. They will be useful for testing your knowledge and for practicing exam-taking. You should read and analyze the questions, write out your answers in essay form and then check your answers against our sample answers. Remember that while our sample answers demonstrate one good way to approach the questions, they are not the only good way.

Here are some suggestions for answering an essay exam question:

1. Keep in mind that you are dealing with an essay examination, which requires extended answers. The complete essay examination answer must contain not only the "answer" to the question, but of greater importance, the **analysis** which led you to the answer, the applicable **black letter law,** and an **explanation** of how you have applied the black letter law to the facts and reasoned your way to the "answer."

2. If your professor has indicated on the exam how much time you should spend on a particular question (most professors do), note that time carefully. Allocate 25% of the total time to steps 3-10 below. The balance of time should be used for the actual writing of your answer (steps 11-18).

3. Begin by **reading the question** thoroughly.

4. Next, **reread the question;** make sure that you look for all the details and nuances; read it as often as necessary to make sure you know what the author intended, not what you may have thought at first.

5. As you read, spot **key concepts, ideas, issues** and applicable **legal terms,** principles and concepts. Make notes in the margin to help you organize the facts and issues.

6. **Organize your thoughts** into an orderly, logical sequence.

7. **Analyze** the fact pattern and the key issues, terms, principles and concepts which you have spotted.

8. **Work out a game plan** for your answer, including the sequence you intend to follow in your answer, giving effect to the logical priority and

progression of ideas, the space to be allocated to each and the time to be spent on each.

9. Make a brief **word-phrase outline** of your proposed answer.

10. If you've spent at least 25% of the time allotted for answering the question on all of the steps outlined above, you're ready to **begin writing** the answer. An organized answer can be written quickly. If you are not organized when you begin your answer and haven't predetermined the time you intend to spend on each element, you'll waste time adding issues, crossing out parts of your answer, and committing too much time to minor issues.

11. Begin writing in short, clear, **decisive** sentences. Answer the question **precisely as it is asked**. For example, if the question reads: "Rule on plaintiff's motion," your answer should begin: "Motion granted," or "Motion overruled." The balance of your answer should explain how you reasoned to that conclusion.

12. Write your answer in **clear, concise, professional English prose,** using **legal terminology** whenever appropriate. Remember: this is an essay examination in the English language, at the graduate level, in a learned profession.

13. Be certain to cite the **black letter law** in full sentences on each of the key issues. The failure to do this is the most frequent mistake made by students.

14. **Do not rehash the facts.** A complete answer requires analysis from fact to rule or principle, as well as black letter law and a description of the way in which the black letter law applies to the facts in the question. Rehashing of the facts without the rest will get you nowhere.

15. *Write in s*hort, complete, simple sentences—confining each sentence to one basic thought or principle*. Avoid at any cost long, wandering, convoluted sentences which deal with several issues and subjects.

16. **Reason to a lawyer-like conclusion.** If you have time and space, add a wrap-up concluding sentence to your answer.

17. **Reread your answer** to make certain that you have made no unintended errors or omissions, and to ensure clarity and completeness.

18. **Use the full time allotted** for the question—no more and no less.

ESSAY QUESTIONS

QUESTION 1

Henry, eccentric and wealthy, died. His will provides, in relevant part, as follows: " I bequeath my country manor, Blackacre, to my daughter, Virginia, for life, and then to her husband, should he survive her, for life, and then to Virginia's children who are then alive and their heirs, in equal shares for life, and then to the Audubon Society for so long as my worthless grandson, Louis, does not kill any of the ducks on Blackacre Pond, but if so, then to my faithful butler, Jeeves, and the heirs of his body, and then to the Czar of Russia. The rest and residue of my estate I bequeath in trust to Quick, my lawyer, to hold as trustee for the benefit of my son, Mortimer, for life, then for the benefit of Mortimer's children for their lives, and then outright to such of Virginia's children who reach the summit of Mount Everest."

Henry was survived by his 57 year old daughter, Virginia, and her 59 year old husband, Lester, their children, Paula (a jockey), Roger (a mountain climber who has recently successfully ascended Everest), and William (a law student), his 72 year old bachelor butler, Jeeves, and Mortimer's only child, Louis, a forty year old hard-drinking outdoorsman and big-game hunter.

For many years prior to his death Henry's town house was adjacent to a studio occupied by Horst Sprockets, a German post-modern artist. Sprockets would frequently throw up his window in the dead of night, screaming "Ist Krap!", and then hurl paintings out the window into a public street. Henry would frequently get out of bed, go out into the street and collect these paintings. Virtually every morning after these midnight outbursts, Sprockets would go outside and collect all the paintings he could find, taking them back into his studio, but he made no other effort to find his paintings.

Quick, the executor of Henry's estate has hired Sotheby's to auction Henry's "valuable collection of 132 paintings and mixed-media works by the important German post-modernist Horst Sprockets."

Please identify who owns what in connection with Henry's estate.

ANSWER TO QUESTION 1

The following interests are created at Henry's death:

1) Virginia has a present possessory life estate in Blackacre.

2) Virginia's "surviving husband," a person as yet unknown, has a contingent remainder in a life estate in Blackacre.

3) The class of "Virginia's children" has a contingent remainder in a life estate in Blackacre. The class of "Virginia's children" is not yet closed and so we do not yet know the identity of every *possible member* of this class. Also, ultimate possession of Blackacre is dependent upon satisfaction of a condition precedent — surviving Virginia's widower, if any. Paula, Roger, and William are tenants in common with respect to this contingent remainder.

4) The Audubon Society has a vested remainder in a fee simple subject to an executory limitation in Blackacre. The interest is defeasible in favor of Jeeves, another transferee, so it is subject to an executory limitation. The nature of the executory limitation is determinable, producing automatic forfeiture of the Audubon Society's interest should the limitation occur.

5) Jeeves has an executory interest in fee tail in Blackacre, if the jurisdiction permits creation of a fee tail. If so, the Czar of Russia, an unknown person, has a contingent remainder. If the jurisdiction converts purported fees tail into fees simple absolute, the Czar of Russia has nothing. And if the jurisdiction converts this into a fee simple subject to an executory limitation in favor of the Czar of Russia, the Czar has an interest that will vest under the statute if Jeeves dies without surviving issue, but otherwise will lapse.

6) Depending on the jurisdiction's treatment of purported fees tail, as outlined above, the Czar of Russia, a non-existent person, either has nothing, a contingent remainder in fee tail, or an executory interest in fee simple absolute in Blackacre. The most likely answer, in order of decreasing probability, is either nothing or an executory interest.

7) Quick has a legal fee simple absolute in the residue of Henry's estate, subject to his fiduciary obligations to manage those assets for the benefit of the beneficiaries of the trust created by Henry's will.

8) Mortimer has nothing because he has predeceased Henry (he isn't listed as a survivor of Henry). If he had been alive he would have had an equitable (or beneficial) possessory life estate in the residue of Henry's estate.

9) The class of Mortimer's children is closed around one person — Louis. Louis owns an equitable (or beneficial) possessory life estate in the residue of Henry's estate.

10) The *class* of Virginia's children (not yet definitively known) who reach the summit of Everest (a condition precedent to vesting) has a contingent remainder in fee simple absolute in the residue of Henry's estate. One member of that class, Roger, has a vested remainder subject to open (or partial divestment) since his siblings might reach the summit of Everest.

Neither a reversion nor possibility of reverter is created by the *will*.

The effect of the rule against perpetuities on the interests created by the will is as follows.

1) Virginia's possessory estate is, of course, vested.

2) The uncertainty as to the identity of Virginia's surviving husband will be removed upon Virginia's death, as she will either have a surviving husband or not. Virginia is a life in being at Henry's death, so she serves as the validating life for this contingent remainder. It is good under the rule.

3) The contingent remainder in Virginia's children who survive her widower is void. The class of Virginia's children cannot serve as a validating life because it is open at Henry's death, and there exists the possibility that Virginia could have another child after Henry's death. That possibility destroys the utility of this class as a validating life, since it leaves uncertain whether or not all members of the class are lives in being. The person who turns out to be Virginia's widower cannot serve as the validating life since Lester may die first and, 20 years later, Virginia may marry an 18 year old who would end up answering the description of Virginia's surviving husband. There is no other validating life that can be used to prove timely vesting. This interest could be saved if we interpret the reference in Henry's will to "her husband" to mean Lester, since then Lester, a life in being, could serve as the validating life for the contingent remainder in Virginia's children. Henry may have meant "Lester" when he said "her husband," but Henry is obviously eccentric and so it may be inappropriate to assume he meant to do what a rational person would. But if he is rational enough to have the capacity to make a will, perhaps we ought to assume that the reference to her husband is a reference to the only husband of Virginia that Henry knew.

4) The vested remainder in the Audubon Society is valid since it is vested at creation.

5) The executory interest in Jeeves is good since the divesting condition that would shift the interest from the Audubon Society to Jeeves must occur, if at all, during Louis's life, and Louis is a life in being at Henry's death.

6) The contingent remainder or executory interest in the Czar of Russia is void. We have no idea when, if ever, a person will come into existence answering the description of the Czar of Russia. If the Czar holds an executory interest, while the divesting condition — Jeeves's death without surviving issue — will either occur or never occur at the moment of Jeeves's death, and Jeeves is a life in being, the existence and identity of the Czar of Russia will not necessarily occur then and may never occur. Depending on the jurisdiction's treatment of purported fees tail, the destruction of this interest leaves fee simple absolution Jeeves's or a possibility of reverter in Henry, which passes by intestate succession to Virginia and Louis, as tenants in common. Mortimer, Henry's son, has predeceased him so Louis takes his father's share by right of representation. The possibility of reverter does not pass under the residuary clause because the will disposes of the property that Henry owns at his death. Henry owned fee simple absolute in Blackacre at his death. His will disposed of the entire fee simple absolute, but the Rule Against Perpetuities operates *after his death* to destroy the final executory interest in the Czar. Thus the possibility of reverter that results from this destruction is created *after Henry's death* and so cannot be a part of Henry's estate. If the jurisdiction con-

verts purported fees tail into fees simple absolute, Jeeves has an executory interest in fee simple absolute, the Czar has nothing, and so no possibility of reverter would ever be created.

7) Quick's interest as trustee is possessory and so valid.

8) Mortimer's interest has lapsed because he predeceased Henry and so is irrelevant.

9) Louis's equitable life estate is possessory and so valid.

10) The contingent remainder in the class of Virginia's children who summit Everest is void. Although Roger has a vested remainder subject to open, the class gift must be good as to all possible members of the class in order to be good as to any. The uncertainty as to the identity of Virginia's children will be removed upon Virginia's death, but the uncertainty as to which of Virginia's children will reach the summit of Everest will persist until all of Virginia's children have died. Unfortunately, the class of Virginia's children is not closed at Henry's death. Virginia may have another child (call him Hercules), then Virginia, Paula, Roger, William, Lester, Louis, Jeeves and Quick all die. Twenty one years and a day later Hercules reaches the summit of Everest, only to moan in despair, "Too late, too late by a day." This unlikely possibility renders the entire class gift invalid. This is a poor rule and the judges or the legislature ought to change it. But even without alteration of the law it is possible to save this interest by construing the reference to "such of Virginia's children who reach the summit of Mount Everest" to refer to Roger. This feat is relatively unique. If Roger had scaled Everest before Henry wrote the will it is even more likely he meant to identify Roger and only Roger, thus making this remainder indefeasibly vested in Roger. But there is evidence against this interpretation. Henry said "*such of* Virginia's children" — if he meant to refer to the only one who had scaled Everest he would have said "to Virginia's child who has ascended Everest" (maybe he couldn't remember Roger's name) or, better yet, "Roger." Henry didn't do these things, so perhaps he did intend to leave the gift open for Paula or William (or even the fanciful Hercules) to share in the loot by climbing Everest. Moreover, the odds are against Henry knowing of Roger's feat when he wrote the will, since (1) Henry wrote it when Mortimer was still alive (he bequeathed a life estate to Mortimer), (2) Mortimer died an unknown time prior to Henry, and (3) Roger has "recently successfully ascended Everest."

The ownership of the Sprockets Collection is subject to dispute. The paintings were created by Sprockets and thus, whether by Locke's labor theory or the principle of first possession or recognized rights of a creator to his creation, they are Sprockets's paintings when created. But Sprockets may have abandoned them by flinging them out of the window in the dead of night. His midnight actions suggest that he voluntarily relinquished any claim of ownership to the paintings, but his regular actions of the following morning suggest the contrary. Perhaps he abandoned them for the period from midnight until the early morning, when he changed his mind and took possession of them once again as a finder.

If abandonment occurred when Sprockets hurled them out of the window, Henry became their owner by finding them and taking possession. Their ownership passes under the residuary clause of Henry's will into the trust. The state has no viable claim as the owner of the locus in quo because the paintings are surely neither mislaid nor lost, they are not imbedded in the soil, they do not constitute "treasure trove," and there is no employee or other servant-type relationship between the state and Sprockets. If abandonment did not occur Sprockets remains the true owner. However, Henry has possessed the paintings for "many years." A typical New Jersey-style jurisdiction has a six years limitations statute for recovery of personal property, commencing when Sprockets either knew or should have known by exercising due diligence, who had his paintings. Perhaps Sprockets was so exhausted by his midnight outbursts he never observed Henry gathering up the paintings in the night. But he certainly knew that his paintings were disappearing from the street. Is it reasonable for a painter who wanted to recover his paintings not to inquire of his neighbors or to make other inquiries as to their whereabouts? Surely not. Henry's residuary estate is the owner of those paintings that Henry has possessed for longer than six years. Sotheby's can auction away and deliver clear title to the purchasers. Sprockets may sit in the audience and get progressively more depressed as the hammer falls on millions of dollars that flow, not to him, but primarily to benefit the apparently dissolute Louis.

On the other hand, if the jurisdiction applies traditional adverse possession principles, the limitations period may not have run against Sprockets (assuming, again, no abandonment). Nor may the elements of adverse possession be present. While Henry had actual possession, it is not likely that his possession was open and notorious. The difficulty of over proving open and notorious possession of chattels argue against the use of the traditional real property-based adverse possession principles and use of the New Jersey approach of focusing upon the true owner's efforts to learn the facts that would enable the true owner to recover the property.

QUESTION 2

In 1972 Aura purchased a 200 acre tract, Nirvana, in a remote rural area in the hopes of living with minimal impact upon the Earth. She immediately moved into a tipi on the western edge of her acreage, built a house by hand of materials indigenous to the site, but soon learned that her wood-burning fireplace was inadequate to keep the house warm. Aura found a geothermal spring on the eastern edge of her property and constructed a buried pipeline to carry scalding hot water to her house, where it circulated in radiators, heating her home to a comfortable temperature. Aura's access to her homesite was by way of a visible footpath she had worn down, running from her home across the adjacent Turner-Fonda Ranch to a public highway. From there she hitchhiked. Aura used the footpath at least twice each week, ignoring the ranch's "No Trespassing" signs.

In 1990, desiring to create a community of like-minded low impact travelers upon Earth, Aura divided Nirvana into three parcels. Lots 1 and 3 divided Nirvana in half on a north-south axis, extending about two-thirds of Nirvana's depth. The only public road runs along the southern edge of Lots 1 and 3. Lot 2, the back third of Nirvana is bounded by Lots 1 and 2, the Turner-Fonda Ranch, the Ponderosa Ranch, and United States Forest Service land. In 1991 Aura conveyed Lot 3 by a deed that stated: "to Kayak and Rolf, a married couple, and their heirs, as co-tenants with right of survivorship, if Lot 3 is used only in a 'minimal impact' manner, and Aura, Kayak and Rolf agree, on behalf of themselves, their heirs, successors, and assigns, that 'minimal impact' means that motor vehicles will never be permitted on Nirvana, nor will any meat or tobacco ever be consumed on Nirvana." In 1992 Aura conveyed Lot 2 "to Rainbow and his heirs, subject to existing encumbrances." The following year Rainbow conveyed Lot 2 to Willow and Aspen, sorority sisters, as "tenants by the entirety." Rainbow told Willow and Aspen that he was selling out because he was "tired of living next door to a crazy eco-freak who wanted to run his life and control use of his property."

Problems emerged almost immediately. Willow and Aspen brought in building materials by a four-wheel drive "sport-utility vehicle" over the footpath formerly used solely by Aura and a few ranch hands. Willow constantly smoked large black Cuban cigars and was fond of grilling steaks outside. The mixture of cigar smoke and aroma of burning flesh wafted onto Aura's lot and produced nausea and headaches in Aura. In 1997 matters came to a head. In January Kayak and Rolf diverted all the flow from the geothermal spring to their hot tub. In February Rolf died in the hot tub. In March Aspen moved out, telling Willow she could no longer stand the constant cigar smoke. Willow replied, "Come back anytime, but I can't give up my stogies." In April the Turner-Fonda Ranch erected a large fence, blocking the footpath. Willow immediately demanded that Aura permit her to drive her Toyota Land Rover over Lot 1 to reach the road. Aura refused. Willow then purchased Rolf's interest in Lot 3 from Rolf's estate, by quit claim deed, and created a road over Lot 3, which she used for her Land Rover.

The jurisdiction in which Nirvana is located has a ten year statute of limitations for actions to recover possession of real property.

Please analyze the rights and obligations of the parties involved.

ANSWER TO QUESTION 2

The various servitudes and other interests in land created by these events are as follows.

1. *Prescriptive easement:* Aura must have acquired fee simple absolute in Nirvana in 1972, since there is no indication to the contrary. She started to use the footpath immediately after moving onto Nirvana, apparently without permission (since she ignored the "No Trespassing" signs). Her usage has likely ripened into a prescriptive easement. Her use was actual, open and notorious (she wore down a "visible" footpath), continuous ("at least twice a week" with no indication of any interruption). Was it exclusive? If the jurisdiction applies the sensible rule that "exclusivity" means only that the general public is excluded this element is met, since at least until the arrival of Willow and Aspen in 1993 Aura "and a few ranch hands" were the sole users. But if the Texas rule (see *Othen v. Rosier*) applies, Aura's use may not be exclusive since she was not the sole user. In any case, usage by "a few ranch hands" and the implied toleration by those hands of Aura's use does not constitute permission from the owner of the Turner-Fonda Ranch for Aura's use. Under the objective test of "hostility" Aura's use is exactly what a "true owner" of an easement for foot travel would do. If the jurisdiction applies the aggressive trespass standard her use would also be "hostile" since she ignored the "No Trespassing" signs. Only if the jurisdiction applies the "good faith" standard would Aura lack "hostility." The majority rule is said to be the objective test, though some academics claim that good faith is the *sub rosa* majority rule. The better rule is the objective test because it avoids subjective state-of-mind inquiry. The prescriptive period is almost certainly the same as the limitations period applicable to claims for recovery of possession — 10 years — so Aura's use ripened into a prescriptive easement in 1982. The easement is appurtenant since Aura's use was entirely in connection with her ownership of Nirvana. The servient estate is the Turner-Fonda Ranch and the dominant estate was Nirvana.

   a. *Scope of the easement:* Does the benefit of the prescriptive easement attach to Lots 2 and 3, once Aura has divided Nirvana? Normally, the scope of an easement depends on what the parties intended, but this rule is of no help when the easement is by prescription. The scope of the easement ought to depend on whether the division of Nirvana imposes a substantially increased burden on the ranch. The additional use of four more people as pedestrians is modest, although it does represent a four-fold increase in quantity. But the use made by Willow and Aspen — vehicle access — is much more burdensome and destructive. This use may be enjoined by the Turner-Fonda Ranch as beyond the scope of the prescriptive easement. But the Turner-Fonda Ranch is not entitled to block the footpath entirely, preventing Aura, Kayak, or even Willow from using the path as a footpath.

2. *Title to Lot 3:* There are two issues concerning the initial title to Lot 3.

   a. *Joint Tenants or Tenants in Common:* The usual presumption is that title is as tenants in common, but the deed explicitly recites a "right of survivorship." Moreover, Kayak and Rolf are a married couple, which may indicate some intention to create joint tenancy. Joint tenancy is most common among married couples, as a cheap and easy method to avoid probate. Without knowing more this issue can be reasonably resolved either way, though the married status of Kayak and Rolf argues slightly in favor of rebutting the tenancy in common presumption and finding a joint tenancy.

    b. *Fee Simple Determinable or Servitude:* The deed conveys Lot 3 "if" it is used only in a "minimal impact manner," defined negatively to exclude motor vehicles, meat or tobacco use. The word "if" might suggest a limitation on the duration of the grant, and hence fee simple determinable, but it also suggests that the grant is conditional upon the grantees' promise to abide by the use restrictions, and hence a use covenant is created. Since forfeitures are generally to be avoided in cases of ambiguity, it is better to conclude that a covenant, rather than a determinable limitation, was created.

    3. *Easement reserved by implication from prior use:* When Aura started piping scalding hot water from the spring to her house she created a "quasi-easement." When she sold Lot 3 did she impliedly reserve an easement in her favor for the piped water? It was in use at the time, but was it apparent or reasonably necessary? The pipeline was buried and, unlike the buried sewer in *Van Zandt,* there are no surface indications on Lot 3 of the existence of the pipeline. This is not very apparent. Is the easement necessary? If the jurisdiction adheres to strict necessity it may not be — however imperfect her wood-burning fireplace, it provides some heat; Aura can install a more efficient wood stove, or maybe she can use more technologically advanced methods of heating. These arguments are useful, but of lesser force, even if the jurisdiction adheres to reasonable necessity. Aura probably does not have an implied easement for the pipeline. This easement has not ripened into one by prescription because only six years have elapsed from the sale and, in any case, Aura's use is not open and notorious. Cf. *Marengo Cave.*

    4. *Reciprocal Covenant?* The conveyance from Aura to Kayak and Rolf raises the issue of whether a reciprocal covenant was created, either impliedly or by express agreement.

    a. *Implied from common scheme:* Aura intends to create a "minimal impact" community on Nirvana, and the initial deed reflects a version of that vision. Is a single deed enough to create a common scheme? In a development of three rural lots of roughly 67 acres each, one of which is to be retained by the developer, the single deed represents half the development. This is probably enough, when taken together with Aura's intentions and her joinder with Kayak and Rolf in promising to keep Nirvana "minimal impact." But the jurisdiction may not recognize the creation of implied reciprocal covenants, since this doctrine certainly carries the disadvantage of being difficult for a later purchaser to detect its existence.

    b. *By express agreement:* Aura has agreed with Kayak and Rolf to confine Nirvana to "minimal impact" uses. This agreement is made at a time when Aura owns Lot 1 and 2, so it is clear that she intended to burden both Lots 1 and 2 with this use servitude and did so via the agreement.

    5. *Rainbow's Title to Lot 2:* Rainbow acquires fee simple absolute "subject to existing servitudes." This is probably adequate notice to him of the existence of the "minimal impact" covenant. At the very least it puts him on inquiry notice — a few questions to Aura and the whole scheme will be revealed, if Aura has not already done so, which is more likely the case. So

Rainbow takes with notice. Moreover, in jurisdictions following the *Guillette* rule Rainbow would have constructive notice of the Aura to Kayak and Rolf deed; in those rejecting this rule he would not have constructive notice from the record.

6. *Willow's and Aspen's title to Lot 2:*

a. *Form of co-ownership:* Although the deed recites that Willow and Aspen take title as tenants by the entirety, they are not married and so their title is presumed to be as tenants in common. The evidence in favor of joint tenancy is meager — practically the only evidence is the fact that tenancy by the entirety contains a right of survivorship. But given the fact that Willow and Aspen could never be tenants by the entirety, it is hard to conclude that they intended to create a joint tenancy unless, perhaps, there is evidence (not before us) that Willow and Aspen are a lesbian couple desiring to replicate marital property rights to the extent that they are able to do so under common law. In that case, joint tenancy ought to be preferred simply because it is reasonably clear that they intended to create a survivorship right.

b. *Does the covenant run with the estate?* Assuming that the minimal impact covenant was created by express agreement or by implication from a common scheme, will it run at law or in equity?

i. *Law:* The original parties surely intended for the burden to run — the agreement purported to bind successors and the common scheme was surely designed for the same purpose. Horizontal privity is not present if the jurisdiction adheres to the restrictive Massachusetts rule of mutual interests, but this is the minority rule, so the jurisdiction probably recognizes horizontal privity when the relationship between the original parties is that of grantor and grantee. Vertical privity is surely satisfied. Rainbow acquired fee simple absolute from Aura and conveyed the same estate to Willow and Aspen. Willow and Aspen probably have notice — Rainbow's deed is explicitly subject to existing servitudes and Rainbow informs Willow and Aspen that Aura is asserting some control over use of his land, which ought to be enough to trigger a duty to inquire. The most uncertain issue is whether the use covenant "touches and concern" the land. The ban on motor vehicles probably does — the presence or absence of motor vehicles affects the relations of the Nirvana residents as landowners, has an effect on land values, although that effect is probably subjective. To most people, the vehicle covenant depresses the value of both parcels. Whether or not the vehicle covenant touches and concerns, the meat and tobacco covenant is much more problematic. These activities are legal, and they have little impact on land values or on the relations of landowners as landowners. Nor are they the type of promise that landowners might create to control externalities of land use. They probably do not touch and concern the land and thus do not run with the estate acquired by Willow and Aspen.

ii. *Equity:* Intent is present, and perhaps notice, but the same touch and concern problems as discussed above may prevent the covenant from running as an equitable servitude, at least as to the meat and tobacco covenants.

c. *Easement implied by necessity:* When Aura conveyed to Rainbow did she create an implied grant of an easement for access by necessity? Aura was the owner of Nirvana who created the landlocked situation, but before the division

Aura had secured the footpath easement by prescriptive use, and that footpath leads directly onto Lot 2. So there is no necessity unless vehicular access is deemed necessary, and the parties have agreed not to permit vehicles (if the no vehicles covenant runs). But if the no vehicles covenant is unenforceable, then an easement for vehicle access is indeed necessary and thus implied. The benefit of that appurtenant easement passed with the estate Rainbow transferred to Willow and Aspen.

d. *Easement reserved by implication from prior use:* Aura's access to Lot 1 is by the footpath, which cuts across a corner of Lot 2. This easement, upon division, is apparent, in use, reasonably permanent, but is it necessary? It is surely not strictly necessary, if the jurisdiction adheres to that view, because she could make the longer walk down Lot 1 to the road. It may be reasonably necessary since it is the more direct route, and the one that she has maintained for 20 years or more. Since the theory behind these implied easements is to create them where there is evidence of the parties' intentions, this is a good case for finding reasonable necessity. The parties apparently intended to perpetuate the footpath since Aura, Willow and Aspen each used it after division.

The present rights and obligations of the parties are as follows.

1. *Turner-Fonda Ranch:* The Ranch is obligated to remove the obstruction of the footpath and can be compelled to do so by injunction sought by any of Aura, Willow or Aspen. The Ranch has a claim for damages against Willow and Aspen for their trespass, consisting of driving their vehicle over the footpath, if the limitations statute applicable to trespass claims permits.

2. *Aura:* Aura must permit vehicle access across Lot 1 in favor of Lot 2 if the no vehicles covenant does not "touch and concern" the land, but if it does, she may deny such access and either enjoin Willow from using her vehicle on Lot 2 or Lot 3, or recover damages. Aura may insist upon continuing footpath access across Lot 2 should Willow or Aspen contest that right. Aura may have a claim for nuisance against Willow stemming from the cigar and meat odors but she is probably unduly sensitive to them and so no nuisance likely exists. On the merits of the nuisance claim the social utility of meat and tobacco usage, while probably not high, is probably not outweighed by the gravity of the harm inflicted. Aura probably has no recourse against Kayak and Rolf's estate for their diversion of the hot water, since it is unlikely that an implied easement from prior use was created.

3. *Aspen:* Aspen is jointly liable with Willow for the trespass upon the Ranch. Aspen may have a claim against Willow for half the fair rental value of Lot 2 if (1) she has been ousted by Willow, or (2) the jurisdiction does not require ouster to trigger such liability. Willow has not denied Aspen permission to enter Lot 2; indeed she invites her to come. The problem, of course, is the cigar smoke. Is cigar usage so obnoxious and offensive as to constitute ouster? Maybe in a small apartment, but probably not in the context of 60+ acre parcel. The jurisdiction may adhere to the minority rule that no ouster is needed, since that rule has much to be said for it — encourages negotiation between parties, avoids litigation over ouster, but does inhibit productive use by one co-owner without consent of the others.

4. *Willow:* Willow is jointly liable with Aspen for the trespass upon the Ranch. Willow is probably not liable for nuisance. Willow's rights and obligations with respect to her creation of a road across Lot 3 depends upon whether she owns any interest in Lot 3. If Kayak and Rolf owned as joint tenants (which is the preferred outcome) then Willow has purchased nothing from Rolf's estate and Willow is a trespasser liable to Kayak for damages. If K&R were tenants in common then Willow owns a 1/2 interest in Lot 3 as a tenant in common with Kayak, but Willow is still liable to Kayak for breaching the no vehicle covenant (and also to Aura) and (possibly, depending on unknown facts) for waste if the location of the road permanently impaired the land value.

5. *Kayak:* If Kayak is a tenant in common with Willow, she is liable to Aura in law and equity for breach of the no vehicles covenant, though she will be able to recover from Willow. If Kayak is the sole owner of Lot 3, she may pursue a trespass claims against Willow. Kayak probably has no liability concerning the hot water pipe.

6. *Rolf:* Rolf doesn't care any more, but his estate has no liability to Willow for breach of one or more deed covenants of title since the deed to Rolf's interest in Lot 3 (if any) was a quit claim deed, which contains no covenants of title.

QUESTION 3

Josie owns a 100 acre vegetable farm which has gradually been surrounded by an expanding city. Beset by rising property taxes, in 1985 she decided to subdivide the property into twenty 5-acre lots and offer them for sale as residential "farm and home" sites. Josie hoped to entice purchasers who would enjoy life in a mixed environment of farm and residence. But, having subdivided the property she continued to operate her farm as before. Among other things this involved the maintenance of a network of irrigation ditches which transport water from a canal at the western edge of the farm throughout the farm. The irrigation water is essential to the farming but it does produce an ideal breeding ground for mosquitoes. When Josie began to sell lots in the subdivision (in 1987) she constructed one road (for minimal disruption to the farming) and bridged all the areas where the road crosses the irrigation ditches. Josie told all purchasers that home construction was to be done in a manner that had the least impact on farming. Every lot that was sold was transferred by a deed which provided that "purchaser, for himself and his assigns, will use the property for residential and farming purposes only."

Bert purchased a lot in 1988 and promptly constructed a house on it. In doing so, he filled in the irrigation ditch which runs across his lot. The following year Bert sold his house and lot to Ernie. In 1994 the adjacent lot to the east was sold by Josie to Tim. Tim, a real estate speculator, promptly resold the lot to Aurelia. Aurelia, who wishes to grow arugula on the property, demands that Ernie re-open the irrigation ditch which would bring water to Aurelia's lot. Ernie refuses. Aurelia consults you, a lawyer, about her rights and obligations. Please advise her.

ANSWER TO QUESTION 3

Aurelia has several legal theories upon which she might rely to force Ernie to open the irrigation ditch or, alternatively, permit her to do it.

Implied Easement from Prior Use. Josie was a common owner of the two parcels. She subdivided the farm and then burdened Ernie's lot for the benefit of Aurelia's lot by transporting essential irrigation water through a ditch across Ernie's lot. An easement may be impliedly created, permitting Aurelia to use Ernie's lot for a ditch to transport irrigation water.

The transfer to Bert, Ernie's predecessor, occurred when Josie still owned what is now Aurelia's lot. The easement thus putatively created was by reservation in favor of the grantor. In those jurisdictions (like the UK) which insist on a showing of strict necessity when the implied easement from prior use is for the benefit of the grantor, Aurelia might have some trouble. Irrigation water is essential for farming but is the ditch network the only way to obtain irrigation water? Is a well feasible? What about the fact that this development is surely as much (if not more) residential than agricultural? It may be strictly necessary to farming but is it strictly necessary for a mixed use environment? Given Josie's apparent commitment to farming even in the midst of a residential environment, Aurelia might sustain her burden of proving this point. Fortunately for Aurelia, most American jurisdictions do not insist upon strict necessity. If the land is located in one of those states she need only show reasonable necessity. Surely, irrigation water from the canal is reasonably necessary to farming.

The prior use may be apparent. Even though Bert filled in the ditch, presumably Ernie could observe a network of ditches from which his lot was exempt. That might trigger an obligation on Ernie's part to inquire about the nonexistence of irrigation ditches. On the other hand, there was in fact nothing for Ernie to observe on the lot he purchased. If anything was apparent, it was the absence of any irrigation ditches.

The prior use was continuous while Josie was maintaining the quasi-easement but ceased when Bert filled in the ditch. There is some doubt whether continuity is really a separate element or simply an indicator of the apparent requirement. The reason for these elements (apparent and continuous) is to be assured that (i) the original grantor/grantee must have intended to create the easement and (ii) that the subsequent taker takes with notice of the burden. Rationale (i) is satisfied on these facts but probably not rationale (ii), unless you care to impose on Ernie the obligation to discover the existence of an easement obliterated by his predecessor in title entirely from the fact that there seems to be an irrigation ditch running up to either boundary line of the property interrupted by Ernie's lot.

One of the four common law negative easements was interference with an artificial stream. But the existence of this easement must still be established in one of the familiar ways. Like the affirmative easement it may be implied from prior use. Negative easements could not be created by prescription.

If an implied easement is established, Aurelia may still lose because the easement has been extinguished by prescription. Bert eliminated the ditch in 1988, seven years ago. We don't know the prescription period in the jurisdiction but prescriptive periods are often quite short, usually shorter than the analogous adverse possession period. Five years is fairly common. Ernie can tack his possession on to Bert's if he needs to since he was a consensual transferee. Ernie can surely establish that he actually occupied the easement, denying use of it to Josie, Tim, and Aurelia. His occupation is open and notorious, being clearly visible to the adjacent landowner. It's not clear whether Ernie is a good faith or bad faith occupier, but on the preferred theory of hostility that it doesn't matter what his state of mind was, Ernie's occupation is hostile. It is clearly continuous and exclusive. Unless the prescriptive period is longer than seven years, Aurelia has likely lost any easement created by implication from Josie's prior use.

Equitable Servitude. An equitable servitude might be enforced by Aurelia. There are two possibilities: (1) based on the express deed covenant and (2) implied from a common development scheme.

Based on an Expressly Created Covenant. The express servitude created, limiting use to residential and farming purposes, does not address the specific problem. Ernie's use is not necessarily inconsistent with the covenant. Perhaps Aurelia can contend that the promise to restrict use to residential *and* farming implies the continued maintenance of the ditches, since even Bert or Ernie would be unable to farm without irrigation water. By filling in the ditch Bert was using his property for residential use only, not residential *and* farming use. This construction of the covenant is consistent with Josie's intent and, if applied, would avoid the notice problems. But one can live *and* farm on five acres without irrigation. If the scope of the covenant is broad enough to encompass an obligation to keep the ditch open, it is clear that the covenant was intended to run ("for assigns") and that it touches and concerns land. Assuming the deed was recorded, Ernie had constructive notice. But, even if Aurelia would prevail on this theory she might likely lose her request for an injunction mandating Ernie to open the ditch because of laches — the equitable analogue to the statute of limitations.

Based on an Implied Covenant from a Common Development Scheme. If the express covenant is simply not broad enough to cover the problem Aurelia faces, she needs to establish the existence of another servitude, one requiring each lot owner to permit the unimpeded flow of irrigation water through the preexisting ditches. There is no such covenant expressly created; can one be implied? Josie, the common owner, certainly manifested an intention to keep the entire subdivision devoted to both farming and residential occupation. Although the covenant does not say it, Josie told each purchaser that residential construction was to be done with the least impact on farming. That indicates an intention to create a use restriction that would assure the continued flow of irrigation water, essential to farming. But the problem here is that this intention is never expressed in a covenant. The intention to burden the lots with this restriction is entirely implied from Josie's oral comments to prospective purchasers. This may well be insufficient to overcome Statute of Frauds problems; moreover, even if the Statute of Frauds is not an obstacle, there is a real problem with notice. Ernie has constructive notice of the covenant in the deed but surely has no actual or constructive notice of Josie's oral admonitions. The only notice that can be inferred is inquiry notice, based on the fact that the other lots all seem to have irrigation ditches crossing them. But even in *Sanborn,* a case relying on inquiry notice, the content of the implied covenant was clear, unlike this case, since the restriction at issue had been recorded with respect to other lots in the scheme. There seems little doubt that the implied promise to keep the ditches flowing is one that touches and concerns the land, either under the *Neponsit* formulation (altering the relative rights and obligations as landowners) or the more modern tests of what covenants are reasonably connected to land usage and of the sort that subsequent landowners might be expected to impose in order to address external costs of land use. The most difficult issue is whether to extend *Sanborn* and imply the existence of a covenant from Josie's sales pitch. That seems to abandon all pretense that subsequent landowners can have any certainty of knowing what restrictions burden their land.

Real Covenant. Aurelia probably does not want money damages but, if she does, she can recover them only if the elements of a running real covenant are present and she can establish that the broad construction of the express covenant is appropriate. If she were to fail in that effort, all is lost on this front. Horizontal privity, to the extent required, is present. The covenant was contained in a deed from Josie, grantor, to Bert, grantee. Ernie apparently succeeded to the identical durational interest that Bert had (probably both are fees simple absolute), thus establishing vertical privity on the burden side. Aurelia has probably also succeeded to the identical interest of Tim, though she need only acquire some interest. So long as Aurelia is successful in her broad interpretation of the covenant, it would appear that the covenant runs with the estates. But, as with the express equitable servitude, she may encounter a roadblock in the form of the statute of limitations or laches.

Nuisance and Termination. Aurelia may have to defend against Ernie's claim that the irrigation ditches constitute a nuisance by reason of the mosquitoes that result. Aurelia's best response to the nuisance claim is to contend that Ernie came to the nuisance and that he voluntarily accepted the nuisance by virtue of his purchasing a property restricted to residential *and* farming use, for which irrigation water is essential. Aurelia could also assert that the social utility of continued irrigation water in a mixed-use development is greater than mosquito abatement. Resolution of that may depend on the health hazards posed by the mosquitoes. If they are malaria carriers, nuisance may be established. If they are just the normal blood-sucking pests, nuisance is probably not present, given the apparent necessity of irrigation water for farming.

Similarly, Ernie may contend that, if the covenant is construed to require keeping the ditches open, the covenant should be terminated by virtue of changed circumstances. The city has grown up around the development and the presence of a mosquito breeding ground, even if not malarial monsters, is sufficiently inimical to residential inhabitation that it should be eliminated. But there is no change within the development that is inimical to irrigation and the value of the covenant is not entirely destroyed by the surrounding changes.

QUESTION 4

On January 1, 1985, Helen leased Blackacre to Albert for a term of years, expiring December 31, 1994, under a written lease signed by both of them. In the lease Albert agreed to pay rent of $36,000 each year, payable in monthly installments of $3,000, and to pay any amount by which the real property taxes exceed $5,000 in any year. Helen promised to keep Blackacre in good repair. Blackacre consisted of a single warehouse, in which were located some offices. Blackacre is located in an area that is zoned by the City "for commercial or industrial use only."

In 1986 Albert assigned his interest in the Blackacre lease to Althea, who promptly converted the warehouse into two "artist loft spaces," which she advertised as "suitable for an artist's studio and residence." Althea then entered into identical subleases for the lofts with Mike and Vaughan. Each sublease expired December 31, 1994, obligated the tenant to pay rent of $2,000 per month, and incorporated by reference "all terms of the lease between Albert and Helen, dated January 1, 1985, which are not inconsistent with this sublease." Mike and Vaughan moved all of their possessions into their respective units.

In 1987 Helen conveyed and assigned her interest in Blackacre to Melvin. In 1988, both Mike and Vaughan complained to Althea of leaky plumbing, lack of heat, broken windows, and inoperable electrical wiring in the lofts. On Sept. 1, 1988, both Mike and Vaughan vacated their lofts, leaving a note for Althea that they were "terminating the lease because of the atrocious living conditions." Althea advertised for new tenants and engaged the services of a rental broker but had no success. On January 1, 1989, Althea notified Melvin that she was vacating Blackacre and treating the lease as terminated. The 1989 property taxes for Blackacre are $10,000. Melvin has paid $5,000 of those taxes; the remainder is due and unpaid.

Discuss the rights and obligations of the parties.

ANSWER TO QUESTION 4

There are three major issues presented: (1) Is Althea liable to Melvin for unpaid rent or taxes? (2) Are Mike and Vaughan liable to Melvin for unpaid rent or taxes? (3) Are Mike and Vaughan liable to Althea for unpaid rent or taxes?

1. *Althea's liability to Melvin.* Althea's liability depends on whether she is in either privity of contract or privity of estate with Melvin.

Privity of Contract. Privity between Althea and Melvin hinges on whether Albert assigned his interest to Althea and she assumed the lease. (An assignment from Helen to Melvin, also needed, is stipulated in the facts.) Althea did not expressly assume the lease, and although an assumption might be inferred from Althea's conduct, the prevailing view is that an assumption will not be found unless it is made expressly.

Privity of Estate. Privity of estate between Althea and Melvin hinges on whether Althea has subleased or assigned her interest to Mike and Vaughan. (Helen has assigned her interest to Melvin, which transfers to Melvin the estate formerly held by Helen.) If Althea subleased to Mike and Vaughan, her privity of estate with Melvin (standing in Helen's shoes) continues and Althea is liable for rent. If Althea assigned her lease to Mike and Vaughan, then privity of estate is destroyed and Althea has no liability on this theory for any unpaid rent after the date of the assignments.

The argument for assignment is that though the transactions with Mike and Vaughan are denominated subleases they expire at the moment of expiration of the master lease. Since Althea lacks any reversionary interest, the transactions are functionally assignments.

The argument for a sublease is that even though Althea failed to retain any reversion in the subleases, the difference in rent and use of the term "sublease" is an indication that Althea intended to keep a reversionary interest necessary to earn the sublease profits. It is in Althea's economic interest to owe Melvin $3,000 per month in rent and collect $4,000 per month in rent from Mike and Vaughan. Nonetheless, many courts (perhaps most) will treat Althea's failure to retain a reversion, coupled with the entry into possession of Mike and Vaughan, as an assignment that places Mike and Vaughan in privity of estate with Melvin and extinguishing the intervening purported leasehold through merger.

Assuming that Althea subleased, and thus is in privity of estate with Melvin, she has either abandoned the lease or has been constructively evicted. Althea has been constructively evicted if Melvin's failure to discharge his duty of repair so deprived Althea of the enjoyment of the property that the leased premises were rendered unsuitable for the purposes for which they were intended. But the intended purposes of the premises were not residential (indeed, that use is illegal). Nevertheless, the problems (no electricity, no heat, broken windows, inoperable plumbing) would appear to make the premises unsuitable for most commercial purposes. If so, the lease is terminated and Althea has no further liability. If there is no constructive eviction, Althea has abandoned and Melvin may either accept her offer of surrender of the lease (thus terminating the lease) or may leave the premises vacant and continue to hold Althea liable for the rent. Since the lease to Althea is commercial, Melvin does not have to seek out new tenants on behalf of Althea.

Althea's defenses. If Althea is in privity of estate with Melvin and she has not been constructively evicted, she may assert as a defense to her liability for rent or taxes that Melvin has breached the covenant of repair. The covenant runs with the estate and Melvin acquired Helen's entire estate. There are several subsidiary issues. Are the covenants to repair and to pay rent mutually dependent? Courts are more apt to view residential leases through the contract lens, and thus regard lease covenants as mutually dependent, but this lease is commercial. Courts are less willing to do so with respect to commercial leases, and unless the lease specifically makes the covenants dependent Althea may not be able to suspend rent payments to Melvin. But Althea will be entitled to recover damages from Melvin's breach of the duty to repair. These damages are limited to the cost of repair, rather than the lost profits to Althea that might be a consequence of Melvin's failure to repair.

Althea has no ability to assert breach of the implied warranty of habitability since she is a commercial user. If anyone can assert this claim, it's Mike and Vaughan.

Althea's liability on the tax covenant. As with the rent covenant, Althea's liability for taxes depends on whether there is either privity of contract or estate with Melvin. Assuming privity of estate, the only additional issue is whether the covenant to pay taxes runs with the estate. Does its substance touch and concern the estate burdened? Property taxes are a burden of land ownership; while the covenant is an affirmative obligation to pay money, the payment is inextricably linked to the land itself. Even though the promise is for the benefit of the landowner it is one that shares the burdens of land occupation and so touches and concerns the burdened leasehold. Althea has the same defenses to this covenant as to the covenant to pay rent.

2. *Mike's and Vaughan's liability to Melvin.* Mike and Vaughan are liable to Melvin only if either privity of contract or privity of estate are present between them. Mike and Vaughan are in privity of contract with Melvin only if the "sublease" with Althea was really an assignment (which it probably is, given Althea's failure to reserve a reversion) and they assumed the master lease. Their "subleases" did obligate them to perform all of the covenants of the master lease and that may be enough to constitute assumption, on the theory that Melvin was the intended third party beneficiary of that promise.

It won't matter too much whether privity of contract is present because privity of estate almost surely is present. The purported subleases are very likely to be seen as assignments, thus creating privity of estate between Mike and Vaughan and Melvin. If the agreements are truly subleases, there is no privity of estate with Melvin because there was no promise to pay the rents directly to Melvin.

Assuming that Mike and Vaughan are in privity of estate with Melvin, the issue arises whether they have abandoned or been constructively evicted. Melvin's failure to repair is the cause of their problems and the substance of the problems are sufficiently severe that it seems likely that Mike and Vaughan have lost all beneficial use of the property for the purposes they intended to devote the leasehold toward. Of course, those purposes are partly residential and so illegal, but even the commercial use as an artist studio would seem to be virtually impossible to achieve. They have probably been constructively evicted and so the lease has terminated. If not, they have abandoned and Melvin has the same options as described with Althea.

Mike and Vaughan have the same defenses that Althea has to liability for either the rent or tax covenants. But, in addition, it may be that once the residential use was established Melvin acquiesced to the residential use and is in breach of the warranty of habitability. If so, by leaving, Mike and Vaughan have elected to terminate the lease and may also be able to recover their relocation costs.

3. *Mike's and Vaughan's liability to Althea.* Liability on the part of Mike and Vaughan to Althea depends on whether the "subleases" are really subleases or whether they are assignments. If the subleases are assignments the purported subleases have been extinguished by merger. Mike and Vaughan then have no liability to Althea for anything, but are liable to Melvin in accordance with the master lease. If the "subleases" really are subleases, then Mike and Vaughan are in privity of contract and privity of estate with Althea, but only as to the terms of the subleases. As discussed above, the purported subleases are most likely assignments and so Mike and Vaughan probably are not liable to Althea.

Assuming that Mike and Vaughan are in privity of contract and estate with Althea on the subleases, Mike and Vaughan have either been constructively evicted or abandoned. Constructive eviction is pretty clear here, since Althea rented the spaces for residential habitation, the landlord's duty to repair was incorporated by reference in the subleases, and Althea's failure to keep the premises in good repair deprived Mike and Vaughan of virtually all utility to the premises. Moreover, the warranty of habitability is surely implied into these subleases, since the purpose of Mike's and Vaughan's occupation was partly residential. Even though the residential occupation is illegal the policy underlying the implied warranty of habitability is to provide minimum residential living standards, and this policy seems applicable to any living arrangements. Mike and Vaughan have terminated the lease but still may recover their relocation costs from Althea.

In the unlikely event that Mike and Vaughan have not been constructively evicted and have abandoned, it appears that Althea has discharged her duty to mitigate damages by seeking to relet the premises.

QUESTION 5

In January 1990, Albert, the true owner and actual possessor of Blackacre, conveyed Blackacre by quit claim deed to Muriel in receipt of $10,000. In July of 1990 Albert conveyed Blackacre by special warranty deed to Vernon, who paid $10,000 to Albert and knew nothing about the prior deed to Muriel. In August 1990, Muriel took possession of Blackacre, recorded her deed and conveyed Blackacre by general warranty deed to Jane, who paid Muriel $15,000. In September 1990, Vernon recorded his deed. In October 1990, after learning of Vernon's recordation, Jane recorded her deed and took possession of Blackacre, which is located in a jurisdiction which has enacted the following statute: "Every conveyance of real property is void as against any subsequent purchaser of the same property, or any part thereof, in good faith and for a valuable consideration, whose conveyance is first duly recorded."

ANSWER TO QUESTION 5

Jane prevails over Vernon because Jane purchased from Muriel, who recorded before Vernon, and Jane obtains the shelter of Muriel's recordation before Vernon. At the time Jane purchased from Muriel, Muriel had recorded her deed from Albert, which was prior to the time that Vernon, a subsequent purchaser without notice, recorded. Thus, even though Vernon records before Jane it does not matter; Jane stands in the position of Muriel, whose claim is superior to that of Vernon. Since Jane is asserting Muriel's title, Jane's notice is irrelevant. This is an application of the "shelter rule," which is rooted in the idea that for Muriel to have the full benefit of her prior recordation she must be able to convey that benefit for value. For that to occur, her purchaser (Jane) must receive what Muriel had.

Vernon may recover $10,000 from Albert for breach of the deed covenants. By special warranty deed Albert has promised Vernon that he, Albert, has taken no action contrary to the six deed covenants contained in the deed. But Albert has breached three covenants: (1) seisin, because at the time Albert conveyed to Vernon he no longer owned Blackacre; (2) right to convey, because having parted with title to Blackacre Albert no longer had a right to convey it; and (3) general warranty, because Jane (through Muriel) has a paramount title. Quiet enjoyment isn't breached because Vernon never had possession; future assurances isn't breached because there is nothing further Albert could have done to perfect title in Vernon; encumbrances isn't breached because the property is not encumbered — it's a relative title problem.

QUESTION 6

Brownacre is located in a state which has enacted the following statute: "Every conveyance or mortgage of real property is void as against any subsequent purchaser or mortgagee of the same property in good faith and for a valuable consideration, whose conveyance or mortgage is first duly recorded." Harold, the owner of Brownacre, borrows $10,000 from First Bank and gives First Bank a mortgage to Brownacre in order to secure repayment of the loan. First Bank fails to record the mortgage. Harold then borrows $14,000 from Segundo Finance, and after telling Segundo of the prior mortgage in favor of First Bank, gives Segundo a mortgage to Brownacre. Segundo Finance promptly records the mortgage. Harold then borrows $5,000 from Third-Rate Credit and gives Third-Rate a mortgage to Brownacre. Third-Rate has no notice of First Bank's mortgage and Third-Rate records its mortgage. An adjacent chemical plant begins to leak toxic polychlorinatedbiphenyls (PCBs) and the value of Brownacre plummets. Harold defaults on all the mortgages. After the foreclosure sale, there is $20,000 to distribute among First Bank, Segundo Finance and Third-Rate Credit. How much should each creditor receive and why?

ANSWER TO QUESTION 6

This is a "circular priority" problem. First Bank is prior to Segundo, since Segundo has notice of First Bank's mortgage, but is junior to Third-Rate, since Third-Rate recorded first and had no notice of First Bank's lien. Segundo is ahead of Third-Rate since Third-Rate had constructive notice but behind First Bank. And Third-Rate is ahead of First Bank but behind Segundo. Just about the only rationale that serves to cut this Gordian knot is to deliver to each party his reasonable expectations. Segundo expects to be in second position (behind First Bank's $10,000 lien), so give Segundo the $10,000 which would be left if First Bank was prior to Segundo. Third-Rate expects to be junior only to Segundo's $14,000, so give Third-Rate its full $5,000 (there is $6,000 left after deducting $14,000 from the $20,000 available). What's left goes to First Bank, since First Bank can not expect to have priority over anyone, given its failure to record. So, First Bank should get $5,000; Segundo $10,000; Third-Rate $5,000.

TABLE OF CASES

21 Merchants Row Corp. v.
    Merchants Row, Inc. 94
3 W Partners v. Bridges 242

Abbott v. Herring 207
Abbott v. Nampa School District No. 131 218
Abo Petroleum Corp. v. Amstutz 140
Abramowitz, Estate of 33
Adrian v. Rabinowitz 82
Ailes v. Decatur County
    Area Planning Commission 274
Albert M. Greenfield & Co., Inc.
    v. Kolea 99
Albright v. Fish 233
Albro v. Allen 168
Alexander v. McKnight 302
American Book Co. v.
    Yeshiva Univ. Dev. Found. 94
American Oil Co. v. Leaman 225
Amphitheaters, Inc. v.
    Portland Meadows 255
Anderson Drive-In Theatre v.
    Kirkpatrick 109
Anderson v. Gouldberg 5, 9
Angle v. Slayton 338
Anthony v. Brea Glenbrook Club 238
Arlington Heights, Village of v.
    Metropolitan Housing
    Development Corp. 281
Armory v. Delamirie 9, 36
Armstrong v. Maybee 96
Arnel Development Co. v.
    City of Costa Mesa 279
Aronson v. Board of
    Appeals of Stoneham 276
Art Neon Co. v.
    City and County of Denver 274
Associated Home Builders v.
    City of Livermore 272
Ayer v. Philadelphia &
    Boston Face Brick Co. 337
Aztec Ltd., Inc. v.
    Creekside Investment Co. 217

Bagko Development Co. v. Damitz 250
Baker v. City of Milwaukie 272
Baker v. Weedon 63
Baliles v. Cities Service Co. 295
Ballard v. Alaska Theater Co. 118
Banach v. Lawera 211
Barash v. Penn. Terminal
    Real Estate Corp. 107
Barnes v. Glen Theatre, Inc. 283

Barr v. Eason 183
Barton v. Mitchell Co. 108
Becker v. IRM Corp. 117
Beiser v. Hensic 221
Bell v. Town of Wells 214
Belle Terre, Village of v. Boraas 287
Berg v. Wiley 103
Berkeley, State ex rel. Stoyanoff v. 270
Berman v. Parker 348
Berzito v. Gambino 112
Bi-Metallic Investment Co. v.
    State Board of Equalization 282
Blackett v. Olanoff 107, 108
Board of Education of Minneapolis
    v. Hughes 336
Board of Education v. Hughes 307
Boomer v. Atlantic Cement Co. 263
Borelli v. Brusseau 188
Boucher v. Boyer 198
Bradley v. Fox 173
Brant v. Hargrove 170
Braswell v. Braswell 147
Bremmeyer Excavating, Inc.
    v. McKenna 237
Bridges v. Hawksworth 12
Broadmoor San Clemente
    Homeowners' Ass'n v. Nelson 250
Broadway Building v.
    City Investing Co. 233
Broadway National Bank v. Adams 68
Brown v. Heirs of Fuller 246
Brown v. Independent Baptist
    Church of Woburn 156
Brown v. Lober 317
Brown v. Southall Realty Co. 97, 110
Brown v. Voss 218
Brunswick-Balke Collender Co.
    v. Seattle Brewing &
    Malting Co. 98
Buffalo Academy of the
    Sacred Heart v.
    Boehm Bros., Inc. 244, 335, 338
Bushmiller v. Schiller 296
Butler v. Haley Greystone Corp. 341
Buttolph v. Erikkson 213

Cameron v. Barton 216
Camp v. Milam 203
Campbell v. Great Miami Aerie 208
Cappaert v. Junker 117
Castle Associates v. Schwartz 223
Caulfield v. Improved
    Risk Mutuals, Inc. 306
Causby, United States v. 350

Causey v. Lanigan 213
Centel Cable TV Co. of Ohio v. Cook 220
Chambers v. North River Line 96
Chandler v. Smith 238
Charles E. Burt, Inc.
    v. Seven Grand Corp. 107, 109
Charter Township of Delta
    v. Dinolfo 287
Cheney Brothers v.
    Doris Silk Corp. 6
Cheney v. Village 2 at New Hope, Inc. 290
Chesapeake Ranch Club v.
    CRC Members 238
Chicago, Burlington & Quincy Ry.
    v. Chicago 345
Choisser v. Eyman 237
Church of the Lukumi Babalu Aye
    v. City of Hialeah 285
City of — see name of city
Clark v. Maloney 9
Cleburne, City of v.
    Cleburne Living Center, Inc. 280
Coe v. Clay 82
Cohan v. Fleuroma, Inc. 215
Cohen v. Adolph Kutner Co. 225
Cohn, In re 32
Collard v. Incorporated Village
    of Flower Hill 277
Columbus-America Discovery
    Group v. Atlantic Mutual
    Insurance Co. 8
Commons v. Westwood Zoning
    Board of Adjustment 276
Commonwealth Building Corp.
    v. Hirschfield 77
Concerned Citizens of Brunswick
    County Taxpayers Ass'n v.
    Holden Beach Enterprises, Inc. 213
Conklin v. Davi 297, 298
Construction Industry Ass'n
    v. City of Petaluma 272
Cook v. Cook 193
Cooke v. Ramponi 204
Cooper v. Leverhulme 154
Cope v. Inhabitants of the
    Town of Brunswick 276
Cotting v. Boston 224
Cousins v. Alabama Power Co. 220
Crane Neck Ass'n v.
    New York City/Long Island
    County Serv. Group 250
Crechalle & Polles, Inc. v. Smith 79
Crosdale v. Lanigan 204

D'Ercole v. D'Ercole 175
Danielson v. Roberts 10, 11
David Properties, Inc. v. Selk 79
Davidow v. Inwood North
    Professional Group 111
Davidson Bros., Inc. v.
    D. Katz & Sons, Inc. 236
Davis v. Vidal 92
Day v. Clark 338
Daytona Beach, City of v.
    Tona-Rama, Inc. 214
Delfino v. Vealencis 177–178
Dickhut v. Norton 114
Dill v. Excel Packing Co. 261
Dolan v. City of Tigard 289, 352, 353
Dolata v. Berthelet
    Fuel & Supply 256
Double D Manor, Inc. v.
    Evergreen Meadows
    Homeowners' Ass'n 250
Duke of Norfolk's Case 149
Dumpor's Case 95
Duncan v. Vassaur 173
Dunlap v. Bullard 92
Dwyer v. Skyline Apartments, Inc. 116

Eagle Enterprises, Inc. v. Gross 237
East St. John's Shingle Co.
    v. City of Portland 261
Eastlake, City of v.
    Forest City Enterprises, Inc. 279
Easton v. Strassburger 303
Edwards v, Habib 114
Elkus v. Elkus 187
Enterprises, Inc. v. Gross 237
Erickson v. Sinykin 10
Ernst v. Conditt 92
Estancias Dallas Corp. v. Schultz 262
Estate of — see name of party
Euclid v. Ambler Realty Co. 285
Euclid, Village of v.
    Ambler Realty Co. 256, 266

Farmer v. Kentucky Utilities Co. 217
Fasano v. Board of County
    Commissioners of
    Washington County 275, 279
Favorite v. Miller 8, 9
Fick v. Weedon 250
Fidelity Fed. Sav. & Loan Ass'n
    v. De La Cuesta 322
Figarsky v. Historic District Comm. 288
Fink v. Miller 253
First American Nat'l Bank
    of Nashville v. Chicken
    System of America, Inc. 89
First English Evangelical
    Lutheran Church of Glendale
    v. County of Los Angeles 354
First Federal Sav. Bank
    v. Key Markets, Inc. 94
First Nat'l Trust & Savings Bank
    v. Raphael 225
Fischre v. United States 176

Fitzwilliam v. Wesley United
    Methodist Church.................................. 250
Flying Diamond Oil Corp.
    v. Newton Sheep Co. 232
Fox v. Smidt.. 249
Fox, State ex rel. Haman v. 213, 214
Fristoe v. Drapeau...................................... 217

Gabel v. Drewrys Ltd., U.S.A., Inc. 333
Gallagher v. Bell.. 233
Ganz v. Clark... 82
Garner v. Gerrish.. 75
Gazzolo v. Chambers.. 84
Gemma v. Gemma... 191
Gibbs v. Kimbrell.. 251
Gilbert v. Showerman...................................... 261
Gilkinson v. Third Ave RR Co. 33
Gion v. City of Santa Cruz 214
Glenn v. Poole.. 217
Goddard v. Winchell.. 11
Golden v. Planning Board of Ramapo 272
Gore v. Blanchard... 213
Gower v. Waters.. 103
Grady v. Schmitz 245, 254
Grange v. Korff... 246
Greenblatt v. Toney Schloss
    Properties Corp................................... 275
Groninger v. Aumiller...................................... 249
Grose v. Holland.. 173
Gruen v. Gruen.. 32
Guillette v. Daly Dry Wall, Inc. 244, 335, 338
Gulstine, Estate of... 191
G-W-L, Inc. v. Robichaux 303

Hadachek v. Sebastian..................................... 349
Haldeman v. Teicholz....................................... 245
Hamaker v. Blanchard....................................... 10
Hamel v. Gootkin.. 170
Haner v. Bruce... 332
Hannah v. Peel.. 12
Hannan v. Dusch.. 83
Harms v. Sprague... 171
Harper v. Paradise... 335
Harris v. Griffin... 324
Hartman Ranch Co. v.
    Associated Oil Co................................... 92
Hatch v. Riggs National Bank 148
Hausmann v. Hausmann....................................... 64
Hawaii Housing Authority
    v. Midkiff.. 348
Hawkinson v. Johnston...................................... 104
Hay, State ex rel. Thornton v. 214
Heinzman v. Howard... 305
Henry v. Dalton... 204
Herpolsheimer v. Christopher 83
Herter v. Mullen... 77
Hester v. Sawyers... 211
Hewitt v. Hewitt.. 194
Hickerson v. Bender 224, 226
Hickey v. Green... 295

Hilder v. St. Peter................................... 111, 113
Hinds v. Phillips Petroleum Co......................... 219
Hochstein v. Romero....................................... 332
Hocks v. Jeremiah... 33
Hoffman v. Capitol
    Cablevision System, Inc. 220
Hohman v. Bartel... 253
Holbrook v. Taylor................................... 203, 204
Homan v. Hutchison... 198
Howard v. Kunto... 19
Hrisomalos v. Smith....................................... 252
Hughes v. Washington...................................... 345
Hurley v. City of Niagara Falls.......................... 12

In re — see name of party
Ink v. City of Canton..................................... 126
International News Service
    v. Associated Press................................. 6
Irvin L. Young Foundation, Inc.
    v. Damrell... 171
Ivons-Nispel, Inc. v. Lowe 213

Jaber v. Miller.. 91
Jack Spring, Inc. v. Little............................... 103
Jack v. Hunt... 207
Jackson v. Williams.. 249
James J.F. Loughlin Agency, Inc.
    v. Town of West Hartford......................... 274
James v. Valtierra... 271
Javins v. First National
    Realty Corp. 110
Jee v. Audley.. 156–157, 160
Jensen v. Schreck.. 324
Jinks v. Edwards.. 82
Johnson v. Davis.. 302
Johnson v. Hendrickson................................... 178
Johnson v. M'Intosh....................................... 5–6
Johnson v. Mt. Baker Park
    Presbyterian Church.............................. 242
Johnson v. State... 238
Jolliff v. Hardin Cable Television Co................. 220
Jones v. Alfred H. Mayer Co. 119
Jones, State v... 270
Jordan v. Talbot... 103
Jordan v. Village of Menomonee Falls................ 290
Jordon v. Nickell.. 104
Jost v. Dairyland Power Cooperative 256
Julian v. Christopher....................................... 94

Kanefsky v. Dratch Construction Co. 218
Kanter v. Safran... 104
Kassan v. Stout... 103
Keeble v. Hickeringill....................................... 5
Kelly v. Neville.. 63
Kendall v. Ernest Pestana, Inc 94
Keppell v. Bailey..................................... 228, 237
Keystone Bituminous Coal Ass'n
    v. De Benedictis................................... 351
Kilbourne v. Forester....................................... 80
King v. Moorehead... 111

Case	Page
King v. Reynolds	83
Kline v. 1500 Mass. Ave. Apt. Corp.	116
Krieger v. Helmsley-Spear, Inc.	94
Ladue, City of v. Gilleo	284
Land Developers, Inc. v. Maxwell	244
Landen Farms Community Services Ass'n v. Schube	253
LaSara Grain v. First Nat'l Bank of Mercedes	303
Lawton v. Steele	285
Leach v. Gunnarson	315
Leeco Gas & Oil Co. v. County of Nueces	126
Lempke v. Dagenais	303
Leonard v. City of Bothell	279
Lewis v. Searles	60
Lindsey v. Clark	223
Lindsey v. Normet	280
Lingsch v. Savage	302
Logan v. Citizens Nat'l Bank	35
Lohmeyer v. Bower	298
London County Council v. Allen	238
Loretto v. Teleprompter Manhattan CATV Corp.	350
Lucas v. South Carolina Coastal Council	266, 288, 349, 351
Luthi v. Evans	332
Mahoney v. Mahoney	187
Mahoney v. Middleton	338
Mahrenholz v. County Board of School Trustees	52
Mains Farm Homeowners Ass'n v. Worthington	250
Malley v. Hanna	245, 246
Mamalis v. Bornovas	172
Mann v. Bradley	172
Mannillo v. Gorski	15
Marengo Cave Co. v. Ross	15
Marini v. Ireland	111
Marriage of Brown, In re	191
Marriage of Elam, In re	192
Marriage of Graham, In re	187
Marsh v. Pullen	221
Marvin v. Marvin	194
Massey v. Prothero	183
Matcha v. Mattox	214
Matthews v. Bay Head Improvement Ass'n	214
McAvoy v. Medina	12
McCurdy v. McCurdy	191
McCutcheon v. United Homes Corp.	117
McGuire v. City of Jersey City	105
McMillan v. Iserman	250
Melms v. Pabst Brewing Co.	65
Members of the City Council of Los Angeles v. Taxpayers for Vincent	284
Mercury Investment Co. v. F.W. Woolworth Co.	85
Messersmith v. Smith	331
Metromedia, Inc. v. City of San Diego	273
Metropolitan Nat'l Bank v. United States	331
Metzner v. Wojdyla	250
Michalski v. Michalski	179
Midland Valley R.R. Co. v. Arrow Industrial Mfg. Co.	198
Mid-State Equip. Co., Inc. v. Bell	241, 244
Miles v. Shauntee	109
Miller v. Lutheran Conference & Camp Ass'n	220, 222
Miller v. Schoene	349
Mills v. Damson Oil Co.	331
Miniat v. McGinnis	242
Minneapolis Star & Tribune Co. v. Minnesota Commissioner of Revenue	285
Mississippi State Dep't of Public Welfare v. Howie	81
Mitchell v. Castellaw	207
Moore v. City of East Cleveland	286
Moore v. Megginson	248
Moore v. Phillips	64
Moore v. Regents of the University of California	6–7
Morgan v. High Penn Oil Co.	255
Morris v. Ulbright	50
Morse v. Aldrich	232
Morse v. Curtis	338
Moseley v. Bishop	237
Mountain Brow Lodge No. 82, Ind. Order of Odd Fellows v. Toscano	67
Mountjoy's Case	220
Mueller v. Bankers' Trust Co.	239
Nahrstedt v. Lakeside Village Condominium Association	194
National Bellas Hess, Inc. v. Kalis	72
Nectow v. City of Cambridge	266
Neponsit Property Owners Ass'n v. Emigrant Industrial Savings Bank	235
Neuberger v. City of Portland	279
New Jersey v. Baker	287
Newcomb v. Congdon	236
Newells v. Carter	16
Newman v. Bost	32
Newman v. Hinky-Dinky Omaha Lincoln, Inc.	94
Nicholson v. 300 Broadway Realty Corp.	237
Nollan v. California Coastal Commission	289, 353
Northpark Associates No. 2, Ltd. v. Homart Development Co.	198
Northwestern Nat'l Bank v. Daniel	35

Norton v. Duluth Transfer Ry. 224

O'Brien v. O'Brien 187
O'Keeffe v. Snyder 25
O'Reilly v. Frye 76
Ogilvie v. Idaho Bank & Trust Co. 171
Old Dominion Iron & Steel Corp.
     v. Virginia Electric
     & Power Co. 234
Omega Corp. of Chesterfield
     v. Malloy 250
Orange & Rockland Util.
     v. Philwood Estates 233
Otero v. Pacheco 207
Othen v. Rosier 209

Page v. Bloom 213
Pagelsdorf v. Safeco Insurance Co. 117
Paine v. Meller 305
Paradine v. Jane 98
Parise v. Citizens Nat'l Bank 324
Parker & Edgarton v. Foote 215
Parkhurst's Estate, In re 33
Pasadena v. California-Michigan
     Land & Water Co. 221
Patterson v. Reigle 17
Patton v. Madison County 249
Penn Bowling Recreation Center, Inc.
     v. Hot Shoppes, Inc. 218
Penn Central Transportation Co.
     v. City of New York 288, 352
Pennell v. City of San Jose 119
Pennsylvania Coal Co. v. Mahon 348, 351
People v. Nogarr 171
People v. Stover 269
Pernell v. Southall Realty 103
Peterson v. Superior Cour 117
Pierson v. Post 4
Pioneer Trust & Savings Bank
     v. Village of Mt. Prospect 290
Pollock v. Ramirez 251
Posner v. Davis 302
Preble v. Maine Central Railroad 18
Pross v. Excelsior Cleaning
     & Dyeing Co. 97
Public Access Shoreline Hawaii
     v. Hawaii County
     Planning Comm. 214

Redarowicz v. Ohlendorf 303
Reed v. King 302
Regency Homes Ass'n v. Egermayer 238
Reno, City of v. Matley 233
Renton, City of v. Playtime Theatres 283
Reste Realty Corp. v. Cooper 108
Rhue v. Cheyenne Homes, Inc. 250
Rick v. West 254
Riddle v. Harmon 169
Riley v. Bear Creek Planning Comm. 243
Riley v. Griffin 309

Robroy Land Co. v. Prather 162
Rockafellor v. Gray 316
Rodgers v. Reimann 248
Rodgers v. Village of Tarrytown 277
Rogers v. Yellowstone Park Co. 191
Romanchuk v. Plotkin 208
Rose v. Chaikin 255
Rothschild v. Wolf 225
Ruckelshaus v. Monsanto Co. 251, 345
Rumiche Corp. v. Eisenreich 97
Runyon v. Paley 232, 234

S.S. Kresge Co. of Michigan
     v. Winkelman Realty Co. 218
Sabo v. Horvath 337
Sakansky v. Wein 221
Sanborn v. McLean 241, 242, 244,
                                          245, 335
Sanderson v. Saxon 168
Santa Barbara, City of v. Adamson 287
Sargent v. Ross 117
Save Our Rural Environment
     v. Snohomish County 274
Sawada v. Endo 176
Schad v. Borough of Mt. Ephraim 283
Schley v. Couch 11
Schulman v. Serrill 249
Schwenn v. Kaye 319
Sellentin v. Terkildsen 213
Sensenbrenner v.
     Rust, Orling & Neale 303
Shanks v. Floom 211
Shapiro v. Thompson 280
Shelley v. Kraemer 67
Shelley's Case 143–146, 148
Shippan Point Ass'n
     v. McManus 252
Shorter v. Shelton 103
Skendzel v. Marshall 324
Smiley v. Van Winkle 93
Smith v. Chanel, Inc. 6
Smith v. McEnany 106
Smith v. Zoning Board of Appeals
     of the Town of Greenwich 287
Smith's Transfer & Storage Co.
     v. Hawkins 72
Snider v. Deban 83
Snow v. Van Dam 247
Sommer v. Kridel 105
South Staffordshire Water Co.
     v. Sharman 11
Southern Burlington County
     NAACP v. Township of
     Mount Laurel 271
Southern California Edison Co.
     v. Bourgerie 251
Spencer's Case 228, 231
Sprague v. Kimball 243
Spur Industries, Inc. v.
     Del E. Webb Development Co. 264

Stambovsky v. Ackley 302
Standard Livestock Co. v. Pentz 82
Stanton v. T.L. Herbert & Sons 219
State ex. rel. — see name of party
Stephens & Co. v. Albers 5
Stewart v. AmSouth
       Mortgage Co., Inc. 170
Stoner v. Zucker 203
Streams Sports Club, Ltd.
       v. Richmond 238
Suttle v. Bailey 248
Swartzbaugh v. Sampson 171

Taltarum's Case 47
Tefft v. Munson 337
Tenhet v. Boswell 171–172
Thomas v. Johnson 172
Thompson v. Baxter 76
Thompson, Estate of v. O'Tool 80
Thomson, Estate of v. Wade 205
Tindall v. Yeats 172
Tindolph v. Schoenfeld Bros., Inc. 242
Toledo Trust Co. v. Simmons 10
Totten, Matter of 35
Townsend v. Singleton 78
Trustees of Columbia College
       v. Thatcher 252
Tulk v. Moxhay 240

Union Bond & Trust Co.
       v. Blue Creek Redwood Co. 324
Union Nat'l Bank of Lowell
       v. Nesmith 226
United States National Bank
       of Oregon v. Homeland, Inc. 105
United States v. — see name of opposing party

Van Sandt v. Royster 207, 208
Van Sant v. Rose 238
Van Valkenburgh v. Lutz 15
Village of — see name of party

Waldorff Insurance & Bonding, Inc.
       v. Eglin Nat'l Bank 334
Waldrop v. Town of Brevard 226
Walner v. City of Turlock 226
Ward v. Mattuschek 294
Wardlow v. Pozzi 172
Warshawsky v. American
       Automotive Products Co. 99
Washington Hydroculture, Inc.
       v. Payne 96
Washington v. Davis 280
Webb v. Russell 93
Webb's Fabulous Pharmacies
       v. Beckwith 350
Werner v. Graham 243, 249
West v. City of Portage 279
Westbrook v. Gleason 338
White v. Brown 60
Whitinsville Plaza, Inc. v. Kotseas 236
Willard v. First Church
       of Christ, Scientist 206
Winthrop v. Wadsworth 207
Witteman v. Jack Barry Cable 220
Wolfe v. Shelley 143–146
Woods v. Garnett 338
Wright v. Horse Creek Ranches, Inc. 217

Young v. American Mini-Theatres 283

Zimmer v. Sundell 336

TABLE OF REFERENCES TO THE RESTATEMENTS (1st, 2nd, 3rd) OF PROPERTY

Restatement (1st) of Property
§ 534	233
§ 535	233
§ 537(a), comment c	238
§ 537, comment h	236
§ 541	234, 247
§ 543, comment c	238
§ 547	234
§ 547, Illus. 3	234

Restatement (2nd) of Property
§ 1.5	73
§ 5.1	110
§ 5.4	99
§ 5.6	113
§ 6.1	106, 109
§ 6.2	83
§ 9.1	97
§ 9.2	99
§ 11.1	112
§ 11.3	111
§ 12.1	96, 100
§ 12.1(3)	105
§ 12.1, statutory note	105
§ 12.5	97
§ 13.1	102
§ 14.8	114
§ 14.9	114
§ 15.1, comment i	92
§ 15.2	93
§ 16.1	95
§ 17.3	117
§ 17.5	116

Restatement (3rd) of Property (proposed)
Servitudes, § 2.4	233
Servitudes, § 2.6	238

TABLE OF REFERENCES TO THE UNIFORM RESIDENTIAL LANDLORD & TENANT ACT (URLTA)

§ 1.403	83, 101, 117	§ 4.105	113
§ 2.104	113	§ 4.106	99
§ 4.103	113	§ 4.301(c)	80
§ 4.104	113	§ 5.101	114

SUBJECT MATTER INDEX

ABANDONMENT
See also LEASEHOLD ESTATES
Easements, 223–224
Equitable servitudes, 252–253
Finders keepers, 8

ABORTIONS
Zoning, 287

ABSTRACTS OF TITLE
Sales and transfers of real property, assistance of attorneys, 292

ACCELERATION OF RENT
Leasehold estates, 100

ACCEPTANCE OF GIFTS, 34

ACCESSION, 27

ACCOUNTING
Concurrent ownership, 179–183

ACQUIESCENCE
See CONSENT AND APPROVAL

ACTUAL AND EXCLUSIVE POSSESSION
Adverse possession, 14
Prescriptive easements, 212–213

ADULT ENTERTAINMENT
Zoning, freedom of speech, 282–284

ADVERSE POSSESSION
Generally, 13–27
Accrual of cause of action, 23–24
Actual and exclusive possession, 14
Aggressive trespass, 16–17
Boundary disputes, 18, 26–27
Color of title, 18–19, 21–23
Concurrent ownership, 183
Consent, lack of, 15–19
Continuous possession, 19–21
Co-owners, 25
Cultivation or improvement, 15
Disclaimers of ownership, 17–18
Earning theory, 13
Elements, 14–21
Extent of property acquired by adverse possession, 21–23
Future interests, holders of, 24
Good faith belief in ownership, 16
Hostility or adverse claim of right, 15–19
Length of limitations period, 23
Lienholders, 24

Minor encroachments, 15
Objective appearance of ownership, 17, 18
Open and notorious possession, 14–15
Ouster, tacking of possession, 20–21
Personal property, 25
Property acquired by adverse possession, 21–23
Quiet title action by adverse possessor, 26
Rationales, 13–14
Real covenants, vertical privity, 234
Recording acts, interests created by operation of law, 332–333
Sales and transfers of real property, proof of marketable title, 297
Sleeping theory, 13
Stability theory, 13–14
Substantial enclosure, 15
Subsurface minerals, 15
Tacking of possessions, 19–21
Taxes, payment of, 21
Tenants, 25
Title acquired by adverse possessor, 25–26
Title insurance, exclusions from coverage, 344
Underground occupation, 14–15

ADVERTISEMENTS
Equitable servitudes, implication from common development scheme, 242

AESTHETIC OBJECTIVES
Zoning, 269–270

AGENTS
Gifts, delivery of, 33

AGGRESSIVE TRESPASS
Adverse possession, 16–17

AGREEMENTS
See CONTRACTS AND AGREEMENTS

AGRICULTURE
Concurrent ownership, profits from land, 181

AIR
Negative easements, 201–202

AMELIORATIVE WASTE
Life estates, 64–65

AMERICANS WITH DISABILITIES ACT, 119–120

AMORTIZATION
Zoning, forced phase-out of nonconforming uses, 273–274

ANIMAL HUSBANDRY
Concurrent ownership, profits from land, 181

ANTENUPTIAL CONTRACTS, 188

APPROVAL
See CONSENT AND APPROVAL

ARCHITECTURAL APPROVAL
Equitable servitudes, 250
Real covenants, 250
Zoning, 270

ARTIFICIAL MONUMENTS
Deeds, construction of description of land, 308–309

ASSIGNMENTS AND SUBLEASES
    Generally, 85–95
Assignments, generally, 85–90
Assumption of performance of obligations, 88–89
Consent of landlord, 93–94
Deeds, present covenants of title, 316
Discrimination, refusal of consent by landlord, 93
Distinctions between assignments and subleases, 91–93
Double rent, 92
Equitable servitudes, 245–246
Implied assumption of performance of obligations, 89
Intent of parties, 86, 91–92
Involuntary transfers, 93
Licenses, 203
Material alteration of lease, assignor tenant excused from suretyship, 89
Merger, 93
Multiple assignments, 89–90
Notice of promise, 86
Obligations of assignee, 85–87
Personal promises, 87
Privity of contract, 85, 86, 87–90
Privity of estate, 85–87, 89–90
Profits a prendre, 202
Reasonableness, consent by landlord, 93–94
Re-entry, right of, 92
Release and novation, 87–88
Restrictive provisions in leases, 93–95
Reversions, 92
Strict construction of restrictive provisions in leases, 93
Subleases, generally, 90–91
Substance of transfer, 92
Surety, assignor tenant as, 89
Touch and concern, 86–87
Waiver of restrictive provisions in leases, 94–95

ATTORNEYS
Sales and transfers of real property, 292

ATTORNEYS' FEES
Uniform Residential Landlord and Tenant Act, willfulness of holdover, 80–81

"AUTONOMY" RIGHTS
Zoning, 286–287

BAD FAITH
See GOOD FAITH

BAILMENTS
    Generally, 27–30
Actual control, 28
Contractual changes to rules, 30
Custody and intent to possess, 28
Duty of care of bailee, 29–30
Elements, 28
Mistakes in identity or composition, 28
Rights and obligations, 28–30
Third parties, rights as to, 28–29

BALLOON PAYMENT MORTGAGES, 321

BANK ACCOUNTS
Gifts, 35–36

BEACHES
Custom, public use by, 214
Public trust doctrine, 214–215

BED AND BREAKFAST
Covenants requiring residential use, 250

BENTHAM, JEREMY, 1, 2

BODY PARTS
Creation *vs.* first possession, 6–7

BONA FIDE PURCHASERS
Deeds, commercial escrows, 311, 312
Sales and transfers of personal property, 36–37
Title, 329–330, 333

BOUNDARY DISPUTES
Acquiescence, 26
Adverse possession, 18, 26–27
Agreed boundaries, 26
Equitable estoppel, 26–27
Title insurance, exclusions from coverage, 344

BROKERS
Sales and transfers of real property, 292, 302–303

CAUSA MORTIS GIFTS, 30

CAVEAT EMPTOR
Sales and transfers of real property, 301–302

CHICAGO
Use of Torrens system, 340

CHILDREN AND MINORS
Adverse possession, accrual of cause of action, 23–24
Fair Housing Act, 119–120

CHOSES IN ACTION
Gifts, delivery of, 33

CIVIL RIGHTS
See DISCRIMINATION

CLAIM OF RIGHT
Adverse possession, 15–19
Prescriptive easements, 210–211

CLOSINGS
Sales and transfers of real property, 293

CLUSTER ZONING, 278

COLOR OF TITLE
Adverse possession, 18–19, 21–23

COMMERCIAL ESCROWS
Deeds, 311, 312

COMMINGLING OF SEPARATE AND COMMUNITY PROPERTY, 190–191

COMMON AREAS
Condominiums, 195
Landlord, tort liability of, 116

COMMON LAW MARRIAGE, 193

COMMUNITY PROPERTY
Generally, 188–193
Agreement transmuting character of property, 191
Commingling of separate and community property, 190–191
Creditors, rights of, 193
Death, rights on, 193
Definition, 189–192
Divorce, rights on, 193
Gifts, devises and inheritances, 189
Income from separate property, 191
Increased value of separate property from community efforts, 191–192
Inflation, increased value of separate property due to, 192
Management, 192–193
Pensions, 191
Personal injury damages, 191
Presumption of community property, 189, 190
Tenancy by the entirety, 174
Tracing of community property, 189–191
Uniform Marital Property Act, 189

COMPENSATION
Eminent domain, 346–347

COMPETITION, COVENANTS AGAINST
Real covenants, 236–237

CONCEALMENT
Sales and transfers of real property, duties of disclosure, 301

CONCURRENT OWNERSHIP
See also CONDOMINIUMS; COOPERATIVES; HUSBAND AND WIFE; JOINT TENANCY; PARTITION; TENANCY BY THE ENTIRETY; TENANCY IN COMMON
Generally, 163–196
Accounting, 179–183
Adverse possession, 183
Cohabitants, contracts between unmarried, 193–194
Coparceny, 163, 177
Exclusive possession by one co-owner, 179–181, 183–184
Fiduciary relationship between co-owners, 183
Improvements, cost of, 182–183
Mortgage, payment of, 181–182
Profits from land, 181
Rental value of exclusive possession by one co-owner, 179–181
Repairs, payment for, 182
Taxes, payment of, 182
Tenancy in partnership, 163, 176–177
Third parties, rents from, 181, 182, 183–184

CONDEMNATION
See EMINENT DOMAIN

CONDITIONAL USES
Zoning, 276–277

CONDITIONAL ZONING, 277–278

CONDOMINIUMS
Generally, 194–195
Common areas, 195
Conversions to condominiums, restrictions on, 195
Conveyance and financing of units, 195
Creation, 194
Owners' association, 194–195
Partition, 195

CONFESSION OF JUDGMENT
Leasehold estates, 101

CONSENT AND APPROVAL
See also ARCHITECTURAL APPROVAL
Adverse possession, 15–19
Assignments and subleases, 93–94
Boundary disputes, 26
Restraints on alienation, 66

CONSERVATION
See ENVIRONMENTAL CONSERVATION

CONSIDERATION
Deeds, 307

CONSTITUTIONAL LAW
See also EMINENT DOMAIN; ZONING
Restraints on alienation, 67

CONSTRUCTIVE DELIVERY
Gifts, 32–33

CONSTRUCTIVE DISPOSSESSION
Eminent domain, 350

CONSTRUCTIVE EVICTION
See also LEASEHOLD ESTATES
Deeds, breach of future covenants of title, 316–318

CONSTRUCTIVE NOTICE
Title, 334–336

CONTINGENT REMAINDERS, 133–136

CONTINUOUS USE OR POSSESSION
Adverse possession, 19–21
Easements, 206, 208, 212

CONTRACTS AND AGREEMENTS
See also EASEMENTS; EQUITABLE SERVITUDES; REAL COVENANTS; SALES AND TRANSFERS OF REAL PROPERTY
Community property, transmutation of character of property, 191
Partition, 67, 179

COOPERATIVES
Generally, 195–196
Financial operation, 195
Limited liability, 196
Transfers, restrictions on, 195–196

COPARCENY
Concurrent ownership, 163, 177

COPYRIGHT, 6

COSTS
Title adjudication under Torrens system, 342

COVENANTS
See EQUITABLE SERVITUDES; REAL COVENANTS

CROPS
Profits a prendre, 202

CULTIVATION OF LAND
Adverse possession, 15

CUMULATIVE ZONING, 267

CURTESY, 186

CUSTOM, 3

***CY PRES* DOCTRINE**
Perpetuities, rule against, 160–161

DAMAGES
See also LEASEHOLD ESTATES; LIQUIDATED DAMAGES; PUNITIVE DAMAGES
Deeds, breach of covenants of title, 318
Easements, enlargement of dominant estate, 218–219
Holdover tenants, 78
Nuisances, 261–262, 263–264
Real covenants, 228
Sales and transfers of real property, 299–301

DATE
See TIME AND DATE

DEATH
Community property, rights to, 193
Deeds, attempted delivery at death, 309–310
Equitable title, 304–305
Gifts, delivery of, 33
Husband and wife, rights of, 187–188
Tenancy by the entirety, termination of, 176

DECLARATORY JUDGMENTS
Eminent domain, regulatory takings, 353

DEEDS
Generally, 306–319
After-acquired title, 318–319
Assignment of present covenants of title, 316
Breach of covenants of title, 314–318
Commercial escrows, 311, 312
Consideration, 307
Construction of description of land, 308–309
Constructive eviction, breach of future covenants of title, 316–318
Damages for breach of covenants of title, 318
Death, attempted delivery at, 309–310
Defense of title, obligation of grantor, 317–318
Delivery, 309–312
Description of grantee, 307
Description of land, 307–309
Encumbrances, covenant against, 313, 315
Equitable title, commercial escrows, 311
Estoppel, delivery by, 311–312
Estoppel by deed, 318–319
Eviction, breach of future covenants of title, 316–318
Formal requirements, 306–309
Frauds, statute of, 306
Further assurances, covenant of, 313, 316–318
General warranty, covenant of, 313, 316–318
General warranty deeds, 312–313
Gifts, delivery of, 31
Granting clause, 307–309
Irrevocable escrow for delivery at death, 309–310
Merger doctrine, 314

Notarial acknowledgment, 306–307, 309
Presumption of delivery, 309
Quiet enjoyment, covenant of, 313, 316–318
Quitclaim deeds, 314
Right to convey, covenant of, 313, 315
Seisin, covenant of, 313, 314–315
Special warranty deeds, 313
Statute of limitations, breach of covenants of title, 315–316
Warranties, 312–319

DEEDS OF TRUST, 323

DEFEASIBLE FEES
See also FEE SIMPLE DETERMINABLE; FEE SIMPLE SUBJECT TO CONDITION SUBSEQUENT; FEE SIMPLE SUBJECT TO EXECUTORY LIMITATION
    Generally, 50–58
Accrual of cause of action for recovery of possession, 57–58
Dower, 185–186
Laches, 57
Perpetuities, rule against, 58, 154–156
Transferability of interest retained by grantor, 56

DEFEASIBLE LIFE ESTATES, 59

DEFICIENCY JUDGMENTS
Purchase money mortgages, 323

DEFINITION OF PROPERTY, 1

DELIVERY
See also LEASEHOLD ESTATES
Deeds, 309–312
Gifts, 31–34

DENSITY ZONING, 267–268

DEPRECIATION
Zoning, forced phase-out of nonconforming uses, 273–274

DESTRUCTIBILITY OF CONTINGENT REMAINDERS
See REMAINDERS

DEVISES
Community property, 189
Fee simple, 45

DISABLED PERSONS
See HANDICAPPED OR DISABLED PERSONS

DISABLING RESTRAINTS ON ALIENATION, 66

DISCLAIMERS OF OWNERSHIP
Adverse possession, 17–18

DISCOVERY
Possession, 5–6

DISCRIMINATION
See also LEASEHOLD ESTATES; RACIAL DISCRIMINATION
Assignments and subleases, refusal of consent by landlord, 93
Restraints on alienation, constitutionality of, 67
Zoning, constitutional validity, 266

DISTRESS/DISTRAINT
Leasehold estates, 105

DIVORCE
    Generally, 186–187
Community property, rights to, 193
Tenancy by the entirety, termination of, 176

DOCTRINE, 3

DOMESTICATED ANIMALS
Possession, 5

DOWER, 184–186

DUE-ON-SALE CLAUSES
Mortgages, 322

DUE PROCESS
Zoning, 266, 281–287

EASEMENTS
See also LICENSES; PROFITS A PRENDRE
    Generally, 197, 198–226
Abandonment by holder of easement, 223–224
Accidental destruction of servient estate, 225–226
Affirmative easements, 201
Alteration of dominant estate, 224–225
Ambiguous grants, 198–199, 200
Apparent use, implication from prior use, 206, 208
Appurtenant easements, 199, 200
Cessation of purpose, 222, 225–226
Changed circumstances in surrounding area, 226
Change in location, 217–218
Claim of right, prescriptive easements, 210–211
Common ownership, implied easements, 206–207, 209
Continuous use, 206, 208, 212
Creation
    Generally, 205–215
    Scope of easement, determination of, 216–217
Definition, 198
Division of benefit of easement, 219–220
Enlargement of dominant estate, 218–219
Estoppel, easements by
    Generally, 206
    Cessation of purpose, termination by, 225
Exclusive use, prescriptive easements, 212–213

Expiration, 222–223
Fee simple, distinguished, 198
Frauds, statute of, 205
Grant, creation by, 205–206, 216
Gross, easements in, 199–200
Implication, creation by
    Necessity, implication from, below
    Prior use, implication from, below
Implied dedication, prescriptive easements, 214
Intended continuation, implication from prior use, 206, 208
Intentional destruction of servient estate, 226
Intent of parties as to scope, 215–216
Interference by servient owner, 221
Interruption of use, prescriptive easements, 212
Leases, distinguished, 70–71
Licenses, compared and distinguished, 202–203, 204
Marketable title, 298
Merger of estates, 222, 223
Necessity, implication from
    Generally, 209–210
    Cessation of purpose, termination by, 225
    Common ownership, 209
    Duration, 210
    Reasonably convenient location, 210
    Recording acts, interests created by operation of law, 332–333
    Scope of easements, 217
    Severance, necessity of, 209–210
    Title insurance, exclusions from coverage, 344
Negative easements, 201–202
Occasional use, prescriptive easements, 212()
"One stock" rule, division of benefit of easement, 220
Open and notorious use, prescriptive easements, 211
Prescription, extinguishment by, 211()
Prescriptive easements
    Generally, 210–215
    Claim of right, 210–211
    Continuous use, 212
    Custom, public use by, 214
    Elements, 210–213
    Exclusive use, 212–213
    Implied dedication, 214
    Interrupted use, 212
    Negative easements, 215
    Occasional use, 212()
    Open and notorious use, 211
    Prescriptive period, 210
    Public land, easements in, 215
    Public prescriptive easements, 213–215
    Public trust doctrine, 214–215
    Recording acts, interests created by operation of law, 332–333
    Scope of easements, 217
    Tacking of uses, 212()
    Termination of easement, use after, 211()
    Title insurance, exclusions from coverage, 344
Prior use, implication from
    Generally, 206–209
    Apparent use, 206, 208
    Common ownership, 206–207
    Continuous use, 206, 208
    Existing use as division, 206, 208
    Intended continuation, 206, 208
    Reasonable necessity, 206, 207–208
    Recording acts, interests created by operation of law, 332–333
    Scope of easements, 216–217
    Subdivision map, implication from, 209
    Title insurance, exclusions from coverage, 344
Public land, prescriptive easements in, 215
Public prescriptive easements, 213–215
Public trust doctrine, 214–215
Real covenants, compared, 229
Release by holder of easement, 223
Reservation of easement in deed, 205–206
Revival after termination of easements, 222–223
Scope of easements, 215–221
Severance, implication from necessity, 209–210
Subdivision map, implication from prior use, 209
Subjacent and lateral support, 201–202
Tacking of uses, prescriptive easements, 212()
Termination of easements
    Generally, 222–226
    Abandonment by holder of easement, 223–224
    Accidental destruction of servient estate, 225–226
    Alteration of dominant estate, 224–225
    Cessation of purpose, 222, 225–226
    Changed circumstances in surrounding area, 226
    Expiration, 222–223
    Intentional destruction of servient estate, 226
    Merger of estates, 222, 223
    Prescription, extinguishment by, 226
    Prescriptive easements, use after termination of easement, 211()
    Release by holder of easement, 223
    Revival, 222–223
    Third persons, acts of, 225
Third party, reservation of easement for, 205–206
Title, Torrens system, 341
Title insurance, exclusions from coverage, 344
Transfer of easements
    Generally, 221–222
    Appurtenant easements, 221–222
    Gross, easements in, 222
Use by servient owner, 220–221
Waiver and estoppel. *See* Estoppel, easements by, above

EJECTMENT
Leasehold estates, 70–71, 103

ELECTIVE SHARE ON DEATH, 187–188

EMBEDDED OBJECTS
Finders keepers, 11

EMINENT DOMAIN
    Generally, 345–354
Compensation, 346–347
Constructive dispossession, regulatory takings, 350
Equitable servitudes, termination of, 251
Executive action, 345
Fair market value, compensation based on, 346–347
Forcible redistribution of property, prevention of, 345
Fourteenth Amendment, 345
Injunctive and declaratory relief, regulatory takings, 353
Judicial action, 345
Leasehold estates, 99
Legislative action, 345
Nuisance, abatement of, 348–350
Public use, 345–346, 347–348
Real covenants, termination of, 251
Regulatory takings
    Generally, 346, 348–354
    Balancing public benefits and private costs, 351–353
    Conceptual severance, 351
    Conditional exemption from regulation, 352–353
    Constructive dispossession, 350
    Damages, 353–354
    Economically viable use, loss of, 350–351
    Injunctive and declaratory relief, 353
    Nuisance, abatement of, 348–350
    Partial destruction of use of property, 351
    Permanent dispossession, 350
    Per se rules, 348–351
    Personal property, confiscation of, 350
    Real property, permanent occupation of, 350
Reverter, possibility of, 126–127
Severance damages, 346
Zoning, constitutional validity, 266

ENCROACHMENTS
Sales and transfers of real property, duties of disclosure, 302

ENCUMBRANCES
See LIENS AND ENCUMBRANCES

ENVIRONMENTAL CONSERVATION
Real covenants, benefits in gross, 239
Zoning, 288

EQUAL PROTECTION
Zoning, 266, 279–281

EQUITABLE DISTRIBUTION, 186–187

EQUITABLE ESTOPPEL
Boundary disputes, 26–27
Equitable servitudes, termination of, 253
Irrevocable licenses, 203–204
Sales and transfers of personal property, 37–38
Sales and transfers of real property, statute of frauds, 295

EQUITABLE SERVITUDES
    Generally, 198, 239–249
Abandonment, 252–253
Actual notice of servitude, 243–244
Architectural approval, 250
Assignment of land retained by promisee, 245–246
Building restriction *vs.* use restriction, 249
Changed conditions in surrounding area, 252
Changed conditions within affected area, 251–252
Common scheme, implication from, 241–243, 247–249
Creation of equitable servitudes, 240, 241–243
Eminent domain, termination by, 251
Enforceability by or against successors, 243–245
Equitable estoppel, termination, 253
Expiration, 251
Frauds, statute of, 241
Frustration of purpose, 252–253
Group home, operation as residential use, 250
Identification of benefited land, 245–249
Implication, creation of negative equitable servitude by, 240, 241–243
Implied waiver or acquiescence, 253
Injunctions, 239–240
Inquiry notice of servitude, 245
Intent, 243
Interest in land, status as, 240
Interpretation, 249–250
Laches, termination, 253
Marketable title, 298
Merger, 251
Negative easement, enforcement of invalid, 202()
Notice of servitude, 243–245
Prior purchasers, enforceability by, 246–249
Privity, 240, 243
Real covenants, distinguished, 229, 239–240
Reciprocal negative easement, 241
Record notice of servitude, 244
Remedy, 239–240
Residential purposes, 249–250
Retention of land by promisee, 245–246
Strangers, enforceability by, 247(), 249
Termination
    Generally, 251–254
    Abandonment, 252–253
    Balance of hardships, 254

Changed conditions in surrounding area, 252
Changed conditions within affected area, 251–252
Eminent domain, 251
Equitable estoppel, 253
Expiration, 251
Frustration of purpose, 252–253
Implied waiver or acquiescence, 253
Laches, 253
Merger, 251
Unclean hands, 253–254
Waiver or release, 251
Third parties, enforceability by, 246–249
Title insurance, exclusions from coverage, 344
Touch and concern, 245
Unclean hands, termination, 253–254
Waiver or release, 251

EQUITABLE TITLE, 304–306

ESCAPED WILD ANIMALS
Possession, 5

ETHNIC DISCRIMINATION
Zoning, equal protection, 280–281

EVICTION
See also LEASEHOLD ESTATES
Deeds, breach of future covenants of title, 316–318
Holdover tenants, 78

EVIDENCE
See also EXTRINSIC EVIDENCE; PRESUMPTIONS
Implied warranty of habitability, retaliatory eviction, 114
Joint tenancy, creation of, 167–168

EXCLUSIONARY ZONING, 270–271

EXECUTORY INTERESTS
Generally, 122, 136–139
Death taxes, avoidance of, 137
Fee simple determinable, interest following, 139
Shelly's Case, rule in, 145
Shifting executory interests, 136–137, 139
Springing executory interests, 136–137, 138–139
Statute of Uses, 137–138

EXTRINSIC EVIDENCE
Fee simple determinable, 53–54
Fee simple subject to condition subsequent, 53–54

FAIR HOUSING ACT, 119–120, 119–120

FAIR MARKET VALUE
Eminent domain, compensation for, 346–347

FAMILY RIGHTS
Zoning, 286–287

FARMING
Concurrent ownership, profits from land, 181

FEDERAL GOVERNMENT
Title, claims under Torrens system, 340–341

FEE SIMPLE
See also DEFEASIBLE FEES
Generally, 43–45
Alienation, 44–45
Common law, 43–44
Creation, 43–44
Devise, 45
Easements, distinguished, 198
Fee simple conditional, 45–46, 50
Fee tail, elimination of, 48–49, 50
Inheritance, 45
Perpetual duration, 43
Words of limitation, 43–44

FEE SIMPLE DETERMINABLE
See also FEE SIMPLE SUBJECT TO EXECUTORY LIMITATION
Generally, 50–52
Elimination of estate, 52
Extrinsic evidence, use of, 53–54
Fee simple subject to condition subsequent, preference for, 54–55
Intent, words evidencing, 51–52
Reverter, possibility of, 51
Transferability, 52

FEE SIMPLE SUBJECT TO CONDITION SUBSEQUENT
See also FEE SIMPLE SUBJECT TO EXECUTORY LIMITATION
Generally, 52–55
Accrual of cause of action for recovery of possession, 57
Action necessary to assert right of entry, 53
Entry, right of, 52–53
Extrinsic evidence, use of, 53–54
Intent, words evidencing, 53
Power of termination, 52–53
Transferability, 53–54

FEE SIMPLE SUBJECT TO EXECUTORY LIMITATION
Generally, 55–56
Automatic termination, 55
Fee tail, elimination of, 49
Optional termination, 56

FEE TAIL
Generally, 45–50
Disentailing conveyance, destruction by, 48
Elimination of estate, 47–50

Fee simple conditional, 45–46, 50
Life estates, relationship to, 49–50, 61
Reversion or remainder, followed by, 46–47

FEMME SOLE AND FEMME COVERT, 183–184

FERTILE OCTOGENARIAN
Perpetuities, rule against, 156–157

FIDUCIARIES
Concurrent ownership, 180, 183
Sales and transfers of real property, duties of disclosure, 301

FINDERS KEEPERS
Generally, 7–12
Abandoned property, 8
Embedded objects and treasure trove, 11
Employees, finding of lost or mislaid property by, 10
Intent to relinquish abandoned property, 8
Invitees, finding of lost or mislaid property by, 10–11
Landowners, rights to lost and mislaid property, 9–12
Lost and mislaid property, generally, 8–12
Prior finders, rights to lost and mislaid property, 9
Private homes, rights to objects found in, 11–12
Public places, rights to lost or mislaid property, 12
Statutory modification of common law, 12
Trespasser, finding of abandoned, lost or mislaid property by, 8, 9

FISH AND GAME
Profits a prendre, 202

FIXTURES
See LEASEHOLD ESTATES

FLOATING ZONES
Zoning, 277

FORFEITURE RESTRAINTS ON ALIENATION, 65

"FOR SALE" SIGNS
Zoning, freedom of speech, 284()

FOURTEENTH AMENDMENT
Eminent domain, 345

FRAUD AND MISREPRESENTATION
Leases, dishonesty of tenant as to intended purpose, 97–98
Sales and transfers of real property, duties of disclosure, 301
Title, Torrens system, 341

FRAUDS, STATUTE OF
See also SALES AND TRANSFERS OF REAL PROPERTY
Deeds, 306
Easements, 205

Equitable servitudes, 241
Leasehold estates, 70, 74

FREEDOM OF PRESS
Zoning, 284–285

FREEDOM OF RELIGION
Zoning, 285

FREEDOM OF SPEECH
Zoning, 266, 282–284

FREEHOLD ESTATES
See also DEFEASIBLE FEES; FEE SIMPLE; FEE TAIL; LIFE ESTATES; RESTRAINTS ON ALIENATION
Generally, 40–68
Escheat, feudal incidents, 41
Feudal incidents, 41–42
Feudal tenures, 40–42
Forfeiture, feudal incidents, 41
Future interests, 40
Marriage, feudal incidents, 41
Possessory estates, 40
Seisin, 40–41
Statute quia emptores, 42
Wardship, feudal incidents, 41

FRUSTRATION OF PURPOSE
Equitable servitudes, 252–253
Leasehold estates, 99–100

FUTURE INTERESTS
See also EXECUTORY INTERESTS; PERPETUITIES, RULE AGAINST; RE-ENTRY, RIGHT OF; REMAINDERS; REVERSIONS; REVERTER, POSSIBILITY OF; SHELLY'S CASE, RULE IN; WORTHIER TITLE, DOCTRINE OF
Generally, 122–162
Adverse possession, 24
Definition, 122

GAS
See OIL, GAS AND MINERALS

GIFTS
Generally, 30–36
Acceptance, 34
Agents, delivery to, 33
Bank accounts, 35–36
Causa mortis gifts, 30
Choses in action, delivery of, 33
Community property, 189
Constructive delivery, 32–33
Death, delivery on, 33
Deed, delivery by, 31
Delivery, 31–34

Intent, 30, 31
Joint tenancy with right of survivorship, bank accounts, 36
Oral trusts, 34
"Pay on death" bank accounts, 35
Possession, donee, 34
Power of attorney, bank accounts, 35
Revocable trusts, 34–35
Symbolic delivery, 31–32
Totten trusts, 35
Trusts, 34–35

GOOD FAITH
Accession, 27
Adverse possession, belief in ownership, 16
Sales and transfers of personal property, bona fide purchasers, 37
Sales and transfers of real property, 296

GROSS NEGLIGENCE
Bailee, duty of care of, 29

GROUP HOMES
Equitable servitudes, operation as residential use, 250
Real covenants, operation as residential use, 250

HABITABILITY, IMPLIED WARRANTY OF
See LEASEHOLD ESTATES

HANDICAPPED OR DISABLED PERSONS
Adverse possession, accrual of cause of action, 23–24
Americans with Disabilities Act, 119–120
Fair Housing Act, 119–120
Leases, 119–121

HAWAII
Use of Torrens system, 340

HAZARDOUS MATERIALS
Sales and transfers of real property, duties of disclosure, 302

HISTORIC PRESERVATION
Real covenants, benefits in gross, 239
Zoning, 287–288

HOLDOVER TENANTS
Generally, 76–81
Control of tenant over circumstances, 77
Delivery of possession at inception of lease, failure to make, 84
Election of new term, 78–80
Eviction and damages, 78
Irrevocability of election of new term, 79–80
Length of holdover term, 78–79
Periodic tenancy, holdover tenancy as, 78
Self-help, eviction, 78
Time for election of remedy, 80

Voluntary nature of holding over, 77
Willfulness of holdover, 80–81

HOMEOWNERS' ASSOCIATIONS
Real covenants, 235, 238

HOSTILITY
Adverse possession, 15–19

HUME, DAVID, 1, 2

HUSBAND AND WIFE
See also COMMUNITY PROPERTY; DIVORCE; TENANCY BY THE ENTIRETY
Generally, 183–194
Abolition of dower, 186
Antenuptial contracts, 188
Common law, 183–186
Common law marriage, 193
Curtesy, 186
Death, rights on, 187–188
Defeasible fees, dower in, 185–186
Dower, 184–186
Elective share on death, 187–188
Equitable distribution, 186–187
Femme sole and femme covert, 183–184
Jure uxoris, 184
Professional skills and credentials, equitable distribution, 186–187
Release of dower, 185
Restitution for financial support while obtaining professional skills and credentials, 187
Spousal contracts, 188
Support of wife, 184

ILLEGITIMATE CHILDREN
Zoning, equal protection, 281

IMPLIED EASEMENTS
See EASEMENTS

IMPLIED WARRANTY OF HABITABILITY
See LEASEHOLD ESTATES

IMPRISONMENT
Adverse possession, accrual of cause of action, 23–24

IMPROVEMENTS
Accession, 27
Adverse possession, 15
Concurrent ownership, 182–183
Partition, 183–184

INDIRECT RETALIATORY EVICTION, 114–115

INFANTS
See CHILDREN AND MINORS

INFLATION
Separate property, increased value of, 192

INHERENTLY DANGEROUS CONDUCT
Nuisances, 256–257

INHERITANCES
Community property, 189
Fee simple, 45
Joint tenancy, taxes, 165

INITIATIVE AND REFERENDUM
Zoning, 279

INJUNCTIONS
Easements, enlargement of dominant estate, 218–219
Eminent domain, regulatory takings, 353
Equitable servitudes, 239–240
Fair Housing Act, 120
Nuisances, 261–262, 263–264

INSANE PERSONS
Adverse possession, accrual of cause of action, 23–24

INSTALLMENT SALES
Sales and transfers of real property, 323–324

INSURANCE
See also TITLE INSURANCE
Sales and transfers of real property, risk of loss, 305–306

INTELLECTUAL PROPERTY, 6

INTENT
Abandoned property, relinquishment of, 8
Assignments and subleases, 86, 91–92
Bailments, 28
Deeds, 308–309
Easements, 215–216, 222, 223–224
Equitable servitudes, 243
Fee simple determinable, 51–52
Fee simple subject to condition subsequent, 53
Gifts, 30, 31
Leasehold estates, fixtures, 117–118
Licenses, irrevocable, 203
Life estates, 60
Nuisances, 256, 257
Partition, agreement not to, 179
Real covenants, 230–231

INVITEES
Lost or mislaid property, finding of, 10–11

JOINT TENANCY
Generally, 163, 164–173
Agreement to sever, 172
Contract to convey interest as causing severance, 169
Conveyance of interest as causing severance, 169
Creation, 165, 167–168
Evidence sufficient to create joint tenancy, 167–168
Gifts, bank accounts, 36
Inference of agreement to sever, 172
Inheritance taxes, inapplicability of, 165
Interests of parties, identity of, 166–167
Lease of interest as causing severance, 171–172
Mortgage of interest as causing severance, 169–171
Murder by joint tenant of another joint tenant, 172–173
Operation of law, severance by, 172–173
Possession, right to, 167
Probate, inapplicability of, 165
Severance, 168–173
Simultaneous death of joint tenants, 173
Straw man conveyances, 166
Theory of joint tenancy, 165
Time, receipt of interests at same, 165–166
Title, receipt of interests under same instrument, 166
Unities of joint tenancy, 165–167

JUDICIAL SALE
Life estates, 63

JURE UXORIS, 184

LABOR THEORY, 1

LACHES
Defeasible fees, 57
Equitable servitudes, termination of, 253

LANDLORD AND TENANT
See LEASES

LATENT DEFECTS
Landlord, tort liability of, 115–116

LATERAL SUPPORT
See SUBJACENT AND LATERAL SUPPORT

LEASEHOLD ESTATES
See also ASSIGNMENTS AND SUBLEASES; HOLDOVER TENANTS
Generally, 40–41, 69–121
Abandonment by tenant
Generally, 103–105
Damages, 104
Rejection of surrender and leaving premises untouched, 105
Retaking and reletting for tenant, 104–105
Acceleration of rent, 100
Accrual of rent, 95–96
Amount of rent, 95
Attached chattels, 118
Civil rights. *See* Discrimination, below
Common areas, tort liability of landlord, 116
Conditional legality of use, 99
Confession of judgment, 101
Constructive eviction
Generally, 106–109

Complete vacation of premises, 109
Remedies after vacation of premises, 109
Ripeness of claim, 109
Substantiality of interference, 108–109
Third party, interference by, 107–108()
Wrongful action by landlord, 107–108
Contingent remainders, destructibility of, 142–143
Cure, reasonable time for, 102
Damage, duty to avoid, 96–97
Damages
    Abandonment by tenant, 104
    Delivery of possession of leased property, failure to make, 83
    Fair Housing Act, 120
    Implied warranty of habitability, 111–113
Default by tenant, 100–105
Defeasibility, 71
Delivery of possession
    Generally, 81–85
    Actual possession, delivery of, 82–84
    American Rule, 83–84
    Continuing nature of obligation, 82
    English Rule, 82–83
    Implied obligation to deliver possession, 81–82
    Landlord remedies, 84
    Modification of obligations, 84
    Partial possession, 83
    Power to demise, 81
    Quiet enjoyment, covenant of, 81–82
    Tenant remedies, 83, 84
    Tenant's obligation to take possession, 84–85
    Waiver by parties, 82, 83
Destruction of property, 99
Discrimination
    Generally, 119–121
    Civil Rights Act of 1866, 119, 120
    Fair Housing Act, 119–120
    Owner-occupied rental housing, Fair Housing Act, 120
    Proof of discrimination, 120
    Single-family dwellings, Fair Housing Act, 120
    State and local laws, 120–121
Dishonesty of tenant as to intended purpose, termination of lease, 97–98
Distress/distraint, 105
Dual nature as estate and contract, 69–70
Easements, distinguished, 70–71
Ejectment, 103
Eminent domain, exercise of, 99
Eviction
    Generally, 101–103
    Constructive eviction, above
    Cure, reasonable time for, 102
    Determinable leases, 102
    Ejectment, 103
    Implied warranty of habitability, defense based on, 113
    Notice to quit, 102
    Procedural prerequisites, 101–102
    Quiet enjoyment, below
    Re-entry, right of, 102
    Retaliatory eviction, implied warranty of habitability, 113–115
    Self-help, 103
    Summary proceedings, 102–103
    Unlawful detainer, 102–103
Excusing tenants from obligations, 98–100
Fair Housing Act, 119–120
Fixtures
    Generally, 117–118
    Attached chattels, 118
    Damage caused by removal, 117–118
    Intent of tenant, 117–118
    Trade fixtures, 118
Frauds, statute of, 70, 74
Frustration of intended purpose, 99–100
"General repair" clauses, 96
Habitability. Implied warranty of habitability, below
Handicapped or disabled persons, 119–121
Honesty of tenant as to intended purpose, 97–98
Illegal use of property, 97, 98–99
Implied warranty of habitability
    Generally, 109–115
    Amount of damages, 112–113
    Damages, 111–113
    Eviction action, defense of, 113
    Inception of lease, condition of property at, 109–110
    Indirect retaliatory eviction, 114–115
    Notice to landlord, 111
    Proportionate reduction of rent, 112–113
    Punitive damages, 113
    Rent, withholding of, 111
    Repair, continuing duty of, 109–110
    Repair and deduct, 111
    Retaliatory eviction, 113–115
    Scope of warranty, 111
    Tenant's remedies for breach, 111–113
    Termination of lease, 111
    Waiver by tenant, 113
Indeterminate term, 72
Indirect retaliatory eviction, 114–115
Intent of tenant, fixtures, 117–118
Joint tenancy, severance of, 171–172
Knowledge of landlord of intended illegal use of property, 97
Latent defects, tort liability of landlord, 115–116
Length of term, 72, 78–79

Licenses, distinguished, 70–71
Liens on tenant's personal property, 105
Liquidated damages, 101
Modification of requirements for notice of termination, 74
Noise, commission of nuisance, 98
Notices
    Implied warranty of habitability, 111
    Quit, notice to, 102
    Termination of periodic tenancy, 72–74
Nuisances, 70–71, 98
Obligations of landlord, 105–117
Obligations of tenants, 95–100
Operation of law, periodic tenancy created by, 74–75
Ordinary wear and tear, 96
Origins and development, 69
Partial possession, delivery of, 83
Periodic tenancy, 70, 72–75, 78
Prepaid rent, default by tenant, 100
Profits a prendre, distinguished, 70–71
Punitive damages, implied warranty of habitability, 113
Quiet enjoyment
    Generally, 81–82, 106–109
    Actual partial eviction, 106, 106
    Actual total eviction, 106
    Constructive eviction, above
Real covenants, horizontal privity, 231
Re-entry, right of, 102
Remedies of landlord, 100–105
Remedies of tenants, 105–117
Rent
    Acceleration of rent, 100
    Obligation to pay, 95–96
    Prepaid rent, default by tenant, 100
    Quiet enjoyment, actual partial eviction, 106
    Rent control, 118–119
Repairs
    Generally, 96
    Implied warranty of habitability, above
    Tort liability of landlord, 116–117
Retaliatory eviction, implied warranty of habitability, 113–115
Ripeness of claim, constructive eviction, 109
Security deposits, 100
Seizure of tenant's personal property, 105
Self-help, eviction, 103
Summary proceedings, eviction, 102–103
Surrender of premises. Abandonment by tenant, above
Tenancy at will, 70, 75–76
Termination
    Abandonment by tenant, above
    Delivery of possession, failure to make, 83

Destruction of property, 99
Dishonesty of tenant as to intended purpose, 97–98
Eminent domain, exercise of, 99
Frustration of intended purpose, 99–100
Illegality of sole use, 99
Implied warranty of habitability, 111
Periodic tenancy, 72–74
Tenancy at will, 75–76
Term of years, 71–72
Third party, constructive eviction caused by interference by, 107–108()
Tort liability of landlord
    Generally, 115–117
    Common areas, 116
    Exculpatory clauses, 117
    Latent defects, 115–116
    Possession by tenant, conditions that arise after, 116
    Pre-existing dangerous conditions, 115–116
    Public use of property, 116
    Repair, covenant of landlord to, 116
    Repair, statutory or judicially created duty to, 116–117
Trade fixtures, 118
Unilateral terminability, 75–76
Waiver
    Delivery of possession, 82, 83
    Implied warranty of habitability, 113
Warranty of habitability. Implied warranty of habitability, above
Waste, avoidance of, 96–97

LICENSES
Generally, 202–205
Assignment, 203
Easements, compared and distinguished, 202–203, 204
Equitable estoppel, irrevocable licenses, 203–204
Intent to make license irrevocable, 203
Irrevocable licenses, 203–205
Leases, distinguished, 70–71
License couple with an interest, 204–205

LIENS AND ENCUMBRANCES
See also MORTGAGES
Adverse possession, 24
Deeds, covenant against encumbrances, 313, 315
Leasehold estates, tenant's personal property, 105
Sales and transfers of real property, defective title, 298
Title insurance, exclusions from coverage, 344

LIFE ESTATES
Generally, 58–65
Affirmative/voluntary waste, 64

Ambiguous grants, 60
Ameliorative waste, 64–65
Deed effective upon death of grantor, distinguished, 310
Defeasible life estates, 59
Equitable *vs.* legal life estates, 61–63
Fee tail, relationship to, 49–50, 61
Group or class of people, life estates in, 59–60
Intent of grantor, 60
Judicial sale of life estate, 63
Life estate *pur autre vie,* 59
Necessity, judicial sale of life estate for, 63
Permissive/involuntary waste, 64
Preservation of use of property, ameliorative waste, 64–65
Remainders, 141
Restraints on alienation, 68
Reversions and remainders, 58–59
Shelly's Case, rule in, 144–145
Third person, measurement by life of, 59
Transferability, 60–61
Trustees, duties of, 62
Valuation, 60–61
Waste, 63–65

LIGHT
Negative easements, 201–202

LIMITATION OF ACTIONS
See STATUTES OF LIMITATION

LIMITED LIABILITY
Cooperatives, 196

LIQUIDATED DAMAGES
Leasehold estates, 101
Sales and transfers of real property, 300–301

LOCKE, JOHN, 1

LOST PROPERTY
See FINDERS KEEPERS

MAPS
Deeds, construction of description of land, 308–309

MARRIED WOMAN PROPERTY ACTS, 175

MECHANICS' LIENS
Title insurance, exclusions from coverage, 344

MEDICAL RESEARCH
Creation *vs.* first possession, 6–7

MERGER
Assignments and subleases, 93
Deeds, 314
Easements, 222, 223
Equitable servitudes, 251
Real covenants, 251

METES AND BOUNDS
Deeds, description of land, 307–309

MINERALS
See OIL, GAS AND MINERALS

MINNEAPOLIS
Use of Torrens system, 340

MINORS
See CHILDREN AND MINORS

MISLAID PROPERTY
See FINDERS KEEPERS

MISREPRESENTATION
See FRAUD AND MISREPRESENTATION

MISTAKES
Bailments, 28
Zoning, necessity of amendment to correct mistake, 275

MONOPOLIES
Zoning, forced phase-out of nonconforming uses, 273–274

MORTGAGES
Generally, 292–293, 319–323
Assumption of mortgage on sale of property, 322
Balloon payment mortgages, 321
Concurrent ownership, 181–182
Deeds of trust, 323
Default by mortgagor, 322–323
Defective title, 298
Deficiency judgments on purchase money mortgages, 323
Due-on-sale clauses, 322
First and second mortgages, 320–321
Fully amortized mortgages, 321
Joint tenancy, severance of, 169–171
Purchase money mortgages, 321
Redemption, 320, 323
Sale or transfer by mortgagor, 321–322
Title, 321, 333

MULTIPLE DAMAGES
Holdover, willfulness of, 80–81

MURDER BY JOINT TENANT OF ANOTHER JOINT TENANT, 172–173

NATURAL LAW THEORIES, 1

NATURAL MONUMENTS
Deeds, construction of description of land, 308–309

NATURAL RESOURCES
Concurrent ownership, profits from land, 181

NECESSITY, EASEMENTS BY
See EASEMENTS

NEGLIGENCE
Bailee, duty of care of, 29
Nuisances, 256–257

NEGOTIABLE INSTRUMENTS
Sales and transfers of personal property, 37

NEW HOMES
Sales and transfers of real property, implied warranty of quality, 303–304

NOISE
Leasehold estates, commission of nuisance, 98

NONCONFORMING USES
See ZONING

NOTARY PUBLIC
Deeds, acknowledgment of, 306–307, 309

NOTICES
See also LEASEHOLD ESTATES
Assignments and subleases, 86
Equitable servitudes, 243–245
Real covenants, 230
Title, 329, 334–336
Zoning, procedural due process, 281–282

NOVATION
Assignments and subleases, 87–88

NUDE DANCING
Zoning, freedom of speech, 282–284

NUISANCES
Generally, 255–264
Bilateral monopolies, transaction costs, 259
Damages, 261–262, 263–264
Economic theory, 258–262
Eminent domain, 348–350
Free riders, transaction costs, 259–260
Gravity of harm, 256
Holdouts, transaction costs, 260
Inherently dangerous conduct, 256–257
Initial entitlement, award of, 260–261
Injunctions, 261–262, 263–264
Intentional conduct, 256, 257
Leases, 70–71, 98
Negligence, 256–257
Private nuisances, 255–257
Public nuisances, 255, 257–258
Recklessness, 256–257
Sales and transfers of real property, duties of disclosure, 302
Special injury, abatement of public nuisances, 257
Substantial interference, 255–256
Transaction costs, 259–260
Trespass, relationship to, 258
Unintentional conduct, 256–257
Utility of conduct, 256

OIL, GAS AND MINERALS
Adverse possession, 15
Concurrent ownership, profits from land, 181
Profits a prendre, 202
Title, Torrens system, 341

"ONE STOCK" RULE
Easements, division of benefit of, 220

OPEN AND NOTORIOUS USE OR POSSESSION
Adverse possession, 14–15
Prescriptive easements, 211

OPPORTUNITY TO BE HEARD
Zoning, procedural due process, 281–282

OUSTER
Adverse possession, tacking of possession, 20–21
Concurrent ownership, rental value of exclusive possession by one co-owner, 180

PARKS
Zoning, 289

PARTITION
Generally, 177–179
Agreement not to partition, 179
Agreements among co-owners, 67
Condominiums, 195
Equal shares, division in, 178, 179
Improvements, cost of, 183–184
In kind partition, 177–178
Repairs, payment for, 182
Sale, partition by, 178–179

PARTNERSHIP, TENANCY IN, 163, 176–177

PATENTS, 6

"PAY ON DEATH" BANK ACCOUNTS, 35

PENSIONS
Community property, 191

PERMISSION
See CONSENT AND APPROVAL

PERPETUITIES, RULE AGAINST
Generally, 148–162
Applicability, 149
Artificially relevant people, class of persons as measuring or validating lives, 154
Charity-to-charity exemption, 155–156
Class gifts, 151
Class of persons as measuring or validating lives, 153–154

Commercial transactions, 161–162
Construction of instruments, 160
Cy pres doctrine, 160–161
Defeasible fees, 58, 154–156
Fertile octogenarian, 156–157
In utero, measuring or validating lives, 153
Measuring or validating lives, 152–154
Period of uncertainty permitted, 149
Re-entry, right of, 155
Reformation of instruments, 160–161
Reverter, possibility of, 155
Savings clauses, 161
Time for testing validity, 150
Unborn widows, 157–158
Vesting, 149, 151
"Wait-and-see" statutes, 158–160

PERSONAL PROPERTY
See also BAILMENTS; GIFTS; SALES AND
TRANSFERS OF PERSONAL PROPERTY
Generally, 27–39
Adverse possession, 25
Tenancy by the entirety, 176

PLANNED UNIT DEVELOPMENTS, 290

POLICE POWER
Zoning, 279

POSSESSION
See also ADVERSE POSSESSION; FINDERS
KEEPERS
Generally, 3–27
Accession, 27
Actual possession of wild animals, 4
Creation of intangible property rights, 6–7
Discovery, 5–6
Domesticated animals, 5
Escaped wild animals, 5
Exclusivity of right to exploit intangible property, 6
Relative title to wild animals, 4–5
Wild animals, 4–5

POWER OF ATTORNEY
Gifts, bank accounts, 35

POWER OF TERMINATION
See RE-ENTRY, RIGHT OF

PRESCRIPTIVE EASEMENTS
See EASEMENTS

PRESS, FREEDOM OF
Zoning, 284–285

PRESUMPTIONS
Community property, 189, 190
Deeds, delivery of, 309
Easements, ambiguous grants, 198–199

Tenancy by the entirety, 174
Tenancy in common, 163, 164
Zoning, validity of amendment, 274–275

PRIOR USE, IMPLICATION OF EASEMENTS FROM
See EASEMENTS

"PRIVACY" RIGHTS
Zoning, 286–287

PRIVITY
Adverse possession, tacking of possessions, 19–21
Assignments and subleases, 85–87, 87–90
Equitable servitudes, 240, 243

PROBATE
Joint tenancy, 165

PROFITS A PRENDRE
Generally, 202
Division of benefit, 219–220
Leases, distinguished, 70–71
Transfer of profits, 222

PROMISSORY RESTRAINTS ON ALIENATION, 66

PUBLIC POLICY
Implied warranty of habitability, waiver by tenant, 113
Leases, obligations of tenants, 98

PUBLIC PRESCRIPTIVE EASEMENTS, 213–215

PUBLIC TRUST DOCTRINE, 214–215

PUNITIVE DAMAGES
Fair Housing Act, 120
Leasehold estates, implied warranty of habitability, 113

PURCHASE MONEY MORTGAGES, 321

QUIET ENJOYMENT
See also LEASEHOLD ESTATES
Deeds, 313, 316–318

QUIET TITLE
Adverse possession, 26

QUITCLAIM DEEDS, 314
Title, 336

RACE ACTS
Title, 328–329

RACE-NOTICE ACTS
Title, 329–330

RACIAL DISCRIMINATION
Restraints on alienation, constitutionality of, 67
Zoning, equal protection, 280–281

REAL COVENANTS
Generally, 197, 227–239
Abolition of horizontal privity requirement, 233
Adverse possession, vertical privity, 234
Architectural approval, 250
Benefit and burden, 227
Building restriction vs. use restriction, 249
Competition, covenants against, 236–237
Conveyances, horizontal privity, 232–233
Creation, 229
Damages, 228
Definition, 227
Easements, compared, 229
Eminent domain, termination by exercise of, 251
Enforceability by or against successors, 229–230
Equitable servitudes, distinguished, 229, 239–240
Expiration, 251
Gross, benefits and burdens in, 238–239
Group home, operation as residential use, 250
Homeowners' associations, 235, 238
Horizontal privity, 230, 231–233
Intent, 230–231
Interpretation, 249–250
Landlord and tenant, horizontal privity, 231
Marketable title, 298
Merger, 251
Money, covenant to pay, 238
Mutual interests in burdened estate, horizontal privity, 231–232
Negative easement, enforcement of invalid, 202()
Notice of covenant, 230
Remedy, 228
Residential purposes, 249–250
Running with the land, 227–228
Termination
    Eminent domain, 251
    Expiration, 251
    Merger, 251
    Waiver or release, 251
Third party beneficiaries, vertical privity, 234–235
Touch and concern, 230, 235–239
Utilities, provision of, 237
Vertical privity, 230, 233–235
Waiver or release, 251

RECIPROCAL NEGATIVE EASEMENT, 241

RECKLESSNESS
Bailee, duty of care of, 29
Nuisances, 256–257

RECORDING OF TITLES
See TITLE

REDEMPTION
Mortgages, 320, 323

RE-ENTRY, RIGHT OF
See also DEFEASIBLE FEES; FEE SIMPLE SUBJECT TO CONDITION SUBSEQUENT
Generally, 122, 127
Abolition of determinable estates, effect of, 127
Assignments and subleases, 92
Eminent domain, 127
Fee simple subject to condition subsequent, 52–53
Leasehold estates, 102
Perpetuities, rule against, 155
Termination, 127
Transferability, 127

REFORMATION OF INSTRUMENTS
Perpetuities, rule against, 160–161

REGISTRATION OF TITLES
See TITLE

REGULATORY TAKINGS
See EMINENT DOMAIN

RELATION BACK
Deeds, commercial escrows, 311

RELEASES
Assignments and subleases, 87–88
Dower, 185
Easements, 223
Equitable servitudes, 251
Real covenants, 251

RELIGION, FREEDOM OF
Zoning, 285

REMAINDERS
Generally, 122, 128–136
Alienability, 136
Artificial or natural termination of life estate, 141
Class-closing rules, 133
Class gifts, 133
Classification, 128–136
Conditions precedent, contingent remainders, 134–135
Conditions subsequent, vested remainders subject to complete divestment, 130–131
Contingent remainders, 133–136
Definition, 128
Destructibility of contingent remainders
    Generally, 139–143
    Artificial or natural termination of life estate, 141
    Executory interests, 142
    Freehold estates, applicability to, 140–141
    Leaseholds, 142–143
    Life estates, 141
    Trusts, 143
    Vested remainders, 141–142

Executory interests, destructibility of contingent remainders, 142
Indefeasibly vested remainders, 130
Leaseholds, destructibility of contingent remainders, 142–143
Life estates, 58–59, 141
Natural expiration of preceding estates, 130
Reversions, distinguished, 124–125
Rule of convenience, class-closing rules, 133
Shelly's Case, rule in, 145
Trusts, destructibility of contingent remainders, 143
Vested remainders
    Generally, 129–133, 135
    Destructibility of contingent remainders, 141–142
    Vested remainders subject to complete divestment, 130–131
    Vested remainders subject to open, 131–133

RENT
See LEASEHOLD ESTATES

REPAIRS
See also LEASEHOLD ESTATES
Concurrent ownership, 182
Partition, 182

RESCISSION
Sales and transfers of real property, 299

RESTATEMENT OF TORTS
Repair, covenant of landlord to, 116

RESTITUTION
Equitable distribution, financial support while obtaining professional skills and credentials, 187

RESTRAINTS ON ALIENATION
    Generally, 65–68
Consent to alienation, 66
Co-owners, agreements among, 67
Disabling restraints, 66
Equitable life estates, 68
Forfeiture restraints, 65
Legal life estates, 68
Life estates, 68
Partial restraints, 66–67
Promissory restraints, 66
Spendthrift trusts, 68
State action, unconstitutional restraints, 67
Total restraints, 66
Unconstitutional restraints, 67
Use restrictions, 66–67

RETALIATORY EVICTION
Leasehold estates, implied warranty of habitability, 113–115

REVERSIONS
    Generally, 122–125
Assignments and subleases, 92
Automatic creation, 123
Lesser estate, conveyance of, 124
Life estates, 58–59
Possession in future not necessary, 123–124
Remainder, distinguished, 124–125
Reverter, possibility of, distinguished, 124–125
Vested interest, status as, 124

REVERTER, POSSIBILITY OF
See also DEFEASIBLE FEES; FEE SIMPLE DETERMINABLE
Generally, 122, 125–127
Abolition by statute, 127
Determinable estate, conveyance of, 125–126
Eminent domain, 126–127
Fee simple determinable, 51
Perpetuities, rule against, 155
Reversions, distinguished, 124–125
Termination, 126
Transferability, 126

RIPENESS
Leasehold estates, constructive eviction, 109

RISK OF LOSS
Sales and transfers of real property, 305–306

ROOT OF TITLE
Sales and transfers of real property, proof of marketable title, 297, 338–340

RULE AGAINST PERPETUITIES
See PERPETUITIES, RULE AGAINST

RULE IN SHELLY'S CASE
See SHELLY'S CASE, RULE IN

SALES AND TRANSFERS OF PERSONAL PROPERTY
    Generally, 36–39
Bona fide purchasers, 36–37
Entrustment to merchant for sale, 38
Equitable estoppel, 37–38
Good faith, bona fide purchasers, 37
Good value, bona fide purchasers, 37
Negotiable instruments, 37
Voidable title, 38–39

SALES AND TRANSFERS OF REAL PROPERTY
See also DEEDS; EASEMENTS; MORTGAGES; TITLE
    Generally, 292–324
Adverse possession, proof of marketable title, 297
Attorneys, 292

Benefit of the bargain, damages for breach of contract, 299–300
Brokers, 292, 302–303
Closings, 293
Conditions on sale, statute of frauds, 294
Cooperatives, 195–196
Damages for breach of contract, 299–301
Deeds of trust, 323
Default and remedies, 298–301
Defeasible fees, 56
Defective title, 297–298
Disclosure, duties of, 301–303
Encumbrances, defective title, 298
Equitable estoppel, statute of frauds, 295
Fee simple determinable, 52
Fee simple subject to condition subsequent, 53–54
Fiduciary relationships, duties of disclosure, 301
Frauds, statute of
    Generally, 293–296
    Conditions on sale, 294
    Equitable estoppel, 295
    Exceptions, 294–296
    Formality of contract, 293–294
    Part performance, 294–295
    Reasonable reliance, 295
    Revocation of contracts, 296
    Single or multiple writings, 294
    Unequivocal reference to contract, 294–295
Good faith, 296
Implied obligations, 296–298
Implied warranty of quality, 303–304
Installment sales, 323–324
Insurance proceeds, risk of loss, 305–306
Latent material defects, disclosure of, 302
Life estates, 60–61
Limitations period, implied warranty of quality, 303–304
Liquidated damages for breach of contract, 300–301
Marketable title, 296–298, 338–340
New homes, implied warranty of quality, 303–304
Nuisances, 302
Out of pocket expenses, damages for good faith breach of contract, 300
Partition, 178–179
Part performance, statute of frauds, 294–295
Proof of marketable title, 297
Reasonable reliance, statute of frauds, 295
Rescission, 299
Reverter, possibility of, 126
Risk of loss, 305–306
Seller-created conditions, disclosure of, 302
Specific performance, 298–299
Time of closing, 296
Unequivocal reference to contract, statute of frauds, 294–295
Zoning restrictions, defective title, 298

SALVAGE VALUE
Zoning, forced phase-out of nonconforming uses, 273–274

SCHOOLS
Zoning, 289

SECURITY DEPOSITS
Leasehold estates, 100

SEISIN, COVENANT OF, 313, 314–315

SELF-HELP
Eviction, 78, 103

SERVITUDES
See EASEMENTS; EQUITABLE SERVITUDES; REAL COVENANTS

SETBACK REQUIREMENTS
Zoning, variances, 275–276

SEVERANCE
Joint tenancy, 168–173
Tenancy by the entirety, 173

SEX DISCRIMINATION
Zoning, equal protection, 281

SHELLY'S CASE, RULE IN
    Generally, 139–140, 143–146
Avoidance of rule, 146
Executory interests, applicability to, 145
Heirs, 145–146
Life estate, applicability to, 144–145
Remainders, applicability to, 145
Worthier title, doctrine of, distinguished, 148

SHELTER RULE
Title, bona fide purchasers, 333

SHIFTING EXECUTORY INTERESTS, 136–137, 139

SIGNS
Zoning, freedom of speech, 284(,)

SIMULTANEOUS DEATH
Joint tenants, 173

SLAVERY, 1

SLEEPING THEORY
Adverse possession, 13

SOLAR COLLECTION
Negative easements, 201–202

SPECIAL DAMAGES
Holdover tenants, eviction, 78

SPECIFIC PERFORMANCE
Sales and transfers of real property, 298–299

SPEECH, FREEDOM OF
Zoning, 266, 282–284

SPENDTHRIFT TRUSTS, 68

SPOT ZONING, 274, 278

SPOUSES
See HUSBAND AND WIFE

SPRINGING EXECUTORY INTERESTS, 136–137, 138–139

STABILITY THEORY
Adverse possession, 13–14

STATE ACTION
Restraints on alienation, constitutionality of, 67

STATUTE DE DONIS
Fee tail, 46, 47

STATUTE OF FRAUDS
See FRAUDS, STATUTE OF

STATUTE OF USES, 137–138

STATUTE QUIA EMPTORES, 42

STATUTES OF LIMITATION
See also ADVERSE POSSESSION
Deeds, breach of covenants of title, 315–316

STRAW MAN CONVEYANCES
Joint tenancy, 166

STRICT LIABILITY
Bailee, duty to return property, 30
Subjacent support, 265

STRUCTURAL DEFECTS
Sales and transfers of real property, duties of disclosure, 302

SUBDIVISIONS
See ZONING

SUBINFEUDATION, 40–41

SUBJACENT AND LATERAL SUPPORT
Generally, 264–265
Land, support of, 264, 265
Negative easements, 201–202
Structures, support of, 264–265

SUBLEASES
See ASSIGNMENTS AND SUBLEASES

SUMMARY PROCEEDINGS
Leasehold estates, eviction, 102–103

SUPPORT OF PROPERTY
See SUBJACENT AND LATERAL SUPPORT

SUPPORT OF WIFE, 184

SURRENDER OF PREMISES
See LEASEHOLD ESTATES

SURVEYS
Deeds, description of land, 307–309

TACKING OF USES OR POSSESSIONS
Adverse possession, 19–21
Prescriptive easements, 212

TAXES
Adverse possession, 21
Concurrent ownership, 182
Rule against perpetuities, savings clauses, 161

TENANCY AT SUFFERANCE
See HOLDOVER TENANTS

TENANCY AT WILL
Leasehold estates, 70, 75–76

TENANCY BY THE ENTIRETY
Generally, 163, 173–176
Alienation of interest, 175–176
Common law, 174–175
Community property states, 174
Creation, 173–174
Operation of tenancy, 174–176
Personal property, 176
Presumptions concerning creation, 174
Severance, 173
Termination, 176

TENANCY IN COMMON
Generally, 163–164
Possession, rights to, 164
Presumption of equal shares, 164
Presumption of tenancy in common, 163
Uneven shares and different estates, 164

TENANCY IN PARTNERSHIP, 163, 176–177

TENANT-IN-CHIEF, FEUDAL TENURES, 40–41

TENANT IN DEMESNE, FEUDAL TENURES, 40–41

TENANTS
See LEASES

TERMINATION
See also EASEMENTS, EQUITABLE SERVITUDES, LEASEHOLD ESTATES, REAL COVENANTS, RE-ENTRY, RIGHT OF

Reverter, possibility of, 126
Tenancy by the entirety, 176

THEORIES OF PROPERTY, 1–3

TIMBER
Concurrent ownership, profits from land, 181
Profits a prendre, 202

TIME AND DATE
See also ADVERSE POSSESSION; STATUTES OF LIMITATION
Partition, agreement not to, 179

TIME OF THE ESSENCE
Sales and transfers of real property, 296

TITLE
See also TITLE INSURANCE
    Generally, 325–345
Abstracts of title, assistance of attorneys, 292
Actual notice, 334
Adjudication of title, Torrens system, 340–341
After-acquired title, 336–337
Bona fide purchasers, 329–330, 333
Character of neighborhood, duty to inquire arising from, 335
Common grantor, deeds from, 335, 338
Common law, 325
Consequences of recordation or lack thereof, 330
Constructive notice, generally, 334–336
Cost of title adjudication under Torrens system, 342
County recorders, 326–327
Creditors, protection of, 333–334
Death of party, equitable title, 304–305
Equitable title, 304–306
Federal government, claims under Torrens system, 340–341
Fraud, Torrens system, 341
Grantor-grantee index, 327
Ineligible instruments, 331
Inquiry notice, 334–336
Invalid conveyances, 332
Joint tenancy, 166
Judgment creditors, protection of, 333–334
Lien creditors, protection of, 333–334
Marketable title acts, 297, 338–340
Mortgagees, protection of, 333
Nonindexed instruments, 331–332
Notice, 334–336
Notice acts, 329
Omnibus clauses, 332
Operation of law, interests created by, 332–333
Possession, duty to inquiry of person with, 334–335
Quit-claim deed, duty to inquire arising from, 336
Race acts, 328–329
Race-notice acts, 329–330
Recording acts, generally, 325, 326–340
Record notice, 334
Registration. See Torrens system, below
Scope of protection under recording acts, 332–334
Shelter rule, bona fide purchasers, 333
Stranger to chain of title, recording of conveyance by, 336
Title searchers, 327–328
Torrens system
    Generally, 325–326, 340–343
    Adjudication of title, 340–341
    Comprehensiveness, lack of, 342
    Cost of title adjudication, 342
    Defective notice in initial adjudication, 341
    Errors by recorder, 342, 343
    Federal government, claims of, 340–341
    Fraud, 341
    Possessory title registration, 343
    Public records, 341–342
    Scope of certificate of title, 340–341
    Transfers of title, 342
Tract index, 327
Unrecorded instrument, record reference to, 335
Wild deeds, 336

TITLE INSURANCE
    Generally, 326, 343–344
Coverage, scope of, 343–344
Easements, 344
Exclusions from coverage, 344
Liability of insurer, 344

TORRENS SYSTEM
See TITLE

TORTS
See LEASEHOLD ESTATES

TOTTEN TRUSTS, 35

TOUCH AND CONCERN
Assignments and subleases, 86–87
Equitable servitudes, 245
Real covenants, 230, 235–239

TRACING OF COMMUNITY PROPERTY, 189–191

TRADE FIXTURES
Leasehold estates, 118

TRADE SECRETS, 6

TRANSFER OF REAL PROPERTY
See SALES AND TRANSFERS OF REAL PROPERTY

TREASURE TROVE
Finders keepers, 11

TREBLE DAMAGES
Holdover, willfulness of, 80–81

TRESPASS
Abandoned, lost or mislaid property, finding of, 8, 9
Leases, 70–71
Nuisances, relationship to, 258

TRUSTS AND TRUSTEES
Contingent remainders, destructibility of, 143
Gifts, 34–35
Life estates, 62

UCC
See UNIFORM COMMERCIAL CODE

UNBORN WIDOWS
Perpetuities, rule against, 157–158

UNCLEAN HANDS
Equitable servitudes, termination of, 253–254

UNCONSCIONABILITY
Implied warranty of habitability, waiver by tenant, 113
Leases, obligations of tenants, 98

UNDERGROUND TANKS
Sales and transfers of real property, duties of disclosure, 302

UNFAIR COMPETITION, 6

UNIFORM COMMERCIAL CODE
Entrustment of personal property to merchant for sale, 38
Voidable title, 38–39

UNIFORM MARITAL PROPERTY ACT, 189

UNITED STATES CODE
Civil Rights Act of 1866, 42 U.S.C. § 1982, 119–120
Fair Housing Act, 119–120

UNNECESSARY HARDSHIPS
Zoning, variances, 275–276

UTILITARIAN THEORY, 1–2

UTILITY AND EFFICIENCY, 2, 3

VALUATION
Life estates, 60–61

VARIANCES
Zoning, 275–276

VESTED REMAINDERS
See REMAINDERS

VIEW
Negative easements, 201–202

WAIVER AND ESTOPPEL
See also EASEMENTS; EQUITABLE ESTOPPEL; LEASEHOLD ESTATES
Assignments and subleases, restrictive provisions in leases, 94–95
Deeds, 311–312, 318–319
Equitable servitudes, 251
Real covenants, 251

WARRANTIES
See also LEASEHOLD ESTATES
Deeds, 312–319

WASTE
Leasehold estates, 96–97
Life estates, 63–65

WATER AND WATER RIGHTS
Negative easements, 201–202

WIFE AND HUSBAND
See HUSBAND AND WIFE

WILD ANIMALS
Possession, 4–5

WILD DEEDS, 336

WILLFULNESS
Holdover tenants, 80–81

WILLIAM OF NORMANDY, 40

WINKFIELD DOCTRINE, BAILMENTS, 29

WORTHIER TITLE, DOCTRINE OF
Generally, 146–148
Heirs of grantor, 147
Operation of doctrine, 147–148
Rule of construction, status as, 146–147
Shelly's Case, distinguished, 148
Trust, revocation of, 147–148

WRITINGS
See FRAUDS, STATUTE OF

ZONING
Generally, 266–291
Abortions, performance of, 287
Abusive amendments, 274–275
Aesthetic objectives, 269–270
Architectural review, 270
Authorization for zoning, 268–272
Changed conditions, necessity of amendment to respond to, 275
Cluster zoning, 278
Comprehensive plan, requirement of, 272, 274–275
Conditional uses, 276–277
Conditional zoning, 277–278
Constitutional law

Generally, 266, 279–288
Abortions, performance of, 287
Bill of rights, incorporation into due process, 282–285
Due process, 266, 281–287
Economic substantive due process, 285–286
Eminent domain, 266
Environmental preservation, 288
Equal protection, 266, 279–281
Family rights, 286–287
Freedom of press, 284–285
Freedom of religion, 285
Freedom of speech, 266, 282–284
Historical preservation, 287–288
Intermediate scrutiny, equal protection, 281
Police power, 279
"Privacy" or "autonomy" rights, 286–287
Procedural due process, 281–282
Strict scrutiny, equal protection, 280–281
Subdivisions, validity of conditions, 289–290
Substantive due process, 282–287
Suspect classifications, equal protection, 280–281
Takings clause of Fifth Amendment, 287–288, 289–290
Cumulative zoning, 267
Density zoning, 267–268
Discretion and restraint, 272–279
Due process, 266, 281–287
Economic substantive due process, 285–286
Enabling acts, 268–272
Environmental preservation, 288
Equal protection, 266, 279–281
Exclusionary zoning, 270–271
Expansion of nonconforming uses, 273
Family rights, 286–287
Floating zones, 277
Forced phase-out of nonconforming uses, 273–274
Freedom of press, 284–285
Freedom of religion, 285
Freedom of speech, 266, 282–284
Growth controls, 271–272
Historical preservation, 287–288
Initiative and referendum, 279

Mistake, necessity of amendment to correct, 275
Mutually exclusive zoning, 267
Nonconforming uses
    Generally, 273–274
    Expansion of use, 273
    Forced phase-out, 273–274
    Rebuilding after destruction, 273
Objections to zoning, 290–291
Parks and schools, dedication of land for, 289
Planned unit developments, 290
Police power, 279
Practical difficulties, variances, 275–276
Presumption of validity of amendment, 274–275
"Privacy" or "autonomy" rights, 286–287
Procedural due process, 281–282
Public need for amendment, 275
Rebuilding after destruction of nonconforming use, 273
Sales and transfers of real property, defective title, 298
Special uses, 276–277
Spot zoning, 274, 278
Subdivisions
    Generally, 288–290
    Conditions, validity of, 289–290
    Constitutional law, validity of conditions, 289–290
    Infrastructure, creation of, 289
    Parks and schools, dedication of land for, 289
Substantive due process, 282–287
Takings clause of Fifth Amendment, 287–288, 289–290
Ultra vires local action, 269–272, 278
Unnecessary hardships, variances, 275–276
Variances, 275–276
Voter discretion, 279

Products for 1997-98 Academic Year

emanuel®

Emanuel Law Outlines

Steve Emanuel's Outlines have been the most popular in the country for years. Twenty years of graduates swear by them. In the 1996–97 school year, law students bought an average of 3.0 Emanuels each – that's 130,000 Emanuels.

Civil Procedure ◆	$18.95
Constitutional Law	23.95
Contracts ◆	17.95
Corporations	18.95
Criminal Law ◆	14.95
Criminal Procedure	14.95
Evidence	17.95
Property ◆	17.95
Secured Transactions	14.95
Torts (General Ed.) ◆	17.95
Torts (Prosser Casebook Ed.)	17.95
Keyed to '94 Ed. Prosser, Wade & Schwartz	
Also, Steve Emanuel's First Year Q&A's (see below)	$18.95

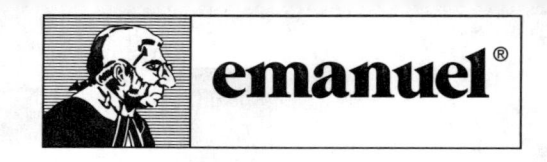

The Professor Series

All titles in these series are written by leading law professors. Each follows the Emanuel style and format. Each has big, easy-to-read type; extensive citations and notes; and clear, crisp writing. Most have capsule summaries and sample exam Q & A's.

Agency & Partnership	$14.95
Bankruptcy	15.95
Environmental Law	15.95
Family Law	15.95
Federal Income Taxation	14.95
Intellectual Property	15.95
International Law	15.95
Labor Law	14.95
Neg. Instruments & Payment Systems	13.95
Products Liability	13.95
Professional Responsibility (*new title*)	15.95
Property (*new title*)	15.95
Torts	13.95
Wills & Trusts	15.95

◆ *Special Offer*...First Year Set

All outlines marked ◆ *plus* Steve Emanuel's First Year Q & A's *plus* Strategies & Tactics for First Year Law. Everything you need to make it through your first year.

Complete Set $97.50

First Year Special Joint Offer...Get the Emanuel First Year Set and the *Law in a Flash* First Year Set together.

$192.50 *if purchased separately* $177.50

Question & Answer Collections

Siegel's Essay & Multiple–Choice Q & A's

Each book contains 20 to 25 essay questions with model answers, plus 90 to 110 Multistate-style multiple-choice Q & A's. The objective is to acquaint the student with the techniques needed to handle law school exams successfully. Titles are:

Civil Procedure	Evidence
Constitutional Law	Professional Responsibility
Contracts	Real Property
Corporations	Torts
Criminal Law	Wills & Trusts
Criminal Procedure	

Each title $15.95

The Finz Multistate Method

967 MBE (Multistate Bar Exam)–style multiple choice questions and answers for all six Multistate subjects, each with detailed answers – *Plus* a complete 200 question practice exam modeled on the MBE. Perfect for law school and **bar exam** review.

$33.95

Steve Emanuel's First Year Q&A's

1,144 objective–style short-answer questions with detailed answers, in first year subjects. A single volume covers Contracts, Torts, Civil Procedure, Property, Criminal Law, and Criminal Procedure.

$18.95

For any titles not available at your local bookstore, call us at 1-800-EMANUEL or order on-line at **http://www.emanuel.com**. Visa, MasterCard, American Express, and Discover accepted.

Law in a Flash

Law In A Flash Flashcards

Flashcards

Civil Procedure 1 ◆	$16.95
Civil Procedure 2 ◆	16.95
Constitutional Law ▲	16.95
Contracts ◆▲	16.95
Corporations	16.95
Criminal Law ◆▲	16.95
Criminal Procedure ▲	16.95
Evidence ▲	16.95
Future Interests ▲	16.95
Professional Responsibility (953 cards)	32.95
Real Property ◆▲	16.95
Sales (UCC Art.2) ▲	16.95
Torts ◆▲	16.95
Wills & Trusts	16.95

Flashcard Sets

First Year Law Set   95.00
(includes all sets marked ◆ *plus* the book
Strategies & Tactics for First Year Law.)

Multistate Bar Review Set   165.00
(includes all sets marked ▲ *plus* the book
Strategies & Tactics for MBE)

Professional Responsibility Set   45.00
(includes the *Professional Responsibility* flashcards
plus the book Strategies & Tactics for the MPRE)

Law In A Flash Software
(for Windows® 3.1 and Windows® 95 only)

Law In A Flash Interactive Software combines the best features of our flashcards with the power of the computer. Just some of the great features:

- Contains the complete text of the corresponding *Law In A Flash* printed flashcards
- Side-by-side comparison of your own answer to the card's preformulated answer
- Fully customizable, savable sessions – pick which topics to review and in what order
- Mark cards for further review or printing
- Score your answers, to help you spot those topics in which you need further review

Every *Law In A Flash* title and set is available as software.

Requirements: 386, 486, or Pentium-based computer running Windows® 3.1 or Windows® 95; 16 megabytes RAM; 3.5" high-density floppy drive; 3MB free space per title; Windows-supported mouse and printer (optional)

Individual titles	$19.95
Professional Responsibility (covers 953 cards)	34.95
First Year Law Set*	115.00
Multistate Bar Review Set*	195.00
Professional Responsibility/MPRE Set*	49.95

* These software sets contain the same titles as printed card sets *plus* the corresponding *Strategies & Tactics* books (see below).

Your bookstore sells flashcards and software together in a Combo pack, at a special discount price

---

Strategies & Tactics Series

Strategies & Tactics for the MBE

Packed with the most valuable advice you can find on how to successfully attack the MBE. Each MBE subject is covered, including Criminal Procedure (part of Criminal Law), Future Interests (part of Real Property), and Sales (part of Contracts). The book contains 350 actual past MBE questions broken down by subject, plus a full-length 200-question practice MBE. Each question has a *fully-detailed answer* which describes in detail not only why the correct answer is correct, but why each of the wrong answer choices is wrong.

☞ Covers all the new MBE specifications tested on and after July, 1997.

$34.95

Strategies & Tactics for the First Year Law Student

A complete guide to your first year of law school, from the first day of class to studying for exams. Packed with the inside information that will help you survive what most consider the worst year of law school and come out on top.

☞ Completely revised for 1997.

$12.95

Strategies & Tactics for the MPRE

Packed with exam tactics that help lead you to the right answers and expert advice on spotting and avoiding the traps set by the Bar Examiners. Contains actual questions from past MPRE's, with detailed answers.

$19.95

Prices effective through 7/31/98. Visit our website at **http://www.emanuel.com** for the latest product information.

LEXIS·NEXIS
NOW brings to you...

SHEPARD'S UPDATED DAILY!

LEXIS-NEXIS is your best online source for SHEPARD'S legendary history and treatment analysis. New citing references and analyses are updated every day upon receipt from SHEPARD'S.

Wider Coverage
This unsurpassed level of SHEPARD'S currentness extends to all citations series on LEXIS-NEXIS...and LEXIS-NEXIS gives you wider coverage than any other online source, including all 50 state statutes, the U.S. Code, the CFR, patents, Federal Rules of Court, law reviews, and of course caselaw.

Quick Rating Codes
Take advantage of the SHEPARD'S Signal on LEXIS-NEXIS—three concise codes that quickly rate the strength of your cited case.

Faster Research
SHEPARD'S on LEXIS-NEXIS has been streamlined to reduce research steps, improving your productivity like never before.

Be sure you've built your case on a solid foundation by using SHEPARD'S on LEXIS-NEXIS. For a free brochure or to learn more,

CALL 1-800-528-1891.

LEXIS·NEXIS
A member of the Reed Elsevier plc group

SHEPARD'S

It's all you need to know

and NEXIS are registered trademarks of Reed Elsevier Properties Inc., used under license. The INFORMATION ARRAY logo is a trademark of Reed Elsevier Properties Inc., used license. SHEPARD'S is a registered trademark of SHEPARD'S Company, a Partnership. © 1997 LEXIS-NEXIS, a division of Reed Elsevier Inc. All rights reserved.